BLOOD BROTHERS

BLOOD BROTHERS

The Criminal Underworld of Asia

Bertil Lintner

BLOOD BROTHERS

First published 2003 by PALGRAVE MACMILLAN™
175 Fifth Avenue, New York, N.Y. 10010 and
Houndmills, Basingstoke, Hampshire, England RG21 6XS.
Companies and representatives throughout the world.

PALGRAVE MACMILLAN is the global academic imprint
of the Palgrave Macmillan division of St. Martin's Press,
LLC and of Palgrave Macmillan Ltd. Macmillan® is a registered trademark in the United States, United Kingdom
and other countries. Palgrave is a registered trademark in
the European Union and other countries.

ISBN 1-4039-6154-9

Library of Congress Cataloguing-in-Publication Data
available from the Library of Congress.

First published in 2002 by Allen & Unwin.

First PALGRAVE MACMILLAN edition: March 2003.

10   9   8   7   6   5   4   3   2   1

Printed in the United States of America.

CONTENTS

A NOTE ON NAMES

It is almost impossible to be consistent in Romanising Chinese names, but I have used Pinyin in most cases, except for familiar names more commonly spelled according to the Wade-Giles system (for instance, Chiang Kai-shek instead of Jiang Jieshi). The names of Malaysian Chinese and Indonesian Chinese have been spelled according to the local systems of Romanisation. In all cases, the surname comes first followed by given names. For Japanese names, which actually follow the same pattern, I have used the system with which most non-Japanese are familiar: the given name first, followed by the surname. All amounts in dollars ($) mean US dollars, unless otherwise indicated.

ACKNOWLEDGEMENTS

I am grateful to a large number of people who have directly and indirectly assisted me in writing this book. I received extraordinary help from my friend Ko-lin Chin, the world's foremost expert on illegal Chinese migration and ethnic Chinese gangs in North America who also shares my interest in Burma and the Golden Triangle, as well as Harald Bruning of Reuters and the *South China Morning Post* who knows more than any other westerner about all aspects of life and society in Macau, and Leung Yat-chan of Hong Kong's *Oriental Daily News*, whose insights into the underworld in Hong Kong and Macau are unique.

Lynn Pan's accounts of old Shanghai were extremely helpful for my attempts to reconstruct events in that city in the 1920s and 1930s. Investigative reporter David Kaplan of *US News and World Report* and Tokyo's best-known foreign writer, Mark Schreiber, guided me through the maze of the Japanese underworld. Pasuk Phongpaichit of Bangkok's Chulalongkorn University has described the relationship between organised crime and officialdom in her own country in a scholarly and professional way, without moralising and through research that is free from sensationalism. My old friend Alfred W. McCoy of the University of Wisconsin at Madison also provided inspiration, and his books on the Golden Triangle opium trade and organised crime in Australia remain the best sources of information about those subjects. Greg Bearup, the *Sydney Morning Herald*'s prime crime reporter, helped me update McCoy's research with more recent material about the Australian underworld.

Many other individual sources have to remain anonymous, but I pay tribute to their courage and determination when it comes to researching one of the shadiest aspects of life in the Asia-Pacific region. Former and serving officers from the Australian Federal Police, the Royal Hong Kong Police, the Royal Canadian Mounted Police and various other law enforcement agencies also helped me obtain information.

I am grateful to Simon Robson and Andrew Marshall for proofreading the manuscript and tidying up my English. But, above all, I wish to thank the John D. and Catherine T. MacArthur Foundation for providing a research grant, which enabled me to take time off from my regular work as a journalist to write this book.

Finally, I would like to note that nothing contained within this book should be regarded as an allegation of corruption, malpractice or other misconduct, but merely as re-statements of others' views, included here simply to reflect the nature and tone of current debate.

INTRODUCTION

It was execution day in Shanwei, an isolated town on the rugged, pirate-infested coast of China's Guangdong province. Thirteen men, handcuffed and shackled, had already been herded into the town's courtroom on charges of piracy. They staggered out soon after with their fates sealed: death by firing squad. 'Doomsday arrives for "evil monsters" of the sea' declared the local authorities with medieval relish, although afterwards they mellowed somewhat, and allowed the pirates to drink a large amount of wine, 'to help take away the tension of being executed' as one official put it. Thousands of people gathered outside the courthouse for a glimpse of the damned men as they were led away to the execution grounds. By then, most of the pirates were profoundly drunk and singing loudly.

To the people of Shanwei—indeed, to anyone familiar with the dark traditions of the South China Sea—there was nothing unusual about this scene. At the beginning of the nineteenth century, hordes of men and women were organised in confederated fleets of thousands of junks which dominated the entire coastal region of southern China. They were at one and the same time immortalised in local folklore—which often depicted them as Robin Hoods who stole from the rich and resisted the oppressive authority of the Emperors—and, less romantically, feared by their victims, most of whom were actually ordinary people living along the coast.

The spectacle in Shanwei, however, was not taken from ancient history. It happened in January 2000—as was obvious to anyone who heard the drunken pirates sing. Jumping up and down in his rattling chains, Yang Jingtao, a 25-year-old pirate, led the chorus with a boisterous rendition of Ricky Martin's theme song for the 1998 World Cup, ironically called 'The Cup of Life':

Go, go, go!
Ole, ole, ole!

Go, go, go!
Ole, ole, ole![1]

Before Yang and his fellow convicts had time to sober up, they were trucked away to an open field on the outskirts of Shanwei, forced to kneel in a row, and dispatched one by one by an executioner with a Kalashnikov—one bullet through the back of the head, one bullet through the heart. A coroner was on hand to certify the deaths. Then, in the Chinese tradition, the families were billed for the ammunition costs.

The thirteen pirates were among 38 defendants who had been convicted of hijacking the Hong Kong-owned *Chang Sheng* cargo ship on 19 November 1998. Dressed up as officers from Chinese Customs and the Ministry of State Security, China's powerful secret police, they had boarded the ship off Kaohsiung in Taiwan while it was on its way from Shanghai to a port in Malaysia to unload thousands of tonnes of furnace slag. All members of the 23-man crew of the *Chang Sheng* were bludgeoned to death and dumped in the sea. The ship was later sold to an unknown foreign buyer for about $300,000, and the pirates divided the money between them.

It was no mean feat on the part of the Chinese authorities to track down and arrest the pirates. But Beijing was eager to show that it was serious about the alarming rise in various types of crime, one of the most worrisome side-effects of the free-market reforms which were introduced in the early 1980s to replace the old socialist system.

Piracy is only one tradition of China's dark history that is back with a vengeance after years of rigid communist rule. In October 2000, China admitted for the first time the existence in the mainland of crime related to the country's legendary secret societies, the so-called Triads, bands of outlaws who were even more powerful than the pirates before Mao Zedong's revolution of 1949—and certainly more revered by the public as they claimed to be true Chinese patriots who owed their origin to the struggle against the 'foreign' Manchu Dynasty that seized power from the more indigenous Ming line of emperors in the seventeenth century. According to legend, the Triads claim as their founders a secret sect of monks and avengers at the equally mythical Shaolin monastery, which was located 'somewhere' in southern China.

Today's Chinese Triads are involved in drug trafficking, extortion, kidnapping, the stealing of cultural relics, smuggling illegal aliens, gambling and prostitution, a report said. It went on to state that 'there are at least one million Triad members in China' today.[2] This is hardly surprising. For modern China's teeming hordes of millions of migrant workers, finding jobs is not easy in a competitive labour market, and the tightly knit criminal fraternity that the Triads offer means both economic survival and mutual protection for many drifters who find themselves lost in a hostile environment. 'Triad activities,' the report went on, 'are not only rampant in the vast countryside but also in leading cities such as Shenyang and Tianjin in the north, Guangzhou in the south, and in Shanghai.' It blamed corrupt officials and policemen for providing the criminals with a 'protective umbrella', which made it difficult to deal with the situation.

The rise in organised crime in China is reflected in the number of executions all over the country. The total number of executions remains a state secret, but Amnesty International was able to record at least 1263 executions in 1999 and 2088 death sentences that year—more than in the rest of the world combined.[3] Drugs, yet another scourge of pre-revolutionary days, have become a serious problem, with millions of addicts in all parts of China, but especially in Yunnan province, which borders the infamous Golden Triangle in northern Burma and Laos, the world's most important source of illicit opium and pure, white, Number 4 heroin.

In most countries, the United Nations' annual anti-drug day—26 June—is celebrated with awareness campaigns in schools and perhaps public rallies against narcotics. But in China, the day is marked by mass executions in major cities and towns across the country. In 1996, for instance, 110 people were shot on the day, with most executions carried out in Chengdu in Sichuan and in Kunming, capital of Yunnan, which borders the Burmese sector of the Golden Triangle where most of the world's heroin is produced. Twenty-nine people were executed in Guangdong province, with six of them shot in the special economic zones of Shenzhen and Zhuhai opposite then-British Hong Kong and Portuguese Macau respectively. Additional sentences were passed on 1725 drug traffickers, while a large quantity of confiscated drugs was publicly destroyed.[4] But such harsh measures seem to have little or no effect; China's criminals are only becoming more daring, better organised—and more numerous.

The situation in Russia is even more out of control. Following the collapse of communism in 1991, there was no new system to replace the old one, which—for all its flaws and shortcomings—had provided a functioning administrative structure. The new Russia that emerged in the 1990s was not the democratic state which many had hoped for: gangsterism reigned, and corruption and abuse of power followed, precipitating the breakdown of social and civil order. The old system was overthrown, but organised crime, not the people, became the new overlords. Russian gangs are usually called *Mafiya* (to distinguish them from the Italian and American 'mafia'), and international law enforcement agencies estimate there are between 3000 and 4000 such gangs in Russia today, with a total membership of maybe 100 000 people. Most of the gangs are fairly small and loosely organised, and their activities—as well as members—often overlap.[5]

Viktor Ilyukhin, chairman of the Parliamentary Security Committee, believes that criminal cartels, despite their haphazard structures, control as much as 45 per cent of capital in the country, and 80 per cent of all voting stock, while another estimate has them controlling 15–25 per cent of Russia's banks.[6] The *Mafiya* has managed to turn crime into the only really profitable growth industry in the post-Soviet era. As the optimism engendered by the dismantling of communism turned sour, the hopeful term *demokratiya* practically disappeared from everyday talk in Russia. People now talked about *demokratura*—a combination of *demokratiya* and *diktatura* (dictatorship)—to emphasise that the new system was little more than another form of authoritarian rule.

Japan may appear orderly, but powerful organised crime gangs lurk under its smooth surface. Japan's mobsters, the so-called *yakuza*, are in fact the world's most successful—and powerful—criminal entrepreneurs. The main gang alone, the Yamaguchi-gumi, boasted 16 500 full-time members in 1999, or five times the size of the entire Italian-American mafia at its peak in the 1950s. Taking into account other members and associates, the syndicate may have as many as 23 000 followers. Total membership of all *yakuza* gangs across Japan may be as high as 80 000.[7]

The Yamaguchi-gumi's main base is in the port city of Kobe, but the gang has branches all over Japan and, like other organised crime groups, it is active in traditional gangster pursuits of drug trafficking, prostitution, blackmail, extortion, gambling and murder. But, in the 1970s, a new type of businessman-gangster emerged: the *sokaiya* ('general meeting fixer'), who would extort protection money from companies by threatening to disrupt their annual general meetings and by publishing 'financial journals' which would contain damaging information about certain firms if they did not pay the gangs. Or big corporations would be coerced into paying huge fees to subscribe to these useless news sheets.[8]

Another type of gangster, the *jiageya* ('land-turners'), exploited the Japanese real estate boom in the 1980s. When the government in the 1990s moved to bail out Japan's special housing loan companies, *jusen*, it was discovered that they owed billions of dollars to *yakuza*-related outfits, money that no one expects will be repaid.[9] The *jiageyas* were largely responsible for the collapse of the bubble economy in the early 1990s. On the other hand, the *yakuza* are reported to generate some 1.4 trillion yen, or $10 billion, annually from their various criminal activities.[10]

The *yakuza* are active not only in Japan but also in Hawaii, where they own hotels, resorts and golf courses. Working with gangs in the Philippines, they have expanded into gambling, fraud, money laundering and gun-running. Their international connections stretch to Hong Kong, Southeast Asia, Australia—and even to Brazil and other Latin American countries where there are large numbers of Japanese immigrants. *Yakuza* mobsters have arrived in Los Angeles, San Francisco, New York and Europe and blended in with huge numbers of Japanese travellers and businessmen.[11]

In more recent years, the *yakuza* has established links across the Sea of Japan—with Russian gangs in Vladivostok and other cities in Siberia. In Vladivostok today, most cars have their steering wheels on the wrong side, indicating that they have been brought in from Japan across the sea. In return for shipping secondhand Japanese cars to Siberia, the *yakuza* has taken back hand-guns, assorted machinery and Russian girls to service the night clubs in Tokyo's notorious entertainment district of Kabuki-cho, and in other cities where Japanese salarymen are looking for sexual encounters with a European girl.

Russian prostitutes are cheaper—and much more plentiful—than American, Dutch or Swedish ones.

Russian prostitutes—and gangsters—have also found their way down to Macau, where long-legged blonde girls became popular with Asian and other local customers in the 1990s. Russian prostitution in Asia—and the crime that comes with it—became front-page news in Hong Kong's papers in June 1994, when a well-respected lawyer from the then-British colony, New Zealander Gary Alderdice, was found dead in a dingy flat in Vladivostok, together with Natalia Samofalova, a 20-year-old beauty who had just returned from a stint as a prostitute in Macau. Both had been shot at close range, execution-style with bullets through their heads. The 47-year-old Alderdice had met Samofalova in a disco in Macau, and flown to Vladivostok to meet her—perhaps to start a new life after having gone through a belated midlife crisis.

It was long assumed that Alderdice had gone to Russia to buy her freedom from the syndicate that had brought her down to Macau—and that both of them were punished for 'breaking the rules of the game'. In the end, however, it turned out to be a robbery gone awry: some of Samofalova's friends knew that she had brought back at least $20 000 from Macau, but shot the couple before they had learned where the money was hidden.[12] The tragic case nevertheless represented a watershed for the media and law enforcers in Asia, who for the first time were compelled to take a serious look at the rise of Russian crime in the region. For months, the press was full of reports about Russian gangsters, former KGB agents and prostitutes, and the connections that were assumed to exist between them.

Some of the weakest links in the criminal web that spans the Asia-Pacific region, and includes the Russian *Mafiya*, are to be found—incongruously enough—in the Pacific islands. Long a haunt of buccaneers, beachcombers and missionaries, the South Pacific has become a new kind of paradise: for crooks and money launderers flocking to take advantage of the secretive financial regimes of some of the tiny island states. All the South Pacific islands have little arable land or natural resources, and small populations. Unable to develop industry or agriculture, they have been forced to seek other sources of income. Most have sold fishing licences to fleets from Japan, Taiwan,

South Korea and the United States. More imaginatively, tiny Tuvalu until recently earned 10 per cent of its national revenue by selling its telephone country-code (688) to American sex hotlines. Tonga and the Marshall Islands have sold passports, mostly to Hong Kong Chinese, and Kiribati has marketed its prime location near the Equator to sell satellite tracking services.

But it is the Pacific states' recent entry into the ranks of the world's tax havens that has caused the most concern in the West. The best-established South Pacific tax haven is Vanuatu, whose one-street capital, Port Vila, abounds with nearly 80 private banks, 2000 trust companies and numerous insurance agents, accountants and solicitors. A list of Vanuatu's banks reveals a motley collection of mostly unknown and strangely named financial institutions, such as the 'Spec Bank', the 'Fidutia Bank', the 'Yorker International Bank' and the 'Worldwide Guaranty Bank'. But the identity of bank owners and the nature of their assets remain secret to both the public and foreign investigators.[13]

For many years, international law enforcement officials have been concerned about the flow of 'hot' money from China, Hong Kong and Taiwan through Vanuatu's offshore banks. Alarm bells rang in 1996, when it was discovered that seven Russian banks had shown interest in opening 'representative offices' in Port Vila.[14] The South Pacific attracted the interest of Russian 'bankers' in the mid-1990s, at a time when the US government began to step up pressure on financial centres in the Caribbean. After Vanuatu came Nauru, one of the world's smallest republics covering an area of 21 square kilometres, with a population of just over 10 000.

Few, if any, Russians have ever visited Nauru, but the Internet has made it possible to move money across the globe in cyberspace by using (for a fee) an exotic domain name. Many international law enforcement officials identify it as their most serious challenge in the twenty-first century, along with increased globalisation of organised crime. Russian gangs now operate all over the world, as Japanese and Chinese gangs have done for decades—and there are signs of growing cooperation between the gangs rather than rivalry and competition.

One of the most startling examples of the globalisation of international crime was found in September 2000, some 2600 metres up in the Andean Mountains in South America. The police discovered a

Russian-designed submarine that was being built to smuggle drugs out of Colombia and, presumably, on to North America. It was not clear why work on the submarine had been started near landlocked Bogota, hundreds of kilometres from the sea, but Russian-language documents were found alongside the partially completed vessel, which led the authorities to conclude that the Russian *Mafiya* was involved in a deal with Colombian drug cartels. The submarine was big enough to carry 150 tonnes of cocaine or heroin.[15]

In December 2000, a US government report identified 'well-connected networks of international criminals' as the main and most rapidly 'growing security threat' in the post-Cold War era, perhaps even more than global terrorism. A dominant theme in the report was that organised crime had diversified internationally and 'become even more intertwined with political elites in home countries, making it especially hard to combat'. Well-connected Russian gangs are bringing in heroin from Southwest Asia and selling it in the west, while the Dai Huen Jai, or 'the Big Circle Boys'—the most powerful crime syndicate in China today—'deals in drugs, alien smuggling, vehicle theft, financial crimes, and computer hacking as part of a worldwide network that links cells in nearly every Chinatown worldwide'.[16]

As the execution of the pirates in January 2000 and the introduction of mandatory death sentences for drug traffickers are meant to show, China's communist leaders want to be seen to be moving with a firm hand to crush the resurgence in crime in a country that is still struggling with the difficult task of establishing the rule of law in place of ideologically motivated campaigns against 'counter-revolutionaries'—the main enemies of the state over the past several decades. But how deep does the commitment go? And to what extent are other pre-revolutionary phenomena—such as the age-old Chinese tradition of a symbiosis between officialdom and organised crime—also re-emerging?

On 8 April 1993, just as the people of the then still British Hong Kong were starting to get used to the idea of a return to the 'motherland', Tao Siju, chief of China's Public Security Bureau, gave an informal press conference to a group of television reporters from the colony. After making it clear that the 'counter-revolutionaries' who had demonstrated for democracy in Beijing's Tiananmen Square in 1989 would not have their long prison terms reduced, he began talking about the Triads: 'As for organisations like the Triads in Hong Kong, as long as these people are patriotic, as long as they are concerned with Hong Kong's prosperity and stability, we should unite with them.'[17] Tao also invited them to come to China to set up businesses there.

The statement sent shockwaves through Hong Kong's police force and there was an uproar in the media. Since 1845, Triad membership had been a crime in the territory, and the rule of law was considered one of the pillars that made it an international city. Claiming to be 'patriotic' was no excuse for breaking the law. But the people of Hong Kong should not have been surprised. Deng Xiaoping, the father of China's economic reforms, had over the years hinted at the existence of connections between China's security services and some Triads in Hong Kong. In a speech in the Great Hall of the People in October 1984, Deng pointed out that not all Triads were bad. Some of them were 'good' and 'patriotic'.[18]

While Deng was making those cryptic remarks in Beijing, secret meetings were held between certain Triad leaders and Wong Man-fong, the deputy director of Xinhua, the New China News Agency, China's unofficial 'embassy' in Hong Kong. Wong told them that the Chinese authorities 'did not regard them the same as the Hong Kong police did'. He urged them not to 'destabilise Hong Kong' and to refrain from robbing China-owned enterprises. But they could continue their money-making activities.[19]

In the years leading up to the 1997 handover—and especially when the British on Hong Kong's behalf argued for more democratic rights to be included in its mini-constitution, or when the Hong Kong people themselves demonstrated their support for the pro-democracy movement in China—certain 'patriotic' Triads were there as Beijing's eyes and ears. They infiltrated trade unions and even the media. Hong Kong—and increasingly even China—experienced a paradoxical throwback to Shanghai of the 1930s, when the former rulers of the country, the Guomindang, had enlisted gangsters to control political movements and run rackets to enrich themselves and government officials alike.

A few days before security chief Tao made his stunning public statement to the reporters from Hong Kong, a new, glitzy nightclub called Top Ten had opened in Beijing. One of the co-owners was Charles

Heung of the Sun Yee On, one of Hong Kong's most notorious Triad societies—and another was Tao himself.[20]

The interrelationship between criminals and powerful people in China is even more blurred when it comes to maritime piracy. According to numerous reports, many ships on the high seas were boarded by personnel from military gunboats bearing the markings of the Chinese navy, and the 'pirates' were dressed in genuine Chinese naval uniforms. The same reports suggest that, while piracy may not be condoned by the Chinese navy as such, the temptation to participate in attacks on foreign ships, or to turn a blind eye to sea-robbery in exchange for bribes or part of the loot, appears to be very strong.[21]

In the light of such reports, some foreign observers have been quick to jump to the conclusion that 'organised crime' and colourful 'secret societies' are about to take over China. But Chinese organised crime is not, as many people surmise, a cross between the Free Masons and IBM, well-organised corporate structures shrouded in Masonic ritual. While the criminals may live outside the law, they have never been outside society. In Asia, there has always been a symbiosis between the law and crime—but only with respect to a particular kind of criminal underworld. For instance, organised crime helps the authorities police more unpredictable, disorganised crime to keep the streets safe.

There are also certain things that governments—and big business—just can't do. A certain company may want to eliminate a competitor, but is unable to do so by normal, legal means. An organised crime gang can then be employed to make life difficult for the other party. When in 1984 the Guomindang's security services in Taiwan wanted to get rid of a dissident, troublesome journalist in exile, Henry Liu, they delegated the task to hitmen from the island's most powerful crime syndicate, the United Bamboo gang. The gang was more than willing to carry out the killing, not on account of any concern about Liu, but because in exchange they would get unofficial protection for their own businesses: gambling, prostitution and loan sharking.

With Taiwan developing into a democratic—and therefore more transparent—society, the United Bamboo thugs are clearly on the defensive. But as chaos prevails in the Southeast Asian nation of Cambodia following decades of civil war and genocide and an extremely fragile democracy, the Taiwanese mobsters found a new haven for their activities.

Chinese gangs from the mainland have also established themselves in Cambodia, and turned the country into a base for illegal immigration of Chinese nationals to the West, drug smuggling, illegal capital flight through the country's many shady banks, and weapons trafficking. But in order to police the gangsters in Cambodia, the Chinese authorities turned to an even bigger Godfather-type to police the petty criminals: Teng Bunma, the unofficial head of the local Chinese business community. In late October 2000, Guo Dongpo, director of Beijing's Office of Overseas Chinese Affairs, met Bunma in Phnom Penh and asked him to help control the unruly gangs in the Cambodian capital. Bunma is not only the honorary president of both the Chinese Association of Cambodia and the Phnom Penh Chamber of Commerce—he is also on Washington's blacklist of suspected drug traffickers, and has been denied entry to the United States.[22]

In Hong Kong, certain business tycoons have always used Triad gangs to enforce their will on ordinary people who cannot be 'persuaded' to cooperate by legal means. In early 2000, young men dressed in black T-shirts, with their chests and biceps adorned with tattoos of dragons and phoenixes, suddenly appeared in the quiet village of Pak Tin in the New Territories. They would swear and kick doors as they demanded exorbitant rents from local residents. A car was parked in the village, with a sign on its dashboard clearly indicating that its owner belonged to the well-connected Sun Yee On Triad. When that message was not clear enough, a funeral van—an obvious sign of bad luck—was parked in Pak Tin.

The problem was that the local villagers, who had lived in Pak Tin for generations, had refused to give up their homes to a Hong Kong 'developer' who wanted to turn the rural area into a complex of 600 flats in four high-rise towers. Thanks to the brave efforts of Law Yuk-kai, a local human rights activist and law graduate, the villagers resisted both the initially formal request from the 'developer' and the more forceful methods of the hired hoodlums, which began when 'normal' means did not seem to work. Law had the courage to assist his fellow villagers to prepare to fight for their homes.[23]

Given the Sun Yee On's well-placed connections, Law's chances of success are difficult to determine. It is those connections that enable the Sun Yee On, and other Triads, to run prostitution, illegal gambling rackets and 'protection' of street hawking, minibus services and the film industry, which often idealises the 'secret societies' and their mythical origin. Yiu Kong Chu, a professor in the Department of Sociology at the University of Hong Kong, argues that the Triads are an integral, rather than a merely predatory, element of many sectors of the local economy.[24]

During the Sydney Olympics in September 2000, many Australians became aware of how well-placed and influential some alleged mobsters can be. Two members of the 'Olympic family', senior Uzbekistan boxing official Gafur Rakhimov and International Basketball Federation vice-president Carl Ching, were refused visas. The *Weekend Australian* reported on 9–10 September that the immigration authorities referred to a Russian government report, kept by the US Federal Bureau of Investigation (FBI) and the Australian Security and Intelligence Organisation (ASIO), which linked Rakhimov to organised crime figures in Central Asia. Rakhimov himself has always denied such allegations, but they were considered strong enough by the Australian authorities to refuse him a visa.[25]

Hong Kong-based Ching was suspected of being closely linked to Triad gangs and the Australian press reported at the time that he had also been 'refused a visa by Canada when trying to attend the 1994 World Basketball Championship in Vancouver due to reasons of "national security"'.[26] The president of the International Olympic Committee, Juan Antonio Samaranch, wrote to Australian prime minister John Howard in which he protested against the ban, calling it 'a matter of most serious concern for the Olympic movement'. But the Australian authorities refused to give in, and immigration minister Philip Ruddock insisted that the ban on Rakhimov and Ching was related to 'the safety and security of the Australian community'.[27]

Ching, it transpired, was a close associate of Eddie T.C. Chan, a former Hong Kong police officer who fled the territory during a crackdown on corruption in the 1970s. A document from the Royal Canadian Mounted Police identifies Chan as an organised crime figure in New York, whose first main company in the United States, the Continental King Lung Group, was a major money-laundering outlet for the Triads. But, officially, the 'Group' was engaged in 'banking and financing, trading in bullion, trading in securities, computer parts manufacturing, real estate development, insurance business, international trading and entertainment'.[28]

Chan's son Chan Wing-po later became an assistant to Ching's company, Frankwell Holdings, which in the 1990s was closed down in the United States and Britain as a result of investigations into various illegal activities. In 1992, Ching had been one of the organisers of a gangster summit in Hong Kong which brought together representatives from Taiwan's United Bamboo gang, the 14K and Sun Yee On of Hong Kong, the United States-based Ghost Shadows and the On Leong Merchants' Association, a Triad cover organisation in New York. But the Hong Kong police raided a couple of rooms in the hotel where the meeting was going to be held, and many mobsters fled the scene.[29]

On other occasions, Ching and Chan have travelled together to China, wining and dining government officials. High-level connections were established, and a company in which Ching was a director and shareholder traded as a sauna in Hong Kong's main entertainment district, Tsim Sha Tsui. According to the territory's police, one of the owners, behind a nominee, was believed to be the son of China's then military leader, Yang Shangkun.

This symbiotic relationship between China's military establishment and gangland figures went beyond such mutually beneficial business deals—and even further than low-level espionage on pro-democracy activists in Hong Kong—and this became clear when a major scandal broke in the United States in the late 1990s: the so-called Donorgate saga, the revelation that mainland Chinese interests had used shady 'businessmen' in Macau to channel funds to the Democrats and former president Bill Clinton's election campaigns in 1992 and 1996, leading to suspicions that Beijing was trying to buy its way into the White House to gain political influence and acquire advanced technology. None of these 'businessmen', who all had a stake in the murkier side of Macau's casino industry, had any personal interest in Clinton being re-elected but, in exchange for acting as conduits for mainland money they would receive unofficial protection from the Chinese military for their own business interests.

A similar partnership exists between the *yakuza* and Japan's ruling circles. The Japanese government has not used mobsters for espionage to infiltrate the United States, for instance. But since the beginning of the last century, gangsters have colluded with 'mainstream' Japan. In the post-World War II era, powerful backstage fixers and power brokers have brought the *yakuza* together with senior politicians in the ruling Liberal Democratic Party (LDP), Japanese business interests and ultra-right wing groups. The *yakuza*—'patriots to the core', according to themselves—has been used to control the activities of Japanese left-wingers, and in 1960 the LDP enlisted some 28 000 gangsters—and 10 000 extreme rightists—to provide security for a planned visit to Japan by then US president Dwight Eisenhower which was eventually cancelled.[30]

Despite an official police crackdown on the *yakuza* in recent years, the Yamaguchi-gumi discreetly helped raise money and secure votes for scores of politicians in the election to the Lower House of the Japanese parliament as late as June 2000. A regional weekly magazine quoted one beneficiary of mob largesse as saying: 'There isn't a single Japanese politician who doesn't know his local yakuza boss.'[31]

Success in politics and business in Asia depends on powerful contacts, who are often above the law and adept at bending it. It is contacts rather than the courts which serve as arbiter; who you know, not how many lawyers you employ, which decides the outcome of difficult business undertakings and political careers. The same factors decide how successful you will be as an extortionist, a pimp or a pirate. In Chinese society especially, there has existed since ancient times a collaboration between open and secret societies, whereby mainstream business and governments and their various agencies—and even ordinary civil society—coexist with darker forces in a mutually beneficial relationship.

My own interest in this symbiotic relationship goes back to the time in the early 1980s when I researched the Golden Triangle opium trade and the politics of the narcotics business in Burma, which is the focus of one of my previous books. Gradually, I came to understand that organised crime and the illegal trade in narcotics and arms in East Asia are a much broader phenomenon than just Burma's civil war and ethnic conflict. I discovered linkages between the Chinese Triads, the Japanese *yakuza*, Korean and Vietnamese gangs and—the most recent addition to the plethora of organised crime groups in Asia—the Russian *Mafiya*. With a grant from the John D. and Catherine T. MacArthur Foundation, I set out to investigate crime, politics and business in the Asia-Pacific. My travels took me to China, Taiwan, Japan, Vietnam, Australia and several of the Pacific islands over a period of nearly five years, from 1997 to 2001, and this book is the result of that research. But one cannot hope to understand the networks behind organised crime in the Asia-Pacific—the tangled web of bankers, gangsters, soldiers and spies—without first understanding the past. And the most perfect example of this began almost a century ago in the grandest city ever built in East Asia: Shanghai.

• 1
WHORE OF THE EAST

Good-bye to all that: the well-dressed Chinese in their chauffeured cars
behind bullet-proof glass; the gangsters, the kidnappers; the exclusive foreign
clubs . . . Good-bye to all the nightlife: the gilded singing girl in her
enamelled hair-do, her stage makeup, her tight-fitting gown with its slit skirt
breaking at the silk-clad hip . . . The hundred dance halls and the thousands
of taxi dolls; the opium dens and gambling halls . . . the sailors in their
smelly bars and friendly brothels on Sichuan Road; the myriad short-time
whores and pimps busily darting in and out of the alleyways . . . gone the
wickedest and most colourful city of the Orient: good-bye to all that.
—Edgar Snow, 1961.[1]

It was already over when the first communist troops marched into
Shanghai on a quiet Wednesday morning, 25 May 1949. Chiang Kai-
shek and other top leaders of the nationalist Guomindang—who
boasted of turning Shanghai into a new Stalingrad and would 'fight to
the end'—had fled on a gunboat to Taiwan weeks before the city
finally fell after a long siege by Mao Zedong's army of peasant revolutionaries. According to Sam Tata, an Indian Parsi and a native of the
city who witnessed its fall: 'At the same time, the vaults of the Bank
of China were secretly emptied of their stocks of bullion and the
entire gold reserves of the country were spirited after him. The President had pulled off the biggest bank robbery of all time'.[2]

Most of the wealthy Chinese and the Europeans living in Shanghai
had fled by any means possible: with shiploads of rice and cotton,
planeloads of gold and money, truckloads of jewellery and tobacco,
until the city was stripped bare. The few remaining Guomindang
troops surrendered without putting up any resistance. Mariano
Ezpeleta, the Philippine consul general, spotted the first communist

soldiers at seven o'clock in the morning from the window of his offices in the Hamilton Building in the city centre: about a hundred troops were patrolling the old European-style City Hall and the Police Headquarters. Officers and soldiers were indistinguishable, garbed in the same unmilitary uniform, but Ezpeleta took those giving orders to be the commanders. He noticed that the soldiers looked calm and composed: 'They walked slowly; not martially, not nervously, but deliberately. At all street intersections within sight, including the one under our windows, platoons of soldiers were standing at ease with fixed bayonets'.[3]

But Ezpeleta was somewhat disappointed by the initial impression of the communist troops. He had expected to see 'tough, weather-beaten soldiers, swaggering with assertive sureness, steel-helmets at rakish angle, sub-machineguns under the arms and hand-grenades dangling from their pockets'. But here they were, the feared enemy—'mostly teenagers in the first blush of youth, slightly built boys still awkward in gait; others, almost adult country bumpkins trying to steady first one foot, then the other. They stood at street crossings, casually holding their carbine at rest, looking around open-eyed, obviously bewildered by the ornate and magnificent buildings of the city'.[4]

Most of them came from the countryside deep in China's interior, and their scraggy faces betrayed years of toiling in the fields and fighting in the mountains. Their rice-green uniforms were of coarsest cotton, tailored without any regard to size and length. For army boots, they had flat rubber shoes and their headgear was patterned after a baseball player's cap. People came running out of their houses to offer them water, fruit and noodles. They declined everything except for water.[5]

Merging into a solid column, they continued down The Bund, the city's main street with its stately European-style banks, hotels and trading houses. The Bund began at the Garden Bridge north of the British Consulate and stretched for about half a mile along the banks of the Huangpu river. The neoclassical buildings along the way housed the premises of Jardine, Matheson and Company—the Scottish-founded firm that began trading along the China coast in the early nineteenth century—the Hong Kong & Shanghai Bank, Butterfield and Swire, the Asiatic Petroleum Company and the Glen Shipping Line.

There was also the grand Cathay Hotel, owned by the Sassoon family, Jewish merchants from Baghdad who had grown prosperous on the trade in cotton and opium. At the lower end of The Bund, a tall European-style clock tower faced the nearby Shanghai Club, where membership was confined to uppercrust British men only—or, at least, to rough business tycoons and assorted adventurers who liked to see themselves as such—and which boasted the longest bar in the East at 33 metres. The final fall of Shanghai may have been peaceful, but the sight of Mao's partisans marching down the streets of the greatest colonial city the world has ever known, with their red flags and portraits of their Chairman and Zhu De, their military commander, clearly showed that an entirely new era had arrived.

Later that day, red flags appeared over factory buildings and government offices throughout the city. According to Lynn Pan, a Chinese author who was born in Shanghai:

> The People's Liberation Army had simply walked in in their sneakers and straw sandals the night before. You could see them the next morning lying quietly in rows on the pavement, young soldiers curled up as though they might be under a tree by a river, but spread out with almost geometrical neatness all down the sidewalks. But for these, and for the announcement on the radio on the twenty-seventh that the People's Liberation Army had taken Shanghai over, you could hardly have known that Shanghai had fallen to the Reds.[6]

In line with their wanton attitude to life in general, the citizens of Shanghai did not at first let the Communist takeover worry them too much. When the new rulers staged a victory parade a few weeks after the 'liberation' of the city, the same trucks and buses that were used in the victory parade for Chiang Kai-shek just a few weeks previously were again in the streets as the main participants; the same faces shouted themselves hoarse again for the Red Commissars, only more so.[7] Bookstores and footpath stalls which before did a thriving business in selling dime-novels and pornographic literature suddenly became philosophically minded, offering the works of Marx, Engels and Lenin. The sellers of nude pictures changed to selling portraits of Stalin and Mao.

But no matter how lightly people took the communist takeover of the city, they could not, in their hearts, deny that such events signalled the demise of old Shanghai. There had never been a city quite like it. Shanghai had been known to some as the 'Paris of the Orient' for its gaiety and stylishness, and by others as the 'Whore of Asia', where every sin imaginable was permissible. Shanghai was a city where vice and virtue were bedfellows, remembers Consul General Ezpeleta, 'a city of contrasts: the rich were so wealthy they could afford to buy anything at any price; the poor so miserable they had to sell anything, property or person, at any price'.[8] According to Lynn Pan:

> The whole gamut of Western and Asian humanity was there, from Jewish tycoons and self-styled White Russian 'countesses' to Annamese gendarmes and Filipino band leaders. One shopped at Hall and Holtz; Lane, Crawford and Company; Laidlaw and Company; and Kelly and Walsh. One read the *North China Daily News, Shanghai Times, Shanghai Mercury, L'Echo de Chine, Der Ostasiatische Lloyd*, and the *Shanghai Nippo*. One danced in the chic ballroom of the Cercle Sportif Français and partied at cabarets like the Casanova, Del·Monte and Ciro's.[9]

There were also American cars, American cigarettes and American movies all over town, and Clark Gable broke as many hearts in Nanjing Road as he did in Beverly Hills.[10]

Rewi Alley, an idealistic young New Zealander who arrived in the city in 1927, was:

> struck by the contrast of wealth and poverty . . . If you got away from the main streets with their palatial buildings, you were soon in a maze of narrow, stinking, congested lanes where everyone spat—95 per cent of the population seemed to have chronic catarrh. Beside the general high living in the foreign residential section, the town seemed to be full of beggars. The Shanghai of luxurious clubs, sleek cars and well-trained servants was the Shanghai in which one slept and ate one's food. But one's working and emotional life was spent up and down the alleyways where the vast majority of the Chinese people lived—where every tiny room held a family, and where rows of night pots lined the streets.[11]

Alley worked as a factory inspector for the Shanghai Municipal Council, and he was shocked by what he saw. It was sights such as these that eventually made the farm boy from the Canterbury plains on New Zealand's South Island a fervent supporter of Mao's revolutionaries. One of his most miserable experiences was to see the incredible torture of the young children working on the system in silk filatures. The children, many not more than eight or nine years old, stood for twelve hours at a time over boiling vats of cocoons, with swollen red fingers, inflamed eyes and sagging eye muscles.

Alley noted that the children would be crying from the beatings of the foreman, who would walk up and down behind their long rows with a steel wire as a whip. Their tiny arms were often scalded in punishment if they passed a thread incorrectly. Conditions of work in the other factories were no better. Antimony poisoning in the enamel works and lead poisoning, especially in places where battery plates were made, were two extremely vicious industrial hazards. Alley recalled 'the small boys who stood wearily, day and night, over buffing wheels, their pitiful limbs encrusted with the grime of emery powder, sweat and metal dust'.

The children worked over open chromium vats without exhausts for the poisonous fumes around them, sores ate into their flesh, and their hands and feet were pitted with 'chrome holes' that were nearly impossible to cure under their deplorable working conditions. Children toiled for incredibly long hours in a desperate situation, and were denied the most elementary rights. 'Emaciated little bodies fought for life against great odds to bring swift profit to their masters', Alley noted wryly.[12]

Girls from poor families fared no better. In the tea houses and bordellos on Fuzhou Road, the Chinese institution of the singsong girl—a hostess, a geisha, an escort, a whore—was perfected. Shanghai had hundreds of such plush 'tea houses', where wealthy Chinese—and foreigners—not only sipped tea, but more specifically could buy any sexual service or fantasy they could dream of. Almost half of the singsong girls hailed from Suzhou, a town further inland which was renowned for its sweet, soft-spoken women. They filled the establishments on Fuzhou Road and elsewhere.

But many also came from other parts of China. During the 1930s, Shanghai had 35 000 prostitutes, the largest concentration per capita anywhere in the world. The first-class prostitutes were called 'long-gowns' because their customers wore long gowns, a sign of prosperity among Chinese males at the time. Some of these prostitutes were well educated, and good at singing, poetry and painting.[13] Next in line came prostitutes who were called 'six-yuan-to-bed'—six yuan was what a month's food would cost. Many of these girls were very young, barely in their teens. A late nineteenth-century poem expressed sympathy for all these girls:

> The stuck-up madam is called the *benjia*.
> She spares no expense to buy sweet young things.
> Pitiful girls of twelve and thirteen
> Dance and learn singing until the moon sets.[14]

Lowest of all in the hierarchy of brothels were the so-called 'flower-smoke rooms' and 'nail sheds'. The first were places where a customer could smoke opium and sleep with girls—'flowers'—at the same time. They were small, filthy and barely furnished, and the crude beds were covered with smelly quilts. Droves of 'flowers' would stand or sit in a narrow doorway singing lascivious songs like 'Ten Cups of Wine'. When a customer showed interest, they would rush over and pull him up the stairs like a prisoner of war.[15]

'Nail sheds', scattered throughout the poorer northern districts of the city, were brothels housed in shacks made from roughly hewn planks or grey bricks. They were patronised by 'simple-minded labourers of limited economic means', and the prices ranged from ten cents for quick sex to one yuan for the whole night. Intercourse in such places was called 'driving a nail', with none of the finesse, or pretence, of the more upmarket tea houses.[16]

Foreign sailors usually ended up in Rue Zhu Baosan, a block away from The Bund and the river front. Better known as Blood Alley (and now as Xikou Road), it was only about a 100 metres long—but lined with smelly, fetid bars, a place of drunken brawls where many foreigners simply disappeared. Even long before the notorious joints in Blood Alley opened, numerous foreign visitors to the city had been 'shanghaied', as it became known—that is, robbed and murdered by bar girls, or the thuggery that usually controlled them.

The more fortunate customers just caught venereal diseases, which were so prevalent that the municipal council dispensed free treatment to western sailors—and White Russian prostitutes, of whom there were also many. Chinese prostitutes patronised by Chinese customers were not included in any of these measures. Just before the fall of Shanghai, it was estimated that 10–15 per cent of the Chinese urban population had syphilis, and nearly half had been or were infected with gonorrhea. This meant approximately half a million people with syphilis and two million with other venereal diseases.[17]

Nowhere was Shanghai's taste for vulgar pleasure more striking than in the Great World, a massive amusement centre on Avenue Edourad VII (today's Yan'an Road). Hollywood film director Josef von Sternberg visited this remarkable place in the mid-1930s:

> The establishment had six floors to provide distraction for the milling crowd, six floors that seethed with life and all the commotion and noise that go with it, studded with every variety of entertainment Chinese ingenuity had contrived. When I entered the hot stream of humanity, there was no turning back had I wanted to. On the first floor were gambling tables, singsong girls, magicians, pick-pockets, slot machines, fireworks, bird cages, fans, stick incense, acrobats and ginger. One flight up were the restaurants, a dozen different groups of actors, crickets in cages, pimps, midwives, barbers, and earwax extractors. The third floor had jugglers, herb medicines, ice-cream parlors, photographers, a new bevy of girls their high-collared gowns slit to reveal their hips, in case one had passed up the more modest ones below who merely flashed their thighs; and under the heading of novelty, several rows of exposed toilets, their impresarios instructing the amused patrons not to squat but to assume the position more in keeping with the imported plumbing. The fourth floor was crowded with shooting galleries, *fan-tan* tables, revolving wheels, massage benches, acupuncture and moxa cabinets, hot-towel counters, dried fish and intestines, and dance platforms serviced by a horde of music makers competing with each other to see who could drown out the others. The fifth floor featured girls whose dresses were slit to the armpits, a stuffed whale, story tellers, balloons, peep shows, masks, a mirror maze, two love-letter booths with scribes who guaranteed results, 'rubber goods' and a temple filled with ferocious gods and joss sticks. On the top floor and a roof of that house of multiple joys a jumble of tightrope walkers slithered back and forth, and there were seesaws, Chinese checkers, mah-jong, strings of firecrackers going off, lottery tickets, and marriage brokers. And as I tried to find my way down again an open space was pointed out to me where hundreds of Chinese, so I was told, after spending their coppers, had speeded the return to the street below by jumping off the roof.[18]

The owner of the complex, Huang Chujiu, had made his first fortune selling a miracle potion that he promised would tone up the brain. But the Great World would eventually pass into the hands of a squat, pock-marked gangster called Huang Jinrong. Better known as 'Pock-Marked Huang', this notorious mobster boss also happened to double as a senior Chinese police officer. This special relationship between gangsters and officialdom was partly due to the peculiarities of Chinese culture, where 'the rule of law' has never had the same meaning as in the West—but also because of the extraordinary circumstances under which Shanghai was founded and grew.

The city was first noticed as an 'excellent entrepôt for commerce' by Hugh Hamilton Lindsay of the British East India Company, whose ship, *Lord Amherst*, docked there in 1832. He had sailed to Shanghai from the Portuguese enclave of Macau on the South China coast, then a centre for European trade in the Far East. But there was only one problem: foreigners were allowed to trade only in the southern port city of Guangzhou, and Lindsay was advised to return there as soon as possible.[19] These restrictions, imposed by the Chinese government, infuriated the British, who saw China as a huge, almost untapped market. Business was flourishing in Guangzhou, but the overall China trade was nowhere near its potential. Britain's interests were soon to collide with those of the Imperial Court in Beijing— over the most valuable commodity that the British exported to China: opium.

Opium and opium smoking had been known in China for centuries, and small quantities were grown domestically, primarily in the southwestern provinces of Sichuan and Yunnan. But India was the main producer of the drug for international trading. Some of India's Mughal emperors had tried to tax opium sales to raise revenue for the state. However, no single organisation in any part of Asia had the will, the networks or the political and naval power to create new markets before the advent of the colonial powers.

Britain's move to colonise India and other parts of Asia heralded a new era in international opium trading. In 1600, the East India Company had been formed with the aim of expanding trade contacts between Britain and Asia, and between British spheres of influence in the Far East. In subsequent centuries, this trade was pursued with much vigour. The stalwart mariners of the East India Company fought their way into the highly competitive markets of Asia, followed by the armies of Britain's expanding colonial empire.

China, with its teeming millions, held the greatest attraction. It ought to be a great market for the products of the growing British Empire and, more importantly, China could supply goods that were becoming popular in Europe itself—especially tea. Britain, however, faced severe problems in its trade relations with China. At first the British had little to offer that the Chinese wanted. In fact, the Chinese showed interest in only one item from Britain and British India: silver. By the late eighteenth century, every British ship that sailed from India to Guangzhou carried a cargo composed of 90 per cent silver bullion.[20]

By the early nineteenth century, India faced a shortage of silver and another commodity had to be found. The answer was opium, which was abundant in India and which was gradually becoming popular in China. Opium replaced silver as the currency of trade with the Chinese. The flow of silver from India to China was effectively halted, and after the mid-nineteenth century the silver trade completely reversed direction. Silver was now going back to India from China to pay for opium. India had also begun its own tea production, and the loser in this game was China. India's income from the Chinese opium trade paid for constructing grand, imperial buildings in Calcutta, Madras, Bombay and other cities established by the British in India. An opium tax soon produced more than one-fifth of government revenue in the vast empire of British India.[21]

But Britain was far from being China's only opium supplier. Americans also sold Turkish opium to the Chinese. Clipper ships belonging to well-respected firms such as Perkins & Company and Russell & Company of Boston transported immense quantities of opium from the Middle East to China.[22] Persian opium was later imported by any trader in a position to do so. The American merchant W.C. Hunter used one simple phrase to describe the Chinese opium trade between 1835 and 1844: 'We were all equally implicated'.[23]

The Chinese government tried, at least officially, to suppress the trade. Opium was devastating China's population: millions of people became addicted to the drug. Opium smoking had actually been prohibited in China in 1729; cultivating and importing opium was specifically banned in 1799.[24] But these edicts were ignored by all western merchants—and the ruling Qing Dynasty was too weak to enforce its policies. Moreover, local officials were too corrupt to obey orders from the Court in Beijing, or unwilling to follow directives from a dynasty of foreign emperors which originated in Manchuria.

The Qing Emperors tried time and again to stop the inflow of opium and the outflow of hard currency. Then, in March 1839, Emperor Xuanzong appointed an unusually vigorous official, Lin Zexu, as commissioner for foreign trade and sent him down to Guangzhou to stamp out the opium business. Lin demanded that the merchants sign bonds promising never to bring opium to China again, on pain of death. Some American merchants signed, but the British refused. In a series of letters to Queen Victoria, commissioner Lin appealed to the British to stop the trade. There was no response, and Lin wrote in a final, carefully worded letter to the Queen:

> Let us suppose that foreigners came from another country and brought opium into England, and seduced the people of your country to smoke it. Would you not, the sovereign of the said country, look upon such a procedure with anger, and in your just indignation endeavour to get rid of it? Now we have always heard that Your Highness possesses a most kind and benevolent heart. Surely then you are incapable of doing or causing to be done unto another that which you should not wish another to do unto you.[25]

Moral persuasion has never proved very effective in dealing with drug smuggling or rulers who sanction it, and the British in Guangzhou were no exception. When diplomacy did not help, Lin decided to use force. In June, he destroyed 20 000 chests of opium, weighing 133 pounds each, which had been seized from foreign merchants' warehouses. Lord Palmerston, the British Foreign Secretary, decided to retaliate: a powerful fleet, with 4000 soldiers aboard, was assembled. An official proclamation said that the fleet would 'protect British interests'. Admiral George Elliot was in charge of the overall operation, with Vice-Admiral Sir William Parker and military commander Sir Henry Gough sailing with the warships.[26]

High-powered British naval cannon bombarded the ports along the South China Sea to force the Emperor to open them to British merchandise—which was primarily opium from India. But not everyone agreed with this policy. William Gladstone, a young Liberal politician who later became prime minister of Britain, said: 'A war more unjust in origin, a war more calculated to cover this country with permanent disgrace, I do not know and I have never read of.'[27]

The British fleet laid siege to Guangzhou, took Amoy (Xiamen) and Ningbo, and finally occupied Shanghai in July 1842, cutting off supplies to Beijing which were delivered via the Grand Canal, a massive, ancient man-made waterway that connected the Yellow River—the Huanghe—with the Yangzi. China was defeated, and on 29 August the first treaty was signed with Britain on board the *Cornwallis*. Known as the Treaty of Nanjing, it required that the Chinese pay $21 million in reparations, open five ports—including Shanghai—to British trade, and cede the island of Hong Kong to Queen Victoria.[28]

The new colony of Hong Kong gave the British a tremendous advantage over other opium merchants. Trade with China became a virtual British monopoly, and Hong Kong emerged as the most important transfer point for Indian opium entering the vast Chinese market. By 1854, yearly British sales of opium amounted to nearly 80 000 chests, and China's opium smokers numbered in the millions.[29]

New trading houses were also built in Shanghai where, although it remained nominally under Chinese sovereignty, British and other foreigners enjoyed extraterritorial rights: they could be tried only by their own courts, and they had their own police forces and customs officials. The opium trade, organised from Hong Kong and Shanghai, laid the foundation for many personal fortunes. The most successful entrepreneurs of all were two young Britons: William Jardine and James Matheson. Veteran Australian journalist Richard Hughes described them as 'both Scottish, both religious in the stiff Calvinist way, both scrupulous in financial and personal matters, both indifferent to moralistic reflections on contraband and drugs'.[30] Jardine-Matheson became one of the biggest trading firms in Shanghai, and remains so in Hong Kong. Its present-day executives are conventional members of the Hong Kong business world, and few of them would like to be reminded of the origins of their company's wealth and influence.[31]

Frictions between the Chinese and the foreigners continued after the acquisition of Hong Kong and the opening of Shanghai to foreign trade. A second opium war was fought from 1856 to 1860, and its final phase saw the Anglo-French forces charging into Beijing, where they looted and burned the Emperor's famous summer palace. China had lost again, and more territory was ceded to the British. The Kowloon

Peninsula was added to the British colony of Hong Kong. The British also proposed the legalisation of the opium trade, to which the Chinese agreed reluctantly. According to the terms of the new agreement: 'the importer was to sell [opium] only at the port. It was to be carried to the interior by Chinese only . . . and the transit dues were to be arranged as the Chinese government saw fit'.[32]

But this was on paper only. Opium continued to be the most important commodity foreigners traded with China. Following its military defeats, the Chinese were too weak, and local officials too corrupt, to stop the drug flow into their country. Britain continued to export increasing amounts of Indian opium. In the peak year of 1880, China imported more than 6500 tonnes, most of which was produced in India. But then, in the 1860s, China began to grow her own on a massive scale. After 1880 the demand for foreign opium decreased, and by 1905 imported opium amounted to roughly half the amount of 1880. By the early twentieth century, China's annual opium production had risen to 22 000 tonnes.[33]

Opium merchants flocked to the British Settlement in Shanghai to cash in on this lucrative business. Other fortune seekers also arrived, as Shanghai grew at a tremendous pace: western Protestant and Catholic missionaries, teachers, newspapermen, and assorted carpetbaggers and adventurers. Most westerners preferred to live south of the Suzhou Creek, so when a separate 'American Settlement' emerged north of it, most of its inhabitants were actually Japanese. Nevertheless, in 1863, the so-called American concession area was amalgamated with the British enclave, and the city's famous International Settlement came into existence, governed by a foreign-appointed municipal council.

The French, wary of the Anglo-Saxon dominance of the foreign community in Shanghai, built their trading houses and churches on a separate stretch of the Huangpu riverfront between the International Settlement and the original Chinese city. This became the so-called French Concession, where the French ruled and the streets had French names. In effect, Shanghai became three cities—the International Settlement, the French Concession and the Chinese city—each with its own administration and law enforcement. The British brought in turbaned Sikhs from India to maintain order in the International Settlement, while the French depended on their Vietnamese—or Annamese as they were then called—gendarmes with French officers.

With the British came also an unusually enterprising group of people: Jewish merchants who hailed from Baghdad but had moved to Bombay to avoid persecution. As naturalised British subjects in India, the Sassoon family, especially, built up a thriving business in cotton and opium. They soon discovered that nowhere were the prospects for the two commodities better than in Shanghai—and their business contacts in India were unparalleled. Their two family companies, David Sassoon and Sons and E.D. Sassoon, became the biggest opium trading firms in town—and the Sassoons some of the wealthiest merchants on the entire China coast.[34]

Silas Hardoon, another Jew from Baghdad, first worked for the Sassoons, but later built up his own empire. Ralph Shaw, a British journalist who lived in Shanghai in the 1930s, wrote:

> Among those who had made immense fortunes by bringing in opium was the 'Baghdad Jew', Hardoon. Starting life as a watchman, he had risen like a phoenix from the ashes of the millions of pipefuls of the drug he had provided for the emaciated sots who were in its deadly grip. But, as if to atone for the misery his trading success had caused, he adopted a family of about nine orphaned children of many races who lived with him in a palatial mansion on Bubbling Well Road [today's Nanjing Road West].[35]

At the turn of the twentieth century, $40 million worth of opium came into the port of Shanghai every year. The city had more than 80 opium shops where raw opium was sold under licence, and there were 1500 opium dens which catered to people of all social classes. The poor usually smoked a mixture of opium and opium residue, which cost only 10 cents per pipe. James Lee, a western writer, visited such a place in 1906 and wrote:

> When my eyes became accustomed to the dim light of the place, I saw that we were in a large room entirely bare of furniture. On the boards of the floor were stretched, alongside of each other, about a dozen grass mats, and on most of them there was a Chinese coolie. Some of them were already lying insensible like dead bodies, while others were still smoking opium . . . Some were filthy and in rags, and I noticed that some were quite young boys, although there were old men too.[36]

However, voices were being raised against the opium trade, especially by foreign missionaries but also by educated Chinese. Drug addiction was crippling the country, and in September 1906 an edict was issued from the Imperial Court in Beijing which stated the country's predicament:

> The cultivation of the poppy is the greatest iniquity in agriculture, and the provinces of Sichuan, Shaanxi, Gansu, Yunnan, Guizhou, and Shanxi abound in the product, which, in fact, is found everywhere. Now that it is decided to abandon opium smoking within ten years, the limiting of this cultivation should be taken as a fundamental step . . . opium has been in use so long by the people that nearly three-tenths or four-tenths of them are smokers.[37]

'Three-tenths or four-tenths' of the Chinese population at the turn of the century meant 150 million opium users, four or five times the population of Great Britain, and more than that of the United States at the time. At least 15 million were considered incurable addicts.[38] The first proposal for drastic action against this appalling situation came in 1906 from Charles Brent, an American missionary who was serving as the Episcopal bishop of the Philippines. Having seen for himself the terrible effects of opium abuse in Asia, he wrote to President Theodore Roosevelt suggesting the time was ripe to call for international action against the opium trade.[39] Britain agreed in 1908 to restrict the import of Indian opium into China to 60 000 chests annually, down from more than 100 000 the year before.[40]

In February 1909, representatives of thirteen countries met in Shanghai for the first international congress to discuss the opium problem. Presided over by Bishop Brent, the meeting led to the formation of the International Opium Commission and a resolution that urged governments to halt the drug trade, which in Shanghai now included not only opium but also morphine, a refined derivative which was used both as a 'cure' and a narcotic. But the Commission was toothless, as no one was bound by any definite policy, and some key countries such as Turkey and Persia did not take active part in it.[41] Ironically, the Sassoon family later built their famous Cathay Hotel across the street from the office where the Opium Commission had met in 1909.

Nevertheless, another opium conference was held in The Hague, the Netherlands, in 1911–12. Britain agreed to halt all importation of Indian opium by 1917, and the Shanghai Municipal Council closed down opium houses in the International Settlement. It was not a big loss. By then, Shanghai's economy had sufficiently diversified into banking, shipping and manufacturing so that opium, which had provided the main income during the first years of the city's existence, was no longer necessary. With opium providing the initial capital, Shanghai had become China's most industrialised city. Hong Kong had developed in a similar manner: by 1917, about a third of the colony's revenue was derived from its Opium Monopoly.[42]

But many still craved the drug, and the supposed ban only pushed most of the opium trade into the French Concession, where the authorities had a much more flexible attitude to all kinds of vice than the superficially more moralistic Anglo-Saxons in the International Settlement. For outlaws, who had flocked to the city with everyone else, its division into three parts was the ultimate dream arrangement: a few miles could put them beyond the reach of one set of authorities and into the territory of another, with neither knowing or caring much about what happened over the 'border'.[43] And crime flourished in the city—or the three cities. Lynn Pan observed:

> Touts and small-scale hoods [were] recruited to the ranks of the Green Gang, a secret society which, like the Mafia, had historically been a patriotic fraternity and which initiated its members in time-honoured ceremonies with oaths and symbolic acts. Like the Mafia too, it specialised in enterprises like drug-peddling and gambling, businesses in which the enormous profits bought official connivance, but also attracted gangland rivalry and violence. The French Concession harboured a roaring opium trade, the highest-ranking Chinese officer in the gendarmerie having a bigger stake in it than anyone. He was Huang Jinrong, running with the hare and hunting with the hounds. The French had cynically recognised the world of Shanghai for what it was, a jungle of bums, adventurers, opportunists and swindlers, where one culture had to dictate to another with neither side remotely understanding the other. To the French there were worse sins to a police force than having as its Chinese head a man who, by virtue of his influence in the underworld, kept the level of crime from brimming over.[44]

Huang was, of course, 'Pock-Marked Huang', who later took over the Great World Amusement Centre. Hiring gangsters as detectives—at the same time they controlled the gambling and narcotics rackets—was simply a matter of convenience to the chief of police in the French Concession, Etienne Fiori, who otherwise had only a handful of French officials to control a native population of nearly one million Chinese.[45]

Huang had joined the French Concession police at the age of 24 in 1892. He was already thick-set as a young man, and a bout of small-pox had left distinct marks on his cheek, which gave him the nickname that stayed with him throughout his life. However, the pock-marked policeman did not rise to prominence until World War I, when a large number of the French officers were sent back to Europe for war duties. The French consul general gave greater responsibilities to the Chinese members of the force, and Huang was promoted to chief superintendent.[46]

The promotion was no coincidence. Huang had developed excellent relations with the Shanghai underworld, the Green and Red Gangs, and their leaders who held sway over an intricate web of smaller, associated groups such as the Big Eight Mob and the Thirty-Six Mob. Huang at first stayed above the street gangs, but became a formal member of the Green Gang in 1923.[47] These criminal networks were simply too complex for any European officer to understand. The easiest solution was to let the stronger gangsters police the weaker ones. Thanks to his connections throughout the Shanghai underworld, Huang was able to assist the French Sûreté in their occasional clean-ups of disorganised, or loosely organised, crime. In 1922 alone, Huang smashed thirteen vicious gangs, which were not playing by the rules. He was also able to help the French control the volatile political scene in the Concession. In 1919, Huang broke up a shopkeepers' strike in the wake of the launch of the May Fourth Movement of that year, a series of student demonstrations across the country which gave birth to China's modern nationalist movement, and later the Communist Party.[48]

From his headquarters in the Ju Bao Teahouse in the French Concession, Huang regulated the activities of robbers, kidnappers, gambling den operators and drug traffickers. The French were satisfied with pretending not to notice as long as crime was kept within tolerable limits—and provided they themselves received a share of the proceeds.[49] While the arrangement between crime and the law was blatant in the French Concession, it was actually not unique. The chief Chinese detective in the Shanghai Municipal Police in the 1910s and 1920s was a man called Shen Xingshan—who was also the principal leader of the Big Eight Mob, which controlled the city's narcotics traffic.[50]

By the mid-1920s, Huang had become Shanghai's best-known gangland celebrity, or *wenren*, and dominated all the other crime bosses. He has sometimes been compared with Chicago's legendary Mafia boss, Al Capone, but there are significant differences between the two godfathers. Al Capone began and ended his career as a gangster—Huang combined his duties in the detective squad with his criminal enterprises from the very beginning. His position was also much stronger; it was as if Al Capone had been not only an outlaw, but also the chief of the Chicago police. One striking similarity, however, is that Chicago's gangsters made their fortunes by selling bootleg liquor during America's Prohibition; Huang and his men refined and sold narcotics during a period when the authorities were attempting, ostensibly, to fight the opium trade and drug abuse.[51]

Huang needed a trustworthy lieutenant to run his opium rackets, and in the mid-1920s he found him: a man with big, protuberant ears who was always dressed in an ill-fitting robe. His name was Du Yuesheng, an almost illiterate urchin from the slums of Pudong across the Huangpu. In 1902, when 'Big-Eared Du' was only fourteen, he had left his mud hovel in Pudong and gone across the river to Shanghai proper to look for a job. After working as an errand boy for a fruit vendor, he drifted into gambling. Being extremely fond of both sex and opium, he spent a lot of his youth in the 'flower-smoke rooms'. Those two addictions were to follow him throughout his life.

In the early 1910s, Du joined the Green Gang and became a follower of Chen Shichang, an opium trafficker in the Shiliupu area. Like so many other petty criminals, he combined his opium peddling with being an informer for the police—and that was how he had met the pock-marked Inspector Huang. They were members of the same gang, although Du belonged, through the lineage connected with his surname and background, to a younger generation than Huang. Notwithstanding this, the powerful gangland detective decided that he liked the urchin from Pudong, and let him sleep in a room behind the kitchen in his mansion in a lane off Boulevard des deux Républiques.

Being at least officially a police inspector, Huang kept a certain distance from overt crime—his *de facto* wife, 'Miss Gui', looked after such activities. A former brothel keeper from Suzhou, she was also known as *baixiangren saosao*, or 'Sister Hoodlum', and ran an army of bandits.[52] Du became one of her foot soldiers, and soon proved his worth when a consignment of opium went astray. In the middle of the night, Du set after the culprits in a rickshaw, brandishing his pistol. He caught up with the thieves, and returned the opium to a delighted Sister Hoodlum. She persuaded her husband to take the brave young man into the inner circle of their family company, the Collective Prosperity Club, one of the largest gambling establishments in the French Concession which also effectively monopolised Shanghai's burgeoning narcotics business.[53] Under Huang's patronage, Du came to control a string of theatres, opium dens, bathhouses, gambling joints and brothels in the French Concession.[54] The French officers did not interfere, and their Annamese gendarmes just kept on patrolling the streets.

The almost surreal quality of the French Concession was further enhanced by the presence of large numbers of Russian refugees. The Communist victory in the Russian civil war had forced tens of thousands of people who remained loyal to the Tsar—hence the nickname 'White' Russians—to flee. The wealthiest ended up in Paris, London and New York, but those without money and contacts, and thousands of soldiers who had been trapped in the Russian Far East, crossed into Manchuria to settle in the city of Harbin. Some continued down to the new international metropolis Shanghai.

By the end of 1922, what so far had been a trickle became a flood. A Russian fleet of 27 ships—with 8000 men, women and children on board—left Vladivostok in October of that year, as the whole of Siberia was falling to the communists. Many of the children were orphans whose fathers had been killed in the civil war; they were, it could be said, Asia's first 'boat people', looking for a refuge from civil war and oppression. The Russians first landed in Pusan in Korea, but the Japanese authorities there did not allow them to stay. After encountering a violent storm, in which one ship was lost, they sought refuge in the Yangzi and anchored off Wusong just north of Shanghai.[55]

With Christmas fast approaching, the fate of the refugees—and the presence of a large number of children among them—softened the hearts of the foreign community in Shanghai. Despite some initial hostility, the refugees were permitted to stay. Soon, more 'boat people' arrived from the Russian Far East, and the Bureau of Russian Affairs was set up to deal with what was becoming a crisis. Although no one was pushed out of Shanghai, the stiff-upper-lipped British did not consider the Russians 'real' Europeans, and treated them with disdain.

The situation became even more complicated in 1924 when China, now a republic, recognised the new Soviet regime in Moscow. The Russian Consulate near Suzhou Creek in the old American Settlement area was handed over to the Soviets, much to the chagrin of the White Russians, and even other foreigners in the city. Victor Grosse, the Tsar's consul who had performed his duties for a regime that no longer existed, was forced to vacate the building.

The White Russians became citizens of nowhere, and never enjoyed the extraterritorial rights granted to other foreigners; the Russians were subject to Chinese laws, courts and prisons. There was also the question of where in the city they should live. The Anglo-Saxons did not want them, but the pragmatic French opened their Concession for Russian settlement, and before long its main street, Avenue Joffre (today's Huaihai Road), was full of shops with signs in Cyrillic script. The street became known as 'Little Russia'—or, in Russian, 'Nevskaya Avenue'—a nostalgic reminder of Nevsky Prospekt in St Petersburg. Portraits of the Tsar and the Tsarina hung in the sitting rooms of Russian homes in the French Concession, several Russian Orthodox churches were built, two Russian newspapers appeared—the *Shanghai Zaria* ('Shanghai Dawn') and *Slovo* ('The Word')—and there were Siberian fur shops and Russian sausage factories.

By the mid-1930s, some 25 000 Russians lived in Shanghai, forming the single largest foreign community after the Japanese. Dispossessed and deprived of citizenship, socially they occupied a gray area between white expatriates and Chinese.[56] Former officers in the Tsar's cavalry became riding instructors for wealthy European families or, more often, bodyguards for anyone willing to hire them—including Big-Eared Du's sons, who had trusted Russian gunmen following them wherever they went. The women became hairdressers, cabaret dancers and prostitutes, selling their services to all buyers, Chinese and Europeans alike.

White Russian men and women worked in nearly every night club in the city, from the most expensive to the sleazy bars in Blood Alley, as jazz musicians, bouncers, bartenders and 'taxi girls'—a euphemism for high-class prostitutes. Although many of them, especially when they applied for jobs in more upmarket night clubs, claimed to be generals, counts and princesses, the vast majority were actually former merchants, ex-army officers, cadets, rich peasants and university teachers.[57] But whatever their actual backgrounds, some of the White Russians were now so poor that they pulled rickshaws. White Russian and Chinese beggars died together in the streets.[58]

It was into this murky, permissive world of the French Concession that a 28-year-old school teacher arrived in the summer of 1921. He was Mao Zedong, a peasant-born revolutionary leader from Hunan, and he had come with some comrades to formalise the founding of the Communist Party of China. Shanghai's French Concession was one of the most lightly policed, and therefore safest, places in the country for any band of dissidents or outcasts to meet. The communist revolution, which they wanted to instigate, also had to be based on the proletariat—and Shanghai was the only city in the country that had a sizeable working class. And, thanks to western education, there were also intellectuals who had received modern, egalitarian influences from abroad.

In the last week of July that year, twelve delegates met in a non-descript, grey brick building on Rue Wantz (now Xingye Road) which belonged to one of the founding members of the party. But even though regulations were lax in the French Concession, the unusual meeting of these twelve dedicated revolutionaries attracted the attention of the authorities. After a few days, it was interrupted by a stranger whom the delegates suspected was a spy from the French police. They hurriedly moved the meeting to Jiaxing county, 113 kilometres south of Shanghai, where they resumed their discussions on a pleasure boat on Nan Lake.[59]

The Communist Party of China was born, and the first resolution promulgated by the new party began with the sentence: 'The basic mission of this party is to establish trade unions'.[60] In other words, Shanghai had to be the base, and the CPC founded the Chinese Labour Secretariat in the city as well as left-leaning labour unions. Clandestine party cells were established in factories and other workplaces to coordinate the activities of the unions, which operated openly. These unusual movements among the Shanghai working class led to immediate, and inevitable, clashes with the interests of organised crime, which controlled the lives of most poor people in the city.

According to an early labour activist in Shanghai: 'Our work met with many difficulties . . . Hardest to handle were the Green and Red Gangs. Finally we decided that several comrades should infiltrate their ranks'.[61] A meeting was arranged between Li Qihan, a young student who had helped set up the Labour Secretariat, and a Green Gang boss. Surprisingly, he welcomed Li as a disciple, and a useful connection was established.

At first, relations with the Guomindang were also good. The party had been set up by a young Chinese doctor, Sun Yat-sen, who became the father of the Chinese Republic and its first president. He was not opposed to leftist ideas, and in 1919 the new Bolshevik leaders of Russia had relinquished all old claims to railways and mining rights in Manchuria, together with 'all other concessions seized from China by the government of the Tsars, and by the brigands Horvath, Semyonov, Kolchak, the Russian ex-generals, merchants and capitalists'.[62]

No other foreign power had treated China with such respect, and in 1923 the Soviet-directed Communist International, the Comintern, sent a high-ranking operative to work with Sun and the Guomindang. His name was Mikhail Borodin, and he urged Sun to form a united front with the CPC.[63] From 1923 to 1927, the two parties cooperated and Mao himself also served in various positions in the Guomindang, including a stint as the party's propaganda director.

But the situation in China was chaotic. Sun had replaced the mediaeval Qing Dynasty with Asia's first modern republic, a contradiction that led to warlordism and civil war. After a period of chaos, Sun died in March 1925 in Beijing at the age of 59. But Borodin had begun to groom a possible successor, whom he thought would carry on the special relationship the Soviet Union had managed to establish with the young Republic of China: a 36-year-old former clerk with the Shanghai Stock Exchange called Chiang Kai-shek.[64]

Like Mao, Chiang came from a peasant background. He was born in Fenghua on the outskirts of Ningbo south of Shanghai, and had studied in Japan. In August 1923, Borodin had sent him off to Moscow for military training, from which he returned, quite disillusioned, in

December.[65] Nevertheless, Chiang became superintendent of the newly established Whampoa (Huangpu in *pinyin*) Military Academy near Guangzhou, where an entire generation of republican army officers was trained.

On 1 July 1926, Chiang felt that the time was ripe to make an attempt to unify China. He set off from Guangdong with a combined force of Guomindang and CPC troops on a long military expedition north to defeat the local warlords, who were running their own fiefdoms all over the country. Changsha, the main city of Hunan, was captured on 11 July, and Wuhan in September. In December, Fuzhou was brought under the control of the United Front, followed by Shanghai and Nanjing in March 1927.

But Borodin had made a serious miscalculation if he really thought that Chiang Kai-shek could be useful for the Comintern's interests in China. Mao never denied his peasant origins. Chiang felt ashamed of them and was no social revolutionary. Later in life, he even claimed that he was a descendant of the ancient Zhou Dynasty that had ruled China in the first millennium BC. With such pretensions, it was hardly surprising that his days in Moscow had turned him against the Russians and their suffocating communist beliefs.

As a Shanghai stockbroker, Chiang had befriended Chen Qimei, boss of the city in the first years of the Republic. Chen had mobilised the Green and Red Gangs to capture Shanghai during the 1911 revolution, and introduced Chiang to his gangland associates. Chiang was an avid but reckless gambler, winning a fortune just to lose all of it a year later. To fend off his creditors, Philippine consul general Ezpeleta remembers that Chiang:

> turned to his loyal friends in the underworld and in the underground. There, he was always a brother . . . The initiation of Chiang into the secret societies in Shanghai was in later life of immense and incalculable use to him. It opened his eyes to new vistas, sharpened his mind to sly intrigues, toughened his heart to underground cabals and taught him the gentle art of eliminating prospective rivals.[66]

Whether Chiang himself also became a member of the Green Gang is disputed, but he himself did admit in a letter written to two colleagues in 1924 to having led a wild and dissolute life when he was a stock broker in 1919 and to becoming familiar with, as he put it, the 'playboy world' of Shanghai.[67] Huang Zhenshi, a former Green Gang mobster boss, has asserted that Chiang indeed became a close associate of Pock-Marked Inspector Huang during his time in Shanghai. Moreover, Chiang's name appears on a list of members in a Green Gang manual.[68]

Frictions had already emerged between the two parties in the United Front, and in January 1925 the Communists had stated at their fourth national congress that 'one can easily find all sorts of reactionaries even in ordinary labour unions. The Guomindang is now plotting to amalgamate these anti-Communist elements under its own control'.[69] The Communists responded by launching labour strikes in Shanghai, led by their left-leaning trade unions and their own militia. The bankers and the industrialists were grumbling and, in spring 1927, Chiang decided to strike against his rivals, the hated communists. It was going to be an urban campaign, making regular troops unsuitable for the task. Chiang turned to his old comrades in the Green Gang.

By then, Big-Eared Du had become one of Shanghai's most prominent gangland bosses, and two British journalists described him as being 'tall and thin, with a face that seemed hewn out of stone, a Chinese version of the Sphinx. Peculiarly and inexplicably terrifying were his feet, in their silk socks and smart pointed European boots, emerging from beneath the long silken gown. Perhaps the Sphinx, too, would be even more frightening if it wore a modern top-hat'.[70]

His mansion on Rue Wagner was one of the most famous in the French Concession, but it also had some very bizarre features. Big-Eared Du, who now was also known by an even less flattering nickname—'Snake Eyes'—was a highly superstitious man who adhered to his own interpretation of ancient Chinese beliefs. For instance, he was born in 1888—the Year of the Rat—and therefore refused to let his servants disturb, let alone kill, any rodents in his house. As a result it was full of rats, and the stench and continual scratching noises were quite disturbing for important visitors who occasionally had to go there to see Shanghai's boss of bosses.[71] Many Shanghai oldtimers dismiss this story as fiction, which may well be the case.[72] But it is nevertheless part of the legend that surrounded the wily urchin from Pudong.

As the conflict between the Communists and the Guomindang deepened, the Godfather of Shanghai did not hesitate to come to the rescue of his old comrade Chiang Kai-shek. Big-Eared Du mobilised hundreds of his and Pock-Marked Huang's hijackers, kidnappers, bodyguards, pimps, masseurs, manicurists, pick-pockets, gunmen, hawkers, waiters and beggars, dressed them in blue and wrapped a band marked with the Chinese character for 'labour' around their arms. Guns were provided by Chiang's high command. The attack began an hour before dawn on 12 April 1927, as the mobsters attacked the Commercial Press buildings where the workers' militia were headquartered. The pickets surrounding the building were cut down by a hail of machine-gun fire. Almost simultaneously, the gang-sters—supported by Guomindang artillery—assaulted the workers encamped at the Chinese Tramways Company.[73] Rifle fire rang out again, and more pickets fell to the ground, bleeding profusely.

Seven hundred unionists were killed before the end of the day, and it took eight truckloads and several hours to cart away the dead and the litter. With them went the last of the alliance between the Guo-mindang and the communists; Chiang was the new overlord and Du his loyal lieutenant. They continued to hunt down Reds, and sus-pected Reds, until August of that year. A whirlwind of house searches followed. The British and the Japanese defence corps assisted too, delivering prisoners to the Guomindang garrison by the armoured truckload.[74] Scores of communists, union workers and leftist intellec-tuals were arrested, tortured and shot, their heads kept in cages hung on telegraph poles along the streets.[75]

On 16 April, Chiang and his Guomindang established a new gov-ernment, based at Nanjing further inland. From there, he continued the White Terror in Shanghai, which he called a 'purification'. It was carried out 'with the help of local labour unions and chambers of commerce [which] disarmed the Red labour pickets and kept Com-munist saboteurs under surveillance'.[76] When the worst excesses came to a halt in August, it was estimated that over 5000 leftists, commu-nists, members of the Guomindang 'left wing' and other activists—real or imagined—had been killed by the police and Green Gang mobsters.[77]

In the midst of it all sat Big-Eared Du, directing this army of hoodlums from his luxury residence in the French Concession and receiving congratulatory messages from the Chamber of Commerce. To the business community, the gangsters were 'national saviours', and Du was a hero. He drew closer to the Guomindang government and to politics. In 1929 he founded his own bank—the Chung Wai Bank—and later became director of the Shanghai Stock Exchange, several commodities exchanges and a string of established financial institutions. He also sat on the board of the Shanghai Bankers Association, the Shanghai Chamber of Commerce, the Bank of China, the French Municipal Council and the Chinese branch of the Red Cross. But more precisely, his alliance with Chiang Kai-shek ensured his position as the undisputed overlord of Shanghai's underworld[78]—not bad for a barely literate, opium-smoking street urchin from the slums of Pudong.

But as Chinese history has shown time and again, the secret societies have served as vehicles for upward social mobility even for the dispossessed and the outcast—and, from time to time, politicians have found it expedient to use their forces for their own ends. 'The mandarin [Chinese official in the imperial period] derives his power from the law, the people from the secret societies' goes an old Chinese proverb.[79] Despite elaborate rituals and secret initiation ceremonies, the Green and Red Gangs, as well as other secret societies, were neither philosophical-religious groups like the Freemasons and the Rosicrucians, nor outright criminal societies like the Mafia. In a Chinese context, the secret societies should be seen as a phenomenon, not as properly organised groups, or even disorderly gangs of street thugs.

Secret societies have been part of Chinese history and folklore for almost a thousand years. One of the oldest, the White Lotus Society, was founded by monks and scholars in the twelfth century and played an important role in the struggle against Mongol occupation in the thirteenth and fourteenth centuries. Zhu Yuanzhang, who eventually drove out the Mongols in 1368 and established the native Ming Dynasty, was probably a leading member of the White Lotus.[80] When the Manchus ascended the throne in Beijing in the mid-seventeenth century, and established another 'foreign' dynasty—the Qing—the White Lotus Society organised several insurrections in the hope of restoring the Ming.

The White Lotus combined in its dogma and rites Buddhist ceremonies, Confucian virtues and Taoist beliefs in sacred numbers, the correspondence between colours and the points of the compass. But the entire history of China's fabled secret societies is a blend of fact and legend, often more legend than fact. And nowhere is that more obvious than in the story of the formation and evolution of the *Tiandihui*, or 'the Heaven and Earth Society', to which most modern Triads, or Chinese gangster bands, trace their origins.

According to the legend, a barbarian tribe called the Xi Lu rebelled in the 1670s during the reign of Kangxi, the second Qing Emperor. He promised a reward of 10 000 ounces of gold to anyone who could defeat them. The Buddhist monks of the Shaolin monastery—sometimes placed in the Jiulian Mountains of Fuzhuo prefecture in Fujian, sometimes in the Zhongshan Mountains in Hunan or other locations—took up the challenge. The monks, who were also martial arts masters, killed so many Xi Lu soldiers that their bodies filled the mountain streams and created a river of blood. Within three months, the foreign invasion had been repelled without the monks losing a single soldier or weapon.

But the Manchu Emperor suspected that the victorious monks, inflated with pride because of their victory, might rebel against his rule as well. He invited all 128 monks at Shaolin to an imperial banquet in their own monastery, where they were offered wine which contained drugs to put them to sleep. At midnight, 3000 palace guards set fire to the monastery. One hundred and ten monks burned to death, but the eighteen who were still alive ran to the back hall, where they knelt down to implore the gods of Heaven and Earth to save them. High in the clouds appeared the Damo Buddha, the founder of the Zen sect of Buddhism, and then a road suddenly cut through the fire. They managed to escape, but the Emperor's troops set after the monks. Another thirteen of them were killed. The five surviving monks made it to the Gaoxi temple in Shicheng county, Huizhou prefecture in Guangdong, and settled there.

The gods had not abandoned them. When the monks reached the sea, they fainted from hunger. When they awoke, they saw an object float to the water's surface. It was a white ingot-shaped incense burner. They did not think much of its significance, but that night the burner glimmered in brightness, and the monks could see that on its bottom were the four characters *Fan-Qing Fu-Ming*: 'Crush the Qing, Restore the Ming'. They were very happy, and swore a blood oath of loyalty. 'The Qing Emperor is not just,' the monks declared, 'he turned our gratitude into revenge by burning the Shaolin monastery to the ground and killing our monks. We are now raising troops to get our revenge.'[81]

While they were discussing the matter, a boy in his early teens showed up unexpectedly. According to one version of the legend, 'his face was like peach fuzz, his lips like rouge; his two ears extended to his shoulders, and his two hands to his knees. He had all the appearances of royal and noble bearing'.[82] The youth declared that he intended to join the monks' army. Perplexed, they asked: 'You are so young, you don't have any weapons with you, yet you dare to come join the army. What special ability do you have?'. The boy replied: 'I am no other than the grandson of Emperor Chongzhen, son of the Western Palace Concubine Li Shen and the crown prince. Seeing that the country of my great ancestors was being invaded by Qing beasts, if I am not able to recover the Central Plain, how will I be able to face my ancestors in the other world?'.

This hitherto unknown descendant of the last Ming Emperor eventually starved himself to death, but the five monks went to Muyang, the imaginary City of Willows, which seems to have been another name for Paradise. There they founded a secret society to lead an uprising against the Manchu emperors of the Qing Dynasty. These monks—Cai, Fang, Ma, Hu and Li—became known as 'the Five Ancestors', and vowed, to the death, to avenge the injustice done to them. Their brotherhood was the beginning of the Tiandihui, or the Heaven and Earth Society, which was later to spread its tentacles all over China and the world.

Its various offshoots became known as Hong Men, or the Hong Gates. ('Hong' referred to 'Hongwu', the reign title of the first Ming Emperor, Zhu Yuanzhang.) Entering 'the Hong Gates', or sometimes 'the City of Willows', has become synonymous with going through the increasingly Masonic initiation rites of the secret society. The popular name 'Triad' was first coined by Dr William Milne, principal of the Anglo-Chinese College in Malacca, who in 1821 wrote the first systematic account of what was also known as the 'Three Unities Society'.[83]

To these tightly knit brotherhoods, bound together by almost religious rituals in order to avoid betrayal by fellow members of the group, the number three was of central significance. Numerologically, it was a magic number. Three multiplied by three equals nine and any number whose digits add up to nine is divisible by nine. To the Chinese, three was also the mystical number denoting the balance between Heaven, Earth and Man. Each society, or lodge of a larger society, became headed by a *shan zhu*, or Mountain Master, assisted by a *fu shan zhu*, or Deputy Mountain Master. These two men were frequently referred to as *da lao* (*tai lo* in Cantonese, a language more commonly spoken by the Triads), Elder Brother and *er lao* (*yee lo* in Cantonese), Second Elder Brother.[84]

After the two elder brothers came two officials of equal standing: the *xiang zhu* (*heung chu* in Cantonese) or Incense Master, and the *xian feng* (*sin fung*) or Vanguard. These two controlled the Rites Department of the society and were responsible for its elaborate initiation ceremonies. Every new member of the Triad society had—and to this day still has—to obey a series of 36 oaths. The penalty for breaking any one of these has, since the formation of the Tiandihui, been the same: death. The first pledge states solemnly—and menancingly—that 'after having entered the Hong Gates I must treat the parents and relatives of my sworn brothers as mine own kin. I shall suffer death by five hundred thunderbolts if I do not keep this oath'. (For a complete list of the 36 oaths see the Appendix on pp. 388–391.)

While those oaths and the organisational structure of the Triad are real, the creation myth is not. Recent research into the origin of the Tiandihui, or the Hong Men Society, based on original Qing Dynasty archives, shows that it was formed almost exactly a hundred years after the supposed burning of Shaolin, a monastery that probably never existed in real life. Nor did the original Triad society aspire to overthrow the Qing Dynasty, or have any other political aims.

The Tiandihui was first mentioned in official Chinese records in March 1787, when the Qing Dynasty had been in power for more than a century. In that year, the governor general of Guangdong reported to the Emperor in Beijing that they had interrogated a man called Xu Axie, who confessed to belonging to a secret society called 'Tiandihui', or 'Heaven and Earth'. Xu had been to Raoping County in Guangdong to buy yeast, but had been robbed of all his silver on the way. When he reached Raoping, the yeast seller told him: 'If you join the Tiandihui you can avoid being robbed on the road in the future, and I can also get back the silver that was robbed from you'.[85] Xu was told that if he encountered robbers while on the road, he should hold up the thumb as a signal for Heaven, and then the person about to rob him would point downwards with his little finger to indicate Earth.

The most detailed account came a year later, when the authorities in the southern coastal province of Fujian interrogated a cloth seller from Yunxiao township called Yan Yan. In his first statement before the Imperial Commissioner in the province, Yan Yan said that 'there is a kind of vagabond or travelling strongman who moves around creating disturbances and harassing the people . . . They all join the Tiandihui because, with its large number of followers, it gives them more advantage in conducting robbery. They rob anyone who is not a member of the society'.[86]

The Commissioner stated in his report to the Emperor that 'we have personally interrogated Yan Yan in a very severe way', and the culprit was sent to Beijing for further questioning. Grand Secretary He Shen of the Board of Punishment reported to the Emperor on 19 July 1788 that 'we, Your Officials, interrogated Yan Yan under torture to obtain a confession', and a remarkable tale followed. Yan Yan said that not only had he become a member of the Tiandihui, but that he had also helped establish a branch of it in Taiwan in 1783. The society, it transpired, had been founded in or around 1767 by Ti Xi, a monk, who together with his companion Ma Jiulong specialised in the practice of magic arts and the expulsion of ghosts.

Not much is known about Ti Xi other than that he was a leader of a band of 48 monks and resided in the Guanyinting, or Goddess of Mercy pavilion, in Gaoxi village in Zhangpu county of Fujian. He died in 1779, almost a decade before his activities came to the attention of Qing officials. On his deathbed, Ti Xi—who was also known as Zhang Kai, Monk Hong Er and Mong Wan—imparted the secrets of his society and the name of his followers to his son, Zheng Ji, and his band lived on and expanded to other places in Fujian and neighbouring Guangdong province.[87]

Ti Xi was deeply influenced by a milieu in which secret societies were emerging all over Fujian. Zhangzhou, the southernmost of

Fujian's coastal prefectures, where Zhangpu is located, was a damp and vaporous area 'full of snakes and worms'.[88] The situation in Quanzhou, another prefecture trapped between the sea and the mountains further up the coast, was similar. Proximity to the sea gave rise to a highly commercialised, outward-looking trade culture. Foreign silver flowed into Fujian's coastal prefectures, but they were also hard hit by an inflationary cycle that pushed land prices to the highest levels in Fujian. The result was a mass emigration by the dispossessed which was so extensive that, as early as 1600, half of the Fujianese earned their living away from home.[89] That meant either in other provinces in China or, increasingly during the centuries to come, in Southeast Asia.

Conditions worsened during the Qing Dynasty, when the introduction of new crops such as peanuts, corn and sweet potatoes led to an unprecedented population growth and, indirectly, land scarcity and high rice prices. Zhangpu, the real birthplace of the Tiandihui, was especially hard hit and became known as a region where 'the land is barren and the people are poor'.[90] The situation was exacerbated by rising absentee landlordism and a large number of landless farmers. Many of those without land or other resources became priests, martial arts teachers, beggars, pirates, or thieves. According to a local saying, 'whenever people in Zhangzhou or Quanzhou got hungry, pirates emerged'.[91] Fujian had always been an unruly province, and Zhangzhou prefecture in particular was characterised as being *hua wai*, 'outside of civilisation'.

Others were pushed out of their traditional homeland, and crossed the sea to Taiwan, a huge, rugged island off the Fujian coast which was then populated by non-Chinese, Austronesian aboriginals. Because of Taiwan's location near the Chinese mainland and on the sea route to Japan, the Portuguese had established trading posts there in the sixteenth century. They called the island Ihla Formosa, 'Beautiful Island', but had to give up their bases there to the Dutch who in turn were driven out in 1661 by a Fujianese rebel called Zheng Chenggong. Better known as Koxinga, 'Lord of the Imperial Surname', he was a Ming loyalist and a member of a prominent Fujian trading family. When the Qing armies attacked his base in Amoy (Xiamen), he moved over to Taiwan, where he continued the resistance. Koxinga died at the early age of 38, but his family held on to

Taiwan. It was not until 1683 that the Qings succeeded in taking over Taiwan and converted the island into a prefecture of Fujian.

But central control over Taiwan was tenuous at best, and the island continued to serve as a safety valve for the overflow of mainlanders, mainly Fujianese, who for economic or political reasons were looking for a way out. In the mid-seventeenth century, the population of Taiwan was no more than 100 000; a century later it had increased to two million. Among those who stayed behind on the mainland, feuds between different lineages erupted, and the situation became so bad that, according to one report, 'in Tongan county, Quanzhou prefecture, and Zhangpu county, Zhangzhou prefecture, the lines of enmity have been drawn for many years. Grudges over murdered fathers and elder brothers are everywhere ... There is not one feud-free county in Quanzhou or Zhangzhou, nor is there one feud-free year.'[92]

Local semi-religious, syncretic sects called *shenminghui* often financed these feuds and allowed their temples to be used as bases for feud operations. Sworn brotherhoods were also used by both the elite and the commoners as vehicles through which to wage struggles for economic survival or political resistance, or both. Oaths were sealed by drinking a mixture of blood and wine, and it was in this wild and insecure frontier environment that the Tiandihui was born. Mutual aid, not politics or Ming restorationism, was the *raison d'être* for the Tiandihui as well as for many similar societies which emerged at about the same time.

Being a member of a strong secret society such as the Tiandihui had many advantages, especially for the dispossessed, the poor and other vulnerable elements of society. In a society where family or clan associations were well established as mutual-aid organisations, the Tiandihui provided similar services for dispossessed people with different surnames. Despite its millions of people, China has less than 150 surnames, and those indicate huge clans rather than families. Most clans have their own associations which look after the social needs of people with the same surname. But in times of upheaval and distress, many dispossessed people of different surnames formed sworn brotherhoods to protect their interests. Secret oaths and rituals then replaced actual family ties through the established clan system; the blood-and-wine-drinking ceremony was a substitute for real blood-ties.

Belonging to a secret society also made travel along roads and highways in the region safer. According to the testimony of Yan Yan, the cloth seller who was arrested in the 1780s:

> Originally, the reason for people's willingness to enter the society was that, if you had a wedding or a funeral, you could get help from the other society members; if you came to blows with someone, there were people who would help you. If you encountered robbers, as soon as they heard the secret code of their own society, they would then bother you no further.[93]

All secret societies practised armed robbery, the kidnapping of children for ransom and piracy. However, banditry was aimed mainly at the rich, the merchants, the landowners and the officials of the hated Manchu Qing dynasty. The societies operated under the slogan *Da-Fu Zhi-Pin*: 'strike at the rich and help the poor'.[94] They claimed to be based on a higher system of justice than the imperial state, and used religious symbolism to enhance their legitimacy among the ordinary people. Constant references to the magic qualities of various mountains related to Taoism, while the establishment of sworn brotherhoods of people with various surnames was deeply embedded in popular culture, as can be seen in two well-known tales from the Middle Ages: *The Romance of the Three Kingdoms* and *The Outlaws of the Marsh*. The latter especially, in which 108 (1+0+8=9) brigand-heroes from Liangshangpo organised a brotherhood of people with different surnames, inspired people to form a multitude of such societies. What made the Tiandihui different was that it transcended all the others in its magnitude, complexity and longevity.

As the society was expanding, it was impossible for one member to know all the others, so certain code words and secret gestures were developed to help them identify each other. The main password was 'five dot twenty-one', a split character code for 'Hong'. The most common gesture involved the use of the three middle fingers, which would be pointed towards heaven or pressed against the chest. Officials would use their thumb, which represented heaven, and the little finger, which stood for earth.[95] Such sign language also facilitated communication between members who spoke different dialects and could not interact verbally.

As soon as the Qing authorities learned about the existence of the Tiandihui, they decided to crush it once and for all. According to an imperial edict issued in 1646, blood-oath brotherhoods were illegal; if any of their members was caught, the punishment was severe. Those who had merely taken the oath were given 100 strokes of the heavy bamboo cane; more active members were executed. Rapacious officials now cracked down heavily on the Tiandihui, and several of its leaders were caught and executed.

The imperial government's attempts to wipe out the Tiandihui may have forced it to become more political in its fight for survival. The famous slogan *Fan-Qing Fu-Ming* was not coined by the monks at the Shaolin monastery in the seventeenth century, but first came into use in Triad parlance in the early nineteenth century. 'Ming Restorationism was more than a heroic echo of the past', argues American historian Frederic Wakeman. 'It gave the Triads political relevance, even providing a form of social respectability that put them a cut above gangsterism, thus the raising of a Ming banner provided its own illegitimate "legitimacy"'.[96]

The earliest known version of the legend of the fighting monks of Shaolin was found among the possessions of a Triad member in Guangxi, and sent to the Emperor in June 1811. Since then, six more versions of the same legend have been recorded. The details vary, but the theme is the same: a band of patriotic monks from Shaolin monastery were betrayed by the Qing Emperor and swore to fight to restore the Ming. It is impossible to know who invented this myth, but it served its purpose: the Tiandihui became a popular movement that claimed firm roots in Chinese history and tradition. It was also in the early nineteenth century that the name 'Hong Men'—another reference to Ming restorationism—became synonymous with the Triad, and the elaborate 36 oaths were introduced. Prior to that, initiation rites had been relatively simple, consisting of drinking a mixture of wine and blood, and making a few pledges in front of an altar where incense was burning.[97]

Although the original Triad—the Tiandihui and its many subgroups—remained the biggest and most powerful, it was by no means the only clandestine group of its kind. Remnants of the White Lotus were still active in various parts of China. Zheng Guancai, a native of Fujian, set up a group called the Small Sword Society, proclaiming itself 'the guardian of the countryside'. This meant it depended on people giving it small fees in exchange for 'protection'.[98] The Small Swords spread to Guangdong and Taiwan and, along with the Increase Brothers, the Ox Heads, the Double Swords and the Golden Coins, also claimed to be Ming loyalists.

By the mid-nineteenth century, secret societies—and especially the Tiandihui and its offshoots—had spread to wherever the Chinese, and the Fujianese in particular, went. Chapters and lodges were established all over southern China, in Taiwan and in Southeast Asia, where large numbers of dispossessed Chinese had migrated. Many Chinese who found themselves adrift in an alien environment endeavoured, through the rituals of sworn brotherhoods, to create pseudo-familial networks as a basis for interacting with other communities.[99]

However, the various societies did not have any kind of centralised organisation. Each of the lodges, no matter where it was located, used the same nomenclature, oaths and rituals as lodges elsewhere, had its own mountain master and incense master, and initiated its own members. Rivalry was often bitter, and it is more accurate to speak of 'the Triads' rather than 'the Triad', even when considering the original Tiandihui. French scholar Jean Chesneaux argues that:

> this factionalism contributed greatly to the Triad's degeneration into purely criminal gangs . . . in 1854, in Singapore, two offshoots of the Triad, the Ghee Hin Society (formed of Cantonese) and the Ghee Hok (made up of emigrants from Fukien [Fujian]) met in a series of bloody street battles which claimed several dozen victims.[100]

Tiandihui and other Triad-style organisations also served as a vehicle for rebellion. The Nanjing Treaty of 1842, with the accompanying loss of Hong Kong and the opening of Shanghai, Ningbo, Amoy, Fuzhou and Guangzhou to international trade, gave the secret societies a new field of action—and an excellent opportunity to demonstrate their patriotism. Insurrections led by the Tiandihui broke out in Guangzhou and, at dawn on 7 September 1853, the Small Sword Society attacked Shanghai. Wearing badges of red cloth on their jackets and caps, they gutted the magistrate's office, killed the magistrate, and liberated the prisoners in a nearby gaol. 'They walk about without the least fear; no one molests them, and they abstain from plunder', the English-language *North China Herald* reported.[101] On all the city gates, the Small Swords posted proclamations announcing the restoration of the Ming, and their leaders assumed honorary titles in the name of the dynasty.

For two years, the Small Swords managed to hold on to Shanghai. The westerners, who had at first adopted a wait-and-see attitude, eventually threw in their lot with the Emperor's forces, and launched a joint military operation against the rebels. Lin Li-ch'uan, the Cantonese commander of the Small Swords, was killed trying to resist the final assault on the city on 15 February 1855.

Shanghai was safe, but in the surrounding countryside another secret society-led rebellion was raging. In 1851, founders of the Heavenly Kingdom of Great Peace—*Taiping tianguo*—organised scattered groups of bandits, pirates and other outlaws in the most serious threat so far to the authority of the Qing.

The initiative came from Hong Xiuquan, a visionary, shaman and failed candidate in the imperial examinations, who presented himself as the younger brother of Jesus. Taiping forces marched north on a crusade to bring the whole of China under the Heavenly Kingdom. They captured Nanjing, only 280 kilometres inland from Shanghai, and introduced new egalitarian concepts, including equality for women and a sweeping land reform. Harvests were gathered into 'heavenly granaries' to be distributed equally to everybody. But rivalry and dissension among the leadership led to fierce infighting among the followers of the Kingdom. Tens of thousands of Taiping soldiers were killed in the internecine strife, and the Emperor took advantage of the weakened state of the movement and crushed it in 1864. Hong Xiuquan died of illness—some say he committed suicide—and many of his men reverted to banditry.

But the China of the Manchu Qing dynasty was getting weaker. Defeat in the Opium Wars against Britain was followed by another humiliating debacle in a war against Japan in 1894–95. Korea, a semi-autonomous peninsula over which the Chinese claimed suzerainty, was captured and, under the Treaty of Shimonoseki in 1895, Beijing was forced to cede the island of Taiwan to Japan. China also agreed to recognise the independence of Korea, although this was actually the beginning of Japanese colonial rule over the peninsula. China was being carved up by various colonial powers; central authority was breaking down as economic depression, famine and banditry swept across the countryside.

To many Chinese, the foreigners—especially the Christians who had undermined Confucian belief and authority—were to blame. A wave of xenophobia spread across China. In 1898, the Yellow River burst its banks and caused disastrous flooding in several provinces. Most rural Chinese were deeply superstitious, and to them the floods were proof that the foreigners had even interfered with nature.[102] Encouraged by several provincial governors, and especially by Cixi, the Empress Dowager during the last years of the Qing Dynasty and the country's *de facto* ruler for several decades, a secret society called Yihequan—the Fists of Righteousness and Harmony—began attacking foreigners, and signs of foreign influence, all over northern China. Dressed in brightly coloured clothing and wearing headbands with Chinese characters and religious amulets to protect them from 'foreign bullets', their battle cry was *sha! sha!* ('kill'! 'kill'!).[103] Entire Christian families, including children, were hacked to death with swords. Churches and railway stations were burned, factories ransacked and telegraph lines cut. Then the Fists marched on Beijing.

On 13 June 1901, the rebels laid siege to the foreign legation quarter in Beijing, which was defended by 340 British, American, Russian, French, Italian and Japanese troops. But since the defenders had firearms, and the rebels only swords, the latter were kept at bay until an expeditionary force of 8000 Japanese, 4800 Russian, 3000 British, 2100 American and smaller numbers of French, Austrian and Italian troops arrived. On 14 August, the siege was finally lifted, and the Empress Dowager and her court fled to Xi'an. She was not allowed to return to Beijing until China had agreed to pay the equivalent of £67 million in reparations over the next 40 years. The Empress Dowager herself was spared, but other officials deemed guilty of involvement in the uprising were brought to court, and several were executed. China's defences were also downgraded, and the imperial court had to agree to let the foreigners station troops in the country permanently.

The Fists of Righteousness and Harmony—or 'the Boxers', as most foreigners called them—were an offshoot of the Eight Trigrams sect, which traced its origin back to the White Lotus Society. Some of their branches were also known as the Big Sword Society—not to be confused with the Small Swords—and gained a reputation for viciousness and strong anti-foreign sentiments. Although the society was used by powerful interests in Beijing in a vain attempt to drive out the foreigners, most of its followers came from the poor peasantry of North China who had suffered from the floods. It also had a strong appeal to the boatmen who had been ruined by the decline in traffic on the Grand Canal in northern China as goods were increasingly being transported by sea, and by foreign ships. Like the founders of the Tiandihui, the members came from marginal elements of rural China and saw themselves as heroes, engaged in a ceaseless struggle against injustice on behalf of the poor, the oppressed and the dispossessed.

Of the two main leaders of the Boxers, one—Zheng Dezhang—was a former boatman, and the other—Zhao Futian—was an ex-soldier who had become unemployed when his unit was disbanded. And their followers did not just include men: special units of girls aged from twelve to eighteen years, called the Red Lanterns and the Blue Lanterns, operated under the command of Huanglian Shengmu, the 'Sacred Mother of the Yellow Lotus'. She too came from a family of boatmen and claimed to possess magic powers.[104]

It was not only the Empress Dowager who realised the revolutionary potential of the secret societies, and the courage and dedication of their members. At the same time, Sun Yat-sen was plotting to overthrow the Chinese Empire and establish his Republic. One of his closest lieutenants, a young Cantonese named Zheng Shiliang, was the son of a wealthy merchant, who is said to have been ruined by an unscrupulous official of the Qing administration and to have died as a result of his misfortune.

Zheng's hatred of officialdom flamed Sun's already smouldering discontent at the misrule of the increasingly corrupt Qing administration. Zheng was also a member of the Tiandihui, and discussed with Sun the possibility of mobilising its members in their struggle for a new China.[105] Eventually, Zheng collected as many as 10 000 Triad supporters as they gathered on Taiwan at the turn of the century, awaiting shipments of arms and ammunition from abroad. The Japanese, who now controlled Taiwan, sympathised with Sun and his movement, but suddenly had a change of heart. They now forbade the supply of munitions to the revolutionaries, and the attempt at an uprising failed.

Sun's interest in the Tiandihui stemmed not only from his friendship with Zheng. He had discovered its strength during his years in exile in Honolulu, Hong Kong, Macau and London, where he had organised resistance against the Qing from abroad. In the Straits Settlements—the British colonies of Singapore, Malacca and Penang—the authorities believed that up to nine-tenths of the population of several hundred thousand Chinese were Triad members. Likewise, almost 90 per cent of the Chinese in the United States—or nearly 80 000 people—belonged to a chapter or lodge known as the *Zhigongtang*. Sun was told that, if he expected to receive contributions from the American Chinese, he had better join one of the lodges himself; he did so almost immediately after his arrival in the United States.[106] On 30 November 1905, Sun travelled to Tokyo where he convened a conference with revolutionaries from all over China. They set up the *Tongmenghui*, or 'United League', which became the nucleus of modern Chinese nationalism.

Within China, Sun's revolutionaries concluded that their most dependable allies would also be the Tiandihui, as well as the Small Swords Society and the allied Elder Brothers Society. But they soon found out that local organisations inside China had their own agendas and were not much interested in driving out the Manchus. *Fan-Qing Fu-Ming* was an empty slogan—but Sun now began to over-emphasise that aspect of the Triad's legend in order to create a stronger anti-Manchu consciousness among its members. Other revolutionaries, such as Sun's contemporary and competitor Tao Changzhang, also began to revive the legend of the monks of Shaolin monastery and their alleged resistance against the Manchus to mobilise the people.

In the end, it was not the Tiandihui but the power of social groups that had developed in the last twenty years of the Qing Dynasty—the tiny, new urban middle-class, a fairly modern-minded gentry and a fledgling new regular army—that took the final step and overthrew the Qing. On the evening of 10 October 1911, units of the New Army based in Wuchang—a part of the modern city of Wuhan on the banks of the Yangzi river—mutinied and took over their garrison. The next day, they seized the city and declared themselves independent of Beijing. The date of this initial rising, the tenth day of the tenth month, or Double Tenth, became the National Day of the republic that was established on 1 January 1912 with Sun Yat-sen as its first president. On 12 February, Henry Pu Yi, the last Emperor, abdicated, ending the rule of the Manchu Qing Dynasty. In August of that year, the Tongmenghui absorbed four smaller parties to become the Guomindang, China's most powerful political party at the time.

The Qing had been overthrown but the Ming had not been restored—and Sun's dream of turning China into Asia's first modern, democratic state died with him in 1925. Under Chiang Kai-shek's new regime, military might reigned supreme. Republican China was still trying to find a common identity after the fall of the last of the dynasties that had ruled the country successively for thousands of years. Chiang was unable to govern the country effectively—and certainly not without help from the secret societies, as the events of 1927 in Shanghai had shown. Just as would happen in Russia after the fall of the Soviet regime many years later, only organised crime had managed to survive the collapse of the old order, and would profit from the disarray of the new one.

The Green Gang became in many ways China's first 'modern' secret society. It followed the same quasi-Masonic rituals as the old societies, and the hierarchical order was similar. But it was an urban-based gang which lent its services to a modern political force—nationalist republicanism—against a leftist labour movement that threatened both the gangsters and the government. It was also the first Triad to get involved in the production and distribution of 'modern' drugs such as morphine and heroin.

At the turn of the century, morphine manufactured from opium produced in the Middle East entered China from Europe and the United States via Japan. To begin with, the addictive qualities of morphine were not recognised. Western missionaries in China used it to cure opium addiction, which earned it the name 'Jesus Opium'. When it was discovered in the 1920s that morphine was even more dangerous than opium, western powers stopped its export to China. But Japanese underworld figures—who were more often than not connected with that country's security services—began to sell it in China and even to manufacture it there.[107]

Heroin was first produced in 1874 by a British scientist, C.R. Wright, who boiled morphine and acetic anhydride over a stove. But tests on dogs soon convinced Wright that it was a dangerous drug, not a useful medicine. Nevertheless, 20 years later, German researchers decided that it was an excellent treatment for almost everything from pain and anger to sorrow and depression. In 1898, the Bayer chemical cartel of Germany began marketing heroin as 'the sedative for coughs', and it was an instant success.[108] In the United States it soon became one of the most popular patent medicines on the market. But, as was the case with morphine, it turned out to be highly addictive and to have devastating side-effects. In 1924, the United States banned the import and manufacture of heroin, and severe restrictions were imposed in Europe.

Those moves only drove the production underground—to China. The secret societies began to produce the drug in clandestine heroin laboratories in Shanghai and Tianjin. Among the buyers were Chinese warlords, European crime syndicates and American mafiosi like Charles 'Lucky' Luciano.' In the southern French port city of Marseilles, syndicates from the island of Corsica opened smaller laboratories which also produced the drug for the European market.[109]

In China, the Guomindang regime in Nanjing had set up an Opium Suppression Bureau, which seized raw opium from smaller merchants and peddlers. The seized goods were handed over to Big-Eared Du's Three Prosperities Company for refinement into heroin.[110] The new drug—and a cheaper version called 'Red Pills'—became immensely popular among many people in Shanghai. A special subsidiary company, the Yah Kee (Xiaji in *pinyin*), was set up to run heroin factories in Shanghai's south market. Business was so lucrative that Big-Eared Du enlisted the support of the Guomindang's finance minister, T.V. Soong—an immensely wealthy banker who was also the eldest son of Chinese Nationalist-Christian patriarch Charlie Soong—to get military protection for his laboratories.[111]

The new French police chief, Lieutenant Colonel Louis Fabre, was less than pleased with these developments, which were going too far even by the freewheeling standards of the French Concession. Unlike his predecessors, Fabre was said to be incorruptible, and he tried to have the Three Prosperities Company removed from the Concession. A bitter conflict ensued, with Big-Eared Du finally orchestrating a strike in the French Tramways Company, timed for the week before

Bastille Day 1932 to maximise its impact on the French authorities.[112] After a few manoeuvres and back-door negotiations, the situation in the French Concession was again depressingly normal.

Part of the problem was that no government was in a position to effectively curb the influence of the Green Gang. Like the original Tiandihui, the Green Gang began as a mutual aid organisation among the lower strata of society. In this case, it was the boatmen on the Grand Canal, who were organised into several *bang* ('fleet' or 'gang') to look after their interests. The decline in traffic on the Canal in the mid-1850s, as goods were increasingly being transported by sea, put 50 000 boatmen out of work. This had led to the formation of the militant Yihequan, or the Boxers, and others joined existing secret societies, among them the Green Gang.

Exactly how the Green Gang—or Qing Bang—got its name is not entirely clear, but by the end of the nineteenth century it was well-established in Tianjin and Shanghai. Before the 1911 revolution, the rival Red Gang—or Hong Bang—was also active in the same cities. But, thanks to Chiang Kai-shek's underground mentor, Chen Qimei, the two gangs merged, and it became common to refer to the two groups in a single name: *Qing Hong Bang*, the Green-Red Gang. Both groups claimed they had their origins in the Tiandihui, which may have been the case as far as the rituals, the incense halls and the blood oaths—and the legends—were concerned. But whether that was true did not matter; the two societies—and the Taiping rebels and the Boxers—had emerged under circumstances similar to the original Triad.

For the hundreds of thousands of migrants from all parts of China who flocked to Shanghai, the Green Gang provided a sense of belonging to a powerful fraternity in a new and alien environment. The Gang could also arrange jobs, housing, women and opium. And, in case regular employment was scarce, the Gang itself always needed robbers, kidnappers, drug peddlers and various helpers at its brothels. The Shanghai gangsters transferred to this mixed Sino-foreign urban environment the rural bandits' classic strategy of establishing 'lairs' in the no-man's land between two or more county or prefectural administrations. Shanghai had become an urban version of Liang-shanpo—the hideout and stronghold of the Chinese 'Robin Hoods', as described in the Ming Dynasty novel *The Outlaws of the Marsh*, which had inspired the legend behind the first Tiandihui.[113] At least 20 000 people—some say as many as 100 000—in Shanghai pledged their loyalty to Big-Eared Du and Pock-Marked Huang.[114]

The campaign against the communists also continued with intense vigour. The White Terror of 1927 had forced the communists to leave the city for the countryside. The communists had to change strategy; what they had thought would be an urban revolution, led by the working class, became a peasant rebellion—not unlike other struggles in the rural hinterland throughout China's long and turbulent history. In August 1927 Mao Zedong and his trusted Sichuan-born comrade Zhu De formed the Workers' and Peasants' Red Army to fight the Guomindang. The Chinese Civil War had begun.

In the countryside, it was often impossible to tell so-called political actions from outright banditry; it was hard to tell who was, or had been, a government soldier, and who belonged to the army of a local chieftain. People were living in mortal terror of disbanded soldiers, plundering warlords and bandits. Tinko Pawley, a young English-woman who herself was kidnapped by bandits in the early 1930s near her home in Niuzhuang in Manchuria, tells that if the bandits suspected anyone of having hidden money, they would light a fire under the household's copper cauldron, and 'then put the poor old grandfather or grandmother naked into the blazing cauldron and burn them until they confessed the hiding-place of the family's savings'.[115]

Wealthy Chinese were often abducted, and brigands would slice off the fingers and ears of their victims and send the grisly tokens to relatives as a hint to pay the ransom speedily. Pawley mentions one case in which the young son of a Chinese merchant had been kidnapped. In due course, a letter was sent by the bandits demanding a preposterous sum of money. The father replied that it was impossible for him to raise the ransom. About a week later, a maimed old beggar arrived at the merchant's house with a basket which he said he had been told to deliver. Upon opening it, the merchant discovered the dismembered and mutilated body of his child.[116]

In these circumstances, it was perhaps hardly surprising that the well-disciplined soldiers of the Red Army stood out as an ideal. What their political commissars preached—human rights, equality and an end to tyranny—made communism seem like a shortcut to utopia.

In October 1934, Mao Zedong and Zhu De, along with 100 000 soldiers, cadres and supporters, left their first stronghold in Jiangxi and marched north. It became the longest military march in history, covering more than 9000 kilometres across twelve provinces. In January 1935, the 20 000 or so survivors reached the northern province of Shaanxi where they set up a new base area in Yan'an. Peasant leaders, underground labour activists, intellectuals, writers and many others flocked to Yan'an, which became a revolutionary bastion exemplifying the promise of a new order, and the hope of release from servitude and economic bondage.

But not even the communists could ignore the secret societies, which were as much a part of China's political and social heritage as the mandarins and the imperial tax collectors. This became especially clear when Japan began to encroach on northern China in the early 1930s. The Japanese war machine was expanding its influence over Manchuria, which in 1932 became a nominally independent puppet state, with Henry Pu Yi—the last ruler of the Qing Dynasty—as its 'Emperor'. In the same year, Japanese forces also marched into Shanghai. In 1937 they bombed the city, and went on to occupy Nanjing, where over 100 000 civilians were slaughtered in one of history's worst blood baths, and women and girls were systematically raped by Japanese soldiers.

The communists and the Guomindang had to unite to fight the Japanese, and a second United Front was formed. But help was needed from other quarters too, and in a surprisingly candid appeal to one of the most powerful of the secret societies—the *Gelaohui*, or the Society of Elder Brothers—Mao Zedong himself stated:

> Following its principles—*Fan-Qing Fu-Ming*: 'Crush the Qing, Restore the Ming', *Da-Fu Zhi-Pin*, 'strike at the rich and help the poor'—the Gelaohui participated actively in the anti-Manchu revolutionary movement of 1911. The revolution in northern Shaanxi has also benefitted from the Gelaohui. Comrades such as Xie Zichang or Liu Zhidan are not only leaders of the Red Army; they are also exemplary members of the Gelaohui. This revolutionary spirit, these glorious feats, must be manifested even more widely in today's heroic struggle to save the country and save ourselves . . . The Gelaohui has always been representative of the organisations of the resolute men of our nation, and of the broad masses of peasants and toilers. It has constantly been

the victim of the oppression of the militarists and bureaucrats; its members have been considered 'inferior people' or calumnied as bandits, and it was denied a legal existence . . . The Soviet Government is the government of the oppressed people in China. We have the responsibility to receive and to protect all those who are persecuted and threatened with arrest by the Guomindang government. Consequently, the Gelaohui can exist legally under the Chinese soviet government . . . We proclaim loudly:

> Show the revolutionary spirit that characterised the Gelaohui in the past!
> Let the Gelaohui and the whole of the Chinese people unite to strike at Japan and to restore China!
> Long live the liberation of the Chinese people![117]

Many members of the Gelaohui had actually already joined the Communist Party. Some of their names were inadvertently revealed by westerners, who sympathised with Mao Zedong, but probably did not fully understand the complexities of China's underground movements. These foreigners had become involved in the communist struggle via the party's front organisations in Shanghai. Among them were not only Rewi Alley from New Zealand, but also George Hatem, a doctor from Buffalo, New York, who later joined the Red Army and gained the name Ma Haide, and Agnes Smedley, a young American woman who had been a dedicated Marxist since her teens.

Born in a small mining town in Colorado, Smedley was officially the Shanghai correspondent for the German paper *Frankfurter Zeitung*, but actually worked as an agent for the Communist International, the Comintern. She was very close to China's communist leaders and wrote in her classic biography of Zhu De, the founder of the Red Army and one of the leaders of the Long March:

Foreign and Chinese reactionaries charged that the cell system of the Chinese Communist Party was an alien idea imported from Russian Bolsheviks. When I mentioned this, General Zhu dismissed it as stupid if not a deliberate fabrication . . . The cell system, he said, was as old as the Chinese secret societies.[118]

Zhu had begun his revolutionary career as a Great Elder of a Gelaohui lodge in Sichuan before the 1911 revolution, fighting against the imperial government. The new viceroy of the nearby Yunnan province, Li Ching-hsi, had organised an extensive espionage network against the republican revolutionaries, and Zhu realised that only the secret societies would be able to provide him and his men with the protection they needed. Zhu's initiation took place among a gathering of people at an isolated monastery in the mountains of Sichuan, where he went through the ancient rituals—including kowtowing to the deities and taking the blood oath. Zhu and the members of the society cut a vein in their wrists and let a few drops of their blood fall into a bowl of rice wine. The bowl was passed around and all the participants in the ceremony had to take a sip. Next, Zhu pledged 'deathless loyalty to the society's principles of brotherhood, equality, and mutual aid. He then learned the signs and passwords by which society members can, to the present day, identify one another anywhere'.[119] Apart from Zhu De, party stalwarts He Long, another general in the Red Army, and Liu Zhidan, a peasant leader who joined the communists during the Long March, were also former secret society members.

Mao had recognised the importance of secret societies as early as 1926, when he analysed the class structure of Chinese society:

> The yu-min [rural vagrants] consist of peasants who have lost all opportunity of employment as a result of oppression and exploitation by the imperialists, the militarists and the landlords, or as a result of floods and droughts. They can be divided into soldiers, bandits, robbers, beggars and prostitutes . . . They have secret organisations in various places: for instance, the Triad Society [Tiandihui] in Fujian and Guangdong; the Gelaohui in Hunan, Hubei, Guizhou and Sichuan; the Big Sword Society in Anhui, Hunan and Shandong; the Society of Morality [Observance Society] in Jilin and the three northeastern provinces; the Green Gang in Shanghai and elsewhere . . . These people are capable of fighting very bravely, and if properly led can become a revolutionary force.[120]

Mao was especially interested in the Gelaohui—and also in a society called the Red Spears, which in many parts of the country served as local home guards, protecting local villagers against other bandit gangs and rampaging warlord armies.[121]

The struggle against Japan also encouraged Chiang Kai-shek and the Chinese Nationalists to once again praise the secret societies. The war years spawned a spate of Tiandihui-related popular books that emphasised the patriotic contributions of the societies. The fighting monks of Shaolin were portrayed as heroes, and the relationship of the Tiandihui to Sun Yat-sen and the Guomindang was also high-lighted.[122]

The reliability of the mobsters as allies to either the communists or the Guomindang was, however, questionable. While some of them took part in the guerrilla war against the Japanese, others became col-laborators. A pro-Japanese puppet regime, set up in Nanjing in 1940 and led by a once-respected Guomindang leader, Wang Jingwei, also relied on the support of the secret societies. Wang himself supported the 'Hong Society of the Five Continents', which claimed the cel-ebrated name of the original Triad, the Tiandihui.[123] In Hong Kong, which the Japanese occupied in 1941, various offshoots of the Triad assisted in maintaining order, and reported anti-Japanese activities to the new masters of the colony. According to former Hong Kong police officer W.P. Morgan:

> The local societies in Hong Kong were perfectly willing to collaborate because they were thus invested with power over the ordinary citizen, and also because the Japanese favoured and shared in the open organisation of prostitution, narcotics, and gambling which were the main sources of Triad revenue.[124]

The war forced Chiang Kai-shek to move his administration to Chongqing, deep in the mountainous Sichuan province. This became the new Guomindang 'capital'—and from there, Chiang continued to direct his fight against the Japanese, vigorously assisted by the United States and the Allies. But more money was needed and, luckily for Chiang's government, it had a store of Sichuan opium, seized during the anti-narcotics campaign in the early 1930s. Big-Eared Du, who had followed Chiang up to Chongqing, took charge of shipping the opium to the coast through his clandestine network of Green Gang contacts. The opium was eventually sold in Hong Kong and Macau, with some going to Japan's new opium monopoly in Shanghai.[125]

With Du came another prominent mobster from Shanghai, Dai Li, the leader of the 'special services' section of the so-called 'Blue Shirts', an anti-Communist organisation that had helped secure

Guomindang—and Green Gang—control over the city's labour unions.[126] During the anti-Japanese resistance, Dai Li became head of Chiang Kai-shek's secret service, and was described by an American observer as 'China's combination of Himmler and J. Edgar Hoover'.[127] He was known to be totally ruthless and one of Shanghai's most unsavoury characters. Among his other misdeeds, Dai Li invented a new and efficient method of killing Chiang's enemies. He would line up some locomotives on a siding, get the fireboxes red hot, open their doors, tie down the whistles to shut out the screams, and one after another throw his living victims into the blasting furnaces. In this way, thousands of labour leaders, students and intellectuals were killed in a few days.[128]

The US officer in charge of this peculiar bastion of Allied resistance to tyranny was the legendary General 'Vinegar Joe' Stilwell. Assisted by Guomindang troops and workers and engineers from the British Empire, Stilwell had built a road from India across northern Burma to Yunnan, a distance of over 1000 kilometres, to supply the Chinese forces in their fight against Japan. T.V. Soong, the Guomindang finance minister and also a close associate of Du, built a western-style residence for Stilwell on the edge of the Jialing River near the command headquarters at Chongqing. It had a roof terrace with flowers and a pool, and a magnificent view of the river. Dai Li supplied the servants who looked after Stilwell when he retreated to this odd edifice in the southern Chinese mountains.

The building also served as headquarters for the informal Sino-American Cooperation Organisation (SACO), headed by Dai Li with a US navy officer, Major (later Admiral) Milton E. Miles, as his deputy.[129] Miles, in his days at the Naval Academy, was also called 'Mary', after a movie star named Mary Miles.[130] Milton Miles had been sent to China to prepare the coast for a later landing by the US Navy and, in the meantime, 'to find out what's going on there'.[131] What that was supposed to mean was uncertain, but he ended up going native in the mountains of Sichuan with Du and other gangsters from Shanghai. SACO carried out sabotage behind Japanese lines in China—and, with the help of the Green Gang network, numerous real and imagined collaborators were assassinated in broad daylight inside Shanghai.[132]

Dai Li was so ruthless, however, that even Stilwell began to have second thoughts about the regime he was relying on in the anti-Japanese war. He felt there was something fundamentally wrong with the way in which the United States had manoeuvred itself 'into the position of having to support this rotten regime'.[133] According to historian Barbara Tuchman, Stilwell felt that his closest ally curiously mirrored what the United States was fighting against in Germany: 'a one-party government, supported by a Gestapo [Dai Li's organisation] and headed by an unbalanced man with little education'.[134] Nevertheless, Stilwell did lead Chiang Kai-shek's army into Burma at a later stage in the war, the wisdom of which was seriously questioned by his British allies at the time.

'Mary' Miles and the other like-minded 'cowboys' in the US armed forces were certainly less scrupulous about their connections, and thought more highly of the controversial Guomindang leader. When Stilwell, during a discussion among US commanders, said that Chiang was 'a vacillating tricky undependable old scoundrel who never keeps his word', a fellow US general, Claire Chennault, retorted: 'Sir, I think the Generalissimo is one of the two or three greatest military and political leaders in the world today. He has never broken a commitment or promise made to me'.[135]

Chennault had raised the famous Flying Tigers in China during the war, and later set up the Civil Air Transport (CAT), his own airline which supplied Chiang's troops when they were fighting Mao's communists—for as soon as the Japanese had been defeated in 1945, the Civil War between the Reds and the Guomindang began again. Big-Eared Du, Dai Li and 'Mary' Miles returned one after the other to Shanghai, where they tried to rebuild what had been lost during the war. On 25 October, the island of Taiwan was also formally returned to China after 50 years of Japanese rule.

The British were no longer pre-eminent in Shanghai; the Americans had taken over, and Miles wanted to show who was now the supreme foreign power in the city. The logo of the US Navy was hoisted on the Glen Line Building on The Bund. American servicemen were staying in the Cathay and Park Hotels, and journalists—mostly Americans—set up a meeting place for their Foreign Correspondents Club in the Broadway Mansions, overlooking the Garden Bridge on Suzhou Creek.

From his offices in the Glen Line Building, Miles was driven home in a highly unusual vehicle. It was an armoured car, which Big-Eared

Du had given to him, thinking that it would be fitting for his American friend. It weighed seven tonnes, and the glass in all the windows, front, side and back, was 100 per cent bulletproof. The interior venetian blinds were made of quarter-inch thick steel, and the slits along the top were for the barrels of Thompson submachine guns. It was a 1925 seven-passenger sedan, custom-made for Al Capone in Chicago, who had paid $20 000 for it. Du had taken over the vehicle from its former owner, the chief of police of Shanghai, who had been forced to leave the city because of his collaboration with the Japanese during their occupation.[136]

But the war was going badly for the Guomindang. The communist offensive began in earnest in the summer of 1948. Soon the Reds were closing in on Shanghai. The thuds of distant artillery were becoming heavier, the explosions nearer. Hundreds of military trucks and jeeps rumbled along the streets, most of them headed for the Jiangwan airfield, from where the passengers left for Taiwan. The communists were obviously winning the war and American policy was to give Taiwan to Chiang Kai-shek to enable him to reconquer the mainland. Taiwan, like Korea, could have become independent after the defeat of the Japanese. But instead it was 'reunited' with a country from which it had been separated since 1895—and before that it had only been loosely controlled by the central authorities. Taiwan was going to become Chiang Kai-shek's new fortress, a heavily armed and militarised island that Mao Zedong's armies would have had to pay an extremely heavy price to capture.

Two million mainlanders made it to Taiwan after the communist victory, but most of them came from parts of China other than Shanghai. The indifference of the cosmopolitan Shanghaiers to the outcome of the war was shown by the fact that it was only Chiang Kai-shek, his Guomindang followers and a few business associates who were bound for Taiwan. Most other local Chinese who wanted to leave the city fled to Hong Kong, Singapore and Malaya, where business opportunities were more abundant than on the then-impoverished island of Taiwan. 'The jokes being circulated at the time were all at the expense of Mao and Chiang,' Philippine consul Ezpeleta recalls. 'Songs and couplets were in vogue and these were not complimentary to either of them.'[137] One such song that swept the night clubs, dancing-halls and cafés was typical of the local fatalistic attitude. It was originally in Chinese, but its Shanghai English version became more popular:

Me no worry,
Me no care,
Me going to marry a millionaire;
And if he die,
Me no cry,
Me going to get another guy!

Most foreigners were leaving for Hong Kong, or returning home. Surprisingly, some of the Russians went back to the Soviet Union, but most of them no longer had any country (or city) they could call their own. The Geneva-based International Refugee Organisation approached the government of the Philippines, which gave the Russians temporary asylum on Guiuan island, near Samar, until arrangements could be made for them to migrate to other countries. They eventually ended up in Australia, New Zealand, Argentina, Chile, Bolivia and the United States.[138]

For those inhabitants who were relatively wealthy and who remained behind—mostly Chinese, but also a few foreigners who had been unable to leave—the winter of 1948–49 was turning into a nightmare. In August 1948, the Guomindang government had introduced a new currency, the gold yuan, which was pegged at four yuan to the US dollar. The government claimed that the new currency was stable, and demanded that the people surrender all their gold, silver and foreign currencies to the Central Bank of China for conversion into gold yuans. The government proclamation also stipulated that the penalty for non-compliance was confiscation and imprisonment.[139]

The government sat down and waited for the loot. 'Printing Press Yuan' would have been a more appropriate name for the new currency, which by the first week of January 1949 had gone down to more than 150 to the US dollar. By February, it was 750. In March, it had fallen to 3000, and on April Fool's Day one US dollar equalled 30 000 gold yuan. When Labour Day came it was difficult to buy a dollar for six million gold yuan.[140] The gold and silver which was supposed to back up the currency was already locked up in Chiang Kai-shek's vaults in Taiwan. Chiang's bank robbery was obviously well planned.

Chiang knew that he was not popular, but made some last attempts to show that, at the very least, he had some moral principles. He closed down the night clubs, the cabarets and the ballrooms and had them converted into barracks for his soldiers and hospitals for the wounded. If magnanimity was the motive, the move proved counter-productive. It put about 10 000 hostesses and dancing girls out of work—and they countered by preparing to stage a demonstration against the closure of the night spots. The planned mobilisation of the dancing girls from Ciro's Metropole, Majestic, Cosmos and Canidrome was called off only when Shanghai's police chief threatened to have them all arrested.[141]

In a last-ditch attempt to shore up his credibility, Chiang launched a crack-down on crime, which was spreading and making ordinary people's lives insecure. Petty gangsters and suspected communists were rounded up and sentenced to death in a matter of minutes. At the appointed time and place the victims were delivered in police cars with sirens and fire-bells ringing. Huge crowds gathered. The accused were told to kneel and, with a pistol shot at the nape, the execution was over.[142]

The most dramatic execution was that of Xiao Zhang, the 30-year-old chief of the 'Razor Clique', a band of hoodlums who liquidated their enemies with razor blades. Xiao Zhang was one of Shanghai's most feared underground bosses. He terrorised Shanghai for years, openly proclaiming that Al Capone was his hero. This might have annoyed Du, who thought of himself as Shanghai's Al Capone, and Xiao Zhang was arrested. When he was taken from Police Head-quarters at Fuzhou Road to the execution site in Nantao, an unusually big crowd gathered to watch the spectacle.

The car carrying the mobster was followed by three pedicabs. In the first two were crying, screaming women who were waving their arms in despair. In the third was a young, sobbing girl with her face buried in the embrace of a slightly older woman in her late twenties. The two screaming women were concubines Nos 1 and 2. The sobbing teenager was Xiao Zhang's last, and current favourite, concubine being consoled by his loving and understanding wife. At the execution, the three concubines fainted, while the wife, helpful to the last, revived them and took them home.[143]

Old Shanghai was dying, but, for reasons which were not entirely clear, Big-Eared Du decided not to join his political allies in exile on Taiwan. On 1 May, a limousine pulled out from his stately residence on Rue Wagner in the French Concession. Du was accompanied by his fourth and fifth wives, and they boarded a Dutch ship bound for Hong Kong. Before the steamer's foghorn sounded, Du caught a last glimpse of the confusion of ramshackle mud-houses in Pudong across the river where he had grown up. According to Lynn Pan, he 'had a stab of regret, seeing in a flicker of memory the sun striking the flaring roofs of his clan hall—that monument to all that he had won, and all that he was about to lose'.[144]

In Hong Kong, Du rented an apartment on Kennedy Road, and learned from newspaper reports which were read to him that the communists were taking over not only Shanghai but the whole of China. On 1 October 1949, before hundreds of thousands of people who had gathered outside the Gate of Heavenly Peace at the Imperial Palace in Beijing, Mao Zedong proclaimed the People's Republic of China, saying: 'Never again will the people of China be enslaved!'

When the first communist troops had entered Shanghai, people had indeed been struck by their discipline. The Red Soldier's manner was one of:

> uncommon gentleness and modesty; he was honest, courteous and incorruptible. No soldier, it seemed, would think of riding in a tram without buying a ticket or of jumping the queue. And he was, strangely for a man in uniform, not predatory: he did not commandeer rooms but continued to sleep on the pavement; when requisitioning firewood he would weigh it out carefully and then return the exact amount—of a quality that was usually higher; he hesitated even to accept a drink of water, so undemanding was he of the local people.[145]

Then came the changes, gradually at first but with determination and a clear plan behind the transformation. The new rulers were, after all, dedicated communists, and to them the city was a parasitic, criminal place where consumption was greater than production.[146] First to disappear were neon lights and other public advertisements in English. Foreign plaques in public parks and gardens were taken down and translated into Chinese. In the French Concession, where the streets and boulevards were named after French heroes and literati, a litany of communist icons inexorably replaced them. The casinos, cabarets, dance halls and ballrooms ran out of clients and business, and the taxi girls disappeared along with the hustlers, the money-changers and the vendors of forged lottery tickets and quack remedies.

Shanghai was turning austere and, in the autumn of 1950, the communists launched a Campaign to Suppress Counter-Revolutionaries. The targets were identified as the 'dregs of the Old Society, the landlords and their lackeys, reactionary officials and their lackeys, reactionary secret societies, mercenary bandits and thieves and other bullies and hooligans'.[147] One of the first victims of the campaign was, hardly surprisingly, Pock-Marked Huang Jinrong. He was cross-examined for days and nights on end, and eventually signed a long confession, cataloguing all his wrongdoings and 'crimes against the people'.

Then came the main crackdown. In the first half of 1952, 'the Five-Antis Campaign' targeted 'the Five Poisons of bribery, tax evasion and the stealing of State property, cheating on government contracts and the stealing of State economic intelligence, together with the last of the urban business class'.[148] Scores of petty gangsters, black-marketeers, opium dealers and even addicts were rounded up and shot after summary trials. Others were herded away to labour camps, from which few returned. Hundreds of prostitutes were detained in a Women's Labour Training Institute, where they were cured of sexually transmitted diseases and equipped with job skills.[149] For ordinary citizens, endless seminars followed in which *Das Kapital* and Mao's *Selected Works* were the bibles. Business tycoons who cracked under the pressure took their own lives; the earlier benign nature of the Red Army turned out to be a ruse to deceive the population of Shanghai into letting them into the city.

The Green Gang was crushed, and Big-Eared Du kept a loose count of the casualties as news filtered down from Shanghai to his new residence in Hong Kong. The communists viewed the secret societies, with their tightly knit, highly secretive structures, as potential threats to the dictatorship of the proletariat, and the new rulers spared no efforts to hunt them down. Not even the societies which had sided with Mao were spared. After the communist victory, all 'feudalistic and reactionary' organisations were crushed. They had outlived their usefulness now that a new order had been established—a totalitarian order which tolerated no opposition or competition for power. The few former members of the Society of Elder Brothers who survived the purges simply stayed on as loyal members of the Communist Party. Zhu De, for instance, rose to become commander-in-chief of the People's Liberation Army.

Shanghai, with all its contrasts and contradictions, had been a city where, as Lynn Pan says, there existed 'the familiar symbiosis between crime and the law with handsome rake-offs for everyone'.[150] This was where sin, crime, politics and business first coexisted as a new system of government. But now, with the communist takeover, it was time to say goodbye to Edgar Snow's 'all that'. Somewhat surprisingly, however, the communists had decided not to have the former chief of the Chinese Detective Squad of the French gendarmerie put up against a wall and shot. Inspector Huang had to be humiliated, and his punishment was almost bizarre: he was told to sweep the streets in front of the Great World, the entertainment palace he once owned on Avenue Edouard VII. For months he could be seen there, early in the morning, bending over his broomstick. A broken man, he died in obscurity and oblivion in 1953. The Old Shanghai was definitely gone. Or, at least, that was what people thought at the time.

• 2
THE CITY OF THE NAME OF GOD

There is no question that it harbours in its hidden places all the riffraff of the world, the drunken shipmasters; the flotsam of the sea, the derelicts, and more shameless, beautiful women than any port in the world. It is hell. But to those who whirl in its unending play, it is one haven where there is never a hand raised or a word said against the play of the beastliest emotions that ever blacken the human heart.
—Hendrik de Leeuw who visited Macau in the 1930s and wrote *Cities of Sin*.[1]

At the stroke of midnight on 19 December 1999, Portugal's red and green flag was lowered inside a huge pavilion near Macau's outer harbour—and China's red banner was hoisted to the tune of the national anthem of the People's Republic. The last Portuguese governor, Vasco Rocha Vieira, handed over his duties to Edmund Ho, a 44-year-old local banker whom a Beijing-appointed body had selected to become the first chief executive of the Macau Special Administrative Region. Clouds and strong winds had forced the organisers of the historic ceremony to cancel the planned fireworks, but thousands of guests burst into boisterous cheers as the territory changed hands.

Among the cars parked outside the pavilion, which had been built especially for the handover ceremony, was a dark blue Rolls Royce with the auspicious registration number MA 99-99. Everyone knew it belonged to Macau's most powerful man, Ho Hung-sun, better known as Stanley Ho, the flamboyant, Eurasian director of Sociedade de Turismo e Diversões de Macau (STDM). This gambling concern, which covers more than half of the territory's revenues, accounts for nearly half its GDP and employs a quarter of its workforce. To protect him, and other important guests such as China's President Jiang Zemin and Prime Minister Zhu Rongji, uniformed and plain clothes security guards ringed the ceremonial grounds.[2]

Thus ended four-and-a-half centuries of Portuguese rule in Macau. The event went much more smoothly than the handover of Hong Kong did two-and-a-half years earlier, when local Chinese as well as foreign residents worried over that colony's democratic future, and debated whether Beijing would honour its promise to leave it alone for at least 50 years, as it had pledged under the terms of an agreement signed by Britain and China in 1984. Macau was just too small to be able to oppose—or even question—any decisions taken in Beijing. Consisting of only a narrow peninsula and two small islands, the 23 square kilometre territory is 50 times smaller than the former British colony, and has a population of no more than 430 000 people compared with Hong Kong's 6.5 million.

Anyway, many people in Macau were not opposed to the idea of a more authoritarian regime replacing centuries of *laissez-faire* rule and neglect by the Portuguese authorities, which had attracted organised criminals and other shady characters from all over the world. In the years leading up to the handover, Macau had been plagued especially by a vicious turf war between local Triads operating on the fringes of the territory's gaming industry—hence the tight security during the handover ceremony. Since 1997, the fighting had claimed nearly 100 lives, and the murders—often gangland shootings in the streets in broad daylight—had had disastrous consequences for the territory's economy. Many tourists stayed away, especially Hong Kongers from the other side of the Pearl River estuary, whose gambling habits financed Macau.

Conveniently located at the crossroads of Asia, but under European—Portuguese—jurisdiction, Macau in the 1990s had become a unique mix of Chicago in the 1920s, pre-war Shanghai and Casablanca: a sanctuary for gangsters, gunrunners, pimps, prostitutes, gambling tycoons, corrupt officials and secret agents of western as well as Asian powers.

To make things worse, Brigadier Manuel Monge, under-secretary for security, made the mistake of trying to turn the deteriorating law and order situation in Macau into a joke. While addressing the press in 1997, he said that 'our Triad gunmen are excellent marksmen', implying that there was no need to worry because they would not miss their targets and hit innocent bystanders.[3] This particularly insensitive remark did not allay people's fears and, ironically, a year later Monge's own driver was gunned down.[4] By the end of 1999, no one was joking about safety in the streets of Macau; even locals were afraid to go out after dark.

The most spectacular attack had taken place on what seemed to be just another Sunday afternoon in May 1997. A warm drizzle glazed the streets of downtown Macau as three young men drove along the tree-shaded Avenida da Praia Grande, the city's main boulevard. They had not yet reached the traffic lights at Jardim de São Francisco when several motorcycles—some witnesses remember two, others say three—pulled up beside the sedan. Without stopping, the gunmen took aim. Three shots, one for each occupant, were fired through the side windows of the car. Shek Wing-cheung, Fong Mou-hung and Lo Wing-hwa died instantly in a pool of blood. As hundreds of onlookers gathered to gape at the grisly scene, the police found shells from Chinese military-issue 7.62mm semi-automatic pistols. But the gunmen were long gone.

Not even foreigners were spared. On a Sunday night in December 1998, two Portuguese brothers, Carlos and José Ribeiro, had joined their friend Luis Afonso for drinks at the Café Caravela, a popular outdoor bistro that caters to a mainly expatriate clientele. Shortly before 11.00 p.m., a lone man parked his scooter in the street outside. Still wearing his crash helmet, he walked swiftly up to the Portuguese trio's table, whipped out two pistols—one in each hand—and fired at least four well-aimed shots at the three young men. Then he strode away, mounted his scooter and disappeared into the cold December night.

Afonso was hit in the head and died instantly. Carlos Ribeiro took bullets in the neck and hip, and was taken to hospital in a critical condition. Only his brother José escaped injury by ducking behind a table. When the police arrived at the scene, they could do little more than note that it had been 'a very professional job'. It was obvious that, although the victims were foreigners, this attack was linked to the Triad war. The three Portuguese belonged to a group of nine elite prison guards from Portugal who had been carefully selected for their 'incorruptibility' and professionalism, and sent to Macau in October 1998 to boost security at the local penitentiary on Coloane island, the territory's only prison. Their task was to enforce stricter rules in the otherwise rather relaxed prison, where hard-core criminals were known to have access to blue movies, imported liquors and even mobile telephones.

More than 500 of its roughly 720 inmates were believed to have Triad connections.[5] Among the most infamous was Wan Kuok-koi, alias 'Broken-Tooth Koi', the 43-year-old alleged leader of the Macau chapter of the notorious 14K Triad society. Next to the December handover, the trial and conviction of Koi was the main event in Macau in 1999. He had been at the centre of the Triad war, and a movie— appropriately called *Casino*—had been made about his life. Outlandishly dressed in a striped suit, boldly designed shoes and a white shirt, and with at least òne mobile telephone in his belt, he had given interviews to *Time* and *Newsweek* before his career in violent crime came to an abrupt end when he was arrested on 1 May 1998.

On the morning of that day, a bomb had exploded in a mini-van belonging to António Marques Baptista (a.k.a. 'Rambo'), the new crime-busting head of Macau's Judicial Police. In the evening, Koi was picked up in Macau's flashy Lisboa Hotel, suspected of being behind what seemed like an assassination attempt. No evidence was presented to link Koi to the bombing, however, and he was instead brought before the court on an old charge: he had been accused of having intimidated employees at the Lisboa's casino, an offence that carries a five-year sentence on conviction. Koi was also charged with a much more serious crime: suspected membership in 'an illegal organisation'—or, in plain language, a Triad.[6]

To put together enough evidence to make a case again Koi was not an easy task, and it was not until 22 April the following year that he eventually appeared in court on intimidation charges. Predictably, he insisted he was innocent of any wrongdoing, saying that he was just a 'businessman who earned two million [Hong Kong] dollars a month'.[7] Witness after witness denied any knowledge of an alleged attempt to intimidate workers at the Lisboa. 'I don't remember,' said António Garcia, a government casino inspector, with his eyes averted from Koi.[8] Other witnesses simply failed to appear.

The court had no choice but to acquit Koi of 'criminal intimidation', but he could not escape several charges linked to his suspected leadership of Macau's 14K society. In October, the trial resumed after the summer recess. A convoy of heavily guarded cars and vans took Koi and five other defendants from his high-security prison cell on Coloane to the Court of First Instance in the city. The other prisoners were Koi's younger brother Wan Kuok-hung, and two male and two female accomplices. The old colonial courthouse was ringed by police brandishing sub-machine guns—and also by journalists and television crews. Koi had become a celebrity, perhaps Macau's most famous resident after Stanley Ho, and he continued to mock the court. 'I'm not the leader of any Triad faction,' he said. 'I don't know why I am here in court today. I'm just a businessman.'[9] The court, however, insisted that among his 'business activities' were murder, loan sharking, extortion and kidnapping. There was also a grand plan to set up a weapons factory in Cambodia, where he allegedly wanted to buy rockets, missiles, tanks, armoured vehicles and other heavy weaponry from international arms dealers.[10]

The verdict came on 23 November 1999. Armed police stood guard outside the court as Justice Fernando Estrela read out the sentence: fifteen years in gaol. Eight co-defendants, including Koi's younger brother, were gaoled for terms of five-and-a-half years and ten-and-a-half years. Estrela also ruled that all assets of the nine convicted gangsters be confiscated. At first, Koi was speechless. He just stared angrily at the judge—and then began to shout obscenities at him and the prosecutor. At least 50 of his relatives, who were there to hear the verdict, joined in the abuse. 'You have taken dirty money,' Koi screamed at a police officer after jumping up on a bench in the courtroom. But police rushed forward, overpowered Koi and led him away in handcuffs to a newly built top-security wing of Coloane prison. The criminal career of one of the most powerful—but also the most careless—gangsters of the South China coast was over. Four weeks later, as champagne corks popped and glasses clinked across Macau to celebrate the Chinese takeover, Koi, alone in his Spartan cell, was reported to be suffering from deep depression.[11]

Koi's beginnings were just as humble as his end. His father, whose original surname was Tam, was born to a family of poor fishermen in an area which to the Cantonese is known as Hai Lok Fung, and to

Mandarin-speakers as the twin cities of Heifeng and Lufeng. Located close to the Teochew-speaking area of northern Guangdong, this impoverished coastline has over the centuries produced numerous pirates, brigands and emigrants who have gone to Hong Kong, Southeast Asia and beyond.[12]

Koi's grandparents' family was so poor that his father was given away as a young boy to a man surnamed Wan. As an adopted son, he was badly treated and had to work hard as a domestic helper. The moment he could fend for himself, Koi's father, now a Wan, left for Macau, where he found work with the government's water supply company.[13]

Koi was born in Macau in 1956, and thus became a Portuguese citizen. The eldest of six children, the young Koi grew up in one of the territory's shanty towns. As his parents were too poor to support his education, he had to leave school after only two-and-a-half years. As a child and an adolescent, he worked as a coolie before drifting into the street-gang subculture of the poorer strata of Macau society. Koi banded together with six other young hoodlums, who became known as 'the Seven Little Fortunes'. Among them was another teenage drifter, Lai Tung-sang, who later became one of Koi's main business rivals.

Like other juvenile delinquents, they made a living running errands for bigger bosses, powerful and influential people whose identity was known to few. On their bosses' behalf, the youngsters extorted 'pro-tection fees' from shop-keepers, peddled smuggled goods and guarded prostitution rackets. Koi still bears scars from his street-fighting days: he was shot twice and was once attacked and severely wounded by a rival gang, armed with meat-cleavers. He lost nine teeth in another fight—hence his nickname, 'Broken Tooth'.

All young mobsters in Macau in the 1980s, Koi included, had to pay respect to the then over-all godfather of the 14K Triad society, the most powerful gang in both the Portuguese territory and in Hong Kong: Mou Teng-peng—or, in *pinyin*, Mo Dingping. Nicknamed 'Barber' Peng, he oversaw the street battles, proffered loans—at exor-bitant interest—to gamblers who were losing their money at the gaming tables and supplied prostitutes to the few lucky winners. But one day in the late 1980s a shoot-out broke out inside a hotel in town, and a casino inspector was killed. Under pressure from all sides, the police were urged to find the culprits. He heard from his contacts in the police department that he was a prime suspect, and left Macau before he could be arrested. He was sentenced in absentia to 24 years in goal. 'The Barber' disappeared without a trace, although it is believed that he first went to the Philippines and then, like so many other Triad gangsters from Macau and Hong Kong, settled in Thailand under an assumed name.[14]

Rumour has it that a young, ambitious mobster had approached the police, supplied them with crucial information, and even pledged to become a prosecution witness—and to implicate 'the Barber' not only in the shoot-out in the hotel but in many other criminal cases. The youngster who dared to challenge the powerful 'Barber' was said to be Wan Kuok-koi.[15] That has never been proven, but as soon as 'the Barber' was out of the way, street-fighter Koi, with his broken teeth and scarred arms, rose to prominence in Macau's underworld.

However, he was still too·young to become a real Godfather and the casino industry needed an 'enforcer' who could run all the lucrative side businesses connected with the gaming industry. Seemingly by coincidence, a well-known 'local businessman' returned to Macau within months of 'the Barber's' departure. This was the feared Ng Wai, nicknamed Kai-Sze ('Market') Wai because he once allegedly ran protection rackets in Hong Kong's Mongkok market.[16] He had left Hong Kong for the Philippines in the early 1980s to help then President Ferdinand Marcos run his gaming industry, which consisted of nine relatively profitable casinos. Lacking expertise of their own, the Filipinos had actually awarded their casino franchise to Stanley Ho, who cultivated a close relationship with the Marcoses and, it seems, Kai-Sze Wai.

With 'the Barber' ousted from Macau, Stanley Ho's casino monopoly, the STDM, set out to increase the turnover of its casinos. In 1986, the STDM had opened a number of private VIP rooms beside or upstairs from the main gambling halls. There, stakes could be in the hundreds of thousands—or even millions—of dollars. The VIP rooms are officially part of the STDM's operation, but in reality they are run by various gangs who pay a monthly fee, and a percentage of the takings, to the gaming monopoly.[17] To lure people to Macau—especially high-rollers from Bangkok, Seoul, Tokyo and Singapore—the same gangs offer, through their 'travel agencies', junket tours with free air tickets, food and accommodation in exchange for the advance purchase of gambling chips before the prospective clients leave their home countries.

On returning to Macau, Wai soon assumed control over several of the territory's most profitable VIP rooms. He was also allegedly made the new supremo of the local chapter of the 14K, with young Koi as his close aide and lieutenant. By the mid-1990s, Koi had taken over effective control of several 14K-operated VIP rooms. He owned several expensive sports cars, had several wives and numerous girl-friends, and went about Macau surrounded by bodyguards in dark sunglasses. Several hundred mobsters pledged allegiance to Koi—whose teeth by now had been fixed by an expert dentist so he could smile broadly at his female companions—and he controlled an army of young *ma jai*, or 'horse boys', as the street-fighters are called.

Many respected him. He had literally fought his way up in the gangster hierarchy, from the backstreets of Macau to its flashiest VIP rooms. He didn't smoke and he drank only moderately. But he loved dancing, and sometimes used Ecstasy to keep himself awake through-out many wild nights in Macau's discos. He even owned his own spiffy night joint, the neon-lit Heavy Club, just below the Vasco da Gama Garden in downtown Macau. It soon became a popular hang-out for many of his followers, and his younger brother Wan Kuok-hung had worked there as a bouncer before he too was arrested in May 1998.

At the same time, Koi remained loyal to old Triad rituals and, like so many other Chinese mobsters, was a strong believer in occultism. Before making any important decision, he would consult a local soothsayer called San Cha-Kung, and he regularly prayed for guidance from Guan Yu, the Chinese God of War.[18] 'I'm a very old-fashioned guy,' he said in a rare interview a few years ago. 'That means to defend the interests of the society, to fight for your brothers and to uphold the codes of the brotherhood.'[19] Koi also headed several local charities, and organised concerts with well-known singers from Hong Kong. The proceeds went to support needy people in Macau, or so he claimed.

Koi was feeling strong and confident—but his boss, Kai-Sze Wai, was not pleased. He found Koi's behaviour too flamboyant and inap-propriate in a small place such as Macau, where no 'big brother' should become the talk of the town. Discretion was important so as not to upset—or attract too much attention to—the arrangement that existed between the casino tycoons, the government and the Triads. While Wai always remained quietly in the background, supervising the business, Koi was addicted to gambling—and he was a bad loser. Whenever he lost, he would overturn the gambling tables in the VIP rooms and shout abuse at the croupiers. But if he won, he would jump up on the table and perform a wild dance, much to the consternation of other gamblers, who were as amused by the bizarre gangster as they were apprehensive of him.

In December 1996, Koi was banned for four years from Macau's casinos. Wai and others had had enough of his unpredictable temper. Koi was upset. This was a declaration of war. Just as he had challenged his former boss, 'Barber' Peng, he now decided to take on his new boss. Both Koi and Wai belonged to the 14K, but that mattered little. Assassinations, betrayals and the crudeness of the players are the very essence of Triad behaviour—and a spate of gangland killings, bombings and kidnappings soon rocked Macau.

But the war was caused by more than just Koi's anger at not being allowed to gamble. Profits from the gaming industry had begun to slow down when, in the mid-1990s, China's economic tsar, Zhu Rongji—later the country's prime minister—introduced new macro-economic reforms, which included stricter controls over the spending of government money. In the past, government officials from across the border had treated state funds as their own pocket money, and not hesitated to spend it in the casinos of Macau. Zhu clamped down on corruption and the movement of ill-gotten money. It even became harder for local officials to get ordinary bank loans.[20]

The following year, the slump in the economy could also be felt in prosperous Hong Kong. As 1997 was approaching, many people left for Canada, Australia and North America, and others were keeping their savings for what could be an uncertain future after the Chinese takeover. Fewer gamblers were coming to Macau from across the Pearl River—and then the crash of 1997 hit the entire region. As recession spread across East and Southeast Asia, the number of Korean, Thai, Malaysian and Japanese visitors also dropped dramatically. Adding to the uncertainty was the fact that the STDM's decades-long monopoly on Macau's gaming industry expired in 2001. In short, a growing number of gangsters had to compete for shrinking profits from illegal casino-related businesses such as VIP room protection, loan-sharking, extortion and prostitution. And, with uncertainty as to whether the STDM's monopoly would be renewed or not, they also had to position themselves for the post-2001 era, come what may.

In that precarious situation, Koi had made the mistake of being far too selfish—of breaking the unwritten rules by which the underworld rules the seedier side of life in Macau. At first, in 1995, Wan had agreed to form a broader alliance called 'the Group of the Four United', which was made up of the 14K, Shui Fong or 'the Water Room' (a Triad led by Koi's childhood friend Lai Tung-sang), a smaller band known as Wo Shing Yee, and an entirely new secret society that had emerged inside China in the late 1970s, the *Dai Huen Jai*, or the Big Circle Boys.[21] Although the names of three of the Triads were identical to those of groups also operating in Hong Kong, the aim of the alliance was to keep gangs from the British colony out of Macau— or, if they wanted to have a stake in the business, to make them pledge allegiance to the local chapters of the same Triads.[22]

The alliance also agreed to share the income from various casino-related rackets equally between its four members. Koi, however, kept most of the money to himself. His erstwhile mentor, Kai-Sze Wai, linked his 14K faction to the other three groups with Koi as the common enemy. Kai-Sze Wai and his closest henchmen kept a low profile and manipulated events from behind the scenes, while the Shui Fong led the attacks on Koi's men in the streets of Macau and elsewhere. Police investigations revealed that the three gangsters who were gunned down near Jardim de São Francisco on 4 May 1997 were some of Koi's *ma jai*. The 14K retaliated by gunning down any Shui Fong member they spotted in the streets of Macau. The killings had begun.

And the action was not just in Macau. For the first time, what had started as a local Triad war soon spread far away from the South China coast. Koi's main street-level rival, Lai Tung-sang, now known as 'Shui Fong Lai', had in October 1997 managed to escape to Vancouver on a visa obtained at the Canadian consulate in Los Angeles.[23] But, hardly surprisingly, Koi had allies on the other side of the Pacific too. One of them was Simon Kwok Chow, the sole principal of Boss Investment Ltd and the owner of Embassy Billiards in Coquitlam, a Vancouver suburb. More specifically, Chow was also a senior member of the 14K Triad. Nicknamed '426' or 'Red Pole Fighter', Chow controlled numerous Chinese secret society members in Canada.[24]

Meanwhile, Lai settled in a new home in Vancouver's Fraserview Drive and tried—unsuccessfully—to get a casino licence from the British Columbia government. Chow soon heard about Lai's arrival in Vancouver, and in late 1997 sent a band of gunmen to his house. The plot failed, and Chow was arrested and charged with attempted murder. Lai moved to a new house in Richmond. When asked what they planned to do with the 'Dragon Head' of one of Macau's most ruthless Triad societies, Canada's helpless immigration authorities just replied that 'there is no hearing scheduled for this name'. [25]

The Shui Fong were more successful in a counter-attack on the 14K back on the other side of the Pacific. On 17 February 1999, Won Pak-kam, one of Koi's closest lieutenants, was shot dead with a 9mm pistol at a roadside noodle shop in central Bangkok. The killing was carried out by Li Chi-keung, Shui Fong Lai's 'head of operations', who returned to Macau after the assassination.[26] In October, three other members of the 14K were shot on their way to Bangkok's airport in a taxi. They were returning to Hong Kong and Macau from Cambodia's capital Phnom Penh, where they were involved in casino operations.

Macau's gangsters had moved into Cambodia in the mid-1990s, taking advantage of the lawlessness which reigned there as a result of decades of civil war and largely unsuccessful attempts by the United Nations to restore normality. As a legacy of the war, Cambodia also had a thriving black market in arms. On 20 October 1997, the Cambodian police stopped a Mercedes Benz which was leaving the capital for the southern port of Sihanoukville. The car carried two Hong Kong Chinese—and two AK-47 assault rifles equipped with silencers, four Czech-made pistols, a grenade launcher and several cases of ammunition. The two Chinese confessed that the munitions were destined for Macau.[27] They led the police back to their Cambodian suppliers in Phnom Penh, and a gun battle broke out in the street near the French embassy. Two Cambodians allegedly connected with the gang—possibly soldiers—were killed.[28]

That attempt to smuggle guns to Macau was foiled, but other weapons from Cambodia did end up in the territory. On 4 October 1998, a gunman driving a white sports car pulled up near a building in Macau where four alleged 14K bosses close to Koi had just been interrogated. He got out and fired an AK-47 into the air before dumping it on the pavement.[29] A few weeks before that incident, ten journalists and five policemen had been injured by a bomb, probably triggered by remote control. Judicial police spokesman João Manhao described the bombing as an 'act of cowardice' and said the purpose was to 'frighten the press and the police'.[30] It was not the first time the Triads had threatened the media. About a year before the bombing, Macau's eight Chinese dailies and the local television channel each received an unsigned letter stating: 'Warning. From today it is not allowed to mention Wan Kuok-koi (alias) Bang Nga-koi ('Broken-Tooth Koi'), or the 14K, otherwise bullets will have no eyes and knives and bullets will have no feelings.'[31]

Clearly Koi was out of control and his wings had to be clipped. FBI agents arrived in Macau to help the Portuguese police map out the international networks of the territory's Triads. But, more importantly, Stanley Ho—the casino king—decided to speak out against the violence. When, on 31 January 1997, the STDM celebrated its 35th anniversary at the Lisboa Hotel, Ho blasted Macau's police and judiciary for being 'too lenient' on the Triads. 'I have not seen one Triad society member being held and sentenced,' he said, and went on to call for capital punishment for murder and other serious crimes.[32]

Ho had reason to be concerned. That year the number of visitors to Macau had dropped by nearly 5 per cent and the STDM's earnings fell almost 20 per cent to $747 million. The territory as a whole was suffering too, as taxes on gambling account for 59 per cent of all government revenue.[33] Later, the casino king made the startling revelation that there had been a series of unreported kidnappings in Macau involving well-known names. The victims did not inform the police because they had been threatened by their captors. The kidnappings, Ho said, had affected confidence in investment and therefore impacted on Macau's economy.[34]

Ho and others appealed to the Chinese authorities to take on the Triads as the Macau government needed cooperation from across the border to prevent criminals from simply slipping into Guangdong after an assassination, or a robbery, in the Portuguese enclave. The Chinese were also worried that the Triad war would spread to their side of the border. Edgar Snow had jumped a bit too early to the conclusion that 'all that' passed into history when the Communists marched into Shanghai. The new China that emerged following the introduction of economic reforms under paramount leader Deng Xiaoping in the late 1970s was actually quite different from what the peasant revolutionaries of 1949 had envisaged. China advanced economically at a breathtaking speed—and at the same time society began moving back to the gangsterism, piracy and prostitution of pre-revolutionary days.

In June 1998, the Chinese dispatched several thousand soldiers and policemen down to Zhuhai, a special economic zone opposite Macau to tackle these new 'social evils', as vice and crime are called in the official rhetoric. Some security forces were deployed on patrol boats in the waters around Macau, while in Zhuhai itself—and in the towns of Zhongshan, Jiangmen and Foshan—more than 1000 'entertainment places'—barber shops, karaoke bars and massage parlours which often double as brothels and gambling dens—were raided. A total of 108 suspected criminals were arrested, including twelve gang members from Hong Kong, Macau and Taiwan.[35]

But even the sensational arrest of Broken-Tooth Koi in 1998 did nothing to stop the violence. The following year, threats against the authorities and bloody vendettas among the gangsters only escalated. In June 1999, six months before the takeover and possibly in a confidence-boosting measure, the Chinese launched an even wider campaign against organised crime, this time targeting clubs and bars in eight cities in Guangdong, including the provincial capital Guangzhou (Canton), Zhuhai, Shenzhen opposite Hong Kong and Zhongshan. Thousands of 'entertainment centres' were raided, scores of suspected criminals were rounded up and guns, ammunition, knives, axes and icepicks were seized. The stated aim of the operation was to crack down on 'gangs from Macau which have moved operations to Guangdong'.[36]

However, the main problem remained inside Macau, then and now a separate jurisdiction under the same formula as post-colonial Hong Kong: 'one country, two systems'. In Macau, beyond the reach of Chinese law enforcement, the Triads outnumbered the local police by at least two to one. The territory's law enforcement authorities had only 4500 men at their disposal, while 13 000 people were believed to be members of one secret society or another. Most were 'dormant' members—that is, they had taken the oath and then gone back to their ordinary jobs. But an estimated 5000 people worked for the syndicates more or less full time and, if they needed any special services, the 'dormants' could always be called in to help.[37]

When the crackdowns inside China were seen to have little effect on the situation across the border in Macau, Beijing's security apparatus in October 1999 drafted a secret plan to deal with the problem more firmly. According to an internal document, security had to be heightened within 'Macau-based Chinese institutions', efforts to 'recruit agents working in foreign security organisations operating in Macau' had to be intensified and the territory's police department should be infiltrated more effectively.[38]

On the same day as Broken-Tooth Koi was sentenced to fifteen years in prison, another, much less publicised, verdict was also announced by the Provincial Higher People's Court in Guangdong across the border in China. On 23 November, Ye Cheng-jian, a lesser Macau crime boss, and two mainland accomplices, He Jingsheng and Li Xinwen, were sentenced to death for Triad-related offences. As is customary in China, the three convicted criminals were promptly executed with a bullet to the back of the head.[39]

Known in Cantonese as Yin Sing-kin, and nicknamed 'Cunning Kin', Ye Cheng-jian was the number two in the Big Circle Gang, after a shadowy figure known as the 'Four-Eyed Bull', a nickname he earned because of his thick glasses. The execution of Cunning Kin sent shivers through Macau's underworld; the Bull was known to have close links with China's security services, which is hardly surprising as many of its members are former or serving PLA officers.

Cunning Kin, like Broken-Tooth Koi, had broken the rules by being too flamboyant, upsetting the precarious balance of power in the underworld that had existed for decades. Kin was executed on the same day as Broken-Tooth was convicted in Macau which does not have the death penalty. The timing was hardly coincidental. Clearly, the Chinese authorities wanted to send a strong signal to the Macau underworld: if you want to stay in business, then keep a much lower profile.[40]

The violence did not end until a heavily armed convoy of troops from the PLA came across the border on 20 December, the first day of Chinese sovereignty over Macau. But, unlike Shanghai in 1949 when the soldiers had to walk, the PLA drove into the old Portuguese bastion on the South China coast in brightly-painted green trucks and armoured personnel carriers. And, unlike Hong Kong where the PLA's presence was not especially welcome, thousands of Macauites were out to greet the soldiers from the mainland.[41] The expectations were clear: the Portuguese had been hopelessly inept in dealing with the violence; now there would be no more Triads, no more characters like Broken-Tooth.

While major crime gangs had been cowed into submission, Stanley Ho and other wealthy Macau businessmen seemed unconvinced the territory was entering a new era of peace, law and order. To be on the safe side, in October 1999—just two months before the handover—Ho had returned to his and Kai-Sze Wai's old turf in the Philippines and invested $50 million in the Manila-based gaming concern Best World (BW) Resources, becoming its chairman.[42]

Other tycoons with interests in Macau's gaming industry set up a joint venture with private businessmen in Mongolia, the Mon-Macau company, which planned to build a $13.7 million facility in Ulan Bator's most luxurious hotel. That scheme fell through when lawmakers in newly democratised Mongolia accused three members of the government of having accepted 'gifts' for assisting Mon-Macau to win the casino tender.[43] The Hong Kong-based Emperor Group, which also had business interests in Macau, opened a gaming hall in the $180 million Seaview Casino Hotel in the Rajin-Sonbong free-trade zone in the northeastern corner of North Korea. No North Koreans would be allowed to gamble there, but a spokesman for the Emperor Group said the target market was 'rich Chinese and Russians'.[44]

This unusual business conglomerate is headed by Albert Yeung Sau-shing, who was gaoled back in the early 1980s for intimidating witnesses in an assault case. In more recent years, he was arrested both by the Hong Kong police and by the Independent Commission Against Corruption for a similar crime more forcefully applied to someone who had betrayed him in business—with threats to kneecaps. Sadly, the victim—like the witnesses at Broken-Tooth Koi's first trial—suffered an irreversible loss of memory when the case was brought to court, and Yeung remains a free man. He has been associated with several Triads, among them Sun Yee On, 14K and Wo Shing Wo.[45] But the Emperor Group has also had a few more conventional business partners, including a well-known Australian politician who, perhaps out of naiveté, agreed to join its board of directors.[46]

Among the most extreme of the gangs and groups based in Macau were the North Koreans. In the 1980s they had used the tiny territory as a staging post for the most infamous terrorist outrages: a 1983 bombing in Burma's capital Rangoon that killed 21 people, including several visiting South Korean ministers and other officials; and a 1987 bomb attack on a South Korean airliner *en route* from Baghdad to Seoul. Terrorism costs money, and American intelligence agencies have traced large sums of remarkably high-quality counterfeit $100 banknotes to North Korea's main commercial arm in Macau, the Zokwang Trading Company.[47] In June 1994, Zokwang executives were actually arrested after they had deposited $250 000 in counterfeit notes in a local bank—but their Macau office was never shut down.[48]

The North Koreans seemed untouchable in Macau, perhaps because of the close friendship between the governments in Beijing, which in effect ran Macau even when it was a Portuguese colony. They also used the unusual territory as a training ground for their secret agents. Kim Hyun Hee, the young female agent who together with an older North Korean intelligence male operative blew up a South Korean airliner in 1987, killing all 115 passengers onboard, describes in her autobiography how she and another girl were sent to Macau 'to practise our Cantonese and improve our abilities to impersonate Chinese nationals'.[49] In Macau, they also learned how to live in a capitalist society. They had an apartment and a bank account. They paid bills, went to the supermarket and visited night clubs—skills which would prove useful when they were later posted abroad, posing as 'Chinese' from Hong Kong or Macau.

If North Korean agents were at one end of the social spectrum in Macau, Russian prostitutes were at the other. They started coming to the territory in the early 1990s, in the wake of the collapse of the Soviet Union, and were an immediate hit with Asian customers who were willing to pay a lot of money to sleep with well-endowed white girls, especially blondes. By early 1994, more than 200 Russian girls were working in Macau as 'dancers', 'entertainers' and 'nightclub hostesses'. Most had travelled down to the Portuguese territory over-land through China, a 3000 kilometre journey from the Russian Far East. A sordid ordeal, perhaps, but—at least in material terms—a marked improvement on their previous lives in Vladivostok or Khabarovsk. Many were from simple backgrounds, with little to look forward to but unemployment or boring, poorly paid work in post-Soviet Russia. In Macau, even peasant girls from Siberia could afford to buy new fashionable clothes and eat in flashy restaurants. It did not matter that some of their customers were old enough to be their grandfathers.

The tragedy of today's Russia is evident in the scene in certain coffee shops in Macau: they are full of weary, long-legged blonde girls. Nearly all wear thick layers of make-up. One is dressed in a daring miniskirt and leather boots which reach almost to her knees. Many smoke incessantly. 'Yekaterina' is a typical Russian prostitute in Macau.[50] When the Soviet Union collapsed in 1991, she was only nineteen and still struggling with a computer course at a university in Khabarovsk. But she became pregnant and her boyfriend left her. With a newborn son to support—and with parents whose old state pension stood at 20 000 roubles, or approximately $5 a month—she had to take whatever offers came her way. One day she saw a poster on a telephone pole in Khabarovsk: well-paid jobs for women avail-able in the Far East. Yekaterina rang the number listed on the poster. A Russian syndicate escorted her and a number of other girls through China to Macau. Now she is able to support herself, her son, and her parents.

In the mid-1990s, girls like Yekaterina could soon be found all over Macau, where the authorities were much less rigid when it came to law enforcement than their Hong Kong counterparts. Apart from the main source of income—gambling—there has also always been wide-spread prostitution and every sort of vice, all of which is controlled by local Triads. In the beginning, they cooperated with the Russian syndicates which brought the girls to Macau. But, by a curious twist of events, the Russian *Mafiya* was soon squeezed out of the Por-tuguese territory.

The front for the syndicate which had sent Yekaterina and other Russian girls to Macau was the 'tourism department' of a local 'firm' in Siberia called *Dialog Naradov* ('Dialogue of Nations'). When they arrived in Macau, their applications for work as dancers and entertainers were usually handled by a local 'employment agency' called 'The Society of Support to the Enterprises of Macau'. The arrangement worked fine, and the Triads and the *Mafiya* seemed to get along well. But then, on 24 June 1994, a couple was found dead in a small flat in Vladivostok's rundown First of May District, a typical Brezhnev-era suburb of dreary, prefab apartment blocks intersected by pot-holed, muddy streets. The man had been shot once through the eye and the girl had been tortured and then shot in the head.

Such murders were everyday events in the new, post-communist Russia, and usually passed unnoticed in lawless Vladivostok. This time, however, the world's media paid attention. The man turned out to be Gary Alderdice, a 48-year-old New Zealander, a top Queen's Counsel and one of Hong Kong's leading criminal lawyers, as well as a well-known socialite in the British colony. The girl, who was found tied to a chair, was identified as Natalia Samofalova, a 20-year-old Russian prostitute whom Alderdice had first met at the Skylight nightclub in the Hotel Presidente on Avenida Da Amizade in Macau.

The initial police investigation into the case claimed that Alderdice had had $150 000 in cash on him just hours before he and his Russian girlfriend were shot. This led to speculation that he had gone to Vladivostok to buy Natalia's freedom from the syndicate which many suspected had controlled her when she worked as a nightclub dancer in Macau. According to the police investigation, Natalia had entered Macau in August 1993 and first met Alderdice in March 1994. In May, she left her work at the Skylight to live with the New Zealand lawyer.

However, Hong Kong lawyer Michael Lunn, a colleague of Alderdice, went to Vladivostok shortly after the murder to identify the corpse—and to find out more about the case. He returned to Hong Kong with the conclusion that the sole motive for the murder was robbery. He also questioned press reports that Alderdice was carrying as much as $150 000 with him, saying he entered Russia with less than $3000.[51] It was robbery, plain and simple. Life is cheap in Russia today.

Alderdice's corpse was flown back to New Zealand, and a few weeks later in Hong Kong, hundreds of judges, lawyers, stockbrokers and racehorse owners gathered at St John's Cathedral for a memorial service in his honour. Natalia was put to rest without much fanfare in a public cemetery in Vladivostok at a ceremony attended by only a few relatives and friends.

The case appeared to have been buried along with the victims. But then, in August, the Special Branch of the Royal Hong Kong Police called in a number of Russians for questioning about the Vladivostok murders. The first to make the headlines in the colony was Vladimir Ripin, who went by the nickname 'Bob'. He was an alleged former KGB agent born in Vladivostok who had studied economics and Chinese culture at university in Moscow and was fluent in English and Chinese.

Following an unauthorised affair with a female American agent in Beijing, Ripin was allegedly discharged from the KGB. But he remained in China as a businessman and later acquired, for $100 000, a passport from the West African republic of Guinea-Bissau. From Harbin, Manchuria—an old Russian stronghold—he continued on to Macau, where he set up a company called Valta Trading. Using its own freighter, the Russian-registered *Bureya*, Valta Trading imported furniture, wood, steel and even mammoth ivory from Siberia to Macau and China, while exporting fresh fruit back to Vladivostok on the return voyage.[52]

But the Hong Kong Special Branch alleged that Valta Trading was also a front for bringing Russian prostitutes to Macau. Not even Ripin himself denied that he used to work for the infamous China City Night Club as an 'interpreter', and that he helped hire Russian girls to work there. Blond-haired 'Russian Bob' had a $3800 a month income from the night club, but earned money in many other ways as well, as his diamond-studded gold ring and watch testified. The press quoted him as saying that his job was to arrange for 'dancers' and 'hostesses' to work in the thriving night club near Macau's ferry terminal, but he vehemently denied ever having worked for the KGB.[53]

The other Russians questioned by the Special Branch in Hong Kong were his business partners, Igor Deordienko and Nicolai Arzamassov. It transpired that 'Russian Bob', who was alleged to have known Natalia while she was in Macau, had left for Vladivostok a few days before Alderdice—and that he had reappeared in the Portuguese territory within days of the murders. All three denied any involvement in the murder, and even the Hong Kong police had to set them free after a brief interrogation. But the publicity to which 'Russian Bob' and his colleagues were subject prompted them to reach the conclusion that discretion was the better part of valour. They shut down their Macau branch of Valta Trading and moved on to Bangkok and Jakarta, taking some of the Russian girls with them.

The publicity which the case attracted also led to a crackdown on Russian prostitution in Macau—in true Macau style. Not only 'Russian Bob', but all Russian males associated with the 'Dialogue of Nations', were forced to leave along with over 100 girls who were rounded up and expelled from the territory. Then local Chinese gangs took over the entire operation. The Russian males were not allowed to return, but the girls soon reappeared in Macau, in the Lisboa Hotel coffee shop, a popular meeting place for people who have just won some money in the establishment's casino downstairs, and in the glitzy China City night club, a massive entertainment complex in the same street ás Hotel Presidente, where Natalia once worked.

The famous Tonnochy Nightclub in Rua Da Praia Grande in central Macau was another popular place and its supply of girls actually read like a real 'dialogue of nations'. Apart from Russians, there were also Chinese girls from every province on the mainland, Koreans, Thais, Filipinas and, as a result of shared colonial heritage, Brazilians. The decor seemed to be out of a Chinese Kung Fu movie: chrome, glass and red silk—and private rooms where the customers could meet the 'hostesses' of their choice to discuss the price for further activities.

The 'new' prostitution scene in Macau demonstrated both the weaknesses of the chaotic, ill-organised Russian *Mafiya* as well as the strength and power of the Chinese Triads. The Russians were no match for well-organised local gangs. They had to be content with playing second fiddle if they wanted to get any share of the cake in Macau's part of the world. The Russian gangsters failed to gain a foothold in the territory. But Triads of all descriptions continued to run night clubs and strip joints. They operated junket-tour companies, 'protected' VIP rooms and ran loan-sharking rackets. Drug traffickers with connections in Burma's sector of the Golden Triangle laundered money through the territory's banks and casinos. Only the Japanese *yakuza* never showed much interest in Macau, perhaps because it was somebody else's turf—and the *yakuza's* main stomping ground outside Japan, in any case, had always been Southeast Asia, Hawaii, the west coast of the United States and Australia.

Macau is a place that strikingly resembles the thirteenth-century Venetian explorer Marco Polo's novel idea of what he termed a 'model city: a city made up only of exceptions, exclusions, incongruities, contradictions'.[54] Even China's communist rulers have had to recognise that fact, and the brutal idealism which guided the first decades of revolutionary rule in Shanghai has given way to a more 'pragmatic' approach, which is more in tune with China's own centuries-old political and criminal traditions.

The founding and development of Macau provide a shining example of this heritage, and how local authorities—indigenous as well as foreign—have not always been the upholders of the formal rule of law. In the Portuguese version of the history, China gave them the peninsula in the mid-sixteenth century in gratitude for suppressing piracy in the South China Sea.[55] In reality, the first Portuguese reached the Chinese coast in 1513 when explorer Jorge Alvares sailed to the mouth of the Pearl River estuary, landed at the Bay of Tun Men (now called Tuen Mun in Hong Kong) and set up base on Lin Tin island. From their foothold in Malacca, the Portuguese were exploring new markets in the Far East, and went as far as Japan in 1542. As shipping along this route was being established in the following decade, the Portuguese needed a halfway trading station.

The island of Langbaiao (or Lampacão, as the Portuguese called it) in the Pearl River estuary became a base for Portuguese smugglers, where they bought silk and other commodities which were exported to Japan. In 1553, Leonel de Souza, the commander of the fleet that traded with Japan, reached an agreement with local Chinese authorities to establish a permanent trading site in the area.[56] Four years later, the Portuguese found a suitable place: a narrow rocky peninsula. At its tip was a small fishing village known as Hou Kong, and a temple dedicated to A-Ma, the Chinese goddess of seafarers and fishermen. When the Portuguese asked the villagers the name of the place, the legend goes, they were told it was 'Amakau' ('Bay of A-Ma'), which they corrupted to 'Macau' or 'Macao'.[57] No treaty was signed, and the status of the Portuguese settlers in Macau was closer to that of squatters than proprietors. They simply moved in—and eventually agreed to pay anchorage fees and ground rent to the local authorities in Guangdong.

But the imperial court did not relinquish its rights over the peninsula.[58] Zhang Mingwang, the governor-general of Guangdong, argued that endeavouring to control and confine the Portuguese in one place was preferable to expelling them from the coast altogether. And, rather than being 'grateful' to the Portuguese for 'suppressing pirates', he and other local representatives of the Emperor were concerned the foreigners were harbouring them in their settlements. Chinese records show that some Portuguese colluded with a notorious pirate chieftain in Guangdong called He Yaba and wantonly looted coastal areas of the province.[59] However, it was not until 1887—46 years after Britain took over Hong Kong—that a formal treaty was finally signed in Beijing, according to which the Portuguese were given 'perpetual occupation and government' of Macau, and the outlying islands of Taipa and Coloane, which Portugal had occupied by force of arms in 1846.[60]

Nevertheless, Macau flourished for centuries under Portuguese *de facto* rule as an entrepôt for European trade with China and Japan. It also became the centre for the spread of Christianity in Asia: churches and convents were built, and Jesuit fathers and other Catholics used Macau as a base for their missions to China. In the seventeenth century, Lisbon rewarded Macau with the grand title of *Cidade do Nome de Deus, não há outra mais leal*, or 'the City of the Name of God, None More Loyal', to honour it for its dedication to Portugal, even when the motherland was under Spanish rule from 1580 to 1640.[61]

But it remained, in many ways, an exceptionally ungodly place. Its importance for the China trade declined in the mid-nineteenth century with the opening of new treaty ports and the establishment and growth of Hong Kong following Britain's victory over China in the Opium Wars of 1839–42 and 1856–60. Alternative sources of income had to be found in order to prosper in the shadow of its younger and much more dynamic neighbour. Macau has always celebrated all that Hong Kong forbids—gambling, prostitution or whatever—but the first big business in the enclave after the establishment of the new British colony was the export of human labour. In the mid-nineteenth century, Macau became the infamous centre of the trans-Pacific coolie trade, which was as inhuman as the earlier African slave trade across the Atlantic. Edward Fuller, a western traveller who visited Macau in 1866, described how it worked:

> A planter in need of men in South America, or Cuba, sends an agent here to 'hire' five hundred Chinamen. This agent employs compradores (Chinese) to go into the interior after his men. Mr. W. this evening gave me an instance of how they get them. One of these well paid compradores entered the hut of a poor wretched coolie a few days since, gave his children a [little] cash, and told him he was a foolish fellow for lying idle—that if he would come with him to town, he would insure him $4 (good wages here) per month. The poor devil swallowed hook and line at a gulp and that night found himself on board a coolie ship, bound for Havana . . . The Capt, when he gets his 'freight' on board, gives them $8 each in money, two suits of clothes—more than they (half of them) ever had before in the world. While this is fresh in their minds the Harbour Master comes off, and (it is said) asks each if he is willing to go. The poor wretches, bewildered with the 'advance' and having not the most remote idea of what they are acceding to, generally say yes, upon which the ship receives her papers—sets sail—and coolie is a slave for life—unless he dies on the voyage, which is about the same. Contracts have been entered into for delivery—this year—of twenty thousand coolies![62]

The Portuguese authorities turned a blind eye to this human traffic, or even actively supported it, hoping it would bring in badly needed cash. In the free-wheeling legal climate of Macau, it was obviously easier to engage in such activities than it was in more strictly regulated Hong Kong, and a powerful underworld controlling opium, slavery and prostitution emerged in the Portuguese settlement. The coolie trade was especially lucrative, as prices of Chinese 'labourers' in Cuba or Peru ranged from $120 to $1000. More than 140 000 people were exported through Macau from 1845 until the Portuguese eventually put an end to the practice in 1873.[63]

The Portuguese had a problem, however. Apart from looking after the needs of its own citizens, Macau also had to support the eastern half of the island of Timor, one of Lisbon's poorest colonies in Asia. This was a severe drain on the local economy. But fortunately, by the time the lucrative labour trade was halted, Macau had discovered a source of income that would enrich it to the present day: gambling. Licensed gambling was first introduced in the 1850s by Governor

Isidoro Francisco Guimarães. Gambling houses, it was hoped, would bring in much-needed revenue in a manner that was not quite as shameful as the coolie trade. By 1866, sixteen regular gambling houses provided an annual income to the government of $165 000.[64]

In the wake of the Taiping Rebellion and throughout the gradual weakening of the Qing Dynasty in China in the mid-nineteenth century, the first modern Triads were also emerging, mainly in Guangdong and Fujian provinces. When, and how, they arrived in Macau is uncertain, but by the turn of the twentieth century they were well established in the territory, where they helped the authorities to 'police' the gambling houses, collect debts and enforce the official and unofficial rules according to which the 'system' operated. Macau became a gamblers' paradise, especially for people from Hong Kong, and in 1911 the governor of the British Crown Colony estimated that one million dollars were being transferred to Macau annually to pay for lottery tickets alone.[65]

The gangs, in collusion with the Portuguese authorities, also ran brothels and opium dens. The opium trade was not in itself illegal and, until 1927, was carried out under what was called a 'farm system'. Like gambling, it was a government monopoly that was 'farmed out' to local syndicates. Opium was imported from Persia and India, then processed in Macau, where it was consumed locally or re-exported to third countries such as China, the United States and Mexico. The increase in China's own opium production from 1919 onwards, and the fall of the trade into the hands of local warlords, was a disaster for Macau. The Portuguese abolished their 'farm system', and the entire opium business was taken over by the state.

Officially, Portugal had ratified the 1925 Geneva Agreement, which was meant to put an end to the opium trade. But there were plenty of loopholes in that agreement, and Portugal continued to import Persian opium and resell it, legally or otherwise, to China and Japan.[66] Financial transactions for the purchase and sale of opium were handled by Banco Nacional Ultramarino, or BNU, the first—and for many years the sole—European bank in the territory, and the only one that had the right to issue local bank notes in the local Macau currency, the Pataca.[67]

But, as campaigns by Christian missionaries and other moral authorities mounted against the opium trade, its future was becoming uncertain. The risky trade also involved smuggling to territories where no one knew who was in charge. Gambling was a better bet for Macau, and in 1934 the government granted for the first time monopoly rights in the form of a franchise to a single firm. This was the Tai Hing Company, which for a fee of 1.8 million *leung* of gold acquired the monopoly.[68] Subsequently, Tai Hing opened its first 'casino' in Hotel Central behind the central square on Avenida Almeida Ribeiro in the middle of the city. Other casinos were located in Rua de Felicidade, or 'the Street of Happiness', then Macau's most notorious red-light district, and in Rua de Cinco de Outubro near the Inner Harbour.[69]

Gambling in those days was mostly on Chinese games such as *fan-tan* and *dai siu*. In the former, a pile of several hundred white porcelain beads is placed in the centre of a table. A croupier then plunges a silver cup upside down into the pile and slides it to the side of the table. Players then bet on how many beads will remain in the cup after they are divided by four. It is said that *fan-tan* was invented by a Chinese general who could not afford to pay all his troops. He paid half of them, won it all back at *fan-tan*, and then paid the other half. The many losers at Macau's *fan-tan* tables paid for government bills, and made the Tai Hing Company relatively rich by pre-World War II standards.

In *dai siu*, Cantonese for 'big and small', three dice are thrown under a covered glass container. Players bet by guessing what number will come up on the dice. Macau was no Monte Carlo, and a visitor to the city's gambling houses in the 1920s said 'there is in fact no casino in Macau, but there are twelve dingy opium-reeking dives, the patrons of which wear no formal dress . . . on a warm summer day you may rub elbows with half-naked coolies, road-dusty farmers, and fugitive embezzlers as you lay your bets on the gaming tables'.[70]

But, despite the simple nature of the games—and the roughness of the establishments—taxes and levies on gambling and the opium trade amounted to 60 per cent of Macau's total revenue in the period before World War II.[71] The Tai Hing Company, and its gambling franchise, remained in the hands of the influential Fu family, but as usual various Triads controlled related pursuits such as loan-sharking, drug peddling and prostitution. A centre for their activities—women, gold and opium—was the Grande Hotel at the west end of Avenida Almeida Ribeiro, where wild orgies were held when the bosses met among themselves, or entertained their police contacts.[72] Official-dom, licensed gambling and Triad activities formed a symbiotic existence that continues to this day.

Reaching an accommodation with the Triads had always been vital for the survival of tiny Macau. The remote Portuguese outpost in the Far East was located in a lawless region, where the colonial authorities had more important and dangerous enemies to deal with. Since the Por-tuguese first arrived on the South China coast, piracy had been a major problem. And, although the early colonialists no doubt cooperated with the pirates, following the establishment of some kind of lawful authority in Macau, the issue had to be addressed in a different way.

Between 1790 and 1810 especially, the South China coast saw a spectacular growth in piracy. Pirates dominated the entire coastal region and, at their peak, had 50 000–70 000 men and women organ-ised in a confederation of six fleets and 2000 junks.[73] They came from the same milieu of dispossessed frontier people as the members of the Tiandihui Triad. From their headquarters in the town of Chiang-ping near the Vietnamese border, they held sway over the huge island of Hainan off the coast of southern Guangdong.

Most of the pirates were outcast, semi-nomadic, Cantonese-speaking 'water people', perjoratively referred to by the clansmen of Guangdong as *tanka*, or 'egg families'. They were basically an illiter-ate, loosely organised community without a gentry, whose lives were marked by religious ceremonies and the worship of the sea-goddess Tien-hou, Hung Hsing, the reincarnation of the Dragon King who ruled the South Seas, a local weather saint called Tam-kung and Guan Yin, the Buddhist Goddess of Mercy. The pirate community lacked both firm roots and any real manifestation of permanence. Neverthe-less, their headquarters at Chiang-ping attracted a large number of non-*tanka* people, mainly urban failures and social misfits.

The pirates could sail from their base on the Vietnamese border, raid coastal settlements in southern China and be back at Chiang-ping before the Chinese authorities could assemble their water forces or instruct the Vietnamese to organise an attack from their side. Large amounts of money were extorted from villages and towns along the coast, and even upriver in Guangdong. Those who refused to pay had their houses burned down.

A woman in her thirties called Cheng I Sao soon emerged as the leader of the pirates. Also known as 'the Dragon Lady of the South China Sea', she was a former prostitute who inherited the command of the fleets from her male companion, a pirate chieftain called Cheng I (Cheng I Sao = wife of Cheng I) who, according to one version of the story, had died while fighting other pirates off the Vietnamese coast. A less dramatic version maintains that he was blown overboard in a storm. But he was gone, and Cheng I Sao took on a new male consort, Chang Pao, the teenage son of a fisherman. Together, they transformed what had been a loose confederation of fleets into a well-organised fighting force.[74]

In late March 1804, a fleet of pirate junks took possession of Taipa, then not yet under Portuguese jurisdiction but dangerously close to Macau. They were eventually driven off, but the waters around Macau were never safe. To explain who they were, and why they had taken to burning and looting as a means of survival, the pirates posted a declaration in Macau and Guangzhou in June 1809. It was a sweeping attack on the repressive and corrupt nature of the Chinese state:

> We who live on the seas weeping declare that the reason why we are Pirates has been no other but for that in past times all the Mandarins being persons of tyrannical hearts sought for naught but money . . . The Military Mandarins great and small are all afraid of Death. They ask for nothing more than the money of others with the purpose that at a future time when they shall not be able any longer to exercise the charge on Mandarin, being under the necessity of returning to their homes, they shall have by that time amassed money for the expenses of subsistence. If they were not such kind of men as thus specified they ought forthwith to have come out to the open sea in order to fight with us, when they know of our arrival in these parts, instead of seeking for various pretexts as for instance of repairing their Boats, mending their sails, setting this and that to rights, and pretending all this notwithstanding their being aware of our arrival . . . We hope that the Pai Chim Tien [the Viceroy] may chastise and deprive all these Mandarins from their offices which they exercise, listening to our first suggestions and complaints; we will then no longer be pirates . . . We who live upon the Seas with Lamentation have spoken.[75]

They were a formidable organisation, and the government eventually realised that it could not treat piracy as solely a law and order problem. In 1810, the government introduced a policy of pardon and pacification, and thousands of pirates surrendered. Some of their leaders stepped ashore into new lives with much of their proceeds from piracy intact. A few were even awarded high positions in the government and the military. Chang Pao, for instance, was given the rank of lieutenant in the Chinese Navy, and was allowed to retain a fleet of 30 junks. Shortly afterwards, he was received as a visitor of state in Macau, where he met the commanders he had previously encountered in battles on the seas.[76] Cheng I Sao spent her last days quietly in Guangzhou, 'leading a peaceful life so far as [was] consistent with the keeping of an infamous gambling house'.[77] She died in 1844 at the age of 69.

The big fleets were gone, but the pirates did not disappear. Coloane remained a haven well into modern days, and the island's last pirate raid was repulsed by the Portuguese army in 1910. A monument in Coloane village outside the Chapel of St Francis Xavier commemorates the pirates' final defeat in that year.[78] But piracy continued to fester in the waters around Macau and Hong Kong. In an almost unbelievable undercover action in the 1920s, an early investigative journalist, Finnish-American Aleko E. Lilius, posing as a White Russian mercenary and freelance bodyguard from Shanghai, managed to infiltrate one of the most powerful pirate gangs in the South China Sea, and later wrote a book about his exploits.[79]

Once again, the pirates were led by a remarkable woman, Lai Choi San. She had inherited her business and ships from her father, who had died in a fight with a rival gang. He, and his daughter, had been given refuge in Macau, with the tacit understanding that their gang should protect the colony's enormous fishing fleets and do 'general police duty on the high seas'.[80] The new Queen of the Pirates owned twelve junks, fully armed with cannon and manned by rifle-toting pirates. When not protecting Macau's fishing fleets, she and her men plundered every ship or village they came close to, kidnapped men, women and children for ransom, ransacked homes and burned junks and sampans. Lilius would romanticise her as 'a female Chinese version of Robin Hood'.[81]

The outbreak of the Pacific war put an end to piracy in the South China Sea. Now, war ships sailed the high seas—and war and destruction swept the Chinese hinterland. The Japanese invaded Hong Kong in 1941, but Portugal remained neutral and Macau was spared occupation. Entirely surrounded by the Japanese, but still a non-aligned territory, Macau became the hub of all sorts of intelligence agencies: communist, Guomindang, British, American, Portuguese and Japanese. Even so, Macau's infamous cabarets suffered from a lack of patrons, and business was down in the gambling houses and opium dens. Then food prices soared, and throughout 1942 Macau suffered a severe famine. Many of the unemployed were reduced to begging and died in the streets, and there were even reports of cannibalism.[82]

But Macau survived as a separate entity and, somewhat paradoxically, the first serious threat to the territory's survival came when the war was over. Chiang Kai-shek's Guomindang began to show interest in taking over the colony. Being on the winning side in the war, nationalist-ruled China had regained Taiwan and the Penghu islands from the Japanese as well as the Zhanjiang leasehold in southern Guangdong from the French. Chiang Kai-shek had visions of a greater, united China without foreign settlements and concessions. On 16 September 1945, General Wat Yuen-chak, commander of a former guerrilla force that had operated behind Japanese lines in Guangdong, marched into Macau through the old border gate, Porta do Cerco, on the narrow isthmus that separates the Portuguese colony from China proper. He and his men lodged themselves in the Hotel Grande, and were only disarmed after intervention by the Macau police.[83]

The threat of a nationalist takeover was real. Guomindang affiliated guilds and 'sporting associations' were already active in Macau, including a local chapter of the fiercely nationalistic secret society Hong Men, which was just another name for the Tiandihui. But China's republican government never conquered Macau, perhaps because Portugal became a close ally of the United States after the war. Then came the communist victory in China in 1949, and many people once again thought Macau was doomed. Hong Kong was too important, and Britain too powerful, for China to instigate a challenge. But Macau? It would have taken the Chinese only a few hours to take over the tiny territory. It never happened, though. Surprisingly, the Chinese communists showed much less interest in claiming sovereignty over Macau than the Guomindang. It was years before the reason for China's acceptance of Portuguese rule over Macau became known—and the explanation was as incongruous and extraordinary as the territory itself.

At the outbreak of World War II, Portugal had 63 tonnes of gold in its bank vaults. When the war was over, Portugal's reserves had risen to 365 tonnes.[84] Germany's Nazis had used gold pillaged from all over Europe—especially from the Jews, including wedding rings and tooth fillings from holocaust victims—to pay for wartime supplies. A 1998 study by US government historians concludes that Portugal, together with Spain, provided Germany with 'almost 100 per cent' of the essential minerals needed to produce 'machine tools and armaments, especially armor-piercing shells'.[85]

Other Nazi gold was also stored in neutral Portugal for safe-keeping, and was left there when Germany surrendered.[86] In 1945, Britain compiled a report of Nazi gold, ingot by ingot, that had ended up in Portugal. After years of haggling, Portugal gave up four tonnes. But when Portugal in 1949 became a founding member of the North Atlantic Treaty Organisation (NATO), the Allies became less interested in the gold; Portugal's anti-Soviet stand—and, more importantly, NATO's air bases on the Azores—were more crucial than settling what was becoming an old wartime score.

The international gold trade had been regulated when a number of developed nations, led by Britain and the United States, met at a conference in Bretton Woods, New Hampshire in July 1944. An agreement was signed to set up a framework for the postwar international monetary system with fixed exchange rates and a gold exchange standard under which currencies were convertible into gold at stable rates. It also banned the importation of gold for private use. The Bretton Woods conference led to the establishment of the International Monetary Fund (IMF) and, after the war, more and more governments gradually ratified the treaties that had been agreed upon. Portugal was one of them—but Lisbon conveniently 'forgot' to include Macau in the list of its dependent territories.

Somehow, through an exceptional set of circumstances, Macau had found a way to survive both the economic crisis caused by the war, and the new threat posed by communist rule in China. The colony became the centre for the world's unofficial gold trade. Ingots marked with the coats of arms of the Soviet Union, the Netherlands, South Africa and even the republic that lost Spain's civil war ended up in

Macau, along with other gold bars marked with the Nazi eagle and swastika.[87] Macau merchants bought gold at $35 an ounce from any bank, the price stipulated under the Bretton Woods Agreement. The bullion was then shipped to Macau and sold at a premium to whoever wanted to buy it. This violated the Bretton Woods Agreement, but satisfied people who wanted to own gold but could not acquire it legally.

To facilitate the movement of gold, the traders in Macau set up the Macau Air Transport Company (MATCO) which, despite its grand name, had only one aircraft: an old seaplane left over from the war which they named *Miss Macau*. On 16 July 1948, the plane took off from Macau's outer harbour, headed for Hong Kong. Eight minutes after it became airborne, *Miss Macau* lost contact with the ground. Two days later the wreckage was found floating in the sea. Only one person survived out of 23 passengers and four crew members. It turned out that the survivor was a man who had heard that the plane was going to carry gold, and had hijacked it.[88]

But new seaplanes were acquired and subsequent flights went smoothly. Much of the gold arrived from Bangkok. After landing in the outer harbour, the gold was taken under police escort to the Almeida Ribeiro branch of a 'bank', or money-changer and pawn shop, called Seng Heng on the other side of the peninsula.[89] There the gold was weighed and checked against the cargo manifest, and the Macau authorities levied a tax of 44 cents an ounce on all imported bars. But they knew nothing—or claimed to know nothing—of gold being melted down, reshaped and exported from the territory.[90]

Reports in the British press in 1998 first revealed that Macau did indeed serve as a centre for laundering Nazi plunder. Much of the controversial Nazi gold seems to have ended up in China, which could explain why Beijing, strangled by a United States-led trade boycott after the Korean War, let Portugal keep its toehold on the South China coast.[91] If this theory is true, then an extraordinary scenario emerges: capitalist Macau, ruled by then fascist Portugal and equipped with Nazi gold, helped communist China survive throughout its first difficult years of existence.

The gold traffic continued until 1974, when a new system for the pricing, sale and exchange of bullion was introduced, making the arrangement through Macau superfluous. But as long as it went on,

$40–50 million worth of gold passed through the narrow door of the Seng Heng Bank annually. That China in the 1950s and 1960s had a secret gold supply was something that western intelligence had long suspected. Ian Fleming, the creator of James Bond and a sometime informant for the British Secret Service, was on the trail of the story when he visited Macau in the 1950s. Fleming found no evidence, but his investigations inspired him to write a book centred around China's desire to build up its own gold reserves. He called it *Goldfinger*.[92]

A leading candidate for the hugely wealthy protagonist of any Bond movie was an ethnic Chinese gold trader called Ho Yin. [93] More than anyone else in Macau, it was Ho Yin who profited from the territory's status as China's window to the capitalist world. He would soon emerge as Beijing's most trusted ally in the colony.

Initially, Macau's gold syndicate was run by Dr Pedro José Lobo, a locally born Sino-Malay-Eurasian who before the war had served as president of the Comissão Administrativa do Opio, or Macau's opium regulating body, and later became head of the colony's Economic Department as well as a famous local composer of classical music.[94] But, before long, control over the gold business passed into Ho Yin's hands. A native of Panyu in Guangdong, he had been a skilled gold trader since his teens. When the Japanese invaded Guangzhou in October 1938, he left for Hong Kong where he and a few other young entrepreneurs set up the business that eventually was to become the Hang Seng Bank, now one of that territory's biggest financial institutions.[95] In 1941, when Hong Kong also fell to the Japanese, Ho Yin and his friends moved their base to Macau. Once there, Ho Yin set down roots and never left.

Less than a year after his arrival in the Portuguese colony, Ho Yin had became acquainted with many of its movers and shakers, and was hired by the Tai Fung Silver Shop as a manager. Although Macau was never occupied, the war that was raging around the enclave meant hardships even for the Portuguese authorities, who were desperately short of funds. But Ho Yin's business acumen had caught their attention, and they approached him for help. Using his gangland connections, Ho Yin began to smuggle currency from Hong Kong to Macau to end the shortage.[96] In 1943 Ho Yin and a few partners founded the Wo On Gold Company—pioneers in what was to become a multi-million dollar business—and linked up with Lobo. Together, they held a virtual monopoly on the gold market even before the end of the war. When the war was over, the syndicate benefited enormously from restrictions imposed under the Bretton Woods agreement.

Another partner was the Ng Fuk Tong, or the Five Good Fortunes Association, a branch of the Tai Hing Company that held the colony's gambling franchise.[97] And, although Ho Yin never joined any Triad society, he knew all the big brothers and gangland leaders in town.[98] Macau's indigenous business community—above ground and underground—was tiny and its inner circle even smaller. Ho Yin was emerging as the most powerful power broker in the colony.

The gaming industry picked up again after the war, but the opium trade—which before the war had been the other main source of revenue in Macau—did not. The Portuguese authorities had laid down regulations banning opium smoking. After half a year's grace period, the new laws came into effect on 1 July 1946. Opium and smoking paraphernalia were confiscated and destroyed in public.[99]

In order to stay in business, it was important for Macau's traders and merchants to show they were important to China. Smuggling thrived, and secret deals were made between Ho Yin, his associates and the authorities across the border. Macau was not Hong Kong. It was too small and vulnerable. Pleasing the Chinese became especially important when the communists took over the mainland, and Macau's future should have become even less certain had Mao Zedong and his comrades adhered to their Marxist principles of anti-colonial struggles. Fortunately, gold had taken over from opium as one of the territory's two most important sources of income—and that, of course, helped Macau's merchants to establish a good rapport with China's new rulers. Already, within months of the communist victory, Ho Yin had managed to meet both Mao and Zhou Enlai, and an understanding was reached.[100]

This special relationship earned the Macau merchants the nickname 'Red Fat Cats', and one of the fattest was Ho Yin. His business empire included the old Seng Heng 'bank', a new bank, the Tai Fung—which had emerged from the old silver shop with the same name—hotels, restaurants, and bus and taxi companies. He chaired several public utility companies and served as president of the

Chinese General Chamber of Commerce, vice-president of Macau's Legislative Assembly and, later, as a member of the Standing Committee of the Chinese National People's Congress in Beijing.[101]

Portugal had no official diplomatic relations with China at the time, so a system of working through intermediaries had been established involving powerful local businessmen like Ho Yin. That Nazi gold ended up in China through these connections has only recently been revealed, but it was known even at the time that Macau served as a trans-shipment centre for petroleum and munitions into China during and after the Korean War in violation of a United Nations-imposed embargo.[102]

The United States put pressure on Portugal to fall into line, but the trade continued using local Chinese business fronts. One of the most successful players was Fok Ying-tung, better known as Henry Fok. Born in 1923 on a small fishing boat owned by a *tanka* family, Fok was in his late twenties when he organised a smuggling ring that broke the United Nations embargo.[103] Six months after the end of the Korean War in 1953, he set up Fok Hing Yip Tong Estates Ltd, specialising in real estate development. Within a year, he had established a whole string of real estate and construction companies, owned by himself, his mother, his two wives and their children.

Fok's smuggling activities on behalf of China led to his being awarded an exclusive concession to import sand from the mainland to Hong Kong—an extremely lucrative business in the 1950s and 1960s, when land was reclaimed along the colony's waterfront and new houses had to be built to accommodate the thousands of refugees who had come there after the communist victory in the mainland. Fok freely admits to shipping everything from steel to food to China during the Korean War, but denies ever smuggling arms.[104]

The future had even more surprises in store for the poor *tanka* boy who by 1960 was already a multi-millionaire. In the following year, he entered into a partnership with Yip Hon, a sworn member of the Hong Men society whose grand plans were to change the face of Macau forever. Yip had grown up in Jiangmen, Guangdong province, where his family owned a porcelain shop. They were quite well off, and in 1922, when Yip was in his early teens, they sent him to Guangzhou to continue his schooling. But he was already addicted to gambling, and he moved down to Macau. Yip had a number of nicknames, one of the earliest being 'Devil King', which is the Chinese term for the Joker in a deck of cards. It is said that in an early game with friends, Yip drew two Jokers in a row, thereby earning his new name.

According to one story, gambling tycoon Fu Tak-yam, whose family had acquired the gaming monopoly franchise in 1934, recruited Yip to open another casino operation in Shanghai three years later. But competition was fierce, and the operation ended in failure, causing a fall-out between Fu and Yip.[105] A relative of one of Yip's partners disputes this, saying that Yip never worked for Fu, although he spent a lot of time in his gambling houses, winning a great deal of money through 'listening' to the dice and predicting how the game would turn out. Whatever the case, Fu took Yip aside one day in the 1940s and offered him $200 000 to leave Macau for good. Yip took the money, opened a casino in Saigon's Chinese sister town Cholon and then brought the proceeds back to Hong Kong and invested in property.[106]

Although the details are ·unclear, Yip's poor relationship with Fu Tak-yam is not disputed. Yip began plotting to take the Macau gambling concession away from the Fus. Then the old Fu died and Yip put in several bids against his sons, but failed to get the monopoly. More powerful allies were needed, so Yip began to look around for an influential Chinese businessman to be his partner. He settled on Teddy Yip, with whom he shared the same clan name, but was otherwise not related. Teddy Yip was born around 1910 in what today is Indonesia. In the 1940s he had migrated to Hong Kong where he started out as a salesman for a cash register company run by an Englishman. By then he was already fluent in English, French, German, Dutch, Malay and several Chinese dialects, including Mandarin, Fujianese, Teochew, Cantonese and Shanghaiese. He was also a classic playboy and, in his youth, a well-known car racer.

Teddy Yip was rapidly promoted to be the British company's primary agent. His talent as a salesman soon came to the notice of others, and he was offered a job by a sugar company, Jianyuan, as manager of its office in Burma's capital, Rangoon. Again Teddy Yip showed his talent, quickly gaining Jianyuan a 5 per cent share of the Hong Kong market, and he rose to become general manager for Hong Kong and Southeast Asia.[107]

Then, in 1961, Teddy Yip got a phone call from Yip Hon. The Devil King asked him to join forces to win the Macau gambling franchise from the Fu family. Teddy was not enthusiastic. The Fus were rich and influential and had controlled Macau's gambling industry for almost three decades. But he consulted with his former English boss at the cash register company, who introduced him to a good American lawyer. The lawyer helped the Yips send a letter to the Portuguese government, requesting 'an opportunity to consult the criteria for a gambling licence'.[108]

Teddy and his wife also made a secret trip to Lisbon to check the records to find out why Yip Hon had been rejected in his previous bids. They came back with the answer: Yip Hon was not a Portuguese citizen, nor did he have a business of his own in Macau. Once the reasons were clear, Teddy thought of one of the brothers of his wife Ho Yuen-yuen: Ho Hung-sun, or Stanley Ho, who did have business in Macau and whose wife was a Portuguese citizen. Although Stanley had run a kerosene refinery in Macau in the late 1940s together with two followers of the Fu family, he was known to be a smooth operator with considerable diplomatic skills. Once some rival gangsters who wanted a piece of the action in the kerosene business had threatened Stanley with hand grenades. But Ho had stood up to them, injuring one of the gangsters. Worried about the long-term ramifications of the confrontation, Stanley offered to pay the thug's hospital bill.[109]

Stanley's intermediary when he negotiated with the gangsters was Ho Yin, the banker. Stanley had many other friends in the Macau government, among local businessmen and in the underworld. One of them was Korean War trader Henry Fok, who was brought in on the casino deal to provide funding to match that of the Fus. Stanley also believed—and rightly so—that Fok's special standing with the mainland Chinese authorities was a factor that the Portuguese could not ignore. Further, Fok was a native of Panyu—just like Ho Yin, whose support was needed if they were going to get the contract.[110]

At first, Ho Yin was opposed to the idea, and tried to talk Stanley and his friends out of bidding for the casino franchise. Ho Yin said that Stanley's life would be in danger if he pushed the proposal, and that even if he managed to open a casino, his enemies would ensure that Macau was cast into chaos, that hotels would be closed, ferries stopped, thugs posted at the casino door and hand grenades hurled.[111] But Stanley would not give in, and in January 1962 the STDM was born.

Fok suggested that, in addition to the bid for the licence, the consortium should offer to develop a port and speedboat service to reduce the travel time between Hong Kong and Macau, and better hotels and infrastructure to encourage more tourism to the territory. It also helped that the newly appointed governor, Antonio Lopes dos Santos, had let it be known that he felt the authorities were not getting enough revenue from gambling.

Nevertheless, to challenge the Fus' monopoly was a formidable and potentially dangerous task, as Ho Yin had emphasised in his talks with Stanley Ho. At the last minute, the STDM's local lawyer, responsible for drafting the bid, got cold feet and disappeared. Teddy Yip sent four of his race car drivers to look for him. The errant lawyer was eventually located in a side street and 'persuaded' to finish his work. A few weeks later, the STDM won the licence—and the transformation of Macau began.[112]

Until the 1960s, ordinary people could reach Macau only by an old-fashioned ferry, which took three to four hours to sail across the Pearl River estuary from Hong Kong. Now hydrofoils were introduced, reducing the travel time first to 75 minutes and later, when replaced by Boeing jet foils in the late 1970s, to less than an hour. The Fu family's scruffy gambling dens in the Hotel Central and elsewhere, where croupiers wore singlets and slippers, gave way to new, Las Vegas-style casinos complete with roulette, slot-machines, blackjack and baccarat. Later, dog and horse racing were added, and each November the Macau Grand Prix attracted world-class drivers to a dare-devil race through the city. This was Teddy Yip's idea, and he himself took part every year until 1966 when, at 56 years old, he decided that further participation would be a risk to his health.

Better accommodation than the dilapidated Central and the Grande was also needed, and in 1970 the STDM opened the Lisboa Hotel and Casino. Macau gossip has it that the architect had been told to create something unforgettable, and that is precisely what he did. The garish, high-rise hotel is shaped like a giant bird cage, sup-posedly—according to Chinese *fengshui* beliefs—to keep money flowing in, but not out.[113] In the Mona Lisa Hall downstairs, half-naked dancers at the revue-style Crazy Paris Show entertained gamblers and tourists who wanted to see something different from the casino next door. More luxury hotels were built, and the STDM had finally converted gambling in Macau from a sleazy pastime which barely provided enough revenue to maintain basic government services into a massive growth industry.

But the first years of operation were not without problems. Towards the end of 1966, China's Cultural Revolution spilled over into Macau. In November, over 200 policemen were called in to stop the demolition of an old building on Taipa, which a pro-communist neighbourhood wanted to replace with a community-run school. A scuffle erupted, and baton-wielding police charged the crowd. A few days later, Maoist youths, Mao's *Little Red Book* in hand, forced their way into Government House, sacked the Leal Senado—the City Hall—and also occupied the Catholic charity centre, Santa Casa de Misericordia, in Macau's main square. The security forces were overwhelmed, and Red Guards in effect took over the city. Across the border in Zhuhai, tens of thousands of Red Guards and others held mass meetings, denouncing 'the Portuguese imperialists' and holding banners with slogans such as 'Resolutely support our patriotic compatriots in Macau for their struggle against brutality!'.[114]

Had the Chinese government one morning ordered the crowds in Zhuhai to march into Macau, the territory would have been taken over before lunch. No one would have stopped them and there would hardly have been any international condemnation. After all, the Indians had occupied Goa and the other Portuguese colonies on the coast of the Subcontinent in December 1961, and annexed them to their union the following year. But in Macau nothing happened. The territory, though tiny, was too important as China's conduit to the rest of the world for trade and commerce—and the gold business was still bringing in enough money for everyone to silence even Beijing's most diehard communist leaders.

In the end, China's main man in Macau, banker Ho Yin, intervened and defused the situation. He went on the radio and announced: 'I am Ho Yin, I am Ho Yin, please will everybody calm down. The situation is now being resolved. Please stay inside unless absolutely necessary'.[115] Both the public and the government heeded his advice. The demonstrators went home—though the governor, José Nobre de Carvalho, was forced to apologise for the brutality of the police, and the families of eight demonstrators killed in the rioting were compensated. On

29 January 1967, the Portuguese signed a protocol which stated that from now on their administration would function 'in accordance with the instructions of the Guangdong Provincial Foreign Affairs Bureau'—and of the Macau Chamber of Commerce, whose chairman was Ho Yin.[116] The Portuguese could stay, but the bottom line was that Macau would remain, at least in name, a separate jurisdiction, and therefore would still be useful in Beijing's quest for foreign exchange and trade. Colonial authority had been fundamentally weakened.

In April 1974, another crisis broke out, when Portugal's fascist government was overthrown by progressive army officers who had returned from the unpopular colonial wars in Africa. A racy democracy replaced fascism, and all the African colonies—Mozambique, Angola, Guinea-Bissau, Cabo Verde and São Tomé e Príncipe—became independent republics. Then the Portuguese eastern half of Timor was invaded by Indonesia in December 1975. Portugal tried to give Macau back to China, but the Chinese did not want it—at least not yet.

The new, democratic Portugal, which wanted to shed its image as a colonial power, stopped calling Macau an 'overseas province of Portugal'. Under a new constitution, promulgated in 1976, Macau was reclassified as 'a territory under Portuguese administration'. When Lisbon and Beijing established diplomatic relations in 1979, the Chinese version of the protocol described Macau as a 'Chinese territory under Portuguese administration'.[117] Portugal retained its own wording in its constitution, but did not object to China's way of interpreting it. In effect, Portugal had relinquished sovereignty, but continued to govern the territory. Macau—and the STDM—had survived two revolutions, and the goose continued to lay golden eggs for both the Portuguese and the Chinese.

Although the STDM had been Yip Hon's idea, and Henry Fok and Teddy Yip had provided most of the initial capital to set up the enterprise, it was Stanley Ho, a flamboyant, cosmopolitan ballroom dancer, who became its manager and main front man. Born in 1921 in Hong Kong, Stanley—the story goes—fled to Macau when the Japanese invaded the British colony in 1941. He arrived with only ten Hong Kong dollars—or $1.28—in his pocket, and the dashing young man then went on to become another of Asia's many rags-to-riches stories.

Other sources tell a different story, saying that he actually came from a wealthy Eurasian family in Hong Kong. One of his grand-uncles was

Sir Robert Ho-tung, a compradore of Jardine Matheson, the colony's biggest trading house. In those days, Sir Robert was considered the richest man in Hong Kong. But then disaster struck the family. When Stanley was thirteen, his father, Ho Sai-kwong—a compradore to one of Shanghai's wealthiest families, the cotton and opium-trading Sassoons—lost all his fortune in share speculation and fled to Saigon in French Indochina. Young Stanley finished high school on a scholarship and continued his studies at Hong Kong University. Then World War II broke out, the Japanese took over Hong Kong, and neutral Macau became a centre for trade with both the Japanese and the Chinese. Stanley, with the help of an English-speaking Japanese whom he had met in Hong Kong, was offered a job at a Japanese-owned trading firm in Macau.[118] It was involved in barter trade, supplying machinery and spare parts to the Japanese army in China in return for food, which was in great demand in Macau because of the influx of tens of thousands of refugees from adjacent provinces.[119]

Initially, part of Stanley's job was to accompany the firm's ships when they carried goods between Macau and the Japanese-occupied territories in China. On one of these trips Stanley's ship was attacked by a band of well-armed pirates. Some of Ho's men were shot in the chase and, having boarded the ship, the pirates took all the money, cargo and personal belongings of everyone on board. Ho and his remaining crew returned to Macau in their underwear.[120]

Two years after his arrival in Macau, Stanley was a fluent Japanese speaker—and also one of the richest men in town. When the war was over, he returned to Hong Kong, where he diversified his businesses into real estate, shipping and construction. In fact, the man who had once acted as go-between for Japanese occupation forces began to make big money from the British army garrison by building quarters for the troops.[121] When he later became manager of the STDM, the handsome Eurasian's glamorous lifestyle—he was often seen with gorgeous Chinese film actresses and ballerinas—enhanced his image of being 'the last swashbuckling merchant prince of the South China Sea, thirsting for adventure and fun'.[122] He loved to sing love songs and dance the tango, and he was good at both.

His taste for adventure, and his willingness to take a gamble, led Ho to look for 'export' markets for his gaming enterprises in the 1970s. His biggest investment was in Iran, where the Shah was still in power.

In 1973, he was granted a 25-year horse racing franchise in conjunction with the Shah's Royal Horse Society, and embarked on a $25 million project to build two racecourses and a greyhound track.[123] But only six years later, the Islamic revolution swept Iran, and horse racing was, of course, banned. He was equally unsuccessful in Timor, where the Portuguese authorities in the early 1970s granted him a gambling franchise. He had nearly completed a three-storey hotel in the territory's capital, Dili, when civil war broke out in August 1975, leading to the Indonesian invasion four months later.[124] Similarly, a contract to open a casino in Karachi was nipped in the bud when Pakistani leader Zulfikar Ali Bhutto was overthrown in a coup staged by general Zia-ul Haq in 1977.[125]

He fared somewhat better in Indonesia proper, where president Suharto allowed him to operate a stadium for *jai-alai*—a cross between squash and lacrosse—in a 50:50 partnership with the government. He also built bowling alleys in Jakarta, but this was not really big business. Nor were his attempts to break into the Australian gambling market a great success. In 1972, he bought a stake in Australia's first casino, Wrest Point, in Hobart, Tasmania, but failed to get a contract to operate it more extensively. That was when he turned to the Philippines, where the kleptocratic and deeply corrupt Marcoses invited him to run the country's first gaming establishment, the government-owned floating casino in Manila Bay. 'President Marcos asked me to help. How could I refuse?' Stanley later told a foreign journalist.[126] But in February 1986, Marcos met the same fate as the Shah of Iran, and was ousted by a popular uprising.

Ho's attempts to branch out in the region had failed, so he turned his attention to further expanding his influence in tiny Macau, where no one was in a position to challenge him or his business empire. After keeping its books closed for 35 years, the STDM in 1997 had to abide by new disclosure laws, and revealed a massive $595 million profit in 1996. Government statistics showed that tourism and gambling generated 43 per cent of Macau's GDP in the same year.[127] Profits had also been invested in Hong Kong, where Stanley Ho had built up another concern, Shun Tak Holdings. Listed in the British colony, it showed a market capitalisation of more than $1 billion.[128] Shun Tak's business interests included real estate development, hotels and catering, as well as a fleet of hydrofoils and jetfoils which shuttled between Macau and Hong Kong.

Macau prospered because of its casinos and related services. Stanley Ho was also a generous man on a more personal level. He became the main benefactor of a number of charities, ranging from a few thousand dollars towards Christmas parties for the poor organised by Macau's best-known Roman Catholic Father, the legendary Manuel Teixeira, to generous donations to the Duke of Edinburgh's Award International Foundation. When the Foundation's refurbished London offices were opened in June 1966, Prince Philip and Stanley Ho posed for a photograph together.[129] The Pope conferred on him the Papal Insignia of 'Knight Commander of the Equestrian Order of Saint Gregory the Great' in 1989 in appreciation of the 'magnanimity and humanitarian gestures of the Macau and Hong Kong Impresario towards the Catholic Church'.[130] The dining hall in Macau's prestigious Clube Militar was named after the gambling tycoon, and the green banner of the STDM fluttered beside the Portuguese national flag at the entrance of the landmark Lisboa Hotel.

A joke began to circulate among cynical Macau residents: Stanley Ho sits on the right-hand side of the Portuguese governor and a senior representative of the Chinese government sits on the left. When the governor needs permission to spend money, he turns to the left. But for the money itself, the governor always turns to his right.[131]

Other founders of the STDM did not fare as well. Teddy Yip sold his 10 per cent stake in STDM to Stanley Ho in 1992, but has retained a major shareholding in Shun Tak Shipping—which owns the jetfoils—and has property in Britain, the United States and Canada. His accumulated wealth is estimated at more than $250 million. The old playboy and former car-racer also claims a bevy of beauties all over the world as his 'girlfriends'. In 1983, he invited 52 of his current and former fiancées to a big party in Acapulco, Mexico, along with their husbands and children who all were given free air tickets and five-star hotel rooms. Teddy Yip claims that his wife—who happens to be Stanley Ho's sister—tolerates his admitted infidelities because he has always made it clear that he 'values his family'.[132]

He also keeps a collection of vintage race cars in his garages in Hong Kong and London, and makes a point of inspecting his prized possessions every day. Teddy Yip freely admits that women and cars are the only things that give life meaning. 'It isn't blood flowing in my veins, it's petrol!' he once told some journalists from Hong Kong.[133]

Yip Hon remained rich but never made a comparable fortune. He was the only real gambling expert among the founding fathers of the STDM, but never felt entirely comfortable with the partnership. Stanley Ho and Henry Fok increased their stake in the venture, giving them more leverage over Yip Hon. Finally, in 1975, Yip announced his withdrawal from the STDM, selling off all of his shares by 1982 for $40 million to Cheng Yu-tung, the director of New World Development, who became a new partner in the gaming enterprise.[134] At the same time, Henry Fok stood down as STDM director and chairman of Shun Tak in favour of Stanley Ho, who was already running much of the show anyway.[135] But Fok retained a 28 per cent share in the STDM, and continued to oversee its operations from behind the scenes.[136]

Despite much bitterness, business ties between Yip Hon and Stanley Ho were not completely severed. Yip's eldest son, Yip Ping-yan, remains a director of companies in Ho's Shun Tak Group. And Yip Hon himself never gave up his interest in gambling. In 1980, he built a European-style trotting track on Taipa island. However, this style of horse racing did not prove popular in Macau, and by the end of January 1988 Yip had lost nearly $14 million. He sold the company to Taiwanese interests, who changed it into a regular horse racing establishment. Exactly four years later, a subsidiary of the STDM bought a 51 per cent share of the company, which effectively put Stanley Ho in control of all of Macau's gambling venues. Yip philosophically noted that, although he had been mistaken about trotting, at least his company had finally brought some prosperity to Taipa. Before the track was built, Taipa was a small rural community, living on farming and commuting to work in Macau. Today, its many high-rise condominiums, hotels and casinos makes it almost indistinguishable from the city on the peninsula across the bridge.

In his waning years, Yip Hon made a last attempt to re-enter the gambling business. In 1988 he announced plans to buy a floating casino, called the Orient Princess, which would not be bound by Macau's monopoly and franchise laws. Through his wide range of underworld contacts, he also ganged up with the Heung brothers from one of Hong Kong's most notorious Triads, the Sun Yee On, to regain a foothold in Macau through the Kingsway, a hotel with a casino—and VIP rooms—located behind the Lisboa. One of Yip's nephews joined another Sun Yee On leader, Ki Ming-po, in operating the floating casino. Stanley Ho put pressure on the governments of China, Hong Kong and Macau to ban floating casinos, but when that failed he invested in one of his own to compete with Yip Hon directly. Yip decided that it was not worth a fight, and when the lease on the ship came due, he did not renew it. The floating casino was gone and with that move Yip effectively retired from the gambling business.

But he continued to gamble for his own personal pleasure. He visited Las Vegas every year on the first day of the Chinese Lunar New Year. He once spent 32 hours gambling non-stop at Caesar's Palace and, over the Lunar New Year of 1996, lost $5 million at the tables of another casino. Even so, he enjoyed Las Vegas and became acquainted with major American casino operators such as Steve Wynn and Donald Trump. Wynn used to welcome Yip's New Year visits to his Mirage Casino with a red carpet, and lion and dragon dances—and a beautiful blonde wishing him *Kung Hei Fat Choi*, or 'Happy New Year' in Cantonese.

When Trump opened his Trump Plaza Casino in Atlantic City, he took Yip Hon's advice and included games such as *fan-tan* and *pai-kau* to attract Chinese gamblers. And a Chinese restaurant in Las Vegas still serves a dish called 'Yip Hon Fried Rice', which was first invented when the ageing gambling tycoon ordered rice to be fried with gravy from a roasted duck. Yip Hon died in May 1997 of a heart attack at his home in Hong Kong's Mid-Levels. He was studying a horse-racing sheet at the time.[137]

Henry Fok fared rather better. The STDM's financier and first director—and still believed to be its single biggest shareholder—became the honorary chairman of the Hong Kong Chinese Chamber of Commerce. Due to his excellent connections in China, he also emerged as the territory's undisputed kingmaker. When in the mid-1990s the Chinese government was looking around for candidates to lead the Hong Kong Special Administrative Region after the departure of the British, they sought Henry Fok's advice. His recommendation was shipping magnate Tung Chee-hwa. The Chinese liked the idea, and Tung was selected in November 1996 by a Beijing-appointed electoral body to become the first chief executive of the Hong Kong SAR.[138]

Fok's connections with the Tung family go back many years. The Tungs, entrepreneurs from Shanghai who fled to Hong Kong after the communist victory on the mainland in 1949, owned Orient Overseas International (OOI), one of East Asia's biggest shipping companies. The company was a main beneficiary of the 1956 Middle East War and the Vietnam conflict in the 1960s and 1970s. But in 1985, it was so heavily in debt that it had to seek court protections from its creditors.[139] Fok came to the rescue. He arranged a $120 million loan from the Chinese government—although connections between Tung and Chiang Kai-shek's Guomindang had been so close that OOI had become known as 'Taiwan's shipping company'.[140] Now the communist government in Beijing stepped in to prevent OOI from going bankrupt. This bail-out became a hotly debated issue in Hong Kong when Beijing selected Tung as chief executive. Where would Tung's loyalties lie: with the people whose interests he was supposed to represent, or with Beijing?[141]

Beijing's selection of Edmund Ho as chief executive of the new Macau SAR was based on the same concept of finding a person who had a strong standing in the local business community—and a very special relationship with the Chinese authorities. On 15 May 1999, 163 out of 199 members of the China-appointed selection committee, headed by Beijing's vice premier Qian Qichen, voted in favour of Edmund Ho, general manager of the Tai Fung bank, vice president of the Macau Chamber of Commerce, vice president of Macau's Legislative Assembly and a member of the standing committee of the National People's Congress in Beijing.[142]

More significantly, Edmund Ho is also the son of 'Red Fat Cat' banker Ho Yin, Beijing's main man in Macau until his death at the age of 74 in December 1983. Edmund, who was educated partly in Canada, worked as an accountant in Hong Kong until his cancer-stricken father called him back to take over the management of the Tai Fung Bank. Ho Yin's age and ill-health were not its only problems. The bank's name, which means 'Great Abundance', was beginning to sound more and more hollow, as it was facing severe liquidity problems and perhaps was even on the verge of bankruptcy.

Edmund managed to overcome that with a hefty injection of capital from the Bank of China. The mainland-owned bank also reportedly acquired at least a 50 per cent stake in Tai Fung.[143] The exact details of the deal have never been made public, but Tai Fung is now the second largest bank in Macau after the local branch of the Bank of China. To demonstrate his impartiality in politics and business, Edmund Ho resigned from all the bank's positions after his election as Macau's future chief executive—but cynical observers could not help but notice that China had managed to fill the post of chief executive in both Hong Kong and Macau with local businessmen they had helped bail out at roughly the same time.

The near-collapse of Tai Fung was blamed on outdated management and accounting practices, which almost wrecked what should have been a solid bank. Each year since 1976, the STDM deposited 10 per cent of its receipts into a development fund which by 1982 stood at around $40 million—and the money was kept in Ho Yin's bank. Until July 1981, interest on the fund had gone only to the STDM. With Yip Hon acting as an intermediary, that changed as the STDM agreed to share the interest earned with the government.[144] This may have caused confusion, and possibly also unauthorised loss of funds, before the new rules had been finalised and put into practice.

Whatever the case, STDM 'development funds' continued to generate controversy. A major dispute centred around a 'cultural fund' called *Fundação Oriente*, or the Orient Foundation. Set up in 1986 by Carlos Monjardino, financial affairs secretary under Macau's then governor Joaquim Pinto Machado, the foundation received its initial capital of $3 million from the STDM. The gambling monopoly also agreed to pay 1.6 per cent of its receipts directly to the foundation for 'cultural and social uses', in addition to a 30 per cent gambling tax paid to the government.[145] In Macau, the foundation built public housing and supported hospitals and schools, exhibitions and concerts.

But the statutes of the foundation stated that its headquarters had to be in Lisbon, with only a 'delegation' in Macau. Consequently, tens of millions of dollars were transferred to Monjardino's Lisbon-registered foundation every year. This money, which had originally been generated at the gaming tables in Macau, was spent on various enterprises in Europe. The foundation report for 1994 stated that investments in France, Britain, Switzerland and Luxembourg alone amounted to $70 million. Large sums of money reportedly also found their way to Portugal's ruling Socialist Party. Monjardino had been appointed to his post in Macau by Mário Soares, Portugal's then president. Soares had reason to repay a favour to Monjardino. Before he was swept to power after the 1974 revolution, Soares had spent years in exile in France—with a house and funds from Monjardino's father, a medical doctor.[146] Now Monjardino became a 'fundraiser' for Soares.

By 1993, the Orient Foundation's listed assets were worth $270 million—a sum too huge for the Chinese to ignore. Beijing charged that the foundation was nothing more than a conduit for channelling capital from Macau out of the territory and, more importantly, out of Chinese hands before the 1999 handover.[147] China wanted to control both the foundation and the 1.6 per cent it was receiving from the STDM's net profits—and began to put pressure on Stanley Ho. The Chinese started to insist that his gambling concession, which in 1986 had been renewed for another fifteen years, was 'still under negotiation'. Ho and Monjardino countered by paying a visit to 'the Macau Basic Law Promotion Association', which was responsible for drafting a mini-constitution for the post-1999 era. They came to hand over a $65 000 'charitable donation' on behalf of the Orient Foundation—but were left waiting for hours, just to be told that the association could not accept 'outside money'.[148]

The dispute was eventually resolved in June 1997, just a few days before the Chinese takeover of Hong Kong. Ho agreed to stop funding the Orient Foundation, while the 'Sino-Portuguese Joint Liaison Group', which was to oversee the 1999 handover of Macau, confirmed that the STDM's gambling monopoly would not be terminated before its stipulated franchise expired in 2001. At the same time, the gambling tax was increased to 31.8 per cent—and the STDM pledged to contribute an additional 1.6 per cent of its takings—the same as it had paid to the Orient Foundation—to a new Macau-based outfit called the Macau Co-operation and Development Foundation. As STDM manager, Ho applauded the decision to let his monopoly continue even beyond the handover of Macau.[149]

Ho's business acumen, negotiating skills and remarkable ability to fight off the many challenges to his grip on Macau's economy have won him respect in all quarters—including the Chinese criminal underworld. To them, he is known as 'Sun Gor', which is Cantonese for 'Big Brother Sun' and adapted from his Chinese name, Ho Hung-sun. That respect can sometimes be personal. In the early 1990s, someone broke into a car in Macau and stole a million dollars worth of jewellery. This was nothing unusual in Macau, but it became big news because the car belonged to one of Ho's daughters. The day after local papers ran the story, the jewellery was returned with an unsigned note of apology.[150]

Stanley has always vehemently denied he has any relationship with the Triads, who nevertheless run the STDM's VIP rooms. In August 1992, US Senate Committee hearings named Ho as an 'entertainment industry participant not known to be involved in organised crime' but linked to 'former associates' who were.[151] This has usually been interpreted as a reference to Yip Hon, who was a member of the Hong Men society. A Hong Kong government report in 1994 also linked Ho to a series of corporate transactions involving some high-flying Australian businessmen, which had become the subject of a police investigation into violations of securities regulations in the colony.[152]

The investigation was inconclusive, but links such as these became a problem when Ho tried to expand his interests in Australia's gambling industry beyond his stake in Hudson Conway's Wrest Point casino in Hobart, which he had acquired in 1972, and stakes in the same company's casinos in Darwin and Launceston. In 1992, Stanley had tried and failed to buy a 50 per cent stake in Perth's Burswood casino. A year later, he tendered—unsuccessfully—in Sydney for the Pyrmont Bay casino, which later became Star City. Stanley did not show his frustrations openly, but another executive of his Shun Tak Group spoke at an Australian business lunch in 1995 and warned that 'racist policies' could be damaging to Australia's foreign investment potential.[153]

The now defunct licensing board of New South Wales, however, saw it in a different light. Its report on Ho is stamped 'never to be released', but it is clear that he was deemed 'an unsuitable person to hold a casino licence' in Australia.[154] That assessment continued to haunt Ho when, in 1998, he once again attempted to buy into Australia's lucrative casino business, this time negotiating to buy Cairns' Reef Casino. The talks fell through when the Queensland government refused to initiate probity checks.

But most allegations levelled against Ho and his supposed connections to Chinese organised crime failed to take into consideration that it would have been impossible to run a gambling enterprise in a place like Macau without reaching some kind of understanding with the Triads. Casinos inevitably attract criminals, who see opportunities for loan-sharking, extortion, prostitution and drug peddling. Casinos are also well-known vehicles for money laundering. Regular visitors to Macau's Triad-controlled VIP rooms, which are not subject to the same regulations as the public casinos, sometimes bring in suitcases containing several million Hong Kong dollars, which the managers willingly, but for a commission, convert into tokens—and then into cheques, which can be declared as gambling winnings and deposited in any bank.[155] Disclosures are minimal. Money moves in and out of Macau fast enough to make an accountant's head spin.

Triad-related activities have been part of life in both Macau and Hong Kong for more than a century. But the early Triads in European-ruled towns on the South China coast were somewhat different from both the original Chinese Tiandihui, which organised outcasts and misfits against the capricious rule of the Emperor's corrupt Mandarins, and the Shanghai Green Gang, which virtually ruled the city in which it operated. However, they were born out of the same distrust of governments, and the need for vulnerable segments of society to band together in secret guilds and associations to protect their own group interests in an alien and sometimes hostile environment. Ultimately, of course, they became criminal associations that formed a lucrative partnership with big business and the law.

Hong Kong's first ordinance 'for the Suppression of the Triad and other Secret Societies' was promulgated in January 1845, less than three years after Britain acquired its new colony. This was hardly surprising. The local Chinese, wary of the foreign rulers whose language and customs they did not understand, naturally turned to their own associations rather than to the established authorities. By 1857, the British had discovered that the societies had gained control of the local labour market. Jobs were 'sold' to people from across the border, and those with jobs were subjected to intimidation and extortion.[156]

As the republican movement gathered momentum inside China, and in overseas Chinese communities in Southeast Asia and North America, Hong Kong's Triad members also met to organise resistance against the Manchu Qing dynasty. In 1895, Chinese nationalist leader Dr Sun Yat-sen tried to stage a revolt in Guangdong, but failed and fled to Hong Kong, along with thousands of supporters. He was not allowed to stay, but managed to whip up more support for his cause among people in Hong Kong. The outcome was the first purely Hong Kong secret society, the Chung Wo Tong, or 'the Lodge of Loyalty and Righteousness', which aspired to unite all local Triad members in support of Dr Sun's republican party. Prior to the 1895 revolt, Dr Sun had also run a surgery in Macau, where he and Zheng Shiliang of the Tiandihui had organised secret societies with links to troops in the service of the Emperor.

Following the overthrow of the Manchus and the establishment of the Republic of China in 1911–12, Hong Kong's and Macau's Triads turned their attention to local issues such as organising and settling labour disputes, extortion, protection rackets and drug peddling. Hong Kong's Chung Wo Tong disintegrated into a whole range of societies, all with 'Wo'—'harmonious' in Cantonese—in their name: Wo On Lok ('Harmony, Peace, Happiness'), which was set up in Mongkok in 1934 and became active in Yau Ma Tei and Sham Shui Po in Kowloon as well as in Yuen Long and Castle Peak in the New Territories; the Wo Shing Yee ('Harmony, Victory, Righteousness'), with a stronghold in Mongkok and Yau Ma Tei; and the Wo Shing Tong ('Harmonious and Victorious Society'), the most powerful Triad in the Western and Central districts of Hong Kong island. The Wo Shing Wo ('Harmonious, Victorious and Peaceful Society') operated inside Kowloon's infamous Walled City, one of Hong Kong's many incongruities.

When, in 1898, China leased out the New Territories to Britain for 99 years, it was agreed that the Kowloon Walled City, just off Boundary Street—the old border—would remain under Chinese sovereignty. Since the British were not allowed to police the area, it became a haven for outlaws who amassed fortunes operating brothels, opium dens and gambling joints. Sanitation, education and health care were almost non-existent, and disease and crime thrived in this lawless, 2.9 hectare enclave of nominally Chinese territory in the middle of Hong Kong. It was not until 1987 that the British and Chinese authorities agreed to clear the Walled City and turn it into a public park, which happened a few years later despite protests from many of its 33 000 inhabitants.

The winding lanes of the Walled City became the main stronghold for the Yee On ('Righteous and Peaceful Society'), the most powerful secret society among the colony's Teochew-speaking residents. At first registered officially as the Yee On Commercial and Industrial Guild, it later resorted to outright criminal activities, operating under the cover of the To Shui Boxing Club and the Tai Ping Shan Sports Association. Another group of Triads, the Chuen, organised coolies, marine store hawkers and mahjong school students and teachers. They also oversaw prostitution in the Yau Ma Tei typhoon shelter, collected protection money from street vendors, and rented out cars and bicycles.

Pre-World War II Triads in Macau were similar in outlook, only smaller and with their attention focused more on opium and gambling. Like their Hong Kong compatriots, they also laid claim to 'righteousness' and 'harmony'. But, despite all the pretense of 'patriotism' and adherence to old Chinese moral values, World War II split both Hong Kong's and Macau's Triad societies into three camps.

Most of the Hong Kong Triads ended up under the command of the Asia Flourishing Organisation, an oddly named outfit that was formed by the Japanese occupying power. Triad members became informers and enforcers for the Japanese, who in return destroyed the members' criminal records in captured British archives, and allowed them to operate gambling dens and opium houses. They were also encouraged to operate prostitution rings for the Japanese soldiers who came to Hong Kong for rest and recreation.[157] A few Triads continued to work faithfully for Chiang Kai-shek's Guomindang, while the third camp consisted of more pragmatic Triads who shifted their allegiances depending on who they thought was going to win at any given time.

In neutral Macau, there were no Japanese troops. But the Japanese maintained a large army camp just a few metres beyond the border gate, and the Japanese 'consulate' in the city was in fact a military command post. Some of the Triad bosses evidently believed that the Japanese were going to win the war, and sided with them. Wong Kong Kit, the leader of one of Macau's main gangs, openly defied the Portuguese colonial authorities by being driven around the city in a black limousine accompanied by eight bodyguards with sub-machine guns. He and his wife became known as 'the Bonnie and Clyde' of Macau, and established their headquarters under the auspices of the Japanese police in a villa on Avenida do Colonel Mesquita where there were sandbags on the veranda, a terrace with mounted machine guns, and a uniformed guard at the garden gate. Their business was espionage for the Japanese, pressuring the Portuguese authorities, and controlling all imports of rice from China so they could levy a tax on the trade.[158]

Another godfather, Siu Keng Siu, who was nicknamed 'the Immortal' because of his ability to manipulate any situation to his advantage, cooperated with the Allied powers as well as the Portuguese.[159] Other less important gangsters made a killing selling scrap metal to the Japanese war machine, or smuggled gold and other hard currencies between Hong Kong, China and Macau.

All that changed after the war—and the 1949 Communist victory in China, which forced thousands of gangsters to flee for their lives. Most of them ended up in Taiwan, but Hong Kong also saw a large influx of hard-core criminals from Guangzhou and Shanghai. When Big-Eared Du Yuesheng arrived in 1949, he tried to re-establish the Green Gang in Hong Kong—but, unable to carve out a niche for themselves in a milieu already dominated by local Triads, the gangsters from Shanghai resorted to armed robberies, and their bands of highly skilled pickpockets roamed the streets. The colonial authorities soon ran out of patience with them, and many were deported to Taiwan.

Big-Eared Du, however, was too rich and powerful to be ordered out. Anyway, his health was failing and he died in 1951. A grand funeral reception was held at the Luk Kwok Hotel in Hong Kong's Wanchai district near the harbour. Countless condolence messages from prominent people and big corporations arrived from Taiwan. Marching bands and Taoist priests led the procession through the city, and the hearse was bedecked with pine and cypress, symbols of mourning and virtue.[160]

But he was not allowed to be buried in Hong Kong. In October 1952, a year after his death, the remains of the Godfather of Shanghai were taken under police escort to Hong Kong's harbour, and put on a ship bound for Taiwan. To express their gratitude to the man who had nurtured Chiang Kai-shek's political career, the Taiwan authorities later erected a statue in his honour in Xizhi village near Taipei. The four-character inscription on the monument praises the dead man's 'loyalty' and 'personal integrity'.[161]

The Green Gang's followers in Hong Kong were left leaderless, and only small bands survived in pockets in Bay View, Eastern District and

Tsim Sha Tsui. But another gang from the mainland soon rose to prominence. In the 1940s, new Triads had been set up by Guomindang officers and the Nationalist government's secret police to fight the communists more effectively. The best known was the 14K Society, founded in 1947 by a Guomindang general, Kot Siu Wong. The gang's name came from its first headquarters, which had been located at No 14, Po Wah Road in Guangzhou. Later, a 'K' was added, derived from the symbol of 'karat' gold, which is harder and stronger than the local soft variety of the metal.[162]

In 1949, general Kot fled to Hong Kong with hundreds of his followers. Many of them settled in Rennie's Mill, a rundown village on Junk Bay east of Kai Tak airport, where Republic of China flags flew over shabby houses until the area was sanitised and redeveloped in the mid-1990s. 14K had obvious political aims, and the mythical slogan of the original Tiandihui—*Fan-Qing Fu-Ming*, 'Crush the Qing, Restore the Ming'—was paraphrased into 'Crush the foreign invader (the communists)—Restore the Chinese (Nationalist) government!'.[163]

Backed by Taiwan's intelligence apparatus and nationalist-minded businessmen, the 14K expanded its influence over the colony, which was a more important non-communist toehold on the mainland than Macau. General Kot was deported to Taiwan in 1950, but even under the leadership of more junior Guomindang officers, the 14K prospered. Within a few years, it had become one of the biggest Triads in Hong Kong with an estimated following of 80 000—of whom many were teenagers and children. The 14K had found a new constituency among juvenile delinquents, drifters and social outcasts who, in a group that seemed inspired by the warriors of ancient China, could find a new identity and place in society. But the rough newcomers were also quick to terrorise shopkeepers and street hawkers for 'protection money', ostensibly to support the anti-communist cause but in reality to enrich themselves. The police had to crack down on the growing menace and, in 1955, 148 of the 14K's most troublesome leaders were arrested and deported to Taiwan.[164]

But such police actions were clearly inadequate as long as the Triads had powerful backing. In October 1956, senior 14K officers held a meeting in Taiwan to discuss ways of absorbing Hong Kong's other, more loosely organised, secret societies. Nothing materialised as riots broke out in the colony at almost the same time: 10 October, or 'double ten', was approaching. On that date in 1911, Dr Sun ignited the struggle that led to the proclamation of the Republic of China on 1 January 1912, and it has since been national day for all supporters of the nationalist cause.

The residents in a Kowloon suburb populated by refugees from the mainland had pasted Republic of China flags on doors and walls all over the neighbourhood. This was technically against the law, which forbids the posting of handbills on places other than notice boards. Usually the authorities ignore this rule on 10.10, but this year one over-zealous government official, in charge of resettling the refugees, tore them down. A scuffle broke out, and he retreated to his office, which was promptly surrounded by an angry crowd. He called the police, who rescued him, but were stoned by angry protesters who went on to set fire to the office.

The riot escalated, and a few thousand protesters clashed with 300 armed policemen. Tear gas was fired, and the crowd dispersed. That day, 10.10 went off relatively peacefully, but on the eleventh, mayhem reigned in Kowloon. As shops and cars were burned, it was now clear the Triads had taken over the protest movement. Young, rough-looking men sold nationalist Republic of China flags at exorbitant prices to pedestrians and drivers, beating up those who refused to pay. This only served to turn the population at large against them, and there was for the first time a public outcry against the Triads in Hong Kong. The police took advantage of the shift in the mood of the public to introduce new, tough legislation against the gangs.[165]

In the aftermath of the 1956 riots, more than 10 000 Triad members were arrested. Five hundred were deported to Taiwan—which turned out to be a serious mistake. They were welcomed as heroes by the authorities on the Guomindang-ruled island, and simply regrouped. Some were later drafted into Taiwan's main Triad, the *Chulian Bang*, or the United Bamboo Gang, which had close links with Chiang Kai-shek's security services.

Back in Hong Kong, it was becoming riskier to be a Triad member. This only prompted the societies to be even more ruthless against police informers and other 'traitors'. Some also adopted a secret language to identify themselves to members of the same Triad. Members of the Wo On Lok, for instance, started to call themselves 'Shui

Fong'—which literally means 'the water room'. Since it was illegal to belong to a Triad, a member could not say that he came from, for instance, the Wo On Lok. But at that time there was a famous fizzy bottled water in Hong Kong called 'On Lok', or 'Peace and Happiness'. It also happened to be the last two words in the name of the Triad. So instead of saying 'I'm from the Wo On Lok', a member would say 'I come from the water room', and it would be understood what he meant. The name of another Triad, the Wo Hop To, sounds almost like the Chinese word for 'walnut'. Its followers began to identify each other by saying *ngan hok*, Cantonese for 'hard seed'.[166]

Tougher circumstances—coupled with the rise of the 14K—prompted other Triads to modernise their structures and activities to match the might of general Kot's followers. Heung Chin, the leader of the old Yee On, which had its roots in Hong Kong's Teochew-speaking community, had been among the gangster bosses who were deported to Taiwan after the 1956 riots. His nine sons took over, revitalised the old society and built up a massive network of contacts in Hong Kong and around the globe. His eldest son, Heung Wah-yim, became the Triad's Dragon Head—and he also renamed the society Sun Yee On, 'the New Yee On'.

The Sun Yee On retained all the traditional Masonic rituals for new recruits, who had to recite the 36 oaths of the old Triad society, burn incense and drink a mixture of blood and rice liquor while kneeling before a Taoist altar. But it also became one of the few Triads that assigned numbers to its sworn brothers, and later kept computerised membership records. Organised along disciplined lines, the Sun Yee On allotted areas of control to its various office bearers, who were solely answerable to a central committee, headed by Heung Wah-yim. His eldest son, Heung Chin-sing, a 'Red Pole', or enforcer in the Sun Yee On, worked as the managing director of Fair Finance, an investment company. Heung Wah-yim's two brothers, Thomas and Charles, put their money into Hong Kong's lucrative film industry, which for years had been Triad-infested. 'Lured by well publicised profits, the vanity of organised crime has always had a taste for the glitz and glamour of the film business', a police report concluded.[167]

But on the street level, Sun Yee On was no different from other Triads. When a man tried to open a home decorating shop in an area which Sun Yee On considered its turf, he was brutally chopped in broad daylight with a 10-inch butcher's knife as horrified staff and customers watched. The Sun Yee On was feared and it continued to grow. Before long, it was reported that its membership had surpassed 47 000.[168]

The extent of the well-drilled organisation stunned even the police when, in 1987, they raided Heung Wah-yim's office where he worked as a part-time law clerk in the legal firm of Samuel Soo and Company. The office was not in some dark back alley in the Walled City, but in the Star House in central Hong Kong. The police stormed into some other offices, and ended up with a set of matching name lists of senior Sun Yee On office bearers. Of the 1267 names, 22 were listed as being based abroad: twelve in Macau, one in Australia, one in New Zealand, three in Britain and four in the United States.[169]

The police were convinced they had a case. Heung Wah-yim and ten other leaders of the Triad were brought before Hong Kong's High Court. It was a sight that stunned many onlookers. Heung, the Dragon Head of the Sun Yee On, one of the colony's most feared secret societies, did not even remotely resemble the stereotype of a gangster. The press described him as 'appearing like a solicitor clerk, who led a life of respectability and humdrum monotony'.[170] At lower levels, young Triad members may look like the thugs they are, complete with tattoos and pagers so that they can quickly respond to the gang's call for muscle in some dark part of Hong Kong or Macau. But the new generation of Dragon Heads, Incense Masters, Vanguards and Red Poles have abandoned their greasy T-shirts and blood-dripping meat cleavers for pinstriped suits and briefcases.

Heung was convicted of various crimes related to his leadership of an outlawed Triad society. The court also found his ten lieutenants guilty of similar crimes—but all convictions were reversed on appeal. To the embarrassment of Hong Kong's law enforcement authorities, Heung and his men were released after serving about two years of their six- and seven-year sentences.[171] Among the gangsters who walked out into freedom was Sun Yee On office bearer Cheung Leung-shing, who had been convicted in Canada in 1977 for conspiracy to import heroin. He had been released on parole in 1981, and returned to Hong Kong the following year. When he stood trial together with Heung in late 1987, the charge was blackmail and assisting in the management of the Sun Yee On.[172]

Out of gaol, Heung and his brothers realised that Hong Kong might not be a good place for business. They had been exposed and disgraced in public. But their fortunes were more or less intact—and they began to invest heavily in China. Deng Xiaoping's reforms had done away with old-style socialism, and opened the world's potentially largest market to foreign enterprise. The Sun Yee On first moved into an area which it knew—the movie industry—and set up a studio in Shenzhen across the border from Hong Kong. As Shanghai was slowly reverting to its former self, the Sun Yee On was one of the first to invest in its reborn entertainment industry. With its knack of making friends in high places, the Sun Yee On soon owned not only the Top Ten night club in Bejing together with China's security chief Tao Siju, but also a whole a string of similar establishments in Shanghai in partnership with various officers from the PLA.[173]

After the startling revelations in the early 1990s about contracts between China's security apparatus and Hong Kong's underworld, and the way the Triads had spied on labour groups, student organisations and other pro-democracy groups in the colony on behalf of China's intelligence service in return for business contracts and protection, people began to ask whether any similar arrangement had been made in Macau. It had. Macau's Triads were off-shoots of major gangs in Hong Kong, but operated independently. The only exception was the centrally controlled Sun Yee On, which had a presence in Macau through VIP rooms at the Kingsway Hotel's casino that were controlled by Jimmy and Charles Heung, two of Heung Wah-yim's many brothers. In April 1993, a couple of hand grenades were found in a garbage bin outside the hotel. After that incident, Jimmy gave an interview to a Hong Kong magazine where he asserted that 'the casino is an investment only'; he said he had never seen himself as a casino king, 'because Stanley Ho is the one'.[174]

But the police began to speculate whether Stanley Ho had granted the Heungs the right to get a stake in Macau's gaming industry due to the Sun Yee On's apparent influence in China.[175] And because of their close links to the Chinese authorities, they also stayed out of Macau's Triad war, which was disturbing the peace in the territory. At the same time, suspicions began to emerge that Broken-Tooth might have been framed after all because his outrageous behaviour was seen as the reason for all the trouble.

'The Group of the Four United' Macau Triads had been revitalised—but Kai-Sze Wai's faction of the local, albeit largely independent, chapter of the 14K had taken over the place previously held by Koi and his men. The mastermind behind the new alliance was said to be the shadowy Four-Eyed Bull, the alleged leader of the Macau chapter of the Big Circle gang.[176] The explosion that blew up judicial police chief Antonio 'Rambo' Marques Baptista on 1 May 1998 was said to have been orchestrated by the Bull to get Koi out of the way.[177]

However, the days of the faction leaders of the Bull's alliance may also be numbered. The master of Wo Shing Yee, Kwong Kwok-leung, is already in gaol, serving a six-year sentence for Triad-related crimes, and Shui Fong's Lai Tung-sang lives in exile in Vancouver. Kai-Sze Wai is too close to the casino establishment to be a major problem. And in late 1999, rumours began to circulate in Macau that even the Bull may have outlived his usefulness after the arrest of Koi, and that he could be dumped by the Chinese—which the 23 November 1999 execution of his right-hand man, Cunning Kin, clearly indicated.

Was a clean Macau emerging? Hardly. What was happening was just a shift in the kind of characters the authorities would want to deal with. The old-fashioned bandits may have passed into folklore, but an entirely new breed of entrepreneurs is emerging on the fringes of China. The businesslike, pinstriped suit-wearing managers of the Sun Yee On have shown where the future lies, which was clearly illustrated during the controversy over Chinese money going to former President Bill Clinton's election campaigns in 1992 and 1996—the so-called 'Donorgate' saga.

The figure at the centre of the controversy, Yah Lin Trie, better known as Charlie Trie, seemed an unlikely candidate to be the link between organised crime, Chinese intelligence agents and American politicians. First, his family had fled the mainland after the communist takeover and Trie was born in Taiwan and grew up there. But in 1975 he moved to Little Rock, Arkansas, where he opened first a fairly popular Chinese restaurant, Nan King, followed by another, Fu Lin. That was when he met Clinton, who would become the governor of Arkansas and the president of the United States.[178]

It is still uncertain when, and how, Trie linked up with mainland Chinese business circles and security services, but in 1984, another

Chinese—Sino-Indonesian tycoon Mochtar Riady, alias Li Wen-zheng—had put $16 million into the stock of Arkansas' Worthen Bank. His son, James Riady (or Li Bai) was sent over to learn the ins and outs of American banking.[179] The Riadys already owned one of Indonesia's biggest banks, the Lippo Bank. At about the same time, the Riadys took over the old Seng Heng Bank in Macau—together with Jackson Stephens, the director of Worthen Bank—and turned what had been an old money changer and gold-dealing front into a proper financial institution. Seng Heng was later sold to Stanley Ho, but the partnership with Stephens was important. The Little Rock lawyer was considered the kingmaker of Arkansas, a position that became very important when in 1992 Clinton launched his first election campaign. A former employee of the Lippo Bank, John Huang, took over fundraising tasks for the Democrats, who did not have nearly as much money as George Bush and his Republicans, whose power they were challenging.

Clinton won convincingly and was sworn in as the 42nd president of the United States in January 1993. The saxophone-playing president was young and popular, a fresh breeze in the White House after years of stifling influence by old-style politicians. He revitalised the American economy, initiated social welfare programs and seemed to be doing quite well—until one scandal after another began to rock his presidency. His enemies managed to dig up details about shady land deals when he was the Arkansas governor. There were allegations of drug abuse and numerous infidelities.

And then came the bombshell. In July 1994, fundraiser John Huang joined the Commerce Department as a senior official with top-secret clearance to oversee foreign trade.[180] He was dismissed during Clinton's 1996 re-election campaign, after growing reports of 'improper campaign solicitations'. It was also discovered that his former employer, Lippo Bank, had served as a conduit for donations to the Democrats from an intricate web of Chinese interests in the Far East.[181] The foreign money had been funnelled through US residents of Asian origin, which is illegal. Alleged linkages between the Riadys and their Lippo Bank and China's intelligence agencies exacerbated the confidence crisis that hit Clinton.[182] On 16 December 1996, Clinton's legal defence fund announced that it had returned $640 000 in suspect donations—from Charlie Trie.[183]

But, for a change, Trie's money did not come from Lippo Bank. He had left his Chinese eatery in Little Rock and moved to Washington. Using an apartment in Watergate as his base, he was busy maintaining contacts with his old friend Clinton, and introducing visiting dignitaries from China to the White House. On 6 February 1996, he had escorted Wang Jun, chairman of Poly Technologies—an arms company owned by the PLA—to a White House reception for donors.[184]

Investigators began to look into Trie's bank records and tax returns, only to discover that he received almost no income other than remittances from a little-known businessman in Macau called Ng Lap Seng.[185] Born in China, Ng's diverse business interests included ownership of one of Macau's hotels in the territory, the Fortuna, whose night club featured 'table dancing' by strippers, a massage parlour and a karaoke room with 'attractive and attentive hostesses from China, Korea, Singapore, Malaysia, Vietnam, Indonesia and Burma together with exotic girls from Europe and Russia'.[186] Its karaoke lounge was regularly frequented by 'big brothers' from the Shui Fong, a local Triad, as well as high-ranking PLA officers. The mother company of Ng's various enterprises, San Kin Yip, was incorporated in Little Rock in October 1994 by his friend and partner Charlie Trie.[187] Ng also paid the rent for Trie's Watergate apartment. The US investigators discovered that more than a million dollars had been transmitted by Ng, who also turned out to be a frequent visitor to the White House, and an honoured guest at several fundraising dinners for the Democrats, hosted by the president.[188]

Other shady players in the Donorgate saga soon emerged, all of them contacts of Trie's in Macau. Chen Kai-kit, who also used the name Chio Ho-cheung, was a prominent Macau politician who owed his 1996 election victory to the 14K Triad, whose goons intimidated voters or bought their votes for $195 each.[189] Obviously Chen was no ordinary businessman. He was actually not a native of Macau, but a Hainanese born in Thailand. But his influence in Macau was not only based on his political muscle in the Legislative Assembly; he was also president of the local association of people of Hainanese descent—and the proud owner of a local 'no hands' restaurant, where waitresses feed customers, thus enabling them to use their own hands to explore the bodies of the young ladies while gulping down the Chinese delicacies which are put in their mouths. His wife, Elsie Chan, had in 1986 been a runner-up winner of the Miss Peace prize of the Miss Asia beauty contest. She later made a mark in the local television and film industry by introducing more full-bodied women on to the screen. In married life, she continued supplying Macau's various 'entertainment' centres with women from her husband's native Thailand. Chen, Elsie and Trie sat at the head table with Clinton at a fundraising dinner at Washington's Sheraton Hotel on 13 May 1996.

What was behind the strange schemes and plots that were being hatched in Macau? Ng and Chen may not have had any personal interest in seeing Clinton re-elected, but in exchange for acting as conduits for money from the mainland they would get unofficial protection from the Chinese military for their own shady businesses. Even so, agreeing to help infiltrate the White House was pushing the envelope, even for people with high-level PLA contacts.

In February 1998, Trie eventually returned to Washington to face charges of illegally funnelling funds into Clinton's re-election campaign. As it turned out, he had spent more than a year in hiding with Ng in Macau, but realised at last that he could not escape American justice. In May, he pleaded guilty and agreed to cooperate with the Justice Department's campaign fundraising investigation in exchange for federal prosecutors dropping the indictments pending against him in Washington and Arkansas.[190]

At the same time, another Taiwan-born Chinese-American fundraiser for the Democrats, Johnny Chung, told federal investigators that a 'large part' of the nearly $100 000 he himself had given to Democratic causes in the summer of 1996, including $80 000 to the Democratic National Committee, actually came from the Chinese PLA through an aerospace executive called Liu Chao-ying, the daughter of General Liu Huaqing, a high-ranking Chinese military commander and a member of the Standing Committee of the Politburo of the Communist Party. General Liu was at the time also vice-chairman of China's Central Military Commission and in charge of China's drive to modernise the PLA by exporting old arms to other countries, and use the money earned in that way to acquire modern western weapons technology.[191]

The donation was only a tiny part of the $194 million that the Democrats raised in 1996, but it came at a time when Clinton was making it easier for American civilian communication satellites to be launched by Chinese rockets. This was important for the PLA—and for Liu, whose own company sold missiles for the Chinese military and also had a space subsidiary. Chung claimed that Clinton's decision—and the fact that he had gained her admission to a fundraising event in Washington where she was photographed with the president—helped her company to do business with American counterparts.

Liu was also a lieutenant colonel in the PLA, and the company she worked for, the Hong Kong arm of China Aerospace Corp., was described as 'a state-owned jewel in China's military industrial complex with interests in satellite technology, missile sales and rocket launches'. But the company had run into trouble when, in 1991 and 1992, the US government barred all American firms from doing business with two China Aerospace units that had sold missiles to Pakistan. The company needed to improve its business relations with the United States; that was, at least in part, achieved. US investigators, on their part, were satisfied with the identification of Liu, which they regarded as a small but important breakthrough in their hunt for more evidence to back up the claim that China was indeed trying to buy influence in the United States.[192]

Ng was one of the most mysterious of the characters in the 'Donorgate' saga. He was not born in Macau but in China, and arrived in the territory in 1979 with a few belongings and the equivalent of $12 in his pocket. He began his business career selling bales of cheap cloth to the local garment industry, and later became one of the most influential businessmen in the territory. But after all the damaging revelations that came out of the 'Donorgate' affair, the enigmatic Ng disappeared from sight in Macau. He refused to answer phone calls from journalists and was rarely seen at dinners in the territory, even though his name appeared beside Stanley Ho's and those of other local dignitaries on a bronze plaque outside the Clube Militar, honouring benefactors who had paid for the refurbishment of the old colonial institution. Ho and Ng, as it turned out, were also partners in Macau's most ambitious construction project: the Nam Van Lakes. This massive $2 billion land reclamation scheme was going to turn the waterway between the peninsula and Taipa into two giant lagoons, surrounded by hotels, apartment blocks and resorts. Launched during the regional boom in the early 1990s, Nam Van Lakes became a favourite site for wealthy

Chinese businessmen and officials looking to move 'hot money' out of Guangdong into the more stable precincts of Macau.[193]

The investments have not yet proven to be wise: the building boom has left Macau with a glut of space, and an estimated 30 000 of the apartments remain empty. Yet, oddly, construction of new property continues—though reports abound that much of the money is being filtered back into Chinese pockets through construction subcontractors, including PLA-owned companies.

Chen Kai-kit, the Triad-connected legislator who had dined with the Clintons, published an autobiography in which he boasted that many international figures had paid him tribute, including the American president, who presented him with 'a signed photograph' which he hung on the wall of the office of his 'import–export' company, called Ang Du, in the Bank of China building in downtown Macau.[194] Such displays may have benefited Chen in his attempts to build up a network of business associates in the territory, and perhaps also in China. But there was one man on whom it was not necessary to make any special impression: Wong Sing-wa. They were already long-time friends and close partners in the management of a VIP room in Macau's Mandarin Hotel. Wong, the head of the Talented Dragon investment firm, was in 1990 appointed Pyongyang's honourary consul in Macau, and the travel arm of his company was authorised to issue visas for North Korea.[195] As such, he worked closely with Zokwang Trading, North Korea's main commercial arm in Macau. In early 1998, a Lisbon-based weekly newspaper, the *Independent*, protested Wong's presence in a delegation from Macau that was being received by the Portuguese president. The paper cited a Macau official as saying that Wong had 'no criminal record, but we have registered information that links him to organised crime and gambling in Macau'.[196]

Wong was also linked to the inner circle of people who had tried to buy their way into the corridors of power in Washington. In 1995, he posed for a photograph outside the White House with Stanley Ho, another local business contact, and two sisters: Anna Chennault and Loretta Fung.[197] Anna, a Chinese, was the widow of the legendary Claire Chennault, who had raised the famous Flying Tigers in China during the war, and later set up the Civil Air Transport (CAT), his own airline which supplied Chiang's troops when they were fighting

Mao's communists. Later, when Deng's reforms changed China, she became as friendly with the leaders in Beijing as she had been for many years with those in power in Taipei. Together with Loretta, she opened a girlie bar called the Volvo Club in Hong Kong's racy Tsim Sha Tsui East district. It became a famous hang-out for visiting PLA officers, although the Swedish car manufacturer lodged a complaint and the club had to change its name to B.Boss. Being true Chinese patriots, the two sisters had facilitated meetings between their friends in Macau and Washington.

Like Ng, Wong Sing-wa continued to keep a low profile after the Donorgate scandal and subsquent disclosures in the American media—just to resurface in December 1997, when he had opened a new VIP room in the Lisboa Hotel in partnership with two other local businessmen, Carl Ching Men-ky and Siu Yim-kwan. Carl Ching is, of course, the same person who ran a sauna in Hong Kong's Tsim Sha Tsui in partnership with the son of China's military leader Yang Shangkun—and who was denied entry to Australia to attend the 2000 Sydney Olympics as an official of the International Basketball Federation. Siu Yim-kwan had been reported as a business partner of the shady wheeler-dealer Albert Yeung of the Emperor Group. Siu was also a major investor in Pearl Orient Holdings, a company that was widely suspected of laundering money for Deng Xiaoping's family.[198]

Chen Kai-kit also resurfaced soon after Donorgate. He landed in the middle of another controversy in early 1998, when it was reported that the Ukraine would sell an unfinished aircraft carrier to a 'leisure company' in the then still-Portuguese territory. The Ukraine had inherited the aircraft carrier after the break-up of the Soviet Union, and badly needed hard currency. The registered objective of the Macau company, Agencía Turistica e Diversões Chong Lot Limitada—which in English means 'Tourism and Amusement Agency'—was to run 'activities in the hotel and similar areas, tourism and amusement'.[199]

But why would such a company need an aircraft carrier? And where would this obscure company get $20 million, which was the price that the Ukraine wanted for the 67 000-tonne vessel? The plot thickened when local journalists discovered that the company's official address was on a major street in downtown Macau, Avenida da Praia Grande, but at a street number—335—that did not exist. The company had indicated that it intended to use the carrier as a hotel and amusement centre, a kind of floating discotheque. But a Macau government official said he doubted whether a giant aircraft carrier could be stationed near Macau because of the enclave's extremely shallow waters.[200]

The 306-metre-long ship was too big to pass through the Bosporus and Dardanelles Straits, and for months the Turkish authorities forced it to remain at anchor in the Black Sea. In September 2001, however, the Turks finally allowed the aircraft carrier to be towed to China, where its fate remains a mystery. Although Cheng Zhen Shu, chairman of Agencía Turistica e Diversões Chong Lot Limitada, denied having bought it for the PLA to enable Chinese engineers to study the secrets of aircraft carrier design, that seemed to be exactly the case. And the Hong Kong media reported that the real boss of the so-called 'tourism company' was Chen Kai-kit.[201] In other words, a man deeply implicated in an American president's fundraising campaign might also have been simultaneously acting on behalf on the Chinese military. One can only wonder how Clinton's voters might have reacted if the disclosures had come during the actual re-election campaign.

But then, in August 1999, Hong Kong's Independent Commission Against Corruption issued a warrant for the arrest of Chen and his wife Elsie Chan. They and six others, including Chen's brother and the accountant of his main company, Ang-Du International, were accused of helping to siphon off millions of dollars from Guangnan Holdings, an insolvent mainland food conglomerate, and of a plan to defraud the Standard Chartered Bank of London of $13.9 million in bogus loans.[202] Eight accomplices were arrested, but Chen could not be apprehended as he was 'receiving treatment for a heart condition in a military hospital on the mainland'.[203]

Ng Lap Seng had better luck. He was featured on the August 1998 cover of *China Today*, a mainland monthly. Not a word was mentioned about his involvement with Charlie Trie's adventures in the United States. Instead, Ng has received lavish praise from the mainland: 'As a successful entrepreneur, Ng hasn't forgotten his homeland. In recent years, in addition to his large investment [in Macau], he has donated 30 million Yuan to education, transportation, poverty relief and aid for the handicapped on the mainland. Regarding this, Ng says with a smile, "That is what every Chinese should do".' Ng also expressed optimism 'about Macau's future after its return to the motherland'.

Some people may have worried about the future when the Portuguese flag was lowered over Macau at midnight on 19 December 1999. But not Ng—and not Edmund Ho, the new chief executive. They knew the rules of the game, the delicate balancing act between the underworld and officialdom which China had also come to accept since old-style communism was discarded in the early 1980s. When Broken-Tooth Koi was arrested in 1998, he was approached by a Hong Kong reporter who asked him if he had had anything to do with Edmund Ho, whose full Chinese name is Ho Hau-wah. Koi replied: 'Oh, Brother Wah! I know him. He's a good man.'[204]

A few months before the handover, Edmund Ho stated that contacts with the Triads 'may be necessary to solve the gang problem'. He hastened to add that he had never been involved in any illegal Triad activity, with the caveat that 'if you say you don't know the Triads, you have no contacts with people with Triad background or business dealings with them, it's impossible'.[205] The only person who reacted publicly against Ho's confession was Antonio Ng, an opposition member of Macau's Legislative Assembly. Ho's comments may have tarnished his image, Ng said, but the lawmaker's biggest worry was 'whether Ho will stand up to Beijing if necessary'.[206]

How could he? Tiny Macau has survived and prospered as a separate jurisdiction—Portuguese colony, Chinese territory under Portuguese administration, a Special Administrative Region of the People's Republic of China—only because it has been willing to bow to higher authority. Unlike the outspoken citizens of Hong Kong, the people of Macau have, over the centuries, learned to deal with the mainland on its terms. The leaders in Beijing may not care if the city they inherited from the Portuguese is 'of the Name of God'. But they can rest assured that there will be None More Loyal.

• 3
THE DARK MASTERS OF KABUKI

In the winter we give the sunny half of the street to common people because we survive on their work. In the summer we yakuza walk on the sunny side, to give them the cool, shaded half. If you look at our actions, you can see our strong commitment to *giri-ninjo* [obligation and loyalty].
—The late Shotaro Hayashi, a top boss of the Sumiyoshi-kai in Tokyo[1]

Neither logic nor money can control a self-willed gangster. But by brandishing the supreme and irrational principle of the 'fatherhood' of the boss, the organisation can make members submit to anything.
—Japanese lawyer[2]

At the break of dawn, the earth began to tremble—and 20 short seconds later thousands of people lay dead or dying in the rubble of their homes. It was 17 January 1995 and the Japanese port city of Kobe, or 'Heaven's Door', had been struck by the most powerful force of nature to hit Japan since the Kanto earthquake in 1923. Homes, shopping centres, office blocks, railway stations, and even elevated expressways which the authorities had assured would withstand any earthquake, collapsed as if they had been built from paper and sticks.

In the city's Nagata ward, a tightly packed collection of flimsy buildings, people had been cooking their breakfasts over open gas flames that fateful morning. The burners overturned when the earthquake struck, and within minutes the whole neighbourhood resembled Tokyo after its 1945 firebombing. People old enough to remember that earlier cataclysm found themselves huddled under blankets on the cold stone floor of Kobe's City Hall. Tens of thousands more camped out in other public buildings, and food, water and medicines were in short supply.[3]

But the Kobe earthquake destroyed more than lives and property. Pictures of a city in ruins and criticism of government rescue efforts badly dented Japan's image as a modern economic power. The whole nation was appalled by the government's lack of leadership and the absence of crisis management in the crucial initial hours after the quake. Private community organisations had to intervene where the government had failed. In Nagata, the worst-hit ward in the city, which was home to at least 15 000 ethnic Koreans, both the pro-Seoul Korean Residents Union of Japan, or Mindan, and the pro-Pyongyang General Association of Korean Residents in Japan, or Chongryun, offered temporary shelter for the victims in relatives' homes and in their respective local headquarters.

In other parts of Kobe, heavy trucks were parked by the side of the devastated roads, and some odd-looking young men with crew cuts and dark sunglasses were seen distributing water and other necessities to the victims—also long before the Self Defence Forces and other government agencies got their act together. They belonged to the Yamaguchi-gumi, Japan's most powerful crime syndicate. The gang is headquartered in Kobe, where its *oyabun*, or leader, Yoshinori Watanabe, resides in a heavily guarded villa on a hillside overlooking the ocean. But he is no local hoodlum. The Japanese mafia, the *yakuza*, are among the mightiest of the world's crime syndicates, whose strength is surpassed only by that of the Chinese Triads. And, just like organised crime in China—whether it was under Chiang Kai-shek in the 1930s or the Communist Party today—the Japanese mobsters also maintain the same informal links with the authorities and big business.

Some old Japan hands would later argue that Watanabe's men gave out bottled water only to people in the *oyabun's* own neighbourhood, not city-wide, and that this was little more than a local colour story played up by the Japanese and foreign media.[4] But the rumour spread, and the Kobe earthquake was a heaven-sent opportunity for the *yakuza* to live up to their Robin Hood image of being honourable outlaws who protect the poor. And that was exactly what the Yamaguchi-gumi and other gangs, or *gumis*, needed at the time.

To some extent, the *yakuza* had been hit by new anti-gang legislation that had been passed in 1991, designed to drive the *yakuza* into the ground. The law might not have been terribly effective, but it had had some harassment value, and it formally recognised for the first time that the *yakuza* were violent, anti-social racketeering organisations which had to be controlled. It also prohibited certain *yakuza* activities, such as extortion and 'negotiating' car accidents, and legislated tough measures for mobsters involved in open gang wars. But the law actually did little to challenge the gangs' existence.[5]

A far more serious blow to the *yakuza* mobs and their image had been the collapse of Japan's 'bubble economy' in 1990. This difficult period showed the true colours of the gangsters, who were anything but noble Robin Hoods. For years, the *yakuza* had evoked images of exotic gangsters, the modern torchbearers of the ancient traditions of the *samurai*, feudal warriors with a deep sense of honour. Covered in tattoos and with missing pinkies, severed in punishment for an offence committed against their boss and brotherhood, the *yakuza* were cult figures often glamourised in novels and movies as misunderstood social outcasts.

All that changed in the 1980s, when the Japanese real estate market exploded. The combined value of the property in Tokyo alone was said to exceed that of the entire United States. The grounds of the Imperial Palace were worth more, at least on paper, than all of California. Based on these inflated values, Tokyo's stock exchange became the biggest in the world.[6] The underworld was quick to cash in on the boom, and at the peak of what would later be seen as the biggest bubble economy in history, the police in Tokyo counted some 740 mobster-controlled offices, which dealt in finance, construction and real estate.[7] A new breed of criminal emerged, the *keizai yakuza*, or the 'economic gangster', who not only collected 'protection money' from other companies, but also ran their own businesses. Gangsters became real estate developers and stock speculators, managing multi-billion-dollar loans from banks and credit unions.[8]

Mainstream companies also began to solicit the services of *yakuza* mobsters to lay their hands on desirable property in a country where the law actually favours the tenant. Known as *jiageya*, 'land-turners' or 'land raising specialists', they induced recalcitrant owners and tenants to vacate land needed for new projects. Although this involved what was euphemistically called 'mental harassment', it was not strictly illegal, and became the biggest grey-zone activity during the bubble economy of the 1980s.[9] In some cases, a mere visit by a *jiageya* agent would suffice to persuade a landowner or a tenant to move. If that were not enough, the *yakuza* would open an office in the neighbourhood, which invariably led to a drop in property prices. As a last measure, night calls, vandalism and physical abuse would follow. Few ordinary people would be brave—or foolhardy—enough to continue to resist such pressures.

The *jiageya* 'professionals' went into high gear just as another, more traditional, *yakuza* activity began to disappear: the *sokaiya* racketeers, who would extort protection money from companies by threatening to disrupt their annual shareholders' meetings. Many big corporations had lost millions to these 'general meeting fixers' but, on the other hand, companies that paid them could in return expect help in suppressing legitimate questions from ordinary shareholders, or other 'services' which could not be obtained by conventional means. In many ways, the *yakuza* filled niches that in the West are occupied by lawyers—which may explain the exceptionally low ratio of lawyers to the general population in Japan. But, while western lawyers slap lawsuits on 'corporate enemies', the *sokaiya* used more forceful methods to 'protect' their clients.[10]

Sokaiya payments were outlawed in the early 1980s, which slowed down the extortion business. But, even so, nearly a third of 2000 companies who responded to a 1991 survey by Japan's National Police Agency admitted that they still paid the racketeers annual amounts of up to 100 million yen, or $800 000, each.[11] The *sokaiya* also used other methods, on the borderline of legality and illegality, to extort money from corporations. Under the cover of 'research institutes', they published journals on economic matters, for which they collected huge subscription fees. If a company refused to pay up, these 'research institutes' could always dig up some dirt about it, and run the damaging 'information' in the next issue of their journal.[12]

But, during the bubble years, *jiageya*-related activities proved far more profitable, and *yakuza*-related lending was channelled through a wide range of financial institutions. At least 24 of Japan's main real estate companies lent heavily to *yakuza*-related construction projects, and even Japan's own housing-loan corporations, called *jusen*, began lending to real estate 'developers' with *yakuza* connections. Set up in the 1970s to serve the public, by the mid-1980s most of them were in the *yakuza*'s grip. Credit cooperatives, once primarily lenders to small businesses, also lent money to gang-linked real estate developers, and agricultural cooperatives lent $52 billion to insolvent *jusen*.[13]

Then the bubble burst. From its record high at the end of 1989, Nikkei, the Japanese stock index, lost nearly half of its value over the first nine months of 1990. Land prices nose-dived as Japan was hit by its worst economic recession since the post-World War II years. But it was not until January 1998 that the Japanese Ministry of Finance announced the first reasonably precise accounting of the magnitude of the bad loans that the bubble had left behind: nearly $600 billion. Who was going to clear up the mess—and, more importantly, how? As much as 40 per cent of the bad loans were believed to be derived from the *yakuza* and its various outfits.[14] Collecting debt had long been a specialty of the gangsters; now the entire nation owed the *yakuza* a sum that was as large as the combined GDP of Singapore and the Philippines.

Part of the problem had been that Japanese banks and other financial institutions lacked the know-how and the resources—and perhaps even the will—to conduct proper credit risk analyses. In the wake of the collapse of the bubble, one scandal after another hit Japan. It was revealed that Nomura Securities and Nikko Securities, Japan's largest and third-largest stockbroking firms, had lent more than $277 million to Susumu Ishii, the late head of the main Tokyo-based *yakuza* gang, the 7000-member *Inagawa-kai*. At the beginning of 1992, as the magnitude of the economic disaster was becoming evident, it was announced that another Japanese giant, the Tokyo Sagawa Kyubin Co Ltd, had ties to a golf course developer affiliated with Ishii's gang.[15]

Where all the money went is still a mystery. Some was undoubtedly siphoned out of the country. American investigators found that *yakuza* money was behind 50 major properties in Hawaii, including hotels, resorts and golf courses. The second-in-command of the Yamaguchi-gumi and Watanabe's deputy, Masaru Takumi, turned out to be the owner of homes, businesses and tourist resorts on Australia's Gold Coast and in Vancouver, Canada. *Yakuza*-related investment was also traced to the Philippines, Thailand, China, Vietnam and other emerging markets in East Asia. But billions of dollars? When asked by American investigative reporter David E. Kaplan what happened to, for instance, Ishii's 'private' money, a Japanese police officer replied: 'Nobody knows where it all went. It just disappeared.' His wealth was estimated at $2.3 billion. And it just disappeared?[16]

Trying to collect the debts proved an insurmountable task. Early one morning in September 1994, Kazufumi Hatanaka, the 54-year-old branch manager of the Sumitomo Bank in Nagoya, an industrial city in central Japan, was awakened by a knock on the door of his flat. Still in his pyjamas, he opened it—and all the neighbours remember was a big bang. Hatanaka was found slumped on the floor, shot through the head. Part of his job for the bank, one of the world's largest, was to collect huge amounts in bad, overdue loans from what the press described as 'unsavoury characters'.[17] More murders were to follow, and the Japanese government finally realised that it had to deal with the *yakuza* problem.

Until the collapse of the Bubble Economy, the *yakuza* had not been illegal. Japan had no racketeering statutes and being a member of a *yakuza* gang was not a crime *per se*. Unlike the Chinese Triads, which are secret organisations, the *yakuza* had for years identified itself with lapel buttons and business cards embossed with the gang's emblem and identifying their syndicate, rank and name as well as phone and fax number. Most gangs had local offices all over Japan, with signboards outside which stated the name of the proprietor. The name of the gang was inscribed on flags and lanterns, and they had their own official songs and emblem-emblazoned cushions, as well as their own magazines containing photos of their members, which they would send not only to those members, but also to the local police.[18]

One magazine, typical of the genre and published by the Yamaguchi-gumi, had inside its front cover a list of what was purported to be the moral principles of the gang: the development of 'our country and our society according to the *kyodo* spirit'. That meant that gang members had to 'preserve harmony in order to strengthen the group, to love and respect people outside the group and remember what is owed to them, to always be courteous and always be aware of senior–junior relationships, to learn from the experience of seniors and work for self-improvement, and to show restraint in contacts with the outside world'.[19] This list of virtues was followed by poems about nature and love, stories about outlaws in Japanese history and a eulogy for a dead gangster, written by his daughter. There were complaints about 'injustices in Japanese society' and articles about how powerless the police were in the face of rape, street robberies and murder—until the gang came to the rescue. The magazine ended with personal information on individual gang members about to be released from gaol, and the kind of welcoming ceremonies which awaited them. Some magazines had legal columns, where lawyers answered questions from the readers: how to avoid getting caught and what to do if that happened.

All this was meant to end when the Japanese parliament in May 1991 passed the new, supposedly tough, anti-gang law. Called the *Boryokudan Countermeasures Law*, it came into effect in March 1992, but it merely allowed the authorities to designate certain organisations as crime groups, based on the proportion of convicted criminals in their ranks. The law defined any organisation in which more than 4 per cent of the members had criminal records as *boryokudan*, a new term which means 'the violent ones'. Evidently, it was far too sensitive to use the name *yakuza*, which many Japanese—despite what had happened during the bubble economy—still associated with honourable societies of misunderstood heroes. Members of gangs designated as *boryokudan* were prohibited from 'practising extortion and the use of coercion or enticement to recruit juveniles'.[20] For the first time, the police began to raid *yakuza* offices in search of illegal weapons and evidence of criminal activities.

Hardly surprisingly, the effect of the law was negligible. In a rare newspaper interview, a member of the inner circle of the Yamaguchi-gumi said that 'because of the new law, I've pretty much stopped wearing my lapel button—I only hand out my business card to other *yakuza*'.[21] The law was so weak that the mobsters also easily found ways around it. One Tokyo gang converted itself into a right-wing political group and held a party to inaugurate the new association, while another suspected crime group declared itself reborn as a new religious sect. More than 70 gangs affiliated with the Yamaguchi-gumi registered their offices as 'private businesses'. The syndicate even published a book entitled *How to Evade the Law*, which was distributed among its members. In the most spectacular protest against the new prohibitions, wives and daughters of *yakuza* leaders marched through Tokyo's flashy Ginza district shortly after the laws had gone into effect.

At a meeting in Kobe before members of the local police, Masaru Takumi declared that his gang, the Yamaguchi-gumi, had nothing to do with 'violent groups'. He informed the police panel that his gang would challenge the constitutionality of the new law since, in his view, it 'violates a person's freedom of association and choice of profession'. As for the Yamaguchi-gumi, 'our spirit is to help the weak and to fight evil. We sent donations to victims of Mount Unzen [a volcano on the southern island of Kyushu that erupted in 1991, killing 44 people and destroying over 2000 buildings] and received letters of thanks from children.'[22] To prove their chivalry, they later helped the victims of the Kobe earthquake.

Japan's unique criminal culture traces its origin to the early seventeenth century, shortly after the Tokugawa shogunate was established. Tokugawa was the name of an old family of noble warriors that were to rule Japan for more than 250 years, and its *shoguns*, military chieftains who exercised unlimited power to which the emperors themselves were obliged to yield, unified and pacified the country following years of civil war. But that also meant that almost half a million *samurai*, or ordinary warriors, found themselves without military duties. Many became *ronin*, or 'masterless *samurai*', roving bandits who made a living robbing travellers and terrorising the countryside. Some of the more eccentric of the former *samurai* became known as *kabuki-mono*, or 'the crazy ones'. Sporting outlandish costumes and unusual haircuts, they evolved into Japan's first organised crime gangs. They were also known as *hatamoto-yakko*, which translates roughly as 'servants of the shogun', but were, in effect, independent gangs with their own argot and criminal code. The well-disciplined *hatamoto-yakko* demanded total loyalty among themselves, and pledged to defend and protect one another, no matter what happened.[23]

The *yakuza*, however, do not consider these to be their forebears. Instead they say their spiritual ancestors are the *machi-yakko*, 'servants of the town'—who took up arms to protect the villages and towns from these renegade *samurai*. The *machi-yakko* recruited clerks, innkeepers, artisans, labourers, homeless warriors and other *ronin*, and anyone who was an adept gambler—which helped them develop a closely knit relationship with each other and their leaders, much like today's *yakuza*.[24] The *machi-yakko* soon became real folk heroes, admired by the townspeople because they defended them against the *hatamoto-yakko*. This Robin Hood image was further embellished by numerous romantic, but not always accurate, eighteenth-century plays and dramas, in which they are portrayed as defenders of the weak. The name *yakuza*, which later came into common use, is the sequence of 8-9-3 in Japanese, 'ya-ku-sa', or the losing hand in a popular Japanese card game. Thus the name roughly translates to 'loser', the underdog image which they have cultivated and exploited over centuries.[25]

Like the Chinese Triads, the *yakuza* developed intricate initiation ceremonies for new members, which also had the trappings of religious ritual. A simple wooden altar stands at the front of a banquet hall, laden with *sake*, or Japanese rice wine, in porcelain decanters, fish, fruit and other offerings to the gods of Shinto, Japan's indigenous religion. Prominently displayed behind the altar are banners with the names of the sun goddess, the patron god of warriors and another god associated with the imperial household. Dressed in black *kimonos*, the new recruits then sip *sake* from the small cups and, to complete their initiation into the gang, they are given their 'regalia': a sword, a map of the gang's turf, seals and some swathes of cotton. A short closing address by the boss follows, and the new members then retire for some less formal drinking—in the company of *kimono*-clad females.[26]

How the *yakuza* developed over the first two centuries of its existence as an organised crime group is not entirely clear, as the Tokugawa *shoguns* closed Japan to the outside world, and Japan's own writers, playwrights and poets almost invariably romanticised the outlaws. The most famous of the gangster-related plays portrays the life of Chobei Banzuiin, who was born into a *ronin* family in the early seventeenth century and rose to become the leader of Tokyo's *machi-yakko*. But before that he worked as a labour broker, recruiting workers to repair the *shogun*'s palace and build roads around Tokyo. In that capacity, he invented a practice that later became a favourite occupation of the *yakuza*. He opened a gambling den, which attracted workers whom he could recruit for his construction projects—and, having employed them, he made sure he could recoup a large portion of their salaries by making them lose at his own gambling tables.[27]

But plays abound depicting Chobei as the ultimate chivalrous commoner—which was how the *machi-yakko* saw themselves—and many have found their place in Japan's rich theatrical traditions. Most dramas about Chobei and other outlaws are played as *kabuki*, a kind of variety show performed by troupes of itinerant entertainers. The creation of this art form is ascribed to Okuni, a female attendant at the Izumo Shrine, a Shinto temple in medieval Japan. She and her mostly female troupe of dancers and entertainers staged their first light theatrical performance on the dry bed of the river Kamogawa in Kyoto in 1603. Their popular style became a tremendous success, and they soon gained nationwide recognition. Okuni's dramas—and later the genre itself—became known as *kabuki*, a term connoting its 'out-of-the-ordinary' and 'shocking' character.[28]

The popularity of *onna*—or women's *kabuki*—which Okuni introduced, was largely attributable to its sensual dances and erotic scenes. But the dancers also doubled as prostitutes, so there were frequent fights over them among potential customers. In 1629, the Tokugawa Shogunate therefore banned women from performing on stage. Young men or boys had to play the roles of females, but the strict *shoguns* disapproved of these shows as well, because the male adolescents also began to sell their favours. Even stricter rules were imposed, and older *onnagata*, or female impersonators, were employed.

After centuries of refinement—and despite its unsavoury aspects—all-male *kabuki* became a highly formalised art form. Its actors were praised for their performance of plays whose stories had essentially remained the same since the early years of the Tokugawa shogunate. For some people, this rarefied art form was a reflection of Japanese society itself: refined, traditional, meticulously ordered. However, just like the polished world of *kabuki*, this view of Japanese society was a grand illusion. It was an entirely different story behind the scenes.

Two different types of 'underworld' character emerged from Chobei's humble beginnings: the *tekiya*, or street peddler, and the traditional Japanese gambler called *bakuto*. Neither phenomenon may appear particularly subversive, but the street peddlers were organised along strict feudal lines to establish control over market stalls outside temples and shrines—and to protect members from the excesses of the Tokugawa shogunate, which in some ways was the world's first genuine military dictatorship. A boss, or *oyabun*, was at the top of the strict hierarchy of the *tekiya*. Below him were one or more under-bosses, other office bearers, enlisted men and apprentices. The home of the *oyabun*, which was not always palatial, served as headquarters for the gang and as a training centre for new recruits. All ranks were obliged to follow what became known as the 'Three Commandments of the Tekiya':

1. Do not touch the wife of another member.
2. Do not reveal the secrets of the organisation to the police.
3. Keep strict loyalty to the *oyabun–kobun* relationship.[29]

The first commandment was introduced because the wives of peddlers were often left alone while their husbands were out selling their merchandise or street food at temple and village fairs. A *kobun* was a follower of an *oyabun*, and a strict father-and-son relationship existed between them. The older and wiser *oyabun* provided guidance and protection for the *kobun*, which was reciprocated with blind loyalty.

The *bakuto*, or gamblers, were somewhat different from the *tekiya*. The first gambling gangs were established along roughly the same lines as Chobei ran his labour rackets in the early seventeenth century: workers were tricked into gambling away their incomes to the boss who had paid them. But, to make up for the boss's losses, other vagrants, misfits, outlaws and day labourers were enticed to join the gambling sessions. Even *samurais* and *sumo* wrestlers joined the fray, and these gambling gangs—not the loosely assembled bands of highway robbers and itinerant *ronins*—became Japan's first organised crime groups.

It was also in the gambling dens that the term *yakuza* (8-9-3) was first used—and that offenders and cheats were severely punished. Those who had completely betrayed the trust of the boss, or cheated a fellow gang member, were killed or—if they were lucky—expelled from the organisation. But it was also possible to beg for mercy, and receive it in exchange for a punishment that would serve to remind the follower for the rest of his life that he had to be absolutely loyal and sincere in his dedication to his *oyabun*. The bakuto introduced the custom of *yubitsume*, whereby the top joint of an errant gang member's finger is severed as an expression of apology to the group for making a mistake. This finger-cutting practice later spread to the *tekiya* as well, and an offender would cut off a digit on his right hand if he had slighted his *oyabun*, or his left hand if he had committed a crime against his *gumi*, or gang. This is an ancient, feudal *samurai* tradition conceived so that the violator would not be able to handle his sword as effectively as if all his fingers had been intact.[30]

This ritual is still being practised, and nearly half of all *yakuza* members have severed finger joints even today.[31]

Another *yakuza* tradition that has lived on into modern times also emerged during these early days of organised crime in Japan: ritual tattooing. Originally meant as a punishment, used by the authorities to ostracise society's outlaws by making it easier to recognise them among ordinary citizens, it developed into an art, of which the *yakuza* became very proud. An estimated 73 per cent of today's *yakuza* bear some tattooing to show their strength and courage. The tattoos often cover their whole body, except for their hands, feet, neck, and head, so that they are not visible when the gangster is fully clothed, but beneath the wide cuffs of their *kimonos*—and, in modern times, trouser-legs—peek the green and purple extremities of tattooed dragons, famous gods and folk heroes, or animals and flowers. Other tattoos may be only a small mark behind their eyebrows, and even more difficult for an outsider to detect.[32]

From the very beginning, both the *tekiya* and the *bakuto* also adhered to *bushido*, the almost sacred code of the *samurai*, which includes the concepts of *giri* and *ninjo*. *Giri* can be loosely translated as a strong sense of duty or obligation, while *ninjo* means 'human feeling', 'emotion' or 'loyalty'. The relationship between these two concepts—and indeed their profound meaning—is almost impossible to explain in western terms, but it reflects a deep moral obligation to superiors as well as a sympathy toward the underdog of society. By combining these two human traits—obligation and compassion—the *yakuza* showed that they, like the *samurai* before them, were not only loyal, noble warriors but also defenders of the weak.

The *yakuza*'s identification with the disadvantaged was not only a ploy to gain respect and sympathy from the population at large—which it actually swindled, robbed and terrorised. The new bands of outlaws that emerged in the seventeenth, eighteenth and nineteenth centuries attracted large numbers of *burakumin*, or Japanese outcasts. The original meaning of the term is just the combination of *buraku* (small hamlet) and *min* (people), but it came to embrace those living in certain squalid quarters on the outskirts of each castle town. The reason why they lived there, and not inside the town proper, was that they were tanners and leather workers—an 'impure' profession, according to both Buddhist and Shintoist belief, because it involved killing animals.[33]

The rest of society looked upon them with disdain. Many were convinced that they were 'non-Japanese'—or, in other words, Korean.[34] But they were not ethnically different from the rest of the population, just treated differently—and, in fact, not considered fully human because of their occupation. Consequently, they were not included in the periodic censuses that were conducted from 1720 onwards. But it is believed that their total number increased more than three times during the period 1720–1850, as many outcasts moved into rural areas to take up farming, often on the least productive land. A major famine in the 1730s had reduced the ordinary farming population, and there was a labour shortage in many agricultural areas. But even out of their traditional *buraku*, the outcasts were confined to certain new villages, and continued to be treated as non-humans.[35]

Becoming a *tekiya* peddler was one way of breaking this vicious cycle of discrimination and rejection by society. As itinerant peddlers, *burakumin* were also able to leave their tainted birthplaces and, to some degree, mingle with the population at large. But they still felt they needed protection, and the gangs and new brotherhoods which emerged during this period provided exactly that—and more: the ability to strike back, and a way to gain respect and upward mobility in a hostile society. Legal discrimination ended with the promulgation of the Liberation Edict of August 1871, but people's attitudes did not change so fast. Even today, the *burakumin* are discriminated against by their fellow Japanese, unless they manage to hide their identity. Private detectives in Japan derive a large proportion of their income from pre-marriage checks into the background of potential spouses to ensure they have no *buraku* blood.

Like the Chinese secret societies, the *yakuza* thus managed to absorb social outcasts, misfits and dropouts and turn them into a formidable underground force that no government—or big business—could afford to ignore. But the outlaws also rejected conventional society by following their own code of conduct, loyalties and rituals. The tattooing reinforced this desire to be different: it marked a misfit for life, always unwilling to adapt himself to society.[36]

Japan's transformation from a strictly feudal society, cut off from the rest of the world, to a formidable regional power began in the early nineteenth century as western colonial powers began to penetrate

East Asia. The British and other 'barbarians' had already established footholds in China, and the Russians were in the process of conquering Siberia, across the Japan Sea. Despite the closed-door policy of the *shoguns*, foreign influences trickled into Japan through the port city of Nagasaki, where the Dutch and the Chinese had been allowed to continue carefully monitored trade throughout most of the Tokugawa era. The floodgates opened wide when American Commodore Matthew Perry arrived in 1853 and concluded a friendship treaty with Japan. But the first American consul, Townsend Harris, had to be backed by the threat of force before he could negotiate the opening of treaty ports, similar to those in China. Japan's days as a hermit kingdom were over.

This humiliation of the Japanese proved a key factor in an upsurge of imperial loyalism, which led to the toppling of the Tokugawa shogunate in 1867. The battle cry was clear: 'Revere the Emperor! Expel the Barbarians!'. A year later, the restoration of the absolute power of the Emperor followed and the new monarch, Meiji, set about modernising Japan—but in his own way. Local domains, or *daimyo*, found themselves under central control, and the *samurai* were deprived of their swords. Modern education was introduced, and the first industries were established to turn Japan into a strong nation able to withstand the onslaught of the colonial powers.

A modern army was also raised, and soon Japan began to have territorial ambitions. In 1879, the Japanese annexed the Ryukyu Islands, formerly a dependency of the *daimyo* of Kagoshima, and established a new prefecture called Okinawa. In 1895, they pushed south and captured the huge Chinese island of Taiwan. Then came Japan's great military success that placed the country on par with the western nations: its victory over Russia in the 1904–05 war. Russia was forced to cede the southern half of the island of Sakhalin as well as Port Arthur on China's northeastern coast, along with control of the Manchurian railway, which ran from the Russian border down to Port Arthur. Japan's status as both an island and mainland power was further enhanced when the Korean peninsula was formally added to its conquests in 1910. Then, in 1931, the Japanese army staged an 'incident' outside Mukden in Manchuria by bombing the South Manchurian Railway—which led to a Japanese takeover of the entire country. To create a façade of legitimacy concerning Japan's new conquest,

Manchuria was proclaimed an 'independent state' in 1932 with the hapless, dethroned last Emperor of China, Henry Pu Yi, as 'Regent'. In 1934, he was proclaimed 'Emperor of Manchukuo' in his new capital, Changchun. But, in effect, the docile 'Emperor' was a puppet of the Japanese, who plundered the rich natural resources of Manchuria.

This rapid and dramatic expansion of Japanese power would not have been possible without the help of the underworld. The Meiji Emperor had been only fifteen years old when the Tokugawa shogunate was overthrown, and he was surrounded by advisers and noblemen who became the new rulers. Although the new power structure that emerged accorded supreme authority to the Emperor, he served merely as the sacrosanct basis for rule by others. The role of the Emperor was to ratify policies and decisions reached by the ministers of state and the increasingly powerful chiefs of the armed forces. But, as a symbol, the Emperor was a potent force, and the *yakuza* gangs, who claimed to be true nationalists who had been suppressed by the Tokugawa *shoguns*, saw a chance to gain more prominence. The new, expansionist state that emerged also needed intelligence—about the movement of the western powers, and of the situation in the territories that Japan wanted to annex before they could. There was also the possibility of a backlash from the ousted Tokugawa *shoguns*, or other forces opposed to the new order.

From the beginning of the Meiji Restoration, as the new era became known, the emphasis was placed on intelligence gathering in almost every sphere of Japanese life. 'Never perhaps in the history of the world has one nation set out upon so comprehensive and broad-based a system of intelligence-collection', writes Richard Deacon, an expert on the world's intelligence services. Nothing was neglected, nothing was allowed to be done haphazardly. The information gleaned was all obtained systematically, some of it openly, but the greater part 'as unobtrusively and secretly as possible'.[37]

And what group would be better suited to perform these important tasks than Japan's own patriotic underworld? Japan's first real external intelligence service was that of the *Genyosha*, or Dark Ocean Society, founded in 1881 and led by Kotaro Hiraoka, a wealthy ex-*samurai* who was also a mine-owner interested in mining prospects in Manchuria. The society established its first base on the southern island of Kyushu and took its name from the strip of water that separates it from the

Korean peninsula.[38] But the name also suggested expansion, and preparations for that became the main preoccupation of the society's most ambitious member, Mitsuru Toyama. The third son to a family of obscure *samurai* ancestry in the city of Fukuoka, also on Kyushu, and a former sweet-potato peddler, he was not nearly as upper-crust as Hiraoka, but far more farsighted when it came to establishing a mutually beneficial relationship with Japan's new nationalistic rulers. Toyama, a grandfather-like figure who later in life sported a long white beard, was an eccentric and lonely character, part-politician, part-mystic. He was noted for his ascetic lifestyle, and spent hours in meditation. At one time, he decided to live on a diet of grass and leaves.[39] And he loved Japan, its rich culture and proud traditions.

In the same year as the Dark Ocean Society was formed, Japan saw the birth of another powerful institution, officially founded by the Army General Staff: the *Kempeitai*, or military police. Initially an elite corps of 349 men, its first duty was to discipline army officers and others who resisted conscription, but it soon developed into an intelligence agency with almost unlimited powers.[40] And, from the very beginning, it cooperated with Toyama. In 1882, the godfather of the Dark Ocean Society sent a hundred agents to China to collect intelligence, and to infiltrate the Chinese secret societies, which were often hostile to Japan. They found out that the familiar 'Crush the Qing, Restore the Ming!' was not the only battle cry of China's fabled Triads—they also shouted the far more revolutionary 'strike at the rich and help the poor!'.[41] Obviously, it was a movement that had to be more closely watched.

The wealth of information obtained by Toyama's agents paved the way for Japan's successful wars against China in 1894–95 and Russia ten years later. Dark Ocean agents had travelled to the port city of Vladivostok as early as 1898 on an undercover photographic expedition, and brought back useful pictures of military installations in the Russian Far East.[42] But Toyama's secret society's greatest success was Korea. Ryohei Uchida, another leading member of the Dark Ocean, was put in charge of a special fifteen-man taskforce called *Tenyukyo*, or the Society of the Celestial Salvation of the Oppressed. Its assignment was to establish contacts with the *Tonghaks*, an obscure religious sect in Korea which propagated eastern learning and Confucian philosophy. Its original aim was to destroy the corrupt Korean oligarchy then in power and to drive the Japanese, who had begun to exert influence over the peninsula, from the country. But it was also fiercely opposed to all kinds of western influences, which suited Japan's interests. Japanese agents managed to infiltrate the movement, split it and set up a new, pro-Japanese front organisation called *Ilchinhoe*, or 'the Advancement Society'. At the same time, other Japanese secret agents walked the Korean countryside to compile detailed maps of the peninsula. These manipulations and clandestine manoeuvres paved the way for the eventual annexation of Korea.[43]

Following a brief period of political liberalism in the 1920s, Japan developed in the same direction as Germany and Italy in Europe: towards unabashed fascism. The ultra-rightist gangster associations played an important role in this development. While the gangs supported themselves by running gambling dens, brothels, protection rackets and blackmail schemes, they also struck with a heavy hand against Japan's fledgling labour movement. The *yakuza* had its own labour bosses, who organised construction and dockworkers in industrial centres and port cities all over the country. In Kobe, several rival gangs recruited workers for the port, but, in the end, one gang emerged victorious from the fights and established a virtual monopoly on labour contracts in the city: the Yamaguchi-gumi. It was named after its founder, Noburu Yamaguchi, but in effect led by a local thug called Kazuo Taoka.[44] Nicknamed 'the Bear', Taoka had joined the Yamaguchi's gang in 1936 at the age of 23, and soon earned a reputation for extreme violence, even to the extent that he gouged his enemies' eyes out with his fingers.[45]

Terror and assassination became the order of the day, and Toyama soon commanded an 'army' of 60 000 gangsters who cooperated closely with Tekejiro Tokunami, the home minister, and, after 1937, with the new prime minister, Prince Konoye Fumimaro, an imperial favourite and a hardliner on China.[46] It was estimated that, by 1941, the imperial Japanese government nurtured between 800 and 900 fanatical, emperor-worshipping, expansionist and proto-fascist secret groupings, which all made their contribution to Japan's militarisation in the 1930s.[47] The *Sakura*, or Cherry Society, was one of the most influential groups within the right-wing militarist network, while the secretive and well-disciplined *Kokuryu-kai*, or Black Dragon Society, began its brief but colourful history by spying on the Soviets for

Colonel Motojiro Akashi, a former Japanese military attaché to Moscow.

The Black Dragon was headed by Toyama's assistant, Uchida, and its very special mission required that it be separate from the old Dark Ocean and its various, thuggish offshoots. The more sophisticated Black Dragon in effect replaced the Dark Ocean, as the ultranationalists felt that a more tightly organised organisation was needed to counter Japan's external threats. Both Toyama and Uchida were convinced that only Russia, and its successor the Soviet Union, posed a serious challenge to Tokyo's attempts to expand its influence in mainland Northeast Asia—and Japan's military establishment was in full agreement. Many army officers joined the Black Dragon, while other, politically less important, gangs were sidelined when World War II broke out and strict discipline became of the utmost importance. The more unruly gangsters could either go to war, or go to gaol. Many served on various fronts in Asia, while, for instance, Taoka of the Yamaguchi-gumi ended up doing time in prison.

Uchida died in 1937, just as Japan's troops made their first advances into northern China and several years before the war spread throughout Asia and the Pacific. Yoshihisa Kuzuo, the director of the Imperial Rule Assistance Association, another rightist outfit, succeeded him as leader of the Black Dragon. Under him, the Black Dragon expanded its function as a central training agency for intelligence operatives, who were sent to the society's two special institutes in Tokyo: the so-called 'Tokyo & Osaka Foreign Language School' and 'the Nationalists' Training College'. The ageing gangster-rightist, Toyama, remained a chief adviser to the Black Dragon, despite its formal separation from the Dark Ocean, until his death in 1944 at the age of 89.[48]

A year later, the coalition between the ultranationalists and certain segments of the underworld—and Japan's brutal attempt to subdue all of Asia—came to a definite end, as the United States dropped its atomic bombs over Hiroshima and Nagasaki. The Soviet Union's Red Army marched into Manchuria, and handed the province back to China. Chinese sovereignty was also restored on Taiwan, and the Korean peninsula was divided between the Red Army and its local allies in the north, and the US army in the south. Japan was defeated. The country lay in ruins: virtually every city and town across the islands had been bombed. People cried in the streets as Emperor

Hirohito announced Japan's capitulation over the radio on 15 August 1945. It was the first time ordinary subjects had heard the voice of the divine Emperor, the Heavenly Sovereign. The humiliation was too much to bear for many Japanese, who committed suicide rather than live the rest of their lives in shame.

The final surrender was signed aboard the *USS Missouri* in Tokyo Bay on 2 September—a solemn event that marked the beginning of the official occupation of Japan. On paper, Japan was placed under the rule of a six-member Allied Council, comprising the foreign ministers of the United States, the Soviet Union, China and the three Commonwealth countries of Britain, Australia and New Zealand. In reality, however, Japan was ruled by General Douglas MacArthur, and the occupation lasted until 29 April 1952, when a peace treaty signed with the Americans came into effect. It was decided that the democracy they had imposed upon the country was going to work without their direct assistance. But first the 'war criminals' had to be tried. Altogether, 5700 Japanese officers, soldiers and collaborators were tried, of whom 920 were executed. It was swift, victors' justice. The most 'hard core' of the 'criminals' were tried in Tokyo, where the trial became a show piece. It was there that the top leaders were sentenced, including Hideki Tojo—prime minister and war minister at the time of the attack on Pearl Harbour on 7 December 1941, which prompted the United States to enter the war—and several other ex-ministers and military commanders.[49] More than 1000 former officials were kept in Sugamo Prison, where the executions were later carried out.

There was not much pride left in Japan. Summer was over and it was getting grey and cold. Hardly a house was left standing in the major cities. Food, firewood, clothes, soap, medicines—everything was in short supply, and the occupation forces provided only a very few basic necessities. But as early as 18 August, only three days after the Emperor's radio speech, an advertisement appeared in a local newspaper, urging factories and other enterprises which were shifting from 'wartime production to peacetime production' to come to 'Shinjuku Market' to sell their products.[50] Beside the railway tracks in Shinjuku, then a northwestern Tokyo suburb, Japan's first postwar black market sprang up, even before the first American soldier had set foot in Japan.

When General MacArthur's administration decided a few weeks later to ration food, the black market business took off, and a new class of entrepreneurs helped kick-start, in their own way, the Japanese economy. Many of the peddlers were *sangokujin*, or 'people of three countries', which meant Korea, Taiwan or China. They had been brought to Japan to work in the factories when almost the entire indigenous workforce had been drafted into the army. The Americans, who still did not trust the Japanese, favoured the 'foreigners'—who also took advantage of their new position to take revenge on the Japanese, who had oppressed them during the Japanese occupation of their own countries. Street fights were common—and the disbanded *yakuza* was reorganised to defend the 'true Japanese' against the 'foreigners'. Once again, they sided with the underdog—and in defence of Japan's national pride and honour. But nor were they entirely disinterested in wresting control of the lucrative black market from the outsiders.

The new and younger *yakuza* was far more violent and vicious than the old prewar gangsters had been. Instead of *samurai* swords, its members used firearms obtained from American soldiers, and they began to emulate American gangsters, whom they had seen in the movies, by wearing flashy outfits such as loud floral shirts and shiny double-breasted suits, and often sporting crew cuts or permed curly hair. The old bosses referred contemptuously to this new breed of thugs as *gurentai*, or 'juvenile delinquents'—adding a third type of gangster to the older two, the *tekiya* peddler and the *bakuto* gambler.[51]

The most prominent of Tokyo's new *gurentai* bosses, Akira Ando, controlled Korean labour in the city, ran a construction company and even managed to get contracts from the US forces to spruce up one of the city's air bases. He was only 44 when the war ended, and saw opportunities in the new era that the occupation had ushered in. He discovered that many Americans took a liking to Japanese girls, and opened a string of nightclubs that catered to the GIs.[52]

Another, more traditional mobster, *tekiya* boss Kinosuke Ozu, was the one who had placed the ad in the paper on 18 August—and the collection of makeshift street stalls outside Shinjuku station even became known as the Ozu market. Other, similar 'blue sky markets' were set up along all other major stations beside the Yamanote railway line that circles Tokyo: Ueno, Tokyo itself, Shimbashi and Shibuya.

Ozu controlled more than 45 000 street stalls over Tokyo, all of which had to pay half their daily profits to the newly powerful *oyabun*. He forced his way into Tokyo's new postwar Chamber of Commerce, but failed to win a seat in the Diet, or Parliament, when he contested the 1947 election from his home constituency in Shinjuku. But he did get 12 000 votes—and he had dared to run for parliament, even though an American journalist, Darrell Berrigan of the *Saturday Evening Post*, had called him 'Tokyo's own Al Capone'.[53]

Ozu's home turf, Shinjuku, became the new stomping ground for the postwar mob. It began with his modest, postwar black market and developed into one of the raunchiest and most spectacular red-light districts in the world, with strip clubs, love hotels, massage parlours—or 'soap lands' as they are called locally—peep shows, porno shops, sex shows where the audience is invited to participate, a wide range of imaginative cabarets, numerous restaurants and bars. As veteran writer Mark Schreiber puts it, it was 'a bustling 24-hour city-within-a-city that defies the rest of Tokyo to keep pace'.[54]

Shinjuku, which means 'New Inn', was founded 300 years ago next to an ancient way station, which at that time was a day's journey on foot from the old city centre. But the old staging post had become too small to accommodate the increasing number of travellers, so another one sprang up next to it. As most travellers in those days were male, this new station was dominated by a collection of brothels, euphemistically called 'inns'.[55] When the map of Tokyo was redrawn in 1947, Shinjuku became one of the capital's 23 new central wards. Its most infamous quarter, Kabuki-cho, was built on the bombed-out ruins behind Shinjuku station immediately after the war. It was originally a residential area called Minami Okubo, but then some local businessmen organised an exposition to make it into a cultural playground and invited the Kabukiza, Tokyo's most celebrated *kabuki* theatre, to open a branch in the neighbourhood. In anticipation of the theatre, they named the area 'Kabuki-cho' (a 'cho' is a city area between a ward and just a few blocks). In the event, a cinema was built instead. But the original name was kept.[56] As for the 'cultural playground', the mob evidently had its own interpretation of what kind of culture the public wanted.

Ironically, Kabuki-cho took off as a red-light area just as the Japanese Diet in 1958 passed a law criminalising prostitution.

'Prostitution' was narrowly defined as 'the sale of sexual intercourse on a repeated basis', which left a wide range of other sexual acts outside the purview of the new law. 'Entertainment services' fell under the Law on Control and Improvement of Amusement Businesses—which had the effect that most of Tokyo's commercial sex became concentrated in entertainment districts such as Kabuki-cho.[57] The *yakuza*, hardly surprisingly, was in charge. Apart from Japanese prostitutes, young women were brought in from the Philippines, South Korea and Thailand to serve a growing clientele of newly rich Japanese businessmen and office workers. *Yakuza* toughs, keeping watch in the neon-lit corners of the narrow streets of Kabuki-cho, made sure there was no random violence, which made it not only the world's wildest but also the safest red-light district. But every bar, club, shop and restaurant in the area also had to pay for order being maintained. This order was brutally enforced: anyone who dared to violate the rules imposed by the gangs was punished severely. A foreign visitor once watched—along with a crowd of about 50 people—as two *yakuza* heavies beat up a hapless salaryman they had just hurled out of a nearby girlie bar. He gripped his briefcase to his chest, curled up and cried, over and over again, 'I'm sorry, I'm sorry . . .'. The two mobsters, with absolutely impassive faces—no trace of anger at all—worked him over for about 20 minutes, stamping on his back and kicking his vital organs while he writhed in agony and apologised. He was lying in the middle of the road, and the witnesses all watched but did nothing. The nearest police box was less than 100 metres away.[58]

But the underworld's business was not only geared to the needs of the new entertainment-hungry middle class. The rapid reconstruction of Japan after the war created a demand for amphetamine-type stimulants. During World War II, many fighting men on all sides had taken stimulants to endure the hardships of the war; when the war was over, the construction workers, dock workers, long-distance truck drivers, students and others needing to work long hours in impoverished conditions continued the trend. Commercial advertising of stimulants after the war used slogans such as 'Shake off sleepiness— become energetic!'. To cope with the epidemic, the *Stimulants Control Law* was passed in 1951.[59] But, as was the case with so many other laws in Japan, there were numerous ways around it.

While amphetamines were first synthesised in Germany in 1887, and first marketed in Europe in the 1930s as 'Benzedrine' in an over-the-counter inhaler to treat nasal congestion, the simpler version—methamphetamine—actually originates in Japan. At about the same time as German chemists were experimenting with amphetamines, Dr Nagai, a Japanese chemist, made a similar drug from a plant he called *mahuang* (in English, ephedra), which grows wild in many parts of Asia. He found that it was effective against asthma, and a pharmaceutical company began mass-producing it.[60]

When the *yakuza* discovered other uses for the drug after the war, it was refined in small kitchen laboratories throughout Japan. But a police crackdown in the late 1950s forced it to move production to South Korea, where controls were not as strict—and where the gangs also had a lot of influence. As regulations were stepped up in South Korea in the 1970s, the gangsters simply moved again, this time to another former Japanese colony, Taiwan. When the Taiwanese authorities in turn cracked down on drug manufacturing a decade later, mainland China was open for business—and the laboratories moved again. By then, the chemists had also discovered a way to produce synthetic methamphetamines, so they were no longer dependent on harvesting the ephedra plant.

The number of drug users in Japan has never properly been documented by the authorities, who have concentrated their efforts on reporting arrests of dealers. Japan's National Police Agency recorded 24 000 such arrests from 1970 to 1984, a steep rise over previous years. But the situation was looking brighter because 'about 100 per cent of the methamphetamine abused in Japan [is] unlawfully imported from foreign countries'.[61]

Fortunes generated from the immediate postwar black market, extortion rackets, drugs, the sex industry and other enterprises enabled the *oyabuns* to buy power and influence in a society which, by the 1960s, had risen like a Phoenix from the ashes of World War II. In the beginning, the US military administration saw the resurgent *yakuza* as a threat to its authority. Underworld links to ultranationalist militaristic circles before and during the war had not been forgotten. But attitudes began to change as leftist forces began gaining momentum in Japan. The Japanese Communist Party grew from 6000 members in 1946 to 100 000 three years later, and its influence over the country's workers was challenged only by the *yakuza* and the far right.[62] World War II had also given way to the Cold War, and the Soviet Union and its real and perceived allies were the new enemy of the United States and the West.

General MacArthur's intelligence chief, Major-General Charles Willoughby—a staunch rightist himself—began to forge ties with Japanese nationalists, including officers who had been in active service during the war against the Allies. One of them, Lieutenant-General Seizo Arisue, former chief of army intelligence, was drafted to serve with the 'Historical Section' of General Willoughby's department. A former aide to General Tojo, ex-Colonel Takushiro Hattori, set up a special agency, the Hattori Kikan (*kikan* means 'agency'), which worked for Willoughby. General Arisue and four other former army officers formed the Katoh Agency, whose job was to collect 'information on the Soviet situations and "Red" activities within Japan'.[63]

It is perhaps not suprising that links between these Japanese 'agencies' and some American officers were strong. One group of former Japanese army officers, the so-called Cannon Agency, was even named after an American colonel, J.Y. Cannon. But that both the Japanese 'agencies' and the Americans established a relationship with the underworld should have been a cause for alarm among western governments, who were supposed to defend not only liberal democracy, but also the rule of law. One of the first mobsters to link up with the occupation forces was Hisayuki Machii, a mean-looking Korean-Japanese *taekwando* expert, who led a gang called the Tose-kai ('Voice of the East Society'), which was made up of 1500 mostly ethnic Korean thugs.[64] With this muscle behind him, and the backing of the Cannon Agency, Machii established an indirect relationship with Willoughby. The Tose-kai used strong-arm tactics to break up communist demonstrations—at the same time as they began to establish a string of 'Cultural Celebration Clubs' all over Tokyo, where 'hostesses' were available to provide sexual services.[65] Later the same company opened up a chain of clubs called 'Seventh Heaven', where former Playboy bunnies and Penthouse pets first introduced lap-dancing to Japan.

But the main turning point in the emerging nexus between the Americans, Japanese war veterans and the underworld was the outbreak of the Korean War. The Soviet forces in the north had refused to cooperate with the United Nations, which had proposed elections all over the former Japanese colony. Nevertheless, elections were held in the United States-occupied south in May 1948, and three months later the UN officially established the Republic of Korea with its capital at Seoul. The leader of the new republic was the staunch Korean nationalist and wartime anti-Japanese resistance leader Syngman Rhee. Moscow branded the move 'illegal' and countered in September by setting up its own puppet state north of the 38th parallel which divided the Korean peninsula: the Democratic People's Republic of Korea, with its capital at Pyongyang and headed by communist leader Kim Il Sung.

Under-estimating the determination of the communists to push on, the United States withdrew most of its forces from South Korea. By June 1949, only a small military advisory group of 500 men remained to assist in the formation and training of Syngman Rhee's armed forces. Exactly a year later, the North Koreans attacked. On 27 June, shortly after meeting with the United Nations Security Council, US president Harry S. Truman decided to send air and sea forces to assist the fledgling South Korean republic. By no means coincidentally, on 7 June the United Nations decided to dispatch additional ground troops from other countries, and it requested that an American take unified command of these forces. Truman's choice was General MacArthur. The United States was now directly drawn into the battle against communism in Asia.

The conflict divided Asia and the rest of the world into opposing camps, for and against communism. Mao Zedong's China, not a member of the United Nations at this time, sent more than 400 000 'volunteers' to fight alongside North Korea's 130 000 men. Soviet land forces did not participate, but it must not be forgotten that Mao had visited Moscow in December 1949–January 1950, six months before the invasion from the north. This was the Chinese communist leader's first and only visit abroad, and it is widely believed that he discussed with Stalin the unification of the Korean peninsula under communist control.[66]

The South Korean army numbered about 100 000 men, assisted by the same number of US troops, with additional contingents from a host of other members of the United Nations. Britain and Turkey sent two regiments each; Australia contributed two infantry battalions; New Zealand provided an artillery regiment; one infantry battalion came from each of Belgium, Colombia, Thailand, the Philippines, Ethiopia, France, Greece and the Netherlands; Luxembourg sent an infantry company; and South Africa and Canada supplied an air unit each. Denmark, Sweden, Norway, Italy and India dispatched non-combat medical teams.

In Japan, the American attitude towards the imprisoned 'war criminals' changed quite dramatically against the backdrop of developments in Korea, and the subsequent massive effort to contain the spread of communism in Asia. In Sugamo Prison, the convicts were separated into two groups. Seven of the 25 who had been tried for war crimes, including Tojo, were hanged on 23 December 1948. Sixteen were sentenced to life imprisonment while the remaining two received somewhat milder prison sentences. But the majority of the so-called 'Class A War Criminals' in Sugamo were never brought to trial. Instead, they were released.[67] Most of them immediately returned to the political arena which, despite its new American-style democratic constitution, was again dominated by the former militarists and ultranationalists, who had held high positions in the pre-1945 administration. One freed Class A war criminal, Nobusuke Kishi, who had effectively run Manchukuo's economy before becoming minister of industry and commerce in Tojo's wartime cabinet, eventually rose to serve as prime minister from 1957–60.

New duties also awaited other former inmates of Sugamo Prison. Two names stand out, as far as the underworld is concerned: Yoshio Kodama and Ryoichi Sasakawa. Kodama had been in China during the war, where he had made a fortune from 'import–export deals', and as a supplier of goods to the Japanese armed forces. Born in 1911, he had been active in ultranationalist groups in his youth and was later sent to China as an 'irregular officer'—a euphemism for intelligence agent. He was only 30 when he arrived in the grand city of Shanghai, where he set up an outfit called the Kodama Kikan, or 'Kodama Agency'. He was awarded an exclusive contract to supply strategic materials to the Japanese Naval Air Force, and his operation financed the Shanghai office of the Kempeitai.[68]

It has also been widely alleged that Kodama was involved in the drug trade in Japan's occupied territories.[69] Given his close connections with the Kempeitai, this seems perfectly plausible. The Kempeitai sponsored and promoted cheap opium dens in China and Manchuria to undermine native resistance. In Manchuria especially, many Kempeitai officers became rich as a result of drug, sex and gambling monopolies, franchising them out for huge fees.[70] In Shanghai, Tokyo's intelligence units had moved to fill the void left when the Godfather of that city, Du 'Snake Eyes' Yuesheng, had left the city together with Chiang Kai-shek at the approach of the Japanese army in the early 1930s. The Japanese arranged for opium from Iran to be shipped to Shanghai, where it was sold for a handsome profit.[71] Du himself even supplied opium to the Japanese in Shanghai, who set up a 'merchant association' called the Kosai zendo ('Hung-chi Benevolent Association') to distribute drugs throughout central China. Officially, the 'association' was an arm of the Japanese-installed anti-Chiang Kai-shek puppet government in China. But no one doubted that it operated at the behest of the Japanese army in Shanghai.[72]

Kodama returned to Tokyo a rich man, but was arrested by the Americans in 1946 and sent to Sugamo. In prison he was interrogated at length, and a report concluded that 'he appears to be a man doubly dangerous. His long and fanatical involvement in ultranationalistic activities, violence included, and his skill at appealing to youth make him a man who, if released from internment, would surely be a grave security risk'.[73] But just over two years later he walked out a free man.

It soon became obvious that Kodama had made a deal with Willoughby's intelligence unit. Not only was he one of the richest inmates in Sugamo, his skills in dealing with the underworld were also needed. In the chaos following the resurgence of the *yakuza* after the war, and in light of the fact that the occupation authorities needed some of their services, Kodama's duty was to discipline the more unpredictable of the gangs. Being anti-communist was an asset in the eyes of Willoughby and his men. But some gangs remained fiercely nationalistic in the old tradition; they were anti-communist, anti-Korean and anti-American at the same time.[74]

The gang that benefited the most from the new criminal order in Japan was the Yamaguchi-gumi. Noburu Yamaguchi had died from natural causes in 1946, and Kazuo 'the Bear' Taoka had succeeded him as the gang's *oyabun*. When Taoka took over, the Yakaguchi-gumi had only 25 devoted members, but he built it up to a massive criminal corporation which, at the peak of its strength in the 1960s, comprised 343 different local gangs with more than 10 000 followers. Its annual turnover from various criminal enterprises was in the hundreds of thousands of US dollars.[75] Although based mainly in Kobe and the nearby industrial city of Osaka, the Yamaguchi-gumi wielded influence all over Japan, even in Tokyo and Yokahama, where another boss reigned supreme: Kakuji Inagawa and his Inagawa-kai. A third gang, the Sumiyoshi-kai, could also count on the support of thousands of street fighters, pimps, drug pushers and extortionists.

Kodama became the broker-behind-the-scenes who would ensure that peace prevailed on the streets of Tokyo and other urban centres. On a more global scale, the Americans felt they needed a new, much more powerful intelligence agency than the small and outdated outfits that had been set up during the war. In 1947, the Central Intelligence Agency (CIA) was created, against the wishes of Willoughby. But Kodama became one of the agency's most important intelligence assets in Japan. His knowledge of China was superb, and he was involved in sending a spy ship to Shanghai to gather intelligence on Mao Zedong's new communist regime.[76] Kodama's ardent anti-communist stance was evident even in the way he sought to control the street gangs. 'The visionary Godfather of the Underworld', as he was called, urged them to 'use your physical strength only when we are in danger of a leftist revolution in Japan'.[77]

As an affluent citizen and a true patriot, Kodama handed over some of his wealth to another ultra-rightist, Karoku Tsuji, a mysterious figure whose role in postwar Japanese politics has never been fully explained. What is known, however, is that he used money that Kodama had amassed in China during the war to set up a new political organisation, the Liberal Party. In 1955, it merged with the Japan Democratic Party to become the Liberal Democratic Party (LDP), which since then has been the country's dominant political force. But, as a western journalist formerly based in Tokyo put it, 'it's neither liberal nor democratic, or even a party'.[78] It rapidly developed into a corporate colossus, which combined the interests of big business, the bureaucracy, the 'reformed' ultra-rightists led by former Sugamo inmate Nobusuke Kishi and the underworld. Kodama became the ultimate *kuromaku*, or Japanese backroom powerbroker and king-maker, who kept it all together. He moved back and forth between open and secret society at ease, at the same time maintaining useful links to foreign intelligence services.

The only person in Japan who could rival Kodama's clout in political circles was the crusty old kingmaker of the ruling LDP, Shin Kanemaru. But even he could not ignore the gangsters and the ultra-rightists, with whom he maintained close links. Later in life, Kanemaru had to answer charges of having offered a huge pay-off to a rival far-right group to stop a smear campaign against one of his political allies. A mobster called Ryumin Oshima, head of the small rightist mobster group Kominto, told prosecutors that Kanemaru had said he would pay three billion yen, or $24 million, to stop using loudspeaker vans to blare out offensive slogans, day and night, outside the home and office of LDP stalwart Noburo Takeshita. Oshima added that Yoshiro Mori, another leading LDP figure, had also proposed giving the group two billion yen, or $16 million.[79] Mori denied that he had made any such offers, but the allegation continued to haunt him even after he had become Japan's prime minister in April 2000.

Connections with the mob and the political right were also maintained by Kodama's former fellow cellmate at Sugamo, Ryoichi Sasakawa. As a young nationalist, Kodama had actually been a follower of Sasakawa, who was twelve years his senior. A native of Osaka and born into a family of extremely wealthy *sake* brewers, Sasakawa was still in his twenties when he started a right-wing newsletter called *Kokubo* ('National Defence'). By then he was already known for his short temper; as a child, he had roughed up his classmate and future winner of the Nobel Prize in literature, Yasunari Kawabata.[80]

Having made millions from speculative investment in rice futures, Sasakawa in 1931 became head of the 1000-strong ultranationalist group Kokusui Taishuto, or the 'Patriotic People's Mass Party' (PPMP). He was then only 32 years old, but under his energetic leadership, the organisation grew to 15 000 members, each one wearing a dark uniform fashioned after Benito Mussolini's Italian Black Shirt. It also had its own airport with 22 aircraft—a possession that enabled him to forge close ties with the military. When the puppet state of Manchukuo was established a year later, he made headlines in the Japanese media by airlifting supplies of pickles, *sake*, sweets and sundries to the troops occupying the territory. His aircraft were lent to the Naval Air Force for pilot training as Sasakawa used his oratorical skills to whip up public support for Japan's expansion into the Asian mainland.

In 1939, Sasakawa piloted one of his planes to Rome where, dressed in a formal black kimono, he met Mussolini. 'A first class person . . . a perfect fascist and dictator' was his assessment of the Italian leader. Years later, he expressed regret about not meeting another European leader of that time: 'Hitler sent a cable asking me to wait for him, but unfortunately I didn't have time'. Late in life, he would continue to look back at his years with the PPMP with no regrets: 'As head of the People's Party, I was interested only in social welfare and public health'.[81]

Like Kodama, Sasakawa spent the war doing business in Shanghai. The two worked together, supplying the Japanese army with whatever it needed and plundering China for gold, diamonds and other minerals which were sold to the military. In 1942, Sasakawa was elected to the Diet on the basis of a 'platform of intensified aggression in Southeast Asia'.[82] When the war was over, Sasakawa was arrested well before Kodama—or, rather, he gave himself up to the occupation forces in a somewhat unorthodox way. 'Please arrest me as a war criminal,' he taunted the Americans in several public speeches. On 11 December 1945, a day before MacArthur's military authorities were about to oblige, Sasakawa drove up to Sugamo Prison in a truck shouting 'Banzai! Banzai!' accompanied by a brass band playing the Imperial Navy march.

As a suspected Class A war criminal, Sasakawa was thoroughly interrogated by the Americans. They did not think any more highly of him than of his Shanghai business partner and now cellmate Kodama: 'He is a man potentially dangerous to Japan's political future . . . He has been squarely behind Japanese military policies of aggression and anti-foreignism for more than twenty years. He is a man of wealth and not too scrupulous about using it. He chafes for continued power. He is not above wearing any new cloak that opportunism may offer.'[83] But, despite such credentials, he was released. The reason was probably the same as that behind the freeing of Kodama: his staunch anti-communism was seen as an asset by the Americans in the early years of the Cold War era.

Legend has it that Sasakawa, while still interned in Sugamo, read an article on US hydroplane racing in *Life* magazine. It gave him an idea that would eventually make him, in his own words, 'the world's wealthiest fascist'. The only kind of gambling that was officially permitted in postwar Japan was poorly organised motorboat racing. But plans were underway to bring the races together under one body, and two of Sasakawa's former cellmates from Sugamo helped him acquire what was to become the most lucrative gambling monopoly in Japanese history. Kishi used his political influences to persuade Prime Minister Shigeru Yoshida, who actually despised gambling, to grant the monopoly to Sasakawa, while Kodama paid off a rival business group with funds left over from his wartime loot.

Later, when Kishi was prime minister, Sasakawa was appointed chairman of the Japan Shipbuilding Industry Foundation (JSIF), a non-profit organisation set up to plough back into industry a share of the income from the boatracing business. Sasakawa now controlled both a government-sanctioned gambling monopoly *and* a foundation responsible for billions of yen of supposedly public funds. Sasakawa used his wealth and influence to boost his right-wing causes. At home in Japan, he actively supported rightist organisations with links to the *yakuza*: the Zen-Nihon Aikokusha Dantai Kaigi, or Zan-Ai Kaigi for short ('All Japan Federation of Patriotic Organisations') and the Seinan Shisho Kenkyu Kai or Saishikai ('Youth Ideology Research Organisation'). The former was created in 1959 by a network of influential rightists including Kodama, who became its first chairman, and Sasakawa, who sat on its governing board. Originally it was a violent, loosely structured organisation with a vague ideology, but after 1968 it was tightened up by its new chairman, ultranationalist Yoshiaki Sagoya, and adopted a 'unified . . . theoretical system' based on the teachings of Toyama, the late but still-revered head of the Dark Ocean Society.[84]

However, Sasakawa's ambitions did not stop at Japan's shores. He linked up with other rightists in the region, including South Korea's Syngman Rhee and his old enemy from the war, Chiang Kai-shek. The common enemy now was communism. Syngman Rhee and Chiang Kai-shek had in 1954 set up the Asian Peoples' Anti Communist League (APACL), probably with encouragement from the CIA, which shared its belief that all anti-communist countries and forces surrounding Mao's China needed an umbrella organisation. In July 1967, the brains behind the APACL broadened their reach and formed a larger entity, the World Anti-Communist League (WACL), which brought together Asian rightists, an array of Latin American Fascists including Pastor Coronel, chief of Paraguay's dreaded secret police, members of Croatia's Ustasha movement which had collaborated with Germany and Italy during the war, former Iron Guards from Romania, Ukrainan Nazis and Ray Cline, a former member of the US Organisation of Strategic Services (OSS) during World War II, CIA station chief in Taiwan from 1958–62 and deputy director of the agency from 1964–67.[85]

From the very beginning, both Sasakawa and Kodama were staunch supporters of the WACL. Sasakawa became the most influential of the old fascist duo, and served as chairman of WACL's 1970 conference in Japan. It was believed that the Red Hordes could be stopped in the front-line state of South Korea and Sasakawa, on behalf of the WACL, began to cultivate the friendship of a bizarre Korean latter-day mystic, 'the Reverend' Sun Myung Moon. The son of middle-class parents from what later became communist-ruled North Korea, Moon's life changed forever when, walking through the hills around his village, he met Jesus. 'You are the son I have been seeking,' Christ told him, 'the one who can begin my eternal history.'[86]

Moon's 'Unification Church' was born. Its theology was a mish-mash of Christianity, Confucianism, mysticism, patriotism, anti-communism and Moon's own megalomania. Israel had rejected Jesus, so it could no longer be God's chosen land, but the geographical shape of Japan and Korea respectively clearly showed that they were made for each other, in a very physical sense: 'It [Korea] is a peninsula, physically resembling the male ... Japan is in the position of Eve. Being only an island country, it cannot be Adam. It yearns for male-like peninsular Korea on the mainland'. America, on the other hand, was 'an archangel country. Its mother is England, another island country in the position of Eve'.[87]

Whether the public at large in Korea and Japan was impressed by this curious take on geopolitics is hard to say, but Moon attracted the attention of not only Sasakawa and the WACL but also the Korean Central Intelligence Agency (KCIA), the most powerful institution behind the scenes in the authoritarian South Korea of the 1960s. Given the strong anti-Japanese sentiment among the Koreans—who had been treated as serfs under Japanese colonialism—an organisation that could bridge the wide gap between the two countries would certainly serve the purposes of the WACL and its more powerful backers in the United States.

A major breakthrough for the 'church' came in 1962, when the KCIA's first director, Kim Jong Pil, travelled to the United States on an official visit. Accompanying him as an interpreter was Kim Sang In, a close associate of the Reverend Moon, while Colonel Pak Bo Hi coordinated the visit from the South Korean embassy in Washington, where he served as assistant military attaché. Pak helped Moon build up a power base among Koreans living in America and later became the Reverend's chief aide.

In 1967, Sasakawa arranged a secret meeting in a house he owned on a lake in Yamanashi prefecture in the mountainous interior of the main Japanese island of Honshu. Among the attendants were Moon, Osami Kuboki—a well-known rightist who headed both the Unification Church in Japan and the Japanese chapter of the WACL—and Shirai Tameo—an underworld lieutenant of Kodama and secretary of an obscure organisation called 'Japan Youth Lectures', which trained young members of *yakuza* gangs. The outcome of the meeting was the creation of a new respectable façade for the *yakuza*: the Kokusai Shokyo Rengo, or the 'International Federation for the Victory over Communism'. Sasakawa was the overall chairman, with Kodama as his chief adviser, but it effectively became the political wing of the Unification Church.[88]

In the early 1970s, Moon and his gang decided to take their crusade to the United States, where he arrived in December 1971. With millions of dollars behind him, he built up an organisation which spanned from Asia to North America and, according to American investigators, resembled 'a multinational corporation, involved in manufacturing, international trade, defence contracting, finance, and other business activities'. It included 'economic enterprises ranging from multi-million dollar industries to small retail stores', mostly in Korea and Japan but also in the United States.[89]

Lee Jai Hyon, a former official of the South Korean embassy in Washington, stated before a House of Representatives sub-committee in 1978 that his government had a 'a curious working relationship' with the Unification Church. He said that: 'KCIA agents at the embassy maintained contact with the Freedom Leadership Foundation (FLF)—another Moon-related organisation in

Washington that had been involved in lobbying for South Korean military aid bills—and that Moon had founded the "Little Angels", a Korean children's dance troupe which had appeared around the world as official representative of the Korean government'.[90] But, despite its dedication to freedom, the Moon organisation was no supporter of the American interpretation of the concept. Moon found 'American-style democracy' to be 'a good nursery for the growth of communism'. His solution was a theocracy, 'because we cannot separate the political field from the religious'. Moon visualised the establishment of a 'unified civilisation' of the whole world, to be centred in Korea and 'corresponding to that of the Roman Empire'.[91]

Criticism of the organisation was out of the question because 'members' objection to political activities was considered infidelity to the Master and was like being disobedient to God'. The report went on to quote a speech by Moon in Seoul, where he proclaimed that God was helping to set up a final battle involving the United States, the Soviet Union, China, North and South Korea, and Japan: 'We shall defeat Kim Il Sung, smash Mao Zedong and crush the Soviet Union in the name of God!'.[92]

The Unification Church did not manage to build any Roman Empire. It is doubtful whether its efforts even had any significant impact on the containment of communism in Asia. But it did succeed in establishing a business empire that included the South Korean defence contractor Tong Il Industries, the Il Hwa Pharmaceutical Co, Hankook and Dong Hwa titanium industries and, in the United States, fishing and shipping enterprises—and the *Washington Times* newspaper. The exact value of Moon's investments and enterprises is anybody's guess, but it is in the billions of dollars channelled through a number of companies, sub-contractors and charities, which from time to time ran into problems with the US Internal Revenue Service. Indeed, Moon himself was imprisoned for income tax evasion in 1984, but released the following year. However, that did not deter his more than three million followers worldwide, who continue to worship 'the Master'. Internationally, he has attracted most attention for his unusual mass wedding spectacles, where tens and possibly hundreds of thousands have been married at the same time—until recently with Moon himself choosing matching partners, and then marrying them in football stadiums and other public venues.

Moon's mentors Sasakawa and Kodama, meanwhile, also fared well back home in Japan. In 1976 the annual revenue from motorboat racing was $4.5 billion, of which a stipulated 3.3 per cent, or $150 million, went to Sasakawa's JSIF. By 1983, the annual take had risen to $8.4 billion, which meant that JSIF's cut was nearly $280 million. By 1991 the revenue had more than doubled, giving Sasakawa's foundation a whopping $550 million to dole out that year. The original idea was to use the money to reinvigorate Japan's shipbuilding industry, but even if some of the money is still used for that purpose, 12 per cent goes to the foundation's overseas projects, which include support for leprosy sufferers in Southeast Asia, a university and a women's shelter in Thailand, needy people in China, Rugby in Fiji and Girl Guides in Kenya. Generous donations have also been given to the world's top universities, among them Harvard, Princeton and Oxford. All the money was, of course, taken from unlucky Japanese gamblers, but it was Sasakawa who basked in fame and publicity. Even the name of the foundation was changed in 1990 to 'the Sasakawa Foundation'.[93]

A man who had been imprisoned as a war criminal now declared that 'the world is one family and all mankind are brothers and sisters', and a section of his philanthropical empire was named 'the Sasakawa Peace Foundation'. The old fascist was trying to buy respect—and, to a great extent, he succeeded. In 1982, the then Secretary-General, Javier Perez de Cuellar, presented him with the United Nations' Peace Medal. A bronze bust of the multi-billionaire adorned the foyer of the World Health Organisation's headquarters in Geneva, in gratitude to the Sasakawa Foundation's yearly contributions of $10 million. Sasakawa's philanthropy won him kudos among high-profile personalities such as former American President Jimmy Carter—the foundation helped build the Carter Centre's library in Atlanta—and AIDS activist Elizabeth Taylor, with whom he liked to pose for photographs. His main regret was that he never received the Nobel Peace Prize, which he had coveted for many years. Sasakawa died at the age of 96 in 1995, but his charities have survived him. They are now managed by his children, who continue to reap praise for distributing funds which are not their own.

Few of those who benefited from Sasakawa's largesse were aware of his previous incarnations. Those who were argued that he was 'just trying to make up for past misdeeds'.[94] But had he really changed?

Koei Kaga, a respected Japanese journalist, received several death threats and had to go into hiding when he investigated Sasakawa's fortunes for *Bungei Shunju* magazine. The outcome, however, was a revealing—and devastating—exposé of corruption and misappropriation of money. And Sasakawa never severed his links with the mob. He once bragged that he was a drinking partner of Kazuo Taoka, the late *oyabun* of the Yamaguchi-gumi, and that both he and Nobusuke Kishi had sent congratulatory telegrams to the 1974 wedding of Taoka's son.[95] A strange shootout in the summer of 1993 at the Sasakawa family residence in Setagaya, an upmarket district of Tokyo, also suggested that he was not immune to gang warfare. The target, it was reported, was his third son and heir apparent, Yohei Sasakawa.[96]

Kodama's career took a different trajectory from Sasakawa's—and ultimately ended in a blaze of scandal. Kodama had largely succeeded in his task of 'taming' the *yakuza* and becoming the undisputed power broker and 'the visionary godfather' of Japan's underworld. But some of the gangs were still fighting each other. Kodama deplored the turf wars, which he saw as a threat to 'anti-communist unity'. Many gangs had proven their usefulness by attacking the leftist student movement Zengakuren, labour demonstrations and individual members of the Socialist and Communist Parties. Through his contacts with the gangsters, Kodama had also managed to mobilise almost the entire mob to protect a planned state visit by American President Dwight Eisenhower in 1960 from possible attacks by Japan's militant leftists. Japanese journalist Koji Nakamura, writing for the *Far Eastern Economic Review*, described the scene:

> Kodama persuaded *yakuza* leaders of organised gamblers, gangsters, extortionists, street vendors and members of underground syndicates to organise an 'effective counter-force' to ensure Eisenhower's safety. The final plan called for the deployment of 18,000 *yakuza*, 10,000 street vendors [*tekiya*], 10,000 veterans and members of rightist religious organisations. They were supported by government-supplied helicopters, Cessna aircraft, trucks, cars, food, command posts, and first-aid squads, in addition to some 800 million yen [about $2,300,000] in 'operational funds'.[97]

Never before had so many gangsters been mobilised for a task that would normally be the duty of a government—or, at least, not since

Du Yuesheng had organised his mobsters to crush the labour movement in Shanghai in 1927. But in the end, Eisenhower's visit was cancelled. Tens of thousands of leftists were still marching through the streets of Tokyo to protest against Nobusuke Kishi's rightist government, which was in power at the time, and the Japan–United States defence treaty. But the mobilisation, as well as demonstrating the potential strength of the *yakuza*, had also inadvertently revealed how strong their links were to the government and the police.

In the early 1960s, Kodama went a step further, and urged the *yakuza* gangs—who were still fighting one another—to join together into one giant coalition. His efforts to unify the *yakuza* bore fruit, which was no mean feat. The Tokyo Metropolitan Police estimated that Japan had a total of 70 000 *yakuza* members in 1958. Five years later, there were 184 000, but many belonged to gangs which were very small. In all, there was an estimated 5200 gangs. The biggest was still the Kobe-based Yamaguchi-gumi, but Tokyo was controlled mainly by the somewhat smaller, but perhaps meaner, Inagawa-kai and Sumiyoshi-kai. Other towns had their own gangs, some with as few as a dozen members. But they all shared the same mythology about their origin, and all of them pledged adherence to 'patriotism' and rightist policies.

Kodama managed to keep the peace between most of these groups, and even went as far as overseeing the formation of alliances between the Yamaguchi-gumi and Kakuji Inagawa, a Yokohama-based gangster, the head of Inagawa-kai, whose influence stretched into Tokyo. He also brought his old friend Yamaguchi-gumi *oyabun* Taoka together with Hisayuki Machii, the leader of Japan's most powerful ethnic Korean gang. Kodama's 'peace efforts' perhaps differed somewhat from Sasakawa's. But the way they perceived themselves was essentially the same: as upholders of traditional Japanese values and anti-communism. And the organisations they represented included thugs in the streets, more uppercrust *yakuza*, powerful business interests and ministers in the government.

Kodama's fall from grace began when he agreed to become the Japanese and Korean agent for the Lockheed Aircraft Corporation. The American aircraft manufacturer had had a relationship with Kodama since the late 1950s, which was perhaps not surprising considering his political connections. According to the postwar peace treaty, Japan was not allowed to keep an army. But Japan's need to re-arm had become of utmost importance after the Korean War, and a way around the restrictions was to transform elements of the National Police Reserve to a 'Self Defence Force'—which eventually comprised 240 000 men, some of the best equipped soldiers in East Asia. Kodama lobbied successfully for the Japanese 'Air Self-Defence Force' to buy Lockheed's Starfighter instead of Germany's F-11F. But his most critical task was to sell the American company's new wide-bodied passenger plane, TriStar L1011, to Japan's All Nippon Airways, a deal that was deemed crucial for the Lockheed's future. Lots of money was sent in cardboard boxes to Kodama to grease the hands of his political contacts.

When the scandal broke in 1976, it was revealed that Lockheed had funnelled the equivalent of $12.6 million into Japan, a large portion of it in yen bank notes.[98] And the names of those who had accepted bribes from Kodama and Lockheed included former prime minister Kakuei Tanaka and several leading ministers and officials in the LDP. Tanaka, who had been forced to resign two years before when the influential monthly *Bungei Shunju* had exposed some of his other shady business dealings, was arrested. There was not enough evidence—or political will—to arrest Kodama, the person at the centre of the bribery scandal. But he was indicted for 'tax evasion', and his house was raided. The stress was too much to bear for the 65-year-old kingmaker and god-father, who suffered a stroke. He made only one appearance in court in June 1977, and was thereafter forced to receive the prosecutors by the bedside in his home. Many were shocked, but it was not because Kodama had bribed his contacts in the government—and, most probably, used some of the millions from Lockheed to shore up the fortunes of the by now troubled LDP. Their astonishment was reserved for the fact that the police had raided the home of one of the most powerful figures in postwar Japan. Kodama himself could not believe that someone like him, who had never had to worry about the taxman, was charged with tax evasion. He broke down and spent the next few years in hospital. On 17 January 1984, he suffered another stroke and died. The Godfather was gone and, at his funeral, another godfather, Kakuji Inagawa of the *Inagawa-kai*, exclaimed: 'The world will never see the likes of Yoshio Kodama again.'[99] Nor had the world ever seen a gangster empire like the one that Kodama had helped create.

It was years before the *yakuza* would recover from Kodama's death. As soon as he disappeared from the scene in the mid-1970s, the gang wars resumed. The long-time boss of the Yamaguchi-gumi, Kazuo Taoka, was shot outside the Bel Ami nightclub in Kyoto in 1978. But he survived for another three years, until a heart attack finally killed him in 1981. Kodama, himself dying in a Tokyo hospital, sent flowers to the funeral. Four years later, it was time for another spectacular funeral, when the new *oyabun*, Masahisa Takenaka, was gunned down in the Osaka home of one of his mistresses. Open war raged between the Yamaguchi-gumi and several other gangs well into the 1980s. The bubble economy opened new business opportunities for the *yakuza*, and that seems to have dampened the street-fighting spirit. The new anti-gang law of 1992 also forced many *yakuza* to concentrate more on legitimate businesses such as the entertainment and film industry, bars, golf courses and property development.

But old habits die hard, as the arrest of former construction minister and LDP stalwart Eiichi Nakao in June 2000 clearly showed. He was charged with accepting $566 000 in bribes from a construction company called Wakachiku to favour the firm with public works contracts. Wakachiku, in turn, was said to have got the money from Heo Young Jong, a property developer connected with the Yamaguchi-gumi.[100] In January of the same year, the shares of Japan's leading yoghurt maker, Yakult Honsha Co, had fallen after a newspaper reported that the company had regularly paid *sokaiya* gangsters to suppress criticism at shareholder meetings.[101]

At about the same time, the former president and chairman of Yamaichi Securities, Atsuo Miki and Tsugio Yukihira, were found guilty of helping to cover up the losses of Japan's oldest security house, which had led to its collapse in November 1997. Among other economic wrongdoings, Miki was accused of having sanctioned more than $1 million in payoffs to a corporate racketeer.[102] This was only a minor part of the total covered-up losses—which amounted to $2.43 billion—but it clearly showed that the days of the *sokaiya* racketeers were far from over.

The internal workings of the *yakuza* also remained strikingly normal, despite changes in other segments of Japanese society. 'We've got respect and traditions,' said a veteran gang leader to the Japanese weekly *Shukan Taishu* in May 1997. 'We're not the "mafia" and never will be. In the twenty-first century, or the twenty-second for that matter, the *yakuza* will always be Japanese *yakuza*.'[103] Perhaps he is right. When the new boss of the Yamaguchi-gumi, Yoshinori Watanabe, took over in April 1989, ending nearly a decade of violent leadership struggles, the elaborate accession ceremony vividly illustrated that the feudal and traditional aspects of the *yakuza* were still alive. A videotape seen by a Tokyo-based foreign correspondent shows the entire leadership of the Yamaguchi-gumi. Wearing traditional Japanese dress and carrying old-style paper fans, each enters the room where the ceremony is to be held, and is identified in subtitles by name, organisational rank and sub-gang.[104] Under Watanabe's able, and some people say charismatic, leadership, the number of *kobun*—or loyal followers—of the Yamaguchi-gumi has risen to 16 500, up a third since he took over in 1989.[105] Despite the new anti-gang law, the Yamaguchi-gumi remains a major player in Japan's lucrative sex and drugs industry. Not since the days of Kazuo Taoka has there been a *yakuza* boss as powerful as Watanabe.

The power structure that Watanabe established followed strict feudal lines. He was the *kumicho*, or 'supreme boss', aided by Kazuo Nakanishi, his *saiko komon*, or 'senior adviser', who resided in Osaka with fifteen sub-gangs and 439 members under his command. Saizo Kishimoto, Watanabe's *so-honbucho*, or 'headquarters chief', stayed with the supreme boss in Kobe, with six gangs and 108 gangsters under his control. Masaru Takumi, who had branched out to Australia's Gold Coast and to Vancouver in Canada, was titled *wakagashira*, or 'the number-two-man', and was in charge of 941 mobsters in 41 gangs in Osaka. In addition to these chief lieutenants, Watanabe appointed various *komon* (regular advisers), *shingiin* (counsellors), *kumicho hisho* (secretaries to the *kumicho*) and *wakagashira-hosa* (underlings of the number-two-man). Then came the footsoldiers, commanded locally by *shatei* ('younger brothers'—or, in effect, street gang leaders) and numerous junior leaders, or *wakashu* ('young men').[106]

For social outcasts—and there are many in Japan even today—this strictly hiearchical structure gives them a place in what amounts to a blood brotherhood, not unlike the Triads but in many ways much better organised than the Chinese secret societies. Thousands of Chinese gangs and sub-groups use the names of well-known Triads to instill fear and respect in the people around them without necessarily being connected with gangs with the same name in other places or countries. But being a *kobun* of the Yamaguchi-gumi meant exactly that, and no one—anywhere—would dare to claim to belong to it if he were not a *bona fide* member.

For many outcasts, the *yakuza* also provides a vehicle for upward mobility in society. Joining the *yakuza* also offers a source of identity, the all-important status of membership in a group that is both feared and revered. Staple recruits include working-class youths who, for one reason or another, fail to make the grade in the pressure cooker of Japan's highly competitive education and examination system, school drop-outs, members of motorcycle gangs, casual methamphetamine users and habitués of Japan's ubiquitous *pachinko*, or pinball, parlours.[107] The allure of the *yakuza* has been enhanced by popular culture, movies and books that elevate the mobsters to the status of cult figures. Yukio Yamanouchi, an Osaka lawyer and former legal adviser to the Yamaguchi-gumi, now earns a living cranking out sensational *yakuza* novels. One of his books, *Kanashiki Hittoman* (or 'Lonely Hitman') even became a blockbuster movie in 1989. Yamanouchi and similar writers have managed to generate public sympathy for the *yakuza* by portraying them as a haven for *burakumin*—Japan's own untouchables—and other disadvantaged groups in Japanese society.[108] From a different perspective, as noted writer Ian Buruma puts it: '*Yakuza* heroes are ultimately the heroic victims of this world, which is exactly the way many Japanese like to picture themselves.'[109]

Burakumin have always made up a disproportionally large percentage of all *yakuza* gangs, as have ethnic Koreans, especially in Kobe and Osaka. Both groups have become scapegoats of Japanese society, a release valve for members of the latter to express their dissatisfaction with their own lot as perhaps successful, but extremely hard-working, 'salarymen' with few real joys in life.[110] Dropout rates of both *buraku* and Korean children have also always been higher than the national average. It may sound paradoxical that such minority groups would join super-Japanese outfits like the *yakuza*, but for some that has been the only way to prove their 'Japaneseness'. The sharp political division between North and South on the Korean peninsula has also created a complex and contradictory set of loyalties. Japanese-Korean gangster boss Hisayuki Machii, for instance, is widely believed to have been involved in the 1973 kidnapping of the well-known pro-democracy oppositionist Kim Dae Jung in Tokyo. The reason may have been that Machii wanted to curry favour with the then-powerful KCIA—and perhaps also with Kodama and his Japanese rightists, who saw Kim as a dangerous political activist, and perhaps even a communist.[111] The incident nearly cost Kim his life—and he was released only after heavy pressure from the Americans, who regarded the incident as disgraceful. Kim lived to be elected president of South Korea in December 1997.

Not all ethnic Koreans in Japan were right-wing extremists. Most Koreans, who had been sent to Japan to work in factories when their country was a Japanese colony, and especially during the war when there was an acute shortage of labour in the factories because of the draft, returned home when the war was over. But several hundred thousand remained in Tokyo, Osaka, Kobe, Nagoya and other industrialised areas. More than 97 per cent of them came from the southern provinces of the peninsula, but the political division of their homeland still separated them into 'South' and 'North' Koreans. The former were organised in the pro-Seoul Korean Residents Union of Japan, or Mindan, and the latter in the pro-Pyongyang General Association of Korean Residents in Japan, or Chongryun. In the mid-1950s, Japanese authorities estimated that about 90 per cent of Koreans in Japan supported the northern regime.[112] This is not as surprising as it may sound today. At that time, South Korea was seen by many nationalistic Koreans as a puppet regime of the Americans— and the hated Japanese. The North, on the other hand, had defended its motherland from the 'foreign imperialists'. Any true Korean patriot had to be thankful to Kim Il Sung and his regime. Stories about atrocities and repression in the Democratic People's Republic of Korea were dismissed as 'imperialist propaganda' aimed at smearing the Korean people and their nation.

Chongryun taught this message in its many Korean schools throughout Japan, and the Japanese government tolerated its activities—as long as the 'North Koreans' did not get mixed up in Japanese leftist politics. In fact, an understanding to that effect had been reached in 1955, when the 'North Korean' leader in Japan, Han Dok Su, broke with the Japanese Communist Party and decided to concentrate his efforts on the education and welfare of the Korean community in Japan. He also, somewhat paradoxically, cultivated close links with the ruling LDP.[113]

As the first chairman of Chongryun, Han moved into a grand home in a quiet residential area of Tokyo. Guards watched his residence around the clock, and he had several luxury cars and personal body-guards to accompany him wherever he went.[114] His lifestyle could hardly be described as proletarian, and was in sharp contrast to that of the often-impoverished members of his organisation, who were expected to donate a large share of their meagre salaries to the organisation. Koreans in Japan were also encouraged to donate money to the regime in Pyongyang, which became especially important when the North Korean economy collapsed in the 1980s—at the same time as the lot of the Japanese-Koreans had improved considerably. Patriotic and affluent Korean residents of Tokyo and Osaka were offered photo opportunities with the 'Great Leader' Kim Il Sung at $20 000 per picture. Anyone with enough sympathy for the North to donate over $1 million was rewarded with a special Kim Il Sung medal. By the early 1990s, hundreds of millions of dollars a year in remittances, cash gifts and investment were flowing from Japan to North Korea, helping to prop up the world's last Stalinist regime.[115] Income for the Chongryun—and, more specifically, for North Korea—also comes from Japanese pinball, or *pachinko*. Many of Japan's 18 000 *pachinko* parlours were and still are operated by ethnic Koreans. No one knows exactly how much profit there is in the shady, mob-connected world of *pachinko*, and how much ends up in North Korea. But in 1994, the Japanese police testified in the Diet that $600 million or more was being sent to Pyongyang, much of it derived from *pachinko*.[116]

Following the death of Kim Il Sung in July of that year, and as more and more Japanese-Koreans have woken up to the bitter realities of life in the country of their dreams, Chongryun is no longer as powerful as it used to be. But it still has between 100 000 and 250 000 members, and thousands of Korean children in Japan still begin their schooldays by singing patriotic hymns under portraits of the late Kim Il Sung and his successor, his son the 'Dear Leader' Kim Jong Il. However, the number of pupils enrolled in Chongryun schools has dropped from 40 000 in the early 1980s to 10 500 in 2001. Remittances have also begun to drop considerably, both as a result of shifting loyalties—unlike many of his predecessors, Kim Dae Jung cannot be accused of being a 'US puppet' or a 'military dictator', and for most Japanese-Koreans it is easier to relate to him than to the erratic Kim Jong Il—and because of the poor state of the Japanese economy since the bubble burst in the late 1980s. This could be one reason why the beleaguered North Korean regime has turned to drug trafficking and the printing of counterfeit dollars to survive, in effect creating the world's first truly criminal state where the government is not just cooperating with criminals, but is itself the criminal. In November 2001, Japanese police raided the Tokyo headquarters of the Chongryun as part of an investigation into alleged embezzlement by one of the association's senior officials. The main suspect, Kang Young-kwan, was apprehended on suspicion that he had diverted about $6.5 million from a failed financial institution serving Korean residents in Japan. After years of ignoring the Chongryun, the Japanese police had at last launched an investigation that could shed some light on the activities of one of Asia's most secretive organisations. But it needed a financial scam to provoke this reaction from the Japanese authorities.

The collapse of the bubble economy can also be felt in the narrow lanes of Kabuki-cho. As many Japanese *yakuza* have been forced by economic circumstances, and to a lesser extent by the 1992 anti-gang legislation, to become more 'legitimate', ethnic Chinese gangs with lower expectations have moved in to run prostitution rackets, illegal gambling dens and the fencing of stolen goods. Many *yakuza* have been driven out—and the more ruthless Chinese gangs have not hesitated to resort to violence.[117]

Small Chinese communities have been living in Yokohama and Kobe and other port cities for generations, but the Chinese in Kabuki-cho are mostly newcomers. After launching a program of economic reforms in 1979, Beijing began to approve overseas travel by Chinese citizens. At about the same time, then Japanese Prime Minister Yasuhiro Nakasone announced a scheme aimed at raising the number of overseas students in Japanese universities to 100 000. More than 30 per cent of those who were granted such visas came from China, and the official number of Chinese students in Japan increased to 22 810 in 1998 from only 23 in 1978.[118] It is anybody's guess how many of them actually were students, but it led to a rapid expansion of the Chinese community in Japan.

In 1998, it was estimated that 230 000 Chinese were residing legally in Japan, while illegals—including 'visitors', 'students' with expired visas, and immigrants smuggled into the country—numbered at the very least 70 000.[119] Incidents of theft, extortion, robbery, abduction and murder by members of new crime syndicates have become endemic in Japan's Chinese communities. Snakeheads, or human smugglers, are making fortunes bringing in illegal immigrants from China by boat, and this new wave is changing the criminal landscape of Japan. Rivalries between gangsters from Beijing, Fujian and Shanghai have erupted into shoot-outs, even in the usually peaceful Kabuki-cho. Guns are smuggled in from China—and from Russia across the Japan Sea. Several clubs in Kabuki-cho now also show a new type of 'hostess' on photo displays outside their well-guarded entrances: blondes from Russia, the Ukraine and Belarus.

While many xenophobic Japanese tend to blame the escalated violence on 'foreigners', it is also obvious that Japan's own gangs are becoming more violent. Teen-bike gangs known as *bosozoku* are responsible for a serious surge in violent crimes, which more than doubled in the last five years of the 1990s. The *yakuza*, which traditionally had depended for new recruits on *burakumin* and Koreans, at first saw the *bosozoku* as unruly teenagers who could not become disciplined, organised gang members. But, as the need to 'tame' the wild *bosozoku* on their noisy motorbikes increased, the *yakuza* realised that the best way to control the youngsters was to absorb them. Japan's notoriously unreliable and inefficient National Police Agency claims that the *yakuza* has links with 'no more than 40 per cent' of the country's thousand or so *bosozoku*. Sources closer to the bikers, however, assert that 80 per cent of them pay cash tributes to various *yakuza* gangs to enjoy their protection, or are affiliated with them in other ways. The *bosozoku* has become not only a pool of potential recruits, but also a source of income for the *yakuza*, at a time when yields from other, more traditional gangster pursuits are drying up.[120]

As the recession continues, gang wars are bound to escalate—and there is even fear that the *yakuza* may become even more unpredictably violent than events at the dawn of the twenty-first century have shown. Watanabe controls his gang with an iron fist, but he is no Kodama who can negotiate truces between different bands of mobsters. The Japanese weekly *Shukan Taishu* also believes that if anti-gang crackdowns by the authorities become real and drive the *yakuza* to desperation, this could conceivably even be extended to attacks against police and other officials. And if those without proper gang affiliation run amok, and try to grab a larger share of the spoils, there is a strong chance that the level of violence will escalate even more, ending once and for all the myth of a 'safe' Japan.[121]

The myth of the honourable gangster is also dead—and no amount of water distributed by Watanabe's men after the Kobe earthquake can revive it. There are no noble outlaws in the new criminal disorder emerging in Japan and across the Asia-Pacific. This is particularly true of Russia, on other side of the Japan Sea, where the latest addition to the region's pantheon of organised crime groups is active—and expanding at a breathtaking pace.

• 4
A COUNTRY WITHOUT LIMITS

In Russia, the brigand is the only true revolutionary. He is a revolutionary without phrases, without bookish rhetoric . . . the brigands of the forests, towns and villages, scattered throughout Russia, together with the brigands confined in the innumerable prisons of the empire—these constitute a single, indivisible, tight-knit world, and in it alone, there has always been revolutionary conspiracy. Anyone in Russia who seriously wants to conspire, anyone who wants a people's revolution, must go into this world.
—Russian nineteenth-century anarchist Mikhail Bakunin.[1]

The *dachas* of the hilly Odintsovo region near Moscow are popular retreats for many people who want to escape the hectic life of the city. But when one big, black limousine after another drove through the snowy countryside in December 1991, they were not carrying the ordinary visitors who come here for a quiet weekend. Thirty of Russia's most powerful men had been summoned to an important *skhodka*, or meeting of underworld figures. They represented gangs from Moscow, St Petersburg (as Leningrad was once again known), Kiev and Odessa. Some had come from as far away as Georgia and Armenia in the Caucasus, and from Vladivostok in the Far East.

Only four months before, a disorganised group of old-time Soviet hardliners had attempted to overthrow the reformist leader Mikhail Gorbachev in Moscow. The coup had failed miserably, and the ruling Communist Party had lost power to the then president of the Russian Federation, Boris Yeltsin, a nationalist and a reformer. The Union of Soviet Socialist Republics had ceased to exist. The collapse of communism also meant dramatic changes in the business arrangements of the godfathers. The unique relationship some of them had enjoyed with the rulers of the former Soviet Union had collapsed too.[2]

Among the most powerful bosses at Odintsovo was a gnome-like man with a pointed beard, Vyacheslav Kirillovich Ivankov, who was better known as 'Yaponchik', or the 'Little Japanese'. His nickname came not from any Asian ancestry but just to harmonise it with that of his mentor, the mighty 'Mongol', a shadowy figure whose real name was Gennadiy Korkov, and who ruled Moscow's underworld in the 1960s.

'Mishka Yaponchik' was also the name of a famous outlaw, immortalised in a 1926 book about Jewish bandits and revolutionaries in Odessa at the turn of the century.[3] This further added to the legend and mystique that surrounded Ivankov. He was born in 1940 in the Caucasian Soviet republic of Georgia, but grew up in a truly criminal milieu in Moscow, engaging not only in black marketeering but also in street fights and extortion—other common callings in Soviet days. His godfather, the Mongol, was eventually arrested in the early 1970s, staging a *razgon*—prison slang for a typical Russian bandit ruse. Disguised as police officers, some of his followers had broken into the home of a well-known black marketeer in Moscow. He had been unwilling to make a 'voluntary contribution' to the Mongol's gang and, to frighten the black marketeer into submission, his wife had been killed before him and his family. But the real police caught up with the gangsters, including the Mongol, and they were all taken into custody.[4] Only Yaponchik managed to elude capture—and fled after a fierce gun battle. He surrendered after six months on the run, but only after one of the biggest manhunts in the history of the Soviet Union, which only added to the romanticism surrounding the wily gangster. But he was soon a free man again, and in 1980 formed his own criminal organisation called the Solntsevskaya. The gang was named after the district of Solntsovo, but operated all over Moscow and earned most of its money from smuggling, protection rackets and dealing stolen goods on the black market.[5] At first, he received protection from the highest levels of Soviet officialdom who benefited from his smuggling activities; among his closest associates was Yuri Churbanov, the son-in-law of the then Soviet leader Leonid Brezhnev.[6]

In 1982, Yaponchik's luck ran out. He was arrested and sentenced to fifteen years for robbery, possession of firearms, forgery and drug trafficking. He was sent to a labour camp near Magadan, a remote town in eastern Siberia surrounded by penal colonies, but was later transferred to the high-security prison in Tulun near Irkutsk after he had stabbed a fellow inmate. That, however, did not mean his influence over the Russian crime scene had diminished. Already, before he was deported to Siberia, Yaponchik had been 'crowned' overlord of the country's gangsters—a title that might not have been recognised by the entire, badly factionalised criminal milieu in the Soviet Union, but was enough for him to command respect from thousands of mobsters across the country. The 'coronation' had taken place in Butyrka prison in Moscow, and enabled him to become—even from behind the walls of his prison—one of the most powerful criminal figures in the entire 'Primorsky Krai', the official name of the maritime region in the Russian Far East.[7]

He continued to play an active role in criminal politics, advocating greater involvement in what he saw as the crime industry of the future—narcotics—and encouraging ethnic Russian gangs to take on the Chechens and other Caucasians, bitter rivals of the Russians. Yaponchik also assumed control over Vladivostok's underworld, and even managed—while still a prisoner but with the help of two Russian co-conspirators in Toronto, Canada—to persuade several Russian banks to invest in a phony Siberian gold mining company.[8]

Yaponchik didn't serve his full fifteen years in Siberia's Gulag. In November 1991 he was released, reportedly following the intervention of a 'powerful politician', and the bribing of a judge on the Russian Supreme Court.[9] Yaponchik flew back to Moscow in a privately chartered jet and was welcomed by fellow godfathers with a lavish banquet at the capital's luxurious Metropole Hotel. During his years in prison, Mikhail Gorbachev had launched his *glasnost* (openness) and *perestroika* (restructuring), which in effect put an end to the old socialist economic and political system. And a few months before Yaponchik walked out into freedom, the Soviet Union had died altogether. The entire country had changed—and the gangsters were about to cash in big time.

This process began at the *skhodka* at Odintsovo. Yaponchik and other godfathers carved out territories and examined new business opportunities. The extraordinary meeting they had organised resembled the

1957 Apalachin Conference of North America's godfathers and it achieved the same dramatic effect: the public, and law enforcers all over the world, became acutely aware of the powerful role of organised crime. More precisely, the meeting enabled the godfathers to survive the collapse of the old order, and to profit from the disarray of the new, much weaker regimes which had succeeded it.

The Russian underworld is not new. As Yaponchik's own criminal career clearly shows, it also existed during the communist regime when he and other well-connected gangsters were running the ubiquitous black market in the then Soviet Union. But, under the old order, gangs had forged well-established arrangements with certain officials. Boundaries between the spheres of influence of the various groups were also relatively well defined. Now many of the godfathers at Odintsovo were concerned that turf wars could be a problem.

Prior to the 'August Revolution' in 1991, there had been very few lucrative pursuits for gangsters other than smuggling and black marketeering. The centrally controlled police state had also regulated crime in a way that made it hard for newcomers and upstarts to rise to prominence in society. Ironically, one of Gorbachev's first free-market reforms had led to the first diversification of criminal activities in the Soviet Union. In 1989, the cooperatives had been allowed to function as private enterprises—which, in turn, had resulted in a new criminal phenomenon that was later to spread across the country: protection rackets.

The breakdown of the old system opened the door to even more opportunities. All the fifteen former republics had become—or were in the process of becoming—independent nations, each with legal jurisdiction only within their own borders. Goods stolen in Russia could be sent to another republic, where they could be traded legally. The collapse of the banking system, and the gradual creation of new currencies for the new states, meant unlimited opportunities for fraud and speculation. The old police state was giving way to a string of new, much more chaotic, law enforcement agencies which simply could not crack down on crime as in the past. The demise of the Soviet-style security services meant that it would be easier for Russian gangsters to operate abroad. Evidently, the godfathers had to work out a new arrangement both among themselves and in relation to the new, post-communist authorities.

The criminals had a new catch-word, *bespredel*—or 'without limits'—prison talk for those who did not comply with the thieves' internal code of conduct. Later, the meaning of the term broadened to describe the whole society. It encapsulates a sense of living in a frontier where all the rules and laws that regulate normal life are absent.[10]

Nowhere was that frontier more evident than in Yaponchik's new 'home town' of Vladivostok—and nowhere in the former Soviet Union was the criminal tradition as strong as in the Russian Far East, which owes its foundation to the penal colonies set up there more than a hundred years ago. Its proximity to Japan and China, and its links with Southeast Asia and even the United States, have also allowed gangs based in Vladivostok to establish contacts with international organised crime in a manner unavailable to gangsters in Moscow and St Petersburg.

Siberia in the late 1980s and early 1990s, when Yaponchik rose to prominence in the Far East, was a strange and cruel place—but nothing compared to its past. Eastern Siberia, Russia's 'Wild East', has long been characterised by a mixture of youthful frontier spirit, heroic colonisation, rampant lawlessness and a tradition of penal servitude. 'Four hundred years of continual human striving chart its course, a drama of unremitting extremes and elemental confrontations, pitting man against nature, and man against man', wrote American historian Benson Bobrick.[11] And it is out of this chaotic history that today's anarchic Siberia has emerged: a country 'without limits', which now gives the rest of the world a limitless supply of girls, guns and drugs.

This wild land was originally inhabited by nomadic and semi-nomadic tribes of reindeer herdsmen, fishermen and hunters, distant relatives of the Lapps of northern Scandinavia and the Samoyeds of Russia's Arctic regions. Chinese chronicles from the Han Dynasty (202 BC–AD 220) mention 'fishskin tribes' (most probably the Nanai), 'hairy people' (possibly the Ainu, who now survive only in pockets of south Sakhalin, the Kuriles, and the northern Japanese island of Hokkaido) and a people called Yi-lou, whose curious habits included washing themselves in urine.[12]

Mongol and Turkic warriors also roamed the vast steppes and forests of northeast Asia until the first Europeans arrived in the late eleventh century. Russian fur traders from Novgorod reached the northern Ob river region nearly 900 years ago, but it was not until the sixteenth century that the Russian expansion east began in earnest. In 1571, Tartar hordes burned Moscow, and Russia needed to secure its eastern frontiers. A third of the government's income depended on the sale and taxation of pelts of Arctic foxes, martens, squirrels, otters, beavers, mink and sables—creatures which the early traders had discovered in abundance in Siberia.

Peasants from impoverished European Russia were attracted by promises of free land. And then came the Cossacks, independent frontiersmen who staked out a life for themselves along the fringes of the Russian empire. They rode east to fight the Tartars, and to see whether the news they had received of a rich country full of precious furs and silver was true. As was the case in America, fugitives of all kinds and members of non-conformist religious sects also migrated to the new Promised Land.[13] In a sense, the Cossack represented the American pioneer, the Tartar the Red Indian and the Russian Army the US Cavalry.[14] By the late 1600s, the European newcomers were as numerous as the indigenous Siberian tribes.

Inevitably, the Russians clashed with the Chinese, who claimed the same territories. Delegations from Moscow and the Manchu Court in Beijing finally met in Nerchinsk in August 1689. Following several weeks of negotiations, the two powers agreed on 6 September that the frontier should run along the Argun, Shilka and Gorbitsa Rivers and the crest of the 'stone mountains' north and east of the Amur River.[15] The Russians' expansion south was halted, but they continued undeterred with their conquest north and east as far as the Kamchatka peninsula, dubbed the 'land of ice and fire' for its harsh climate and many active volcanoes. In 1742 the Russians crossed the Bering Strait and reached Alaska. The biggest land empire in history was forming, and although clashes with the aboriginal population were frequent, there was—unlike in the American West—surprisingly little racial prejudice. The Russians treated the natives no worse than they did each other.[16]

Brutality and killings were not uncommon, but that didn't mean that the local tribes were considered inferior. They were simply called *inorodsty* ('people of different birth') or *inoversty* ('people of different faith'), a barrier which could be overcome by conversion to Christianity. Mixed marriages were common, and as a result many Russians—not only in the Far East—have Mongol features, including the founder of the Soviet Union himself, Vladimir Ilyich Lenin.

In November 1856 the Russians established a new territorial unit along the Pacific coast which they named Primorskaya Oblast, or the Maritime District. Despite resistance from Emperor Xianfeng of the Manchu Qing dynasty in Beijing, Russian sovereignty over all territories north of the Amur River was recognised by the Chinese authorities under the treaties of Aigun and Tianjin in 1858. The following year the governor-general of Eastern Siberia, Count Nikolai Muriaviev, sailed along the coast of the newly acquired regions on a New York-built corvette, the *Amerika*. He reached a spectacular, well-sheltered anchorage which was known to the Chinese as Haishenwei ('the Lofty Sea Cucumber') and to British Seafarers as Port May.[17] He decided to call it Vladivostok, 'ruler of the east', to show that Russia was the new supreme power in the region. But it was not until the summer of 1860 that the Russian imperial standard was raised over a cluster of huts, marking the official birth of what was to become the administrative centre for Russia's new Pacific acquisitions.[18]

Russia's main setback on the eastern frontier was its inability to properly colonise Alaska. Empress Catherine the Great's son, Prince Paul, had in 1799 issued a charter to a new trading firm, the Russian-American Company, granting it monopoly of resources along the North Pacific coast. But the results were disappointing. The territory was large and difficult to control, and separated from mainland Russia by sea. Meanwhile, the British were advancing in Canada, and the Americans were pushing west towards the Pacific. In 1867 Tsar Alexander II abandoned all attempts to expand beyond the Bering Strait, and sold Alaska to the United States for $7.2 million, or less than $5 a square kilometre. It was one of the biggest real estate deals in history.[19]

But the drive to populate Siberia continued, and in 1862 an imperial edict granted 100 *desyatins* (270 acres) of land to each household that moved to the vastness of the Russian Far East. Settlers were also exempted from conscription to the Tsar's army for ten years, and did not have to pay taxes for 20 years.[20] Thousands of poor and landless peasants migrated to Siberia, where they turned the wilderness into fields of grain and vegetables. Later, privileges for new settlers became less generous, but the migration continued.

China, wracked with civil strife and suffering from humiliating defeats by Britain in two opium wars—the first of which led to the loss of Hong Kong—was not in a position to oppose the Russian colonisation of the East. Xianfeng, the Chinese Emperor who at first had refused to ratify the 1858 accords, was forced under the 1860 Treaty of Beijing to recognise finally and formally the Russian acquisition of Primorye. The Amur River became the official border between the two empires.

The new Russian settlers comprised more than just Cossack soldiers and peasants looking for land. Many were non-conformist Christians, such as German Mennonites and Baptists, who settled along the Zeya and Bureya Rivers north of Mongolia. Others were religious outcasts from Russia itself. Following a schism between reformers and traditionalists within the Russian Orthodox Church in 1658, many of those who could not accept the new liturgical forms—called 'Old Believers' or 'People of the Old Faith'—crossed the Urals to continue their worship in freedom.

During the eighteenth century, *Skoptsy* or 'eunuchs'—a sect that stressed sexual abstinence—and *Dukhobors*—literally 'soul strugglers', or people who did not believe in the Holy Trinity—settled in the area. They worshipped the Father and the Son, struggled against the Holy Spirit and founded new communities in the Far East that acknowledged the authority of neither the Orthodox Church nor the Tsar.[21] By 1880, Old Believers accounted for half the population of Amur district, which had more religious sectarians than any other province in the Empire. The long trek to the East could take more than a year, with entire families moving in convoys of horse carts, driving their cattle in front of them.

Prosecuted people and other wretched refuse of Russia's teeming European lands also ended up in Siberia. The most celebrated were the *Dekabristy*, or the Decembrists, aristocratic army officers who had tried to revolt against Tsar Nicholas I in 1825. Five of them were executed, but more than a hundred of Russia's finest minds were sent to rural parts of the East for hard labour. Having served their sentences, they were free to move to the towns, where they had a substantial influence on the educational and cultural life in an area that in many ways resembled the American West.

Large numbers of Polish rebels were also deported following several failed uprisings against Russian rule in their homeland. After the Poles came Ukrainians, Finns, Estonians and Lithuanians who settled on the shores of Peter the Great Bay on the Sea of Okhotsk.

Officials who had fallen from favour in European Russia were sent to administer the new territories in the East.

Some newcomers were not even from the Russian Empire. A Swiss silk merchant from Shanghai, Jules Johann Brüner, settled in Vladivostok where he ran a successful import–export business. He Russianised his name to Yulius Ivanovich Bryner, and his enterprise, Bryner & Co, invested in Amur timber, coal from Sakhalin and lead from the mines at Tetyukhe. Yulius' grandson, who was born in the Russian Far East, added an 'n' to his surname when he later emigrated to the United States: he was Yul Brynner, who played the Thai King Mongkut in the movie *The King and I*.

At the bottom of the social ladder were the convicts. In the mid-seventeenth century, the Russian government began sending criminals to the East. As the demand for labour in the mineral-rich area increased, so did the list of punishable offences elsewhere in Russia: vagrancy, prostitution, prize-fighting and even fortune-telling became grounds for banishment. The death penalty was abolished and replaced with exile and hard labour deliberately to encourage migration to the East. Scores of people were sent to Siberia without even a trial. By 1890, more than 3000 exiles a week were marched in shackles to Irkutsk by Lake Baikal. Only one in ten would survive the journey. Siberia was no Oregon or California.

A penal colony was established on the huge island of Sakhalin, which also belonged to the new Primorskaya Oblast. The author Anton Chekhov visited the island in 1890: 'I have seen Ceylon which is paradise and Sakhalin which is hell'.[22] The ordeal was especially severe for women, who made up less than 10 per cent of the convicts. The best they could hope for was to become the concubines of prison officials; the most unfortunate became the common sexual property of the prison guards and other ruffians.

At that time, political exiles usually fared better than common criminals. One revolutionary recalls that he took along his books and enjoyed freedom of movement within several thousand square kilometres. The government supplied him with writing paper, weather-recording instruments, a Winchester rifle, a pistol and a shotgun.[23] Mikhail Bakunin, the famous Russian anarchist, managed to escape on a barge down the Amur and boarded an American schooner bound for San Francisco. Other exiles included novelist

Fyodor Dostoyevsky, Leon Trotsky, Lenin (who spent three years near Abakan) and a swarthy Georgian seminary drop-out turned revolutionary called Josif Dzhugashvili, who in 1903 was exiled to the tiny Buryat Mongol village of Novaya Uda. He later assumed a name that was to become synonymous with the utmost cruelty: Joseph Stalin, 'a man of steel'.

Bakunin in particular developed a sincere affection for the Robin Hoods, Ned Kellys and Billy the Kids of the Siberian *taiga*, and even saw them, in his own anarchistic way, as potential revolutionaries. A criminal culture called *Vorovskoi mir*, or 'Thieves' World', thrived in the Siberian woods. The roots of these criminal fraternities can be traced back to the seventeenth century and they demanded that their members openly and defiantly follow their own laws. Upon entering the Thieves' World, a criminal would choose from among a number of 'professions' to earn his living. These could be pocket theft, apartment theft, railway theft, safecracking or armed robbery. The Thieves' World was also marked by its own argot, referred to as *blatnaya muzyka*, or 'the music of the *blatnoi*', the criminal elite—a patois drawn from various languages, including Russian, Polish, German, French and Turkish—and by numerous signature tattoos, which indicated rank, profession and time served in prison.[24]

The Russian Far East was to European Russia what Australia was to Britain, and what French Guiana in South America and New Caledonia in the Western Pacific were to France: a remote dumping ground for criminals, political undesirables and human refuse of all descriptions. The difference, however, was that the mighty Russian Empire was bound together by geography. No oceans separated one part of Russia from another. Despite this geographical unity, though, St Petersburg ended up with a mish-mash of a territory which any government would have found hard to control.

Land transport between European Russia and the Far East exacerbated the problem. Travel to Siberia was at least a three-month undertaking by horse cart, while it could take much longer for families of settlers, or chained convicts, to make the same journey. The Chinese threat was also still present despite the weakness of the Manchu Emperors in Beijing. Japan was another problem. Japanese fur traders had reached Hokkaido, where they clashed with Russian trappers. The Russian Empire clearly needed better communications, and the Tsar decided to build what was to become the longest railway in the world, connecting St Petersburg with Vladivostok. It was a trip of 9939 kilometres—or more than twice the distance from New York to Los Angeles.

The construction of the Trans-Siberian railway began in 1891, and the need for quick access to the new territories in the Far East became even more pressing when, in 1904, tensions between Russia and Japan led to war. Such was the urgency of sending troops and munitions to the front that temporary rails were laid across the frozen Lake Baikal. The first train plunged through the ice, making a 22-kilometre-long hole. Undaunted, the Russians relaid the tracks, disassembled the heavy locomotives and used packs of horses and people to pull the engine parts and the carriages across the lake.

Later the same year, travelling became considerably easier as a line was laid around the huge lake. Finally, it was possible to go by train all the way from the Baltic Sea to the Pacific. A side-spur ran through Manchuria to Port Arthur, a Russian naval base on the Yellow Sea. In 1897 the Russians had secured a 25-year lease over the Dalian peninsula, including Port Arthur. A narrow strip of land on either side of the railway was also under Russian sovereignty, thus extending St Petersburg's writ down into Chinese territories—which Japan also coveted. In February 1904, Admiral Togo Heihachiro launched a surprise attack on Port Arthur. The Russian-controlled Manchurian city of Mukden (now Shenyang) also fell to the Japanese, while the Tsar's Baltic fleet was destroyed in the Straits of Tsushima in May 1905 after an epic 28 000 kilometre journey from its base in northern Europe. Russia lost the war, and was forced to cede the Dalian leasehold, the Manchurian railway and the southern half of Sakhalin to Japan.

This humiliating defeat made it even more important to upgrade the Trans-Siberian railway, the cord that bound European and Asian Russia together. But the fact that it was indeed difficult to govern the Far East from Europe, thousands of miles away, became even more evident when the Russian revolution broke out in 1917. Having established the world's first communist republic and moved the capital back to Moscow—somewhat more in the middle of the huge country—Lenin and his Bolsheviks were faced with the daunting challenge of establishing their authority over the former Imperial lands. Some—including Poland, Finland, Estonia, Latvia and Lithuania—managed to break away and become independent. In the Far East, confusion reigned and an extremely bloody civil war erupted.

As revolution swept across the country in 1917, revolutionary councils—called 'soviets' in Russian—were formed in Vladivostok and Khabarovsk. But in May 1918 a general counter-revolution broke out in the Far East, sparked by a force of 45 000 Czech and Slovak prisoners of war who disagreed with the official axis between Russia and the western powers, and who believed in the self-determination of Slavic peoples. They had been caught in Russia by the revolution and feared that the new Bolshevik authorities would hand them over to Germany. In June, the Czech and Slovak legions seized Vladivostok and overthrew the city's communist government.

Meanwhile, the Tsarist Admiral Alexandr Vasilevich Kolchak, who had been stranded in the United States when the revolution broke out, returned via Japan and Harbin, Manchuria to Siberia, hoping to unify the resistance against the communists. Kolchak, a cultured man who played the piano and classical guitar, joined forces with Cossack warlords and assorted armed bands in the Wild East. His army was boosted by the support of 7000 American troops, 72 000 Japanese, 6400 British and 4400 Canadians who were there ostensibly to assist the Czechs.[25] By mid-September, most of Siberia was in the hands of the Whites, and on 18 November Kolchak declared himself 'Supreme Ruler of Russia'. His opponents, however, called him the 'Ruler of Omsk'—the only part of Siberia which he actually controlled—and ridiculed him for wearing Russian epaulets on 'an English uniform' while smoking 'Japanese tobacco'. To his critics, he was little more than a foreign puppet with only limited influence—not a man capable of overthrowing Lenin's new government.

War, revolution and counter-revolution created a very special atmosphere in Vladivostok. The city was a unique blend of provincial Russia, Shanghai in pre-revolutionary days and the American Wild West. Dozens of languages were spoken in the city, and several types of Russian roubles—tsarist, revolutionary and local—were used along with US dollars, Chinese yuan and Japanese yen. News-stands sold papers from New York, Tokyo and London as well as Vladivostok's own Japanese, American, Tsarist, Menshevik and communist dailies and journals, including Russian, English, Japanese and Chinese editions of *Business Siberia*. Chinese guilds and Japanese merchant firms were housed beside the National City Bank, International Harvester, the YMCA, the Knights of Columbus, the American Red Cross and the Chicago Café.[26]

But the war was going badly for the counter-revolutionaries. The White Terror usually surpassed the Red Terror in sheer brutality, as Kolchak's forces were under the leadership of some extremely savage officers. The most notorious of all was Roman Fyodorovich von Ungern-Sternberg, a Baron whose ancestry was as complex as his own personality. He claimed to be a descendant of Attila the Hun, but family records show that he actually came from a prominent Swedish-Latvian family that had been knighted by the King of Sweden in 1653, when the northern Baltic states were ruled by Stockholm.[27] One branch of the family remained behind in Latvia when Sweden was forced to give up the territory to Russia in 1721, and many of them had few employment prospects outside the armed forces.

A former major-general in the Tsar's cavalry, von Ungern-Sternberg arrived in Vladivostok in 1918 to fight the Bolsheviks. Today he would simply have been certified as a psychopath and locked up. But in the desperate days of the Civil War he had won renown among the White armies as a soldier of extraordinary—if reckless— courage as well as ferocious cruelty.[28] During an earlier stint in the Far East, the 'Mad Baron' had adopted Lamaistic Buddhism from Mongol horsemen in his cavalry unit. His Buddhist teachers had taught him about reincarnation, and he now firmly believed that in killing the feeble people he only did them good, as they would be stronger beings in their next life.[29] A Russian eyewitness, Dr Ossendowski, described von Ungern-Sternberg as having 'a skinny exhausted face like those old Byzantine icons. Then everything else faded from view save a big protruding forehead overhanging steely sharp eyes. These eyes were fixed on me like those of an animal from a cave'.[30]

In the autumn of 1920, 'the Mad Baron' led a motley force of 6000 soldiers, among them former members of the Tsar's army, local Cossacks and Mongol horsemen, into Mongolia, where he unleashed a reign of terror. Previously, Bolsheviks and Jews had been the principal victims of his rage. But in Mongolia he killed without discrimination. When his forces invaded Urga, the capital of Mongolia, in January 1921, 'innumerable men, women and children of all ages, races and creeds were hacked to bits and bayoneted and shot and strangled and hung and crucified and burnt alive'.[31] Women offered themselves up for rape to save their husbands—'but were cheated in the end', according to Dimitri Alioshin, a former White officer who left a vivid description of von Ungern-Sternberg.[32]

At the time, Mongolia's status was unclear. A traditional vassal of China, it had gained some measure of independence after the Chinese revolution of 1911 and the proclamation of a weak and fragmented republic in the place of the former Empire. But there were still Chinese troops in Urga when von Ungern-Sternberg arrived. He drove them out, and in return the Bogd Khan—a local political-religious leader somewhat similar to Tibet's Dalai Lama—bestowed on the him the exalted title of Khan. Von Ungern-Sternberg, though, proclaimed himself 'Emperor of all Russia' and vowed to plant 'an avenue of gallows' stretching all the way from Urga to Moscow, from which would swing 'Bolshevik and Jew alike'.[33]

The new Soviet government in Moscow clearly viewed the Baron and his band as a threat—and not only because of the atrocities he committed. The Baron's main benefactors were the Japanese, who saw him as a useful tool to expand their influence in north-central Asia, especially after their victory in the 1904–05 war. The Japanese openly backed his plans for a 'Greater Mongolia', which they had already ear-marked as their own protectorate. These provocations led to a determined intervention by the Red Army. Ten thousand Soviet troops marched into Urga in July 1921. Mongolia, because of von Ungern-Sternberg, became a vassal of Moscow—the first communist-ruled country after the Soviet Union itself.

The Baron fled, but was eventually captured and taken to the Supreme Court in Novosibirsk. He reportedly told his accusers: 'For a thousand years the Ungerns have given other people orders. We have never taken orders from anyone, and I refuse to accept the authority of the working class'.[34] The 'Mad Baron' was executed by firing squad on 15 September 1921. Although not a common crimi-nal, von Ungern-Sternberg left behind a legacy of violence and cruelty that has become part of the folklore in Russia's Far East. And he has not been forgotten. One of his boots is kept in a museum in Ulan Bator—Urga's new name after the communist takeover—where his name still evokes awe and revulsion.

Other counter-revolutionaries in the Far East were almost as bizarre. Grigory Mikhailovich Semyonov, a Cossack of Buryat Mongol descent who had served on the Austro-German front during World War I, proclaimed himself 'Ataman', or supreme chief, of the Cossacks in 1918. He led the strongest anti-Bolshevik force east of Lake Baikal—and, like the 'Mad Baron', was supported by the Japanese. Also like the Baron, Semyonov, together with another Cossack Ataman, Ivan Pavlovich Kalmykov (who was only 27 years old), became known and feared for his barbarism. William S. Graves, a US Army General who commanded the American Expeditionary Force in Siberia from 1918 to 1920, called the two Atamans 'the most contemptible scoundrels I have ever met'.[35] Kalmykov headed a Japanese-supported regime in Khabarovsk—and shot everyone who he thought had destroyed his pre-revolutionary world. Among his victims was an entire musical ensemble which played the 'Internationale' instead of 'God Save the Tsar' in a Khabarovsk café.[36]

One of the few exceptions among the Whites in Siberia was Kolchak himself. But, surrounded by a bunch of military commanders who were at best eccentric and at worst despotic, his attempts at fighting the Soviet regime were doomed to failure. His army was routed by the Reds. Once numbering 800 000, no more than 20 000 remained by the end of 1919. The Czech legionnaires were also in disarray, and eager to return to their families. In January 1920, they handed Kolchak over to a social-democrat coalition that ruled Irkutsk in exchange for freedom of passage home. Soon afterwards, the Bolsheviks seized power in Irkutsk and put Kolchak on trial. He was sentenced to death. The 47-year-old veteran of the Tsar's navy requested a guitar and sang a classical Russian love song before he was shot.

The fall of the Kolchak regime signalled an end to the resistance against the Bolsheviks in the Far East. But another incident pitted the Reds against the Japanese. On 25 March 1920, all Japanese soldiers and civilians—about 700 people, including women and children—in the lower Amur town of Nikolayevsk were massacred on the orders of a Red Army commander and his chief of staff and mistress, Nina Lebedeva, a 25-year-old communist who liked to dress up in dark red leather and, armed to the teeth, gallop about on her horse.[37] The killings prompted the Japanese to send more troops to the Russian Far East.

But the Reds had already won the war in Siberia. Nevertheless, it was too early to incorporate this far-flung and still potentially volatile region into the Soviet Union. The compromise solution was the proclamation on 6 April of the Far Eastern Republic, a buffer state between Bolshevik Russia and other interests in the area: the western interventionary forces, who were still there and, above all, the Japanese. For some, this meant an illusory independence for eastern Siberia.

The president of the new 'republic' was Alexandr Michailovich Krasnoshchekov, a Ukrainian who had once worked with Leon Trotsky and, in 1905, emigrated to Chicago. There he became active in the Industrial Workers of the World (IWW), or the 'Wobblies', a militant American trade union movement formed in the early 1900s. He returned to Russia after the revolution in 1917. His minister of war was a fellow Chicagoan, Vladimir Sergeevich ('Bill') Shatov, another devout anarcho-syndicalist and erstwhile IWW organiser who had also returned to his native land to celebrate the victory of the working class. Recognised officially by Lenin in Moscow as an independent state, the Far Eastern Republic gradually acquired a semblance of authority.[38] At the very least, it managed to convince the Japanese to withdraw from Siberia in exchange for promises of 'containing Bolshevik influence' and turning the region into a 'neutral zone' closed to the Soviet army.

This situation lasted for more than two years—as did sporadic fighting in the area—until, on 18 November 1922, the Far Eastern Republic was finally reunited with Russia and incorporated into the Soviet Union, which was set up in the same year to unite the various communist-ruled republics. The civil war was over and the Bolsheviks had triumphed—but at immense human cost. War, executions and starvation had claimed the lives of an estimated 25–26 million people, or a sixth of the population of the whole of Russia at the time.

Many more were to die as the new Soviet government consolidated its grip over the former Russian Empire. In 1922, Lenin said that 'though Vladivostok is a long way off, it is after all one of our own towns'.[39] But, rather than alleviating strains between the centre in Moscow and the Far East, the fall of the Tsar had exacerbated them. The civil war had kept Siberia cut off from the rest of the country for years, and the creation of the Far Eastern Republic had not instilled in the Wild East a strong sense of belonging to a greater fraternity ruled from far-away Moscow.

The independence the republic enjoyed for a few years was largely fictitious, but its separate status nevertheless meant that it had to fend for itself economically. The people in the Far East knew they had experienced economic recovery without any help from Moscow; by using the enterprise of their own bourgeoisie, and investment from foreign countries which shunned Russia proper. The experience suggested that the region's potential lay in an Asia–Pacific arena.[40]

The task of bringing Siberia into the Soviet mainstream fell on Lenin's successor, Joseph Stalin, who came up with some rather unorthodox solutions to the problem. The most innocent was intended to solve the perennial shortage of women in the Far East. When the Far Eastern Republic was absorbed by the Soviet Union, there were 93 women for every 100 men in the Far East.[41] The imbalance got worse during the next decade as the new Soviet leadership sent tens of thousands of soldiers, construction workers and communist volunteers, most of whom were young males, into the area.

In 1932, a photogenic 18-year-old woman called Valentina Khetagurova left Leningrad to marry a powerful officer in Stalin's Special Far Eastern Army. She threw herself into setting up 'Stalin corners' in army barracks, where 'culture and literacy' were promoted. The young woman caught the attention of higher authorities and, on 5 February 1937, the communist youth paper *Komsomolskaya Pravda* ran an article headlined 'Girls! Come to the Far East!'.[42]

More than 27 000 young Russian women followed Valentina's example. In the army barracks of Siberia, and in the headquarters of the newly established Soviet Pacific Fleet in Vladivostok, they had ample opportunities to meet men of the same age. Some, however, fell foul of alcohol and pimps. Vice had flourished for decades in this wild frontier region, and continued to thrive despite the new revolutionary idealism.

Nothing was ever clear-cut in Siberia, and even the sale of opium had been accepted under the Far Eastern Republic. Its government had actually gone as far as to encourage the trade in narcotics by creating a special office, the Inspection of Opium Affairs, and by licensing poppy cultivation and opium smoking. After all, the original Chinese population had produced opium for export to their homeland well before the Russian conquest. These efforts provided the local authorities with a substantial source of income.[43] Vladivostok was indeed 'a long way off'.

If anything, it had become a haven for assorted mavericks, including enthusiastic young communists who, with a revived pioneer spirit, travelled in vast numbers to the Far East to build socialism in a land full of contrasts and contradictions.

Stalin's main contribution to Siberia's transformation was hardly a novel one. He simply revived and expanded the Tsar's old scheme of turning the region into a penal colony—and, in doing so, helped lay the corrupt foundations of a modern criminal state. The first exiles to arrive were the criminals, waifs and strays who had been rounded up when the new order was established. More came during Stalin's political purges in the 1930s. A plot to overthrow the Soviet government had allegedly been unearthed—and Stalin gave full powers to his secret police—the dreaded NKVD, or 'the People's Commissariat of Internal Affairs'—to track down and punish any opponents to his regime, real or imagined.[44]

Tens of thousands of ethnic Koreans from the Vladivostok area were put in boxcars and sent off to Uzbekistan and Kazakhstan in Central Asia, despite the fact that they, having fled from the Japanese, had good reason to be faithful to the Soviet regime.[45] Numerous party cadres and perfectly loyal army officers were arrested, tried and executed. Among them was the pair from Chicago who had headed the Far Eastern Republic, Krasnoshchekov and 'Bill' Shatov. Polish, Finnish and Estonian communities were thinned out by executions and deportations.

But huge numbers of people were also sent to Siberia under Stalin's new plan. In the year of the Great Terror alone, 1937–38, more than a million were executed—and an estimated 7 million banished to labour camps, many of which were located in the remotest parts of Siberia.[46] They arrived in unheated cattle cars, which were divided into windowless compartments. A prison train could consist of 50 or more 60 ton freight cars, carrying 6000–7000 convicts at a time.[47] Having crossed the vastness of Siberia, they finally arrived at transit camps outside either Khabarovsk or Vladivostok. They were then loaded on to ships for the ten-day voyage to the ports of Nagayevo and Magadan further to the north, where the long march to the labour camps began. Magadan was infamous long before Yaponchik was deported to the remote Siberian town in 1982.

Ironically, the two most infamous ships sailing between the ports of the Far East were American-built and named *Sacco* and *Vanzetti* after two working-class heroes from Boston, who had been sent to the electric chair in 1927 for alleged involvement in a local robbery, and who later became symbols of international solidarity among down-trodden working-class people across the world. How Italian-born, American anarchists Nicola Sacco and Bartolomeo Vanzetti would have reacted to having these two prison ships named in their honour is anybody's guess, but the horrors of the voyage from Vladivostok are well documented. One ship left Vladivostok too late in the year and became stuck in the ice in the Sea of Okhotsk, finally reaching Magadan nine months later; none of its thousands of prisoners survived. Prisoners aboard another ship made the mistake of revolting—and the guards held them back with water hoses, filling the hold. It was 40°C below zero. The 3000 convicts were delivered to Magadan entombed in ice.[48]

Magadan served as the marshalling point for prisoners destined for the camps in the Kolyma region further inland. It was a Gateway to Hell, and the roads leading up to the region's 100 or so camps were littered with human bones and decomposed bodies. Gold had been discovered in Kolyma in 1910, but little was done about it until Stalin, in his own brutal way, decided to open up the area in the 1930s. Prisoners were also used to work the coal mines, logging camps, fisheries and construction sites in the area, all of which became part of the local slave-labour economy.

It was a society in which only the strongest and the fittest survived. Intellectuals who had travelled East during the civil war were marked as 'foreign spies' and executed. Their wives were often sent to camps, and their children placed in special orphanages. Siberia's fledgling intelligentsia, with the Decembrists as its most revered pioneers, was physically obliterated.

Stalin's mass purges saw the labour camps in the Far East expand at an extraordinary rate. In 1927, an estimated 200 000 prisoners languished in the region's camps, most of which were ordinary criminals. By 1939, the figure had risen to three million. Most of the newcomers, however, were innocents or political prisoners. The security apparatus had more confidence in the criminals, who were used as trustees in the camps to keep the 'politicals' in line.[49] Karlo Stajner, a Viennese communist who had left for Moscow full of youthful enthusiasm in 1932, but who was later arrested, accused of being a 'foreign spy' and sent to the camps in the Far East, remarks in his memoirs:

The criminal convicts were better off than the politicals in every respect. Only criminals were employed as administrators, tailors, shoemakers, and barracks janitors. They took it easy and frequently stole from the politicals. If a political prisoner received a package from his relatives, he could expect to have it stolen. Practically every day, you would see a prisoner crossing the yard with a package he'd just picked up, and a criminal holding him up at knife point and taking the package away. It was not only useless to inform the camp police of such crimes (since they were often in league with the criminals), but dangerous; a criminal would murder a fellow prisoner who denounced him to the camp police.[50]

Organised crime has a long and strong tradition in Russian society, but it developed important new characteristics under communist rule. Criminal prisoners banded together to distance themselves from the political prisoners, who were even more feared by the authorities, and whose 'crimes against the state' were considered worse than theft, robbery and murder. After the revolution—and especially after Stalin's purges of his real and imagined political opponents—Bakunin's Thieves' World became led by a criminal elite known as *vory v zakone*, or 'Thieves-within-Code', implying that they followed certain rules and an internal code of conduct. [51]

The establishment of what writer Alexandr Solzhenitsyn called 'the Gulag Archipelago' provided the actual criminals with new opportunities. It has here in the 1930s that they first began to cooperate with the authorities—especially the security services, with which they forged an almost symbiotic relationship. The criminals were often given guns to guard the political prisoners. A woman prisoner who was sent to a labour camp in the Far East in the late 1930s remembers her:

> first meeting with the real hardened criminals among whom we were to live in Kolyma . . . they were the cream of the criminal world: murderers, sadists, adepts at every kind of sexual perversion . . . [a] half-naked, tattooed, ape-like horde . . . [that] without wasting any time . . . set about terrorising and bullying the 'ladies'—the politicals—delighted to find that the 'enemies of the people' were creatures even more despised and outcast than themselves.[52]

The new power structure emerging in the labour camps—even the existence of the camps themselves—was known to few outsiders. World War II, and the alliance between the Soviet Union and the

United States, further obscured the vision of many otherwise critical observers as to what was actually happening in Siberia. When President Franklin D. Roosevelt met Stalin in Teheran in 1943, they discussed security and common interests in the North Pacific, and a second, somewhat more low-level, meeting was arranged in the region itself. Vice-President Henry A. Wallace was sent to the Far East for talks with the chief of the NKVD's prison system, Sergei Goglidze, who almost overnight turned Magadan and Seimchan into glitzy Potemkin villages. Watchtowers came down, and stores were painted and stocked with provisions flown in from Moscow. Prisoners were removed from sight, their places in the mines taken by NKVD guards and office girls.[53]

During his three-day stay in Kolyma, Vice-President Wallace enjoyed himself, dining on caviar and salmon, vodka and champagne—and was impressed with what he saw. He remarked: 'Goglidze is a very fine man, very efficient, gentle and understanding with people'.[54] Thanks to Goglidze, his secret police—and millions of slave labourers—by 1945 Siberia accounted for most of the Soviet Union's gold, 21 per cent of its steel, 18 per cent of its cast iron and 32 per cent of its coal.[55]

But the society which the pioneers of the seventeenth and eighteenth centuries had dreamed of establishing in the Siberian wilderness was shattered: Russia's frontier was not going to develop like British Columbia, California or Hokkaido. The intellectuals were gone, and even the most idealistic of the Party's own cadres had been eliminated. The new elite that emerged was made up of political opportunists, corrupt apparatchiks, hardened executioners and violent criminals. Hardly surprisingly, the criminals were the most cunning of them all.

During World War II, some of the criminals had volunteered to join the army, either as a way of getting out of the camps or to show their patriotism. Entire battalions were made up of criminals, who were sent to the front. Some fought heroically against the Germans, and thus earned their freedom, while others—who had been less brave—had to return to the camps when the war was over. The returnees, like the trustees, were branded *suki*—'bitches'—by the orthodox *vory v zakone*, who viewed them as upstart collaborators, and who themselves would never work with the authorities. The late

1940s and early 1950s saw the whole Soviet prison system ravaged by what became known the 'scab wars', as these 'bitches' took on the traditional, more uncompromising criminals, and eventually won. It was a hidden war in which thousands died, and which the government either was unwilling or unable to prevent. Consequently, the country's prisons became dominated by criminals who realised the advantages of cooperating with the authorities.[56]

Stalin's death in 1953 changed the situation dramatically. Some camps were opened, and eight million prisoners of an estimated twelve million interned at the time were released—although most of them appear to have been common criminals. The political prisoners were not set free until much later. Disillusioned, and with their lives destroyed, they eventually returned home to their broken families. The criminals, on the other hand, began to consolidate their position in the new Soviet society. In 1956, a year before the Apalachin meeting in the United States, *vory v zakone* from all over the Soviet Union even held a secret *skhodka* in the town of Krasnodar in southern Russia, near the Black Sea and the Georgian border, where they divided up the country between them for smuggling and protection purposes. Territories were allotted, and their sanctity safeguarded under mutual agreements. The whole purpose of the gangster summit was to avoid costly, and potentially disastrous, turf wars.[57]

Unlike the traditionalists before them, the 'bitches' also sought to cultivate alliances of convenience with members of the political elite and the officials of the state, from the NKVD's successors—the MVD, the MGB and the KGB—and the police to Communist Party civil servants.[58] This was the case especially during Brezhnev's lax rule in the late 1960s and 1970s, when the worlds of organised crime and politics became so close that it was almost impossible to distinguish the two. 'The Mongol' and others became semi-public figures, who quite openly ran gyms and wrestling clubs. 'Pupils' from those 'athletic centres' could, of course, be used as enforcers in extortion rackets.[59]

But the cooperation had to be fine-tuned, and in 1979 the godfathers met again. Their second nationwide *skhodka* was held at Kislovodsk, another town on the fringes of the Caucasus, and their main interest this time was control over the flourishing black market in the Soviet Union: foreign cigarettes and whisky, American blue jeans and the illegal trade in foreign currencies. Leading black marketeers—mostly petty traders and enterprising individuals—were also invited to attend the meeting. The latter had to agree to pay the *Mafiya* 10 per cent of their takings in return for protection.[60]

The style and direction of the Soviet Union's godfathers had changed, but not the basic structure of their organisations. Entry into *Vorovskoi mir*, the 'Thieves' World', demanded the fulfilment of strict sponsorship requirements and a swearing-in ceremony for new recruits. At this initiation, the gangsters were given nicknames based on their professional and personal qualities. They were told to be tough, cunning, fierce with traitors and honest with their peers. *Vory v zakone* was led by an inner council which met to decide on strategy. There was even—before the Soviet Union descended into chaos—a thieves' court which gangsters presided over to mediate in disputes and to mete out punishments against 'traitors' within their own ranks.

Profits from their criminal activities were kept in a common treasury called *obshchak*, funds from which were used for loan-sharking, bribing officials, investing in new ventures and looking after members in need and families of imprisoned or deceased gangsters.

The internal organisation of the gangs has always been—and still is, even after the collapse of the system—strictly hierarchical. At the top are the *vory v zakone*, followed by their own personal 'advisers'. Middle-ranking supervisors come next; they are responsible for issuing orders, recruiting new members, providing protection and collecting payments, and for paying off corrupt police and other officials. Under the supervisors are gangs of ordinary street fighters who pay tribute in return for protection from other criminals. Throughout the communist era, the main breeding ground for the criminal underworld remained the Soviet prison system.[61]

In the 1960s, criminal organisations began to surface in all major cities. This was when the obscure 'Mongol' emerged as the undisputed *vor v zakone* of Moscow's underworld. Following his arrest in 1972—and Yaponchik's first stint in prison—a member of the 'Mongol's' gang, a 24-year-old Moscow-born wrestler of Georgian origin called Otari Vitalievich Kvantrishvili, began his rise to power. 'Otarik', as he was nicknamed, had been imprisoned for a brutal gang rape when he was only eighteen. He was released two years later, and became a coach for an Olympic team of wrestlers at the Dynamo Sports Club, an establishment run by the security services.

After the arrest of his godfather, Otarik forged an extraordinary array of contacts and made a point of courting the police and influential politicians. He co-founded a charitable foundation to help the families of injured police officers and established the first hard-currency casino in Moscow.[62] The casino not only earned hard cash for Otarik, but also laundered money; the sports club trained his enforcers. Otarik soon became one of the youngest, and most powerful, *vory v zakone* in the country.

The Mongol's other prominent follower, Yaponchik, was still in prison at that time. But even without his direct participation, the changes could be felt in the Far East as well. In July 1986, Gorbachev had paid a visit to Vladivostok where, in a highly publicised speech, he had focused on the region's disappointing growth rate. 'Much of what was mapped out has, unfortunately, been badly carried out', he lamented—and went on to announce an ambitious development scheme for the Far East.[63] Gorbachev had promised to plough 232 billion roubles ($359 billion at official mid-1980s rates, $38.7 billion at the black market rate of the time) into developing the infrastructure in the Far East, and to increase electricity production and oil exploration. The Far East, he said, would become more autonomous and be given a larger role in the processing of its raw materials. The idea was to link the Soviet Far East with the booming economies of East Asia: Japan, South Korea, and perhaps even Taiwan.

For years, Vladivostok had been closed to the rest of the world. The headquarters of the Soviet Union's Pacific Fleet tolerated few outsiders, but gradually Vladivostok began to end its hermetic existence. By 1989, more than 700 foreign delegations had visited the city. Some foreign countries—among them the United States and South Korea—set up consulates in the city. Vladivostok was going to become Moscow's window on Asia. Some enthusiastic researchers produced plans for turning the Tumen River basin around Vladivostok into a 'future Hong Kong'.[64]

Then came the August 1991 revolution. In the Far East, as elsewhere, social disorder and a severe economic crisis followed the collapse of the Soviet Union. It was not only the Soviet republics which asked for separation from the Union. In March 1992, Siberian politicians met at Krasnoyarsk, a city on the Trans-Siberian Railway between Novosibirsk and Irkutsk, and called for an independent

Siberia. On the Pacific coast, the outspoken mayor of Sakhalin Island, Valentin Fyodorov, suggested a return to the 1920–22 Far Eastern Republic.[65]

But with the collapse of communist rule in 1991—and the subsequent breakdown of civil order across the former Soviet Union—it was not only local gangsters who became the new overlords of Vladivostok; organised crime gangs from Azerbaijan, Armenia, Georgia, Chechnya and other Caucasian mountain regions moved in. The dreaded *yakuza* arrived from across the sea and set up shop buying guns and whatever else they could scavenge from the ruins of the erstwhile superpower. Smuggling, gambling, prostitution, fraud, kidnappings, drive-by shootings and Italian mafia-style bombings became commonplace in Vladivostok after 50 years of almost total isolation.

The rapid growth of organised crime, some analysts argued, was due in part to Russia's eagerness to develop a free market before constructing a civil society in which such a market could safely operate.[66] Even some of Gorbachev's most well-meaning schemes had been totally counter-productive and had played into the hands of the *Mafiya*. In 1985, he had launched an anti-alcohol campaign which was as much of a boon for Russian organised crime as the Prohibition had been for its US counterparts in the 1920s and 1930s.[67] Attempts to encourage economic reform through cooperatives had in practice provided new opportunities for racketeering, money laundering and loan sharking.

This was exactly what the *vory v zakone* who met at Odintsovo in December 1991—the third such *skhodka* of Russian crime bosses—wanted to cash in on. Yaponchik, fresh out of gaol and full of new ideas, had some unusually bold proposals, to which the other godfathers agreed. He had himself appointed special emissary of the Russian *Mafiya*—to the West. In March 1992, he boarded a plane in Moscow, bound for New York. He had a regular passport and his American business visa, issued by the US Embassy in Moscow, said he would be working in the 'movie industry'.[68]

Relatively peaceful and law-abiding Russian communities have existed in Brooklyn, Miami and California for decades, although some were carried away by their first encounter with freedom and openness.

Many émigrés became criminals in the United States, where they discovered credit card fraud and other new ways of making money, of which they had been unaware when they lived in the Soviet Union. But following the collapse of the Soviet Union, many new immigrants made it to the United States, bringing more brutal *Mafiya*-style crime with them. In the 1980s, there were more than 65 murders and attempted murders involving Russians and Russian émigrés, dramatically signalling the arrival of Russian organised crime on American soil. Smuggling incidents involving Russian émigrés ranged from aluminum to weapons to currency scams and drugs. The centre of much of this activity was Brighton Beach in Brooklyn, where thousands of Russians had settled in the 1970s and even before. But when the newcomers arrived, there was a dramatic upsurge in extortion, protection rackets and smuggling. An abundance of gangs worked for whoever paid them, and there was no evidence of monopoly control by any clearly defined syndicate.[69]

Yaponchik's assignment in the United States was to establish a relationship with the loosely organised gangs in Brooklyn and elsewhere and, if possible, to take control of their criminal networks. The local police may have been caught slumbering, but New York's leading Russian language newspaper, *Novoye Russkoye Slovo* ('New Russian Word') reported on 26 October 1992: 'To the traditional articles of Russian export to America must now be added organised crime . . . we have begun to see many new crime leaders travelling here from Russia, including *vory v zakone*'.[70]

Two years later, Yaponchik presided over a summit in Miami which tried to carve up North America in very much the same way as the Russian Godfathers had done at home in the former Soviet Union. How well the effort succeeded is hard to determine but, given the chaotic nature of the Russian *Mafiya* today, it seems highly unlikely that achieving such a degree of cooperation and understanding between the gangs would have been possible.

Yaponchik's own criminal career in the United States came to an abrubt end on 8 June 1995. Agents from the Federal Bureau of Investigation (FBI) stormed his girlfriend's 22nd-floor flat in 'Little Odessa', the Russian quarter of Brighton Beach, where they knew he was staying. The Russian gangster boss snarled like a bear and kept on kicking and screaming as he was dragged out of the flat. He even refused to unclench his hands for fingerprinting; the FBI had to pry open his fingers one by one.[71]

Yaponchik was charged with masterminding a scheme to extort $3.5 million from an investment firm run by Russian businessmen, and sentenced to nine years and seven months' imprisonment.[72] In prison, one of Russia's most powerful—and colourful—criminal personalities broke down and became an almost pathetic figure. In 1999, he was found with heroin in his cell; the veteran of Moscow's gang wars and Godfather of Vladivostok had become a drug addict.[73]

Even so, the organisation he established is still expanding, and other Russian *vory v zakone* have set up shop in North America: 'Kats' in Los Angeles, 'Vachigan' in Denver and Vyacheslav Sliva in Canada.[74] In 1996 in Miami, the US Drug Enforcement Administration (DEA) uncovered a trafficking network that shipped cocaine from Ecuador to Florida in cargoes of frozen shrimp. The organisers, who met regularly in a backroom at Porky's, a Russian-owned pink-neon strip club on the fringes of Miami International Airport, also bought Russian helicopters, smuggled cigarettes, alcohol and counterfeit money, and provided prostitutes to local Russian mobsters. Their most extravagant project was an alleged plot to buy a Russian navy submarine to sneak South American cocaine up the West Coast to San Francisco. Kenneth Rijock, a Miami-based financial crimes consultant, commented: 'They've got more money than God. And they are more ruthless than the 1920s Prohibition gangsters'.[75]

Meanwhile, back home in Russia, Yaponchik's old colleague, *vor v zakone* Otarik, had been killed by a sniper on 5 April 1994. He was the main casualty of the gang warfare that everyone had feared would follow the collapse of the old order; the gunman had reportedly been hired by a rival gang from the Caucasus region. The godfather of Moscow was buried at the city's prestigious Vagankovskoe Cemetery, and his funeral was attended by more than a hundred *vory v zakone* as well as a cross-section of Russia's political and artistic elite. After all, he had been a close friend of, and personal tennis coach to, Russia's new president, Boris Yeltsin. The president himself had signed papers granting lucrative tax exemptions to a club Otarik ran.[76]

The *Mafiya* had not only survived the collapse of communism; they had become the country's new secret rulers.[77] In September 1997,

Russian interior minister Anatoliy Kulikov was forced to admit: 'Organised crime has changed qualitatively. Leaders and authoritative figures in the underworld have created a united criminal community. They have at their disposal huge finances, qualified lawyers who consult them and other experts, and extensive corrupt links. Moreover, they have armed militia groups'.[78]

No longer did the old Soviet prison system provide most of the *Mafiya*'s foot soldiers. Economic collapse and social dislocation forced thousands of young people from all walks of life into the Thieves' World: unemployed urban youths, sportsmen with no teams to join, assorted drifters and vagrants, and Afghan war veterans who suffered from the same trauma as their American counterparts who had fought in Vietnam.

The most vicious addition to the pool of new recruits came in 1991, when the old KGB was abolished. Its First Directorate, which had been responsible for foreign intelligence, was replaced by a new, more professional spy agency called the SVR, or the state intelligence bureau. The SVR was modelled on its western equivalents, the CIA and Britain's Secret Intelligence Service: a tightly knit group of analysts attached to embassies abroad. The KGB's other directorates were transformed into Russian equivalents of America's FBI and National Security Agency. This reorganisation meant that tens of thousands of former informers, street detectives and gunmen lost their jobs. Russian criminal organisations hired them as first-class hitmen to carry out 'special assignments'.[79]

The new hero in Russia was the gangster, sometimes outlandishly dressed in a striped suit and dark sunglasses, today's version of the old Russian brigands of the nineteenth century. During the communist regime, it was fashionable for Russian women to have an artist, a rock singer or even a journalist as a boyfriend. Now trendy young girls wanted *Mafiya* boys.

In the Far East, the attempts to integrate the region into the booming economies of the Pacific Rim had failed miserably, mainly because the rest of the world associated it with crime and violence. Vladivostok, the 'Ruler of the East', had humbly begun to seek outside help, especially from Japan—but with little or no response. The influx of hordes of hustlers and dealers from the former Soviet Central Asia made the city not only unsafe, but also dirtier, noisier and more crowded. With more people to support, there were increasing shortages of food, energy and housing. The government was even unable to pay the famous and once well-respected sailors of the Pacific Fleet, whose mighty ships by now were rusting away in the city's harbour, some still loaded with nuclear weapons. To survive, a group of the sailors opened a 'Magic Burger' clone of MacDonald's in Vladivostok. There were other imaginative ideas for making a living. With an eye for tourists—especially wealthy Japanese ones—Magadan craftsmen refashioned skulls from the mass graves in Kolyma into ashtrays, bangles and motorcycle ornaments—an ironic and grisly exploitation of Siberia's violent past.[80]

In the midst of the economic crisis, many Russians began to re-discover their roots. Vladivostok's street names were changed back to those of the pre-revolutionary era. Russian Orthodox churches were suddenly filled to capacity. Descendants of 'the Old Believers'—the few who had survived Stalin's purges—met again to practise their creed. In Irkutsk, some local businessmen announced a plan to erect a monument to Admiral Kolchak. Local Cossacks, dressed in their traditional costumes, held a mass for Ataman Semyonov in the town of Chita. To suggest that Kalmykov and von Ungern-Sternberg were heroes would still be considered too extreme. But it may be only a matter of time before even the 'Mad Baron' is rehabilitated: the Cossack fraternity in the Far East, which he helped establish during the civil war, is growing in strength and is linked to several trans-regional criminal organisations.[81]

Yaponchik was gone from Russia and Vladivostok, but one of his followers, Evgeny Petrovich Vasin—nicknamed *Dzhem* or 'Jam'—became the new godfather of the city. In the classic Russian criminal style, he became not so much the head of a disciplined and monolithic empire as an arbiter and first-among-equals of the heads of the region's reported 194 criminal gangs. However, in his capacity as 'elder statesman', he is able to deal with other godfathers in Moscow, St Petersburg and Central Asia in the name of the underworld of the Far East.[82] Valdivostok's gangsters, disorganised as they may be, are involved in protection rackets against most local businesses, heroin smuggling from Afghanistan and Burma via China to supply the region's growing community of drug addicts—and, of course, in arranging for Russian women to work in 'entertainment centres' all over East and Southeast Asia.[83]

The criminal scene in Vladivostok has been complicated further by the arrival of numerous illegal Chinese immigrants who have brought with them influences from the Triads. Thanks to Stalin's purges, Vladivostok—once a predominantly Chinese town—was the only major port city in the Pacific Rim without a Chinese community. However, when cross-border contacts expanded in the 1990s, so many Chinese poured across the border that the Russians became concerned about the threat of uncontrolled illegal immigration.[84] While there are some 100 million people in China's northeastern region, the population of the Russian Far East—an area two thirds the size of the United States—was less than seven million. The total population of the whole of Siberia was no more than 32 million in the mid-1990s.

In September 1993, a Khabarovsk newspaper published an article by a local scientist, Petr Ivashov, who identified four paths the Chinese were taking to gain a foothold in Siberia: becoming traders; purchasing property; marrying Russian citizens; and finding work in Russian firms and farms. If the Russian press is to be believed, anywhere from 150 000 to two million Chinese now reside in Russia.[85] Western academics estimate that Chinese represent at most 4 per cent of all the people in the Russian Far East, but they are concentrated in the cities of Vladivostok, Khabarovsk and Blogoveshchensk, and in smaller townships such as Pogranichnyi, where they are believed to outnumber the European population.[86] Facing racial prejudice and the threat of deportation, many choose—or are forced—to work for ethnic Chinese gangs, which are linked to the Triads.

Cheap Chinese garments and consumer goods are flooding the markets of the Far East, along with narcotics from elsewhere in Asia. In 1996, the English-language *Vladivostok News* reported that ephedrine, known as *mulka* among addicts, was the most widespread drug in the Far East. A home-made adaptation of methamphetamine, it had begun to arrive 'in huge quantities from China'.[87]

Rising unemployment, particularly in rural areas, was pushing increasing numbers of people into the drug culture. Yuri, a local addict, was quoted by the *Vladivostok News*: 'Young people have nothing to do. Only the old folks don't smoke cannabis. And even babushkas, who used to condemn addicts, now trade cannabis to buy sugar and potatoes'. On 6 March 1997, the paper reported that an old woman had been found with 21 kilograms of amphetamine tablets on her return to Nakhodka from China: 'This is the second time a pensioner from Nakhodka has been involved in smuggling. The first case involved a disabled person who organised a shipment of weapons from the Baltics'.

The opening of borders also saw the arrival of a host of harder substances, such as opium and heroin, brought in from China and North Korea. Some drugs were sold locally, while others were re-exported to other destinations by the local *Mafiya* in Vladivostok. The US DEA reported in July 1996: 'One particular group has been importing kilogram quantities of Southeast Asian heroin to the New York area since 1991'. Coincidentally or not, that was just before Yaponchik arrived in the United States. In January 1993, Australian police seized 6 kilograms of heroin which had been smuggled from Vladivostok.[88]

Even more worrying were suspicions of North Korean involvement in the heroin trade and other criminal activities. As early as 1994, officials in China's Yanbian Autonomous Region had discovered that the North Koreans, or local ethnic Korean gangs with North Korean connections, were using northern China as a trans-shipment point for heroin bound for Japan and the United States. In early 1994, an ethnic Korean from China was arrested as he attempted to smuggle 300 kilograms of heroin from North Korea through China. Chinese border officials are concerned about this cross-border traffic, but feel powerless to stem it as most of it occurs across the Yalu and Tumen Rivers at night. The origins of the drugs that are being smuggled in this way are unknown, but the raw opium from which the heroin was made is most probably from Southeast Asia's Golden Triangle.[89]

On 9 June 1994, the authorities in the Vladivostok area arrested two North Korean citizens carrying 8 kilograms of heroin. A Moscow newspaper reported: 'To smuggle such a large amount of narcotics from North Korea without the deliberate connivance of the authorities appears most improbable'.[90] The value of the heroin seized from the North Korean citizens was $1 million at the going rate on the world drugs market, which is all the more impressive when seen against the backdrop of the economic plight of the Stalinist regime still in power in Pyongyang.

The two North Koreans were later identified as Kim In-Chol and Choe Chong-Su. Both are alleged to be North Korean intelligence officers based in Vladivostok. On 3 January 1995, two more North Koreans—one of them in possession of a Democratic People's Republic of Korea passport—were arrested in Shanghai attempting to sell 6 kilograms of opium.[91]

Any evidence of official North Korean involvement in the East Asian drug trade—and links with the ethnic Korean underworld in the Russian Far East—remained circumstantial, although suspicions were strong. With the economic situation in North Korea also worsening, Pyongyang's reliance on illicit sources of foreign exchange, such as gun running and most probably also drug trafficking, seemed almost beyond doubt—and was, for western law enforcers, a real concern.

Although Stalin had deported most ethnic Koreans from the Far East to Central Asia, many had remained behind, and others had returned when the region was once again opened for settlement. The North Korean consulate in Nakhodka and the new South Korean consulate in Vladivostok began to compete for the loyalty of Siberia's ethnic Koreans—but it was clear that the lifestyle of South Korea was far more attractive than that of the impoverished North. A firm from Seoul set up a hotel while other South Korean interests distributed Bibles or imported reindeer horn, a renowned local aphrodisiac.[92] Smuggling to and from the South Korean port of Pusan has also grown, to the extent that many shops in the city's former entertainment area for American GIs now display signs in Russian.

The tense relationship between the North and the South Koreans surfaced when, in October 1996, the city was shaken by a bizarre, high-profile killing: Choi Duck-Keun, South Korea's arts and culture consul, was found dead in his apartment stairwell. While the official cause of death was bludgeoning, the reported discovery of two pencil-sized insertions on Choi's torso led to speculation that he had been poisoned—with the finger pointing at his political rivals at the North Korean consulate in nearby Nakhodka. It is unlikely that robbery was the motive since he was found with $1200 in cash still in his pocket.[93]

The murder shocked Vladivostok's new diplomatic community. No suspects were arrested, and three representatives from the North Korean consulate in Nakhodka came to Vladivostok to 'protest press reports linking their country to the murder'.[94] Not many were convinced, and people began to ask what Choi might have known that prompted someone to get rid of him. 'Arts and culture consul' was a cover for intelligence work, and the South Koreans had become increasingly interested in North Korea's involvement in drug trafficking and the printing of counterfeit money. But nothing came out of the investigation: the police were tight-lipped and unwilling to cooperate.[95]

Penetration by the *yakuza* has been somewhat more subtle. While heavily involved in smuggling between Russia and Japan, they have otherwise confined themselves to investing in profitable ventures in Vladivostok, Magadan, Sakhalin—where Japanese and Russian gangsters have been cooperating for years—and the Kamchatka peninsula, which has become an important waystation for various contraband. In 1997, Japanese police cracked an organised car theft ring stealing vehicles to order in Osaka and Fukuoka to be shipped to Russia. It was run by a member of the Yamaguchi-gumi, Japan's most powerful *yakuza* gang.[96] In the opposite direction, Russian prostitutes have travelled—some on their own, but others through local, *Mafiya*-run 'travel agencies'—to the honky-tonk districts of Pusan, Seoul, Tokyo and Osaka. Some girls from Russia have gone to Macau, Bangkok and even Jakarta in search of greener pastures. This exodus—the biggest flight of Russians into Asia since thousands of them settled in Shangai in the 1920s—is in many ways incongruous. Siberia's economic potential is enormous and could have been developed, if its history had only been different. Siberia's gold and diamond deposits rival those of South Africa; its natural gas fields surpass those of the United States; the fishing grounds of Sakhalin match those of the North Atlantic; and the timber reserves are as abundant as those of Brazil.[97] But kleptocracy, not democracy and a genuine free-market economy, had succeeded communism. Even the governor of the Far East refuses to leave because there 'is so much to steal here'.[98] The region has become one of the most mismanaged in the whole country—an extremely dubious distinction in today's Russia.

New, palatial mansions have been built next to the old Stalinesque, prefab apartment blocks in the city's suburbs and, as a Canadian journalist who visited the city in 2000 pointed out, ownership of imported reconditioned vehicles with darkened glass was a sure sign of a dishonest fortune. A local prosecutor told the visitor that the *Mafiya* bosses 'are the fathers of the city. They even go to receptions at City Hall.' But neither the prosecutors nor the police can touch them: 'They have connections to the politicians and if we get too close all they have to do is make a telephone call'.[99] In the wake of the collapse of the former Soviet Union, a complex nexus has emerged between politicians, former KGB agents, gangsters, prostitutes and businessmen, and all the players are typical products of this pehnomenon—people who are involved in a variety of legal and criminal businesses to survive in today's Russia where the law has little meaning.

The presence of the *yakuza*, the Triads and the North Korean also shows that the Russian Far East has, at long last, become incorporated in a larger East Asian fraternity—but in a way quite different from that envisaged by development enthusiasts when they thought the region was destined to become a 'future Hong Kong'. While some of the more traditional—and racist—Godfathers resent working with their Chinese and Japanese counterparts, a younger generation of more business-oriented gang leaders sees all sorts of advantages in cooperating with the established, regional networks of the Triads and the *yakuza*. It is rumored that even the somewhat older *Dzhem* shares their views.[100]

Extravagant hopes for the Far East have waxed and waned over the decades, but it is a wild and untamed frontier area whose ethnic mix, cosmopolitan pedigree and legacy of violence have fostered a situation that is unique even in post-communist Russia. Eastern Siberia—a land that could have been Russia's California if its history and politics had been different—is developing into a lawless state, ruled by extortionists, pimps and international gangsters.

Even with a new, more energetic president at the helm of Russia, former KGB Chief Vladimir Putin, Vladivostok remains the new whore of the East—a city thriving on smuggling, prostitution, drug trading and contract murder. The entire Russian Far East has become so volatile that it might even break away from the rest of Russia to become the world's first truly criminal republic. After all, the police, the courts, the banks and most local enterprises are already in the hands of the *Mafiya*, which in turn has managed to establish links with like-minded people and organisations all over Asia, and even as far away as North America. In the 1970s, a Tokyo entrepreneur called for the establishment of a 'Russo-Japanese Magadan Republic' that would thrive on the trade in 'sex and gold'.[101] It may have sounded like a joke at the time. Today, it is almost a reality.

• 5
THE GREAT GOLDEN PENINSULA

Chinese sailors coming to the country note with pleasure that it is not necessary to wear clothes, and, since rice is easily had, women easily persuaded, furniture easy to come by, and trade easily carried on, a great many sailors desert to take up permanent residence.
    —Chou Ta-kuan, Chinese envoy to the court of Cambodia from 1296–97[1]

In 1813 we hear of the Society under the name of . . . T'in Tei Hui [Tiandihui], that is, the Brotherhood of Heaven and Earth. It now tended to concentrate in the South, particularly in Canton [Guangzhou], where we find [it] is using the alias of Sam-ho-hui (the Society of the Three Rivers), and sent Lodges overseas as far as Java and the Indian [Indonesian] archipelago. This marks its entry into what is British Malaya. All attempts to suppress it failed, as such attempts usually do, for history shows that it is practically impossible entirely to stamp out a secret society. Such action is more often calculated to drive it underground and to restrict its membership to desperate, dangerous and unscrupulous men.
    —W.G. Stirling of the Malayan Chinese Protectorate, Singapore, 1925[2]

Royal Air Cambodge, the national airline of impoverished Cambodia, is not exactly renowned for excellent service. But when a passenger called Theng Bunma was asked to pay $4670 in overweight baggage charges on a flight from Hong Kong to Phnom Penh, he decided that enough was enough. The airline had already lost his luggage on a previous flight and offered only paltry compensation. So this time, after his flight had landed at Phnom Penh's Pochentong airport in April 1997, Theng borrowed a pistol from one of the bodyguards sent to meet him. Then he walked across the tarmac, aimed the gun at one of the Boeing 737's front wheels, and fired. The tyre burst and the huge aircraft tilted, but even then Theng wasn't satisfied. 'I'm sorry it was dark, otherwise I could have shot out all the tyres,' he said later.[3]

The incident would have led to legal action anywhere else in the world, but the trigger-happy passenger happened to be the president of the Cambodian Chamber of Commerce and the richest man in the country. His Cambodian investments, which included a hotel, a bank and an import–export business, were worth more than $400 million.[4]

He was also a main financier of the Cambodian People's Party (CPP), which has ruled the country in various guises since 1979. No other Cambodian tycoon enjoyed the same respect as Theng, and his political influence was unparalleled within the country's business community. In December 1997, Theng—and Cambodia's Prime Minister, Hun Sen of the CPP—even received an honorary doctorate in business administration from Iowa Wesleyan College. Bob Prins, the director of the college, presented the award to Theng during an international industrial-commercial conference in Phnom Penh and praised Theng as 'a man who cares for ordinary Cambodians'. Prins cited Theng's success as an entrepreneur, his donation of thousands of tonnes of rice to needy Cambodians, and his 'contributions to the country's road and currency systems'.[5] Theng, on his part, promised to donate $10 000 a year for Cambodian students to study at the Wesleyan College.

There were many red faces in Iowa when the press revealed that Theng was barred from entering the United States because of his suspected involvement in drug trafficking.[6] The doctorate was quickly withdrawn, and Theng was furious. In an interview with Australian journalist Anthony Paul, he lashed out at the press:

> Please do not play games with me. There are journalists who have defamed me by writing that I am the head of a drug-smuggling ring. I would like to tell you that if Theng Bunma does something, he never answers questions about it inaccurately. If I say I will shoot you, I'll really shoot you! Like I shot the plane's wheel. I really shot it . . . I shot the plane's tyre, I think wrongly, in anger.[7]

Theng's outburst came shortly after he had given Hun Sen $1 million in gold to finance the ousting of his main rival, Prince Norodom Ranariddh.[8] This bloody coup claimed scores of lives, and was only one of many sad legacies of the anarchy that has prevailed in Cambodia since 1993, when the United Nations supervised a general election which was—ironically enough—meant to lay the foundation for peace and democracy after decades of civil war and genocide. The United Nations spent $3 billion on the operation—an unprecedented sum—but the country's fragile democratic institutions were soon subverted by the wealth of drug kingpins and other crime lords.

Cambodia has since emerged as a haven for the illicit trade in narcotics and arms as well as money laundering and smuggling of illegal aliens. And in a country that is being shunned by mainstream investors, the new business elite is dominated by characters such as Theng Bunma.

Sam Rainsy, a former finance minister who was ousted in October 1994 for his frank criticism of corruption within the government, bluntly described the lawless situation that has emerged his country:

> Land prices [in Cambodia] are very high because of speculators from Thailand, Hong Kong, Singapore, Malaysia and the many Chinese people in the region, who I think are related to the mafia because they want to launder money. They launder money in three ways: property development, banking and gold smuggling . . . the money comes mainly from Hong Kong and Thailand—mostly from drugs and arms trafficking . . . trafficking in heroin from Laos is increasing. From Thailand and Burma, the drugs go to Laos, and from Laos they go through the whole of Cambodia to Phnom Penh, then to Vietnam and Sihanoukville . . . there are 29 banks in a small country like ours. [Some] are laundering money, making deposits and sending funds to another country and saying that the money comes from Cambodia.[9]

Decades of war had left Cambodia with some of the biggest stockpiles of weapons in Southeast Asia, and there were many rebel movements in the region that were eager to buy: Burma's dozens of ethnic and political insurgents, Sri Lanka's Tamil Tigers, the Naga rebels of northeastern India and armed opposition groups in the Philippines. While some guns were sold at the Thai border, a new route was discovered in February 1993 when a ship carrying 20 tonnes of munitions was detained along the Mekong river while on its way to Vietnam. Only 20 per cent of the weapons were functional. A subsequent investigation showed that private arms dealers in Vietnam bought old weapons from Cambodia, repaired them and then offered them for sale on the illegal arms market in Asia. It turned out that the ship had been hired by a company owned by the wife of Uy Sambath, Cambodia's vice-director of customs and a former minister of commerce.[10]

Among the most affluent of the buyers of weapons from Cambodia were the Tamil Tigers. Their agents, operating under cover as managers of 'South Indian restaurants' in Phnom Penh, acquired for the

Tigers everything from assault rifles to Russian-made SA-7 surface-to-air missiles. The chief arms procurer for the Tigers, Selvarajah Padmanathan—or 'KP' as he is better known—became a frequent visitor to Phnom Penh in the mid-1990s.[11]

But he was not the only internationally wanted terrorist to take advantage of the chaos in Cambodia. In March 1996, Interpol and the Cambodian police had raided an office in Phnom Penh in search of counterfeit dollar bills, which had been discovered in neighbouring Thailand and traced to Cambodia. An Asian man in the office fled—and sought refuge in the North Korean embassy in Phnom Penh. A few days later, a Mercedes with blacked-out windows and diplomatic licence plates left the embassy compound and sped out of the city. A police team decided to follow it as it drove toward the Vietnamese border. The Mercedes tried to evade the police, but the chase continued all the way down to Bavet, the last Cambodian checkpoint before Vietnam. There it stayed for almost two days and its occupants 'ate, slept, shat and pissed' in the car.[12] Eventually a deal was made. The North Korean diplomats in the car were given immunity and allowed to return to Phnom Penh. But the counterfeiter had to be handed over to the police. He had a North Korean diplomatic passport under the name 'Kim Il Suu'—but turned out to be Yoshimi Tanaka, a wanted member of the Japanese Red Army, Japan's most feared terrorist group. As a 21-year-old student, Tanaka and eight other members of the Red Army had hijacked a Japanese airliner to Pyongyang. Apart from a North Korean passport, he was in possession of $40 000 in fake $100 bank notes when he was arrested. Tanaka was extradited to Thailand a few days later.[13] In 2000, he was sent back to Japan, where he was charged with hijacking and other violent acts.

While the North Korean connection attracted the interest of the international media, most new gangsters in Cambodia are ethnic Chinese—from Hong Kong, Macau, Taiwan and mainland China. The presence of Taiwanese gangs was highlighted on 9 July 2000, when Chen Chi-li, 'spiritual leader' of the United Bamboo gang and nicknamed 'Dry Duck', was arrested in Phnom Penh and charged with possessing firearms, including hand-guns, assault rifles, M-79 grenade launchers and thousands of rounds of ammunition. And this transpired even though Chen had managed to be awarded both an honorary royal *Oknha* status—usually acquired through contributions in excess of $100 000—as well as an official adviser's position to Cambodian Senate President and security chief Chea Sim.

Whenever new investors from Taiwan came to Cambodia to set up a business, a visit to Chen's luxury villa in Phnom Penh was obligatory. Investors would offer the mobster a generous gift as 'a gesture of their respect'. Before escaping to Cambodia, Chen ran a string of nightclubs and brothels in Taiwan. Chen's legal difficulties in his new base, Phnom Penh, turned out to be more than a minor inconvenience. In August 2001, he was released from custody along with two of the other suspects. 'He used illegal weapons because of fear of his own security,' said Cambodian judge Yia Sakom. 'The three were not involved with organised crime.'[14] Chen's high-level connections were too powerful for anyone in the government—or business—to challenge.

Among their major achievements, Chen and his fellow gangsters had turned Cambodia into a clearing house for Chinese migrants, mainly from Fujian province on the mainland opposite Taiwan, to go to the United States and other western countries. This traffic is not even illegal in Cambodia. According to Article 10 of the new Law on Nationality, which the parliament passed in July 1996, anyone who invested $500 000 in the Cambodian economy or donated $400 000 in cash to the state budget would be entitled to Cambodian citizenship—and it is a lot easier to enter the United States on a Cambodian passport than on one from the People's Republic of China.[15] That *is* legal. But for much less money, it is possible just to buy a passport from corrupt officials in the Cambodian administration. After being added to the US government's list of countries supporting drug trafficking in 1996, only a year later Cambodia was gaining notoriety as a major transit point for illegal immigration.[16]

The rise in illegal migration through Phnom Penh, and the prominent role being played by Taiwanese gangsters in this business, was the main reason why the government in Beijing in October 2000 decided to pay more attention to crime in Cambodia—by asking Theng Bunma to control the smaller gangs and their unruly members. Theng, a Sino-Cambodian, is also the honorary president of the Chinese Association of Cambodia, which has emerged as a powerful lobby group. Chinese migration to Cambodia is not new— it began 800 years ago—but it has increased dramatically since the 1992–93 UN intervention. This is the third time in China's history that such a massive exodus has taken place, not only to Cambodia but also to Southeast Asia and the rest of the world.

What had over the centuries been a trickle turned into a flood after the fall of the Ming dynasty in 1644. That first wave consisted mostly of non-Mandarin speaking southerners who opposed the Manchu Qing dynasty's seizure of power in Beijing. These migrants— Hokkien, Hakka, Cantonese, Hainanese and Teochew—established overseas Chinese communities all over Southeast Asia. The warmer, fertile countries south of China became known as 'Nanyang', or the 'South Seas'; they were lands of milk and honey beyond the reach of the oppressive Manchu Emperors.[17] The next wave came after the Taiping Rebellion and other upheavals in the mid- and late nineteenth century as the Qings crumbled and warlords tore the country into lawless fiefdoms. Not only did these migrants—again mainly from the southern coastal provinces—swell the existing Chinese communities in Nanyang, but newly invented steamships took them to North America and Australia.[18]

This time, migrants are coming from all over China. Improved overland routes through China and better transportation links worldwide have led to a steady movement of people into northern Thailand, Burma, Laos and Cambodia—and beyond. This third massive exodus stems from policy changes in China after 1978, when Washington and Beijing established diplomatic relations. To qualify for most favoured nation status in the United States, China relaxed emigration regulations in 1979 and the flow south and westwards began. In the 1980s, China's economic 'reform and opening up' under the late leader Deng Xiaoping paved the way for Chinese to go in search of business opportunities abroad. The shift from people's communes to private agriculture, the massive lay-offs at state-owned enterprises, and the rapid industrialisation in coastal provinces all led to dislocation and more migration.

Those without legitimate channels through which to emigrate often turned to people smugglers for help. If land borders and airports were well guarded, the migrants took to boats; if coastguards stepped up patrols, the migrants left by air. Backdoor routes multiplied. For example, would-be migrants trekked overland through Burma to Thailand, flew from Bangkok to Bucharest—the cheapest airfare to Europe—then slipped into the countries of the European Union. People from Manchuria, including a large number of Korean-Chinese, cross the border into Russia, where they either settle or catch the Trans-Siberian express from Vladivostok to Eastern Europe. There are now between 20 000 and 40 000 Chinese in Hungary, where they sell toys, cheap electronics, socks, shoes and underwear at Budapest's Four Tigers market.[19]

While exact figures are not available, western intelligence officials believe that more than a million Chinese have migrated legally and illegally since 1978. They estimate that between 30 000 and 40 000 a year go to the United States—the favourite destination for most illegal migrants—but many prefer to stay in Southeast Asia. In the northern Burmese city of Mandalay, newly arrived Chinese are buying up shops, restaurants, hotels, karaoke bars—and identity papers. Given the relative wealth of the Chinese migrants, and the fact that impoverished Burma is in desperate need of any kind of foreign investment, local officials are reluctant to enforce immigration laws. Indeed, a well-known Burmese novelist, Nyi Pu Lay, was arrested in 1990 and sentenced to ten years' imprisonment after writing a short story called 'The Python', a satire on Chinese migrants—many of whom are involved in drug trafficking, smuggling, gambling and other illegal pursuits—moving into Mandalay and squeezing out the Burmese.[20]

The number of Chinese 'tourists' coming to Thailand rose sharply in the 1990s. In 1998, for instance, arrivals from China rose by 23 per cent over the year before to 432 995, the biggest increase for any nationality entering Thailand. At the dawn of the twenty-first century, more than half a million Chinese were visiting Thailand each year. While many of them were genuine tourists or visiting relatives, a fair number never returned to China.[21] In May 2000, Thai police colonel Wissanu Maungprasee admitted publicly that large numbers of illegal Chinese had used Thailand as a transit point on their journey to the West. The illegal migrants paid $40 000 to cover expenses between China and the United States. About 10 per cent of that went to the racketeer agents who accompanied their clients to their final destination.[22]

Under pressure from the United States, Thai police raided 'safe houses' and dubious 'travel agencies' in Bangkok—and that was when the human-smuggling rackets moved some of their activities to lawless Cambodia. The would-be illegal immigrants wait for their new documents in Cambodia, but the actual forgeries are still done in Thailand, where printing is of much better quality.[23] Once the documents are ready, they continue by air to other destinations, and finally reach the United States, Canada, Western Europe or Australia through a variety of routes and means. By leaving from Phnom Penh's airport rather than Bangkok, the migrants avoid the increased scrutiny of documents by airline personnel who have been trained by US and Australian law enforcement teams. Phnom Penh also reduces the cost; bribes to officials are significantly lower, as are other operating and maintenance costs such as rent for safe houses, food and other living expenses.[24]

But, as recent developments in Mandalay show, not every illegal immigrant continues on to the United States. There is still the lure of Nanyang—the region is now referred to as the Great Golden Peninsula, a land of opportunity—and large communities of illegal migrants from China have also sprung up in Bangkok and Chiang Mai in northern Thailand, in Cambodia and in Laos, where the Chinese population is also increasing. But whatever the destination, the suspicion is strong that the Chinese authorities are actually encouraging people to leave. In this way, China both gets rid of its surplus population and earns foreign exchange through remittances from the migrants once they have found jobs abroad. In May 2000, when the Canadian police decided to send 90 Chinese migrants back to Fujian province, and gave the case wide publicity in order to deter further illegal migration, the Chinese media remained conspicuously silent on the deportations. The return of the illegal immigrants was mentioned in a single paragraph in the English-language *China Daily*, which is read mostly by foreigners. It quoted foreign ministry spokeswoman Zhang Qiyue as saying that the two countries are cooperating so that 'the question of illegal immigrants can be smoothly handled'.[25] Ko-lin Chin, an expert on illegal migration from China, asks rhetorically: 'In such a well-policed state, how could smugglers covertly transport tens of thousands of people and escape the notice of Chinese authorities? They must either be accepting bribes or be actively involved in transporting people out of China'.[26]

Cambodia is one of the few countries which has actually opened its doors to this wave of migration from China, perhaps hoping that the enterprising newcomers will help the economy get back on its feet after decades of turmoil. In the boldest move yet to attract migrants, at least eight Cambodian government bodies—including the National Investment Committee, the office of the Council of Ministers and the governor of Kandal province, which adjoins Phnom Penh municipality—approved a scheme in 1993 to lease a 20 square kilometre area near the capital to a firm called the Cambodia-China City Company (CTGC). In exchange for investments totalling $1 billion, the government would agree to let 200 000 ethnic Chinese settle in the enclave. The Kandal provincial governor argued that the project would help 'reconstruct and develop Cambodia [by bringing] Chinese and overseas Chinese throughout the world to Cambodia'.[27] The proposed contract even called for a Chinese citizen to assume the authority of deputy governor of the new city.

The CTGC, it turned out, had been created by the China Non-Ferrous Metal Company, which was managed by Wu Jianchang. His wife, Deng Lin, was one of the daughters of China's paramount leader, Deng Xiaoping. Wu had set up shop in Hong Kong in the 1980s, and in the early 1990s was in business with some 'local businessmen' widely reputed to be members of the Triads.[28] In July 1994, the Cambodian government eventually rejected the proposal based on concerns over massive foreign immigration. 'I believe that this is not a mere ordinary investment problem but rather a national political issue because it involves 200,000 immigrants,' said Keat Chhon, then minister for reconstruction and development.[29]

But with or without a city of their own, thousands of Chinese immigrants have flooded into Cambodia, legally and illegally. The total Chinese population of Cambodia is estimated at 350 000, of whom 200 000 live in Phnom Penh. Old communities have been joined by doctors, dentists and businessmen from Shanghai, architects from Taiwan and investors from Malaysia and Singapore. Since 1990, a major resurgence of Chinese culture has also occurred, and the largest and most prestigious Chinese school, Duanhua, has more than 10 000 pupils. This makes it the largest Chinese school in any country where Chinese is not one of the official languages.[30]

This 'third wave' of Chinese migration as such is not necessarily connected with criminal networks other than gangs involved in the smuggling of illegal aliens. But the fact that the Chinese Association in Cambodia is headed by a character like Theng Bunma has opened the door for all sorts of unsavoury characters, and many criminals have indeed come in with the tide. Chinese-owned night clubs in Phnom Penh have become meeting places for Chinese gangsters carving up the local entertainment and drugs scene in the capital, and their web of contacts—their own 'bamboo network', as the term goes—seems more akin to the worldwide network of the Triads than mainstream chambers of commerce.[31]

That was why Guo Dongpo, director of Beijing's Office of Overseas Chinese Affairs, met Theng in Phnom Penh in October 2000 and asked him to help control Dry Duck and other unruly gangsters who had flocked to the Cambodian capital, including Macau's Wan 'Broken Tooth' Kuok-koi during his heyday in the late 1990s. And, as Theng's case also shows, the new wave has created entirely new loyalties and upset traditional power structures within the overseas Chinese communities and associations in Southeast Asia, including the underworld networks. A new kind of criminal order—or disorder—is taking root.

That the Iowa Wesleyan College decided to award Theng with an honorary doctorate was not an accident. The man who arranged it was Ted Sioeng, an Indonesian-Chinese businessman and tobacco tycoon who was a key figure in the 'Donorgate' saga in the United States in the 1990s. Sioeng is alleged to have acted on behalf of China in funnelling money to the Democratic National Committee, activities which later were subject to separate congressional and Justice Department investigations. In 1995 and 1996, Sioeng appeared at several glitzy Democratic Party fundraising events in the United States, usually accompanied by delegations of unidentified Chinese 'businesspeople'. On one occasion, he sat next to President Bill Clinton, and on another with then Vice President Al Gore. Sioeng and his family were reported to have donated $250 000 to Clinton's and Gore's re-election campaign.[32]

Sioeng also sat on the board of trustees of the Iowa Wesleyan College from 1994 to 1997. The college, which for its part apparently hoped to get donations from its newly minted doctors, appears to have been used by Sioeng to further his own business. Theng is big in tobacco in Cambodia, and several officials from China's Yunnan province, where Sioeng won the right to distribute the exclusive Hongtashan cigarettes in 1993, were awarded Iowa Wesleyan degrees during his tenure as a trustee. Sioeng also arranged honorary doctorates from the little-known 'American M&N University', a 'religious school' registered in the state of Louisiana, but with no campus, teachers or students. The 'university' was, in fact, headed by a Chinese-American called Nancy Chien, whose company in Monterey Park near Los Angeles runs the M&N Driving School. Among those awarded degrees from this unusual academic institution was the irrepressible Chen Kai-kit, alias Chio Ho-cheung, the Triad-connected Macau legislator who was also implicated in the 'Donorgate' affair. Chen, who sometimes uses the English name 'Tommy', proudly had new business cards printed identifying him as 'Doctor Tommy Chio'.[33]

Sioeng is evidently a much more important person than the mobsters from Macau, and the US Senate investigative committee concluded that he 'worked or perhaps still work[s] on behalf of the Chinese government'.[34] He carries a passport from the Central American country of Belize, where his flagship company, the S.S. Group, is based, even though his wife and children are American citizens. Sioeng had long been buying influence in the United States in ways other than supporting Clinton's and Gore's re-election campaign. In 1995 he paid $3 million for the *International Daily News*, then a politically moderate Chinese-language newspaper in Los Angeles. As soon as he had taken over the paper, its editorial policy switched to a strong pro-Beijing stance. A few years later, it opened a bureau in Hong Kong which was headed by Yeung Hong Man, a former editor of the territory's Beijing run *Wen Wei Po* newspaper. The *International Daily News*, which also distributes a North American edition of *Wen Wei Po* as a free 'bonus' for its readers, is headed by Jessica Elnitiarta, Sioeng's eldest daughter. It was in her name that one of the main donations to the Democratic National Committee was made. At a Senate committee hearing in October 1997, Republican Senator Robert Bennett described Sioeng as being among a dozen witnesses who had 'fled the country rather than be available for either this committee or the Justice Department'.[35]

But Sioeng has remained a regular visitor to China, the site of his main tobacco business—and to Cambodia, where he became a partner in Theng's cigarette factory. In November 1997, Sioeng and Theng together attended an international conference of ethnic

Chinese in the city of Chaozhou in China's southern Guangdong province. The get together was presided over by Li Ruihuan, a member of the standing committee of the Politburo of the Communist Party of China. In his opening address, Li appealed to the congregated overseas Chinese to 'act as a bridge between China and the world'.[36] In fact, Sioeng had done much more than that: as the Donorgate scandal showed, he had even helped build a bridge right into President Clinton's Oval Office in Washington.

The inroads made by Beijing into the overseas Chinese communities in Southeast Asia and the world over the past couple of decades stand in sharp contrast to how those communities were formed hundreds of years ago—and how they developed until Deng Xiaoping launched his new economic policies in the late 1970s, and the third wave of migrants landed on the shores of Nanyang. The first compact and permanent Chinese settlements in the region—as opposed to bands of deserters from the navy, artisans and assorted drifters and adventurers—were established in the fourteenth century at Palembang in Sumatra and at Tumasik, or Old Singapore. From these humble beginnings grew the overseas Chinese communities in Southeast Asia which today consist of millions of people. They came as labourers, coolies and refugees, but soon ran their own schools and temples, and very quickly took over much of the commercial life of the region. Today many are bankers and tycoons, whose economic power and influence stretch far beyond Southeast Asia.

The fall of the Ming Dynasty in the mid-seventeenth century and, equally importantly, the establishment of European outposts in the region prompted many Chinese to look for a new future in Southeast Asia. In 1786, British Captain Francis Light acquired the island of Penang from the Malay sultan of Kedah, to which later was added a strip of the mainland, Province Wellesley. After the foundation of this new colony, Chinese immigration increased dramatically. Penang, however, proved to be only a limited success as a settlement and trading post, and it was not until after the foundation of Singapore in 1819 that the Chinese became really well established in Malaya.[37] Gradually, the Malay sultanates on the peninsula also became British protectorates. Over the years, hundreds of thousands of Chinese—and a smaller number of Indians—were brought in by the British, as it was hard to persuade the native Malays to work in the plantations, the tin mines and the ports. They preferred to stay in their *kampungs*, or villages, with their paddy fields and their mosques, and they paid their respects to the Malay sultans rather than the colonial authorities.

Nearly all the Chinese who migrated to Penang and Singapore, and to the rest of Malaya, came from the south, but were of different language groups: Hokkien (Fujianese), Cantonese, Hakka and so on. They did not form a unified social unit as they had done at home in China, where they had lived side by side in defined districts and regions. Friction was common between the different groups of immigrants, and although the European colonial power protected all of them against the oppression or exactions of native princes and rulers, fear and trade jealousy sometimes brought them into conflict with the British. Nor were the immigrants exclusively composed of enterprising merchants, industrious artisans and hard-working labourers. Some of the worst characters for whom China itself had no room also came with the southward flow of migrants. There were frequent robberies, even in broad daylight, and for the first years of Singapore's history most of these went unpunished as the British had brought with them only a handful of police, mostly Indians from Bengal and Madras.[38]

To protect themselves in this new, alien and sometimes hostile environment, the different groups banded together in secret societies, though it was not until 1831 that there was any reference to the existence of such groupings in official colonial records in Singapore. Twenty years later, in 1854, a series of incidents took place which culminated in a riot in which 400 Chinese were killed. But, for nearly a century after Captain Light had landed in Penang, the British administration was completely unaware not only of the nature of the secret societies, but also of the organisation of the Chinese community in general. In 1857 there were 70 000 Chinese in Singapore, but not a single European who understood any Chinese dialect. It was not until a Dutchman, Gustav Schlegel, published his epoch-making work, *Thian Ti Hui* (*The Hung League* or *Heaven-Earth League*), in 1866 that the colonial authorities came to know anything definite about the secret societies.[39] A 'Chinese Protectorate' under the direction of W. Pickering, a member of the Civil Service who had actually learnt to speak Chinese, was established in Singapore to deal with the Chinese immigrants—and it was discovered that all their societies and community organisations were in one way or another offshoots of the Tiandihui.

Somewhat arbitrarily, however, the British decided to divide these organisations into 'benevolent' *kongsi*, or district and clan associations, and the malevolent *hui*, which were believed to be more prone to violence and crime.[40] *Kongsi*, which over the years have become the Chinese equivalent of 'company limited' in English, sprung up in the many tin-mining towns that were developed during Britain's time in Malaya. They were often groups that had reached agreement on how to divide capital and labour responsibilities, each member having a share. They could also be people of the same surname, or language group. The *hui* took after the *kongsi*, and one of the most influential secret societies in Singapore, the *Ghee Hin* (or *Ngee Hin* or *Ngee Heng*, which is *yixing* in Pinyin; 'the rise of righteousness'), officially called itself Ngee Heng Kongsi.[41] *Hui*, which means 'society' or 'brotherhood', sounded far more Masonic to the British, who introduced a new law in 1889 that recognised the *kongsi* but banned the *hui* as 'unregistered societies'.

That piece of legislation created an artificial division between the two types of organisation by forcing the *hui* underground. What the British did not grasp was the *yin–yang* interaction—the dialectical relationship of interlocking opposites—that has always existed between open and secret societies among the Chinese. *Yin* (female) and *yang* (male) symbolise contrasting qualities corresponding to male and female characteristics, such as hard–soft, forceful–submissive, dry–wet, military–civil, and open–secret. The balance was unequal, *yang* always being the predominant element, but it had to respect the nature of *yin*.[42]

In western terms, *kongsi* and *hui* were two sides of the same coin, and the relationship between them was perhaps even stronger among the overseas Chinese than at home in China. The alien environment, with its many other ethnic groups—and foreign colonialists at the apex of the power structure—required a more flexible communal organisation among the immigrants. At the same time, sworn brotherhoods were the only available basis for social organisation for the male immigrants to Southeast Asia, and in the beginning nearly all of them were male.[43] 'Mutual-aid fraternities' would actually have been a more appropriate term than 'secret societies'.

Both *kongsi* and *hui* groups used symbols such as flags and seals, and the trappings were strikingly similar: Guandi, the god of merchants, was worshipped in both *kongsi* and *hui* temples and lodges, and both groups had initiation ceremonies that involved drinking the blood drawn from either a chicken or from the forefingers of the initiates. But *hui* initiation ceremonies tended to be more elaborate, and were always held in secret. As the *hui* drew their recruits from the lower strata of society, stricter discipline was needed.[44] But, at the same time, the unruly secret societies had a habit of clashing with each other.

In this relationship, the more secretive *hui* were obviously *yin*, a role that the British legal system formalised by outlawing them. Mary Somers Heidhues of the Universities of Göttingen and Hamburg argues that 'colonial policy finally forced (or better, facilitated) a differentiation of these brotherhoods, leaving the fields of extortion, petty rackets, and other criminal activities to the *hui* in the twentieth century'.[45] As the Chinese communities in Malaya grew—by 1911 they accounted for 35 per cent of a total population of 5.5 million, compared with 49.2 per cent Malays and 14 per cent Indians—so did both the *kongsi* and the *hui*. But the influx of more people from different parts of China also led to more factionalism and infighting. Riots and open street warfare between different Triad, or secret society, factions were common in both Singapore and Penang. Different societies repeatedly petitioned the British Governor of the Straits Settlements—Penang, Singapore and Malacca—to help one or the other against its rival, but he declined to take sides in the conflicts.[46] Instead, he charged the colonial police with containing the violence. The police, for their part, almost admitted that they were powerless. According to one internal British report commenting on the secret societies in Malaya:

> Their worst feature is the protection they afford their members, whatever crimes these may have committed. The brethren will risk their lives for each other without hesitation and if one were to betray another vengeance would be very sure. Outsiders who assist the authorities are in little less danger than traitors from within: if they aid in the arrest of a brother they are almost sure to meet vengeance from the society, and the mere ill will of the fraternities can mean ruin. Thus those who disapprove of their aims or methods are usually too cowed to dare to report them to the police.[47]

As far as the British were concerned, what had begun as mutual-aid organisations to assist new immigrants had developed into fierce criminal gangs. According to another report:

> Chinese secret societies' activities in Malaya ... have included the organisation of opposition to the government; the stirring up of anti-foreign feeling; the formation of self-protection units against robber gangs; the 'protection' and extortion of money from hawkers, shopkeepers, hotel-keepers, prostitutes, labourers, opium and gambling dens; kidnapping for ransom; and the operation of rings and rackets.[48]

The Chinese nationalists, however, saw it rather differently, which was why Dr Sun Yat-sen turned to the overseas Chinese for help in the struggle against the Qing Emperors in Beijing. He knew that wherever the Chinese went, they took their secret societies with them—and they were going to form the basis for his revolution. Since most Chinese in Malaya came from the south, many were also Ming loyalists, and opposed to the Manchu Qing. Local branches of his first political organisation, the Tongmenghui, or 'United League', were formed in Singapore, Penang, Kuala Lumpur, Seremban, Malacca and Kuala Pilah. Dr Sun became a frequent visitor to Malaya, and his many articles for revolutionary papers even prompted the British to issue a stern warning; it was important for Britain to maintain good relations with the court in Beijing so as not to jeopardise the security of Hong Kong. But the overseas Chinese listened to Dr Sun, and provided him with financial backing for his struggle. Between 1909 and 1911—just before the fall of the Qing—a Triad society in Malaya even carried out a number of gang robberies, the proceeds of which were sent to China to aid the revolutionary cause.[49] When the Guomindang was formed in 1912, its Singapore branch followed the Triad tradition by calling itself a 'Lodge'.[50]

The political division in China was also reflected in the communities in Southeast Asia: communist cells began to operate in Malaya in 1924, and after Chiang Kai-shek's and Big-Eared Du's massacre of communists and labour union organisers in Shanghai in 1927, a separate Communist Party of Malaya (CPM) was formed. Its members were almost exclusively ethnic Chinese—and they were drawn from the same lower end of society as the Triads and the Guomindang: Chinese coolies, servants and labourers, mainly of Hainanese origin. The clannish, secretive Hainanese remained separate from other immigrant Chinese, comprising a closely knit group with a long and proud anti-establishment tradition.[51] The CPM led the struggle against the Japanese during World War II, only to go underground again in the 1940s to fight the British. Malaya's—and, after 1963, Malaysia's—civil war was bitter and bloody, despite the name the colonial power gave it with typical English understatement: 'the Emergency'.

Intermingling between the CPM and the Triads did exist, but it was more on an individual basis. By and large, they were rivals, because they appealed to the same social outcasts of society who made up the foot soldiers of both. But the CPM thought that perhaps the Triads could be reformed and turned into leftist revolutionaries. A letter written by the secretary of the Selangor State Committee of the CPM, Chan Lo, expressed that sentiment:

> Triad personnel are elements of a decadent society, ostensibly patriotic, but in reality self-seeking. When once tempted by offers of money they will commit all sorts of crime. Care should be taken to avoid arousing their suspicion. They should be given political teaching, and their societies should be recognised under different names, such as the 'Righteous Killer Squad', the 'Blood and Iron Volunteer Corps', and the 'Anti-British Protection Corps'.[52]

But no such alliance emerged. Their ideologies were too different. The CPM preached Marxism and wanted to introduce a Soviet-style government. The Triads offered the protective shield of traditional social organisation, which they hoped to bring back to public consciousness. It was not until the Malayan Chinese Association (MCA) was formed in 1949 that the non-communist Chinese established an organisation that could challenge the CPM—and count on the support of the *kongsi* and the *hui*. A former president of the MCA, and later the Gerakan Party, Dr Lim Chong Eu, was previously a local leader of the Guomindang, to which the societies, guilds and associations remained loyal. Similarly, Tun Sir Colonel Henry H.S. Lee, head of Malaysia's Development and Commercial Bank, co-founder of the Singapore-based Overseas Union Bank and the first finance minister of Malaysia when it was created in 1963, was at one time a Guomindang leader.[53]

At that time, it was impossible to separate open societies from secret ones, and in the House of Representatives on 21 April 1961, the leader of the People's Progressive Party, D.R. Seenivasagam, accused the MCA's Youth Section of recruiting thugs and gangsters of the Wa Kei Society to intimidate voters at elections. Seenivasagam and other politicians went on to reveal that a special fund had been set up to pay the cost of defence of any of the 'brothers' brought to trial, and that an MCA lawyer, Senator Yeoh, was at hand to provide free legal advice. Yeoh vigorously denied any association between the MCA Youth and the secret societies but, according to numerous reports, it did send truckloads of young people to places where elections were being held, ostensibly to 'keep the peace'. Leong Yew Koh, then minister for justice, remarked: 'The steel grip which the secret societies have on the vast bulk of the Malayan Chinese community is really frightening.'[54]

The situation elsewhere in Nanyang was not that different. It was only Thailand's criminal milieu—and history—that had its unique features, mainly because the country was never a European colony. Thailand's role as a front-line state during the Cold War also gave it a very special position, where crime became closely intertwined with politics, covert operations and espionage. And, compared with the Chinese elsewhere in Southeast Asia, those who immigrated to Thailand have become fairly well assimilated into society. But such acceptance has not always been the case with Thailand's Chinese immigrants. No one knows for certain when the first Chinese arrived in Thailand—then called Siam—but migration arose from the centuries-old junk trade between China and Southeast Asia. Nearly all of these seafarers came from Fujian and Guangdong in the south. Frequent natural disasters, famine, epidemics and social unrest forced tens of thousands of Chinese to leave for the more hospitable climes and more peaceful conditions of the south. Many of the newcomers happened to come from Shantou (Swatow in the local dialect), Chaozhou and Chao'an in the Teochew-speaking area in northern Guangdong.

They were so successful that a son of a Teochew immigrant, Taksin, even made himself King of Siam after the Burmese sacked the old capital, Ayutthaya, in 1767. He built a new royal city at Thonburi, which was closer to the sea and therefore easier to defend. Taksin encouraged Teochew immigration to his kingdom, and many arrived by ships which sailed up the Chao Phraya River. When Taksin died in 1782, the capital was moved to Bangkok, across the river from Thonburi. By 1855, Bangkok had grown to accommodate nearly 300 000 inhabitants, of whom two-thirds were Chinese.[55] At first, most of them lived near the river just opposite Thonburi, but they were moved from that area when the new Chakri Dynasty began building the Grand Palace in what was then northern Bangkok. The Chinese were given new homes and shops a few kilometres to the south. This settlement became Sampeng Lane and, over the years, a whole Chinatown grew up around it. But the fabled Sampeng Lane remained the heart of Bangkok's Chinatown and its early history is shrouded in tales of murder, prostitution, gambling dens, a once-booming opium trade and street wars between rival bands of Chinese secret societies.[56]

The Chinese immigrants had brought the habit of smoking opium with them. In 1822, King Rama II had promulgated Thailand's first formal ban on selling and consuming opium. In 1839, his successor Rama III reiterated the prohibition, and he introduced the death penalty for major opium traffickers.[57] These efforts, however, were doomed to failure. Ethnic Chinese traffickers could be arrested and punished—but British merchants were virtually immune to prosecution. Large quantities of opium were brought to Bangkok by British ships from India. Even though it was nominally independent, Thailand did not escape the scourges that followed colonial rule in neighbouring countries. Finally, in 1852, the legendary King Mongkut—played by Yul Brynner in the film *The King and I*—bowed to British pressures. He established a Royal Opium Franchise, to be leased to vice franchises managed by wealthy Chinese, a system that mirrored the 'tax farming' of the Dutch East Indies and other European colonies. Opium, lottery, gambling and alcohol permits were up for rent. By the end of the nineteenth century, taxes on these government monopolies provided 12–22 per cent of Siam's government revenues.[58] Government control was further strengthened in the early twentieth century when it eliminated the Chinese middleman and assumed direct responsibility for the management of the opium trade. Royal administration did not impede progress, however; an all-time high of 147 tonnes of opium was imported from India in 1913; the number of dens and retail shops jumped from 1200 in 1880 to 3000 in 1917; the number of opium addicts reached 200 000 by 1921; and the opium profits continued to provide 15–20 per cent of all government tax revenues.[59]

But, because the Royal Monopoly had always marketed expensive drugs of Indian and Middle Eastern origin, cheaper opium had been smuggled overland from Yunnan and Sichuan since the mid-nineteenth century. There was actually so much smuggling that the Royal Monopoly's prices were determined by the availability of smuggled opium.[60] Despite this lucrative market for opium, poppy cultivation in Thailand itself remained negligible until World War II. Some opium-growing Hmong and Yao hill tribes had started migrating from southern China down to Laos and Thailand in the nineteenth century, but it was not until the late 1940s and early 1950s—during the devastating civil wars first in China and later in Burma—that large numbers of highland farmers started crossing into the country from the north.[61] Poppy cultivation increased significantly in northern Thailand, as the country was now known.

The country's name change was one of many reforms introduced by its military leader during and after the war, Field Marshal Pleak Phibunsongkhram. 'Thailand' meant the Land of the Free, and Phibunsongkhram was determined to modernise its old backward society. An ardent nationalist, he had allied himself with Japan during the war; however, after Mao Zedong's victory in China in 1949, his support for the anti-communist cause was crucial, and the United States and other western powers forgave him for his past loyalties. Phibunsongkhram wanted to create a new 'Thai' identity, and his chief ideologue was a maverick historian called Luang Wichit Wathakan, who became infamous for his staunchly anti-Chinese rhetoric.

He had inherited that from King Vajiravudh, who reigned from 1910–1925. Vajiravudh had carried out an investigation which claimed to have unearthed a plot by 'Siamese subjects of Chinese descent' who wished to topple the king and emulate the republican revolution of Dr Sun Yat-sen.[62] The King subsequently produced a series of polemic texts with titles such as *The Jews of the East* and *Wake up Siam: A Reminder to the Thai*. Luang Wichit went a step further and said in a 1938 speech at Bangkok's Chulalongkorn University—which coincided with *Anschluss*, Germany's takeover of Austria—that the

Chinese were 'worse than the Jews' and that it was high time Siam considered dealing with its 'own Jews'.[63]

Thailand's Chinese did not have to face the same fate as the Jews in Europe, but Phibunsongkhram and his advisers launched a determined drive to make them Thai. They were requested to take Thai names, the number of Chinese schools was limited, and immigration from China was drastically reduced. Phibunsongkhram felt strongly that the Sino-Thais should owe their loyalty and allegiance first to Thailand.[64] And in the 1950s, together with his powerful police chief, Phao Sriyanonda, he crippled the political clout of the Triads among Bangkok's huge Chinese business community.

An entirely new power structure emerged, which had two main elements. The first, and the most important, was a marriage of convenience between the Thai military and bureaucracy and the Chinese oligarchy. The other was that the old secret societies were replaced by a new class of mostly 'assimilated' ethnic Chinese gangster bosses, the so-called *chao pho* (a literal translation of the English term 'Godfather'). These have remained powerful figures in politics and business, but each have influence only over a few towns or provinces; the Thai establishment did not tolerate any nationwide networks of potentially subversive secret societies.

These changes were prompted not only by Phibunsongkhram's and Luang Wichit's extreme nationalism, but also by developments that occurred in the wake of the communist victory in China. Chiang Kai-shek's main Guomindang force had retreated to Taiwan, where his 'Republic of China' lived on after the loss of the mainland. Fighting continued for several months in some remote parts of China, including Yunnan, but the communists emerged victorious even there. Then, in January 1950, hundreds of defeated Guomindang forces from Yunnan—unable to withstand the attacks of the Chinese communists, and also unable to join Chiang Kai-shek in Taiwan—crossed over into northeastern Burma. Later led by wartime hero General Li Mi, they in effect invaded the mountains of the Kengtung region and also ensconced themselves in the hills surrounding Möng Hsat, close to the Thai border. These forces contacted Taiwan through its embassy in Bangkok—and it was decided not to evacuate them to Taiwan, but to turn the remaining Nationalist Chinese soldiers into a 'liberation army', which would build up bases in northeastern

Burma—and from there try to retake China from the communists. The tiny Möng Hsat airstrip, built during World War II, was reconstructed into a formidable air base capable of receiving C-46 and C-47 transport planes, which brought in arms, ammunition and medical supplies. The Guomindang also recruited new soldiers from the border areas—mostly Lahu hill tribesmen—and gave them military training.

The arrival of the Guomindang in northeastern Burma coincided with the Korean War, and on 24 March 1951 the commander of the US forces in East Asia, General Douglas MacArthur, issued a statement from Tokyo calling for a 'decision by the United Nations to depart from its tolerant effort to contain the war to the area of Korea, through an expansion of our military operations to its coastal areas and interior bases [to] doom Red China to risk the imminent military collapse'.[65] So, directly and indirectly, General MacArthur and his security planners were responsible for both revitalising the *yakuza* gangsters in Japan *and* the formation of a formidable renegade army in the Golden Triangle (the area where the borders of Burma, Thailand and Laos intersect), which was soon going to take over the region's trade in illicit opium. And it was all done in the name of defending western democracy!

Another hard-line former US general and World War II veteran, Claire Chennault, now headed the unofficial 'China Lobby' in the United States which advocated close ties with Taiwan and confrontation with Beijing. Hardly by coincidence, Chennault's airline, Civil Air Transport (CAT), had from the very beginning been responsible for air drops of arms and ammunition to the KMT at Möng Hsat.[66] He later admitted publicly that a plan did exist to implement McArthur's idea of a broader war against China, using Burma as a springboard:

> It is reported—and I have reason to believe it is true—that the Nationalist [Guomindang] Government offered three full divisions . . . of troops to fight in Korea, but the great opportunity was not putting the Nationalists in Korea. It was a double envelopment operation. With the United Nations forces in Korea and the Nationalist Chinese in southern areas . . . the Communists would have been caught in a giant pincers . . . this was a great opportunity—not to put the Nationalist Chinese in Korea, but to let them fight in the south.[67]

By April 1951, the Guomindang's force in the area had swollen to 4000 men and by December it was 6000 strong. Officers and cadres were flown in from Taiwan as well, and a strategy was mapped out. After leaving 1000 heavily armed troops to defend Möng Hsat, the bulk of the fighting force marched north to the Wa Hills and Kokang, closer to the Yunnan frontier.

Operations in the Shan states became more secretive after 11 April, when American President Harry Truman decided to relieve General MacArthur as UN Commander and head of all US forces in the Far East. Truman, who wanted to limit the conflict in the Far East, had found himself at loggerheads with MacArthur, Chennault and others who openly advocated an all-out war with China.

The president argued that the hawks of the China Lobby did not pay heed to what he perceived as the greater threat to Europe posed by the Soviet Union. Officially, American involvement with the Guomindang then ceased. Unofficially, the China Lobby continued its activities in the Shan states, ignoring the president's orders. The covert Guomindang operation that followed was the first of many similar 'secret' wars that US security agencies carried out in Third World countries, such as Cuba, Laos, Nicaragua, Angola and Afghanistan.

The Kengtung-based 'secret' Guomindang army tried on no less than seven occasions between 1950 and 1952 to invade Yunnan, but was repeatedly driven back into the Shan states.[68] The Burmese army was sent to the eastern hills to rid the country of its uninvited guests, but was unsuccessful. Burma's prime minister, U Nu, then raised the issue in the United Nations General Assembly which, on 22 April 1953, adopted a resolution demanding that the Guomindang lay down its arms and leave the country. Thousands of Guomindang soldiers were evacuated to Taiwan by special aircraft with pomp and circumstance—at the same time as reinforcements were being flown in to Möng Hsat by nightly flights. Thus the number of Guomindang soldiers in the Shan states increased to 12 000 by the end of 1953.

The Burmese army failed to defeat them, but managed to drive some of the units across the Salween River into the Wa hills and Kokang, traditionally the best opium growing areas of the Shan states, where they set up new bases. The Guomindang had become involved in the Golden Triangle opium trade earlier on, but it was now able to trade more directly. It enlisted the support of Olive Yang (Yang Jinxiu or Yang Kyin-hsui), the leader of a district in the north-easternmost corner of the Shan states, which was dominated by ethnic Chinese. Known locally as 'Miss Hairy Legs', this formidable woman, still in her early twenties, came to command her own army of nearly 1000 men.

Like so many other children of aristocratic Shan states families, Olive Yang had attended the prestigious Guardian Angel's Convent School in Lashio. Former classmates remembered that their parents warned them not to play with the odd little girl: 'Stay away from Olive!' they used to say. 'She's got a revolver in her schoolbag.' When Olive finished her education, she no longer had to hide her gun. She was formally proclaimed ruling princess of Kokang and went about the district in a grey uniform, with a Belgian army pistol on each hip. Backed by the Guomindang, Olive became the first warlord—or, strictly speaking, warlady—to send opium by convoys of trucks rather than mules down to the Thai border. On these occasions, heavily armed Kokang troops called 'Olive's boys' lined the roads to provide security.

The money she earned from these operations was used to arm and equip her army—and to buy lavish gifts for her lover, the famous Burmese film actress Wa Wa Win Shwe. Olive's troops traded with the Guomindang, and their armed support added to the general insta-bility of the frontier areas. This kept the Burmese army split up on several different fronts, which benefited the Guomindang.

To help finance its secret war against Mao Zedong's communists in China, the Guomindang also turned to almost the only cash crop of any significance in the Shan hills: opium. In 1950, when the Guomindang first entered the area, the annual production there amounted to a mere 30 tonnes. The Guomindang persuaded the hill tribe farmers to grow more opium, and they introduced a hefty opium tax that forced the farmers to grow even more in order to make ends meet. By the mid-1950s, opium production in the Burmese sector of the Golden Triangle had shot up ten or twenty times, to an annual yield of 300–600 tonnes. And more sons of the hill tribe farmers were recruited to fight for a cause they knew little about.

The Guomindang conducted a reign of terror from its strongholds in the Shan hills. According to Elaine T. Lewis, an American missionary who was working in Kengtung state in the 1950s: 'For many years, there have been large numbers of Chinese nationalist troops in the area demanding food and money from the local people. The areas in which these troops operate are getting poorer and some villagers are finding it necessary to flee'.[69] Thousands of opium-farming hill tribesmen from the mountains north of Kengtung close to the Chinese frontier, where the Guomindang has its secret bases, left their homes and settled in Chiang Rai province in northernmost Thailand, where they remain.

The Guomindang effort in the Golden Triangle also involved the US Central Intelligence Agency (CIA), and institutions and individuals who were later prominent in other covert operations got their first experience and training in the Golden Triangle. The best known of them was Colonel Paul Helliwell, who operated the local transport company that flew supplies from Thailand to the Guomindang in Möng Hsat. In the late 1950s, he moved to Miami where he became an important figure in the failed Bay of Pigs invasion and other CIA battles against Fidel Castro in Cuba.[70]

The secret war in the Golden Triangle was also a failure. The Guomindang's forces and special agents could not ignite any rebellion in Yunnan and, frustrated, they increasingly turned their attention to the more lucrative opium trade. The secret war may have had little influence on China, but the Guomindang's and the CIA's covert operations in the Golden Triangle had resulted in large-scale poppy cultivation all over Burma's northern mountains. They also led to a rebellion among the Shan ethnic minority against the central government in Rangoon. Squeezed between two forces, both of which were perceived as foreign—the Burmese army and the Guomindang—the Shans, ethnic cousins of the Thais, rose in a rebellion that has continued to this day.

Thailand's role in the whole affair was mostly that of a conduit for supplies going to the Guomindang in Burma. Thai police and army officers were closely connected with the Guomindang network—and the CIA. Helliwell's dodgy 'transport company', SEA Supplies, also helped build up the Thai police, then headed by the powerful General Phao who American researcher Alfred McCoy said resembled 'a cherub with a Cheshire cat smile'.[71] Arms, armoured vehicles, aircraft and even naval patrol boats were supplied. Thailand's cooperation in the 'secret' war against communist China was crucial, but both the

United States and Taiwan felt that Phibunsongkhram could not be relied upon because of his extreme nationalism. Phao, on the other hand, was easier to deal with, and he became the Guomindang's main backer in Thailand. Phao's influence far exceeded even that of the chief of the Thai army, General Sarit Thanarat, who frequently complained to his American advisers that the SEA Supply Company never gave him the same fancy equipment as it did Phao.

The wily police general also established close links with pro-Guomindang elements within Bangkok's Chinese business community. According to American scholar G. William Skinner, among them was an especially influential person who was described as 'one of the richest and most pro-Guomindang Chinese in Bangkok . . . virtually a member of one of the most powerful cliques in the Thai ruling class. In a sense, he is the banker and business agent of the Police General, for whom he speaks in Chinese councils'.[72] This banker, who had arrived virtually penniless in Bangkok to look for a job in 1928, was Tan Piak Chin. He came from Chua Aw, a small, insignificant village in impoverished Shantou, and later became better known under the name he assumed when he settled more or less permanently in Thailand a few years later: Chin Sophonpanich.

Chin remained in Thailand during World War II and joined the Allied-sponsored resistance, the Free Thai movement, at the same time as his Asia Company was supplying the Japanese war machine with daily necessities. Using the income from these activities, Chin went on to speculate in war bonds and gold. In 1943, the Thai Ministry of Finance had issued 30 million Thai baht worth of war bonds at 3 per cent interest per year over an eight-year maturity period. The most attractive feature of the issue was a redemption option in gold at 86 baht cash per one *baht* (15.2 grams) weight. When the bonds finally matured in 1951, the value of gold was more than six times higher than stipulated at the time of issue. Chin invested his gold profits in a new company called Asia Trust, which quickly became the centre of all foreign exchange dealings in Thailand.[73]

In 1952, Chin and some of his friends floated the Thai Financial Syndicate, which was involved in money lending, discounting bills, foreign exchange transactions, dealing in stocks, bonds and precious metals, and importing gold. The board chairman of the new company was General Phao himself.[74] This marriage of convenience between

Bangkok's Chinese plutocrats and Thailand's men in uniform set the tune for many other similar alliances in the future: the Chinese provided the money, and the police and the army secured protection and status in Thai society.

General Phao's police also protected SEA Supplies' shipments of arms to the Guomindang in Burma—and, in return, opium poured out of the Shan hills in increasingly larger quantities. The London *Times* gave a rare look into the Thai network in an article dated 6 April 1953. Its correspondent had travelled up to Chiang Mai in northern Thailand, then a small but rapidly growing provincial centre:

> This little town near the Burmese frontier is, in effect, a rear base for the Chinese Nationalist troops operating in the Shan state. In spite of denials in Bangkok, essential supplies are sent by road to the Nationalist headquarters at Möng Hsat and in return opium caravans escorted by Nationalist troops bring into Siam [Thailand] about 500 kilograms of drugs a week, according to conservative estimates . . . traffic across the border has been going on either from here or from Lampang [90 kilometres south of Chiang Mai] for two years, and it has become rather obvious as well as efficiently and ruthlessly run. Three attempts were made to assassinate a local newspaper editor who objected.[75]

Half a ton of opium every week for two years makes 52 tonnes. Where all that money went is not certain, but the resultant Guomindang operation destabilised not only Burma but also Thailand. While local Chiang Mai dealers with roots in China's southwestern Yunnan province, and direct access to growers and merchants in the Sino-Burmese borderlands, were responsible for smuggling opium down to the Thai border, it was groups of Teochew in Bangkok who financed and controlled the major drug shipments destined for the international market. According to an official US document:

> These men are the bankers of the narcotics trade. Operating behind legitimate business covers and using Thai names, the major Chao Chou [Chiu Chao or Teochew] financiers in Thailand are regarded as respectable businessmen, and have been immune from arrest and prosecution, largely because they rarely, if ever, personally touch narcotics. Only fellow members of a Chao Chou [Chiu Chao] secret society know when and how a narcotics deal is being put together and who is involved.[76]

Journalist Melinda Liu summed up the new drug pecking order in a few words: 'Hill tribes in Burma grow the opium. Insurgents in Shan State transport it. Yunnan Chinese tax it. And Chaozhou [Teochew] Chinese buy and export it.'[77]

The business relationship that developed between the Yunnanese and the Teochew—and the different roles which the two Chinese communities came to play—had its roots in the recent history of northern Thailand. The socio-economic structure of that region had first been altered by the arrival of the railway in the 1920s. After more than ten years of hard work, sweat and blasting through the hills, the first train steamed into Chiang Mai, and the King in Bangkok could expect to control his northern Thai subjects more effectively. But with the railway came, not surprisingly, thousands of Teochew-speaking Chinese from Bangkok. With trading partners already well established in the capital, they swiftly took over most of the commercial activities in the north as well. They were soon seen in shops and company offices all over Chiang Mai, though bearing Thai names and just as assimilated as their cousins in Bangkok.

The next major change came with the influx of the Yunnanese, who had arrived with the Guomindang after the communist victory in China. They linked up with ethnic Chinese Muslims from Yunnan, who had fled their home country after an extremely bloody rebellion in the mid-nineteenth century. Called Hui in China and Panthay in Burma, they claimed to be descendants of Kublai Khan's horsemen, whose hordes had swept as far south as Yunnan in the thirteenth century. The Panthays were local traders, the best muleteers in the region, and had business links stretching as far north as Yunnan. But their role in the drug trade ended in Chiang Mai and, to a lesser extent, in Bangkok. The big business—the regional and international networks—was firmly in the hands of the Teochew. A working relationship had to be formed between the establishment and the immensely powerful Teochew underworld in order to neutralise what could have amounted to the subversion and further destabilisation of Thailand—and to make sure a fair share of their profits were re-invested in the Thai economy.[78]

The man who oversaw this development, General Phao, had accumulated not only political might through his powerful police force, but also economic influence through banking and corporate owner-ship, which owed much to money derived from the opium trade with the Guomindang.[79] The opium trade had become especially impor-tant since traditional sources in other parts of the world had dried up. Iran had agreed, in April 1946, to ban poppy cultivation; Chinese supplies had also ceased after the 1949 revolution, when Mao Zedong's communists wiped out virtually all opium production in Sichuan and Yunnan. According to Thai researcher Surachart Bam-rungsuk:

> While the Iranian and Chinese opium supplies were gradually disappearing in the early 1950s, the Guomindang began to fill the void by expanding opium production in the areas they occupied in the Shan states. In 1954, British customs in Singapore stated that Bangkok had become a major centre for international opium trafficking in Southeast Asia . . . By 1955 the Thai police under General Phao Sriyanonda had become the largest opium-trafficking syndicate in Thailand, and were involved in every phase of the narcotics traffic.[80]

This business was well worth fighting for, and it resulted in an open conflict between Phao and Sarit. The tenuous political and military balance between the two contenders for power and influence was finally upset in September 1957. Army tanks and infantry moved into Bangkok. They encircled the police headquarters in the Thai capital and proclaimed martial law. Phao fled the country to look after his bank accounts in Switzerland, where he later died as one of the richest men in the world. His local banker, Chin Sophonpanich of the Bangkok Bank, was also forced into exile, which he spent mostly in Hong Kong until he eventually returned in 1964.

Thailand's prime minister, Phibunsongkhram, escaped to Cambo-dia and later fled to Japan, where he died in 1964. Sarit and the army had seized power. For the next sixteen years, Thailand was to be ruled by a single group of men: military officers who rose to power when Sarit decided to make his move. The power of the police had been effectively broken and a new elite was emerging.[81] A handsome, silver-haired Field Marshal called Thanom Kittikachorn soon became the most public of these new powerholders. His charming appearance earned him the nickname 'Siamese Smile' in the foreign media. But the most powerful of Sarit's underlings was his side-kick, the plump

Field Marshal Praphat 'Porky' Charusathien, whose 'sunglasses, tiny moustache and coarse features in a heavy face gave [him] a sinister appearance, especially next to Thanom. Whereas Thanom was able to interact easily with visiting foreign leaders, Praphat shied away from such contacts'.[82]

Sarit's rise to omnipotence was not smooth, however. Unruly civilian politicians were still around, as well as parties opposed to his winning the election on 15 December 1957. A second coup had to be staged on 20 October 1958 before he could consolidate his grip on power. In the interim, Sarit had been admitted to Walter Reed Military Hospital in Washington, where he was visited by US Secretary of State John Foster Dulles and President Dwight Eisenhower. They discussed a 'free world defence against Communist pressure', and Sarit promised to turn Thailand into the bulwark that the US needed to halt the communist advance in East Asia.[83]

For obvious reasons, a new, United States-led regional pact, the Southeast Asian Treaty Organisation (SEATO) took great interest in the new order in Thailand. The SEATO secretary-general, Pote Sarasin of Thailand, had even headed a pro-Sarit caretaker government shortly after the first coup. He returned to his old post in SEATO when Sarit was firmly back in the saddle after the second military takeover. Significantly, immediately after this second coup, all political parties were abolished and a large number of arrests were made for alleged breaches of a new Anti-communism Law.[84]

Neutral foreign observers, however, reported that there was no communist danger, and the real reason for the coup was that the government was facing bankruptcy. General Phao had plundered the country, and its foreign exchange reserves were shrinking. Despite the close relationship between Phao and Chin of the Bangkok Bank, anti-Chinese rhetoric under the fiercely nationalistic Phibunsongkhram and Luang Wichit had alienated most of the Sino-Thai business community. Chin had fled the country together with Phao, but Sarit promised to restore the confidence of the Sino-Thai plutocracy in the government when he himself took over as prime minister on 9 February 1959.[85]

With the economic arrangements in order and the army firmly in charge, the United States pledged to take care of Thailand's military needs.[86] It was in this new, much more favourable environment that various cloak-and-dagger types also went to work again—in the Golden Triangle. The equilibrium that had been upset by the removal of General Phao had not only been restored but the murky world of secret agents found themselves with a new, much better organised setup. Praphat was their new man. He had supported Sarit in his power struggle with Phao, and was later awarded the Interior Ministry for his loyalty. In that capacity, Praphat took over the role previously played by General Phao—and added a powerful new security apparatus which was built up under his command in the early 1960s: the Communist Suppression Operational Command (CSOC), which later became known as the Internal Security Operational Command (ISOC). Naturally, this new outfit was in charge of border security, which included liaison with the Guomindang as well as armed ethnic minority groups, which had been encouraged to set up bases along the Thai–Burma frontier.

General Sarit's new government decreed the abolition of the 52-year-old Royal Thai Opium Monopoly shortly after assuming power in 1959. But narcotics-related corruption, and private business activities, were already rampant in Thailand, and no serious attempts were made to stop the enormous traffic from the poppy fields of Burma and northern Thailand down to the sea lanes. The West's crusade against the 'communist threat' in Asia made sure that no one made any real effort to upset 'the arrangement' in Thailand. For several decades, the country remained the most important trans-shipment centre for Burmese opium, and Bangkok was Asia's major drug capital.

General Li Mi, who was considered a scoundrel even by his own men, had been sent back to Taiwan in 1952, and the Guomindang was completely restructured in the early 1960s following dramatic events along the Sino-Burmese frontier. Chinese Premier Zhou Enlai had visited Burma for a week in the beginning of January 1961 to ratify a long overdue demarcation of the common frontier. China also pledged to afford Burma an interest-free loan of £30 million. What was not announced, however, was that Burma had secretly agreed to allow Chinese forces to enter Burma and attack the Guomindang.

On 26 January, a combined force of three divisions of regulars from the Chinese People's Liberation Army (PLA), a total of 20 000 men, crossed the frontier between Sipsongpanna and Kengtung state. In human waves, they swept down across the hills surrounding Möng

Yang, Möng Wa and Möng Yawng. The campaign, code-named 'the Mekong River Operation', broke the back of the Guomindang in northeastern Burma. Beaten Nationalist Chinese forces retreated towards Möng Pa Liao on the Mekong River, where 5000 Burmese troops launched an attack. Their base was captured without much resistance—but when the Burmese troops marched in, they found large quantities of US-made arms and ammunition.

When the news hit the papers in the Burmese capital Rangoon, there were violent demonstrations outside the US Embassy on Merchant Street. Neither the Burmese nor the Chinese, however, have ever acknowledged that the PLA formed the core of the force that drove the Guomindang out of the eastern border areas.[87]

Soon after the Mekong River Operation, the CIA reported that Taiwan had evacuated 3371 soldiers and 825 dependents from the Burma–Thai–Laos border area to Taiwan between 17 March and 12 April.[88] But, even so, the agency estimated that approximately 3000 Guomindang 'irregulars' remained in the border areas. Some 1500–2000 of them reportedly based themselves in northern Thailand, and the remainder in Burma and Laos. Some 400–500 Guomindang troops were said to have been recruited by the Laotian army to patrol the area between Luang Prabang and Ban Houei Sai, and the government in Vientiane was attempting to enlist more to garrison Nam Tha province further to the north.[89] The interests that supported the Guomindang were determined not to let it disappear: the Guomindang was simply too useful for intelligence gathering, economic benefits and outright mercenary activities.

The Guomindang could come and go as it pleased along Thailand's northern frontier and, in accordance with the reorganisation of the Guomindang, one unit called 'the 3rd Army', led by General Li Wenhuan, set up base at Tam Ngob in the mountains north of Chiang Mai. A '5th Guomindang' led by General Duan Xiwen established a prosperous community at Mae Salong northwest of Chiang Rai, which had its own schools, army barracks, tea plantations and helicopter landing pads. General Li was even allowed to build an impressive residence in Chiang Mai. Their main contact within the Thai authorities was Field Marshal Praphat, who reportedly encouraged the Guomindang to increase the volume of opium it brought down to the Thai border to finance its activities. This benefited the

Thai authorities as well, as it infused millions of dollars into the local economy.[90]

Li's 3rd Guomindang army at Tam Ngob was the best-organised drug trafficking group in the region, while the 5th Army sent troops to Laos, where they were guided by the CIA and assigned to collect intelligence from across the border in Yunnan. As Asia's new major conflict, the Vietnam War, was escalating, it was becoming of the utmost importance to find out about, and if possible to disrupt, the flow of Chinese weapons and other supplies to North Vietnam.

Apart from General Duan's troops, there was also a little-known elite unit known by its French name 'Bataillon Spécial 111'. Commanded by the highly competent Li Teng, it was manned mainly by ex-POWs from the Korean War. The Allied forces had captured more than 20 000 Chinese PLA troops from the human waves of young conscripts which the communists had sent down across the 38th parallel. More than two-thirds of these Chinese POWs were violently opposed to the idea of returning to their communist homeland and, after careful vetting by Taiwanese intelligence agents, a fair number of them were resettled on the Nationalist Chinese island. The most trustworthy were given special training and had slogans like 'Death to Communism!' tattooed on their arms to prevent defection. They were sent to the Chinese frontier in northern Laos, where they remained for years as the most secretive of all the mercenary groups deployed there during the so-called 'Secret War'.[91]

The most important Guomindang contingent in northeastern Burma was the 1st Independent Unit, led by a Yunnan-born Chinese, Ma Jingguo. Directly controlled by the Intelligence Mainland Operation Bureau of the Ministry of Defence in Taipei, Ma built up an impressive espionage network along the Yunnan frontier. From a string of eight bases in the Thai–Lao–Burma–China quadrangle, Ma's 1500 specially trained Guomindang troops used an even wider web of informants in towns and villages on all sides of the borders in the area to collect vital intelligence for both Taipei and Washington.[92]

Modern radio equipment was installed in the small town of Vingngün in the wild Wa Hills and other remote mountainous areas adjacent to China, and at Loi Sae south of the Burmese garrison town of Tang-yan in central Shan state. The green, fertile valley of Möng Wa in eastern Shan state, close to the Mekong River, served as a third major staging point. The Vingngün base, however, was perhaps the most important because of its proximity to an area of Yunnan where even the central Chinese government exercised little control. The base was led by Colonel Sao Tuen-sung, a high-ranking intelligence operative. His main assistants were three enterprising brothers who had fled Yunnan after the communist takeover: Wei Hsueh-long, Wei Hsueh-kang and Wei Hsueh-yin. Popularly known as 'the Wei Brothers', they were engaged in both espionage and opium trading.[93]

Ma reported directly to the CIA base at Nam Yu in northwestern Laos, passing on vital intelligence on the movement of Chinese supplies to Hanoi and to the pro-Vietnamese Pathet Lao guerrillas in Laos. He was also able to verify the field information gleaned from aerial photography and satellite images. French researcher Catherine Lamour observed: 'Ma Ching-ko [Ma Jingguo] had built up the grandest infiltration operation of secret agents that ever took place in any country after World War II'.[94]

The coexistence of drug trafficking networks and espionage rings with US connections has led many authors and journalists to jump to the conclusion that drug money was used to finance covert operations, and that the CIA was somehow behind the traffic. People with years in the field deny such allegations. US covert operations, they say, were financed by secret funds from Washington. Drug money provided extra income, or 'pocket money', for some of the people who were involved in these operations. In the case of the Guomindang, drug money was also undoubtedly used to buy equipment and rations, and to pay soldiers. In a surprisingly candid interview with a British newspaper in 1967, General Duan of the 5th Guomindang declaimed: 'We have to continue to fight the evil of communism and to fight you must have an army, and an army must have guns, and to buy guns you must have money. In these mountains the only money is opium'.[95]

That other creation of Thai nationalism and the Cold War—the high-profile *chao pho*—was by and large excluded from the well-organised drug trade. Even though they also operated with the protection of local government and military officials, their activities were concentrated on illegal gambling, sponsorship of 'charity boxing matches', real estate development, and the entertainment industry.

But, in pursuing these activities, they accumulated immense wealth, and in the process became influential power brokers. They would throw their weight behind certain candidates in elections, and were rich enough to buy votes to secure the victory of 'their man'. In return, they enjoyed powerful protection for their own businesses.

The power and influence of Thailand's *chao pho* could be observed at the spectacular birthday party that one of them, Somchai Khunpluem, held in 1989. Some 25 000 guests, including cabinet ministers and several members of parliament, came to pay their respects to Somchai, whose only official title was *kamnan*, or district chief, of Saen Sukh municipality near Chonburi on the coast southeast of Bangkok.[96] Nicknamed *Kamnan* Poh, he began his career as an operator of a fishing fleet in Cambodian waters—and by trading US dollars between the American base in Sattahip east of Chonburi and the black market in Cambodia. He put his profits into massage parlours, and made more money from an underground lottery—as well, it was alleged, as the transportation of contraband along the coast.[97]

But he made his real fortune in real estate dealing in the 1980s, when the Thai government launched an ambitious plan to develop what was termed the Eastern Seaboard. Saen Sukh, near the town of Chonburi, benefited from the plans, and *Kamnan* Poh soon had a finger in every pie in the area. Chonburi is also a major centre for vice, smuggling and drug operations, as well as extortion and murder—almost all of which goes unpunished.[98] *Kamnan* Poh, who is referred to as 'the Godfather of Chonburi' by the Thai media, has always denied being involved in illegal activities, and police raids on his homes and properties have turned up nothing. 'Like the television crews who joined the raids, he had been forewarned', stated a regional magazine.[99] And his municipality, Saen Sukh, has remained a prosperous model community. In 1997 it won the 'Thailand's Cleanest City' award, and was nominated by the Thai government for the German Konrad Adenauer Local Government Award of 1998.[100] *Kamnan* Poh did not get the award, but he became a prominent member of the Chat Thai Party. Three of his sons, Sonthaya, Vidthaya and Ittiphol Khunpluem, stood for parliamentary elections in January 2001—all of them were elected.

Relatives of other *chao pho* did not fare quite as well. In Samut Prakarn province, *chao pho* Wattana Asavahame—who was denied a visa to the United States in July 1994 for being on a narcotics watchlist—saw all three of his relatives defeated at the polls. They ran under Wattana's own party banner, Rassadorn, which was no match for the bigger and much wealthier Thai Rak Thai Party—which won the election with a nationwide landslide and was able to pay 300 Baht ($7.00) per vote.[101] The controversial *chao pho* Chalerm Yubamruang, who has been a minister and deputy minister in several governments, also had to accept that his two sons were defeated. The influential Angkinan family—long-time Godfathers of Phetburi, a town best known for Thailand's infamous gunmen—also failed to be elected.

Part of the reason for the decline of the power of the *chao pho* is, of course, that Thailand has developed into a more modern and sophisticated society. Another is that the *chao pho* have been hurt by Thailand's economic crisis, which they actually helped engineer through unscrupulous property speculation and by extracting huge bank loans. Thailand's boom in the late 1980s and early 1990s, and the subsequent bust of the late 1990s, is closely linked to the dubious activities of the *chao pho* and the cutthroat culture that they have fostered—and it actually began with an attempt to crack down on the crime bosses. On 23 February 1991, the Thai military staged its last successful coup, overthrew the government of Chatichai Choonhavan and set up a junta called the National Peacekeeping Council (NPKC). The new military government, which claimed it had seized power because of widespread corruption and abuse of public funds by the Chatichai government, launched a campaign to 'tame' the *chap pho* by persuading them to invest their ill-gotten gains in legitimate businesses such as real estate development, golf courses and the construction of hotels and resorts. But, lacking financial acumen and real business skills, the outcome was (perhaps not surprisingly) pure speculation and an unprecedented waste of money and resources. When the bubble burst in July 1997, Thai banks and financial institutions found that up to 30 per cent of all their loans, or a total of $30 billion, were 'non-performing'—a euphemism for the banks being unable to recover them.[102] When foreign companies were called in to restructure insolvent companies, they faced the same danger as the Japanese bankers who tried to clean up the mess in their country after the collapse of its bubble economy: on 10 March 1999, Michael Wensley, an Australian insolvency expert, was gunned down near the central Thai town of Nakhon Sawan. The gunmen struck as he and four other executives from South Sathorn Planner, a local affiliate of the international consultancy firm Deloitte Touche Tohmatsu, were on their way to a debt-ridden sugar mill near the town.[103] Not a single suspect who was arrested immediately after the murder remains in police custody.

Sia Leng, the *chao pho* of Thailand's northeastern region, even went public and complained in January 2001 that he was broke, and only had debts. Sia Leng, an ethnic Chinese whose Thai name is Charoen Patanadamrongkit, was for years known as the 'Dragon of the Northeast', and party leaders always turned to him when they needed to tap his huge pool of funds for candidates on the campaign trail. Now he has given away his Rolls Royce to a friend 'because imported parts were too expensive', and he has been forced to cancel his yearly gambling trips to Las Vegas and Atlantic City in the United States.[104] But all is not lost. His son Jakrin joined Thai Rak Thai, and was elected to parliament in January 2001. The new constitution under which Thailand went to the polls was meant to introduce a new tough stance on corrupt politics, including diminishing the influence and power of the *chao pho* who treated politics as business rather than a national duty. But, even so, election commissioners described the polls as the dirtiest and most expensive ever.[105] It will take a long time before money politics fade from Thailand's political scene.

One of the few *chao poh* who has survived the crisis more or less unhurt is *Kamnan* Poh, mainly because he had access to the local bureaucracy through his sons' political positions. He was also far-sighted enough not to waste his money on speculative real estate deals, but to invest it in whisky—for which there is always a steady demand—and in Pattaya tourism, which has flourished as a result of the falling value of the Thai baht. When it was time for him and his sons to open their local campaign office a few months before the January 2001 election, more than 5000 well-wishers showed up, including deputy prime ministers Virote Pow-in and Somboon Rahong, as well as education minister Somsak Prisnanuntakul, agriculture minister Prapat Pothasuthon, and numerous deputy ministers and other high-ranking politicians.[106]

Thailand's tight criminal structure has made it almost impossible for outsiders to break in and get a share of the action. Nonetheless, the country's policy of encouraging tourism has been abused by criminals, and its easy-going tolerance of foreign visitors has made it a favourite haven for all sorts of criminals, international terrorists and people smugglers. But the Chinese Triads have played only a peripheral role in Thailand since deals were made between the Guomindang and its associates, and the authorities, in the 1950s and 1960s. The Russians started coming in large numbers as tourists after the collapse of the Soviet Union, and Russian prostitutes are frequently picked up by the Thai police in Bangkok and the seaside resort of Pattaya. A high-profile murder in Pattaya in March 1998 led to a flurry of writings in the Thai media about 'the Russian *Mafiya*' making inroads in Thailand. Kostantine Povoloski, a Russian restaurant owner in Pattaya, was gunned down in broad daylight in the beach resort by a hired assassin who had flown in from Estonia.[107] But that was an exception from an unwritten rule among the Russian mobsters vacationing in Pattaya or doing small business in Bangkok: no violence in Thailand. Everyone wants to enjoy Thailand's bars and the beaches, even the gangsters. And violence on Thai soil would only make it difficult for everyone.[108]

The Japanese *yakuza* has for years imported young women from Thailand to work in bars, massage parlours and brothels in Japan, but always through local middlemen. Guns were also bought in Thailand, before it became easier—and cheaper—to buy any kind of weapons in Russia and China. And extortion activities tend to be directed at fellow Japanese, who never report the incidents to the Thai police. The main area of operation is Thaniya Road in downtown Bangkok, next to the better-known Phatpong red light area. Literally hundreds of karaoke lounges, bars and Japanese restaurants line Thaniya. The Thai hostesses there are said to be the most beautiful, best-trained and best-paid in the business, and the 'private clubs' where they work are off limits to Thais, other Asians and westerners. All customers come from Bangkok's large Japanese business community, or they are tourists. These bars are said to have to pay 'protection money' to local *yakuza* operatives—in addition to 'fees' to Thai gangsters and local police.[109] It is also common for *yakuza* extortionists to rig up hidden cameras in the bars, take pictures of wealthy Japanese businessmen in compromising situations and use these for blackmail.

But, apart from such activities—which do not affect the Thais or Thai society—reported *yakuza* 'crimes' in Thailand tend to be minor, or outright bizarre. In September 1992, the Thai press reported the arrest of a Bangkok-based Japanese businessman who was accused of being a *yakuza* member. The man, Kenji Shinahara, had a company called Bangkok Koeiki, which had been hired by another company, Taniyama, to demand damages from a third company, NYK (Thai), that was alleged to have sent Thai asparagus to Japan by air instead of by sea over a period of two years. Taniyama claimed the more expensive route cost the company nearly $9 million.[110]

The *yakuza*, on the other hand, almost managed to gain absolute control over foreign investment in Burma in 1990. A little known company called Daichi ('Big Earth'—not 'Dai-ichi', or 'Number One', which is a big and well-established corporation) signed a deal with Burma's new, embattled military government, which came to power in September 1988 after killing thousands of pro-democracy demonstrators in the streets of Rangoon and elsewhere. Together they would develop a 'future city' outside the capital. The deal was supposedly worth $15 billion and Daichi, through a subsidiary called the 'Myanmar Concord Development Organisation', or MCDO, secured a 90-year lease on 1600 square kilometres of land outside Rangoon. Burma's trade and planning minister, Brigadier-General David Abel, said the plan would take ten to fifteen years to complete, and would include housing estates, hotels, convention centres, a new airport, highways and 4000 man-made lakes.[111]

A glossy brochure produced by the company was described in the following manner by a western diplomat based in Rangoon at the time: 'As an exercise in fantasy it would be hard to beat. It is as though some rich and overindulgent uncle had given his cranky nephew, possessed with a lively imagination, free-range with a computer, a pair of scissors and a pile of in-house architectural magazines, and told him to play away to his heart's content'.[112] The MCDO organisation chart folded out to a full metre and had at its top a picture of the 'Chief Executive of the Nation President of Prime Minister' [sic]. Another pull-out revealed a 'bird's eye view of the new Rangoon resort city', comprising ringroads, an assortment of skyscrapers, industrial estates—and a gathering of hot-air balloons floating over the city with 'Aska' or 'Aska 21' painted on them.[113]

When the executives of the mother company, Daichi, arrived in Rangoon, they did not look like ordinary businessmen. Dressed in dark suits and with short-cropped hair, they resembled characters in a cheap gangster movie.[114] The head of the company, an ethnic Korean called Bernard Choi, was a US citizen. A prominent member of the Korean community in California and a strong Christian, he had pictures of himself with former president Ronald Reagan and the Pope. It was obvious that he had been used as a conduit to make a deal with Brigadier-General Abel, a fellow Christian. The text on the hot-air balloons indicated who the real power behind the scheme was: ASKA is a company owned by a *yakuza*-connected Japanese loan-shark, Yasumichi Morishita, nicknamed 'the Viper'. The idea was not to build a space city in Rangoon, but to direct all new investors to the MCDO's 1600 square kilometre 'development area', where they would be under the control of Morishita. The Japanese government had to intervene and tell Brigadier-General Abel and other officials in the Burmese junta that they had been conned.[115]

The military first came to power in Burma through a coup in March 1962. The Guomindang invasion, and numerous ethnic insurgencies, had made the army the most powerful institution in the country. General Ne Win, the commander in chief, eventually ousted U Nu's democratically elected government and set up a Revolutionary Council that ruled by decree. He also introduced a new economic system which he termed 'the Burmese Way to Socialism'. In effect, everything in sight was nationalised—that is, handed over to a number of military-run state corporations. The outcome was that Burma, once the richest country in Southeast Asia, was plunged into ruin. Out in the areas where the ethnic minorities lived, insurgencies flared anew, and China—long wary of the unpredictable general—began to support the Communist Party of Burma (CPB). With massive Chinese assistance, the CPB soon took over a 20 000 square kilometre swathe of land near the Yunnan frontier in the northeast, where it established a revolutionary base area with its own administration, hospitals, schools and army barracks. The Chinese even sent thousands of 'volunteers' to fight alongside the CPB as artillery instructors, advisers and strategic planners. This was during the Cultural Revolution, and many of them were hot-headed young Red Guards from Yunnan who wanted to spread the revolutionary gospel to Southeast Asia.[116]

The area which the CPB took over included Kokang and the Wa Hills—the best opium-growing areas in the Golden Triangle. The

CPB taxed the growers and the merchants, but did not have to depend on the drug trade as long as the Chinese were sending in everything from anti-aircraft guns and army trucks to medical supplies and even cooking utensils. But when Deng Xiaoping returned to power in Beijing in the late 1970s, Chinese aid was drastically reduced, and most of the volunteers were recalled. The old Maoist policy of supporting revolutionary movements in the region was abandoned under Deng's new policies, and the CPB suffered badly as a result. It began to show a keener interest in the opium trade, which at that time was in the hands of the remnants of the Guomindang, and a half-Shan half-Chinese upstart called Zhang Qifu in Chinese, and Khun Sa in Shan.

An orphan from the opium mountain of Loi Maw in northern Shan state, Khun Sa formed his own armed band in 1950, when he was only sixteen years old. Ten years later, his 'army' was even recognised officially as the 'Loi Maw *Ka Kwe Ye*', a home guard unit under the Burmese army. *Ke Kwe Ye* (KKY), which literally means 'defence' in Burmese, was Rangoon's idea of a local militia to fight the Guomindang, the CPB and the ethnic rebel armies. The plan was to rally as many warlords as possible—mostly non-political brigands and private army commanders—behind the Burmese army in exchange for the right to use all government-controlled roads and towns in Shan state for opium smuggling. By trading in opium, Burma's military government hoped that the KKY militias would be self-supporting.[117] The warlords, who were supposed to fight the insurgents, strengthened their private armies and purchased with opium money all the military equipment available on the black market in Thailand and Laos: M-16 and Browning automatic rifles. M-79 grenade launchers and 57mm recoilless rifles. Some of them, including Khun Sa, were soon better equipped than the Burmese army itself.

When Khun Sa was only 33, he decided to challenge the supremacy of the much more senior opium warlords, Guomindang generals Li Wenhuan and Duan Xiwen. In May 1967, he set out from the hills of northern Shan state with a large contingent of soldiers and a massive, 16 ton opium convoy, destined for an Khwan, a small Laotian lumber village across the Mekong River from Chiang Saen in Thailand. More traders joined his convoy, so by the time it reached the town of Kengtung, its single-file column of 500 men and 300 mules stretched along the ridges for almost 2 kilometres.[118]

The convoy crossed the Mekong River on 14 and 15 July—and the Guomindang rushed to intercept it. Hundreds of fighters came down from Tam Ngob and Mae Salong on the Thai-Burma border and, on 29 July, they attacked. Fierce fighting raged for several days, and wounded soldiers from both sides were treated in hospitals in Chiang Rai, where they often ended up in the same wards, chatting with each other and sharing cigarettes.[119]

The outcome of the battle is still somewhat obscure. General Ouane Rattikone, the commander-in-chief of the Royal Lao Army, ran several heroin refineries in the nearby Ban Houey Sai area at this time, and he sent the Lao air force to bomb the battle site. Officially, he cheated both Khun Sa and the Guomindang, and made off with the opium. Other sources say the opium had already been sold, and that Khun Sa subsequently made his first significant investment in Thailand.[120] And, despite his 'defeat' at Ban Khwan, Khun Sa grew stronger and more powerful by the day. In 1969, he was eventually arrested by the Burmese government, not because of his involvement in the opium trade—which he was doing with official blessings anyway—but because he had been in touch with the very forces he was supposed to fight: the Shan rebels.

Khun Sa spent four years in gaol, until his men, who had gone underground following his arrest, managed to negotiate his release in exchange for two Soviet doctors, who had been kidnapped from the hospital in the Shan state capital of Taunggyi. Khun Sa returned to the Thai border, where he set up a new camp at Ban Hin Taek north-west of Chiang Rai, actually well inside Thailand, where a powerful new armed force emerged: the Shanland United Army, or the SUA. The force was dominated by ethnic Chinese opium merchants, and—somewhat ironically, given the battle-lines at Ban Khawn in 1967—ex-Guomindang officers. But by adding 'Shan' to the name of their army, they evidently hoped to gain favours from the closely related Thais, who refer to the Shans as 'Thai Yai', or 'Big Thais'. The new base was developing fast—too fast—and it became an embarrassment for the Thais. In January 1982, the Thai army attacked Ban Hin Teak and drove Khun Sa back across the border into Burma. However, within a year, Khun Sa had not only rebuilt his shattered forces, he had also extended his influence right along almost the entire border between Thailand and Burma's Shan state. He established a new headquarters at Homöng, until then a small village of about a dozen ramshackle bamboo huts. Homöng was soon transformed into a bustling town boasting well-stocked shops, spacious marketplaces and a neatly laid-out grid of roads, incuding street lights. The township's 10 000 or so inhabitants lived in wooden and concrete houses amid fruit trees, manicured hedges and gardens adorned with bougainvillea and marigolds. Huge sign boards indicated where travel permits to Mae Hong Son across the border in Thailand were issued.[121]

Khun Sa also managed to capitalise on Shan nationalism, and recruited thousands of young Shans into his army, which he now called the Möng Tai Army, or the MTA (Möng Tai being Shan for Shan state). But the organisation, especially its drug business, remained firmly in the hands of ex-Guomindang officers and other ethnic Chinese. The chief of staff of both the SUA and its successor MTA was Zhang Suquan, who used the Shan name Sao Hpalang, or 'General Thunder'. But he was actually a Manchurian who had joined the Guomindang during World War II. He was among the Guomindang Chinese who had retreated to Burma after Mao Zedong's victory, and then evacuated to Taiwan in 1952. He served briefly as an intelligence officer in Korea, but returned to Southeast Asia in 1960 to join the CIA-supported Bataillon Spécial 111 in Laos. He later linked up with Khun Sa, and became his most able commander. Number two in the SUA/MTA's military hierarchy was Liang Zhongyin, or 'Leng Seün' in Shan, a former Guomindang officer from Beijing.[122] The drug business had become a far more serious affair in the 1960s and 1970s, as new refineries had been set up in the Golden Triangle where raw opium was processed into white, Number Four heroin, which is very addictive and far more dangerous.

To get away with his drug trafficking activities, Khun Sa played up not only Shan nationalism but also anti-communism, which struck a chord with the Thais and others. His army, and his 'liberated area' along the Thai–Burma border, was the buffer that blocked any attempts by the CPB to move south, and possibly link up with other Communist Parties in Southeast Asia. Although Khun Sa lived with a million-dollar reward on his head, courtesy of the US Drug Enforcement Administration (DEA), he remained throughout his career the most unwanted wanted man in the world. His connections with high-ranking Thai and Burmese military officers were impeccable, and the Unification Church of South Korean religious maverick Moon Sun Myung contacted Khun Sa to establish churches inside his territory. This was turned down, the Shans being ardent Buddists and not Christians, but 'missionaries' from the Reverend Moon's church became frequent visitors to Homöng. The related Sasakawa Peace Foundation, founded by former Japanese war criminal Ryoichi Sasakawa, also expressed interest in Khun Sa's activities, maybe with the prospect of supporting educational projects in the area then under Khun Sa's control. 'Rich people' in Taiwan supported a Chinese language school at Homöng.[123] None of them seemed to be bothered by the fact that they were dealing with the word's biggest opium and heroin dealer. But soon the days of the swashbuckling Khun Sa were to be over—though not because of any crackdown on his trafficking activities by international police agencies.

Burma's annual opium production in the 1980s was in the order of 400–600 tonnes annually. In the late 1980s, however, production shot up to over 1000 tonnes and by 1995 it had increased to 2340 tonnes. Satellite imagery showed that the area under poppy cultivation increased from 92 300 hectares in 1987 to 142 700 in 1989 and 154 000 in 1995.[124] The potential heroin output soared from 54 tonnes in 1987 to 166 tonnes in 1995, making drugs the impoverished and misman-aged country's only growth industry.[125] At the same time, a string of new heroin refineries were set up in Kokang and the Wa hills, conveni-ently located near the main growing areas in northern Burma and, equally important, close to the rapidly growing Chinese drug market and seemingly easier routes through Yunnan to the outside world.

In the early 1990s, the same laboratories in northern Burma began to produce methamphetamines. Khun Sa's old network was effectively undermined, and it was further affected when, in December 1993, several divisions of government troops encircled Homöng, placing an effective stranglehold on his operations. In January 1996, Khun Sa eventually surrendered to the authorities in Rangoon without a fight. He abandoned Homöng, moved to the capital, and left his 15 000-man strong army to fend for itself. Many soldiers went home to their vil-lages, while others continued to roam the hills of the Thai–Burmese border, some as bandits while others claimed to be fighting for some nationalist ideal. Zhang Suquan established himself as a prominent businessman in Rangoon, while Khun Sa went into retirement in the capital with three new wives, all teenage girls from the Shan hills.

These dramatic changes in the pattern of opium production and the location of heroin refineries, the introduction of new drug scourges and the opening of new smuggling routes have all emerged in the wake of two recent political events in Burma: the crushing of a popular uprising against military rule in 1988, and an unrelated mutiny the following year among the rank and file of the CPB.[126]

In August and September 1988, millions of people from virtually every town and major village across Burma took to the streets to demand an end to 26 years of stifling military rule and the restoration of democracy which existed before Ne Win's army took over in a *coup d'etat* in 1962. The protests shook Burma's military establishment, which responded fiercely. Thousands of people were gunned down as the army moved in to shore up a regime overwhelmed by popular protest. The crushing of the 1988 uprising was more dramatic and much bloodier than the better publicised events in Beijing's Tiananmen Square a year later.

In the wake of the massacres in Rangoon and elsewhere in the country, more than 8000 pro-democracy activists fled the urban centres for the border areas near Thailand, where a multitude of ethnic insurgencies, not involved in the drug trade, were active. Significantly, the main drug gang operating along the border, Khun Sa and his private army, refused to shelter any dissidents who had fled the urban areas; his main interest was business, not to fight the government.

The Burmese military now feared a renewed, potentially dangerous insurgency along its frontiers: a possible alliance between the ethnic rebels and the pro-democracy activists from Rangoon and other towns and cities. But these Thai border-based groups—Karen, Mon, Karenni and Pa-O—were unable to provide the urban dissidents with more than a handful of weapons. None of the ethnic armies could match the strength of the CPB, whose 10 000 to 15 000 troops still controlled a vast base area along the Sino–Burmese border. Unlike the ethnic insurgents, the CPB also had vast quantities of arms and ammunition, which were supplied by China from 1968 to 1978. Although the aid had almost ceased by 1980, the CPB had enough munitions to last through at least ten years of guerrilla warfare against the central government in Rangoon.[127]

Despite government claims of a 'communist conspiracy' behind the 1988 uprising, there was at that time no linkage between the anti-totalitarian, pro-democracy movement in central Burma and the orthodox, Marxist-Leninist leadership of the CPB. However, given the strong desire for revenge for the bloody events of 1988, it is plausible to assume that the urban dissidents would have accepted arms from any source. Thus it became imperative for the new junta that had seized power on 18 September 1988—the State Law and Order Restoration Council (SLORC)—to neutralise as many of the border insurgencies as possible, especially the CPB.

A situation which was potentially even more dangerous for the SLORC arose in March and April 1989 when the hill tribe rank-and-file of the CPB, led by the military commanders who also came from the various minorities in its northeastern base area, mutinied against the party's ageing, mostly Burman political leadership. On 17 April 1989, ethnic Wa mutineers from the CPB's army stormed party headquarters at Panghsang on the Yunnan frontier. The old leaders and their families—about 300 people—escaped to China while the former CPB army split along ethnic lines and formed four different, regional resistance armies. The biggest was the United Wa State Army, or the UWSA, but another powerful faction maintained control over the hills north of Kengtung in easternmost Shan state. This group was led by Lin Mingxian (Sai Lin) and Zhang Zhiming (Kyi Myint), two former Red Guards from Yunnan who had joined the CPB as volunteers during the Cultural Revolution and stayed.

Suddenly there was no longer any communist insurgency in Burma, only ethnic rebels, and the SLORC worried about potential collaboration between these four new, well-armed forces in the northeast and the ethnic minority groups along the Thai border, as well as the urban dissidents who had taken refuge there. The ethnic rebels sent a delegation from the Thai border to Panghsang to negotiate with the CPB mutineers soon after the breakup of the old party—but the authorities in Rangoon reacted faster, with more determination, and with much more to offer than the ethnic rebels. Within weeks of the CPB mutiny, the chief of Burma's military intelligence, Major-General (now Lieutenant-General) Khin Nyunt, helicoptered up to the border areas to meet personally with the leaders of the mutiny.

Step by step, alliances of convenience were forged between Burma's military authorities and various groups of mutineers. In exchange for promises not to attack government forces and to sever ties with other rebel groups, the CPB mutineers were granted unofficial permission to engage in any kind of business to sustain themselves—which, in Burma's remote and underdeveloped hill areas, inevitably meant opium production. Rangoon also promised to launch a 'border-development programme' in the former CPB areas, and the United Nations and its various agencies were invited to help fund those projects.

The success in striking those deals with the ex-CPB forces was largely due to the efforts of Lo Hsing-han, a Kokang Chinese ex-warlord who acted as an intermediary with the mutineers. Lo, another former KKY commander who controlled the drug trade before Khun Sa took over, had been arrested in 1973 and sentenced to death. But Rangoon had been farsighted enough not to execute Lo, despite the death sentence against him; that would have been tantamount to destroying a useful political tool. He was released during a general amnesty in 1980 and given two million Kyats in Burmese currency to build a military camp at the so-called 'Salween Village' in the Nampawng area southwest of Lashio. This became the base for his own private militia.[128]

But it was several years before Lo Hsing-han regained his former strength and prominence. The 1989 mutiny within the CPB came at the right time, and on 20–21 March 1989, only a week after the first uprising in the CPB's Northern Bureau headquarters at Möng Ko, a small town on the Sino-Burmese border opposite Mangshi in Yunnan, Lo Hsing-han paid his first visit to his native Kokang area, which had been under CPB control since 1968. This visit paved the way for Khin Nyunt's first meetings with the mutineers—and the remarkable ceasefire agreements which were struck between Burma's military government and thousands of former insurgents. Another intermediary who helped initiate contacts between the CPB mutineers in Kokang and the government in Rangoon was Olive Yang, the old warlady who had been instrumental in building up the opium trade in the late 1950s and early 1960s.

The CPB mutiny also provided Lo with a golden opportunity to rebuild his former drug empire, which he had lost to Khun Sa more than fifteen years earlier. Apart from being a local home-guard commander, Lo had until the mutiny been little more than a small-scale entrepreneur, running bus companies, video parlours and liquor franchises. Since the CPB mutiny, and his role as a mediator between the government and the former CPB forces, he and his son Steven Law have grown to become two of Burma's most prominent businessmen with interests in the hotel industry, transport, road construction, timber, gems, and the import and export of various legal commodities. The evidence may be circumstantial, but it is beyond doubt that the initial capital for their legitimate businesses must have come from the drug trade; there is simply no other possible source, and the timing of their rise from obscurity to prominence seems far more than a coincidence.

Within a year of the CPB mutiny, intelligence sources were able to locate at least seventeen new heroin refineries in Kokang and adjacent areas, six in the Wa Hills and two on Lin Mingxian's area north of Kengtung, where the town of Möng La opposite Daluo in Yunnan developed into one of the most important drug-running centres in the country. The ceasefires had enabled the CPB not only to rapidly increase poppy production, but also to bring in chemicals, mainly acetic anhydrite—which is needed to convert raw opium into heroin—by truck from India. The heroin trade took off with a speed that caught almost every observer of the Southeast Asia drug scene by surprise.

Ironically, at a time when almost the entire population of Burma had turned against the regime, scores of former insurgents rallied behind the ruling military, lured by lucrative business opportunities and unofficial permission to run drugs with impunity. With the collapse of the communist insurgency in 1989, several smaller ethnic armies also gave in and signed a formal ceasefire deal with Rangoon in February 1994.

The threat from the border areas was thwarted and the regime was safe, but the consequences for the country—and the outside world—have been disastrous. Enormous quantities of heroin, and now also methamphetamines, are pouring out of Burma in all directions, providing incomes for criminals way beyond the country's own borders. Furthermore, what began as alliances of convenience between a beleaguered government and various political and ethnic insurgents in Burma has over the past three years been compounded by a new, totally unexpected regional crisis: the Asian economic meltdown. Private companies and banks may be faltering all over East Asia and unemployment is on the rise. But the drug trade, it seems, is the only really lucrative business that is left in Burma and elsewhere in a crisis-hit region. The inevitable outcome is that the drug trade will continue to grow in magnitude and importance, despite international criticism and efforts to curb the menace.

In April 1999, the UWSA and the Burmese junta, now renamed the State Peace and Development Council (SPDC), decided to invite a group of journalists to attend the 10th anniversary celebrations of the CPB mutiny and the subsequent ceasefire agreement between the rebels and the government. The foreign visitors were taken first to Möng La, and then to UWSA headquarters at Panghsang, where they were introduced to Möng La commander Lin Mingxian and Wa leader Pao Yuqiang. The purpose of the trip was to show the foreigners that great headway had been made in the war on drugs. Officially, they were eradicating drugs, not dealing in them. According to Reuters, whose reporter was present at the occasion, Lin and Pao denied any involvement in the drug trade, and claimed that 'our consciences are clear'.[129]

It was perhaps hardly surprising that the drug traffickers themselves denied that they were running heroin refineries, methamphetamine laboratories and regional smuggling networks. But when the reporter began to quote official reports from the US State Department's Bureau for International Narcotics Matters, which named Lin, Pao and several other leaders of the ceasefire groups as some of the most prominent drug traffickers in Burma, he was rebuffed by a high-ranking Burmese military intelligence officer who was also present: 'I think they [the Americans] are just making it up—it's politically motivated.' When asked who, if that was so, was running the refineries obviously located in areas which no doubt were controlled by Lin, Pao and other ceasefire leaders, the officer replied: 'We are at a loss about that. But I think the real culprits are Chinese organised crime groups. They are very secretive and we don't know who is actually doing the trade.'

When the officer, and Lin and Pao, went on to claim that their eradication efforts had been extremely successful, the reporter asked them why, in that case, countries in the region were still being flooded by cheap heroin from Burma. The officer replied that the heroin must have come from 'old stocks' which had been warehoused somewhere. The reporter pointed out that, while raw opium can be warehoused, heroin has a limited shelf-life. Only when an order has been made is raw opium taken out of the warehouse and refined into heroin. The officer said that this was wrong, and insisted that the heroin must have been refined years ago.

These statements could have been dismissed as uninformed jabber—if they had come from some low-ranking, local Burmese army officer somewhere in a remote border area. But the officer in question was Colonel Kyaw Thein, head of Burma's Committee for Drug Abuse Control, the country's leading drug enforcement agency and the main contact man for the United Nations' drug control program and international police agencies. Kyaw Thein was accompanied by Lieutenant-General Khin Nyunt, the head of Burma's military intelligence apparatus, and Lieutenant-Colonel Hla Min, the SPDC's main spokesman, and he was only conveying the official version of the situation. Khin Nyunt himself went on to praise 'development efforts' in the former CPB area, and to hit out at 'neo-colonialist countries' for failing to support them and 'levelling false accusations'.[130]

When Khin Nyunt had personally negotiated the ceasefires with the rebels, he had issued their leaders with special ID cards, which made them—and their vehicles—immune from police and customs searches at all checkpoints in Shan state. It is clear that the drug lords in the northeast are enjoying protection from the highest level of Burma's military establishment, and not just from some corrupt local commander. This became even more evident when Kyaw Thein was asked about Wei Hsueh-kang, or Wei Xuegang in Pinyin, a UWSA leader who has been indicted by the United States for drug trafficking. The reply was that Wei was 'not under government control'. Wei is, of course, one of the Wei brothers who had ironically worked for the CIA at the Vingngün base in the early 1960s. As the celebrations were taking place, Wei was busy building up a 'legitimate' business empire in the northern Burmese city of Mandalay. Over the past two years, Wei has invested millions of dollars in the lumber business, mineral smelting, pig farming and the retail trade through what one western drug-enforcement official called 'the biggest money-laundering operation in Southeast Asia today'.[131]

The close cooperation between Burma's drug lords and the SLORC/SPDC has led many to speculate that the government may be more closely involved in the trade than just providing protection for the drug lords and their various businesses. Suggestions were made that drug money had been used to finance the massive buildup of Burma's armed forces that has taken place since the upheavals of 1988. In the late 1980s, the three services of Burma's armed forces totalled 185 000–195 000 men. According to Maung Aung Myoe, a Burmese army researcher, the size of the armed forces has now reached 450 000.[132] Vast quantities of military hardware have also been bought, mainly from China. Where did the money come from? Judging from official statistics issued in Rangoon, there was no source of foreign hard currency listed that could have financed arms purchases totalling more than a billion US dollars.[133]

Burma had no external enemy to justify a buildup of its armed forces of that magnitude—but the 1988 uprising shook its military leadership out of its complacency. Something had to be done about the economy—why not free-market reforms to attract foreign capital and raise the living standard at home so the people would not rebel again and to finance this massive expansion of the army to perpetuate military rule over the country? According to persistent reports from Burma's Shan state, systematic taxation of opium growers and heroin producers exists on the local level. The government usually collects 10 per cent in cash or in kind of any drugs produced in a certain area, but it is uncertain whether this goes to the central coffers in Rangoon, or the money is used to finance local government activities in areas which hardly receive any support or subsidies from the central administration. What can be said with certainty, though, is that the drug trade, and the arrangement between the drug lords and the central government, are important for Burma in three respects.

The first is purely political. The ceasefire agreements of 1989 helped save the government when it was under pressure from both urban dissidents and ethnic insurgents. This is also why it would be extremely difficult for the government to move against the drug trade, even if it intended to do so: any serious attempts to curtail the involvement of the Was, the Kokang army or Lin Mingxian's group could lead to a renewed civil war. The Wa army, for instance, consists of nearly 20 000 men, heavily armed with machine-guns, mortars and recoilless rifles.

The second aspect is personal. Hardly surprisingly, the ceasefire agreements have created new bonds of friendship between the drug traffickers and the Burmese military—and even the highest-ranking officers in the Burmese army and military intelligence have official salaries of no more than $10–15 per month. While those officers do not live lavishly by Southeast Asian standards, it is clear that all of them must have some additional source of income. Lin Mingxian, especially, is reported to have given generous contributions to high-ranking officers in Burma's military intelligence. In exchange, he enjoys protection from the government, which has enabled him to invest heavily in legitimate businesses.

Third, the booming drug trade, now coupled with Asia's financial crisis, has made the overall Burmese economy heavily dependent on income derived from narcotics. As early as 1989, the year of the first ceasefires, the then SLORC decided to no longer confiscate bank deposits and foreign currency earnings of dubious origin. It instead opted for a 'whitening tax' on questionable repatriated funds, levied first at 40 per cent and since reduced to 25 per cent. Equally significantly, in early 1993, *de facto* legalisation of the black market exchange rate (300–350 Kyats per US dollar, as opposed to the official rate of $6 Kyats to the dollar) took place and narco-funds previously held in Bangkok, Singapore and Hong Kong flooded back into Burma.[134]

In June 1996, the US Embassy in Rangoon released a detailed account of Burma's black economy in its yearly Foreign Economic Trends Report. It highlights statistical discrepancies, or what economists call 'errors and omissions', in the country's balance of payments. By comparing Rangoon's official trade figures with statistics from a variety of sources—including the United Nations Conference on Trade and Development, the International Monetary Fund, the Australian National University and the Centre Français du Commerce Exterieur in Paris—the author of the report discovered $400 million in unexplained foreign financial inflows during 1995–96, up from $79 million the previous year. The economist explains that this is basically money which came into the legal economy, and which was not recorded by any of Burma's trade partners in official export–import statistics: in short, it came from smuggling. In addition, Burma spends $200 million annually on foreign-currency denominated defence expenditure, which is not recorded in official reports. This, the economist argues, has to be added to the total amount of money in circulation which cannot be explained in terms of official trade. Thus the actual figure for money that could not be accounted for in fiscal 1995–96 was $600 million.

But why must hundreds of millions in proceeds from smuggling necessarily be drug money? The answer is that the only two other items which Burma produces and which could generate large sums of foreign exchange—jade and precious stones—are no longer smuggled to neighbouring countries in large quantities. The jade trade was previously in the hands of·ethnic Kachin rebels who controlled the mines around Hpakan in Kachin state, from where the jade was smuggled to Yunnan, or down to Thailand. But in 1993–94, the government took over the jade mines, and the trade now goes through official channels via Rangoon. The same applies to the gemstone mines in the northeast: mining rights in the region are subcontracted to private entrepreneurs by the military-controlled Union of Myanmar Economic Holdings, which collects duties on the trade.

A number of other companies also benefited, directly or indirectly, from the new arrangements. In 1992, Lo Hsing-han and his family set up the Asia World Company, which a diplomatic report from Rangoon describes as 'Burma's fastest growing and most diversified conglomerate'. It is involved in the import–export business, bus transport, housing and hotel construction, a supermarket chain, Rangoon's port development and the upgrading of a national highway between Mandalay and Muse on the Chinese border. Its Memorandum of Association under the *Myanmar Companies Act* identifies Lo Hsing-han and his son Htun Myint Naing (Steven Law) as major shareholders. Other shareholders include known drug traffickers from Kokang. In 1996, Steven Law was refused a visa to the United States on suspicion of involvement in narcotics trafficking.

Other companies with known drug connections include the Myanmar May Flower Group. Its ethnic Chinese chairman, Kyaw Win, has emerged as Burma's new high-profile entrepreneur. A Rangoon business magazine names his 'old benefactor', an 'immensely wealthy Thai entrepreneur'[135] who is listed in internal documents from the US Drug Enforcement Agency as a major drug trafficker. Kyaw Win has also, from his old base at Tachilek on the Thai–Burma border, done business with Khun Sa and Lieutenant-General Maung Aye, vice chairman of the ruling junta. In 1990, Kyaw

Win moved to Rangoon and established the May Flower Trading Company, and in 1994, the May Flower Bank. In 1997 the May Flower Group took over Yangon Airways, one of Burma's two private domestic airlines.

Another company, the Peace Myanmar Group, is a rapidly expanding business empire controlled by the Yang brothers from Kokang. Both Yang Maoliang and Yang Maoan are listed in the US State Department's reports as major drug traffickers; their younger brother Yang Maoxian was arrested in China on drug trafficking charges in 1994 and executed in Kunming. The Peace Myanmar Group holds the franchise for Mitsubishi Electric in Burma, and operates a paint factory and liquor distillery producing well-known brands such as Myanmar Rum and Myanmar Dry Gin. It has a large consumer electronics showroom on Merchant Street in Rangoon in a joint venture with the Ministry of Commerce.

The World Group of companies is owned by Wa interests and has investments in construction, retail trading, import–export and the tourist industry. Another Wa-controlled company, Myanmar Kyone Yeom (Group)—which once ran a finance company that foreign analysts described as 'a thinly disguised money-laundering vehicle'—fell out with the government in 1998, and its chairman, Kyaw Myint (aka Michael Hu Hwa, a 'colonel' in the UWSA), escaped to Thailand. He is now back in business in Rangoon.

The Good Shan Brothers International Ltd is a company controlled by surrendered drug lord Khun Sa and his family. In February 1996, a month after Khun Sa's surrender, ten new companies were registered at an obscure address in Rangoon, a virtually empty room in a townhouse with little more than a sign and a mailbox outside. The registered owner of the premises is this company, which is engaged in 'export, import, general trading and construction', according to the official *Myanmar Business Directory*. In two surprisingly candid interviews with a correspondent from the Austrian daily *Die Presse*, Khun Sa stated that he was investing in real estate, the hotel business in Rangoon and a new motorway from Rangoon to Mandalay.[136]

The Union of Myanmar Economic Holdings (UMEH), Burma's biggest holding company, is 40 per cent owned by the Defence Ministry's Directorate of Defence Procurement, with the rest belonging mainly to senior military personnel and their families. Known locally as the 'U-paing Company', it is involved in the gems trade, banking (the Myawaddy Bank), logging, timber processing and coal mining, and is the joint-venture partner in several projects involving foreign investment. Officially, its capital comes from the Burmese army's pension funds, but drug lords such as Lin Mingxian have invested heavily in this company, often in partnership with high-ranking army officers.

While all those companies are flourishing, foreign investment is drying up. During a visit to Japan in June 1999, Burmese foreign minister Win Aung said that Southeast Asia's currency crisis was responsible for a 53 per cent drop in foreign direct investment commitments in the fiscal year which ended in March 1998. Since then, even more foreign businesses have pulled out, or failed to fulfil their commitments. Apart from the oil industry, where the major investors are US and French firms, nearly all other foreign investment in Burma comes from Singapore, Malaysia, Thailand and South Korea.

The clearest indication of the importance of drug money in the overall economy is the value of the Burmese currency. The free-market rate fell dramatically in 1997, down to less than 300 to the dollar from 160 the year before. But since then, it has been stable at 320–340 Kyats to the dollar—despite the huge trade imbalance and the departure of most foreign investors. By comparison, Laos, a country in a very similar situation, has seen its currency, the Kip, nose-dive to 7500 to the dollar in March 2000 (from 1350 in September 1997). Evidently Burma still has a large hard-currency reserve which props up its currency, and that reserve can only consist of drug money. The dramatic increase in drug exports from Burma over the past decade—heroin and now also methamphetamines—lends credence to this suggestion. Burma has become Asia's first and only state which survives on the export of narcotics.

The extent to which the Chinese authorities had a hand in the 1989 CPB mutiny and subsequent events along the Sino-Burmese frontier is uncertain. But it is clear that China, as early as in the mid-1980s, began to have plans for Burma other than support for the CPB's increasingly anachronistic struggle for revolutionary change. In an article in the official *Beijing Review* on 2 September 1985, Pan Qi, a former vice minister of communications, outlined the possibilities of finding an outlet from China's inland provinces of Yunnan and

Sichuan down to the Indian Ocean. He emphasised that it would be easier for those provinces to export their goods through Burma than the much longer route to China's own ports, which in any case were clogged with goods from the booming coastal provinces. Pan mentioned the Burmese railheads of Myitkyina and Lashio as possible conduits for goods from China's southwest—but he conveniently refrained from mentioning that all relevant border areas, at that time, were not under central Burmese government control.[137] However, Pan argued that, in order for the Chinese inland to develop at the same speed as the coastal provinces, such an outlet was essential.

Then, on 6 August 1988—when mass demonstrations shook Rangoon almost daily and only two days before a general strike crippled the entire country—China and Burma signed an agreement, allowing official cross-border trade to take place between the two countries. The timing could not have been more unfortunate; the rest of the world was watching what they thought were the last days of the old regime. Almost the entire 2171-kilometre Sino-Burmese frontier was in any case controlled by the CPB and other rebel forces. But then, in the following year, came the CPB mutiny—and the border trade took off. Cheap consumer goods from China flooded the Burmese market, and the other way went timber, precious stones and drugs. From 1988 to 1994, cross-border trade between Yunnan and Burma swelled from $15 million annually to around $800 million.[138]

With the border trade booming, ties between Burma and China were strengthening gradually. By 1990, Burma had also become China's principal political and military ally in Southeast Asia. Chinese arms poured across the border into Burma to help the extremely unpopular military regime in Rangoon survive. China also soon became involved with upgrading Burma's badly maintained roads and railways. By the mid-1990s, Chinese experts were working on a series of infrastructural projects in Burma. Chinese military advisers arrived in 1991, the first foreign military personnel to be stationed in Burma since the 1950s. Burma was, in effect, becoming a Chinese client state; what the CPB failed to achieve for the Chinese on the battlefield has been accomplished by shrewd diplomacy and flourishing border trade. And with the trade came the migrants—and the new concept of the Great Golden Peninsula, which first appeared in Chinese newspaper and magazine commentaries in 1994. They referred to a vast region stretching from Yunnan to Singapore in the south and India and Vietnam in the west and east. Commonly cited in such analyses are three main 'routes' along which Chinese commerce could penetrate the region: one through Burma, the others through Vietnam and Laos.[139]

Burma has been the most successful of these three 'routes'—and it should also have been the most controversial. China's links with the Rangoon government have caused consternation in many international human rights circles. But its links with the drug-trafficking armies of the former CPB are even more stunning. Despite several ostensibly determined anti-drug campaigns in China—where drugs spilling over the border from Burma have become a major problem— the UWSA buys most of its weapons, including surface-to-air missiles, from China, and Chinese engineers have been observed helping the drug armies build a network of new roads from the mountains along the Yunnan frontier down to Thailand.[140] China's strategic interests in the region are evidently more important than preventing its own youth from being destroyed by narcotics.

A central figure in this new drug empire along the Sino-Burmese border is Lin Mingxian. Under his stewardship, his headquarters at Möng La have been transformed into an even bigger boom town than Homöng ever was. It now receives busloads of Chinese tourists every day. One of the main attractions is the Royal Myanmar Casino, where scantily clad Russian and Ukrainan female dancers entertain the visitors. Lin has also brought in Chinese strip shows and a special domed venue has been built for the Tiffany's transvestite cabaret imported from Thailand. At the 'Möng La Cultural Show', Padaung (or Kayan in their own language) women, who elongate their necks with brass rings, perform traditional dances for the Chinese tourists. The Kayan are not native to that part of Burma, and the show amounts to a virtual human zoo.[141]

Möng La has also become a centre for human trafficking to the West. One illegal Fujianese, who was interviewed in the United States in 1993, recounted the difficulties of leaving China. After having made a down-payment to agents of a well-organised syndicate in Fujian, they set off:

> There were about seventeen of us, all male. The youngest was about eighteen, the oldest in his mid-forties. There were smugglers taking us

from town to town. After we had reached Kunming in Yunnan, we waited for about a month for a person to take us across the China–Burma border. We were all afraid of being arrested by Chinese border patrols. We were lucky: we all went through without any problem. After we crossed the border, we walked through the Golden Triangle to northern Thailand. A tribal soldier carrying a rifle guided us through mountains and forests. We travelled at night and slept during the day. It was raining most of the time and we could do nothing but lie on the dirty wet ground to try to sleep. We ate twice a day, mostly dried food. We saw some corpses along the way and believed that these people, like us, had tried to go to Thailand.[142]

Lin has assigned one of his most experienced officers, a former CPB commander called Bo Tin Win, to organise the escort of these people to Thailand. The fee is 10 000 Chinese Yuan per head. Lin and his gang may not be the main players in the trade in humans, but they are a link in the long chain from the villages of Fujian to the Chinese restaurants and factories in New York and San Francisco, where most of these illegal immigrants end up. And Lin no doubt has made several million dollars from this business. In more recent years, people fleeing the Three Gorges Dam project and the 1998 floods in the Yangtze River Basin have also sought refuge in Lin's area, where they have been given special ID cards, which Lin—in accordance with the ceasefire agreement with the government in Rangoon—is authorised to issue.[143]

It's not a bad career for someone who in his youth was a Red Guard. And his connections are not confined to military officers in Rangoon. The United Nations International Drug Control Programme (UNDCP) maintains a presence in his area, and has also praised his efforts to eradicate drugs. 'Anti-drug plan on track in Wa' read the headline in the *Myanmar Times & Business Review*, an English-language Burmese weekly, in February 2000. It quoted UNDCP officials as saying that 'the drug eradication project was running smoothly and according to schedule'.[144] Another high-ranking UNDCP official, Sandro Calvani, stated at a meeting in Bangkok in January 2001 that Burma's ruling junta 'is serious about fighting drugs, and its commitment is showing good results in controlling opium and amphetamine production'.[145]

More level-headed observers are more interested in a fundamental difference in the organisation of the various ex-CPB drug armies. In the Wa hills and in Kokang, trade is free and there are many private drug traffickers and dealers, while in the Möng La area the business in monopolised by a tightly knit committee of thirteen former CPB commanders headed by Lin and including Zhang Zhiming. Another former Red Guard, Zhang is reportedly still close to China's security service and, like Lin, enjoys an excellent relationship with local Chinese police, army and intelligence officers. Lin and Zhang's group has issued an order banning the export of narcotics to China, where drugs spilling over from Burma have become a major social problem. Private traders who have tried to use the China route have even been arrested by Lin.[146]

With trade to China closed for obvious political reasons, Lin and his group began sending large quantities of heroin down to the Thai border in 1989–90. But something apparently went wrong in May 1991 when Thai police seized 550 kilograms of pure heroin from a fishing boat off the coast of Chanthaburi. It was the biggest drug haul in Thailand for years, and the heroin could be traced back to Lin's former CPB forces in the mountains north of Kengtung. Immediately after the seizure, Lin rushed down to Tachilek on the Thai border opposite Mae Sai. But he returned empty-handed. He had been double-crossed somewhere along the line.

It was after this incident that Lin began turning his attention to Laos—just to the east of his base area, which stretches all the way to the Mekong River, the border between Burma and Laos. The first documented case of Burmese heroin arriving there occurred in August 1991, when Laotian security forces, pursuing a group of unidentified rebels who had crossed the border from Burma, captured two of them and seized 15 kilograms of heroin. After this abortive attempt to open a route through Laos, Lin and his group may have decided to approach elements within the Laotian military instead. Some time in 1992 he reportedly made an agreement with the army-run Mountainous Areas Development Corporation, a corrupt outfit that was set up to make the Laotian armed forces self-sufficient. According to several reports from the now defunct but once Paris-based *Observatoire Géopolitique des Drogues*, the drugs could then be transported down to southern Laos and across the border into Cambodia, where military helicopters would fly the goods to Phnom Penh's military airport. Cambodia, it seems, comes next to Burma as an established narco-state.

But drugs still pour across the border to China, and according to reports from both the Australian Federal Police and the police in Hong Kong, links have been established between the UWSA and Triads based in the former British colony. In late 2000, Australian police led a raid that intercepted 79 kilograms of methamphetamines on a ship from China, while the Hong Kong police captured 184 kilograms of Burmese-made heroin as smugglers tried to bring the consignment in from China. In November 2000, 357 kilograms of Burmese heroin was intercepted in Fiji, suggesting a completely new route from the Golden Triangle to countries around the Pacific Rim.[147]

But it was Australia—the Golden Triangle's closest western-style market, where profits were higher—which would pay the dearest price, not just for the complex opium politics of Burma, but also for the unending turmoil in Cambodia and the endemic corruption in China.

• 6
THE PIRATE REPUBLIC

[In] the old days . . . there used to be robbers, thieves, burglars, that sort of thing, pickpockets in the market, and so on. And for the most part they were just making a living, satisfying basic needs . . . But criminals nowadays, it's certainly not just about livelihood. Instead, it's to throw around lots of money, to show off, getting drunk, gambling. It's clear that this kind of thing's increased. What's even more serious is that this criminal activity is very often tied, either directly or indirectly, to the *aparat* (officialdom), whether it's the military or the police.

—A Javanese lawyer, 1996[1]

When one of Suharto's student followers approached the enormously influential Sultan Hamengkubuwono of Yogyakarta in early 1966 and asked if he would back the general, the Sultan reportedly laughed and asked 'if he was still in the habit of stealing'.

—Michael Vatikiotis, 1994[2]

Ussulau de Jesus Cepeda cast the first vote of his turbulent young life from a stretcher—his chest swaddled in bandages, a drip dangling from his arm. The East Timorese student arrived at the polling station in an ambulance driven by a Catholic nun. A huge crowd, which had begun to form well before sunrise outside the polling station—actually a dilapidated schoolhouse in a suburb of the East Timorese capital of Dili—parted respectfully to let his stretcher through. It was 30 August 1999 and Ussulau was about to vote in the referendum on East Timor's future which would plunge the territory into violence and chaos.

Ussulau de Jesus Cepeda was one of several East Timorese students who had been shot when Indonesian soldiers opened fire on pro-independence demonstrators only a few days before. 'I want freedom. It's now or never,' he whispered to a western journalist as the nun and another sister carried him into the old school house.[3] Many people in the crowd were visibly moved. Some had tears in their eyes as they clenched their fists to salute the wounded student.

In some ways, Ussulau was lucky. He had a couple of gunshot wounds to his chest. Dozens of other independence supporters had been hacked with rusty machetes by 'pro-integration militias', East Timorese who supposedly wanted to remain with Indonesia. These militiamen were, it was said at the time, supported by 'rogue elements' within the Indonesian military who did not want to see East Timor break away, contrary to the government's pledge to honour the outcome of the referendum, no matter what it would be. So, of course, it was not government policy to support these hoodlums. The United Nations (UN), which was there to supervise the referendum, even had the full backing of the Indonesian authorities when meetings were held between 'the two sides' to facilitate a badly needed 'national reconciliation'.

But then all hell broke loose. An overwhelming majority—nearly 80 per cent—of the East Timorese opted for independence, and the militias went on a rampage. They killed, raped and burned down Dili and almost every other town in the impoverished territory. Heads of pro-independence supporters and ordinary civilians were stuck on bamboo stakes along the roads. Rape and torture before death was commonplace, and the only East Timorese who were safe from the systematic slaughter were those who were evacuated at gunpoint to an uncertain fate in closely guarded camps in West Timor. Hundreds of others were herded on to boats, ostensibly also to be taken to 'camps elsewhere'. But within hours the boats returned—empty, save for the crew and the Indonesian soldiers onboard.[4] Town after town was systematically burnt, shops were plundered and livestock killed. Not a single community in the entire territory was left unscathed; even the UN compound in Dili was attacked by 'militias' as Indonesian soldiers and policemen conveniently looked the other way. An estimated 70 per cent of all buildings in East Timor were destroyed along with most of the infrastructure, electricity, water supply and telecommunications.[5]

The carnage continued until 20 September, when the Indonesian authorities, under severe international pressure, were forced to admit an Australian-led and UN-approved international force into the territory to put an end to the killing. No one really knows how many people were killed in the aftermath of East Timor's referendum. Bodies are still being discovered, often in mass graves, and many more are believed to have been dumped in the shark-infested waters around the island.

According to some reports, as many as 80 000 people have still not been accounted for, apart from more than 100 000 people who remain in camps in West Timor. The Indonesian authorities are as unlikely to help shed light on what happened in East Timor in those three bloody weeks in 1999 as they have been to let the world know what actually went on during Indonesia's 24-year occupation of the former Portuguese colony. Ahead of the landing of the first International Forces to East Timor (INTERFET), Dili's 'high-walled intelligence and interrogation centres were emptied and documents hastily dumped on to bonfires . . . Two decades of evidence went up in flames'.[6]

But those bonfires could not destroy numerous eyewitness accounts asserting that the 'rogue elements' within the Indonesian military who cooperated with the 'local pro-integration militias' were none other than the top echelons of the Indonesian armed forces. And the so-called militias have turned out to be little more than juvenile delinquents, petty gangsters and assorted hoodlums who had been hired by the high command of the Indonesian military for tasks which were just too unsavoury to be carried out by its regular forces.

The idea for a referendum in East Timor had been developed in early 1999 between President B.J. Habibie, Suharto's successor, and his British-educated adviser, Dewi Fortuna Anwar. Indonesia was in dire straits after the economic crash in 1997, which led to the downfall of the Suharto regime the following year, and the country needed all the international goodwill it could get. Indonesia would shake the United Nations and the international community off its back if it took the grandiose gesture of letting the East Timorese decide their own future. And the East Timorese would in any case surely not opt for independence—not after all that Indonesia had done to develop the territory since snatching it from the Portuguese in 1975. But the armed forces, who had direct experience of East Timor and knew the sentiments of the local population, were not so sure. Two days after Habibie's surprise announcement, a 'Crisis Team on East Timor, was formed to wage a covert war against pro-independence groups. Headed by Major-General Zacky Anwar Makarim, a former head of military intelligence, the Crisis Team set up a series of 'militias' comprising around 6000 paid and press-ganged East and West Timorese divided into thirteen different, mostly local, groups.[7] Key officers in Jakarta included the armed forces commander and defence minister,

General Wiranto; his chief of staff, General Subagyo Hadisiswoyo; former East Timor commander Major-General Kiki Syahnakri; Major-General Muchdi Purwopranjono, commander of the special forces, Kopassus; intelligence chief Major-General Tiasno Sudarno; and the national police chief, General Ruhsmanhadi.[8]

Some of the top leaders of the 'militas', who loved Indonesia so much that they would kill, torture and maim their own countrymen to convince them that independence was not an option, were sub-district chiefs and East Timorese who had served with the Indonesian armed forces. The self-proclaimed head of all the militia groups, João Tavares, had actually sided with the Indonesians as early as 1975 and, as a reward for his loyalty, had been appointed to serve as chief of Bobonaro, a mountainous ,district bordering West Timor, from 1976–86. He owned houses in East and West Timor as well as an apartment in Jakarta, and one of his sons became an Indonesian diplomat while another, nicknamed 'the King', served as chief of Balibo, the small hilltop town where five foreign newsmen from Australia, New Zealand and Britain had been killed by the Indonesian army almost two months before the actual invasion of East Timor in December 1975.[9] Tavares and his family ran western East Timor as their own private fiefdom, and he liked to boast that, when he was district chief, 'the roads were good and the people were happy'.[10]

His thousands of foot-soldiers had been mostly village youths who had been forced to join the militias in the months following Habibie's announcement. They were kept in check with harsh methods, and those who resisted orders given by their commanders were beaten or punished in other ways. A popular method was to tip an 'offender' upside down in an oil drum full of water from which he had to extricate himself. Their training included weapons drills, marching and physical exercise—and how to deal with the 'foreigners' who had descended on the territory to supervise the referendum. The militias were given colourful names like the *Besi Merah Putih* ('Red and White Steel', after the colours of the Indonesian flag), which took part in a gruesome massacre of more than 60 independence supporters sheltering in a church in the town of Liquica in April 1999; the *Armui Merah Putih* ('I'm Ready to Die for Integration'), led by José Amaral Leite, a long-time protégé of Tavares' son Panglima; and the dreaded *Aitarak* ('Thorn'), a vicious gang that conducted a reign of terror in Dili itself.

The middle-level cadre, who acted as intermediaries between the old leaders and the foot-soldiers, were often real gangsters who were issued with motorcycles and walkie-talkies—and a licence to arrest, torture and kill. Eurico Guterres, the *Aitarak* commander, soon emerged as the best-known of those mid-level leaders. With his long, wavy hair and dark sunglasses, he looked like an extra in a cheap rock 'n'roll movie, but he and his band of thugs were some of the most callously brutal in the territory. They took over the Tropical Hotel, a run-down building in Dili, and turned it into a military-style headquarters, complete with cells and a torture chamber.[11] Around the building, at all times, young men dressed in black t-shirts with *Aitarak* written in white on the back, kept guard. Indonesian army vehicles were also often seen parked outside the Tropical as officers and intelligence agents came to order Guterres to send out his men to attack Indonesia's 'enemies'. On 17 April, *Aitarak* thugs armed with machetes, spears and bows and arrows killed and wounded as many as 30 people in the home of pro-independence leader Manuel Carrascalão. Among the dead was his seventeen-year-old son, Manuelito.[12]

Direct Indonesian involvement with the so-called 'pro-integration militias' was supposed to be a secret. But, a few months after the raid on Carrascalão's home, the cover was inadvertently blown. Guterres had been given a large sum of cash to pay the members of his militia, but instead he tried to deposit it into his own private bank account. The bank handed the money back, saying it was counterfeit. Guterres turned to his paymaster, the Indonesian army, and complained. He was told that the bank notes were to have been given to his men, who would not have known the difference. The money was not supposed to contribute to his personal fortune.[13]

This unusual patriot was born in 1974, a year before the Indonesian invasion, and he became famous for his flaming, anti-independence rhetoric during the campaign in 1999. But Guterres is, in the words of East Timorese leader José Ramos Horta, actually 'a very tragic individual'.[14] His father was killed in front of his eyes by Indonesian troops when he was four years old. That could have been the reason why, in his teens, he joined the independence underground. He is also said to have been part of the crowd demonstrating at the Santa Cruz cemetery in November 1991, when Indonesian troops opened fire and killed scores of mourners. Guterres, then only seventeen, was picked up by the police, thrown in gaol and severely bashed and tortured. He emerged from the ordeal as a fervent supporter of the integration of East Timor within Indonesia. To thank him for his turn-around, the security agencies put him in charge of a youth gang that ran gambling and protection rackets in Dili's central market. Drugs may also have been part of the deal, but not prostitution—an activity that was never widespread in staunchly Catholic East Timor. And, in return for all these favours, he and his men acted as informants for the security services. Thus Guterres was a natural choice when the Indonesian military authorities needed a henchman to counter the pro-independence forces in 1999. His relationship with the security services was solid and well entrenched, and there was no risk that he was going to defect back to his old comrades on the other side, who despised him as a turn-coat and a traitor.

On 26 August, four days before the referendum, Guterres addressed a crowd of 15 000 people in Dili and stated that East Timor would 'become a sea of fire' if independence was declared.[15] True to his word, he led the rampage in Dili, supported by the Indonesian military, and was only forced to leave the territory when INTERFET arrived on the scene. From his new base in Kupang, West Timor, Guterres joined forces with other fugitive militia leaders to form a new organisation called UNTAS, which is not a UN agency but the acronym in Tetum (the most widely spoken dialect in East as well as West Timor) for 'the United Timorese Knights'. Some time later, he was also appointed chief of the *Banteng Pemuda*, the paramilitary youth wing of the Indonesian Democratic Party-Struggle (PDI-P) of then vice president—and since July 2001 the country's president—Megawati Sukarnoputri.[16] Under international pressure, the Indonesian authorities arrested Guterres in October 2000, and he was brought to trial in May 2001. But his sentence was the lightest possible: a six-month gaol term, which was suspended with immediate effect. His cozy relationship with the authorities remained unaltered and Amien Rais, chairman of Indonesia's highest constitutional body, the People's Consultative Assembly, stated publicly: 'He's our friend. He's the leader of the pro-integration militia, and he has lost his homeland. If he's arrested for the sake of the UN, then what a nasty country that makes us'.[17]

Others would argue that what really makes Indonesia 'a nasty country' is its frequent use of hoodlums for political ends. Long before Guterres rose to fame in Indonesia and infamy in the rest of the world, another young East Timorese had performed similar duties for the security services. His name, or nickname, was Hercules and he is reputed to have saved the life of Suharto's son-in-law, (then) Lieutenant Colonel Prabowo Subianto, when he served in East Timor in the late 1980s and early 1990s. To show his gratitude—and realising that young Hercules could be useful for a number of different purposes—Prabowo brought him and some of his followers to Jakarta. They were promised jobs by Suharto's eldest daughter, the immensely wealthy Hardiyanti 'Tutut' Rukmana, but then left to fend for themselves. This was not unusual, and perhaps even intentional. The Yayasan Tiara, a foundation controlled by Tutut, was known for recruiting and then abandoning East Timorese youths, in some cases forcing them to first undergo military training at the Kopassus-run complex in Cijantung, West Java.[18] In that way, they were recruited into 'the system', but the state did not have to spend any money on them. Hercules, a diminutive but vicious-looking street thug, assumed control of Tanah Abang in Jakarta, the largest textile market in Southeast Asia, where he and his boys ran protection and extortion rackets. Hercules and his gang also led attacks on other East Timorese whenever they approached western embassies in Jakarta to seek asylum. They even tried to 'outbid' the staunchly nationalistic paramilitary youth organisation Pemuda Pancasila when it came to mobilising support for East Timorese integration and other activities in favour of the government and the military. Like Hercules' gang, the Pemuda Pancasila was also widely reported to be involved in extortion, debt collecting and providing security at bars. In exchange for its 'concrete support' of the government, Pemuda Pancasila expected 'concrete concessions' such as control of the revenues generated in the 'informal economy'—or, in other words, a regulated symbiotic relationship between itself and the authorities.[19] This was not unlike the situation elsewhere in Asia but, in the case of Indonesia, that relationship became institutionalised in a way that was unusual even for this part of the world.

The Pemuda Pancasila was originally formed in the late 1950s by General A.H. Nasution and other right-wing military commanders as a militant, mass-based youth organisation to counter the growing communist movement.[20] *Pemuda* means 'youth' and *pancasila* was the state ideology until the collapse of the Suharto regime in 1998. Originally spelled out by his predecessor, Indonesia's founding father Sukarno, in 1945, *pancasila*—or the 'five principles'—encompassed a fuzzy belief in one supreme God; justice and civility among peoples; the unity of Indonesia; democracy through deliberation and consensus among representatives; and social justice for all.[21] The original Pemuda Pancasila was a subordinate wing of Nasution's own party, Ikatan Pendukung Kemerdekaan Indonesia, the IPKI, or the League of the Supporters of Indonesian Independence, which was especially powerful in Medan in northern Sumatra. A boxer from that town called Effendi Nasution, known as Effendi Keling and 'the Lion of Sumatra', became its first chairman. He already had his own gang that employed street thugs in extortion and private security as night guards, primarily for rich ethnic Chinese businessmen in Medan. He also controlled the black market sale of cinema tickets at the Medan Theatre, which was located across the street from the local IPKI office. Assorted vagrants and unemployed youths were recruited into Effendi's new, powerfully backed organisation, and they demonstrated their usefulness when a group of right-wing generals, including Suharto, seized power in October 1965, ostensibly to pre-empt a communist takeover. The whole of Indonesia was turned into a slaughter house as hundreds of thousands of real or imagined communist sympathisers were hunted down and shot—or more often hacked to death. The Pemuda Pancasila was particularly active in butchering suspected communists in Aceh and Medan in north Sumatra, while the Islamic organisation Nadhlatul Ulama did its job in Java and adherents of the Partai Nasionali Indonesia (PNI), or the Indonesian Nationalist Party, carried out most of the killings in Bali.[22] Pemuda Pancasila militants in the capital Jakarta seemed more interested in looting the homes of suspected communists than in killing them, but the groundwork was laid for a bigger role for the new organisation as General Suharto emerged as the undisputed leader in the wake of the orgy of mass murder that swept Indonesia for several months.

The 1970s is usually described as a quiet period for the Pemuda Pancasila, but US researcher Loren Ryter has discovered that it was a time of consolidation as the group deliberately recruited a majority of the street thugs and juvenile delinquents in Medan. They gained control over nearly all cinemas in the city and later expanded into entertainment complexes and gambling as sources of revenue.[23] The big breakthrough came in the early 1980s, when the police decided to crack down on disorganised crime in Jakarta. During the so-called *petrus* (acronym of *penembak* or 'shooting' and *misterius* or 'mysterious') campaign in 1982–83, thousands of corpses of tattooed wild street youths called *gali-gali* turned up in public places. Most of them were shot with silencers, which only the security forces were equipped with, and their bloodied bodies were left in the streets for everyone to see. Many of these *gali-gali* had actually been close to the police and the security services, and even campaigned for Golkar during elections. But Suharto felt that they had gone out of control: 'Stability had been shaken,' he said. He later boasted in his autobiography that the *petrus* killings were 'a necessary response to a persistent problem':

> Doesn't that demand action? Automatically we had to give it the *treatment* [in English], strong measures. And what sort of measures? Sure, with real firmness. But that firmness did not mean shooting, bang! bang! just like that. But those who resisted, sure, like it or not, had to be shot. Because they resisted, they were shot.[24]

With most of the petty criminals out of the way, the Pemuda Pancasila was now granted a 'national franchise' on the underworld. A new charismatic leader of the organisation had also emerged: Yapto Soerjosoemarno, a young Jakarta street fighter who was the son of a Dutch-Jewish mother and a Javanese army officer. He was also a distant relative of Suharto's wife, Ibu Tien, and his father, General Soerjosoemarno, was a personal friend of the president's family. His predecessor as Pemuda Pancasila leader—whom he had defeated at the organisation's congress in March 1981—later concluded that 'the Suhartos needed their own force'.[25] Yapto was soon credited with a prominent role in roughing up opponents of Suharto and his regime, as well as providing 'protection' for night clubs and illegal gambling dens. Smaller gangs were pushed aside or crushed—or absorbed into the new nationwide and officially recognised crime syndicate.

Dressed in their red and orange fatigues and wielding big machetes, the Pemuda Pancasila's militants became a familiar sight whenever there was political trouble in Indonesia. In July 1996, hired gangsters—now without their uniforms—invaded the headquarters of opposition leader Megawati Sukarnoputri, who had just been ousted as leader of the Indonesian Democratic Party, the PDI, in a coup orchestrated by the authorities. Nearly a year later, Seno Bella Eymus, a thug from an organisation related to the Pemuda Pancasila, actually filed a law suit against Soerjadi, who the government had installed as new chairman of the officially recognised PDI, accusing him of having promised them 200 million rupiah ($85 000 at the time) but only giving them 5.5 million rupiah ($2300) and a Toyota Kijang light truck. In return, they were to throw out Megawati's supporters from their new 'opposition' headquarters. The assault sparked massive rioting in Jakarta for the first time in years, but Bella's main concern was that he had not been paid properly. Since he had no money to pay his followers, they suspected him of having pocketed it for himself. He now wanted to prove that it was not the case. It was a question of honour.[26]

In another incident in the mid-1990s, when dissident parlamentarian Sri Bintang Pamungkas was brought to trial, youths gathered outside the courthouse shouting: 'We love our nation and our country!' and 'Hang Bintang!' Later, they were spotted in a nearby McDonalds hamburger restaurant receiving 10 000 rupiah notes from a uniformed officer.[27] Yapto and his boys were doing well. He claimed that he had 6 million followers, which may have been a gross exaggeration, but Suharto himself showed up to give the group his blessing at its sixth national congress in June 1996, which was held in a stadium seating tens of thousands in the centre of Jakarta.[28] By then, Yapto had also acquired a deputy to match his own colourful personality and past: Yorrys Raweyai, a half-Chinese, half-Papuan former crocodile hunter and Phillips Petroleum manager from Irian Jaya, the Indonesian western part of New Guinea. Yorrys was given the task of raising funds for the organisation because of his connections with the Chinese community and gambling-den operators. He also managed to strengthen the Pemuda Pancasila's grip over the capital's nightclubs when, in the mid-1990s, he served as head of the Jakarta Tourist Industry Association, which supervised various entertainment centres.[29] Yorrys was arrested on gambling charges twice, but never convicted. After all, he was a main leader of what had become the unofficial youth organisation of the ruling party of the Suharto regime, Golkar, and later even one of its members of parliament.[30] To shore up their political credibility, both Yapto and Yorrys published collections of essays on subjects such as truth, human resources and national awakening, complete with quotes from Socrates, John F. Kennedy and Francis Fukuyama.[31]

The Pemuda Pancasila that re-emerged under Yapto's and Yorrys' new dynamic leadership became a formidable political and criminal force, bound together by a code of conduct resembling that of most other underworld organisations in the Asia-Pacific. Group solidarity expressed itself in a strict chain of command, and every member had to pledge his or her loyalty to a set of regulations and by-laws which specified matters such as terms of office, formal organisational structure, the measurements and layout of branch sign posts and letter seals, and the kind of uniform that would be appropriate for a certain function or duty.[32] Sometimes they would also have to act out of uniform—for instance, when the group needed to gain control over the security at a night club that so far had refused to cooperate. The Pemuda Pancasila would first send in a group of obnoxious drunkards who would make their association with the group loud and clear. The owner would then complain to the Pemuda Pancasila leadership, which in turn would send in other members, who for a fee would make sure that this 'would be the last such incident'.[33] In between such activities, the Pemuda Pacasila made patriotic pledges and declarations of support for Golkar. The Pemuda Pancasila always asserted that it was the only youth organisation in the country brave enough to stand up for 'the youth of the informal sector', embracing them 'not for criminal purposes, but to raise their nationalist consciousness and return them to society'.[34]

Occasionally, some over-zealous police commander would arrest the thugs on gambling, assault and gun charges, and some of them were even gaoled from time to time. But the influence of the Pemuda Pancasila during the Suharto years also reached into Indonesia's prisons. According to Arswendo Atmowiloto, a critical Indonesian writer who was gaoled in the early 1990s on trumped-up charges of 'blasphemy': 'Want a decent cell? Want to go on a day leave? Want your girlfriend to visit? Only Pemuda Pancasila can fix it'.[35]

Indonesia's practice of using hoodlums to discipline unorganised crime and control political opponents is as old as the country itself, and in some respects it even predates the formation of the Indonesian republic in August 1945. Indonesia's own version of Japan's *yakuza* and the Chinese Triads, the so-called *preman*, have roamed the archipelago for hundreds of years. The word is derived from the Dutch *vrijman*, or 'free man', and was the lowest of the five broad categories into which the colonial power divided the population of Batavia, now Jakarta. The first, of course, comprised the white settlers. The second consisted of Asian immigrant workers, mainly Chinese, in the employ of the Vereenigde Oost-Indische Compagnie (VOC) or the [Dutch] East India Company. The third category were women and indentured labourers—practically slaves. The fourth were children of VOC workers and the fifth were 'other residents'. The last category also became known as *vrijman*, most of whom were former workers of the VOC who were permitted to remain in the capital but could not obtain legal employment. They were forced to eke out a living as best they could, technically in violation of colonial laws and practices. From the very beginning, the *preman* and the subculture of *premanism*, as it became known, were born of poverty and exclusion from the legal economy.[36]

Much later, *preman* came to mean borderline criminals and marginilised youths, who often bore the epithet with pride. A *preman*, they pointed out somewhat erroneously, was a freed plantation slave. Some even claimed it referred to youths who did not want to be bound by any dependencies, including a job or a contract.[37] These days, the term has come simply to mean criminals, but in a class of their own. They are not just petty thieves, purse snatchers and burglars, but have their own organisations and leaders who regularly cooperate with the security forces and authorities in expressly political matters.[38] The nature of premanism has best been expressed by Yapto himself:

> *Preman* means a free person, exactly *free-man*. I am one of these. A *preman* is a person who is free, not tied by any knot, free to determine his own life and death, as long as he fulfils the requirements and the laws of this country. But I am free to choose, to carry out the permitted or the not permitted, with all of its risks. For example, if you're a thief, you

take the risks of being a thief, meaning if you're caught, you're finished. If you aren't caught, you're no thief right? Legally that's the way it is; we hold to the principle of the presumption of innocence.[39]

In modern Indonesian history, the usefulness of the *preman* was recognised long before Yapto and Yorrys, or even Effendi, rose to prominence. The Dutch used Eurasian gangsters to control other gangsters, but the indigenous thugs had their revenge when the Japanese invaded in March 1942. Dutch- and Chinese-owned shops and homes were raided before the new Japanese masters decided that they had to restore 'law and order'. This was done partly by setting up a variety of neighbourhood associations modelled on similar organisations in Japan. Each such organisation consisted of ten to twenty households and was supposed to take care of everything from carrying out the policies of the occupying power to distributing goods in their respective neighbourhoods and arranging funerals. Anti-Dutch nationalists such as Sukarno, later the founder of modern Indonesia, were put in charge of some of these groups while others came under the control of the local underworld. Thus the nationalists and the gangsters worked hand in hand from the very beginning, and this special relationship was further strengthened in the chaos that prevailed during the so-called 'revolutionary period' after the war, from Sukarno's declaration of independence on 17 August 1945 until the Dutch finally gave up on 27 December 1949.

The Dutch had returned in September 1945 to reclaim their colony in the East Indies, and the nationalists—predictably—decided to resist. A number of 'people's armies' and 'militias' emerged, which were largely made up of petty criminals and labour bosses from the slums of Jakarta. Their relationship with the authorities, even under the Dutch, had always been ambiguous. According to Australian Indonesia scholar Robert Cribb:

> In some respects at least, the criminal underworld even enjoyed an almost symbiotic relationship with the forces of law and order. To the authorities it provided, of course, a multitude of bribes, kickbacks and other benefits in exchange for overlooking a wide variety of misdemeanours. It was also a source of information and intelligence which enabled the authorities to keep tabs on the level of crime in order to maintain it at an acceptable level.[40]

One of the most patriotic of the gang bosses was undoubtedly Haji Darip from Klender outside Jakarta. His father, too, had been a local boss in the area and was aptly named Gempur, which literally means 'pound' or 'attack'. As a young boy, Darip had been sent to Mecca to study, and he returned to Klender after three years as a religious authority who was believed to possess magical powers. In the immediate postwar era, Darip formed the Barisan Rakyat Indonesia, the Indonesian People's Brigade, which controlled the traffic on the main road west of Jakarta where he, according to Cribb, 'successfully blended brigandage with patriotism by plundering only those whose skin was too light (Chinese, Eurasians and Europeans) or too dark (Ambonese and Timorese). Those more fortunately coloured had only to pay two guilders in Japanese occupation currency and shout "Merdeka!" ("Freedom!") to be allowed past'.[41] The Cibarusa area southeast of Jakarta was controlled in a similar manner by an infamous local bandit leader, Pa' Macem, or 'Father Tiger'. He sold amulets which he asserted made the bearer immune to bullets, but otherwise ruled his turf by a mixture of plunder, terror and patriotic pledges.

In late 1945, many of these smaller gangs merged into the Lasykar Rakyat Jakarta Raya (LRJP), the People's Militia of Greater Jakarta. Among those who joined this new joint command organisation was Imam Syafe'i, the leader of a band of patriotic thugs from the Senen market area in Jakarta. When the Dutch cracked down on the movement, Imam Syafe'i rode out of the capital on a white horse at the head of his followers, promising to return and drive out the colonialists.[42]

But to succeed in their efforts, the Indonesian nationalists needed funds. The initial capital for the freedom struggle came from an unusual source: the sale of raw opium both at home and across the sea in Singapore. The Dutch colonial authorities before the war had imported large quantities of opium from Turkey, Persia and British Bengal which was sold in shops supervised by a government department, Opium Regie. Its main factory, where raw opium was processed before it was sent out to various local outlets, was located in Salemba, a Jakarta suburb, which of course the Dutch lost to the Japanese when they invaded the colony. The Japanese simply took over the factory and the distribution network, which survived the war intact. There were 22 tonnes of raw opium and 3 tonnes of newly processed drugs left in the Salemba factory when the Japanese surrendered in August 1945.[43] This fell into the hands of the indigenous revolutionaries. Some of it was sold, as it had been before the war, through government-licensed shops to addicts as well as pharmaceutical companies. This generated 6.83 per cent of state revenue in 1946, more than four times its proportion of taxes under the Dutch in 1938.

Domestic sales continued until 1947, when the revolutionary government—a parallel administration to the Dutch who were desperately trying to re-establish their rule—decided to sell the remaining opium abroad to earn foreign currency. Much of it was sent to Singapore, concealed in coffins and false-bottomed kerosene drums. The minister of finance, A.A. Maramis, took an active role in supervising the opium export, and recruited the services of a dashing young ethnic Chinese football player, Tony Wen, who had extensive contacts with Chinese businessmen in Singapore. Wen took half a ton of opium, loaded it into a speedboat and set off for Singapore. He returned with $225 000 in Straits Settlements currency, which was returned to the young Republic and also used to finance nationalist operations overseas, as the struggle against the Dutch was far from over.[44]

Indonesia's government-sanctioned opium business ended in 1948, when the Dutch managed to apprehend some of the main dealers. Tony Wen was also arrested, but by the British in Singapore, who suspected him of being involved in weapons smuggling in Malaya. He was released before the Dutch could begin extradition procedures, and disappeared to China. It was only safe for him to return home after the Dutch finally recognised Indonesia's independence in 1949. He joined the Nationalist Party (PNI) and, being an excellent footballer, he became a member of Indonesia's national Olympic Committee.[45] By then, the militias had also been dissolved. Haji Darip's magical powers had not been of much use; he had been forced from Klender by the Dutch, and subsequently lost most of his influence over the area. But the colourful Imam Syafe'i was appointed Minister of State for People's Security after Indonesia gained full independence.

The rise and fall of the postwar gangster militias emphasised the difference between the Jakarta gangs and, for instance, Japanese and Chinese organised criminals. As Cribb has pointed out, the *yakuza* and the Triads have always possessed a sense of 'corporate identity, an abstract notion of the organisation to which they belonged [whereas] the Jakarta gangs seem to have remained creatures of their founders and leaders. The frequent changes of name which the gangs underwent reinforces this sense of organisational flux'.[46] It was not until the Pemuda Pancasila was revitalised in the early 1980s that Indonesia gained a disciplined and centrally controlled criminal organisation.

But where were the Chinese gangs in the Dutch East Indies and Indonesia—which, after all, was part of the fabled Nanyang, the land of milk, honey and golden opportunities? The Chinese represented a much smaller percentage of the population than in, for instance, British Malaya, but the social structures were the same. In the early nineteenth century, any Chinese—especially from Fujian—settled in the sparsely populated southern and eastern part of Borneo now known as Kalimantan. They quickly took over the gold-mining areas around the Sambas River in western Borneo, and formed Triad-style *kongsi*, or district and clan associations, to organise the labourers and divide the profits. These community *kongsi* in fact became self-governing and autonomous entities, which some scholars call 'village republics'. Their inhabitants were bound together by oaths of brotherhood, based on secret society rituals.[47]

These Triad-run mini-states often fought each other, but occasionally also formed 'federations', which managed to break completely free of the control of the Malay sultans, the traditional rulers of Borneo's coastal areas. Apart from running mining operations, the *kongsi* federations also had their own administration, courts, food production and armed forces. Regular soldiers were organised in *khie*—flags or pennants—of about 80 men each. Altogether, the *kongsi* armies totalled up to 7000 fighting men. They smuggled opium and other goods along rivers not controlled by the sultans, and they fought Dayak tribesmen in the jungle and the Malays along the coast. A major problem along Borneo's coasts in the nineteenth century was piracy, which was carried out mostly by indigenous Malays and Sea Dayaks, who lived in 'pirate republics' somewhat similar to the Chinese Triad republics but not nearly as well organised. The situation was so grave that the Sultan of Brunei, the main ruler on the west coast of Borneo, asked a British explorer and adventurer, James Brooke, for help to suppress the pirates. In 1841 Brooke was appointed governor of Sarawak, a dependency of Brunei north of the

Sambas River. A year later, Brooke became the Rajah of Sarawak, and he turned his fiefdom into an independent state which steadily expanded along the north coast at the expense of Brunei. But Brooke managed to put an end to piracy in the sea off Borneo, and his family continued to govern Sarawak as hereditary rulers until the end of World War II, albeit as a British protectorate from 1888.[48]

The Dutch arrived on the scene in the 1850s, and were met with stiff resistance from the armies of the *kongsi* republics.[49] But the Dutch were able to take advantage of the rivalry between various groups of *kongsi* over diminished gold reserves. The manipulations and the superior firepower of the Dutch eventually brought colonial rule to the rest of Borneo, but it was not until the late nineteenth century that the huge, wild island was 'pacified'. *Kongsi* republics similarly also existed on the tin-mining islands of Bangka off the southeastern coast of Sumatra, but were never quite as powerful—or independent—as those in Borneo. Nevertheless, an early nineteenth-century western visitor to Bangka noted that the people there 'live in a kind of republic, which is presided over by the head of the mine'.[50]

Elsewhere in the vast archipelago, the Dutch favoured the Chinese because of their hard labour and business acumen—and because they needed intermediaries to control the natives. The Dutch also depended on the revenue collected through the so-called 'farming system', whereby colonial monopolies—opium sales, pawnshops, salt-making, ferry services between the islands, and taxes on local markets—were 'farmed out' for a fee.[51] Gradually, some of these franchises were reclaimed by the colonial state, such as opium under the Opium Regie. But pawnshops and the retail sale of opium—the most lucrative of the franchises—remained in the hands of the elite within the Chinese community until the 'farming system' was abolished altogether in the early twentieth century.[52] Local opium merchants profited from people's addiction to the drug, and one of the wealthiest of the entrepreneurs was Oei Tiong Ham, who held the profitable opium franchise in both central and east Java. His profit in the period 1890–1903 was 18 million guilders—a fortune at that time—and he used some of his wealth to set up the Oei Tiong Ham Bank and four other private companies. He also contributed generously to various Chinese scholars and schools in both the Dutch East Indies and Singapore. When he died in 1924, his property was inherited by the 26 sons and daughters of his eight wives.[53]

After the demise of the Borneo and Bangka *kongsi* republics in the late nineteenth century, there is little evidence of widespread Triad activity in the East Indies. Forming a much smaller part of the population than the Chinese in British Malaya, the East Indies Chinese were perhaps too dependent on Dutch goodwill to organise secret societies. They were also divided in two different categories. More than 85 per cent of the Chinese on Java were *peranakan*, locally born people of Chinese descent who had lived on the islands for generations and were relatively assimilated in their new homeland. The other category, *totok*, had arrived more recently and were more 'Chinese' than the *peranakan*. Most of them had settled on the outer islands, where they ran shops and small businesses, while the *peranakan* in Jakarta and elsewhere were landowners, 'revenue farmers', sugar planters and even officials.

Clan and welfare organisations existed among both the *peranakan* and the *totok*, notably the Tiong Hoa Hwee Koan, or THHK (*Zhonghua huiguan*, in *pinyin*, 'the Chinese Association'). But its main preoccupation was education for children in the Chinese communities and the promotion of Confucianism, mainly among the *peranakan* Chinese. Later, the THHK dropped 'Confucianism' from its constitution and replaced it with 'Chinese nationalism'.[54] Many young Chinese became increasingly nationalistic after Sun Yat-sen's revolution in China, and Kwee Hing Tjiat, a Dutch-educated editor of a major *peranakan* newspaper, *Sin Po*, was even expelled to China in the 1920s for his anti-colonial stand.[55]

Secret societies had been outlawed as early as 1851, but some smaller groups continued to exist as mutual aid organisations throughout the colonial era. They were tolerated as long as they did not engage in open violence and intimidation, and the Dutch looked upon them as rather innocent Asian versions of the Freemasons. The Hoo Hap (Hehe), originally a secret society in Java with a strong *peranakan* following, openly staged a congress in 1935 announcing plans to form a political organisation.[56] But little came of it, and the Chinese remained by and large faithful to the colonial masters who guaranteed their welfare and protected them against possible hostility from 'the natives'.

The Japanese occupation, and even more importantly the subsequent struggle against the Dutch, brought to the fore an entirely new kind of Chinese entrepreneur with a different set of loyalties. The Chinese filled the economic vacuum that emerged after the departure of the Dutch. They prospered, but they also often bore the brunt of xenophobic attacks by ultra-nationalistic Indonesians. This was especially the case under the Suharto regime, which banned Chinese schools and newspapers along with Chinese writing on shop signs, and even public celebrations of Chinese New Year. They were—and still are—discriminated against, but they continued to control 73 per cent of all listed firms by market capitalisation although they made up only 3.5 per cent of the population.[57] Despite their status as second-class citizens, or just 'residents' and not even citizens, the Chinese have managed to remain the wealthiest ethnic group in the country—and, paradoxically, the richest of them were closely connected with Suharto and his family throughout the years of his dictatorship.

No Chinese in Indonesia could match the wealth of Liem Sioe Liong (Lin Shaoliang in *pinyin*)—or, as he later called himself to show his loyalty to his new homeland, Sudono Salim. Born in 1916 in Fuqing, Fujian, he is the second son of a small farmer and has always been proud of his humble origins. When civil war broke out in the 1920s his elder brother, Liem Sioe Hie, emigrated to the Dutch East Indies where he set up a clove and peanut oil business in Kudus in central Java. At the age of 20, the younger Liem also left China and joined his brother in Kudus. They were not privileged like the 'old' Chinese hands in the East Indies, but made the right move during the revolutionary period from 1945–49. Liem realised that the days of the Dutch were numbered, and he had in any case never benefited from colonial rule. He began to supply the revolutionary forces with medical supplies and, although he strongly denies it, some sources say he also provided weapons.[58]

In 1952, Liem left his brother's shop in rural Kudus for Jakarta, where he began to expand his business through contacts in the capital as well as in Singapore and Hong Kong. But it was not until after Suharto had established himself in power in the late 1960s that Liem's businesses really took off. Liem had become a business associate of Suharto when the latter was the chief supply and financial officer at the regional army headquarters in Semerang, Central Java in the 1950s—and Liem was the main supplier of whatever the army needed.[59] This mutually beneficial partnership was further strengthened after Suharto became the leader of the country after the 1965 coup. In 1968, Liem was given the monopoly right on clove importation—a lucrative business as cloves are used in Indonesia's popular *kretek* cigarettes—and he soon also set up the country's biggest flour mill. The income from these two businesses provided him with the capital he needed to establish his giant cement company, Indocement, in 1973. If anyone had doubted that he had close links with the Suharto regime—which Liem himself always denied—the connection became obvious when Indocement faced bankruptcy in 1985 and the government took a 35 per cent stake in the company at a cost of $330 million. Four years later, the government took over Liem's 40 per cent share in the loss-making PT Cold Rolling Mill Indonesia Utama.[60]

Thanks to the government's interventions, Liem remained the richest Chinese in Indonesia. He also became a major shareholder in the Bank Central Asia, which for a while he ran in partnership with another wealthy *totok* Chinese with top-level connections, Lie Mo Tie (Li Wenzheng in *pinyin*), who is better known by his Indonesian name, Mochtar Riady.[61] The son of a Chinese immigrant, Riady was born in Surabaya in 1929 and was educated both there and in China. Like Liem, he linked up with the nationalist militias in the 1940s, and was even gaoled for his anti-Dutch activities. In 1947, the colonial authorities deported him to China, where he studied at the University of Nanjing until the communists took over and he had to flee to Hong Kong. By then Indonesia had become independent, and he returned home in 1950 with the assistance of Sukarno, as did the flamboyant footballer Tony Wen.

Riady claims to have started his career as a worker in a bicycle shop in Jakarta, where he moved in 1959.[62] In the early 1960s, he ran various kinds of mildly successful businesses: a provision shop, a shipping agency and a small import firm. It was not until Suharto seized power that Riady was able to amass a real fortune through contacts with the government and the president's family. He went into banking, and in 1975 he succeeded in fusing three small banks into the Pan-Indonesian Bank, or PANIN Bank—which later, however, changed its official domicile to the tiny Pacific island republic of Nauru, a major tax haven and money-laundering centre. Exactly how and where Riady linked up with Liem is not clear, but they soon made a swap that changed the entire banking scene in Indonesia: Riady exchanged his shares in Bank Central Asia with Liem's in the Lippo Group. The outcome was that Liem became the largest shareholder in Bank Central Asia while Riady controlled the Lippo Group, including its huge banking sector.[63] Between them, they assumed effective control of a large part of private banking in Indonesia, and both became billionaires under the patronage of the Suharto regime.

Lippo was the first Indonesian group of companies to transform itself into a multinational conglomerate. It all began, of course, when Riady joined hands with Jackson Stephens of Stephens Inc. and Worthen Bank in Little Rock, Arkansas, in March 1978. Six years later, Riady sent his son James Riady, or Li Bai, to Little Rock, where Stephens introduced him to his close friend Bill Clinton. The Riadys' role in the Donorgate saga has never been fully exposed. And what was Riady's relationship with the shadowy Ted Sioeng, the Sino-Indonesian entrepreneur who has been linked to Cambodian mobster boss Theng Bunma? And gambling tycoon Stanley Ho, who bought Riady's and Stephens' Seng Heng Bank in Macau? The plot thickened when it was discovered that Stephens Inc. had been replaced in 1988 by Continental Finance, a company registered in the Pacific tax haven of Vanuatu, a major regional centre for money laundering and strictly secret offshore business registration. Furthermore, company secretary John Huang—who was later implicated in the Donorgate scandal as a collector of improper contributions to Clinton's re-election campaign—had been replaced by a Lippo associate and possible Riady relative, Lee Man-cho. Back in Hong Kong, where the Lippo Group had established its main pan-Asian base, Lee lived in the same low-rise apartment block as Wong Sing-wa, North Korea's honorary consul in Macau and another character who figured in the Donorgate scandal.[64] In the 1980s, Wong shared his Hong Kong office with the honorary 'Trade Commissioner' of the Republic of Vanuatu.

It was not only Sioeng who was suspected of working 'on behalf of the Chinese government'. Almost all the characters in the drama were linked to China's intelligence services or the People's Liberation Army. The Senate Committee investigating the Donorgata saga stated about the Riadys:

> The Committee has learned from recently-acquired information that James and Mochtar Riady have had a long-term relationship with a

Chinese intelligence agency. The relationship is based on mutual benefit, with the Riadys receiving assistance in finding business opportunities in exchange for large sums of money and other help. Although this relationship appears based on business interests, the Committee understands that the Chinese intelligence agency seeks to locate and develop relationships with information collectors, particularly persons with close connections to the US government. The Riadys are central figures in the campaign finance scandal for several reasons. First, they have close ties with President Clinton. James and Mochtar Riady have known President Clinton since the mid-1980s when they held a controlling interest in the Worthen Bank. The Riadys have visited Clinton in the White House on several occasions. They have made significant contributions directly in connection with the 1992 elections; subsequently, various Riady businesses, associates, and employees did likewise. Third, they were the employers of John Huang, whom they helped place at the Department of Commerce, then the DNC (the Democratic National Committee).[65]

So the Lippo Bank agreed to act as a conduit for Chinese funds going to buy power and influence in the White House. And Lippo continued to invest heavily in various enterprises in China.

While the Riadys' relationship—and those of Liem and others—with China were based on business as well as intelligence and covert activities, links to the Suharto regime were based solely on financial deals. It is even doubtful whether the Suhartos—the president and his incredibly wealthy children—were aware of the Riadys' shady dealings in China and the United States, or if they would have cared. They appeared much more interested in making as much money as possible. In fact, Suharto and his family ran the biggest kleptocracy the world has ever seen. By the time he was driven from power in May 1998, the value of their collective fortune was estimated at $15 billion—even more than the riches former Philippine dictator Ferdinand Marcos had stolen from his country. A *Time* investigation in 1999 revealed that they actually owned, on their own or through corporate entities, 3.6 million hectares of land and other real estate (an area larger than Belgium). That included 100 000 square metres of prime office space in Jakarta and nearly 40 per cent of the then still Indonesian province of East Timor, most of which had been acquired through pure theft, or at best with income derived from various family monopolies.[66]

The wealth of the eldest son, Bambang Trihatmodjo, was estimated at $3 billion, including interests in everything from oil and gas to telecommunications and animal feed. His elder sister, Hardiyanti 'Tutut' Rukmana, owned $700 million worth of companies, houses and tollways. Hutomo 'Tommy' Mandala Putra was the proud owner of the Humpuss group of companies, a ranch in New Zealand, and various golf clubs, worth an estimated $800 million. Another son, Sigit Harjoyudanto, was also worth $800 million, with homes in London's exclusive Hampstead area, Los Angeles and Geneva. An avid gambler, he was a frequent visitor to Las Vegas until he suffered a bad run there in the late 1980s. He is known to have lost up to $3 million in a night. The two youngest sisters, Siti Hutami Endang Adiningsih, nicknamed 'Mamiek', and Siti Hediati 'Titiek' Hariyadi, were worth only $30 million and $75 million respectively.[67] Titiek is the wife of Lieutenant General Prabowo Subianto, who had fostered a relationship with Hercules and other East Timorese street goons. Not to be outdone, his brother-in-law Bambang was a personal friend and hunting partner of Pemuda Pancasila leader Yapto Soerjosoemarno.[68]

While the cream of Indonesia's kleptocracy had more money than they could ever dream of spending in a lifetime, the ordinary people suffered political repression and economic hardships. The Asian economic crisis of 1997 hit Indonesia harder than any other Southeast Asian country, mainly because of the gross anomalies in the economy. Within months, the Indonesian economy collapsed like a house of cards; the rupiah lost more than 50 per cent of its value, banks became insolvent, construction ground to a halt across the country, factories closed and tens of thousands of people lost their jobs. People began to talk openly about corruption and abuse of power, the immense wealth of the president's family—and the need for radical political and economic changes.

It all came to a head in May 1998 when the students at Jakarta's Trisakti University demonstrated against the government—and were fired upon by the security forces. Four students were killed, but that only provoked even more people, including large numbers of urban poor, to take to the streets. In an attempt to deflect public attention from the real culprits of Indonesia's economic malaise, the security services then orchestrated attacks on Jakarta's vulnerable Chinese community. Stores were torched, homes were ransacked, people were hacked to death and women were raped by mobs as the military and the police stood idly by. After the carnage, an Australian TV team discovered mysterious colour-coded markings on houses and shops in Jakarta's Chinatown. They were told a green-painted spot on a wall meant 'loot', red stood for 'burn', and black was the go-ahead for 'loot and rape'.[69] The systematic nature of the attack on Chinatown, which became known as Jakarta's own Crystal Night, lent credence to the suggestion that it was not a spontaneous outburst of anti-Chinese sentiment, which is always there under the surface in Indonesia. And the finger pointed at Lieutenant-General Prabowo and Jakarta military commander Major-General Sjafrie Sjamsoedin, who were both named in a government report that was released in November 1998, six months after the eventual fall of Suharto and his regime.[70] In any event, the attack on Jakarta's Chinatown was an incredibly short-sighted move. Most of it was burnt down—which meant that a main source of income for groups such as the Pemuda Pancasila was gone. Chinese shop owners and businessmen had been the largest contributors of 'protection money', as a Pemuda Pancasila leader once confessed: 'We have to admit, whatever else, that Pemuda Pancasila lives from the Chinese'.[71] The riots also got out of hand. A huge and angry crowd ransacked and burned down Liem Sioe Liong's house, and smashed windows of offices of Bank Central Asia in several Jakarta neighbourhoods. Liem and other wealthy Chinese moved millions out of Indonesia, and the country's already severe economic crisis took another turn for the worse.

The collapse of the old order was welcomed by scores of cheering students and other demonstrators, but the euphoria was short-lived. Indonesia opened up, political parties were formed and the press became more outspoken than ever before. But the old forces of evil were still active, and before long it became clear that the country was entering a new era of chaos and disorder, similar to the revolutionary period after World War II. Bands of *preman* and shady militia groups became active again, spreading terror among the people. And these new groups seemed to have nothing to do with the Pemuda Pancasila, which had outlived its usefulness as most people associated it with the disgraced Suharto regime. Suharto's successor as president, B.J. Habibie, opened its congress in May 1999, but it was held under vastly different circumstances from the 1996 stadium party. Only 1000 people showed up this time, and it was obvious that they were concerned about the future of their organisation. Not long after the downcast congress, Yorrys, the swarthy Chinese-Papuan deputy leader of the Pemuda Pancasila, decided to join the independence movement in his native province, Irian Jaya.[72]

The Pemuda Pancasila had made a threatening appearance outside the parliament building during the demonstrations in May 1998, dressed in their orange and black uniforms and brandishing machetes, but someone must have ordered them to restrain themselves.[73] 'Someone' was also busy building up new militias, and the formation of one of them, a vigilante group known as Pam Swaraksa (Pengamanan Swaraksa or 'Voluntary Security Guard'), was endorsed publicly by General Wiranto, the armed forces commander and Prabowo's rival. These hired thugs, mostly desperately poor slum dwellers who were willing to do anything for money, 'guarded' the parliament and were involved in clashes with students and other pro-democracy activists. In one case, hundreds of 'vigilantes' armed with knives and sickles were mobilised to protect the military headquarters in Surabaya from a large student demonstration. Pam Swaraksa also became associated with a string of bizarre murders of religious teachers and practitioners of black magic in late 1998. Eventually, the public turned against the hired thugs and killed and mutilated at least four of them in public. Seven students were killed and hundreds were injured when the military attacked the demonstrators on 13 November. The killings sent shock waves through the nation as many saw the use of the Pam Swaraksa as a desperate act by Habibie's beleaguered and illegitimate regime; the bands were soon dissolved.[74]

But even since the election of 1999, and the formation of a democratic government, the use of militias has continued. Almost every political party has its own 'youth group' dressed in military fatigues and marching boots, and armed with rudimentary weapons, not to mention the private gangs which roam the markets in Jakarta extorting 'protection money' from shop and stall owners, more aggressively now the cake had become smaller and the competition between the gangs had grown fiercer. In April 2001, Jakarta governor Sutiyoso and the city's Leaders' Council eventually declared 'war on the thugs'. Their illegal activities would no longer be tolerated, and a 70 per cent increase in crime compared with the year before was cited as justification for spending 30 billion rupiah (approximately $3 million) on the growing problem. The date for the campaign to begin was set as 16 April. The independent Indonesian website Laksamana.net reported:

> On that Monday morning, the Governor and entourage headed to Tanah Abang, Central Jakarta, where the *preman* are notoriously strong and fearless. Wearing his military uniform emblazoned with three stars as a sign of his authority as Lieutenant General, Sutiyoso brought out more than 100 'troops'. Only thing was, there wasn't one *preman* to be found at the bus terminal or intersection. They simply 'disappeared' when the Governor wished to launch the costly operation. For the benefit of the media, the police then set upon the very people targeted by the *preman* in their extortion rackets—petty traders and road-side food stall owners in the area. Not one *preman* was arrested or even seen but the police trucks were loaded full of poor *pedagang kaki lima* [a nickname for street sellers]. They said the *preman* would be wiped out, but they only got the soup sellers.[75]

Was it just outright incompetence, or could it be, as a voluntary social worker in Jakarta suggested, 'merely a guise for the provincial government, notorious for its links to the Jakarta underworld, to spend 30 billion rupiah?'. The figures did not add up, he claimed. Even if every single one of the city's 5623 employees were involved in the operation over six months, the costs would only amount to around 20 billion rupiah. 'The opportunity for diverting funds into other areas was considerable indeed,' concluded the activist, who works on the laudworthy but almost hopeless task of improving the lives of Jakarta's poor.[76]

The *preman* were never removed from Jakarta's markets, but they have adopted new styles and 'ideologies', which make them different from Hercules' old gang and the Pemuda Pancasila. Many of the new, so-called independent, militias profess a belief in Islam, and there have been attacks on 'godless sinners' selling liquor in the capital's many bars and discoteques. Bearded and turbaned militants have smashed bottles in the name of Allah—but, in reality, the main reason for such raids has been that the bar owners have failed to pay 'protection money' to the right gang. Other 'Islamic' gangs of unemployed youths—and there are hundreds of thousands of jobless young people in Indonesia today—have been hired by the military for specific political purposes, such as the Lasykar Jihad, which deployed some 3000 followers to the predominantly Christian island of Ambon in May 2000.[77] Whatever the reason for action, Islam is a better 'cause' to rally people behind these days than the old state ideology, *pancasila*. And these new Islamic *preman* are only one of many signs of the social fragmentation and dangerous uncertainty that has emerged in the wake of the fall of Suharto's regime. His institutionalised kleptocracy has given way to a chaotic pirate republic, where freebooters of all kinds are trying to grab as much money, power and influence as possible, and where poor people do anything to survive.

Both phenomena are also reflected in the rise of actual sea piracy in Indonesian waters. Nearly two-thirds of the world's pirate attacks in 1999 occurred in Asia, with 113 of the 285 reported cases taking place in Indonesia's waters and ports, compared with only 22 in 1994.[78] Most attacks take place when the merchant vessels are anchored in ports, usually in the middle of the night when the sea is calm and most crew members have fallen asleep. The perpetrators are often just bands of impoverished fishermen wearing face masks and armed with knives, who board larger vessels and threaten the crew before making off with cash and valuables in their own small speed boats. A second, more serious type of piracy usually targets tankers or larger vessels and steals the entire cargo. In this instance, after hijacking a ship, a second pirate-directed vessel moors alongside the captured ship to siphon off the oil, to collect the cargo, or both. This type of piracy requires a higher degree of planning than the first, and is orchestrated by well-organised gangs who follow shipping schedules on the internet. The third type of piracy involves stealing both the cargo and the ship, often killing the crew. The ship is later repainted, renamed and re-registered under a flag of convenience—typically in Panama, the Bahamas or Belize, or other countries with relaxed registration regulations. These 'phantom vessels' can subsequently be used to smuggle drugs or illegal aliens, or are put into service as apparently legitimate commercial vessels, which in turn seize the cargo shipped abroad.

Here, large crime syndicates, with worldwide connections are involved. The most-publicised case of such highly-organised piracy was, of course, the hijacking of the *Chang Sheng* in November 1998, which led to the mass execution in Shanwei in January 2000 (see the Introduction to this book). Among the thirteen pirates who were shot at Shanwei, most were mainland Chinese, but at least one of them, was an Indonesian Chinese. He and a Shanwei native, Wong Siliang, were found to be the ringleaders and the chief organisers of the hijacking.[79]

Rampant corruption within Indonesia's law-enforcement agencies makes it almost impossible for international maritime organisations to control these new forms of piracy.[80] And there may not even be the will to stop it, as more sophisticated forms of piracy often involve the cooperation of greedy security forces. Andreas Harsono, a prominent Indonesian investigative reporter, concluded in April 1999 that 'modern piracy is controlled by a dark alliance between pirates and the Indonesian coastal patrol and other maritime officials'.[81]

The same can be said for another activity that has flourished in Indonesia since the collapse of the old regime and the general economic crisis in Asia: people smuggling. Since mid-1998, shiploads of refugees have arrived on Australia's shores, presenting both the government in Canberra and the Australian public with a difficult dilemma. On the one hand, the vast majority of them come from Afghanistan, Iran and Iraq, countries with extremely repressive regimes, and their claim to be genuine refugees cannot be ignored. The Australian government has been criticised for being inhuman in its handling of the new 'boat people' crisis.[82] But on the other hand, they are not groups of desperate people who have got together and seized a ship with which to flee to Australia. This is another aspect of the highly organised and very lucrative trade in human beings. 'Travel agents' and fixers of Pakistani origin, who work out of carpet shops in Jakarta, arrange passages to Australia in ramshackle boats which leave ports on the southern coast of Java as well as Bali, Lombok, Flores, West Timor and other outlying islands. Whatever travel documents the refugees have are thrown in the sea during the voyage. In 1998, 47 boats and 200 passengers reached Australia. In 1999, it had increased to 80 boats and over 3000 people. The figure for 2000 was even higher—and it all reached a climax in August 2001, when Australian authorities challenged the Norwegian ship *Tampa*, near Christmas Island. The ship was carrying 450 refugees from the Middle East, who had been rescued when their own rickety vessel began to sink. Australia refused to accept the asylum seekers, and sent them on to Papua New Guinea and the tiny Pacific Island republic of Nauru for processing. But not even this harsh treatment has stopped the flow of boat people coming via Indonesia from the Middle East. In October 2001, a boat sank in Indonesian waters and more than 350 people drowned. The survivors—mostly Iraqis—claimed that they had at first refused to board the old vessel, because they feared it was not seaworthy enough to reach Australia. But Indonesian police officers, armed with pistols and automatic weapons, forced the frightened passengers onto the boat. Following an international outcry, Indonesian authorities arrested two of the officers involved, but they were not brought to trial.[83]

In late 2001, it was estimated that as many as 4000 people from the Middle East, Afghanistan and Pakistan were stranded in Indonesia, waiting for ships to take them to Australia.[84] And all of them pay thousands of dollars to the Pakistani-led, Jakarta-based syndicates so that they can escape the stone-age lunacy of Afghanistan as it was under the now deposed Taliban, or the wicked *ayatollahs* of Iran, for greener pastures in Sydney and Melbourne. According to a western investigative journalist: 'After the cost of purchasing a boat and paying off the Indonesian police, one vessel laden with 100 people can translate into a $100 000 profit.'[85] A 'travel agent' in Jakarta told the journalist what he and his colleagues thought of Australia's latest headache: 'Do you know what they think of Australia round here? I'll tell you: After Timor they don't give a f--k about Australia's problems. I know people in the police and military delighted to see you have to deal with this business'.[86] So much for Canberra's pleas for increased regional cooperation against illegal practices—and so much for Indonesia's pursuit of law and order in the post-Suharto era.

•7
WIZARDRY IN THE LAND OF OZ

Tell tale tit,
Your tongue will split.
And all the puppy dogs,
Will have a little bit.
                    —An old Sydney schoolyard rhyme reflecting traditional Australian
                    working-class loyalty to one's 'mates', contempt of police informers,
                    and hostility towards authority[1]

Australia's eastern seaboard has some of the busiest sea lanes in the
world, with hundreds of cargo ships, tankers and pleasure boats
sailing through its waters at any one time. But in October 1998, when
a 40-metre freighter took an unusual course towards Port Macquarie
in northern New South Wales, the police were watching carefully.

For almost two months, some 25 agents from the Australian
Federal Police had been keeping close tabs on a group of people from
Hong Kong who had rented an empty building in Carlton, a faceless
outer suburb on the railway line near Sydney's international airport.
In August, one of their companions had been arrested on suspicion of
being a heroin courier. Now it seemed the gang was waiting for a
major shipment from the Golden Triangle. On 7 October, they had
hired two Toyota vans from a firm in Kings Cross, Sydney's raffish,
most crime-infested 'entertainment' area, and driven north to North
Haven, a sleepy town 20 kilometres south of Port Macquarie.

The police shadowed them as they continued down a dirt track to
the ocean at Grants Beach. The gang stopped, looked around for half

an hour—and then drove back to Sydney. Over the next three days, the police looked on in amazement as the men from Hong Kong went shopping for jackets, wading boots, large sports bags, broomsticks and torches. When the Toyotas headed north again, police helicopters and boats were placed on full alert. The men made several more night trips to Grants Beach, obviously waiting for a signal.

At 9.45 p.m. on 13 October, it came. Exactly how the 40 metre vessel, which had already caught the attention of the police, identified itself is not clear, as it was anchored 20 nautical miles out in the ocean. But the men knew, and at the same time as they arrived at the beach, a small fibreglass dinghy was lowered into the rough sea. The dinghy had a powerful outboard motor, but the weight of its load was so great that it took five hours to reach the shore. Then, just as the dinghy emerged from the darkness, something spooked the men who were waiting for it. It could have been the lights from a passing trawler, or maybe an unusual sound in the dark. They ran back to their vans and sped away. It was now just before 3.00 a.m. The police had to pretend that they were the men who were supposed to be on the beach. A plainclothes officer flashed a torch. As the dinghy slowed down, a high-powered customs boat moved discreetly into position behind it. The men on board the dinghy waved to the plainclothes officer holding the torch, taking it for granted that he was one of them. They must have been shocked when about a dozen police officers stormed forwards. The smugglers did not even have time to reach for the Austrian-made Glock semi-automatic pistol that was on board the dinghy. Three men were arrested on the spot, before the police turned their attention to the dinghy.

It was loaded with 31 bags, each containing 14 kilograms of pure, white heroin. The cache was worth 400 million Australian dollars ($256 million at the time) and represented 20 million hits—or more than one for every person in Australia. It was the country's biggest heroin seizure ever.[2]

Out in the open sea, the 40-metre mother ship, the *Uniana*, was surrounded by naval patrol boats. As daylight broke on 14 October, Federal Police agents boarded the vessel and took the entire crew into custody. At the same time, the men who had escaped in the Toyota vans were arrested on their way back to Sydney. Altogether, seven Hong Kong Chinese and eleven Indonesian seamen were arrested following the bust near Port Macquarie, and the Hong Kong police—who had worked closely with the Australians since the first arrest had been made in August—conducted simultaneous raids across the former British territory, seizing documents relating to the drug-smuggling operation. It was concluded that, although the gang was based in Hong Kong, the freighter that carried the drugs had not passed through the territory, or through mainland Chinese seaports.

The ship, the investigations showed, had sailed directly from Burma. This curious detail would reveal the sheer extent of the syndicate's contacts, which stretched from the remote hills of the Golden Triangle to the mean streets of Australia's cities.[3] Furthermore, as the audacity of the *Uniana* operation showed, the Chinese smugglers had acted with the confidence of a well-established gang that had found an honoured home in Australia. This they owed in part to a criminal culture in their adopted country that began more than 200 years ago, when the first convict ships arrived on the very same shores. For, despite its western-style image, Australia has one striking similarity to its Asian neighbours: it had also long boasted a pragmatic collaboration between business, politics, law enforcement and the underworld, which has allowed crime of every description to flourish.

More immediately, the *Uniana* affair showed how the politics of Southeast Asia directly affect the drug scene in Australia. Although the Burmese sector of the Golden Triangle has always produced most of the world's number four grade heroin, drugs have traditionally been smuggled through Thailand and, since the late 1980s, via China. The drug bust near Port Macquarie made it clear that the alliances of convenience forged between Burma's military government and the drug armies in the Golden Triangle had enabled the smugglers to use the country's own roads and ports to ship out heroin.

The 40 metre vessel was escorted into HMAS *Platypus* Naval Base in Sydney, flanked by two customs boats and a Navy frigate. Further investigations revealed more about the extent of the drug syndicate's contacts. The ship was registered in the Central American tax haven of Belize, but it was originally a Panama-registered vessel called *Ming Star*, which the gang had purchased in May the same year from Shun Tak Shipping S.A.—an arm of the business empire of Macau's casino king, Stanley Ho. Placed in the dry-dock at the Kao-Gang shipyards in Kao-hsiung, Taiwan's main port, it was renamed, reregistered and refurbished. Despite its scrappy exterior, it was equipped with high-tech navigation gear and radar, indicating that it had been outfitted expressly for international drug-running.[4] Then it set off for Burma to pick up the heroin.[5]

The *Uniana* sailed with its valuable cargo down through the Andaman Sea and the Strait of Malacca, through the Indonesian archipelago and the east coast of Australia. Because of its proximity to Southeast Asia, and the fact that the country is the richest in the region, Australia has become the most lucrative destination for Burmese heroin in the Asia-Pacific, rivalled only by Canada's west coast. It is also relatively easy to smuggle drugs into Australia, a huge island country with a long coastline and many international airports. Supplying Australia's 45 000 addicts and approximately 600 000 occasional users with heroin is a multi-million dollar business, and there have been some dramatic changes in the pattern of organised crime gangs which direct this traffic in death and misery.

In March 2001, Australia's retiring police chief, Mick Palmer, stated that there was no point in denying that ethnically based gangs, mainly East Asian and Lebanese, were responsible for most of the problems. Two months before, New South Wales state police commissioner Peter Ryan warned that more than 40 gangs—mostly Chinese, Vietnamese and Lebanese—were battling for control of Sydney's heroin, extortion and prostitution markets. His comments were immediately condemned as 'discriminatory' by ethnic leaders, but the state's director of public prosecutions, Nicholas Cowdery, retorted: 'Why not call a spade a spade? It helps us identify the problem and to address it.'[6]

This was a controversial statement in a country which takes pride in its 'multi-culturalism'—and which, at the time, was grappling with the return to the limelight of its most controversial politician, Pauline Hanson, the fish-and-chip shop owner from Queensland and her One Nation party whose policies effectively demonised Asian immigrants and Australia's own Aboriginal population. Hanson's jingoistic ramblings severely damaged Australia's reputation in the region, and further 'anti-Asian' statements would only make the situation worse. But no one, not even Hanson, would claim that all Australians of Asian origin were criminals. In fact, the ethnic gangs first and foremost terrorise their own kinsmen. Drugs are sold to anyone who wants to buy them, but when it comes to 'protection money' and other forms of extortion, it is a lot easier for Vietnamese gangs to demand it from Vietnamese shop owners than from, for example, merchants of Romanian or Maltese origin. Many members of Australia's Asian communities live in fear of the gangs, and few dare to report anything to the police. The retribution would be swift—and harsh.

The most vicious of Australia's new ethnic-Asian street gangs is without doubt the '5T', which rules the underworld in Cabramatta, a western Sydney suburb. It is made up of ethnic Vietnamese, and they are reputed to be younger and more ruthless than any other crime group in New South Wales. Some are as young as twelve, well below the age at which they can be prosecuted under the law—and that is exactly the point. The older gang leaders remain in the background, out of sight and out of reach of the police. Surveillance cameras on street corners in Cabramatta have made little difference; whenever the police arrive at the scene, no one—not even those easily identifiable on film—can remember seeing anything unusual. But it is crystal clear from surveillance that a large portion of the buyers of heroin are Asian-Australians. Even Asian-Australian dealers who previously only sold drugs, mostly to Anglo-Australian users, have become addicts themselves, and now have to sell even more heroin to finance their habits.[7]

According to popular belief, '5T' stands for the Vietnamese words *tinh, tien, tu, tu, toi* (love, money, prison, death and conviction). Another interpretation is *tinh, tien, tu, toi va, tra thu* (love, money, prison, crime and revenge). But it can also be read as *tuoi tre thieu tinh thuong*—young people who lack love and care.[8] The founders of the gang came to Australia as young refugees when the country decided to accept for resettlement tens of thousands of Vietnamese boat people in the early 1980s. The first Vietnamese refugees were processed at the old immigration camp of Villawood and then moved down a few blocks to Cabramatta, a suburb which had grown up when Australia opened up to non-Anglo-Saxon immigrants in the late 1940s. Today, 80 per cent of Cabramatta's 30 000 to 40 000 inhabitants are of Vietnamese origin, with a sprinkling of Laotians and Cambodians.[9]

A huge Asian-style arch at the entrance to the suburb's main shopping centre states proudly 'Freedom and Democracy' in English, Vietnamese, Lao and Khmer. To some of the new immigrants, this freedom meant that they could resume activities from the old war days in Vietnam. Shady characters from the old Saigon moved in, and with them came the heroin business and other criminal activities. They recruited orphans and juvenile delinquents to distribute the drugs—and the 5T was born. Many of the youngest refugees had been sent away by their parents, who wanted them to have a better future than Vietnam could offer. But they ended up staying with uncles, aunts and distant relatives, who did not pay as much attention to them as they did their own children. They were lonely, angry and full of resentment, and they certainly lacked 'love and care'. All this made them easy prey for gangs looking for new recruits.[10]

The 5T rose to notoriety in September 1994 when John Newman, a local politician, was gunned down outside his home in Cabramatta. The son of a European immigrant who had settled in the suburb after World War II, Newman had spoken out against Vietnamese crime in his constituency. But a year after the murder, the police in New South Wales were no closer to solving it. By that time the police themselves were also the subject of a Royal Commission into corruption and drug-related crime, at the highest and the lowest levels of the force.[11]

Then, in August 1995, Tri Minh Tran, the 20-year-old key commander of 5T, and a nineteen-year-old member of his gang were murdered by a gunman who fired more than a dozen rounds when they opened the door to their Cabramatta home. One was shot at least six times in the head and the other several times in the face.[12] The execution-style slaying shocked the public, and the rising level of gang violence brought more police into Cabramatta to get the drug dealers off the streets. The local police commander, Alan Leek, had already warned in late 1994, well before the killing of Tran and his lieutenant: 'The reality is there is firmly entrenched organised crime in the area . . . Organised criminals have established illegal gaming clubs and coerced shopkeepers to install electronic poker machines which provide millions in untaxed cash . . . this money is used to import heroin and Asian prostitutes.'[13] The attention of the media and the public focused in on the 5T and its culture of murder, extortion and drug dealing.

Tran became almost a media celebrity after the violent end to his young life.[14] He was atypical in that he actually came from a well-to-do family that had arrived in Australia intact, although they—like all other boat people—went through terrible experiences at sea before they eventually reached Sydney. He was seven when he came to Cabramatta, and he did not suffer the same deprivations as most other Vietnamese youth gang members, whose path to crime is easier to understand.[15] Resentment at being abandoned by their families, difficulties in being assimilated into society—being neither Vietnamese nor Australians—led many of the 'Lost Boys' of Cabramatta to find a new identity in the 5T. The gang became their new parents, and it gave them mobile telephones, fashionable clothes, money to spend and heroin to smoke or inject. And there were always lots of girls around the 5T.

This false glamour could have been what lured Tran into joining a street gang, which he did at the age of thirteen. He had actually first come to the attention of the police when he was only eleven, when he was apprehended for carrying a sawn-off rifle and had to spend six months in a children's institution. By the time Tran was seventeen he had been accused of heroin trafficking, extortion and murder. The police charged, but were unable to prove in court, that he had gained respect from his peers by killing two gangland rivals, one with a machete and the other with a gun.[16] He was acquitted on all criminal charges, but many wondered why the social services had not taken better care of a boy whose ruthlessness made him the undisputed leader of the 5T. All its rivals were either eliminated or absorbed, and by 1994 the 5T controlled the streets of Cabramatta and had made it the heroin capital of Australia.

The 5T became notorious for its random selection of targets and predilection for extreme violence. This explained why the police always had great difficulty finding witnesses to crimes committed in Cabramatta, despite the surveillance cameras. 'We haven't seen anything', was the standard answer when the police visited shop owners and others who were clearly identifiable on the cameras. But the vicious nature of the 5T took its toll on the gang's own ranks as well. By the late 1990s, early gang members were either dead or had themselves become leaders, or 'enforcers'. Now a new generation of Australian-born Vietnamese roam the streets of Cabramatta, many of them hooked on heroin. The suburb has such a bad reputation that many law-abiding Vietnamese—the vast majority of the community—do not even want to say that they come from Cabramatta when they apply for jobs elsewhere in the city.[17]

Before the arrival of the Vietnamese, Sydney's heroin market was dominated by another Vietnam War legacy: the gangs that ruled the city's old and seedy entertainment area of Kings Cross, which in the late 1960s began to receive American GIs on 'rest and recreation' from the war in Indochina. Heroin was first introduced by American GIs from Vietnam, and soon the Teochew syndicates in Southeast Asia began to export large quantities of heroin to Australia. But they were only involved in the production of heroin back in the Golden Triangle and, perhaps, some stages of the smuggling. The trade as such was run locally by Sydney's own syndicates, which for decades had controlled prostitution, and illegal bookmaking and gambling.

However, as US researcher Alfred McCoy has pointed out, neither Teochew export operations nor the Sydney distribution networks could have been successful if Australia had not had what he terms 'the five basic requirements any society needs to sustain the mass marketing of heroin'. These are a reliable source of supply, a tradition of political tolerance for some sort of organised crime, a modicum of police corruption, and an informal alliance between the drug syndicates and some influential leaders of established political parties, senior public servants and skilled professionals.[18]

One of the first clubs in Kings Cross catering to American GIs was the Roosevelt Club at 32 Orwell Street. It was operated by Abraham Gilbert Saffron, who had risen from being a petty criminal to becoming Sydney's leading liquor retailer—as well as a bookmaker with interests in seedy nightclubs. Born in 1919 into the Jewish community in Bondi, a Sydney locality more famous for its beach than organised crime figures, Saffron is described in an Australian police report as 'a man who by reputation has for many years dominated the Kings Cross vice scene. He has been referred to in the Parliament of his State [New South Wales] and elsewhere as "Mr Sin", and is reputedly involved in vice and other questionable activities in his state and other states of this country ... His activities are carefully hidden behind complex corporate structures'.[19]

In 1978, the South Australian attorney general called him 'one of the principal characters in organised crime in Australia', and the *National Times*, a leading Australian news magazine, said in 1982: 'The New South Wales Licensing Courts over 30 years have heard police officers rise to their feet to argue against Saffron, his family or associates getting one more liquor licence—yet he and his associates still own or control a string of licenced bars, restaurants, clubs and hotels throughout the country.'[20]

He obviously had connections in high places and, appearing before the 1973 Moffitt Royal Commission into Organised Crime, he demonstrated remarkable reticence. When the Commission asked whether he was aware that he was commonly known in the press as 'Mr Sin', Saffron replied: 'I have seen the references you have and you have informed me for the first time that I might be commonly referred to as such'. He did admit that his companies controlled two clubs, the Pink Parrot and the Pink Pussycat, but asserted he was unaware of their striptease shows—a remarkable statement since the latter club was, at the time, the most famous strip joint in the whole country.[21] Similarly, Saffron would deny any knowledge of the drug trade, although it flourished in the very entertainment area where he was the most influential figure, Kings Cross.

Saffron could afford to mock the law enforcement agencies. His private solicitor and business partner, Morgan Ryan, was a close friend of Lionel Murphy, a High Court Judge and a passionate civil libertarian who had also served as a Labor government minister. In the early 1980s, the deputy police commissioner of New South Wales, Bill Allen, was forced to resign after it had been revealed that he had accepted free trips from gambling and crime figures, had large amounts of unaccounted-for income, had tried to bribe a junior officer and was friendly with Saffron.[22]

Another of Saffron's business associates was a colourful and mysterious American called Bernie Houghton. A Texan who had fought in Asia in World War II, and then in Korea, he established the Bourbon and Beefsteak Restaurant in Kings Cross in 1967 which helped supply the 'recreational needs' of GIs on leave in Sydney.[23] Houghton also maintained links with the then New South Wales premier, Sir Robert Askin, and operatives of the US Central Intelligence Service (CIA) in Laos. In the early 1970s, a former contract agent for the CIA in Laos and Vietnam, Michael Hand, set up the Nugan Hand Bank together with Francis Nugan, the son of a fruitpacker from Griffith, a farming town 1400 kilometres southwest of Sydney. The bank brought together a cast of American army and intelligence characters who were later to appear during the Iran-Contra affairs, and whose names kept cropping up when another banking scandal broke: the infamous Bank of Credit & Commerce International (BCCI), which collapsed in 1991 amid accusations of fraud and money laundering, and reports that the bank had been used as a conduit for secret CIA funds going to cover operations in Central America and the Middle East.[24]

The Nugan Hand Bank was in many ways a smaller and earlier version of the BCCI. Its saga came to an abrupt end when Francis Nugan was found dead in his Mercedes in January 1980. 'Suicide' said the reports, but the mystery was never solved. The bank went into liquidation, and a series of dramatic and unexplained events followed. Robert Clines, a former CIA agent who had specialised in covert operations, flew into Australia and two days later left with Houghton on a trip to Manila. Michael Hand left Australia less than a month later, never to be seen again.[25] Brian Toohey, the editor of the *National Times*, commented later: 'Nugan Hand was a tremendous story but so complicated and with so many elements, it never was going to run'.[26] But the names of both Houghton and Saffron kept cropping up throughout the largely inconclusive investigations into the murky affair. Houghton later returned to Australia to continue to run the Bourbon and Beefsteak, but kept away from the public eye because of his association with the Nugan Hand scandal. He had perhaps even more reason to keep a low profile when one of his former associates and a Nugan Hand Bank affiliate, a renegade former CIA operative called Edwin Wilson, was sentenced to 25 years in gaol for conspiring to sell 20 tonnes of high explosive to Libya.[27]

Houghton passed away on 22 July 2000, just a few days before his 80th birthday. The Bourbon and Beefsteak laid out a condolences book for guests to sign, and many old mates came to pay their last respects to a man whose real identity remained a mystery until the day he died. Saffron, however, is still alive and active. In March 2001, the 81-year-old entertainment king appeared on television, complaining bitterly over unfair treatment because he had failed in his attempt to gain a liquor licence for an outlet in Crown Street in Sydney's Surry Hills. Police commissioner Peter Ryan and the Licensing Court objected on the basis that Saffron had been gaoled in November 1988 for tax evasion and had spent the next eighteen months inside.[28] But that was his first conviction since 1940.

That Saffron has remained more or less untouchable throughout his career should not surprise anyone. As soon as the first settlers—the convicts—arrived, the curious mix of hostility towards police, and links between criminals and law enforcement also emerged. Sydney was where the 'First Fleet' of eleven storeships and transports carrying more than a thousand felons and their gaolers landed on 26 January 1788, and the city would soon contain all the elements needed to create a political climate open to systematic corruption and the growth of a criminal underworld. McCoy argues that the natural tendency of the early convicts to regard its gaoler government with disdain was perpetuated in later decades by the character of the New South Wales police. They were corrupt, brutal and despised. The first constables were recruited from among the convicts, and 'not the best prisoners but the worst'.[29] By joining the widely hated police force, they also betrayed the cardinal rule of mateship, and lost the respect of the citizenry. Police informers were scorned in Australian English as 'phizz gigs' and 'police pimps', and anti-authority sentiments were strong among the urban poor.

Many Australians resent being reminded of how their country was first settled, and it is true that it has developed in a direction entirely different from, for instance, Russia's huge penal colony, Siberia. But the traditional hero is still the outlaw, and the most celebrated of them all—even today—is Ned Kelly, a native-born, bush-bred horse and cattle rustler. Like so many other descendants of convicts and poverty-stricken Irish exiles, Kelly had failed to make a living by lawful means. When four policemen tried to capture him and his gang, three were killed in cold blood. That turned him into a folk hero, and he and his followers went on to rob banks—though legend has it that he, like Robin Hood, shared his booty with the poor. Kelly and his men boasted that they had never harmed a woman or robbed a poor man. He was eventually captured and brought to Melbourne, where he was tried and hanged on 11 November 1880. According to legend, Kelly's last words were 'Such is life'.[30] Whatever the case, he has been immortalised in Australian folklore and ballads, which are still sung today. Even pubs have been named after him.

In the criminal milieu that the colonial era created, new rules of loyalty and mateship emerged—but to survive one also had to have connections in high places. The main voice of the urban poor became, hardly surprisingly, the Australian Labor Party (ALP). When the conservatives wanted to crack down on prostitution, gambling and betting in pre-World War II Australia, the ALP objected strongly, arguing that the perpetrators were not criminals but victims. To suppress illegal gaming was 'gross class discrimination against the poor'.[31]

Many criminals took advantage of the social conscience of the labour activists, and strange and often contradictory alliances were formed between ALP politicians and some leading mobsters. In the early years, the ALP felt sympathy for the underdog, but often in a misguided way. Later, the ALP had to readjust to a new reality of organised crime, while certain of its members may have discovered the mutual benefits of a relationship with the netherworld, which over the years had changed from a working-class phenomenon in Sydney to something richer, more powerful and more regional.

There is no other way to explain why some former ALP politicians would agree to sit on the board of powerful Hong Kong-based companies with links to the Asian underworld.[32] Or why Paul Keating, a former ALP prime minister would, as Australian writer John Pilger asserts in his book, *The Secret Country*, have as one of his closest mates the multi-millionaire property developer Warren Anderson, who was renowned for hiring strongmen with criminal records to pay unsolicited 'visits' to opponents of his many real estate schemes. One of them, Tom Domican, is a much feared 'enforcer' who has bragged about 'stacking' and 'rigging' ALP pre-selections in Sydney on behalf of right-wing members of the party. Anderson owned five luxury homes, including an imitation English manor in the Northern Territory called *Tipperary*, which had a chandelier worth several hundred thousand dollars and a real hippopotamus. According to Pilger, he shares a passion for antiques with his mate, Keating, who is often flown by helicopter to one of Anderson's estates.[33] Certain members of a party created to champion the rights of the downtrodden had apparently discovered the benefits of being close to the rich and famous.

But the ALP was not alone. Joh Bjelke-Petersen, an extreme right winger, ran Queensland from 1968 to 1987. Over the years, Queensland became a police state where corruption and abuse of power were rife. One of his closest lieutenants, Russell Hinze, was appointed the state's racing minister at the same time as he owned one of Queensland's largest racing stables. He later became police minister, until

Bjelke-Petersen's successor, Mike Ahern, dropped him from the new cabinet that took over in 1987. Hinze later appeared in court to answer charges that his family companies had received millions of dollars in loans, advances and other cash benefits from companies doing business in the state.[34]

Compared with most other western-style countries, Australia has had a remarkably high degree of corruption cases, involving politicians at both national and state levels—as well as police constables and officers, solicitors and big businessmen. This is not to say that the entire police force is corrupt. The vast majority today are officers and constables of high integrity. But the problem of corruption was serious enough for Australia to hire an outsider, Peter Ryan (who is British), to replace the unfortunate Tony Lauer, who did not accept that systemic corruption existed among his men. In 1997, the ugly findings of the Wood Royal Commission's investigation of police corruption in New South Wales prompted a local journalist to comment: 'Shakedowns, beatings, extortion, stealing, recycling drugs, tipping off dealers, running interference for organised crime, gutting prosecution cases, supplying heroin. Okay—so while the police were busy, what were the criminals doing?'.[35]

The situation in Australia has further been complicated by the fact that, although the original six colonies were brought together into a Commonwealth in 1901, law enforcement remained a state issue until 1979 when the police in the Australian Capital Territory, which includes the country's capital Canberra, were transformed into the Australian Federal Police (AFP). Until then, Australia had had no equivalent of the Federal Bureau of Investigation (FBI) in the United States. For the first time in its history, the country got a law enforcement agency with nationwide jurisdiction. This has worked quite well in many cases, but friction has also—perhaps unavoidably—erupted between the state police forces and the newly created federal unit, which also has branches in all Australian states and territories. The Federal Police often get in the way of corrupt state police, and sometimes—but much less frequently—vice versa. Effective, coordinated law enforcement is seriously lacking in Australia, and the country's criminals have been quick to take advantage of this weakness. But, at the same time, Australia's crime scene discloses no real 'Mr Big', no well-structured mafia-style organisations; only the professional criminal, the corrupt policeman and the crooked solicitor or politician out to make a comfortable living in this freewheeling society.[36]

Australia's new outlaws of Asian origin may be oblivious to the country's specific criminal traditions and, even if they are aware of them, could not care less. But they have nevertheless prospered thanks to McCoy's five basic requirements, which make life easier for drug peddlers—and pimps and illegal gaming operators. They were also, inadvertently, helped by a series of successful police raids in the mid-1980s when the new AFP managed to smash many of the old, disorganised Australian crime gangs. Many of the Australian-born crime bosses, who were household names in the 1970s, either ended up in gaol or died, violently or otherwise. Leonard 'Lenny' McPherson, regarded as one of the main mobsters of the 1960s, died in Cessnock Gaol in 1996 at the age of 75. Another major drug trafficker in the 1960s and 1970s, Stan 'the Man' Smith, disappeared from the scene Arthur 'Neddy' Smith, who controlled the Sydney heroin trade from the late 1970s until the 1990s—and whose men ventured to Asia to try to bring back heroin themselves—is currently serving life for murder.[37]

These successful police actions left a vacuum that was quickly filled by newly arrived, sophisticated syndicates from Singapore and Malaysia. And that development was the outcome of several completely unrelated events: crackdowns on the Triads in Singapore in the 1960s and in Malaysia in the early 1970s, which by sheer coincidence happened a few years before Prime Minister Gough Whitlam's ALP government ended the 'White Australia' policy in 1973 by introducing new legislation that abolished all racial quotas. Since 1974, immigrants from anywhere have been judged equally. The outcome was a surge in Asian immigration. By 1986 the population of Australian-Chinese born in China, Taiwan, Hong Kong, Malaysia and Singapore had risen to 133 000, compared with 43 100 in 1971.[38] Most were ordinary immigrants, and the Asians soon became known for their hard work, diligence and strong commitment to family values and education for their children. But there were also many criminals among them.

Singapore was the first Asian country to launch a determined campaign to crush organised crime. When Lee Kuan Yew's People's Action Party (PAP) came into power in May 1959, it made a concerted effort to break the power of the secret societies. Gang fights were common and people were killed in broad daylight. The PAP government, which from the very beginning was known for its authoritarian methods, increased the police's powers of arrest and the use of detention without trial. A 'Work Brigade' of young, mostly teenage, Triad members was also set up to reform the juvenile delinquents. As many as 5000 boys and girls lived in rural camps of usually 50–100, where they received vocational training—and some rough treatment as well. In 1963, the 400 inmates of one of the main facilities, which was located on a 200 acre island 20 kilometres south of Singapore called Pulau Senang, revolted. Armed with homemade weapons, they killed the camp superintendent and burned down the barracks. The police were sent in and, without much mercy being shown, all the camp's residents were hauled to the mainland where a four-month long trial followed. In March 1964, eighteen rioters were sentenced to death for murder, eleven were sentenced to three years' incarceration for 'rioting with deadly weapons', and another eleven received two-year sentences.[39]

The Pulau Senang riots prompted the police to intensify their campaign against the secret societies. But it was not an easy task. Singapore historian Irene Lim remarked that, in a study, 'one of the biggest difficulties the Police faced was finding credible witnesses. Most witnesses refused to cooperate or simply stayed in hiding for fear of reprisal from the secret societies'.[40] But non-cooperation with the police also became a crime, and the number of secret society-related incidents fell from 416 in 1959 to twelve in 1983 and only five in 1996, which made Lim conclude: 'The blood brotherhood had been broken'.[41]

In Malaysia, the delicate ethnic balance between indigenous Malays and descendants of Chinese immigrants finally erupted into bloody riots in the capital Kuala Lumpur. The election campaign in May 1969 had resulted in severe losses for the ruling alliance of traditional Malay, Chinese and Indian parties, and gains for more radical opposition parties such as the Chinese-dominated Democratic Action Party (DAP), which was modelled on Singapore's PAP, and the left-wing Malay and Indian Gerakan, which stressed economic and labour issues over communal ones. The day following the election, DAP and Gerakan staged a 'victory parade' in Kuala Lumpur. The demonstrators, believing that the government's pro-Malay policies were about to be overturned, jeered at Malay onlookers—which only heightened Malay anxiety and rage. In response, Dato Harun bin Haji Idris, the Malay chief of the government of the state of Selangor, which surrounds Kuala Lumpur, staged a pro-government demonstration. Thousands of Malays from many parts of the country flocked to the capital, determined 'to teach the Chinese a lesson'.[42]

Many demonstrators were armed with traditional jungle knives, or *parangs*, and other weapons. The rally turned into a rampage of killing, looting and burning against Chinese residents and homes in Kuala Lumpur. The carnage continued for two days, creating about 6000 refugees, 98 per cent of them Chinese. The authorities claimed that 178 were killed, but correspondents on the scene estimated the total killed to be much higher.[43] A national emergency was declared—and the government took two important steps to prevent a recurrence of violence. A so-called 'New Economic Policy', or NEP, was introduced to redress the economic deprivation of the Malays as compared to the non-Malays. And the police, including the special branch, expanded rapidly.

Under the NEP, the Malays were favoured at the expense of the Chinese. But that did not immediately curb the influence of the secret societies. On the contrary, as the NEP also included large-scale government support for investment and development, a construction boom followed, especially in Kuala Lumpur where new high-rise buildings sprang up in the early 1970s. There were rich pickings for the secret societies in the protection of building sites. But in Kuala Lumpur, as well as in upcountry tin-mining towns, new private security firms like those in the West also emerged to service the needs of rich people, especially Chinese. So the wealthy could now buy their own professional protection, and Malaysia's increasingly powerful law enforcement agencies began to take a keener interest in policing the Chinese communities.[44] As in Singapore, many Chinese gangsters decided to leave the country, even if this exodus of criminals had been the indirect outcome of political events rather than the police cracking down specifically on Chinese organised crime.

Australia was not far away—and with the new immigration policies, it seemed the gates were wide open—even for many gangsters. It is also quite possible that Australia did not want to submit the new immigrants to thorough investigations into their past lives. Many

Australians had a bad conscience over the way in which the early Asian immigrants had been treated, and a new wave of liberalism and tolerance was to replace the old 'White Australia' policy. Nothing that could be perceived as racism was accepted. In an Australian context, that was perhaps fully understandable.

The first Chinese immigrants had arrived after the discovery of gold in 1851. Tens of thousands of Chinese flocked to the gold fields in New South Wales and Victoria, where they soon became the target of violent attacks by white miners and discriminatory legislation introduced by the colonial authorities. Local newspapers described them as 'a swarm of Mongolian locusts' and 'moon-faced barbarians'.[45] In 1861, more than a thousand miners marched on a Chinese work camp at Lambing Flat in New South Wales carrying pickhandles, spades, bludgeons and hammers. They were led by a band playing:

Rule Britannia! Britannia rule the waves!
No more Chinamen shall land in New South Wales![46]

The census conducted in the same year showed that, of the total population of 1.1 million people, nearly 40 000 were Chinese. But the sexual imbalance was astounding: there were only eleven Chinese women in all of Australia—two in New South Wales, eight in Victoria, and one somewhere else.[47] Unlike other immigrant communities, the Chinese had little prospect of expanding. When the gold rush was over, many Chinese were repatriated while a small number moved to the cities where they worked in furniture manufacture, market gardening and the retail trade. But, as unwelcome residents, they compacted themselves in squalid slum areas where the presence of gambling halls and opium dens damned them all by association. The anti-Chinese movement in Sydney in the late nineteenth century was led by an ALP politician, George Black, whose 'Anti-Chinese Gambling League' claimed that the Chinese were destroying 'white' commerce in lower George Street and that they gambled, trafficked in opium, corrupted the police and seduced innocent white women.[48]

The discrimination against the Chinese was almost as bad as the treatment of the Aboriginal people, and racist cartoons in the newspapers showed 'The Evil Mister Sin Fat'—a fat ugly Chinese—introducing white women to opium and putting money into the pockets of constables patrolling the streets. Other cartoons depicted the Chinese as a spider about to devour an honest working man, a dragon, or just a head with big fangs.[49] This attitude did not change for decades, and Australia's Chinese population remained small and unremarkable. It is possible that some kind of traditional 'mutual aid societies' existed among the Chinese communities in Sydney and elsewhere in the early years, and there were occasional outbreaks of gang-related fighting over the control of gambling in Sydney at the turn of the last century. But there would be no large-scale, organised Asian underworld until the 1970s.

With the Vietnam War and the related growth of Sydney's entertainment industry came heroin—and by the end of the 1970s, social workers were already talking about a 'heroin plague of serious and growing proportions'.[50] The import of opium, mostly from India, had remained legal until 1907. The smuggling of small quantities of the drug continued until the 1950s, when the derivative heroin, manufactured in laboratories in Hong Kong, became more popular than opium among Chinese addicts in eastern Australia. In the 1960s, the distribution networks supplying Sydney's Chinatown with heroin began to divert some of their supplies to Kings Cross. From dealing almost exclusively with their own kinsmen, the ethnic Chinese dealers found new customers among the American GIs—and young Australians who also liked to hang out at 'the Cross'.[51] Only the Chinese had the necessary contacts to buy drugs from Hong Kong, and directly from the source in the Golden Triangle, where the raw opium was harvested and to where the refineries moved when the police clamped down on heroin manufacturing in the Crown Colony in the late 1960s. But the street dealers in the Kings Cross area belonged to local 'white' Australian syndicates.

The AFP's crackdowns in the 1980s changed that picture dramatically, mainly because the police action had concentrated on street activities and overlooked the gangs that imported the drugs from Southeast Asia. With the massive Asian immigration that followed the end of the 'White Australia' policy, an entirely new gang culture also arrived, mainly from Malaysia and Singapore, and the law enforcement agencies were ill-equipped to deal with a phenomenon they knew almost nothing about.

Through several stages of couriers, the heroin finally reached the street dealers, who now were neither Chinese nor traditional Australian mobsters, but mostly ethnic Lebanese and, increasingly, Romanians. Lebanese gangs have been active in Sydney since the freewheeling days of the Kings Cross era in the 1960s. But it was only after a brutal civil war tore Lebanon apart in the 1970s that Lebanese night-club owners, dope dealers and wheeler-dealers began to look for new business opportunities in the East. Until then, Beirut had been the place where rich Arabs from strictly Islamic countries such as Saudi Arabia and the Gulf states went on vice-filled holidays.

The war forced Beirut's famous night clubs to close, and many operators moved first to Bombay and later to Bangkok, where an entirely new, Middle Eastern-dominated entertainment area grew up around the Grace Hotel off the city's busy Sukhumvit Road. The Grace was a notorious hangout for prostitutes, which had catered first to American GIs and then to foreign tourists, until the Arabs moved in during the mid-1980s. Now, restaurants serving Arab food, clubs with belly dancers from Egypt, coffee shops complete with hookahs—or hubble-bubbles—and bars with prostitutes from North Africa and the former Soviet republics in Central Asia proliferate in the narrow lanes behind the Grace. Many of the owners of these establishments are ethnic Lebanese. While some Lebanese drug dealers in Sydney buy heroin from Chinese wholesalers, drugs are also acquired through their own contacts in Bangkok, and sometimes carried by African couriers to Australia.[52]

The Romanians, like so many other East Europeans, started arriving in Australia after World War II, but there has been a marked increase in both legal and illegal immigration since the fall of Nicolae Ceausescu in late 1989. The end of his dictatorial regime did not result in any rebirth of Romania as a nation; it had been too devastated by Ceausescu's misrule. But thousands of citizens took advantage of the lifting of restrictions on foreign travel—and left the country for good. Ethnic Romanians are an emerging criminal group, controlling a large portion of the heroin market in Queensland. They have even been involved in marketing heroin as far away as Alice Springs in the middle of Australia's vast desert interior. Some Anglo-Australians also remain active in the supply and distribution of heroin, notably members of the country's vicious Outlaw Motorcycle Gangs, always a breeding ground for all sorts of crime.[53]

But these largely disorganised gangs proved no match for the Vietnamese once they moved into the heroin business in the early 1990s. Rather than buying poor-quality drugs in Kings Cross, addicts began to take the suburban train to Cabramatta, where they got purer heroin at the same price.[54] Australia's prisons also helped form seemingly unlikely alliances. Heroin, violence and desperation have come to dominate life in Redfern, an area in central Sydney with a large Aboriginal community. Australia's Aboriginal people have always had an uneasy relationship with the law, and in the early 1990s some of their youngsters teamed up with Vietnamese juvenile delinquents they met in Sydney's Yasma and Minda detention centres to form a common front against other, mostly Caucasian, detainees. These bonds of friendship outlasted their time in prison, and by the late 1990s many of the Vietnamese had become street gang leaders in Cabramatta, while their Aboriginal former cellmates were now drifting around Redfern, unable to support themselves and with few employment opportunities available to them. As the police presence in Cabramatta increased, many Vietnamese street dealers began to look for other and safer outlets, and it was perhaps only natural that they would choose Redfern, where they would be protected by their Aboriginal mates—who were also willing to sell heroin to make a living. As a consequence, heroin addiction has become the new curse in a community already devastated by alcohol abuse.[55]

However, while the 5T sold heroin in the streets, moved drugs around Sydney and even to other cities in Australia—and had to compete with Lebanese and Romanian street gangs—the importation continued to be dominated by ethnic Chinese. In more recent years, Vietnamese gang leaders have shown increasing interest in influencing the importation, and some of them are known to have gone to Bangkok and Ho Chi Minh City to establish direct links between the Golden Triangle and Cabramatta.[56] But such ethnic boundaries may be difficult to define in the context of Asian organised crime in Australia. Ethnic Chinese from Vietnam, called Viet-Ching, often play an important role as members of Vietnamese gangs or as links between Vietnamese and Chinese crime groups.

Vietnam's own criminal culture—like so many other political and social structures—also mirrors China's, albeit on a smaller scale.

More importantly for Australia, the sect-and-gang culture from which Vietnamese organised crime has sprung is, to say the least, quite different from the romantic traditions of the outlaw bushranger Ned Kelly, the pure sleaze of Abe Saffron's night club-based Kings Cross syndicates, or the crudeness of Stan 'the Man' and his mates. This made it extremely difficult for Australia's law enforcement agencies to tackle the problem with the extremely vicious Vietnamese gangs, when they began to terrorise their own communities as well as other segments of Australian society. The police were largely unaware of the complex background to Vietnam's criminal milieu, which is a product not only of Chinese influence, but also of French colonial rule—and the corrupt and brutal legacy of the Vietnam War.

From the very beginning of the French era, Saigon was, as one observer put it, 'a sink, a cesspit of corruption and malfeasance'.[57] At an early stage, the French had turned to opium to finance their conquest of Indochina. The cities of Hanoi, Hue and Saigon already had large opium-smoking populations—primarily the Chinese merchant class—and they were initially supplied with opium imported from China. Once in power, the French licensed several opium trading houses, which all operated by the same rules. Merchants paid a tax to the colonial government on opium, both bought in the hills of Laos and Tongkin and imported from India and the Middle East. The drug was then sold to local consumers through shops or in opium smoking parlours.

In the late nineteenth century, the various French drug interests were consolidated under a single government-administered opium monopoly, a powerful agency called the Régie de l'Opium. Profits soared and trade was brisk. By 1900, tax on opium accounted for more than half of all revenues in French Indochina. In 1930, the territory had 3500 licensed opium dens, or one for every 1500 adult males. Drug abuse had spread from the upper strata of society down to coolies in the ports. A. Viollis, a French writer, describes an opium den he saw in Saigon in the 1930s:

> Let's enter several opium dens frequented by the coolies, the
> longshoremen for the port. The door opens on a long corridor; to the
> left of the entrance is a window where one buys the drug. For fifty
> centimes one gets a small five gramme box, but for several hundred, one

gets enough to stay high for several days. Just past the entrance, a horrible odour of corruption strikes your throat. The corridor turns, turns again, and opens on several small dark rooms, which become veritable labyrinths lighted by lamps, which give off a troubled yellow light. The walls, caked with dirt, are indented with long niches. In each niche a man is spread out like a stone. Nobody moves as we pass. Not even a glance. They are glued to a small pipe whose watery gurgle alone breaks the silence. The others are terribly immobile, with slow gestures, legs strung out, arms in the air, as if they had been struck dead. The faces are characterised by overly white teeth; the pupils with a black glaze, enlarged fixed on God knows what; the eyelids do not move; and on the pasty cheeks, this vague, mysterious smile of the dead. It was an awful sight to see walking among those cadavers.[58]

In this lugubrious environment, several gangs were active, and to ensure the loyalty of the most powerful of them, the Bihn Xuyen, the French allowed its members towards the end of their colonial rule in the early 1950s to organise a variety of lucrative criminal enterprises, and paid them an annual stipend of $85 000 as well.[59] The Bihn Xuyen was named after an old province in southern Vietnam, and consisted mainly of river pirates who preyed on boats plying the Saigon River. Its leader, a swarthy, heavy-set and illiterate man called Le Van Vien, or Bay Vien as he was more popularly referred to, had collaborated with the Japanese during World War II, and his greedy green-clad followers had led savage attacks on the French in Saigon in September 1945. Following a brief alliance with the communist Viet Minh, Bay Vien teamed up first with the French and then with the last Emperor of Vietnam, Bao Dai. By 1954, Bay Vien had extended his control to include the police in Saigon and its Chinese sister-city Cholon.

The Grande Monde, a huge gambling establishment in Cholon, catered to rich and poor alike, and raked in millions, which Bay Vien shared with Bao Dai. He also acquired the Noveautés Catinat, Saigon's best department store, 20 houses in the city, a hundred shops, a fleet of river boats and an establishment which became known as the Hall of Mirrors because of its unusual and spectacular maze of cubicles. It was, in fact, Asia's biggest brothel. A stone's throw away from his head-quarters, his opium factory supplied the dens which the police had officially put out of business. The headquarters itself was one of the most unusual complexes in the Saigon-Cholon area. Crocodiles lived in the moat between Bay Vien's living quarters and his offices and a full-grown leopard on a chain stood guard outside his bedroom door.[60] Bay Vien was promoted to the rank of general and appointed minister of national security.[61]

But, in the turbulent mid-1950s, Bay Vien ended up on the wrong side in a power struggle, and was defeated by troops loyal to the new Catholic president, Ngo Dinh Diem. The Bihn Xuyen's headquarters and military barracks were burned to the ground. Bay Vien, however, managed to escape to France and never returned to Vietnam. The American media at the time described the conflict between Diem and Vien as a 'clash between the honest, moral Premier . . . and corrupt dope-dealing "super bandits"'. US researcher McCoy, on the other hand, argued that the clash was 'only a superficial manifestation of a deeper problem', and that the eviction of the Bihn Xuyen from Saigon produced little substantive change.[62]

In fact, Diem's brother and chief of the secret police, Ngo Dinh Nhu, revived the opium trade to raise funds for his intelligence apparatus in collusion with the Corsican mafia in Saigon. Opium was flown from Laos down to Saigon by air force colonels Luu Kim Cuong and Phan Phung Tien, while customs services under Nguyen Van Loc facilitated the entry of the drugs into the country. Nhu built up a virtual army of pedicab drivers, prostitutes, drug peddlers and other pickpockets through whom the secret police held a tight surveillance over rallies and other anti-government activities in the city.[63] The corruption, brutality and intrigue led to the downfall of the two brothers, Diem and Nhu, who at first had been hailed by the United States—which was becoming increasingly involved in the Vietnam conflict—as rigidly pious Catholics. America's attitude changed when Diem and Nhu launched a vicious campaign against the country's Buddhists—and the entire world was shocked to see a picture of a 66-year-old Buddhist monk, Thich Quang Duc, who burned himself to death at a busy Saigon intersection on 11 June 1963. The United States signalled to the generals in Saigon that it would 'accept a change in government'.[64] The two brothers were overthrown on 1 November, and brutally murdered.

But the drug market remained and now heroin was introduced, as a new pool of tens of thousands, and later hundreds of thousands, of potential customers—the American GIs—arrived with (by local standards) lots of money. Heroin was brought down first from Hong Kong and later from laboratories in the Golden Triangle, and the massive drug trade soon spilled over even into the entertainment areas of Kings Cross. The trade remained in the hands of corrupt army and police officers, and their gangs of street thugs, until North Vietnam's tanks smashed through the gates of the presidential palace in Saigon on 30 April 1975, ending one of the longest, bloodiest and dirtiest wars in modern Asian history.

The Binh Xuyen was gone already by the late 1950s, but it was not the only military-style, non-governmental group in Vietnam at the time. Bigger and much more powerful was the Cao Dai, a politico-religious sect that claimed more than a million members. More importantly, it also controlled an army of 25 000 men. It was founded in 1919 by Ngo Van Chieu, a criminal investigator who had turned to spiritualism because there was little else to do on Phu-quoc, the peaceful, large crime-free island in the Gulf of Siam where he was based. Among the spirits he says he was able to communicate with was one 'Cao Dai'. The meaning of this name is not clear, but Chieu believed that he recognised the surname of God in it, and began to worship Cao Dai in the form of a huge human eye.[65] Chieu's administrative duties brought him back to Saigon in 1925. He and some other spiritually minded Vietnamese—mostly young clerks from customs, public works, the railways and various private business houses—began to meet in a run-down shop house near Saigon's bustling Central Market, a seemingly unlikely place for seances where taking a table was one of the main forms of receiving messages from the spirits of their own ancestors as well as dead philosophers and religious teachers.

In 1926, Cao Dai was officially formed. However, Chieu, the first 'Pope' of the new religion, was quite annoyed with the large numbers of newcomers who flocked to the seances. He retired to be able to spend his entire time in solitude, with the spirits as his only companions. Some of his first disciples, including Pham Cong Tac, who was later proclaimed 'ruling pontiff' of the Cao Dai, took over and led a large number of followers to a remote jungle area in Tay Ninh province near the Cambodian border. There, they established their

'Holy See', an impressive complex of buildings combining the architectural idiosyncrasies of all the old religions that the new creed said it had amalgamated into one: the French Roman Catholic Church, Buddhism, Taoism and Confucianism. Some would argue that it looks like a combination of a mini-version of the Vatican, Singapore's gaudy Tiger Balm Gardens and an Oriental Disneyland.[66] Their priests dressed in striking white, red, blue and saffron robes, and they worshipped Confucius, Jesus, Buddha, Lao Tzu and all the Hindu gods. Their many 'spiritual guides' included Trang Trinh, a Vietnamese diviner, Chinese nationalist leader Sun Yat-sen, and the French writer and poet Victor Hugo. Caodaist mediums also asserted that they were able to communicate with the spirits of Joan of Arc, the French philosopher René Descartes, who died in Sweden in 1650, and René de Chateaubriand, a writer and politician who greatly influenced early nineteenth-century Romanticism in France.

To protect its Holy See in the midst of the wild jungles near the Cambodian border, Cao Dai formed its own armed forces, which enjoyed Japanese patronage and training during World War II. After a brief flirtation with Ho Chi Minh's communists in the Viet Minh, the cardinals and commanders of the Cao Dai threw in their lot with the French. They were encouraged by the colonial power that had returned after the war, to establish physical control over provinces in which they were numerous in order to prevent the increasingly powerful Viet Minh establishing control over the south Vietnamese countryside. By 1950, Cao Dai ran its provinces like an autonomous state. Five years later, Diem, Vietnam's first president, told them to lay down their arms and revert to their former purely spiritual status. Most of them agreed, but those who resisted were eliminated. The pontiff, Pham Cong Tac, fled to Cambodia, taking some church funds with him. He died in 1963, but Cao Dai remained a potent religious and political force, even after the communist victory in 1975. In recent years, it has actually seen a dramatic revival, especially in Tay Ninh—a development which Vietnam's communist authorities are viewing with extreme unease.

The third significant group of politico-religious warlords consisted of the leaders of the sect Hoa Hao. Founded in 1939, it was led by a mustachioed illiterate peasant called Huynh Phu So and named after his birthplace, a small village in the That Son mountain range of

An Giang province near Cambodia. Huynh Phu So was known as a great miracle healer, and he was so successful, it was said, that he attracted over 100 000 followers within one year. The number eventually grew to almost 2 million, and the sect is an offshoot of Buddhism without all the expense of that religion. Hoa Hao became the poor man's Buddhism, and it taught that 'it is better to pray with a pure heart before the family altar than to perform a lot of gaudy ceremonies in a pagoda with an evil heart'.[67]

Early in 1944, Huynh Phu Son raised his own military force, which—like the Cao Dai—received Japanese support to oppose French colonialism. Armed bands and home-guard units soon appeared in the Mekong delta region southwest of Saigon. When the war was over, one of the most prominent of the Hoa Hao's military leaders, 'general' Tran Van Soai, began discussions with the Viet Minh to form a united front against the French. But because of its appeal to the poor peasantry, the Hoa Hao's interests clashed with the communists, who in September 1945 massacred hundreds of the sect's followers in the delta town of Can Tho. Tran Van Soai responded vigorously, and the rich rice-lands around Can Tho became a scene of fearful butchery. The French intervened, but that only forced the bitter enemies, the Hoa Hao and the Viet Minh, to unite against them. Like the brief alliance between the Viet Minh and the Binh Xuyen river pirates, though, this partnership did not endure. The communists, extremely suspicious of the charismatic peasant leader Huynh Phu So, arrested the prophet and executed him in April 1947. Tran Van Soai immediately rallied to the French, taking with him an armed force of 2000 men.[68]

The communists did not ban the Hoa Hao when the south fell in 1975, but by then the sect's influence was more or less confined to the province where it was born in the late 1930s, An Giang, and the neighbouring province of Dong Thap. There, the Hoa Hao has survived and, in March 2001, the 75-year-old leader of the women's league of one of its dissident wings, Nguyen Thi Thuu, set herself on fire to protest against the detention of the head of her faction of the group, the 81-year-old mystic Le Quang Liem. The Vietnamese authorities then accused the sect of having planned a mass suicide at a demonstration in Ho Chi Minh City (the new name of Saigon since 1975). They alleged that Hoa Hao leaders had ordered their followers to 'go to Ho Chi Minh City' carrying petrol-soaked cotton. Exiled Hoa Hao members based in Derwood, Maryland, on the other hand, issued a statement saying that they had only planned a rally to oppose religious prosecution in Vietnam.[69]

There is also an officially recognised, pro-government faction of the Hoa Hao, but it is the dissidents who matter—and Vietnam's communist rulers are fully aware of the political potential of sects such as the Hoa Hao and the Cao Dai. Vietnam's crackdown on Hoa Hao dissidents in some ways resembles China's vicious campaign against the Falun Gong meditation society, in which the communist rulers apparently see the reborn ghosts of the early Triads, the mystical Taiping rebellion, the Boxers or any similar politico-religious group or syncretic sect that in the past has appealed to the masses and threatened dynasties. The conflicts—and sometimes symbiosis— between open and secret polities in Chinese as well as Vietnamese societies has never been fully understood by outsiders, who usually make the mistake of viewing them from a clear-cut, black-and-white perspective: for or against the law, society and the authorities. It has never been that simple.

While it may be far-fetched to trace the origin of vicious Vietnamese-Australian street gangs such as the 5T to the Binh Xuyen, the Cao Dai and the Hoa Hao, it must be remembered that secret societies and syncretic sects have always been an important way of life among the Vietnamese as well as the Chinese. Both share a deep-rooted mistrust of the ruling elite, and the police are seen as an extension of the corrupt and tyrannical rule of the emperor and his mandarins, or whatever their modern equivalents may be called today. The Vietnamese are even more tight-lipped about what they may have seen in the streets than the Anglo-Australians, and much less prepared to cooperate with the police.

And, on the extremely rare occurrence of someone being willing to talk, Australia's own legal system has prevented them from doing so. In May 2001, a seventeen-year-old ethnic Vietnamese boy was gagged from giving evidence into drug and policing issues in Cabramatta for, as the hearing committee put it, 'his own protection as a minor'. Just as he said he wanted to recount his experience in teen gang drug-running, the teenager was told that the inquiry could not protect him from 'defamation'. He was the first youth claiming to have been active in drug dealing in Cabramatta to seek and give evidence to the committee, only to be told by ALP politician Ron Dyer that the 'community consultation' in Cabramatta was 'not subject to privilege of Parliament'.[70] Thus the Australian law enforcement authorities, and the public at large, never received a first-hand account of the new gangs that had emerged in Cabramatta after the murder of Tri Minh Tran and fall of the 'old' 5T: the 5T New Generation, the Red Dragon Gang, the Sing Ma and the so-called 'Thin War'.

But what is the actual relationship between Australia's new Chinese syndicates and these Vietnamese gangs? Are they rivals, competitors or partners in crime? While some mobsters from Cabramatta may have gone to Southeast Asia to set up their own importation networks, the big bust near Port Macquarie in October 1998 indicates quite clearly that the main business remains in the hands of the Chinese syndicates. The Vietnamese would not have such solid connections stretching from the poppy fields of the Golden Triangle to China, Hong Kong, Taiwan, Malaysia, Singapore and down to the backstreets of Sydney— not to mention contacts in New York, San Francisco, London and Amsterdam. The Vietnamese diaspora is far smaller, and not nearly as spread out all over the world. In an Asian context, cross-ethnic alliances are also, if not rare, always shaky. The division of labour seems clear: Chinese syndicates remain the main importers, while other ethnic gangs, mostly the Vietnamese, sell the drugs locally.

In 1997, the AFP alleged that Duncan Lam, or Lam Sak-cheung, a 43-year-old Hong Kong-born Sydney restaurateur, was Australia's biggest heroin importer, while a 42-year-old Cabramatta business-man, Duong Van Ia, was identified as the country's largest distributor of the drug.[71] In May 1996, Lam narrowly escaped arrest after being implicated in what was then New South Wales' largest heroin seizure, 78 kilograms imported in cans from Yunnan, China. The drugs, of course, originated in Burma across the border. Lam is still on the run and may be out of the picture now. But as the seizure near Port Mac-quarie and several subsequent seizures of nearly the same magnitude show, there is nothing to indicate the import of heroin to Australia has slowed down. After the AFP removed the *Uniana*'s 400 kilograms of heroin from the market in October 1998, some observers expected the street price of heroin to go up. There was no effect at all—not a dent in Australia's $1.5–2 billion a year heroin import trade.[72]

If anything, prices have come down, but there are still very few other commodities which increase as dramatically on being transported from one point to another. This helps explain why so many are willing to take the risk and smuggle drugs. The hilltribe farmer in the Golden Triangle, who grows the poppies sells his raw opium to a local merchant for about $75 per *viss* or *joi* (1.6 kilograms). Ten kilograms of raw opium, plus chemicals (mainly acetic anhydrite), are needed to make one kilogram of heroin, which is done in northeastern Burma's jungle laboratories. The refined product is then compressed into bricks weighing 700 grams each. The average wholesale price at the refineries in northeastern Burma for such a 'unit' is $2500–3200. Seven hundred grams of heroin equals $330 worth of raw opium for the farmer.

Once smuggled across the border into northern Thailand, the price per unit has increased to $4800–7500—if the buyer is a local Chinese merchant with connections across the border. An outside buyer from, say, Nigeria or Lebanon has to pay around $10 000 for the same amount of heroin. Down in Bangkok, 750 kilometres and several police checkpoints away, the local wholesale price increases to what outside buyers have to pay in Chiang Mai, or $7400–9200. Then comes the big jump when someone has managed to smuggle the drugs out of Southeast Asia. In Hong Kong, the same 700 gram unit of heroin fetches at least $15 000, while the price in Taiwan—where controls are stricter and the risk of being caught higher—can be as high as $40 000. In the United States, the same amount fetches up to $70 000.[73] No other commodity in the world increases that much in value when transported from one point to another, which makes the drug trade one of the must lucrative global businesses.

The wholesale price in Sydney for a 700 gram unit is A$75 000–85 000 ($32 500–42 500), if sold by an Asian to an Asian. The importer then sells it to a retailer for A$180 000 ($90 000) a unit. Then the heroin is broken up into 0.02 gram-capsules, which are sold in the streets for A$30 ($15) each—or slightly more than one million Australian dollars ($500 000) for the equivalent of a 700 gram unit. The street dealer's share is A$5 ($2.50) per capsule he sells in, for instance, Cabramatta.[74] With such enormous profit margins, it is no wonder that so many people get involved in the drug trade—and that the police have been so unsuccessful in trying to stop it. The law enforcement authorities catch only 7–10 per cent of what comes into the country.[75]

An Australian police report identifies two Hong Kong-based Triads as being deeply involved in Australia's enormously lucrative heroin trade: the Sun Yee On, which is closely connected with China's intelligence services, and the Wo Shing Wo ('Harmonious, Victorious and Peaceful Society'), which once operated inside Kowloon's infamous Walled City.[76] Both Triad societies have long been associated with influential and powerful business circles in Hong Kong and the region, among them Albert Yeung of the controversial Emperor Group.[77] In Australia, the Wo Shing Wo network especially was reported to be working closely with local drug traffickers of Sino-Vietnamese and Vietnamese origin in Cabramatta.[78]

Judging from the availability of heroin on the streets of Sydney, these alliances seem to have survived almost intact, despite several high-profile drug busts and arrests. Also in 1998, but unrelated to the *Uniana* bust, chief distributor Duong Van Ia was eventually nabbed and sentenced to eight years in gaol for heroin trafficking. His network had overtaken the notorious 5T gang to become the major player in Sydney's retail heroin market. But, as a gang boss, Duong was quite different from the youthful brute Tri Minh Tran. In Cabramatta, Duong was called 'Uncle Six' as he was the sixth of eight brothers who sailed with nothing from Vietnam to Australia in the mid-1970s. But within a decade or so he had acquired a luxury high-security home in Cabramatta. Officially, his wealth came from barbecuing pork for restaurants in the area, but that did not explain how he was able to blow millions at the Sydney Harbour Casino, which later became the Star City Casino. Duong was one of its best customers, unloading more than A$20 million in two years—some say as much as A$90 million—before New South Wales Police Commissioner Peter Ryan banned him from the casino in September 1997. The police suspected that, apart from enjoying himself, Duong was using the casino to launder drug money.[79]

The infamous American-Sicilian gangster Charlie 'Lucky' Luciano once said that 'there is no such thing as good money or bad money. There's just money'.[80] That must have been the attitude of the Casino Control Authority of the state of New South Wales as well. In an interview with national television in April 2000, its head, Kaye Loder, was forced to resign after saying she was 'sorry' the police had banned Duong from the Star City Casino. She made the remarkable statement that 'drug money possibly laundered through the Star City Casino' was returned to the government 'in the form of revenue and it was a "matter of debate whether or not that's a good or unacceptable thing"'.[81] At the same time, the Australian media revealed that representatives from Star City had even gone to Cabramatta to woo high-rollers. Mark Wells, a former employee of the casino, admitted in an interview that casinos around the country, not only Star City, targeted Cabramatta as early as 1992 as a source of gamblers with 'plenty of cash and prepared to get big'. Wells himself had been to Cabramatta to wine and dine potential local high-rollers, hoping they would turn up at Star City.[82]

Australia's traditionally relatively lax attitude to crime and dirty money had been demonstrated before in Queensland, where in March 1981 the extreme rightist Bjelke-Petersen decided to allow legal casinos in the state. This suited the Japanese *yakuza* quite well. The Gold Coast was already immensely popular with Japanese tourists—and the Chinese syndicates were not as strong in Queensland as in New South Wales and Victoria. Southeast Queensland has a tourist economy similar to Hawaii's, and just as the *yakuza* were attracted to that place, they now headed for the Gold Coast.[83]

However, since Queensland did not experience the Japanese-related street crime common in Hawaii—and as the state remained under Bjelke-Petersen's rule until 1987—few took any notice of what was happening in Australia's 'deep north'. It was not until May 1993 that Kathy Sullivan, a federal politician, asked Prime Minister Paul Keating to explain what he knew about *yakuza* property investments and money laundering in Australia. She went on to ask why Masaru Takumi, the second in command of Japan's main crime gang, the Yamaguchi-gumi, had been able to make Australia his second home. Even though he had been gaoled no less than five times in Japan, Takumi had managed to purchase a luxury apartment worth A\$800 000 in Surfers Paradise. According to Sullivan, the 65-year-old deputy of Japanese godfather Yoshinori Watanabe was 'enjoying a casual lifestyle on the sunny Gold Coast, playing golf, fishing, and gambling in the High Rollers Room at Jupiters Casino'.[84] The Australian authorities moved quickly to cancel his visa, but although he now is unable to enter the country, he is still allowed to own his Gold Coast apartment.

A lot of *yakuza* investment has gone into golf courses, hotels and real estate along the Gold Coast as part of its efforts to look for new business opportunities abroad, a drive that intensified after the introduction of new anti-gang laws in Japan in 1992. But, despite colourful stories of men with tattoos and missing pinkies, there is no compelling evidence of widespread Japanese involvement in traditional criminal activities in Queensland, or elsewhere in Australia.[85]

They simply would not stand a chance against the Vietnamese and, especially, the Chinese—and the same can be said for another colourful, but perhaps overrated, bunch of international mobsters: the Russian *Mafiya*. Although many Russians have begun to show up in Australia looking for ways—mostly illegal—of making money, their activities seem to be confined to petty smuggling, credit card fraud, prostitution and acting as couriers for more powerful drug syndicates. But the same cannot be said of Russian activities in the small island states of the South Pacific—the latest haven for black money from Russia as well as Asia. The Pacific islands are also associated with another prime criminal activity in the Asia-Pacific region: the smuggling of illegal aliens, mostly Chinese, to the United States.

Alarm bells rang at the AFP's Canberra headquarters as early as 1996, when it was discovered that seven Russian banks had shown interest in opening representative offices in Port Vila, the sleepy one-street capital of the Republic of Vanuatu. The South Pacific seems to have attracted the interest of Russian 'bankers' when, in the previous year, the US government increased pressure on financial centres in the Caribbean. In February 1997, five of the six offshore Russian banks in Antigua were closed by the authorities. All were suspected of having laundered money for the Russian *Mafiya*.[86] In theory, all members of the South Pacific Forum, the island states' regional grouping, are pledged to respect a declaration signed in 1992 in Honiara, the capital of the Solomon Islands, which encourages them to outlaw money laundering. But the truth is that the small Pacific island states have neither the resources nor the means to carry this out—or the political will, as they are too small, poor in resources and too distant to attract significant numbers of tourists or to find other sources of income.

Vanuatu is actually the oldest tax haven in the South Pacific, which is a direct outcome of the republic's unique colonial background. It was first visited by Europeans in the early seventeenth century, but held few attractions other than sandalwood, sea cucumbers, and its potential as virgin territory for various missionaries. Captain James Cook named the islands 'the New Hebrides', after the islands off the coast of Scotland. Since the Pacific islands, and especially the Melanesian ones, had no concept of nationhood—the 192 000 inhabitants of today's Vanuatu speak 114 different languages—the Europeans saw them all as 'new' lands: New Zealand, New Guinea, New Britain, New Caledonia and so on. And colonisation was often a very brutal experience. The missionaries condemned their indigenous culture as 'pagan' and often ran roughshod over the local population. Measles, gonorrhoea, syphilis and smallpox came with the European sailors, and unscrupulous traders kidnapped the natives and sold them to plantations in Queensland. This practice, called 'blackbirding', continued throughout the nineteenth century, and almost entirely depleted the populations of many of the islands.

Both French and British merchants coveted the New Hebrides, and a compromise was reached in 1906. The islands became a 'condominium' whereby both France and Britain jointly ruled the islands. Any disputes were to be settled by the King of Spain—but since there was no Spanish king after 1931, the result was not a harmonious 'condominium' but, as it became popularly known, a 'pandemonium' where no one knew who was in charge. It was the most confused form of government that the world has ever seen.[87] The house of the French Resident stood on a hill overlooking Port Vila, while the British Resident lived on Irikiri, a small island in a nearby bay. Every morning, both the French Tricolor and the Union Jack had to be hoisted outside schools and official buildings, while a band played the 'Marseillaise' as well as 'God Save the King (or Queen)'. There were French criminal codes and British common law, both British and French currencies were used, and British as well as French policemen patrolled the streets. Hardly surprisingly, the French and the British were unable to agree on anything, not even whether cars should drive on the left- or the right-hand side of the roads, or how the population should be taxed. In fact, there were never any taxes at all. The New Hebrides became by default the first real tax haven in the Pacific.

In the early 1970s, a series of British-style laws were passed to create a 'financial centre' similar to that of the Channel Islands. Trust companies and banks came to the islands to do business, and it was all rather innocent until the turbulent period the islands went through immediately before and after independence in 1980. The British left willingly, but the French were reluctant to give up their cattle farms and plantations, most of which were concentrated on the northern island of Espiritu Santo. Boosted by American 'libertarians' from an obscure right-wing organisation called the Phoenix Foundation and business supporters, a local chieftain of mixed race called Jimmy Stephens, who traced his origin to a Tongan princess and a Scots sailor, declared Espiritu Santo independent as 'the Republic of Vemerana'. Visiting journalists were entranced by the colourful Stephens with his 30 wives and his army of tribesmen armed with bows and arrows. But the rebellion—which became known as the 'Coconut War'—was quickly crushed after intervention by British Commando Royal Marines, combat police from the French Garde Mobile, and Papua New Guinean troops. Stephens and 200 of his men were sentenced to imprisonment, but the seeds of disunity and chaos had been sown.[88] Vanuatu went from crisis to crisis, and became one of the most corrupt and badly governed countries in the Pacific.

This suited crooks and fraudsters of all stripes, and by the mid-1990s Vanuatu had nearly 80 banks, more than 2000 trust companies and numerous dodgy insurance agents, accountants and solicitors.[89] But it is not the absence of taxes, or even the ability to walk into a bank with a suitcase full of cash with no questions asked, that makes an offshore banking centre attractive. It is the strict bank secrecy, the inability of any government to investigate the source of unusual wealth parked in places such as Vanuatu. Although most businesses in Vanuatu may be legitimate, Australian officials believe that millions of dollars worth of dirty money, including drug money, is placed in the banks of Vanuatu and other Pacific 'financial centres' through trusts and shelf companies, protected by an impenetrable web of laws.[90]

Few of Vanuatu's banks are banks in the normal sense—and most of them would make even Australia's infamous Nugan Hand Bank seem almost legitimate. For an initial payment of $9000, a paid-up capital of $10 000 and an annual maintenance cost of $7000, anyone can form a bank in Vanuatu.[91] The ownership of the bank is protected by law, and the bank usually consists of little more than a licence and a plaque on the wall in a Port Vila law office, which would represent dozens of other banks and shelf companies. The 'bank' in Vanuatu can then open a corporate account with a real bank anywhere in the world. Legally, the bank is in Port Vila, but the assets are not physically there.

In practice, someone with a computer in Sydney can transfer money from Hong Kong to his 'bank' in Vanuatu, which is not actually there, and then on to a bank in Sydney, or perhaps round the world a couple of times. With today's specialised banking techniques, including the electronic transfer of money, once the cash enters into the banking system, it can be transferred among dozens of banks within a day, making the paper trail either impossible or extremely time-consuming for the world's law enforcement agencies to follow.[92] If one of the banks through which the money has been transferred is 'located' in Vanuatu or a similar place, no investigator can get any further.

But the trick is to first get the cash into a bank, and proceeds from drug sales usually consist of lots of bank notes in small denominations. The process is usually divided into three phases. The first, which experts call 'placement', is the physical disposal of bulk cash resulting from criminal activity. Then comes 'layering' or the piling of layers of complex financial transactions—for instance, wire transfers—to separate the proceeds from their illicit sources. The third stage, 'integration', involves what John Walker Consulting Services in Sydney, which has investigated money laundering for the Australian police, calls the 'provision of legitimate looking explanations for the appearance of wealth by providing investments in the legitimate economy'.[93]

Only the 'placement' stage is actually vulnerable, and the least risky method is what the police call 'smurfing', or hiring a large number of people to visit banks with cash, where they wire or purchase small drafts just below A$10 000, the minimum amount that the banks are required to report to the law enforcement authorities. All these deposits would then be sent to bank accounts in Hong Kong, Singapore or Bangkok, and then wired back to Sydney as a solid deposit which would be declared as income from a legitimate business in East Asia. Another method is to smuggle money hidden in suitcases or inside machinery to Hong Kong. A courier can then take the hydrofoil to Macau, change cash or small bank drafts into gambling chips in one of the territory's casinos, spend a few at the gaming tables, and then convert most of them back into a 'clean' cheque. The casino will issue an accompanying document stating that the money has been won at the tables.[94]

Or, if the transit point is Vanuatu, the money can be stuffed in a yacht which will sail to Port Vila, where it can be deposited in any of the 'real' banks there—those which have an office and not just a plaque on a wall—and then wired back to Sydney. But, whatever the routing, hundreds of millions of dollars are laundered in these ways every year to pay for hotels, restaurants, real estate deals, luxury homes or simply extravagant lifestyles. To raise funds for such purposes, many prominent—and perfectly respectable—business people may invest in a major drug deal. The financiers will never get close to the actual drugs, but hire smugglers and street gangs such as the 5T to do the dirty work.

In only one case has laundered drug money been seized in Vanuatu. It followed some unusually strong evidence from the United States that money from drug sales in America had been transferred to Australia, and then into offshore trusts in Vanuatu. That happened in March 1995, and the amount, $1.5 million, was forfeited to the Vanuatu government following a US Supreme Court order. It was a small and solitary victory for law enforcers.[95]

Concerns about Vanuatu's secretive banking laws, and the way in which the incongruous island republic is becoming a haven also for fraud and other illegal activities, were highlighted not only by Mochtar Riady's and Jackson Stephens' shady dealings in the republic, which may have been linked to laundering, or hiding, funds for Chinese intelligence. In 1996 a scandal rocked Indonesia surrounding a 'financial institution' incorporated in Vanuatu called the Dragon Bank. It was headquartered in a small downstairs room in a Port Vila office building, but had announced plans to build a 101-storey skyscraper in Jakarta which had been named *Menara Harapan Emas*, or 'Gold Hope Tower', a $4 billion telecoms venture, also in Indonesia, and a $80 million property project on the Malaysian island of

Langkawi. The bank was run by a group of Hong Kong and Malaysian Chinese, who were being investigated for fraud. They had teamed up with a company headed by Ibnu Widoya, a brother-in-law of then President Suharto, which helps explain why they never had to apply for a proper banking licence in Indonesia.[96] But, following disclosures in the international media, the Indonesian government was forced to act and the bank was shut down in June 1996. In January the following year, even its banking licence in Vanuatu was revoked.[97]

Despite the closure of Dragon Bank, Vanuatu had established its reputation as 'the Cayman Islands of the Pacific', and according to Thomas Bayer, the American-born head of Vanuatu's Pacific International Trust Company, most of the shelf companies and banks registered in the republic are Asian, with an increasing number from China. Port Vila and Shanghai are even 'sister cities': China maintains an embassy there and the parliament and local campus of the University of the South Pacific were built with soft loans from Beijing.[98]

China's largesse was not the first, or the last, attempt by Asian interests to 'help' the Pacific nations. In the 1970s, Japan's wartime-criminal-turned-philanthropist Ryoichi Sasakawa courted the King of Tonga, Taufa'ahau Tupou IV, promising to present his country with a brand-new Boeing 737. A new, joint Tongan–Japanese airline was going to be established, and Taufa'ahau Tupou IV visited Tokyo as a guest of Sasakawa, who was appointed honorary consul for the kingdom in Japan. But, in the end, nothing happened as the philanthropist 'discovered' that the capital Nuku'alofa did not have adequate first-class hotel facilities to accommodate all the tourists the new planes were going to bring in.[99] Exactly what the wily Japanese rightist was up to in the Pacific never became clear—and, equally mysteriously, almost 30 years later his associate, the Reverend Sun Myung Moon, began to show a keen interest in the region. In early 2001, one of his organisations, the grandly named 'International and Inter-religious Federation for World Peace' (IIFWP), spent hundreds of thousands of dollars to sponsor conferences in the Marshall Islands, Solomon Islands, Palau and Japan, all which featured heavy Pacific islands participation and all-expenses-paid trips for attendees.[100]

Had this taken place in the 1970s, the IIFWP's initiatives could have been more easily understood, but in the post-Cold War era it was hard to say what Moon's interest in the Pacific could be. But, in his own inimitable language, Moon explained his sudden interest in the Pacific in a message posted on his internet website:

> One nation has only 2000 people, but I want to save it and help it become a member of the world community. America and Japan abandoned such nations, but I work with them. Someone has to pay attention, because the Pacific Ocean is in the position of the mother's womb for the two continents and for the planet Earth . . . There are many resources there. Who will be the owner? Let's march to the Pacific Ocean.[101]

Flying in his own jet, the 81-year-old Moon visited the Marshall Islands in October 2000. He went trawling for tuna and marlin, and a state banquet was held in his honour. Kessai Note, the president of the tiny island republic, lavished praise on Moon's 'international leadership'. But not everybody was impressed. Prominent Marshall Islands leader Wilfred Kendall, the minister of education, publicly called Moon 'a fascist and a liar'.[102]

While the Marshall Islands are emerging as a haven for many of the new adventurers who are descending on the Pacific, Nauru is regarded as the most secretive of the 'financial centres' in the region, which could be the reason why it has become a favourite of the Russians. For years, Nauru was actually one of the world's wealthiest nations, with an economy based on bird droppings which, over millennia, had turned into phosphate. But with the mineral wealth running out, Nauru turned to international banking—or, more precisely, to attracting hot money from Russia. 'Nauru's offshore banking regime, in the absence of proper safeguards, is an open invitation to financial crime and money-laundering', stated the US State Department's Bureau of International Narcotics and Law Enforcement Affairs in its 1998–99 report, which claimed that 'Russian organised crime is increasingly exploiting Nauru's offshore financial sector'. In October 1998, Russia's then deputy central bank governor, Viktor Melnikov, said that $70 billion was transferred from Russian banks to accounts and banks in Nauru to avoid tax.[103] Half of a $7 billion sum that was laundered through the Bank of New York in 1999 also went through Nauru.[104]

Nauru is understood to have licensed electronic banking operation that allows the international transfer of funds on an enormous scale—

at the same time as it remains one of the most difficult countries in the world to visit.[105] Visas are rarely granted, and journalists are considered almost enemies of the state. When revenues from phosphate were high in the 1970s and 1980s the Nauruans had a good time. Air Nauru was one of the world's first all-jet airlines, and vast amounts of money were invested in the Nauru Pacific shipping line and real estate in Australia. But they lived beyond their means, and Nauru's 10 000 inhabitants are today burdened with a heavy foreign debt, and the reality that there is no potential income on the horizon other than taking advantage of the fact that this little speck of land in the Pacific Ocean is a separate jurisdiction that has the right to enact its own laws and prevent 'outside interference' in its 'internal affairs'.

Following the *Tampa* incident, Nauru gained, quite unexpectedly, a new source of income. The Australian government gave Nauru A\$20 million (\$10 million) to take unwanted Afghan, Iraqi and Pakistani refugees off its hands, while their claims were being processed. That may help Nauru survive for a while—but it is estimated that the world's smallest republic has lost a staggering \$1 billion in investments and years of government ineptitude.[106] Nauru is not likely to close down its 'financial centre' any time soon.

Some banking scams originate in countries even less firmly rooted in terra firma than Nauru, such as the elusive 'Dominion of Melchizedek'—which exists only in cyberspace but lays claim to some islands in the Pacific belonging to other, real countries—and 'the Kingdom of EnenKio' which is based on a spurious, supposedly tribal, claim to the United States-administered Wake Island, halfway between Japan and Hawaii. In November 2000, US federal authorities closed down a scam in which the 'Kingdom of EnenKio' was selling 'gold war bonds' on the internet.[107] In June 2000, the Organisation for Economic Cooperation and Development (OECD), said 35 territories worldwide practised 'harmful tax competition'; essentially, these jurisdictions were seen as seeking to attract cash from people or companies driven purely by a desire to avoid paying tax on their money. Seven of them were in the Pacific: the Cook Islands, the Marshall Islands, Nauru, Niue, Samoa, Tonga and Vanuatu.[108] The Group of 7 (G7) economic superpowers said they were preparing tough sanctions against Nauru and Niue over mounting evidence that they were key players for the Russian *Mafiya* and even South American drug cartels.[109]

Niue, a 'self-governing territory in free association with New Zealand', comprises 259 square kilometres and, with a population of only 2103 people, it has the dubious distinction of being the world's smallest tax haven. But, as a separate jurisdiction, it has the right to enact its own laws. Anyone can register their companies there via the internet and, to attract Chinese and Russian customers, Niue allows registration to be made in Chinese or Cyrillic characters. But on 30 January 2001, two United States banks, the Bank of New York and Chase Manhattan, took the first step against such activities and imposed an embargo on transfers of money to Niue, where more than 6000 shelf companies are registered. Commenting on the embargo, Niue's prime minister, Sani Lakatani, said: 'It is a brutal blow to us. The money enables us to survive'. The $1.6 million in registration fees paid annually by companies 'incorporated' in Niue accounts for 80 per cent of the territory's annual budget. The rest comes from the export of sweet potatoes, and the sale abroad of addresses within its top-level internet domain, nu.[110]

But such actions are unlikely to put an end to the skullduggery in the Pacific. An almost equally lucrative business comes from selling passports, and most of the customers are people from China who want some kind of 'legal' document to travel abroad—and hopefully end up in the United States or Australia. The first country to develop a 'passport of convenience' scheme was the Kingdom of Tonga. The idea came in the late 1980s from a Hong Kong-based American investment adviser and former Bank of America employee, Jesse Bogdanoff. He was asked by Taufa'ahau Tupou IV, the King of Tonga, for advice on how to raise badly needed revenue. Bogdanoff's suggestion was to sell passports. Britain had just signed an agreement with China for the return of Hong Kong, and a new category of British passports had been introduced for most residents of the territory. They were 'overseas dependants', which meant that they had no right of abode in Britain, and the new passports were of dubious value even as ordinary travel documents. For $33 000, someone who was otherwise 'stateless' could become a 'Tongan Protected Person' and carry a Tongan passport.[111] And not all of them were Hong Kong Chinese. Among those who became Tongans in this way were ex-President Ferdinand Marcos of the Philippines and his wife Imelda, after they had been forced to flee their country after a popular uprising in 1987.

Tonga stopped the practice in late 1998 and made the fateful decision to place the profits from the sale of passports—an estimated $24.5 million—with an American investment company. Jesse Bogdanoff even persuaded the king to appoint him as the official court jester—just to disappear with the money. In the end, Tonga gained almost nothing from its unorthodox passport scheme.[112] But that has not deterred the Republic of Kiribati, Nauru, Tuvalu and the Marshall Islands from following suit. Vanuatu went a step further and appointed people—some of whom had criminal records or other dubious connections—'honorary consuls' abroad, with the power to sell even diplomatic passports. The first scam occurred in 1997, when Vanuatu's then prime minister, Serge Vohor, appointed a Chinese national, Chen Jianpeng, 'honorary consul' to Macau, and Albert Kao, a Taiwan-born Hong Kong resident, was given the same role in the then British colony. Larry Yu, the director of a Hong Kong-based company called NCI International, which specialises in 'investment and immigration services', was appointed Vanuatu's official representative in Cambodia. Yu, who was born in China, carried a passport from the Marshall Islands, and maintained his 'consulate' in Hong Kong. When asked by Vanuatu's energetic Ombudsman, Marie-Noelle Ferrieux Patterson, why he was there instead of in Phnom Penh, Yu replied that it was for 'security reasons', as the Cambodian capital was so violent.[113] In April–May 1997, a four-man delegation from the Vanuatu government, including foreign minister Willy Jimmy, travelled to Hong Kong and Macau, where their new 'diplomatic representatives' presented them with lavish gifts and promises of investments in Vanuatu. More precisely, plans were made to sell passports to Chinese. Cambodia had by then already become an important transit point for illegal immigration to the West.

A report by the Ombudsman put an end to that racket. But in 2000 and 2001, Vanuatu appointed two new 'honorary consuls'. One of them, a Hong Konger called Chen Hung Kee or Peter Chen, was named Vanuatu's envoy to Britain. He was not unknown to the police. On 9 May 1982, he had organised an armed robbery against a jewellery store in Hong Kong's Wanchai district and escaped with gold and diamonds worth 630 000 Hong Kong dollars ($84 000). He was later captured, and in June the following year a court in Hong Kong sentenced him to fifteen years in gaol. His wife, Lim Suk-wah, received five years.[114] When his criminal record was disclosed, Chen 'resigned' as Vanuatu's 'honorary consul' to Britain.

The other, an Indian living in Thailand called Amarendra Nath Ghosh, was appointed 'honorary consul' to Thailand, Laos and Cambodia.[115] His Centurion Bank is registered in Vanuatu, and he is also associated with another offshore bank in the island republic named GST Bank, which is suspected of having defrauded Banco Ambrosiana Veneto, an Italian bank, of around $50 million. Using his newly issued diplomatic passport from Vanuatu, Ghosh applied for a temporary business visa at the Australian Embassy in Bangkok, but was advised to reapply using his Indian passport.[116] However, Ghosh and Vanuatu's then prime minister, Barak Sope, did pay a highly publicised visit to Laos in February 2001. They were received by the Lao prime minister, Sisavath Keobounphanh, and the delegation from Vanuatu pledged to invest in 'satellite and hydroelectric power' schemes in Laos as well as 'telecommunications and eucalyptus planting'.[117]

Vanuatu does not have the necessary skills, nor the money, to fulfil those obligations, but exactly what the Vanuatu delegation was up to was not clear. It is not only the necessity to make money in any way they can which makes the island states of the Pacific prone to exploitation by fraudsters and international tricksters. The gullibility of their leaders is also astounding, and the combination of these two traits makes the Pacific a perfect playground for Russian as well as Asian organised crime. An Australian foreign ministry document, which accidentally became public in September 1997, described the leaders of the Pacific island states as 'incompetent, drunken, vain and corrupt', and said that their economies 'teeter on the verge of bankruptcy'.[118] The leakage of the document left the embarrassed Australians to explain its contents to their smaller neighbours in the Pacific—but although the assessment was harsh, it was not far off the mark. The Pacific island states are artificial nations and superficially idyllic basket cases with little or no sense of nationhood. It is hardly their fault, but the legacy of years of exploitation, underdevelopment and a lack of proper education for their citizens.

Australia is not perfect either, although its problems are entirely different in origin and scope. Australia has become a magnet for Asian gangs, for which it is ill-prepared, and any determined attempt by the authorities to thwart the trend could easily fuel a racist backlash if handled carelessly. The threat is real, but not along the lines envisaged by populist politician Pauline Hanson. What has become a delicate issue has to be examined without ethnic prejudice. The exact nature of the conspiracy of the blood brothers becomes clearer in the main destinations for both Asian heroin and illegal immigrants: Canada and the United States.

● 8

CLIMBING THE MOUNTAIN OF GOLD

Since the mid-nineteenth century, hundreds of thousands of Chinese have immigrated to the United States. Many think of the country as *Jinshan*, or the Mountain of Gold, a place where the streets are paved with gold, and they believe that everyone who makes it there will make a fortune.
—Ko-lin Chin, Associate Professor of Criminal Justice at Rutgers University, Newark[1]

Cooperation between the Hong Kong tycoons, the Triads and the Beijing leadership adds a new dimension to the well-known 'mass line collection' strategy followed by the Chinese Intelligence Services. This situation substantially raises the level of the potential threat, revealing the effectiveness of Chinese efforts to obtain Canadian technology and their capability to interfere in the management of the country.
—From *Sidewinder*, a secret report prepared for the Royal Canadian Mounted Police and the Canadian Security Intelligence Service, 1997[2]

For San Lwin, the Burmese chief officer of the *Golden Venture*, the low point of a long career on the high seas arrived in the pre-dawn chill of 6 June 1993. The dilapidated 30 metre freighter he navigated was floating only a few hundred metres off Rockaway Point in Queen's, New York. A gun was pressed at San Lwin's head, and he was ordered to run the *Golden Venture* aground. At first, the chief officer bravely refused. But the Chinese gangster meant business. San Lwin had no choice but to order one of his men, a younger Burmese called Banyar Aung, to manoeuvre the ship into position. Then it ploughed full speed through the darkness for the shore.

It was no coincidence that half the crew onboard the *Golden Venture* were Burmese. Chinese crime syndicates actually operate fleets of such ships for insurance scams and to smuggle everything from drugs to tobacco. Given the repressive political climate in their home country, the Burmese are less likely than seamen from other nations to appeal to their authorities for help. Few are organised in trade unions, and most of them are willing to accept low wages and abysmal working conditions—and to do whatever is required of them. Or almost. Chief officer San Lwin would not have grounded his ship without a gun to his head. And this particular ship carried no ordinary cargo—only passengers, whose lives also hung in the balance. When the ship hit a sandbar about a hundred metres off Rockaway Point, they started jumping overboard. The *Golden Venture* was tiny, but nearly 300 people emerged from its cargo hold. Two hundred of them threw themselves into the chilling waves in hope of reaching the shore. It was still in the small hours, and the water was crippingly cold: only 12°C. Many could not swim and ten of them drowned.

The park authorities at Rockaway Point spotted the ship and the unusual visitors, and within an hour officials from a variety of law enforcement agencies were on the scene. They began apprehending the cold, wet swimmers, while the US Coast Guard rescued the 100 passengers who had remained onboard. They all turned out to be natives of China's Fujian province. Apart from the crew, which also included some Indonesians, there were another four men. Two of them carried guns and two sharp knives. They were ethnic Chinese enforcers from a syndicate that specialised in smuggling illegal immigrants to the United States.[3]

It had taken four months for the *Golden Venture* to reach the United States, where its dramatic arrival became headline news. Newspapers were filled with reports of people smuggling rings and the TV networks carried dramatic footage of the illegal immigrants as, shivering and huddling under blankets, they were led away by the police. That this was taking place less than an hour's voyage from the Statue of Liberty made the drama even more emotional and divided the nation between those who thought the poor and oppressed—but daring—Chinese youngsters should be welcomed as heroes in the land of the free, and others who saw the massive illegal immigration as a threat to national security. And who were the so-called 'snakeheads'—the men with tattoos, pistols and knives? Some sensational reports depicted the arrival of the *Golden Venture* as almost a Triad-invasion of America.[4]

The tale that unfolded when the police began to interrogate the crew and the illegal immigrants was as dramatic as it was tragic—and it clearly showed the extent of the syndicate's international connections. They were even more far reaching than the network that five years later brought the *Uniana* and its cargo of 400 kilograms of heroin to Grants Beach in New South Wales, Australia. The 300 Chinese had trekked down from Yunnan along the old opium routes that wind through eastern Burma, crossing the Thai frontier at the official border post at Tachilek–Mae Sai. There they were met by members of the syndicate which they had paid to deliver them to the United States. They were escorted in smaller groups down to the southern Thai town of Songkhla, where the *Gina-III*, a 3532-tonne cargo ship was waiting for them. But that vessel, which was big enough to carry 300 people, was washed ashore when a cyclone hit the area in October 1992. The syndicate and its snakeheads panicked, and a replacement had to be found very quickly, as the Thai authorities were now on the trail of the people smugglers. An almost unseaworthy wreck, the *Naje-II*, picked up 200 of the would-be illegal immigrants and sailed across the Indian Ocean to the Kenyan port city of Mombasa. All the syndicate could find to carry the rest was a small coastal freighter called m.v. *Tong Sern*, which sailed under a Panamanian flag of convenience. It sailed from Bangkok to Ko Si Chang, a small island off Thailand's eastern seaboard. Located a short boat ride from Si Racha on the mainland, the Ko Si Chang harbour is always full of barges, although no more than a few thousand people live permanently on the island. Si Racha is halfway between the town of Chonburi, the centre of much of Thailand's booming smuggling industry, and the sleazy beach resort of Pattaya. Ko Si Chang provides excellent offshore storage for all sorts of contraband and is a centre for all kinds of illegal activities.

It was here that the *Tong Sern* picked up the remaning 95 Chinese from the original group of 300. On 14 February 1993, the ship left Ko Si Chang. The first stop was Singapore. The *Tong Sern* reported to the port authorities that it carried only a few crew members and no cargo. No inspection was made, and the ship sailed up the Strait of Malacca and into the Indian Ocean. Twenty-two days later, it arrived in Mombasa too, where the other 200 Chinese had been waiting for months under the watchful eyes of brutal enforcers. Not surprisingly, the rusty old *Naje-II* had broken down, and was unable to carry them any further. They were stranded in Mombasa, but it had not been an entirely unpleasant stay. Most of them were young, in their late teens or early twenties, and it was their first time out of Fujian. They spent a lot of time exploring the seamen's bars of Mombasa, with their Indian and Somali prostitutes, and the Kenyan police did not hassle them. The enforcers had convinced the local authorities that all of them were Thai workers on their way to Angola[5]

But now the fun was over—and everybody had to cram into the *Tong Sern*. By the time it arrived in Mombasa—in fact, the day after it left Ko Si Chang—it had changed names. '*Golden Venture*' was painted over the old name. No one knows why the armed enforcers chose that name, but perhaps it was considered an auspicious one that would help overcome all the unavoidable hardships on the long voyage to America. And they were, after all, on their way to *Jinshan*, the Mountain of Gold. Whatever it was called, the tiny coastal freighter with a registered crew of only five men was not built to cross oceans, and certainly not to carry hundreds of passengers. But there was more to come.

The *Golden Venture* sailed down the east coast of Africa. It stopped at Infanta, a small port in South Africa, not far from Cape Agulhas, Africa's southernmost point. There, even more American-bound Chinese were waiting. But this time, the crew refused. There was almost a mutiny, and the enforcers had to accept that the *Golden Venture* would sink if there were any more people on board. The ship continued across the Atlantic, heading for the island of Antigua in the West Indies, where it was supposed to rendezvous with another ship. There were too many people on board the *Golden Venture*, and it would be easier to split its human cargo between two ships. The other ship never showed up, however, and the *Golden Venture* continued alone to the United States.

The saga surrounding the *Golden Venture* received broad attention and sparked an intense public debate, but it was not the only ship carrying illegal immigrants from China to the United States at the time. Between 1991 and 1997, the US government either intercepted or was aware of the existence of at least 30 freighters carrying thousands of Chinese into the country. Some sailed directly to US shores while others landed in Mexico or Canada, their passengers continuing overland to New York, Boston or San Francisco.[6] Some routes and methods could be quite ingenious. It is much less difficult for most foreigners to enter Canada than the United States, and the easiest point to cross the border between those two countries is the native Indian Akwesasne Reserve 70 kilometres southwest of Montreal. The St Lawrence River forms the official border, but south of it is another area where law enforcement is the duty of local native police: a 22-hectare Mohawk reserve that spans two provinces in Canada, Ontario and Quebec, and the state of New York in the United States. Once inside the Canadian part of this jurisdictional jigsaw, anyone can cross the river and be in the United States without having to go through any official immigration check. Illicit traffic in this loophole along the US–Canadian frontier began in the 1980s with cigarettes. Since then, the smuggling of drugs, weapons and illegal immigrants via this route has become a multi-million dollar business.[7]

And, once inside the United States, the chances of being sent back to China are very slim. Of the 300 young Fujianese onboard the *Golden Venture*, only about 50 were repatriated while 30 received political asylum, 80 were freed on bond and the rest were incarcerated for various periods of time. Finally, in February 1997, President Bill Clinton released all remaining people from the *Golden Venture*, a move apparently triggered by an article in the *New York Times* published earlier that month describing the plight of the Chinese migrants.[8] And there is no question that the illegal 'boat people' had to go through hell before they reached their final destination. They each paid $25 000–30 000, and would now pay even more, for an entire package which is said to include bribes to local officials in Fujian, the purportedly safe passage to the United States, food during the journey and 'escorts' to look after them. But the ships are usually decrepit Japanese, Chinese or Taiwanese long liners and tuna boats that have been converted to carry masses of people. Paying passengers are kept in the hold where the catch of the day was formerly frozen. Conditions are dark, damp, smelly and filthy. The migrants eat, sleep and defecate in the same quarters. Sea water is often pumped into the hold to flush it clean. Sea water is also used for bathing, washing clothes, being seasick in, brushing teeth and relieving oneself; often all these activities go on simultaneously. Other ships have water lowered into the hold twice a day by bucket. Most migrants are generally given food once a day. Sometimes they are allowed to come above decks for a few minutes of fresh air, but they are usually fed in the holds by having buckets of watery rice gruel lowered down to them from above. Shipboard rats are huge and nasty, and some boats even have bandicoots aboard, proof of landfall in South America.[9]

Back in the safe houses in China, rougher-looking 'passengers' are recruited as shipboard enforcers and given a discount fare. They are allowed to sleep above decks, and given double the rations of food in exchange for crowd control. The enforcers assist the smugglers in keeping the passengers in order by beating them, stealing their belongings and threatening them with death in case they have any plans to run away when they reach their destination in order to avoid paying the hefty fee for their passage. A US law enforcement officer recalls recording cases of migrants being made to drink an enforcer's urine at gunpoint, to give oral sex to an enforcer at gunpoint, and having their limbs broken while strung up by their hands.[10] Females among the migrants—and there are a few—are often raped or coerced into having sex with the enforcers with promises of extra rations of food and water.[11]

If relatives in China or the United States have paid the smuggling fees in advance, which often is the case, the migrants are set free once they reach the shores of America. But if they have any outstanding debts, they are kept in smelly and overcrowded hovels—known as 'safe houses'—in the United States until the payment of their fees has been settled. The basements of these single-family houses are converted into virtual prisons, where the migrants are shackled behind tightly closed windows. Those who are late paying their fees are sometimes struck with iron bars while talking to their relatives over the phone, so that their families can hear them crying in pain. A young girl was raped with a mobile phone next to her mouth—so her parents in Fujian at the other end of the line could hear her cries for mercy.[12]

Although President Clinton pardoned most of the illegal immigrants who had arrived on the *Golden Venture*, intense media coverage of the terrible plight of the migrants immediately after the affair prompted the US government to crack down on the traffic in human beings. The government in Beijing, concerned about the damage to China's international reputation, also launched a campaign against the miserable practice. But, years later, the trade continues unabated. Only the routes and methods have changed. Illegal immigrants are no longer carried in smelly, run-down ships—instead they arrive by air, often via circuitous routes. With false documents obtained in Bangkok or Phnom Penh, they may travel to Mexico or Canada—perhaps via Europe to add a few more stamps to their passports to make them more convincing at immigration checkpoints elsewhere in the world—and then cross the border into the United States. Some travel via countries in Latin America with large Asian populations such as Surinam or Panama. Or they try to enter an outlying US territory such as Guam, the US Virgin Islands or Puerto Rico, from where it is easier to continue to the mainland.

Some buy real passports from Taiwanese associates of the syndicates who get US visas in Taipei and then travel to Bangkok. There they sell their passports with a valid US visa in them to a look-alike from the Chinese mainland, or skilful forgers just change the passport photograph. The Taiwanese then report their passports as stolen to the Taiwanese mission in Bangkok, get new ones and return to Taipei.[13] Others may buy a passport from a country such as Vanuatu, perhaps with a false US visa in it, which sometimes is enough to be allowed by airlines to board a flight, but would not work once the plane landed in Los Angeles or San Francisco, where skilled immigration officials scrutinise all travel documents. However, while in the air, they flush their passports down the plane's toilet. When they land, they apply for political asylum.

The smuggling syndicates coach their clients on how to claim political asylum in the United States. They can say they are political dissidents or Christians who have been subjected to religious persecution. Or that they had to flee because of China's one-child policy. Or that they are homosexuals and therefore undesirable in Chinese society. The variations are endless, but it is estimated that as many as 50 mainly Hong Kong-based Triad groups and other criminal organisations are responsible for sending as many as 100 000 illegals per year to the United States, raking in billions of dollars for their services. Some academics who specialise in Chinese migration predict that this figure will rise to 200 000–300 000 by 2005.[14]

The preferred destination is New York's Chinatown. Working conditions in its many sweatshops and restaurant kitchens may be appalling by western standards, and people may end up in dingy, cockroach-infested, one-room apartments sleeping in shifts because they are too small to accommodate all the tenants at once. But they earn incomes more than 20 times what they would be able to earn back in Fujian, so the illegal immigrants put up with it, hoping that after a year or so they will be as prosperous as everybody else in the United States. And America's modern Chinatowns are not, after all, like black and Hispanic ghettos, which lack jobs and capital. They are magnets which attract immigrants, legal and illegal, because there is money to be made, legally and illegally.[15] Some make it and move out of their dingy lodging houses, marry and buy their own apartments and houses, while others get trapped in a vicious circle of crime and violence.

The flood of Chinese to the United States actually began at about the same time as Japanese Prime Minister Yasuhiro Nakasone launched his scheme to attract overseas students, mainly Chinese, to Japanese universities. But the American decision was based on different considerations. In 1979, a year after Washington and Beijing normalised relations, China liberalised its immigration regulations in order to qualify for most favoured nation status with the United States. Chinese were admitted to American universities, or as trainees at companies in the United States, or simply immigrated under a new quota system—and many more wanted to come but were unable to do so by legal means. Deng Xiaoping's market reforms in the 1980s also led to tens of millions of people being laid off from state-owned farms and enterprises, and if there were no new jobs available in the towns, emigration became the most attractive option.

In the United States, the massive influx of legal and illegal immigrants has become not only a challenge to the country's normally liberal immigration tradition, but has also changed the composition and nature of the Chinatowns in New York, Boston, San Francisco and elsewhere—and, apart from bringing in millions of enterprising and hard-working immigrants, an entirely new kind of organised crime has arrived with the tide. Traditional bands of street thugs have been forced out by newly arrived mobsters with solid connections in East Asia, and they are far more brutal than the old Chinatown gangs.[16] Whereas the first inhabitants of New York's Chinatown—by far the largest in North America—emigrated from the eight counties along the Pearl River delta near Guangzhou, and its post-1965 residents came mainly from Hong Kong, the newcomers come mostly from Fujian, 'China's Sicily' and the birthplace of the original Triads, though many others come from all over mainland China and Southeast Asia.[17] Not surprisingly, many Chinese-American old-timers are watching this development with unease, especially given all the hardships and discrimination they had to endure before they gained acceptance in American society.

The Chinese began migrating to the United States in large numbers in the 1840s. They were brought as coolies—literally 'bitter labour' in Chinese—to mine gold and build the railways. The discovery of gold in California in 1848 led to a great demand for cheap labour, and for workers who could go down into the more dangerous underground mines after white workers had exhausted the rich surface of the gold fields. The way in which they were hired, and their living conditions once they had arrived at their new work sites, were not quite as bad as those facing the thousands who were recruited in Macau at about the same time and sent to plantations in Peru and Cuba. But racial prejudice and unionisation of the white workers prompted the Chinese in California to begin migrating to the East Coast towards the end of the nineteenth century.[18]

By 1880, there were 100 000 Chinese in the United States, not a huge number compared with other groups. But two years later, politicians from the western states, with the support of like-minded colleagues from the south, pushed the *Chinese Exclusion Act* through Congress. It was the first and only federal law ever to exclude a certain group of people by nationality.[19] They became the target of abuse and random violence, and had no choice but to seek refuge in larger cities, where they lived together in what became known as 'Chinatowns'. The administrative structures of these new ghettos were transplanted from nineteenth-century feudal China. Clan and village associations, as well as secret societies, were formed to defend the unwanted migrants from China against racial attacks from the white population.[20] The clannish structure of the Chinatowns was further strengthened by the fact that many of those who settled in one place came from the same part of China. The vast majority of the inhabitants of New York's Chinatown, for instance, came from Taishan (or Toishan, depending on the dialect) in southern Guangdong province, or from nearby districts. But the sexual imbalance was almost as striking here in the United States as it was in Australia at the same time: the male-to-female ratio was 27 to one in 1890.[21] This imbalance gave birth to a bachelor-dominated society where prostitution flourished alongside gambling and opium smoking. The secret societies, which had been set up to care for the migrants, became increasingly involved in providing protection for brothels, gambling halls and opium dens—and in extorting money from their own Chinese communities. Street gangs were often employed to carry out duties that the more established 'community associations' did not want to do themselves.

The umbrella organisation for the various clubs and guilds in New York's Chinatown was the Chinese Consolidated Benevolent Association (CCBA). Founded in 1880, it was structured like a government, declared its right to tax its members, but was hardly a democratic organisation. In the mid-twentieth century, the CCBA's powerful executive committee came under the control of seven permanent members, the so-called 'Seven Major Overseas Associations': two district associations called Ning Young and Lian Chen, the Guomindang or the Chinese Nationalist Party and its now defunct affiliate Ming Chi Tang, the Chinese Chamber of Commerce, and two of Chinatown's most influential grey-zone societies, or *tongs*, the Hip Sing ('United in Victory') and the On Leong (or An Leung in Cantonese pronunciation; 'Peaceful and Virtuous').[22]

The word *tong* (*dang* in *pinyin*, as the last syllable in Guomindang) actually means 'hall' or 'lodge', and these groups are patterned after the original Triad societies.[23] In reality, this means that, although they claim to be patriotic mutual-aid societies, they are in fact involved in and benefit from a wide range of criminal activities through a host of more unruly youth gangs which they control. Since the members of the *tongs* were not related and thus had different surnames, they pledged allegiance to one another as 'brothers in blood oath'.[24] But that oath was confined to members of the same *tong*; in the 1930s, the Chinatowns in both New York and San Francisco were shaken by vicious *tong* wars, where different gangs fought for control over certain streets. Disputes over gambling debts and 'protection money' from local shop owners were the most common reasons for these wars, while other conflicts stemmed from local patriotism. Cantonese groups attacked *tongs* dominated by Hakka or other language groups and so on. The *tong* wars spread to San Francisco and Boston, and at one stage the Nationalist Chinese embassy in Washington sent a first secretary to New York's Chinatown to negotiate a peace treaty between its two main warring *tongs*, the Hip Sing and the On Leong. They refused to acquiesce, and the police, who normally left the

Chinese alone to handle their own affairs and internal disputes, intervened and threatened the *tong* leaders with deportation if the violence did not stop. Open fighting in the streets gradually subsided, but the *tongs* continued to run their extortion rackets, gambling dens, brothels and opium businesses in an easy truce of convenience. They all had an interest in keeping the 'white' police out of their Chinatowns.[25]

In 1943, when the United States and China, then ruled by the Guomindang, fought together against the Japanese in East Asia, Congress found it was time to repeal the discriminatory Chinese exclusion acts. Chinese gained the right to naturalisation, and women from China were allowed to come to the United States to marry. From 1945 to 1950, almost 8000 Chinese women—the overwhelming majority of Chinese arrivals during that time—entered the United States, and the long-suffering Chinese there began to resemble other immigrant communities.[26] But it was not until 1965 that the last vestiges of the country's racially discriminatory immigration policy were dropped and applicants from all nations, including China, were given equal treatment with an annual immigration quota of 20 000 each. However, in those days in the United States, 'China' meant 'the Republic of China', or Taiwan. It was only in 1978 that the United States changed its recognition to 'the People's Republic of China', and established an embassy in Beijing. The 20 000 quota for immigrants from China now applied to the mainland. But to show Taiwan some goodwill after decades of close cooperation, the island was in 1982 given a separate quota of 20 000 immigrants, to which another 5000 from Hong Kong were added in 1987.[27] And then came the flood of illegal immigrants from mainland China, who are not part of any quota system.

New York's Chinatown, more than any other, grew at a tremendous pace. Until the 1970s, it covered about a dozen blocks in lower Manhattan below the intersection of Bowery and Canal Streets. But over the past 30 years the population has at least quadrupled and several hundred thousand people now live in the area. Internal Chinatown estimates place the population at around half a million, and suggest that some 200 people come to live there each day.[28] Chinatown has expanded north into Little Italy, east into an old Jewish neighbourhood, south to City Hall and the court buildings, and west beyond the once-chic galleries on lower Broadway.[29] Although still a small minority of the total population of New York, the Chinese have become one of the fastest growing ethnic groups in the city.[30]

Traditionally, the hierarchy in New York's Chinatown has followed a relatively well-established pattern. The CCBA, which was politically strongly influenced by the Guomindang, was the official forum for community affairs. It was also supposed to control the *tongs*, but often ended up being controlled, or manipulated, by them. The *tongs* did their best to uphold a front of legitimate businesses. The Hip Sing still has its own federally insured loan association called the Hip Sing Credit Union, and the On Leong has among the tenants in its headquarters the United Orient Bank, which was set up with Taiwanese money. The bank has representatives from what is officially called the 'On Leong Merchants' Association' on its board of directors.[31]

However, the muscle of the *tongs* was the street gangs, young toughs recruited from the shadier sides of society in New York's Chinatown. The coordinator who raised and organised the street gangs was called *dai dai lo*, or 'big big brother' and, although he was assigned to that particular duty by his *tong*, his bosses could always deny any knowledge of what he was doing. 'Those youngsters', and 'you know, youth gangs', always got the blame for violence and crime in Chinatown. The *tong*-appointed *dai dai lo* would deal with a street-level *dai lo* ('big brother'), who could be a *yee lo* ('second brother') or *saam lo* ('third brother'). Each street-level brother would be in charge of a band of younger *ma jai* ('horse boys', as in Macau) or *leng jai* ('little kids').[32] Some were barely in their teens, and their gangs were given colourful names such as the Ghost Shadows, the Flying Dragons and the White Tigers, all with their own set of codes and strict oaths of loyalty. But most of these street gangs had a short lifespan because they were reorganised and renamed when one gang had outlived its usefulness, its activities been exposed, or its members arrested or killed. In any event, they served a purpose which the *tongs* could not get involved in under their own names: the 'tamed' juvenile delinquents were sent to protect gambling houses, deal in drugs, collect debts and extort money from ordinary shopkeepers and restaurant owners, as well as operators of theatres, night clubs and massage parlours.[33] Everyone knew that the *tongs* were behind the gangs, so there was no way anyone would complain to the CCBA or—even more unthinkable—the police.

To oppose the politics of the elite in America's Chinatowns could also be dangerous. When Mao Zedong proclaimed the People's Republic of China from the Gate of Heavenly Peace, or the Tiananmen, on 1 October 1949, some Chinese in the United States welcomed it, hoping that the new government would be more idealistic and less corrupt than the old Guomindang regime. On 9 October, a few hundred people in San Francisco's Chinatown gathered to celebrate the event. But the speeches had hardly begun before thugs from two local *tongs*, the Hop Sing and the Bing Kung, stormed the auditorium, tore down the new Chinese flag and sprayed the audience with blue dye. The next day, a list with the names of fifteen of the speakers and organisers of the meeting was posted in San Francisco's Chinatown offering a $5000 reward for the death of each one of them.[34]

But as America's Chinatowns grew with the influx of new people from Hong Kong and the Chinese mainland—and as Deng Xiaoping's economic reforms in the post-Mao era transformed China completely—it became much less controversial to show loyalty to Beijing, or to maintain contacts with mainland leaders and businessmen. Ching Men-ky, or Carl Ching of the International Basketball Federation, who was denied a visa to visit the 2000 Sydney Olympics, had perhaps shown the way when he and Eddie T.C. Chan, or Chan Tse-chiu who was also known as 'Fast Eddie Chan', the Hong Kong police sergeant who had fled the colony in 1974, began to travel to China to wine and dine Chinese officials in the 1980s. Their links to China's then military leader Yang Shangkun, and more precisely his son, proved useful for establishing contacts and influence among China's new leaders—'the capitalist roaders', as Mao had once branded them. But links with Taiwan were still important. The United Orient Bank, which had its offices in the headquarters of the On Leong, was actually founded by Ching and Chan.[35] For a while, the moon-faced Chan was also the executive director of On Leong, and later became the model for one of the main characters in Robert Daley's novel *Year of the Dragon*, which was made into a film.[36]

In August 1990, a grand jury in Chicago finally indicted the national On Leong and its local *tong* branches in Chicago, New York and Houston along with 27 individuals on charges of racketeering, loansharking, extortion, income-tax evasion, illegal gambling, fraud and murder. Chan was among the listed defendants, but he had already lived up to his nickname 'Fast Eddie' and fled the United States in the 1980s after being subpoenaed to appear before the Presidential Commission on Organised Crime. He has reportedly been spotted in China many times since then, and some reports have it that he is living in Vietnam.[37]

But Ching continued to operate more openly, and his 1992 gangster summit in Hong Kong drew some 1000 participants, including overseas representatives from Taiwan, the United States, Britain, Germany, France and Australia. Before the Hong Kong police raided the hotel rooms of some of the more suspect participants, an organisation called the United World Chinese Association had been set up. Its logo consisted of a Chinese dragon draped over a globe. A press release issued by Ching said the meeting had been held to unite all mainland and overseas Chinese with the ultimate goal of 'promoting the excellent heritage of our ancestors in terms of diligence and creativity'.[38] But the police in Canada, where Ching had had businesses, had a different opinion of the highly unusual Hong Kong businessman and promoter of both Chinese solidarity and international basketball. When he was denied a visa to enter Canada in 1994, it was because he was one of sixteen people the Canadian Commission in Hong Kong had listed in a confidential report as being 'among the world's most ruthless criminals'.[39]

Down at street level in New York's Chinatown, the changes were also being felt. In the past, the main event of the year had been 'double ten', which commemorated the outbreak of Sun Yat-sen's first Chinese revolution on 10 October 1911. But, gradually, more and more Chinese—both old-timers and newcomers—found it prudent to celebrate mainland China's National Day, 1 October, as well. For the newcomers, it was, of course, 'their' national day. For the old-timers, it was a way of hedging one's bets and making sure both Chinas were satisfied. The possibility of new business opportunities on the mainland was also a factor that many must have taken into consideration.

There were also new gangs extorting money from ordinary inhabitants in Chinatown—gangs which were much closer to the mainland than to Taiwan. The rapid influx of new people, mainly from Fujian, had changed the demographic pattern of Chinatown, and in many areas the Fujianese already outnumbered the old inhabitants of

Taishan origin. A series of successful police actions against the traditional *tongs* and their affiliated street gangs in the 1980s and early 1990s, such as the Presidential Commission on Organised Crime and the indictment of the On Leong 'Merchant Association', further crippled the power of the old-timers. A vicious attack in February 1983 by a Chinese street gang against a gambling den in Seattle on America's West Coast, in which thirteen people were gunned down, had prompted the law enforcement authorities to pay more attention to crime in the Chinese communities. They made use of a new federal anti-crime statute known as the *Racketeer Influenced and Corrupt Organisations Act* (known as RICO), which had originally been introduced to fight the Italian mafia. By targeting an entire organisation, it was enough to be a member of it to face indictment—and to be forced to testify for the state. Between 1985 and 1995, RICO was used fourteen times against major Chinese groups, shutting them down completely.[40] But the successful convictions did not affect Chinatown's infrastructure, and gambling, prostitution and other criminal activities still existed and needed protection. The vacuum was filled by new groups, which were independent of the traditional *tongs* and drew their recruits mainly from among the newcomers from Fujian. The best known of the new gangs, which emerged as a result of the police's anti-crime drives in the 1980s, was the Fuk Ching, or 'Fuzhou Youth'. Its rise to public fame was due to its direct involvement in the *Golden Venture* affair.

Fuk Ching was actually the name given to the group by the police because the gang consisted of young Fujianese who began to meet regularly in the early 1980s at the headquarters of the Fukien (or Fujian) American Association. The Fujianese were then a tiny minority in New York's Chinatown, and their association was not really a *tong* but more of a traditional community organisation. Among the youths who met there was Guo Liangqi, who was born in China and had come to New York at the age of fourteen in 1980. He and his relatives were virtually penniless and the only job he could get was as a debt collector for richer Fujianese. He soon began to imitate the ways of the Taishanese street gangs in Chinatown. He became known as 'Ah Kay', or 'Brother Kay', and earned notoriety when he was arrested in 1985 for threatening to kill a restaurant owner from whom he had tried to extort money. Ah Kay served nearly two years in prison before being deported back to China. A year later, he re-appeared in New York. He had managed to slip across the United States–Mexico border into Texas—a route that later became very popular with Chinese illegal immigrants.[41] A tip-off led the police to his hideout in Flushing, Queens, where he was arrested in mid-1989. But there was not enough evidence to convict him of any crime other than illegal re-entry to the United States, and he was smart enough to play the card that thousands of other Chinese illegal immigrants have been instructed to use: he applied for political asylum.[42] This was in the aftermath of the June 1989 Beijing massacre, and the dramatic events in Tiananmen Square were fresh in many people's memory. Ah Kay's application effectively suspended his deportation as it had to go through all possible legal channels before it would be either accepted or rejected.

The delay enabled Ah Kay to stay in New York and become the undisputed leader of the Fuk Ching, which by the end of the 1980s had become deeply involved in the lucrative people-smuggling business from Fujian to the United States. It is uncertain what kind of deal Ah Kay had worked out with local gangs—and authorities—in Fujian during his year of exile in China. But when he had to flee New York in 1990 because of an internal conflict within the Fuk Ching, he escaped back to Fujian, where he continued to run the gang's trade in human beings from a fortress-like compound near Fuzhuo, the provincial capital.[43] Police investigations in connection with the *Golden Venture* affair indicated that he had been the main organiser of its voyage, as well as those of many other ships carrying illegal immigrants to the United States.[44]

The vast amounts of money that the smuggling of humans gener-ated inevitably led to bloody disputes over how to divide the spoils between the different 'brothers' of the Fuk Ching, a band of thugs which the police described as 'the most violent and most dangerous of the Chinese gangs'.[45] On 24 May 1993, as the *Golden Venture* was on its way across the oceans to America, four of its members were slain in a shoot-out in Teaneck, a smart New York suburb. The gunmen, all Chinese, had arrived at dusk in a Dodge caravan, and stopped outside a house where some other Chinese had been staying for a couple of weeks. Then the neighbours were startled to hear gunfire in the usually quiet upper middle-class suburb. One man was shot as he tried to run away from the house. When the police later arrived on the scene, they found two young Chinese men, bound and gagged, in the basement. Both had been shot in the head. Upstairs, another two victims were lying on a bloodstained carpet. They had been shot and stabbed. Only one of the five survived, but with permanent brain damage from the bullet that had entered his head. Among the four dead were two of Ah Kay's brothers.[46] Within minutes, the police stopped the Dodge and arrested its occupants, five Chinese aged from 20 to 32. All but one of them were illegal immigrants.

Two weeks later, a wake was held for the dead in the Hong Kong Funeral Home in Chinatown's Canal Street. The four coffins lay open while fifteen young men in loose-fitting double-breasted black suits, black ties and wrap-around sunglasses walked past in silence, some bowing slightly. The young Chinese had arrived on foot in the afternoon, walking down Canal Street in single file. Some had crew-cuts while others wore mousse to make their hair stand taller. They had left their cars at home because they knew that the police were there, carefully noting the registration plates of vehicles that came and left the funeral parlour, just as they used to do at mafia funerals.[47]

Between the shootout in Teaneck and the funeral in Chinatown, the *Golden Venture* ran aground on Rockaway Point. Obviously, Ah Kay was running out of luck, but he felt secure in his walled mansion outside Fuzhou. The 27-year-old gangster was sometimes seen travelling in a convoy of three cars with a dozen bodyguards, and appeared to be at the very least tolerated by local Chinese authorities.[48] But then he made the fatal mistake of over-estimating his untouchability and sneaked into Hong Kong to pursue one of his favourite pastimes: gambling. As dawn broke on 28 August, the Hong Kong police raided the illegal den where he had been gambling all night. Ah Kay was arrested, along with one of his bodyguards who had come with him to Hong Kong.[49] In New York's Chinatown, simultaneous raids were carried out, netting a total of thirteen members of the Fuk Ching gang. Ah Kay was later extradited to the United States, and this time his application for political asylum was ignored. In 1998 he was sentenced to twenty years in gaol and fined $200 000 for 'organising a criminal conspiracy'. Two years later, one of his main accomplices in the human smuggling businesses, a China-town restaurateur called Cheng Chui Ping who was nicknamed 'Sister

Ping', was also arrested in Hong Kong, where she had fled in the aftermath of the *Golden Venture* affair.[50]

A major gang had been smashed, but did it mean the end of people smuggling from China to the United States? The media and the police assumed that the millions of dollars that the Fuk Ching had managed to collect from the illegal immigrants went into their own pockets. However, Ko-lin Chin, an ethnic Fujianese himself but born in Burma and the world's foremost expert on human smuggling and Chinatown gangs, points out that human smuggling is actually a lucrative business controlled by many otherwise legitimate groups, both small and large, working independently—each with its own organisation, connections, methods and routes.[51] The main players, or the 'big snakeheads' as Chin calls them, are generally Chinese living overseas who invest money in a smuggling operation and oversee it, but they are usually not known by those being smuggled. Or, if they are based in China, they are either former or current Chinese government employees.[52] But then there are 'small snakeheads', who are hired by the big ones to guide and move illegal immigrants, to charter boats and to act as enforcers during the voyage to the United States. Other 'small snake-heads' further down the line include support personnel who provide food and lodging to illegal immigrants at transit points on the way and, worst of all, the debt collectors. These are the thugs who collect smug-gling fees in advance and lock up those who have not paid in the so-called 'safe houses' until their debt is settled.[53] The 'small snake-heads' receive all the media attention because of the sensational aspects associated with their 'duties' along the line—but the 'big snakeheads' who hired them can always find new ones. Even the much-feared Fuk Ching consisted of replaceable enforcers, and their fall from grace did not in any way affect the overall people smuggling business.

And then there is the general attitude to the traffic in Fujian itself. Many people Chin met in Fujian thought of snakeheads as 'philan-thropists' and appreciated their services. A 43-year-old male from Tingjiang said: 'I look at human smuggling as benevolent work because a snakehead can help people out of their predicament'. A 19-year-old woman described the snakeheads as 'good people because, in a way, they help China solve her overpopulation problem'.[54] Even a government official admitted:

Frankly, we have an ambivalent attitude towards illegal migration. On the one hand, we hope our villagers will have an opportunity to go abroad and make money, because this will solve our high unemployment rate. Also, money sent back by immigrants helps us to construct the local infrastructure. On the other hand, since migration without proper documents is against our law, we must carry out theorders from above and stop illegal migration. Consequently, when it comes to dealing with illegal migration, we usually keep one eye open and close the other.[55]

For many years, nearly all migrants from Fujian came from three counties near the coast: Lianjiang, Minhou and Changle, each with a population of about 600 000. This is not a particularly poor part of Fujian. On the contrary, the fact that so many young people have gone from there to the United States has made these three counties some of the most prosperous in the whole of China.[56] It is not poverty that drives people to emigrate from Fujian, but a long tradition of migration from this traditionally volatile frontier area; as we have seen, as early as the seventeenth century, half of the Fujianese earned their living away from home.[57] As an old Fujianese saying goes: 'Plant a tree in America—rest in the shade in China'.[58] The same can be said of Toishan in Guangdong province, from which nearly all able-bodied men migrated in the late nineteenth century.

In more recent times, people displaced in the course of China's economic growth have also been leaving the country to reap even higher lifetime earnings for themselves and their relatives still living back home. That means permanently relocating to places such as New York's Chinatown—or Canada, Australia, Japan and 'the Great Golden Peninsula' of Southeast Asia. Douglas Massey, an American expert on illegal immigration, argues that the flood of people leaving China has been created by economic development and market penetration, and that the country's rapid growth and headlong movement into the global market contain the seeds of an enormous future migration.[59]

The current third wave of Chinese migration also differs considerably from earlier migrations. First of all, new migrants have begun to come not only from traditional 'migration centres' such as Taishan and Changle, but increasingly from all over China. And they are going to entirely new destinations. One of them is Budapest. There are now between 20 000 and 40 000 Chinese in Hungary. Ten years ago there were hardly any. But the fall of communism in Eastern Europe opened new markets for private entrepreneurs and, ironically, many of them came from the world's last major communist-ruled country, China. Furthermore, most of them did not come from the southern provinces but from Manchuria in the northeast—and by a very long train ride from Vladivostok across the border in Russia. Pal Nyiri, a Hungarian academic, argues that, unlike earlier Chinese settlers in the United States or Australia, these new settlers in his country—who now supply cheap goods across Eastern Europe—do not feel they have stopped being part of China. They see themselves not as local minorities, but as a 'global majority' with an attachment to China that has nothing to do with territorial nationalism. Not only is China their cultural and ethnic base, but it remains the foundation of their economic success—a place they continue to invest in and draw on.[60]

The same could be said of the recent wave of migration from China to the United States, as more and more migrants are coming from places other than Taishan and Fujian—and in the 1980s and 1990s the five-star flag of the People's Republic of China, rather than that of the Republic of China, began to appear more and more frequently in Chinatowns across North America. Somewhat ironically, it was the leader of the old Hip Sing *tong*, a man called Ong Kai-sui, or Benny Ong, who took the first steps toward creating an 'all-China' aware-ness among the Chinese in the United States. A street fighter who served seventeen years in gaol for murder in the 1930s and 1940s, Ong later rose to become the Godfather of New York's Chinatown, securing the title of 'Adviser for Life' to the Hip Sing. He held court almost daily in the Hong Shoon restaurant in Chinatown's Pell Street, from where he also settled disputes between business rivals, arranged loans for newly arrived migrants from China and secured licences for people who wanted to open a restaurant or a garment factory.

Ong changed the image of the Hip Sing from that of a feudal, sec-tarian organisation to one concerned with the welfare of the entire community.[61] But, at the same time, he tolerated no opposition to his grip on power over Chinatown. When, in the early 1980s, a former Hip Sing member called Herbert Liu founded his own organisation on East Broadway, and even recruited street thugs from the Flying

Dragons to protect a gambling enterprise, the punishment was swift. On 23 December 1982, a group of armed young men burst into the Golden Star, a bar on East Broadway where some of Liu's hoodlums were drinking. The intruders opened fire, killing three members of Liu's gang and wounding eight. Ong was never officially linked to the bloody assault, but he later made a revealing statement to the *New York* magazine: 'Sixty years I build up respect, and he think he [can] knock me down in one day?'.[62] Liu was offered police protection if he would testify against Ong but, in the end, decided that that was a bad idea. Instead, he issued a public apology for disturbing the peace of the community.[63]

Ong, who was popularly known as 'Uncle Seven', always argued that the Chinese should be united and solve their own problems. But he also encouraged Chinese-Americans to enter mainstream politics. In 1984, S.B. Woo, an ethnic Fujianese immigrant from Hong Kong, ran as a candidate for lieutenant governor of the state of Delaware. It was the first time an East Coast Chinese had sought to be elected to a prominent post, and he had the full backing of Uncle Seven. The first to respond to his plea for support was the Fujianese Association in New York, which was openly pro-Beijing and always displayed the five-star flag at major functions. This made other Chinatown groups suspicious, but Uncle Seven branded these as 'narrow-minded'. Once the Godfather had spoken, nearly all the community associations in the East Coast Chinatowns came out in support of Woo.[64]

When Ong spoke, no one in the community dared to challenge him, and even the previously omnipotent Guomindang kept silent. At the 1984 Hip Sing annual convention, Taiwan's main representative in the United States—the head of the Coordinating Council for North American Affairs, as it was called after Washington had changed diplomatic recognition of China from Taipei to Beijing—bowed to Uncle Seven during the public ceremony. But Uncle Seven's public statements about China in general so pleased Beijing that it sent a special delegation to attend the National Convention of the Chinese Freemasons, or the Hung Man (or Hong Men) *tong*, which was chaired by him as the undisputed Godfather of Chinatown.[65]

It was under Uncle Seven's tutelage that Fast Eddie Chan began to transform his *tong*, the On Leong, into a modern organisation capable of engaging in banking and commerce—and, for the first time among the Chinese-Americans, of active participation in mainstream American politics. Before he fled the United States, Chan had established several branches of his United Orient Bank in New York's Chinatown. When one of them—on Mott Street—was opened in 1983, Matilda Cuomo, the wife of New York's governor at the time, was present to cut the ribbon. A self-proclaimed Republican, Chan also contributed generously to the Ronald Reagan/George Bush re-election campaign in 1984.[66] And when Edward Koch launched his re-election campaign in 1986, a Chinatown support committee was formed with Uncle Seven and Chan as its main sponsors.[67]

Chan's disappearance from New York in the 1980s did little to reverse the new initiatives that he and Uncle Seven had taken. Nor did it upset the bonds with the People's Republic of China that Eddie and Carl Ching had forged in the 1980s. Communist (nominally, at least) China had gained a significant foothold in one of the Guomindang's oldest and most solid strongholds in North America. In 1985, even the old-fashioned CCBA had felt compelled to elect Uncle Seven as its 'Honorary Permanent Chairman'. When he died from prostate cancer at the age of 87 in August 1994, a funeral procession of 120 cars drove in a solemn procession through New York's Chinatown. An open-back limousine carried the coffin and a huge portrait of the Godfather resting in a bed of flowers.[68] Thousands of people lined the streets when the motorcade carried the most powerful man in Chinatown to his final resting place—and a hidden surveillance camera at the private funeral ceremony for Uncle Seven showed mourners giving traditional Triad hand signs as a community elder made a short speech.[69]

There is no doubt that Beijing has extended its influence over North America's ethnic Chinese communities through organised crime groups and personalities. Beijing has also made extensive use of what the late paramount leader Deng Xiaoping termed 'patriotic Triads' in achieving the remarkable feat of pushing the old Guomindang into the background in North America's Chinatowns. The close relationship between the authorities in Beijing, especially the Communist Party of China and the People's Liberation Army (PLA)—and organised crime—makes the Chinese underworld very different from other ethnic mobs in North America. The Japanese *yakuza* has long been active in California, Hawaii, Guam and other American Pacific territories, where it has invested heavily in real estate, hotels and golf courses. But, as in Australia, the Japanese mobsters there pose no serious threat to American national security. The *yakuza* has never tried to influence the governance of the United States and, despite its links to domestic Japanese politics and business, it has never acted abroad on behalf of the authorities in Tokyo. Rather, it is believed that some of the huge amounts of money that the *yakuza*'s *sokaiya* racketeers and *jiageya* real estate fixers amassed in Japan were siphoned out of the country and sunk into various investment schemes in the United States.[70]

A similar situation applies in Canada, where Masaru Takumi, the second in command of the Yamaguchi-gumi, became in the early 1990s a major shareholder and president of a Vancouver tour company catering to visitors from Japan. The Royal Canadian Mounted Police also noted that several top-ranking members of various *yakuza* groups met at sushi shops in Vancouver, and that they had purchased multi-million dollar homes.[71] But there was little evidence of gang-related violence, or of political involvement by the Japanese mobsters.

And North America's much feared Vietnamese gangs, which strikingly resemble their Australian equivalents, are little more than just that: vicious street gangs, which are involved in murder, extortion and drug peddling. Very often, also as in Australia, they do some of the dirty work for the much more powerful Chinese gangs—and their members are usually misfits from the refugee communities of boat people that were admitted in the 1970s and 1980s. On account of their propensity for violence, Vietnamese juvenile delinquents were first used by New York's Wah Ching, Flying Dragons and Ghost Shadows street gangs as enforcers. Many of the refugees who went to the United States were, like their Australian counterparts, actually Viet Ching—ethnic Chinese from Vietnam. Their ability to speak both Vietnamese and at least one Chinese dialect allowed them to move freely between ethnic Chinese and Vietnamese in America.[72]

In 1986, some Vietnamese youngsters broke away from the purely Chinese street gangs in New York and set up the Born to Kill gang. The name was borrowed from the slogan that many American GIs in Vietnam had written on their steel helmets in the 1970s, and the misplaced, frustrated and angry Vietnamese youths soon resorted to robberies, extortion and murder. With their black clothing and pony-tails, they were as easily recognisable as they were unsophisticated when it came to establishing well-organised, underground criminal cartels. But, curiously and most probably independently of the emergence of the 5T in Sydney, they also identified themselves with five 'dots', meaning *tien* (money), *tinh* (sex), *thuoc* (drugs), *toi* (crime) and *tu* (gaol)—which could also be read *tuoi, tre, thieu, tinh, thuong* ('Youth Needs Love').[73] As the Born to Kill gang became more sophisticated, some turf battles ensued. These resulted in numerous shootings in New York and Newark but, rather than challenging the traditional Chinatown gangs, the Born to Kill gang began to focus its attention on victims within its own communities. Another gang, Action Packed Vietnamese, and an all-female group called Born to Violence, followed the same pattern of newly arrived immigrant youths who worked hard to establish relations with Chinese gangs, and then tried to operate independently. Vietnamese street gang members were usually between twelve and 25 years old, and most gangs were very small, ranging in size from six to 50 members.[74]

These gangs emerged first in California in the late 1970s, often under the patronage of corrupt former officers in the South Vietnamese army and police. A shadowy society known as 'the Dark Side' was reputed to be led by Nguyen Cao Ky, the immensely corrupt former prime minister and air force officer who supplied American GIs with heroin from Laos during the Vietnam War. His 'Dark Siders' extorted money from ordinary, law-abiding Vietnamese in America, ostensibly to finance an effort to overthrow Vietnam's communist government.[75] After the war ended in 1975, Ky—somewhat surprisingly—had been allowed to settle in southern California where he ran a liquor shop when not terrorising the rest of the Vietnamese community in America. Ky had reportedly fled Vietnam with $8 million in gold, diamonds and currency.[76]

As Russians began to arrive in large numbers in the United States in the 1970s, and to establish new ethnic criminal gangs, the attention of the media—which was always hunting for sensational news—also turned in their direction. Journalists descended on Brighton Beach in Brooklyn, New York, where law-abiding Russian Jews settled in the

1970s, to look for the new exotic gangsters from the former Soviet Union. It was not difficult to find them in their ill-fitting suits and with big gold rings on their fingers. One mobster in particular caught the imagination of the media. His name was Evsei Argon and he was one of some 5000 Russian refugees who were allowed to enter the United States in 1975. He settled in Brighton Beach, or 'Little Odessa' as it became known, where he formed a gang that specialised in extortion and later expanded into prostitution and illegal gambling. By 1980 his followers were wresting more than $50 000 a week from Brighton Beach businessmen. Those who resisted were beaten and tortured with electric cattle prods, often by Argon himself.[77]

Some called Argon 'the first boss of the Russian Mafiya in the United States', and his cruelty became legendary. It was even rumoured that he had been a *vor v zakone* in the Soviet Union—a killer and a black marketeer who had spent ten years in prison before managing to escape to Brighton Beach. According to one journalist, Argon was one of those career criminals dumped in the United States when the Soviet spy organisation, the KGB, weeded the country's prisons in the 1970s.[78] Whatever the case, the balding, diminutive— he weighed less than 70 kilograms—Argon was gunned down outside his apartment in Brighton Beach on 4 May 1985, again emphasising the violent nature of the Russian gangs, a tradition that they had brought with them from the back streets of Moscow and the prison camps of Siberia.

And then came Vyacheslav Kirrilovich Ivankov, the notorious 'Yaponchik', who spread fear and terror in Brighton Beach in the early 1990s. People, even law enforcers, were convinced that a new thriving émigré underworld rivalling that of the Italian-American Mafia, had arrived in the United States. Russian nightclubs and strip joints sprang up not only in New York but also in Philadelphia, Florida and California. When Yaponchik was arrested in 1995, the press called him the *capo di tutti capos* of the Russian *Mafiya* in the United States. His arrest was seen as proof of the existence of a centralised Russian crime structure in the United States, along the lines of the 'real' Mafia.[79]

There is no doubt that the *vory v zakone* of the former Soviet Union were well-connected and that they wielded considerable influence both before and especially after the fall of the communist regime. But there is no evidence of a complex hierarchy or set of hierarchies among them in the United States. Rather, they are criminal individuals with some followers who typically mistrust each other.[80] Some of them cooperate with the Cali cartel, and resell cocaine on behalf of the Colombian gangsters, but as second-fiddle players only. Rather than being organised criminals, they are small groups of opportunists who have taken advantage of America's free and open society to make money. Even the much-feared Argon had no more than twenty followers, hardly evidence of a well-oiled criminal syndicate.[81] And most Russian 'gangsters' would be more aptly described as scam artists who engage in Medicaid and credit card fraud. Kidnapping and extortion in exchange for 'protection'—and murder when people fail to pay—are the most advanced types of crime they are involved in.

Two American criminologists, James O. Finckenauer and Elin J. Waring, describe the Russian gangs in America as 'ad hoc teams of specialists [who] are mustered for specific criminal ventures in an opportunistic manner'.[82] The chaotic nature of the society and culture they come from is reflected very clearly in their émigré communities, and they are not likely to maintain any significant links with the authorities and security agencies back home in Russia other than for specific business purposes such as the smuggling of arms, diamonds and strategic minerals. They are products of a flawed social and political system, which nurtured widespread corruption and thievery. This is not to say they are not a threat. They are brutal; they are prepared to do anything for money; they sell guns and launder money. But they are not organised criminals bound together by almost religious ritual in international networks and complex hierarchies.

The Chinese, by contrast, are exactly that. Billy Ong and Eddie Chan had shown the way, and it soon became clear that China's intelligence services had managed to establish wide-ranging contacts within the ethnic Chinese underworld in the United States. Like Chiang Kai-shek and the Guomindang in Shanghai in the 1920s and 1930s, China's new leaders have come to depend on criminal figures for everything from legal and illegal money-making to intelligence-gathering. It is further believed that it was the Chinese authorities who took the initiative to approach what was to become their favourite Triad, the Sun Yee On, first in Hong Kong and later worldwide.[83]

This was hardly surprising, as it was never only the Guomindang that realised the usefulness of the Triads. Zhu De, the founder of the PLA, was a member of a secret society and Kang Sheng, the first intelligence chief of the Communist Party of China, forged close wartime links with some 'patriotic' Triads.[84] And the Triads, opportunistic as ever, were more than willing to serve any master who would provide them with protection. The much-feared Kang was ambivalent in his attitude to traditional Chinese vices in other respects as well. In the 1950s, the Communist Party of China used drastic methods to create a new, drug-free China. Shanghai was 'swept clean' by Kang's secret police. The dealers were executed, and even opium smokers who refused treatment were shot on the spot. But Kang himself continued to enjoy the drug inside his closely guarded headquarters, and was known to the more puritan communist leader Lin Biao as 'Old Opium Pipe'.[85]

China's security chief in the 1980s and 1990s, Tao Siju, continued the same tradition. While thousands of arrested drug couriers, mostly unemployed youths, were executed across China, he built up a lasting relationship with the Sun Yee On. Links were also established with a new Triad, the Dai Huen Jai, or the Big Circle Boys. They came from the area around Guangdong's provincial capital, Guangzhou, which in China is known as 'the Big City' and is designated on maps with a large circle around the Pearl River estuary.[86] The members were Maoist Red Guards who moved to Hong Kong in the 1970s when the Cultural Revolution was over. And they had good reason to flee. Many of them had taken part in book burnings, public humiliations of government officials and mass executions during the Cultural Revolution, and feared revenge from the relatives of their victims.

With this history of violence behind them, the Big Circle Boys began robbing goldsmiths and jewellery shops in Hong Kong, and soon discovered that there was a world beyond the coast of southern China as well. Dozens of them moved to Europe, mainly the Netherlands with its international drug market, and to Britain, which has a long-established Chinese community. But others went to North America, especially Canada, in the hundreds. Wherever they went, they copied traditional Triad structures, but the Big Circle Boys has never been a unified gang. In Canada, the term essentially refers to all Chinese gangs made up of recent refugees or émigrés from mainland

China. They operate in small bands with interchangeable leadership and membership, and are often hired by established Triads as enforcers and smugglers. It is estimated that there is a pool of some 300 Big Circle Boys in the Toronto area alone, and even more in Vancouver, where they are involved in protection rackets, assaults, robberies, arms trafficking and credit card scams. They have also turned Canada into a trans-shipment destination for Southeast Asian heroin sold in the United States—and increasingly also in Canada itself. Moreover, Big Circle Boys provide forged documents and act as escorts for illegal immigrants moving from China to Canada and the United States.[87] The Big Circle Boys in North America would have some contacts with gangsters who operate under the same name in, for example, Macau or Amsterdam. But, unlike the Sun Yee On, they have no central command structure and are, like the Fuk Ching gang, the typical kind of thugs who the more powerful and much better organised gangs use from time to time to carry out criminal activities with which they themselves do no want to be too obviously associated.

The same could actually also be said of the best known of all the Triads, the 14K. There are 14K 'chapters' all over the world, but they are not necessarily connected with each other. And both the 14K and the Big Circle Boys have been used not only by bigger crime gangs, but also by China's intelligence agencies. They reportedly assisted in the abduction of Chinese-Australian James Peng Jiandong in 1993 from Macau across the border to China, where he was wanted on business fraud charges committed against a niece of then paramount leader Deng Xiaoping and subsequently sentenced to eighteen years in gaol. In the same year, public security chief Tao publicly thanked the Triads for 'protecting a state leader' on an 'overseas trip'.[88] This was an obvious reference to an earlier visit to the United States by Deng, but Tao just wanted to show his gratitude. Better late than never.

In August 1999 there were persistent rumours that 'mainland Triads'—presumably the Big Circle Boys and perhaps also the Sun Yee On—were being employed by China's security agencies to disrupt the presidential elections in Taiwan which were scheduled for March 2000. There were also rumours that Taiwanese Triads had established a presence in Fujian province opposite Taiwan in close cooperation with the security agencies and mainland Triads. An internal document from the local headquarters of the Ministry of Public Security in Hangzhou, Zhejiang province, reportedly stated that such connections were considered 'routine' and part of Beijing's strategy against Taiwan—a country that has gone through some astonishing development since the mid-1980s.[89]

The wily old dictator, Chiang Kai-shek, died on 5 April 1975 at the age of 88 and was succeeded by his son, the plump Chiang Ching-kuo, who was best noted for his brutal but phony suppression of black marketeering in postwar Shanghai. Many street peddlers were shot, while he and his father robbed the national treasury to prepare for their flight to Taiwan. But in 1986, after more than ten years as president of the 'Republic of China', the younger Chiang began to liberalise the old authoritarian system. When he died in 1988, his successor as president and head of the Guomindang, Lee Teng-hui, a native Taiwanese, led the island through a remarkable transition from authoritarianism to democracy. This was not just a ploy to attract international sympathy for the diplomatically isolated island. Its rapid economic development in the 1960s and 1970s had created a new, well-educated middle class that was not going to put up with the ways of the old hard-liners. At first the Guomindang reacted fiercely, and street battles were fought between its police and thousands of protesters. In December 1979, scores of civilians—and policemen—were injured in a street confrontation in the southern port city of Kaohsiung, and even more opposition activists were arrested in the wake of the violent incident.[90]

But, in the end, the ruling nationalists had to give in, and Taiwan embarked on a remarkable, and largely peaceful, political transformation away from the old gangster-dictatorship. As even the old Guomindang reinvented itself as a model democratic party, it is perhaps not surprising that the island's own Triads have emigrated in large numbers and established a presence not only in Cambodia but also in China. While Chen 'Dry Duck' Chi-li, 'spiritual leader' of Taiwan's best-known Triad, the United Bamboo, set up a new base in Phnom Penh, the gang's honorary godfather, Zhang An-lo, who is better known as 'the White Wolf', sought refuge 'somewhere' in southern China.[91]

The White Wolf was the hitman who in 1984 killed Henry Liu in Daly City, California, and he had returned to Taiwan in 1995 after spending ten years in an American gaol—just in time for the Taiwanese parliament to pass a new *Anti-Hooligan Law*. In December 1996, it became possible for the police to arrest anyone who was a member of a so-called *hai dao bang pai*, or 'black society'. The White Wolf scuttled for cover in the mainland, where he furiously lashed out against Taiwan's new rulers. 'I'm not a criminal,' he said in an interview with the monthly *Asia Inc.* in April 1997. 'Secret societies have been a tradition in Chinese culture for thousands of years.'[92] Taiwan's popular, United States-educated minister of state and later justice minister, Ma Ying-jeou, retorted: 'Yes, secret societies have been part of Chinese history. They have their own justice. But that type of justice is part of an agricultural society. We are an industrial, commercial society today. You can't take justice into your own hands. The days of Robin Hood are over'.[93]

The United Bamboo gang traces its origin to 1956, when its predecessor, the Bamboo Woods League, was formed in the Taipei suburb of Yung-ho. Named after the neighbourhood's Bamboo Forest Road, it consisted of seventeen teenagers, mostly sons of senior officers in Chiang Kai-shek's military who had escaped to Taiwan after the communist victory in the mainland. The youngest at the time was the thirteen-year-old Chen Chi-li, the son of a local magistrate.[94] Disenchanted by the humiliation of their fathers, the youngsters formed the gang to fight off other local gangs on Bamboo Forest Road. As long as Chiang Kai-shek was alive, they had little to fear. Dry Duck Chen even socialised with the sons of Chiang Ching-kuo, when he and his 'brothers' were not protecting gambling dens and hostess clubs, or otherwise involved in loan-sharking and debt collection. By murdering Henry Liu, they managed to curry favour with the powers that be in Taiwan at the time. In its heyday in the early 1980s, the United Bamboo gang had up to 40 000 members in Taiwan and overseas cells operated in the United States, Canada, Australia and Europe, as well as throughout Asia.[95]

But those days were over, and attempts by Taiwan's Triads in the 1990s to imitate the *yakuza* by entering the construction business did not fare well. Although they managed to siphon off millions of dollars from public works projects, the authorities struck back. In August 1996, the police launched operation Chih Ping, or 'Clean Sweep', and staged a pre-dawn raid on the home of Tsai Kuan-lun, the leader of another notorious Taiwanese Triad, the Four Seas gang. News footage of his arrest was shown on national television, which also filmed Tsai and some of his bodyguards being whisked by helicopter to Taiwan's Green Island gaol, which previously had been reserved for political prisoners. In the ensuing weeks, the police raided massage parlours and brothels and scores of other criminals were arrested.[96] The Triad problem has not gone away in Taiwan, but times have changed and the public do not accept the old ways any longer. Hardly surprisingly—but somewhat ironically—both the United Bamboo and the Four Seas seem to have more business in Shanghai these days than in Taipei.[97]

However, Taiwan's break with its criminal past also resulted in some unforeseen consequences. Suddenly, heroin became available in the streets of Taipei, and the number of addicts was soon in the tens of thousands, and increasing steadily. The drug invasion of Taiwan coincided not only with the democratisation of the island, but also with the massive surge in heroin production in the Burmese sector of the Golden Triangle since the late 1980s. New gangs and networks emerged from the mutiny in the Communist Party of Burma in 1989 which, unlike many of the older groups, did not have historical and emotional ties to Taiwan. The remnants of the Guomindang in the Golden Triangle, and even the organisation of the Shan-Chinese warlord Zhang Chifu (alias Khun Sa), always refrained from selling heroin if the destination was Taiwan. The new dealers—the United Wa State Army, the UWSA and other groups of fighters from the former Burmese communist rebel army—have no such qualms. To them, Taiwan is only a lucrative market for their produce.[98]

A Taiwanese government document issued in 1993 stated:

Drugs were not a serious problem in the ROC (Republic of China) until five years ago. Now drug abuse has reached major proportions . . . Recent drug busts have pointed to Thailand and the Chinese mainland as the major sources. ROC police estimate that 3,000 kilogrammes of heroin . . . finds its way across the mainland into Taiwan each year, but only one-tenth of this amount is seized by the police.'[99]

Another government publication stated that the amount of heroin seized in Taiwan did not exceed 10 kilograms annually prior to 1990.

In that year, the amount jumped to 22 kilograms, increasing to 76 kilograms in 1991 and 320 kilograms in 1992. The year 1993 saw a record volume of drug seizures: 1110 kilograms of heroin, morphine and marijuana, of which 96 per cent was heroin, and 3357 kilograms of finished and half-finished methamphetamines.[100] The flood has not stopped: in June 1999, 21 kilograms of heroin with a street value of $30.5 million, manufactured in the hills of northeastern Burma and smuggled from Thailand, were seized at Taipei's Chiang Kai-shek airport.

China's relations with the drug-running UWSA seems to go way beyond a mutually beneficial business arrangement. In 2000, Chinese technicians were seen upgrading several roads inside and close to UWSA-controlled areas in eastern Burma. Chinese doctors, teachers and even military personnel have been spotted in the Wa Hills, and the 20 000-strong UWSA is equipped with Chinese-made weapons, including HN-5N surface-to-air missiles.[101] A prominent leader of the UWSA, Ta Thang, has Chinese intelligence and military advisers.[102] Ironically, as China is battling its worst domestic heroin epidemic in decades, with millions of mostly young people turning to drugs to escape from the bitter realities of life in today's society, the country's military and intelligence apparatus is actively cooperating with the biggest armed drug-trafficking organisation in the world. Even among the blood brothers at the grassroot level, the impact of the drug epidemic, and related diseases such as HIV and AIDS, could be felt in a rather curious way. Fear of catching AIDS has forced new recruits to slit their own finger tips simultaneously and suck only their own blood rather than following the age-old initiation rite of drinking the mingled blood of new recruits from a communal tumbler.[103]

The relocation of many gangs to China, the emergence of new ones and the new hold that Beijing seems to have over the Triads—even overseas—are all outcomes of traditional weaknesses in Chinese society. Taiwan has managed to put its state-sponsored criminal past behind it and to create a modern society ruled by law, but it will take a long time for China to achieve the same degree of development—if ever—because China has ambitions to become a world superpower, and the 'spiritual homeland' for the world's new 'global majority'. Without the criminal underworld on its side, it would be almost impossible for Beijing to extend its writ beyond its frontiers, and that is what makes the new nexus between the Triads and China's present leaders so dangerous for the rest of the world. China is, even more than North Korea, a state that feels that it has to engage in criminal activities such as drug running and the printing of counterfeit dollars to survive. And China needs the underworld to help it steal industrial secrets from more developed countries and to influence the politics of what is becoming its main rival, the United States.

The Donorgate saga in 1996 revealed for the first time that Beijing has used gangland figures to funnel money to a presidential candidate in the United States. The affair would most probably have attracted more attention than it did had a certain young lady called Monica Lewinsky not stolen the show. Suddenly, media focus shifted to President Clinton's sordid private life instead of what was the tip of an iceberg of espionage and organised crime. Charlie Trie, Ng Lap Seng, Chen Kai-kit and their like were soon forgotten. But during the trial of Taiwan-born Chinese-American fundraiser for the Democrats Johnny Chung, some vital information was unearthed. He had been involved not only with the aerospace executive Liu Chao-ying, the daughter of General Liu Huaqing, a high-ranking Chinese military commander and a member of the Standing Committee of the Politburo of the Communist Party, but also with General Ji Shengde, a former head of China's military intelligence. Chung admitted that Ji gave him $300 000 in the summer of 1996 for Clinton's re-election campaign.[104] Ji was also widely reputed to have been the contact man between the PLA and the gangsters in Macau. The wily general was later linked to Lai Changxing, the key figure in China's biggest-ever corruption scandal which broke in late 2000. Lai, an influential local businessman in Fujian, had used his connections with senior party cadres and army generals to build up a smuggling empire, based in Xiamen port, that handled everything from crude oil to vegetable oil, rubber, cars, tobacco and electrical appliances. Lai managed to get on his payroll at least one of Xiamen's deputy Communist Party chiefs, Liu Feng, the head of the city's police external liaison department, Wang Kexiang, and a top official in the Fujian Provincial Border Defence Force, Zhang Yongding. The manager of the Fujian branch of the Bank of China and the chief of the Xiamen branch of Industry and Commerce Bank Corp. had also been bought off.[105] Lai was reported to have evaded $6 billion in taxes—before he, like so many other Chinese criminals, managed to escape to Canada.[106] Back home in Fujian, more than 300 people were arrested and tried. Fourteen death sentences (three of them suspended), twelve life sentences and 58 fixed-term prison sentences were handed down. Among those sentenced was General Ji, who was sentenced to twelve years' imprisonment for his part in the corruption scandal, but some western intelligence operatives in East Asia felt that he was perhaps punished more for blowing an important attempt to penetrate the White House.[107]

At the very least, the Chinese authorities managed to shut him up—which was not possible with Lai, who was in Canada. Lai told the Canadian media that China has a network of businessmen in Canada and the United States who acted as its spies to steal industrial and military secrets. The network, he said, was run by the intelligence unit of the PLA and Beijing's Public Security Bureau.[108] Many felt that he was trying to show that he could be useful to the Canadian government to get political asylum in the country. But his revelations were strikingly similar to the findings of a top-secret study prepared for the Royal Canadian Mounted Police and the Canadian Security Intelligence Service as early as 1997. Known as 'Sidewinder', the report detailed an alleged pact between Chinese intelligence agencies, businessmen and criminal gangs operating in Canada. The report was subsequently rewritten and given a new code name, 'Project Echo'. The press accused the Canadian government of trying to water down the damning report so as not to upset relations between Canada and China.[109] The original report specifically mentioned CITIC, or the China International Trust Investment Company, as a major player in both politics and business in North America. CITIC, which is the largest Chinese company operating internationally, had on its first board of directors Hong Kong tycoon Li Ka-shing, and Henry Fok, the *de facto* head of Macau's gambling operations. CITIC and the Lippo Bank of Indonesia, in which Li Ka-shing is a major shareholder, were also implicated in the Donorgate affair.

Among the other major Chinese companies mentioned in the 'Sidewinder' report was the arms manufacturer Northern Industrial Corporation, or Norinco, and Poly Technologies, both of which are owned by CITIC. The Poly Group was until recently headed by one of Deng Xiaoping's sons-in-law, He Ping, and is widely seen as part of the PLA's entrepreneurial drive. Large quantities of arms manufactured by Norinco have been confiscated on Indian reserves in Canada, especially those of the Mohawks.[110] In May 1996, US authorities made what was described as the largest seizure of automatic weapons in the country's history: 2000 Chinese-made AK-47 assault rifles and other military weapons. United States-based representatives of the Poly Group were subsequently arrested. The final destination of all those arms was never determined, but native Indian 'Warriors' and, ironically, some of the extreme right-wing American militias were strongly suspected by US authorities. What is clear, however, is that Chinese guns destined for the North American market are almost always transported by the state-owned China Ocean Shipping Company (COSCO), which has been implicated in many smuggling operations other than gun running.[111] The PLA has come a long way since its teenaged peasant soldiers marched into Shanghai in their sneakers and straw sandals in May 1949.

Smaller firms were also highlighted in 'Sidewinder', such as film production companies which were 'regularly in contact with prominent members of the Sun Yee On Triad'. It also accused China's military intelligence of trying to influence Canadian elections in the same way as it had done in the United States.[112] And the choice of Canada to penetrate North America was not an accident. It is huge and sparsely populated. In the least populated part of the country, the Northwest Territories, there are only 160–170 police officers to maintain law and order in an area larger than Western Europe. And it has an 8000-kilometre, porous border with the United States, over which flow not only illegal immigrants but also drugs and guns. Canada is rapidly becoming the United States' unguarded back door, a key entry point for women and child sex-slaves from Eastern Europe as well as one of the world's centres for Chinese organised crime and espionage.[113]

The 'Sidewinder' report became extremely controversial and was criticised by many as being 'biased against China'. But its basic findings received more credence when the Federal Bureau of Investigation (the FBI) in May 2001 arrested three Chinese-born scientists at the telecommunications giant Lucent Technologies and a smaller related enterprise in New Jersey. Accused of a 'complicated scheme of corporate espionage', the three men were brought in handcuffs before a federal magistrate in Newark and detained without bail. They had stolen voice and data software from Lucent to set up a joint venture with a Beijing company that would become the Chinese equivalent of the US data-networking powerhouse Cisco Systems. The venture received $1.2 million in financing from Datang Telecom Technology, a Chinese-government controlled maker of communications equipment based in Beijing.[114] Rick Fisher, a China expert with the Jamestown Foundation, who served on the Republican Policy Committee of the House of Representatives during a 1998 investigation of US technology transfers to China, described the arrests as 'a signal that the United States needs to "redouble" its efforts to find those persons working in this country for the benefit of the Chinese government'.[115] But was it just a joke that the China-financed New Jersey joint venture formed by the threesome was called ComTriad Technologies? Even if not part of a traditional Triad, the firm clearly saw itself as a high-tech version of China's age-old secret societies.

A string of revelations of Chinese industrial espionage in the United States, and also the Donorgate saga, have had a severe impact on America's racial relations, and threaten to undermine the high level of acceptability that the Chinese-Americans have managed to achieve following decades of discrimination. Frank Ching, a Hong Kong-born Chinese-American, wrote in 1999:

> Virtually every Chinese is tarred—visitors, students, diplomats and business representatives. All are suspected of spying. Similarly, it is suggested that there are no legitimate Chinese companies—every one is considered to be a front for the Chinese military or some intelligence agency. It assumes that every member of every Chinese delegation is on an intelligence mission, as is every Chinese student.[116]

The anti-Asian hysteria has echoes of World War II, when every Japanese living in the United States was considered a spy, and nearly all of them were rounded up and interned in camps throughout the war. It is too often forgotten that it is the Asians themselves—the ordinary law-abiding Chinese in New York's Chinatown, the Vietnamese shopkeeper in Cabramatta, the street vendor or minibus driver in Hong Kong, the student or scientist who comes under pressure to spy for Beijing—who suffer the most from ethnically based organised crime, extortion, threats and clandestine operations within their respective communities. They are trapped in an evil social order, for which few have any recourse.

This is unlikely to change while China does not change—and it is important to remember that, although China wants to learn from the West, there is also a deep feeling of animosity towards western powers. China's defeat in the Opium Wars of the last century, and western drug trafficking to China at the time, have not been forgotten. Nor can the Chinese see why the West should take any moral high ground when it comes to issues such as drugs. Just in time for Hong Kong's return to China on 1 July 1997, the Chinese movie industry even released a mega production called *The Opium War*, which depicted Imperial Commissioner Lin Zexu, who had been sent down to the south to stamp out the British opium trade, as a foresighted national hero defending the honour of the Chinese against the 'western imperialists'.

The many other ways in which the Chinese have been humiliated throughout history—the colonial treaty ports, the slave trade from Macau to Peru and Cuba, immigration exclusion acts directed against Chinese in North America and Australia—have left behind a complex mix of anger, an inferiority complex and a sense that China, with its thousands of years of history, is superior to the rest of the world. China's march to a place in the world community of which it could be proud began when Mao Zedong on 1 October 1949 proclaimed: 'Never again will the people of China be enslaved!'.

But China is today going through perhaps the most difficult period so far in its long history. It is trying to modernise without the necessary institutions in place—and the outcome is a heavy reliance on its traditional social formations, the secret societies. However, not all of them are willing to cooperate with the leaders in Beijing. The opening up of the Pandora's box of reform in the early 1980s has released a host of unforeseen social forces and political developments. An internal police report, published as early as 1985, stated:

> During the past few years, there has been a continuous annual increase in the cases of reactionary sect and society activity throughout the country . . . In every region and province of China with the exception of

Tibet, acts of disruption by the reactionary sects and societies have occurred—most prominently in the provinces of Henan, Shaanxi, Sichuan, and Yunnan. The vast majority of these activities have taken place in the countryside, and particularly in remote mountainous areas along the borders between different counties or provinces.[117]

This has happened before in China's history—and it is how Chinese dynasties have fallen in the past. The 1985 report mentions a host of small secret societies and syncretic sects, ranging from small underground Christian churches and sects such as the Yi Guan Dao ('Way of Unity'), a semi-religious group that is strong in Taiwan, to Hong Kong Triads which have become active in Fujian. In more recent years, the strongest spiritual challenge to the moral authority of the ruling Communist Party has come from Falun Gong, a meditation society which once had millions of members all over China. To the West, it was a somewhat eccentric but basically innocent and peaceful club for housewives and others who were seeking inner strength in the teachings of its spiritual leader, Li Hongzhi from Manchuria. In 1992, when Li first began to preach Falun Gong in China, he was also well received and supported by the Chinese government. But gradually, as the group grew, the authorities panicked. Falun Gong's leadership claims that the organisation has more than 70 million followers, including party members, government officials, scholars and members of the army and police.[118]

It was as if a ghost from the past had suddenly come alive again: the Taiping rebellion revived. China's new rulers reacted in the same way as the old Emperors did whenever their moral authority was challenged: they began arresting Falun Gong members. On 25 April 1999, 10 000 Falun Gong practitioners gathered in Beijing, outside the central government compound behind Tiananmen Square, to protest against the crackdown. The authorities were even more alarmed. Such an 'anti-government manifestation' had not happened since the communists seized power in 1949. Hundreds of Falun Gong followers were arrested at midnight and their homes ransacked. Millions of Falun Gong books, pamphlets and tapes were destroyed and, on 22 June, the group was banned. The world condemned the brutal crackdown on the Falun Gong, and voices were raised in its defence even in China's new Special Administrative Region of Hong Kong.

But in loyal Macau, that new bastion of Chinese patriotism, plain-clothes detectives of the local security forces have continued to monitor the group's activities and the enclave's Buddhist and Taoist communities have dismissed Falun Gong as a 'heretical cult'.[119]

The emergence of Falun Gong, and the government's reaction to its rapid expansion, reflects all that is wrong in China today. Falun Gong is not a 'secret society' in the Triad sense of the word, but a typical non-governmental and, in essence, anti-dynastic syncretic society of the kind China's rulers have always feared the most. And, adversely, it emerged because the government is losing its traditional 'Mandate of Heaven' to rule the country. Secret societies that can be used and controlled have never been a problem for China's rulers. But a spiritual group that becomes a higher moral authority than the Emperors certainly is.

The West has always been slow to understand the undercurrents of Chinese society. Witness the the naiveté of historical figures such as Claire Chennault and Milton 'Mary' Miles or, in recent years, the United Nations International Drug Control Program in Burma, which is providing a shield behind which ethnic Chinese drug traffickers and their UWSA allies in the Golden Triangle operate with impunity. Witness, too, the business opportunists who, prompted by China's huge market—'If every Chinese bought a pair of shoelaces from me', the thinking goes, 'I'd be a millionaire'—shun any criticism of the nation. China may have doubled its gross domestic product in fifteen years—a remarkable performance by any standards—but this has been achieved at tremendous social cost, and many outsiders fail to see that the country development strategy has led to massive corruption. The result is a country where—as in old Shanghai—everything can be bought and sold for a price, there are alarming and ever-widening disparities between rich and poor, a near-complete destruction of the environment has taken place, health services and education for the poor are declining, and there has been a massive displacement of perhaps 100 million people who are constantly on the move, looking for jobs or, even better, a way out of the country. China has also seen a resurrection of characters that should belong to history: pirates, street thugs, drug barons and members of secret societies. Chinese organised crime is spreading across the world. Its links to the government and its agencies make it far more dangerous than organised crime groups in Japan, disorganised gangs in Russia, Indonesia's pirates and street thugs, or the increasingly anachronistic *chao phos* of Thailand.

Perhaps mainland China will solve its problems and become like Taiwan and the Guomindang. The so-called 'renegade state' has transformed itself from a Triad-controlled nation into a civil society with robust democratic institutions. But the prospects for China itself are bleak—and the rest of the world must wake up and tackle a problem that is far more serious than the old Cold War divide between East and West. China's Blood Brothers are part of the new world disorder, and pose a more profound threat to global security and stability than the bad old communists—Russian or Chinese—ever did.

APPENDIX: The 36 Oaths of China's Triad Societies

1. After having entered the Hong Gates I must treat the parents and relatives of my sworn brothers as mine own kin. I shall suffer death by five thunderbolts if I do not keep this oath.
2. I shall assist my sworn brothers to bury their parents and brothers by offering financial or physical assistance. I shall be killed by five thunderbolts if I pretend to have no knowledge of their troubles.
3. When Hong brothers visit my house I shall provide them with board and lodging. I shall be killed by a myriad of swords if I treat them as strangers.
4. I will always acknowledge my Hong brothers when they identify themselves. If I ignore them I shall be killed by a myriad of swords.
5. I shall not disclose the secrets of the Hong family, not even to my parents, brothers or wife. I shall never disclose the secrets for money. I shall be killed by a myriad of swords if I do so.
6. I shall never betray my sworn brothers. If, through a misunderstanding, I have caused the arrest of one of my brothers, I must release him immediately. If I break this oath I will be killed by five thunderbolts.
7. I will offer assistance to my sworn brothers who are in trouble, in order that they may pay their passage fee. If I break this oath, may I be killed by five thunderbolts.
8. I must not cause harm or bring trouble to my sworn brothers or Incense Master. If I do so I will be killed by a myriad of swords.
9. I must never commit an indecent assault on the wives, sisters or daughters of my sworn brothers. I shall be killed by five thunderbolts if I break this oath.
10. I shall never embezzle cash or property from my sworn brothers. If I break this oath I will be killed by a myriad of swords.
11. I will take good care of the wives or children of sworn brothers entrusted to my keeping. If I do not do so I will be killed by five thunderbolts.

12. If I have supplied false particulars about myself for the purpose of joining the Hong family I shall be killed by five thunderbolts.

13. If I should change my mind and deny my membership of the Hong family I will be killed by a myriad of swords.

14. If I rob a sworn brother, or assist an outsider to do so, I will be killed by five thunderbolts.

15. If I should take advantage over a sworn brother or force unfair business deals upon him I will be killed by a myriad of swords.

16. If I knowingly convert my sworn brother's cash or property to my own use I shall be killed by five thunderbolts.

17. If I have wrongly taken a sworn brother's cash or property during a robbery I must return them to him. If I do not I will be killed by five thunderbolts.

18. If I am arrested after committing an offence, I must accept my punishment, and not try to place the blame on my sworn brothers. If I do so I will be killed by five thunderbolts.

19. If any of my sworn brothers are killed, arrested, or have departed to some other place, I will assist their wives and children who may be in need. If I pretend to have no knowledge of their difficulties, I will be killed by five thunderbolts.

20. When any of my sworn brothers have been assaulted or blamed by others, I must come forward and help him if he is in the right, or advise him to desist if he is wrong. If he has been repeatedly insulted by others I shall inform our other brothers to help him physically and financially. If I do not keep this oath, I will be killed by five thunderbolts.

21. If it comes to my knowledge that the government is seeking any of my sworn brothers who has come from other provinces or from overseas, I shall immediately inform him in order that he may make his escape. If I break this oath I will be killed by five thunderbolts.

22. I must not conspire with outsiders to cheat my sworn brothers at gambling. If I do so I will be killed by a myriad of swords.

23. I shall not cause discord amongst my sworn brothers by spreading false reports about any of them. If I do so I shall be killed by a myriad of swords.

24. I shall not appoint myself Incense Master without authority. After entering the Hong Gates for three years, the loyal and faithful

ones may be promoted by the Incense Master with the support of his sworn brothers. I shall be killed by five thunderbolts if I make any unauthorised promotions myself.

25. If my natural brothers are involved in a dispute or lawsuit with my sworn brothers, I must not help either party against the other, but must attempt to have the matter settled amicably. If I break this oath I will be killed by five thunderbolts.

26. After entering the Hong Gates, I must forget any previous grudges I may have borne against my sworn brothers. If I do not do so I will be killed by five thunderbolts.

27. I must not trespass upon territory occupied by my sworn brothers. I shall be killed by five thunderbolts if I pretend to have no knowledge of my brothers' rights in such matters.

28. I must not covet or seek to share in any property or cash obtained by my sworn brothers. If I have such ideas I will be killed by five thunderbolts.

29. I must not disclose any address where my sworn brothers keep their wealth, nor must I conspire to make wrong use of such knowledge. If I do so I will be killed by a myriad of swords.

30. I must not give support to outsiders if so doing is against the interests of any of my sworn brothers. If I do not keep this oath, I will be killed by a myriad of swords.

31. I must not take advantage of the Hong brotherhood, in order to oppress or take violent or unreasonable advantage of others. I must be content and honest. If I break this oath I will be killed by five thunderbolts.

32. I shall be killed by five thunderbolts if I behave indecently towards the small children of my sworn brothers' families.

33. If any of my sworn brothers has committed a big offence, I must not inform upon them to the government for the purpose of obtaining a reward. I shall be killed by five thunderbolts if I break this oath.

34. I must not take to myself the wives and concubines of my sworn brothers, nor commit adultery with them. If I do so I will be killed by a myriad of swords.

35. I must never reveal Hong secrets or signs when speaking to outsiders. If I do so I will be killed by a myriad of swords.

36. After entering the Hong Gates, I shall be loyal and faithful and shall endeavour to overthrow the Qing and restore the Ming by coordinating my efforts with those of my sworn brothers, even though my brothers and I may not be in the same profession. Our common aim is to avenge our Five Ancestors.[1]

NOTES

INTRODUCTION

1   Michael Wong, 'Drunken pirates sing pop hit as they head for firing squad' *South China Morning Post*, 29 Jan. 2000.
2   Pamela Pun, 'Triad activities "out of control"' *Hong Kong Mail*, 24 Oct. 2000. The article referred to the October 2000 issue of the official *China News Weekly Review*, which cited Cai Shaoqing, a professor at Nanjing University and an expert on organised crime.
3   Takahiro Fukaka, 'Asia's legal killing fields' *Agence France-Presse* (Tokyo), in *The Nation* (Bangkok), 27 May 2001.
4   Wu Zhong, '110 executed on UN anti-drug day' *Hong Kong Standard*, 27 June 1996.
5   Handelman, Stephen, 'The Russian "Mafiya"' *Foreign Affairs*, March–April 1994, p. 83.
6   Dr Mark Galeotti, 'Organized crime in Russia: the political view—organized crime's influence on politics and vice versa' (unpublished paper submitted at a conference organised by the Royal Institute of International Affairs and Control Risks Group Limited, The Dorchester, London, 6 March 1995).
7   Velisarios Kattoulas, 'Taking care of business' *Far Eastern Economic Review*, 30 November 2000, pp. 92–5, and Garry W.G. Clement and Brian McAdam, *Triads and Other Asian Organized Crime Groups*, Royal Canadian Mounted Police manual, Hong Kong, 1993, p. 121.
8   Karel van Wolferen, *The Enigma of Japanese Power*, Vintage Books, New York, 1990, pp. 105–6.
9   Brian Bremner, 'Yakuza and the banks' *Business Week*, 29 Jan. 1996, pp. 15–18.
10   John McFarlane, 'The Asian financial crisis: corruption, cronyism and organised crime' *Defence Studies Working Paper No. 341*, The Australian National University, Strategic and Defence Studies Centre, Canberra, October 1999.
11   Clement and McAdam, *Triads and Other Asian Organized Crime Groups*, p. 114.
12   Jonathan Manthorpe, 'The man who loved too much and the woman who loved too many' *The Vancouver Sun*, 16 May 2000.
13   Bertil Lintner, 'Paradise for crooks' *Far Eastern Economic Review*, 6 Nov. 1997, pp. 31–5. A complete list of Vanuatu's banks is in my possession.
14   ibid.
15   'Drug-smuggling sub found high in mountains' *The Weekend Australian*, 9–10 Sept. 2000.
16   Joseph Khan and Judith Miller, 'Getting tough on gangsters, high tech and global' *The New York Times*, 15 Dec. 2000.
17   Frederic Dannen, 'Partners in crime' *The New Republic*, 14 & 21 July 1997, p. 24.
18   ibid.

19 'A Social Contract with Territory's underworld' *South China Morning Post*, 14 May 1997.
20 *The New Republic*, 14 & 21 July 1997.
21 Dana R. Dillon, *Piracy in Asia: A Growing Barrier to Maritime Trade*, paper produced by the Asian Studies Centre and published by the Heritage Foundation, Washington, 22 June 2000, p. 3.
22 'China turns to Cambodia's Bunma' *Far Eastern Economic Review*, 7 Oct. 2000.
23 Glenn Schloss, 'Village Law' *South China Morning Post*, 29 June 2000.
24 Chu, Yiu Kong, *The Triads as Business*, Routledge, London and New York, 2000.
25 'Gangster Ban enrages IOC: organised crime figures refused visas ... but Samaranch calls them family' *The Weekend Australian*, 9–10 Sept. 2000.
26 ibid.
27 ibid.
28 Clement and McAdam, *Triads and Other Asian Organized Crime Groups*, p. 95.
29 Communication with Hong Kong-based law enforcement officer, 12 Sept. 2000.
30 David E. Kaplan and Alec Dubro, *Yakuza: The Explosive Account of Japan's Criminal Underworld*, Addison-Wesley Publishing Company, Reading, MA, 1986, p. 86.
31 Kattonlas, *Far Eastern Economic Review*, 30 Nov. 2000, p. 93.

CHAPTER 1

1 Edgar Snow, *Red China Today*, Vintage Books, New York, 1971, pp. 503–4.
2 Ian McLachlan, *Shanghai 1949: The End of an Era*, New Amsterdam, New York, 1990, p. 13. Technically, Chiang Kai-shek had 'retired' from the presidency in January 1949, and handed over his duties 'temporarily' to vice president Li Tsung-jen. On 1 March 1950, Chiang resumed office in Taipei.
3 Mariano Ezpeleta, *Red Shadows Over Shanghai*, Zita Publishing, Manila, 1972, p. 185.
4 ibid.
5 McLachlan, *Shanghai 1949*, p. 13.
6 Lynn Pan (Pan Ling), *Old Shanghai: Gangsters in Paradise*, Heinemann Asia, Singapore, 1993, p. 221.
7 Ezpeleta, *Red Shadows*, p. 191.
8 ibid., p. 129.
9 'Shanghai yesterday and today' by Lynn Pan in *Shanghai: The Paris of the Orient*, Passport Books, Lincolnwood, Ill, 1995, p. 10.
10 Ezpeleta, *Red Shadows*, p. 8.
11 Rewi Alley, *At 90: Memoirs of My China Years*, New World Press, Beijing, 1986, pp. 45–6.
12 ibid., pp. 46–7.
13 Matthew Miller, 'Witness to history' (an interview with Xue Gengxin, a former police superintendent in Shanghai) *Manager* magazine (Thailand) Nov. 1995.
14 Quoted in Gail Hershatter, *Dangerous Pleasures: Prostitution and Modernity in Twentieth-Century Shanghai*, University of California Press, Berkeley, 1997, p. 75.

15   ibid., pp. 49–50.

16   ibid., p. 50.

17   ibid., p. 229.

18   Josef von Sternberg, *Fun in a Chinese Laundry*, Secker & Warburg, London, 1965. Quoted in Barbara Baker (ed.), *Shanghai: Electric and Lurid City*, Oxford University Press, Hong Kong, Oxford & New York, 1998, pp. 144–5.

19   F.L. Hawks Pott, *A Short History of Shanghai*, Kelly & Walsh, Shanghai, 1928, p. 4.

20   Alfred McCoy, *The Politics of Heroin: CIA Complicity in the Global Drug Trade*, Lawrence Hill Books, New York, 1991, pp. 83–6. See also Maurice Collis, *Foreign Mud*, Faber & Faber, London, 1946, pp. 66–7; and *The Opium War*, no author; Foreign Languages Press, Beijing, 1976, pp. 4–6.

21   Collis, *Foreign Mud*, p. 303: 'In 1850 the Government of India was deriving five and a half millions [pounds] of revenue from opium out of a total revenue of twenty-seven and a half millions. Without these five and a half millions, it was innocently asked, how could the Government continue its beneficent plans for education and hospitals and put the Indians to the road of civilization?'

22   Sterling Seagrave, *The Soong Dynasty*, Sidgwick & Jackson, London, 1985, p. 4.

23   J.M. Scott, *The White Poppy: A History of Opium*, Funk & Wagnalls, New York, 1969, pp. 84–5.

24   McCoy, *The Politics of Heroin*, p. 82; Catherine Lamour and Michel R. Lamberti, *The Second Opium War*, Allen Lane, London, 1974, p. 41.

25   Quoted in Samuel M. Wilson, 'Coffee, tea, or opium?' *Natural History*, 11/93, p. 78.

26   *The Opium War* (Beijing), pp. 37–8. Just in time for Hong Kong's return to China on 1 July 1997, the Chinese movie industry released a mega production called *The Opium War*, which depicted Lin Zexu as a foresighted national hero.

27   Richard Hughes, *Borrowed Time, Borrowed Place: Hong Kong and its Many Faces*, Andre Deutsch, London, 1968, p. 119.

28   Wilson, 'Coffee, tea, or opium?' p. 79; and Pott, *A Short History of Shanghai*, pp. 10–11. '$' in this chapter means the amount in US dollars at the time.

29   Scott, *The White Poppy*, p. 100.

30   Hughes, *Borrowed Time*, p. 105.

31   ibid., pp. 105–6. See also Scott, *The White Poppy*, pp. 22–30.

32   Pott, *A Short History of Shanghai*, p. 46.

33   Leonard P. Adams, 'China: the historical setting of Asia's profitable plague', in Alfred McCoy, *The Politics of Heroin in Southeast Asia* , Harper and Row, New York, 1972, p. 361.

34   Pan, *In Search of Old Shanghai*, pp. 42–3.

35   Quoted in 'Tales of Old Shanghai,' a Shanghai website, 1997, http://www.earnshaw.com/shanghai-ed-india/tales/tales.htm; http://www.talesofoldchina.com.

36   Frederic Wakeman Jr, *Policing Shanghai 1927–1937*, University of California Press, Berkeley, 1995, p. 35.

37   Samuel Merwin, *Drugging a Nation*, Fleming H. Revell Company, New York, 1908, p. 9.

38   Wakeman, *Policing Shanghai*, p. 34.

39 John. M. Jennings, *The Opium Empire: Japanese Imperialism and Drug Trafficking in Asia, 1895–1945*, Praeger, Westport, Conn., 1997, p. 62.

40 Wakeman, *Policing Shanghai*, p. 199; see also Martin Booth, *Opium: A History*, Simon and Schuster, London, 1996, p. 180.

41 Booth, *Opium*, p. 181.

42 Ellen La Motte, *The Opium Monopoly*, Macmillan, New York, 1920, p. 34.

43 Pan, *Gangsters in Paradise*, p. 12.

44 Pan, *In Search of Old Shanghai*, p. 97.

45 Wakeman, *Policing Shanghai 1927–1937*, p. 32.

46 Brian G. Martin, 'The pact with the devil', in Frederic Wakeman Jr, and Wenhsin Yeh (eds), *Shanghai Sojourners*, Institute of Asian Studies, University of California Press, Berkeley, 1992, pp. 273–4.

47 Martin, 'The pact with the devil', p. 274. In *Policing Shanghai* (p. 31), Wakeman says Huang joined the Green Gang in 1927.

48 ibid., p. 274.

49 Pan, *Gangsters in Paradise*, p. 24.

50 Martin, 'The pact with the devil', p. 270.

51 Wakeman, *Policing Shanghai 1927–1937*, p. 34.

52 Brian G. Martin, *The Shanghai Green Gang: Politics and Organized Crime 1919–1937*, University of California Press, Berkeley, 1996, p. 38.

53 Matthew Miller, 'Witness to history' *Manager* magazine (Thailand), Nov. 1995, pp. 28–32; Pan, *Gangsters in Paradise*, p. 30.

54 Martin, 'The pact with the devil', p. 274.

55 Pott, *A Short History of Shanghai*, p. 268. See also Alexander Zhi-Cheng Wang, *A History of the Russian Emigré Community in Shanghai* (in Chinese), Sanlen Publishing House, Shanghai, 1993; and Harriet Sergeant, *Shanghai*, John Murray, London, 1991, pp. 30–67.

56 Lynn Pan with Xue Liyong and Qian Zonghao, *Shanghai: A Century of Change in Photographs 1843–1949*, Hai Feng Publishing, Hong Kong, 1994, p. 90.

57 Sergeant, *Shanghai*, p. 33.

58 Sergeant, *Shanghai*, p. 51.

59 Lynn Pan, May Holdsworth and Jill Hunt, *Shanghai: The Paris of the Orient*, Passport Books, Hong Kong, 1992, p. 68.

60 Elizabeth J. Perry, *Shanghai on Strike: The Politics of Chinese Labour*, Stanford University Press, Stanford, 1993, p. 74.

61 ibid., p. 74.

62 Quoted in Chiang Kai-shek: *Soviet Russia in China*, China Publishing Company, Taipei, 1969, p. 16. More about these 'brigands' in Chapter 2.

63 For an account of his exploits, see Dan Jacobs, *Borodin: Stalin's Man in China*, Harvard University Press, Cambridge, 1981.

64 Although a native of Ningbo near Shanghai, Chiang Kai-shek preferred the Cantonese spelling of his name to the *pinyin* Jiang Jieshi.

65 For Chiang's own account of his time in Russia, see his *Soviet Russia in China*, pp. 21–8.

66 Ezpeleta, *Red Shadows*, p. 13.

67 Martin, *The Shanghai Green Gang*, pp. 80–1.

68 ibid., p. 81. See also Pan, *Gangsters in Paradise*, p. 41, and Perry, *Shanghai on Strike*, p. 89.

69   Quoted in Perry, *Shanghai on Strike*, p. 79.
70   W.H. Auden and Christopher Isherwood, *Journey to a War*, Random House, New York, 1939, p. 170.
71   According to Anthony Paul, a veteran Australian journalist in Asia, Bangkok, 15 Dec. 1999.
72   Personal communication with Lynn Pan, 7 March 2001.
73   Pan, *Gangsters in Paradise*, pp. 56–7.
74   ibid., p. 57.
75   Alley, *At 90*, p. 44.
76   Chiang Kai-shek, *Soviet Russia in China*, pp. 50–1.
77   Martin, *The Shanghai Green Gang*, p. 111.
78   Pan, *Gangsters in Paradise*, p. 59.
79   Quoted in Bernard Martin, *Strange Vigour: A Biography of Sun Yat-sen*, William Heinemann, London, 1944, p. 47.
80   Jean Chesneaux, *Secret Societies in China in the 19th and 20th Centuries*, Heinemann Educational Books, London, 1971, p. 37.
81   For a detailed account of this and several other Triad creation myths, see Dian H. Murray, *The Origins of the Tiandihui: The Chinese Triads in Legend and History*, Stanford University Press, Stanford, 1994.
82   ibid., p. 210.
83   ibid., p. 92.
84   W.P. Morgan, *Triad Societies in Hong Kong*, Government Press, Hong Kong, 1989, pp. 96–7.
85   Murray, *The Origins of the Tiandihui*, pp. 183–4.
86   ibid., p. 185.
87   ibid., pp. 19–20.
88   ibid., p. 6.
89   ibid., p. 6.
90   ibid., p. 7.
91   ibid., p. 8.
92   According to Xie Jinluan, a prominent literatus of the early nineteenth century, as quoted in ibid., p. 11.
93   ibid., p. 34.
94   Chesneaux, *Secret Societies*, p. 61.
95   For a complete list of Triad rituals, see Morgan, *Triad Societies*, pp. 165–7.
96   Frederic Wakeman, 'The Secret Societies of Kwangtung [Guangdong]: 1800–1856', in Jean Chesneaux (ed.), *Popular Movements and Secret Societies in China, 1840–1950*, Stanford University Press, Stanford, 1971, p. 44.
97   Murray, *The Origins of the Tiandihui*, p. 29.
98   ibid., p. 27.
99   ibid., p. 178.
100 Chesneaux, *Secret Societies*, p. 33.
101 ibid., p. 85.
102 For an excellent account of these years and the Boxer uprising that followed, see Joseph Esherick, *The Origins of the Boxer Uprising*, University of California Press, Berkeley, 1987.
103 Michael J. Moser and Yeone Wei-chih Moser, *Foreigners Within the Gates: The Legations at Peking*, Oxford University Press, Hong Kong, 1993, p. 48.

104 Chesneaux, *Secret Societies*, p. 122.
105 Bernard Martin, *Strange Vigour: A Biography of Sun Yat-Sen*, William Heinemann, London, 1944, pp. 38 and 81.
106 Murray, *The Origins of the Tiandihui*, p. 117.
107 Leonard Adams, 'China: The historical setting', p. 366.
108 McCoy, *The Politics of Heroin in Southeast Asia*, pp. 4–5.
109 ibid., p. 5.
110 Wakeman, *Policing Shanghai*, p. 263.
111 ibid., p. 264.
112 *Manager* (Thailand), Nov. 1995.
113 Martin, *The Green Gang*, p. 32.
114 Perry, *Shanghai on Strike*, p. 89.
115 Tinko Pawley (as told to Joy Packer), *My Bandit Hosts*, Stanley & Paul, London, n.d. but most probably printed in the mid-1930s, p. 33.
116 ibid., p. 11.
117 Quoted in Chesneaux, *Secret Societies*, pp. 182–4.
118 Quoted in ibid., p. 141.
119 ibid., p. 143.
120 Quoted in ibid., pp. 70–1.
121 ibid., pp. 173–5.
122 Murray, *The Origins of the Tiandihui*, p. 130.
123 Chesneaux, *Secret Socities*, p. 185.
124 Morgan, *Triad Societies*, pp. 72–3.
125 Leonard, 'The historical setting', p. 374.
126 Martin, *The Shanghai Green Gang*, p. 166.
127 Barbara W. Tuchman, *Stilwell and the American Experience in China 1911–45*, Bantam Books, New York, 1972, p. 334.
128 Richard Deacon, *The Chinese Secret Service*, Grafton Books, London, 1989, pp. 219–20.
129 Tuchman, *Stilwell*, p. 334. This was in March 1942, before the retreat to India. The Soong family produced many prominent leaders and businessmen in Nationalist China: T.V. Soong later became prime minister and his younger brothers T.L. Soong and T.A. Soong became prominent financiers in Taiwan. T.V. Soong's three elder sisters all married prominent people: Ai-ling Soong became the wife of Taiwan's finance minister, H.H. Kung; Ching-ling Soong married Guomindang founder Sun Yat-sen and remained a revolutionary even after the communist victory in China; and May-ling Soong married Chiang Kai-shek. The old SACO barracks outside Chongqing are today a museum called 'the US–Chiang Kai-shek Criminal Acts Exhibition Hall'.
130 Pan, *Gangsters in Paradise*, pp. 154–5.
131 Tuchman, *Stilwell*, p. 314.
132 For an excellent account of Dai Li's activities during the war, see Frederic Wakeman Jr, *The Shanghai Badlands: Wartime Terrorism and Urban Crime 1937–1941*, Cambridge University Press, Cambridge, 1996.
133 Tuchman, *Stilwell*, p. 483.
134 ibid., p. 483.
135 ibid., p. 475.

136 There are many accounts of Al Capone's car in Shanghai, among them Pan, *Gangsters in Paradise*, p. 190; and descriptions posted on 'Tales of Old Shanghai,' a Shanghai website, 1997.

137 Ezpeleta, *Red Shadows*, p. 171

138 ibid., pp. 173–4, and Alexander Zhi-Cheng Wang, *A History of the Russian Emigré Community in Shanghai.*

139 Ezpeleta, *Red Shadows*, p. 178, and Pan, *Gangsters in Paradise*, p. 215.

140 Ezpeleta, *Red Shadows*, p. 178.

141 ibid., p. 108.

142 ibid., p. 150.

143 ibid., pp. 150–1.

144 Pan, *Gangsters in Paradise*, p. 220.

145 ibid., p. 221.

146 ibid., p. 224.

147 ibid., p. 228.

148 ibid., p. 234.

149 Hershatter, *Dangerous Pleasures*, pp. 304–5.

150 Pan, *In Search of Old Shanghai*, p. 97.

CHAPTER 2

1 Hendrik de Leeuw, *Cities of Sin*, Willey Book Company, New York, 1945, pp. 146–7.

2 I was in Macau during the handover ceremonies in December 1999, and stayed at Stanley Ho's Lisboa Hotel.

3 'The killings that shook Macau' *South China Morning Post*, 11 May 1997.

4 'PLA hopes scared public' *South China Morning Post*, 20 Aug. 1999.

5 Interview with Daniel Ferreira, Macau's acting prison chief, Macau, 2 Dec. 1998.

6 'Broken Tooth's trial gets underway' *Associated Press*, 22 Apr. 1999.

7 'Suspected triad chief: I earn $2 million a month' *South China Morning Post*, 23 Apr. 1999. HK$2 million=$265 000.

8 ibid.

9 'I'm a gambler not a triad boss, Broken Tooth tells trial judge' *South China Morning Post*, 12 Oct. 1999.

10 ibid.

11 'Broken Tooth "suffers depths of depression"' *South China Morning Post*, 20 Dec. 1999.

12 The people of the northern coastal region of Guangdong province call themselves Teochew in their own dialect. The Cantonese call them Chiu Chao, and the *pinyin* name for the same people is Zhao Zhou. Many Teochews have migrated to Southeast Asia, especially to Thailand where they outnumber all other Chinese communities.

13 This, and other details about Wan Kuok-koi's early life, were passed on to the author in February 1999 by Leung Yat-chan of the *Oriental Daily News*, a prominent Hong Kong crime reporter who has met and interviewed Koi on a number of occasions. The story basically is Koi's own.

14 Communication with Harald Bruning, Macau, 24 May 1999.

15   Communication with Leung Yat-chan, 25 Feb. 1999.

16   John Comley, 'Tales from the Dragonhead' *Time*, 20 April 1998.

17   Cathy Hilborn, 'Making a killing/just say no/suite deals in Macau' *Far Eastern Economic Review*, 12 Mar. 1998, pp. 26–9.

18   Communication with Leung Yat-chan, 25 Feb. 1999.

19   ibid.

20   Interview with Leung Yat-chan, Macau, 2 Dec. 1998.

21   'Shui Fong' is spelt 'Soi Fong' in the Macau way of Romanising Cantonese. The Dai Huen Jai is also called the *Da Quan Bang* ('Big Circle Gang') in *pinyin*.

22   Interview with Daniel Ferreira, Macau's acting prison chief, Macau, 2 Dec. 1998.

23   'Overworked consulate officers let Macau triad boss slip into Canada' *South China Morning Post*, 6 Nov. 1997.

24   'Cops display guns seized in Asian crime-ring raid' *The Province* (Canada), 17 Oct. 1999.

25   ibid.

26   According to a source in Macau who wants to remain anonymous, 3 Mar. 1999.

27   'Cambodian shoot-out linked to Macau arms smuggling bid' *South China Morning Post*, 21 Oct. 1997.

28   Huw Watkin, 'Shoot-out over gun-running' *Phnom Penh Post*, 24 Oct.–6 Nov. 1997, p. 18.

29   'Macau gunman fires AK-47' *South China Morning Post*, 5 Oct. 1998.

30   'Bombings act of cowardice' *Hong Kong Standard*, 9 Sept. 1998.

31   *Asia Yearbook 1998*, *Far Eastern Economic Review*, Hong Kong, p. 52.

32   'Judiciary "too soft" on crime in Macau' *South China Morning Post*, 1 Feb. 1997.

33   Bertil Lintner, 'End of an empire' *Far Eastern Economic Review*, 24 Dec. 1998, pp. 21–4. The article is based on official government statistics. See also 'Gangland war sees big drop in gamblers and tourists' *South China Morning Post*, 8 Aug. 1997.

34   'Kidnappings going unreported: tycoon' *South China Morning Post*, 3 Mar. 1999.

35   'Police wage war on Macao-based crime' *China Daily*, 25 June 1998.

36   'Guangdong crimebusters cast wide net' *South China Morning Post*, 2 June 1999.

37   Interview with João Guedes, Macau, 5 Dec. 1998. Guedes is a former Macau police officer and the author of a book about the Triads in Macau (in Portuguese: *Seitas: Histórias do Crime e da Polítícaem Macau*, Livros do Oriente, Lisbon, 1991.)

38   'Beijing signals greater involvement in Macau' *Jane's Defence Weekly*, 6 Oct. 1999.

39   'Six held over Hong Kong man's murder' *South China Morning Post*, 23 Nov. 1999.

40   According to Leung Yat-chan, 27 Dec. 1999.

41   I was at the border when the PLA convoy drove into Macau. Even a local motorcycle gang was there to greet them.

42   'Macau casino tycoon' *Far Eastern Economic Review*, 21 Oct. 1999, p. 66; and Cesar Bacani and Raissa Espinosa-Robles, 'Manila rolls the dice: in quest of foreign investment and jobs, Estrada lays out the red carpet for Macau tycoon Stanley Ho' *Asiaweek*, 22 Oct. 1999. However, following negative coverage of

the deal in the Philippine press, and criticism from the Roman Catholic Church, by early 2001 this deal seemed to have fallen through.

43   According to Michael Kohn of the *Mongol Messenger*, 10 April 1999.

44   'North Korea opening (Sh-h-h!) a casino' *New York Times*, 31 July 1999.

45   For a detailed account of Yeung's businesses and underworld connections, see Fredric Dannen, 'Partners in crime' *The New Republic*, 14 & 21 July 1997, pp. 18–26.

46   Michael Backman, *Asian Eclipse: Exposing the Dark Side of Business in Asia*, John Wiley & Sons [Asia], Singapore, 1999, p. 327.

47   'More fake notes surface' *South China Morning Post*, 24 July 1994, AFP 15 July 1994 ('North Korea's traders hold fort in Macau'), and 'Macao called new center of North Korean spying' *New York Times*, 16 Aug. 1987.

48   'North Korea's conduit for crime: cash-poor Pyongyang uses tiny Macau to move its dirty money' *Washington Post*, 25 Apr. 1999.

49   Kim Hyun Hee, *The Tears of My Soul*, William Morrow and Company, New York, 1993, p. 69.

50   This and other accounts of Russian prostitution are based on interviews with several Russian prostitutes in Macau, December 1995.

51   'Robbery was sole motive for Alderdice murder' *Hong Kong Standard*, 8 July 1994. 'Yekaterina', who shared a flat with Natalia in Macau for several months, shares this view: Macau, December 1995. See also Jonathan Manthorpe, 'The man who loved too much and the woman who loved too many' *The Vancouver Sun*, 16 May 2000.

52   'KGB man linked to Alderdice case and Macau' *Eastern Express*, 3 Aug. and '"Bob" admits links to Macau vice trade', 11 Aug. 1994; and 'Ripin yarn from Russia' *South China Morning Post*, 16 Oct. 1994.

53   *South China Morning Post*, 16 Oct. 1994.

54   Quoted in Porter, *Macau: The Imaginary City*, p. 1.

55   See, for instance, *Portugal: Overseas Provinces*, Agência-Geral do Ultramar, Lisbon, undated government publication printed in the late 1960s, p. 150.

56   The best account of the early years of the Portuguese settlement in Macau is in Geoffrey C. Gunn, *Encountering Macau: A Portuguese City-State on the Periphery of China, 1557–1999*, Westview Press, Boulder, Col., 1996, pp. 12–16, and Porter, *Macau: The Imaginary City*, pp. 40–50.

57   Porter, *Macau: The Imaginary City* , p. 41.

58   W. Robert Usellis, *As Origens de Macau/The Origin of Macao*, Museu Marítimo de Macau, Macau, 1995, pp. 136–7.

59   Fei Chengkang, *Macao 400 Years*, The Publishing House of Shanghai Academy of Social Sciences, Shanghai, 1996, p. 20.

60   ibid., p. 6. The first to challenge Portugal's claim to have been awarded Macau by the Chinese Emperor in the sixteenth century was Sir Anders Ljungstedt, Sweden's consul-general in the territory in the early nineteenth century. At the time, he was condemned by the Portuguese, but his findings have now been accepted even by the colonial authorities who in 1998 named a new street in Macau after him. Ljungstedt's research was re-published a few years ago: Anders Ljungstedt, *An Historical Sketch of the Portuguese Settlement in China and of the Roman Catholic Church and Mission in China & Description of the City of Canton*, Viking Publications, Hong Kong, 1992.

61 *Macau: Pequena Monografia*, Agéncia-Geral do Ultramar, Lisbon, 1965, p. 24, and *Macau: City of the Name of God*, Agéncia-Geral do Ultramar, Lisbon, 1960s, p. 20.

62 Edward E. Fuller, manuscript Journal Macau, Sunday, 2 Dec. 1866. Also quoted in Porter, *Macau: The Imaginary City*, p. 56.

63 Porter, *Macau: The Imaginary City*, pp. 56–7, and Gunn, *Encountering Macau*, pp. 72–4.

64 Porter, *Macau: The Imaginary City*, p. 94.

65 Gunn, *Encountering Macau*, p. 88.

66 ibid., p. 86–7.

67 ibid., pp. 82, 87.

68 1 *leung* or *liang* or *tael* of gold equals 37.5 grams. Tai Hing is Cantonese (in *pinyin* Tai Xing) for 'Tranquil Prosperity'.

69 Gunn, *Encountering Macau*, p. 90.

70 Aleko E. Lilius, *I Sailed with Chinese Pirates*, Arrowsmith, London, 1930; and Oxford University Press, Hong Kong, 1991, p. 76.

71 ibid. p. 90, and A. Pinho, 'Gambling in Macau' in R.D. Cremer (ed.), *Macau: City of Commerce and Culture: Change and Continuity*, API Press, Hong Kong, 1991, p. 249.

72 Guedes, *Seitas*, pp. 112–13.

73 For an excellent account of piracy in this period in Chinese history, see Dian H. Murray, *Pirates of the South China Coast 1790–1810*, Stanford University Press, Stanford, 1987.

74 ibid., pp. 71–3.

75 Quoted in ibid., pp. 166–7.

76 ibid., pp. 143–4.

77 ibid., p. 150.

78 'Pirates out, tourists in' *Hongkong Standard*, 25 June 1997.

79 Lilius, *I Sailed With Chinese Pirates*.

80 ibid., p. 39.

81 ibid., p. 39.

82 Fei, *Macao 400 Years*, pp. 344–5.

83 Gunn, *Encountering Macau*, p. 128.

84 'Macau's golden goose: Beijing denies cold-war bullion business' *Guardian*, 7 Feb. 1998.

85 'US says Nazis used gold loot to pay for war' *New York Times*, 1 June 1998.

86 *Guardian*, 7 Feb. 1998. A detailed account of the postwar gold trade in Portugal and Macau was presented in a recent Portuguese television documentary produced by Rui Araujo and António Louçã, which was also translated into French, 'Le Guerre de l'Or'. A transcript of the documentary is in my possession.

87 Communication with João Guedes, 25 Jan. 1999.

88 *Next* magazine (Hong Kong, in Chinese), 23 Apr. 1999.

89 At that time there was only one officially recognised bank in Macau, the Banco Nacional Ultramarino, but several gold dealers, money changers and pawn shops called themselves 'banks' as well: communication with João Guedes, 5 Jan. 2000.

90 *Guardian*, 7 Feb. 1998. See also Richard Hughes, *Borrowed Place Borrowed Time: Hong Kong and its Many Faces*, Andre Deutsch, London, 1976, pp. 149–51.

91 *Guardian*, 7 Feb. 1998.

92 ibid.

93 Alexandra Campos, Cláudia Almeida and Pedro Dias de Almeida, *A Convivial Handbook: Macau from A to Z*, Gabinete de Coordemação da Cerimónia de Transferência, Macau, 1999, pp. 208–9.

94 A street in central Macau is even named after 'the enigmatic doctor', as Ian Fleming called him in Donald Pittis and Susan J. Henders, *Macau: Mysterious Decay and Romance*, Oxford University Press, Hong Kong, 1997, pp. 61–6. Lobo may also have been the model for 'Oddjob' in the James Bond movie *Goldfinger*.

95 The Hang Seng Bank of Hong Kong should not be confused with the Macau-based, gold-smuggling Seng Heng Bank.

96 *Next*, 23 Apr. 1999.

97 Gunn, *Encountering Macau*, p. 134.

98 *Next*, 23 Apr. 1999.

99 Fei, *Macao 400 Years*, p. 349.

100 *Next*, 23 Apr. 1999.

101 Elfed Vaughan Roberts, Sum Ngai Ling and Peter Bradshaw, *Historical Dictionary of Hong Kong & Macau*, The Scarecrow Press, Metuchen, NJ and London, 1992, p. 299.

102 Gunn, *Encountering Macau*, p. 154.

103 Jonathan Friedland, 'A winning streak' *Far Eastern Economic Review*, 6 Sept. 1990, pp. 56–61. See also 'The New Elite' (*Fortune*, Asian edition), 26 May 1997: 'Fok, son of a seamstress and a stevedore, made his first fortune smuggling contraband into China during the Korean war, the legend goes. Today he keeps a low profile. But you can bet he'll have plenty of discreet advice to offer [Hong Kong chief executive] Tung [Chee-hwa] and his team.'

104 *Next*, 13 Dec. 1991.

105 *Eastweek* magazine (in Chinese), Hong Kong, 21 July 1993.

106 *Next*, 16 May 1997.

107 Information supplied by Stacy Mosher, Hong Kong, January 1998.

108 Ditto.

109 *Eastweek*, 2 Nov. 1994.

110 Ling Ha, *The Biography of Fok Ying-tung: The Life and Times of a Red Capitalist* (in Chinese), Hong Kong, July 1997.

111 ibid.; *Next*, 26 June 1997 and *Eastweek*, 16 Nov. 1994.

112 The Fu family moved to Hong Kong, where they invested whatever they had earned from their gambling franchise in a new hotel, the Furama, which is still there near the waterfront in the city centre.

113 Friedland, *Far Eastern Economic Review*, 6 Sept. 1990, pp. 56–61.

114 Afterwards, the Chinese government distributed a booklet with photographs from the riots in Macau and the sympathy demonstrations in Zhuhai: *Opposing the Sanguinary Atrocities Perpetrated by the Portuguese Imperialists in Macao*, supposedly published by the *Macau Daily News*, 1 Sept. 1967, but printed in China.

115 *Next*, 23 Apr. 1999.

116 Gunn, *Encountering Macau*, pp. 156–7.

117 Mary Lee, 'The Portuguese gamble' *Far Eastern Economic Review*, 27 Aug. 1982, pp. 51–4.

118 Rodney Tasker, 'Canny eye on the future' *Far Eastern Economic Review*, 16 July 1976, p. 51.

119 James Leung, 'South China's merchant prince' *Asian Business*, Sept. 1996, pp. 18–26. See also 'The next roll of the dice' *South China Morning Post*, 14 Mar. 1998.

120 ibid.

121 Tasker, *Far Eastern Economic Review*, 16 July 1976, pp. 50–1.

122 Leung, *Asian Business*, Sept. 1996, pp. 18–26.

123 Tasker, *Far Eastern Economic Review*, 16 July 1976, pp. 50–1.

124 ibid.

125 Friedland, *Far Eastern Economic Review*, 6 Sept. 1990, pp. 56–61.

126 Tasker, *Far Eastern Economic Review*, 16 July 1976, pp. 50–1.

127 '$4.45 billion profit as casino boss brought to account at last' *South China Morning Post*, 11 July 1997. The currency quoted in the article is Hong Kong dollars.

128 Leung, *Asian Business*, Sept. 1996, pp. 18–26.

129 ibid. and Allen T. Cheng, 'Macau's big bet' *Asia Inc.*, Aug. 1997, pp. 24–31.

130 Christina Miu Bing Cheng, *Macau: A Cultural Janus*, Hong Kong University Press, Hong Kong, 1999, p. 206.

131 Cheung, *Asia Inc.*, Aug. 1979, pp. 24–31.

132 *Eastweek*, 9 Nov. 1994.

133 ibid.

134 'Yip sells out but the show goes on' and 'Cheng buys into STDM' *South China Morning Post*, 24 Oct. 1982.

135 Friedland, *Far Eastern Economic Review*, 6 Sept. 1990, pp. 56–61.

136 Garry W.G. Clement and Brian McAdam, *Triads and Other Asian Organized Crime Groups*, Royal Canadian Mounted Police manual, Hong Kong, 1993, p. 59.

137 Details about Yip Hon's last years come from an article in *Next*, 10 Nov. 1995; additional information was supplied by Stacy Mosher in Hong Kong.

138 'Who's Who of business in Asia', special issue of *Asia Inc.*, vol. 7, no. 2, 1998, p. 23.

139 *Asia Yearbook 1986, Far Eastern Economic Review*, Hong Kong, 1996, p. 72.

140 K.I. Woo, 'A well-connected man' in *Hong Kong: A New Dawn*, The Nation, Bangkok, 1997.

141 Bruce Gilley, 'Tung will face loyalty conflicts' in *Hong Kong: 1997 and Beyond*, Review Publishing Company, Hong Kong, 1997, p. 218.

142 'Banker Ho to become first leader' *Agence-France Presse* Macau, 15 May 1999.

143 Todd Crowell and Yulanda Chung, 'Brave new era' *Asiaweek*, 14 May 1999. Also communication with Harald Bruning, 30 Oct. 1999, pp. 38–41.

144 Lee, *Far Eastern Economic Review*, 27 Aug. 1982, pp. 51–4.

145 'Macau: China wants more control of gambling' *Inter-Press Service*, Macau, 22 April 1995.

146 'The Macau money trail' *South China Morning Post*, 20 May 1995.

147 *IPS*, 22 Apr. 1995.

148 *Asia Yearbook 1995, Far Eastern Economic Review* Hong Kong, 1995, p. 162.

149 'Stanley Ho accepts casino deal' *South China Morning Post*, 22 June 1997.

150 Leung, *Asian Business*, Sept. 1996, pp. 18–26.

151 *South China Morning Post*, 14 Mar. 1998.

152 'Casino Mr. Big rolls dice again' *The Australian*, 17 June 1999.

153 ibid.

154 ibid.

155 According to several sources in Macau. See also a 1997 report from *Observatoire Géopolitique des Drogues* in Paris: 'Various money-laundering methods'.

156 W.P. Morgan, *Triad Societies in Hong Kong*, Government Press, Hong Kong, 1960, reprinted in 1982 and 1989, pp. 61–2.

157 Ko-lin Chin, 'Triad societies in Hong Kong' unpublished paper from the School of Criminal Justice, Rutgers University.

158 Manuel Teixeira, 'The Bonnie and Clyde of Macau' in Pittis and Handers, *Macau: Mysterious Decay and Romance*, p. 3.

159 Communication with João Guedes, 31 Oct. 1999.

160 Lynn Pan, *Old Shanghai: Gangsters in Paradise*, Heinemann Asia, Singapore, 1993, p. 231.

161 Jules Nadeau, *Twenty Million Chinese Made in Taiwan*, Montreal Press, Montreal, 1990, pp. 271–2.

162 Morgan, *Triad Societies*, p. 80. Other sources say 'K' stands for the initial of its founder's surname: Harald Bruning, 'Gangsters who have forgotten the rules' *South China Morning Post*, 12 Dec. 1999.

163 Clement and McAdam, *Triads and Other Asian Organized Crime Groups*, p. 15.

164 Morgan, *Triad Societies*, pp. 82–3.

165 For a more detailed account of the 1956 riots, see Martin Booth, *The Dragon Syndicates*, pp. 186–8; and Morgan, *Triad Societies*, pp. 86–7.

166 This explanation of the origin of the name Shui Fong comes from Leung Yat-chan. Other sources claim that the Wo On Lok first met in a soft-drink factory in the New Territories, and hence got its popular name. However, Leung's explanation seems more credible, given that the code names of other groups such as the Wo Hop To follow a similar pattern. Some sources speculate that the Shui Fong (Soi Fong in Macau) may have been Macau's only indigenous Triad, set up by gangsters on the territory's outlying islands in the 1930s, and believe the name comes from the gang's exploitation of water carriers, at a time when most households had no running water supply: Harald Bruning, *South China Morning Post*, 12 Dec. 1999.

167 Clement and McAdam, *Triads and Other Asian Organized Crime Groups*, p. 100.

168 ibid., p. 96; and *South China Morning Post*, 30 Oct. 1991.

169 Clement and McAdam, *Triads and Other Asian Organized Crime Groups*, pp. 50–1.

170 ibid., p. 40.

171 ibid., p. 50, and Booth, *The Dragon Syndicates*, pp. 219–20.

172 Clement and McAdam, *Triads and Other Asian Organized Crime Groups*, p. 51.

173 Frederic Dannen, 'Partners in crime' *The New Republic*, 14 & 21 July 1997, p. 24. See also Angelina Malhotra, 'Shanghai's dark side' *Asia Inc.*, Feb. 1994, pp. 32–9.

174 *Next*, 7 May 1993.

175 Clement and McAdam, *Triads and Other Asian Organized Crime Groups*, p. 60.

176 Lintner, *Far Eastern Economic Review*, 24 Dec. 1998, pp. 21–4.

177 According to sources in Macau who want to remain anonymous.

178 This and other details about Charlie Trie's life come from 'Exhibit 13: Statement by Yah Lin Trie', Daihatsu International Trading, Little Rock, Arkansas; and 'The money Trie' *Wall Street Journal*, 18 Dec. 1996.

179 'Who is Mochtar Riady-II?' *Wall Street Journal*, 10 Oct. 1996.

180 Robert L. Bartley, ed., *Whitewater*, the *Wall Street Journal*, New York, 1997, p. 505.

181 'Lessons from Lippo' *Wall Street Journal*, 27 Feb. 1997.

182 'Findings link Clinton allies to Chinese intelligence' *Washington Post*, 10 Feb. 1998.

183 Bartley, *Whitewater*, p. 512.

184 Lippo's Chinese connections' *Wall Street Journal*, 15 Jan. 1997.

185 'US Senate Campaign-Finance Report: Charlie Trie's and Ng Lap Seng's laundered contributions to the DNC', Washington, 26 Jan. 1998.

186 According to a handout by the Fortuna.

187 *Wall Street Journal*, 26 Feb. 1998.

188 'Ng visited White House while wiring funds to U' *Wall Street Journal*, 1 Aug. 1997.

189 *Wall Street Journal*, 27 Feb. 1998.

190 'Fund-raiser Charlie Trie pleads guilty under plea arrangement' *All Politics*, Arkansas, 21 May 1998.

191 Jeff Gerth, David Johnston and Don Van Natta, 'Chinese military gave thousands of dollars fund-raiser says' *The New York Times*, 15 May 1998.

192 ibid.

193 'The Macau Connection' *Wall Street Journal*, 26 Feb. 1998, and Lintner, *Far Eastern Economic Review*, 24 Dec. 1998, pp. 21–4.

194 ibid., and various personal interviews with people in Macau, December 1998.

195 'North Korea to set up travel company in Macau' *Kyodo News International*, 23 Aug. 1990.

196 *Wall Street Journal*, 27 Feb. 1998.

197 The picture appeared on the cover of Hu Sin, *The Biography of Anna Chennault* (in Chinese), Taipei, 1995.

198 Communication with Hong Kong-based law enforcement official, 29 Dec. 1997. The VIP room deal was also covered by the Hong Kong weekly *Eastweek*.

199 Harald Bruning, 'Mystery company in Macau reportedly buys Russian aircraft carrier from Ukraine for $20 million' *Hong Kong Standard*, 19 March 1998.

200 Communication with Harald Bruning, Macau, 18 March 1998.

201 Communication with Hong Kong-based criminal investigator, 19 March 1998.

202 'Eight held over [HK] $200 million fraud on food giant' *South China Morning Post*, 9 Sept. 1999.

203 'No-show by wanted lawmaker' *South China Morning Post*, 21 Aug. 1999.

204 *Next*, 23 Apr. 1999.

205 'Confessions of Macau bank heir don't foil his leadership chances' *Associated Press* (Macau), 11 May 1999.

206 ibid.

CHAPTER 3

1 In an interview with David Kaplan, 1984; David Kaplan and Alec Dubro, *Yakuza: The Explosive Account of Japan's Criminal Underworld*, Addison-Wesley,

Reading, Mass., 1986, p. 29. The quote is reproduced with permission from Kaplan.

2   Quoted in Karel van Wolferen, *The Enigma of Japanese Power: People and Politics in a Stateless Nation*, Vintage Books, New York, 1990, p. 102.

3   I arrived in Kobe the day after the earthquake and remained there for a week to cover the disaster for the *Far Eastern Economic Review* (see 'Bigger than both of us: Kobe can be fixed, but what about Japan?', 2 Feb. 1995, pp. 49–50) and the Swedish daily *Svenska Dagbladet*.

4   Communication with Mark Schreiber, Tokyo, 27 Sept. 2000.

5   Communication with David Kaplan, an expert on the *yakuza*, 22 July 2000.

6   For an excellent outline of this development, see David E. Kaplan, *Japanese Organized Crime and the Bubble Economy*, The Woodrow Wilson Center, Asia Programme: Occasional Paper No. 70, 13 Dec. 1996.

7   ibid., p. 4.

8   Michael Hirsh, 'Tokyo's dirty secret: banks and the mob' *Newsweek*, 18 Dec. 1995, pp. 42–3.

9   Robert Delfs, 'Feeding on the system' *Far Eastern Economic Review*, 21 Nov. 1991, pp. 28–35.

10   ibid.

11   ibid.

12   van Wolferen, *The Enigma of Japanese Power*, p. 106.

13   Brian Bremner, 'Yakuza and the banks' *Business Week* 29 Jan. 1996, pp. 15–18.

14   David E. Kaplan, 'Yakuza Inc.' *US News & World Report*, 13 April 1998, pp. 41–7.

15   Delfs, 'Feeding the system', and Barbara Wanner, 'More eyes of Yakuza's role in the Japanese economy' *Japan Economic Institute*, 8 May 1992 (http:// members.tripod.com/~orgcrime/japeconomy.htm).

16   Kaplan, *Japanese Organized Crime and the Bubble Economy*, p. 5.

17   Hirsh, *Newsweek*, 18 Dec. 1995, pp. 42–3.

18   Garry W.G. Clement and Brian McAdam, *Triads and Other Asian Organized Crime Groups*, Royal Canadian Mounted Police manual, Hong Kong, 1993, p. 120.

19   This quote and following details are from van Wolferen, *The Enigma of Japanese Power*, p. 104.

20   Robert Delfs, 'Legal conduct' *Far Eastern Economic Review*, 21 Nov. 1991, pp. 34–5.

21   Clement and McAdam, *Triads*, p. 120.

22   Wanner, *Japan Economic Institute*, 8 May 1992.

23   By far the best account of the *yakuza*, its early years and development into what it is today is David E. Kaplan's and Alec Dubro's classic, *Yakuza*.

24   Adam Johnson, *Yakuza: Past and Present*, Organised Crime Registry (a Website http://members.tripod.com/~orgcrime/yakuzahistory.htm).

25   Kaplan and Dubro, *Yakuza*, p. 24, and Clement and McAdam, *Triads*, p. 113.

26   This description of what actually is a fairly recent *yakuza* initiation ceremony was given by Eric Talmadge of Associated Press in an article entitled 'Yakuza show tradition in succession', which appeared in many Asian newspapers at the time—for instance *The Nation* of Bangkok, 9 Mar. 1991. The main rituals have remained unchanged for centuries.

27   Kaplan and Dubro, *Yakuza*, p. 16.

28   *Japan: Profile of a Nation* (no author), Kodansha International, Tokyo, New York, London, 1994, p. 277.

29   Kaplan and Dubro, *Yakuza*, p. 21.

30   ibid., p. 25, and Clement and McAdam, *Triads*, p. 113.

31   Clement and McAdam, *Triads*, p. 117.

32   ibid.

33   There are two good accounts in English of the *burakumin* in Japanese society: Michael Weiner, ed., *Japan's Minorities: The Illusion of Homogeneity*, Routledge, London and New York, 1997, pp. 50–78, and Suehiro Kitaguchi, *An Introduction to the Buraku Issue: Questions and Answers*, Japan Library (Curzon Press), Richmond, Surrey, 1999.

34   Kitaguchi, *An Introduction to the Buraku Issue*, p. 79.

35   Weiner, *Japan's Minorities*, p. 54.

36   *History of the Yakuza* from a Website, www.yakuza.hiperlinkcorp.com/historia.htm.

37   Richard Deacon, *Kempeitai: The Japanese Secret Service Then and Now*, Charles E. Tuttle Company, Tokyo 1990, p. 31.

38   ibid., p. 37.

39   Deacon, *Kempeitai*, p. 43.

40   Raymond Lamont-Brown, *Kempeitai: Japan's Dreaded Military Police*, Sutton Publishing, Stroud, Gloucestershire, 1998, pp. 16–17.

41   Deacon, *Kempeitai*, p. 38.

42   ibid., p. 57.

43   See ibid., pp. 40–1, and Carter J. Eckert, Ki-baik Lee, Young Ick Lew, Michael Robinson and Edward W. Wagner, *Korea Old and New: A History*, Ilchokak Publishers, Seoul, 1990, for Korea Institute, Harvard University, pp. 216–50.

44   Kaplan and Dubro, *Yakuza*, p. 38.

45   ibid., p. 91.

46   ibid., pp. 36–7, and Sheldon H. Harris, *Factories of Death: Japanese Biological Warfare, 1932–1945, and the American Cover-up*, Routledge, London and New York, 1995, p. 141. Prince Konoye was one of several members of the Imperial family who was most probably aware of Japan's biological warfare research in Manchuria.

47   Harris, *Factories of Death*, p. 9.

48   Deacon, *Kempeitai*, pp. 43–4 and 140. The same Chinese characters for the 'Black Dragon Society' could also be read 'the Amur River Society', and this was its proper name as it was named after the river that separates Manchuria from Russia. But the name 'Black Dragon' stuck, and that is how it has become known in history. See Kaplan and Munro, *Yakuza*, p. 36, and Deacon, *Kempeitai*, p. 43.

49   Richard H. Minear, *Victors' Justice: The Tokyo War Crimes Trial*, Charles E. Tuttle, Tokyo, 1984, p. 6.

50   Robert Whiting, *Tokyo Underworld: The Fast Times and Hard Life of an American Gangster in Japan*, Pantheon Books, New York, 1999, p. 7.

51   ibid., p. 82.

52   Kaplan and Dubro, *Yakuza*, pp. 49–50.

53   ibid., pp. 50–1 and Whiting, *Tokyo Underworld*, pp. 10, 16.

54 Mark Schreiber, 'City of Light' *Winds* (Japan Airlines inflight magazine), Dec. 1998.

55 Communication with veteran Japanese journalist Michio Matsui in Tokyo, 28 Jan. 2001.

56 Communication with Mark Schreiber in Tokyo, 14 Nov. 2000.

57 *Owed Justice: Thai Women Trafficked into Debt Bondage in Japan*, Human Rights Watch/Asia, Sept. 2000, pp. 24–5.

58 Communication with a Tokyo-based journalist, 7 Feb. 2001.

59 C.P. Spencer and V. Navaratnam, *Drug Abuse in East Asia*, Oxford University Press, Kuala Lumpur, 1981, pp. 53–4.

60 The National Police Agency, Japan, *Methamphetamine/Amphetamine Production and Trafficking*, report to the 14th Asian Regional Conference on Drugs, Bangkok, 20–24 June 1996.

61 ibid.

62 Kaplan and Dubro, *Yakuza*, pp. 55–6.

63 ibid., p. 60.

64 Whiting, *Tokyo Underworld*, pp. 81–1.

65 Kaplan and Dubro, *Yakuza*, pp. 194–6.

66 It has now been revealed that US and Soviet air forces clashed directly in Korea. The Russians admit to having lost 354, while claiming they shot down 1300 American planes: Jon Halliday, 'A secret war' *Far Eastern Economic Review*, 22 April 1993, pp. 32–6.

67 See Minear, *Victors' Justice*, and John L. Ginn, Sugamo Prison, *Tokyo: An Account of the Trial and Sentencing of Japanese War Criminals in 1948, by a U.S. Participant*, MacFarland & Company, Jefferson, North Carolina and London, 1992.

68 Deacon, *Kempeitai*, pp. 197–8, and Kaplan and Dubro, *Yakuza*, p. 65.

69 Kaplan and Dubro, *Yakuza*, p. 66.

70 Lamont-Brown, *Kempeitai*, pp. 71–2.

71 John M. Jennings, *The Opium Empire: Japanese Imperialism and Drug Trafficking in Asia, 1895–1945*, Praeger, Westport, Conn. and London, 1997, p. 94.

72 ibid., p. 95

73 Quoted in Kaplan and Dubro, *Yakuza*, p. 66.

74 ibid., p. 62.

75 ibid., p. 94.

76 ibid., p. 68.

77 Deacon, *Kempeitai*, p. 232.

78 Terzani Tiziano of *Der Spiegel*, Bangkok, 20 Dec. 1994.

79 'Kanemaru "offered billions to rightists"' *Reuters*, Tokyo, 5 Nov. 1992. The alleged incident took place in 1987. In May 1992 Kanemaru was eventually forced to resign from Parliament.

80 This and other details from Andrew Marshall, 'In the name of the Godfather', *Caravan* (Bangkok), Dec. 1994, pp. 83–9. See also Hans Katayama, 'The man who tried to buy respect' *Asia Inc.*, Mar. 1994, pp. 34–7.

81 Marshall, *Caravan*, Dec. 1994, pp. 83–9.

82 John Roberts, 'Ryoichi Sasakawa: Nippon's right-wing muscleman' *Insight* (Hong Kong), April 1978.

83 Marshall, *Caravan*, Dec. 1994, pp. 83–9, and Katayama *Asia Inc.*, Mar. 1994, pp. 34–7.

84　Jeffrey M. Bale, 'Privatising covert action: the case of the Unification Church' *Lobster* (UK), May 1991. The article cites information from Karl Hale Dixon, 'The Extreme Right in Contemporary Japan' (unpublished PhD dissertation, Florida State University, 1975).

85　For a list of individuals associated with the WACL, see Scott Anderson and Jon Lee Anderson, *Inside the League: The Shocking Exposé of How Terrorists, Nazis, and Latin American Death Squads have Infiltrated the World Anti-Communist League*, Dodd, Mead & Company, New York, 1986, pp. 275–85.

86　ibid., p. 64.

87　ibid., p. 64.

88　ibid., p. 69, and Marshall, *Caravan*, Dec. 1994, pp. 83–9.

89　*Report of the Subcommittee on International Organizations of the Committee on International Relations, US House of Representatives: Investigation of Korean–American Relations*, US Government Printing Office, Washington, 31 Oct. 1978, pp. 3, 5.

90　ibid., p. 2.

91　ibid., p. 3.

92　ibid., pp. 3–4.

93　Marshall, *Caravan*, Dec. 1994, pp. 83–9.

94　ibid.

95　ibid.

96　Katayama, *Asia Inc.*, Mar. 1994, pp. 34–7.

97　Quoted in Kaplan and Dubro, *Yakuza*, pp. 85–6.

98　ibid., p. 103. See also Whiting, *Tokyo Underworld*, pp. 189–204.

99　Kaplan and Dubro, *Yakuza*, p. 116.

100　'Away with the rogues' *The Economist*, 23 Sept. 2000, pp. 29–30.

101　'Reported Mob Link Hits Japan Yogurt Maker' the *International Herald Tribune*, 15–16 Jan. 2000.

102　BBC World Service, Asia Pacific, 28 Mar. 2000, 'Yamaichi Chiefs Sentenced'.

103　*Shukan Taishu*, 12–19 May 1997, translated by Mark Schreiber.

104　Robert Delfs, 'Clash of loyalties' *Far Eastern Economic Review*, 21 Nov. 1991, pp. 30–1.

105　Velisarios Kattoulas, 'Taking care of business' *Far Eastern Economic Review*, 30 Nov. 2000, pp. 92–4.

106　*History of the Yakuza*, a Website at http://organizedcrime.about.com/cs/yakuza. See also Garry W.G. Clement and Brian McAdam, *Triads*, p. 122.

107　Clement and McAdam, *Triads*, p. 117.

108　Brian Bremner, 'The Samurai meets the Godfather' *Business Week*, 29 Jan. 1996. p. 18.

109　Ian Buruma, *Behind the Mask: Sexual Demons, Sacred Mothers, Transvestites, Gangsters, and Other Japanese Cultural Heroes*, Pantheon Books, New York, 1984, p. 188.

110　Kitaguchi, *An Introduction to the Buraku Issue*, p. 26.

111　Kaplan and Dubro, *Yakuza*, pp. 189–92.

112　Sonia Ryang, *Northkoreans in Japan: Language, Ideology and Identity*, Westview Press, Boulder, Col., 1997, p. 88. Ryang's book is an excellent account of Chongryun and the Korean community in Japan.

113　Donald MacIntyre and Sachiko Sakamaki, 'Squeeze the little guy' *Time* (Asia edition), 6 Dec, 1999, pp. 20–2.

114 Ryang, *Northkoreans in Japan*, pp. 89–91.

115 MacIntyre and Sakamaki, *Time*, 6 Dec. 1999, pp. 20–2.

116 Mary Jordan and Kevin Sullivan, 'Pinball wizards fuel North Korea' the *Washington Post*, 7 June 1996.

117 Nicholas D. Kristof, 'Chinese gangs dominate Japanese "entertainment" zone' *New York Times*, 18 June 1999.

118 Furumaya Tadao, 'From student to illegal worker: Chinese migrants in Japan', paper from Niigata University, May 2000.

119 Mo Bangfu, 'The rise of the Chinese mafia in Japan' *Japan Echo*, Feb. 1998.

120 Velisarios Kattoulas, 'Young, fast and deadly' *Far Eastern Economic Review*, 1 Feb. 2001, pp. 64–7.

121 *Shukan Taishu*, 12–19 May 1997.

CHAPTER 4

1 Quoted in Stephen Handelman, *Comrade Criminal: The Theft of the Second Russian Revolution*, Michael Joseph, London, 1994, p. 25.

2 ibid., pp. 18–20. Handelman's book is the most authoritative study of the 'modern' Soviet *Mafiya*, and most details about the Odintsovo meeting come from him (although he calls it 'Vedentsovo'; Moscow residents assert that 'Odintsovo' is the proper name of the small town outside the Russian capital where the extraordinary *Mafiya* summit took place in 1991).

3 The book, *Benya Kirk*, was written in 1926 by the Russian-Jewish journalist and author Isaak Babel, according to Bangkok-based Russian journalist Evguenii Belenky, 23 Dec. 1999. See also Robert I. Friedman, *Red Mafiya: How the Russian Underworld has Invaded America*, Little, Brown and Company, Boston, New York and London, 2000, p. 109.

4 Malcolm Dixelius and Andrej Konstantinov, *Maffians Ryssland* (in Swedish), Kommentus, Stockholm, 1999, p. 132. According to other Russian sources, 'the Mongol' eventually died in 1992 or 1993 from old age.

5 James O. Finckenauer and Elin J. Waring, *Russian Mafia in America: Immigration, Culture and Crime*, Northeastern University Press, Boston, 1998, p. 111, and Friedman, *Red Mafiya*, pp. 110–11.

6 Finckenauer and Waring, *Russian Mafia in America*, p. 112.

7 Dixelius, *Maffians Ryssland*, pp. 134–5; Friedman, *Red Mafiya*, p. 111.

8 Friedman, *Red Mafiya*, p. 111.

9 Finckenauer and Waring, *Russian Mafia in America*, p. 112.

10 Handelman, *Comrade Criminal*, p. xiii.

11 Benson Bobrick, *East of the Sun: The Epic Conquest and Tragic History of Siberia*, Poseidon Press, New York, 1992, jacket blurb.

12 John. J. Stephan, *The Russian Far East: A History*, Stanford University Press, Stanford, Cal., 1994, p. 14.

13 Erich Thiel, *The Soviet Far East*, Methuen, London, 1957, pp. 121–2.

14 Bobrick, *East of the Sun*, p. 41.

15 Stephan, *The Russian Far East*, p. 31.

16 ibid., p. 25.

17 ibid., p. 49.

18 ibid., p. 64.

19   For an excellent account of Russia's brief rule of Alaska, see Ernest Sipes, 'Traders and soldiers in Russian America' *History Today*, August 1998, pp. 38–44.

20   Stephan, *The Russian Far East*, p. 64

21   ibid., p. 67.

22   Bobrick, *East of the Sun*, p. 288.

23   Stephan, *The Russian Far East*, p. 68.

24   Judy Mogck, 'Former Soviet-Union-based organized crime: a historical perspective' the *Royal Canadian Mounted Police Gazette*, Oct. 1996, pp. 4–10.

25   For an excellent account of the turmoil in Siberia at the time, see Canfield F. Smith, *Vladivostok Under Red and White Rule: Revolution and Counterrevolution in the Russian Far East 1920–1922*, University of Washington Press, Seattle & London, 1975.

26   Stephan, *The Russian Far East*, p. 132.

27   *Nordisk Familjebok* (a Swedish encyclopedia, Stockholm, 3rd edn, 1933), vol. 19, col. 1077. For a complete history of the von Ungern-Sternberg family, see Gustaf Elgenstierna ed., *Den Introducerade Svenska Adelns Ättartavlor* (in Swedish: 'Genealogical Tables of the Swedish Nobility'), Norstedt & Söners Förlag, Stockholm, 1934, vol. VIII, pp. 546–79.

28   Peter Hopkirk, *Setting the East Ablaze: On Secret Service in Bolshevik Asia*, Oxford University Press, Oxford, 1984, pp. 123–4.

29   ibid., p. 126.

30   Jasper Becker, *The Lost Country: Mongolia Revealed*, Hodder & Stoughton, London, 1992, p. 75.

31   ibid., p. 134.

32   ibid.

33   Hopkirk, *Setting the East Ablaze*, p. 137.

34   Becker, *The Lost Country*, p. 82.

35   Stephan, *The Russian Far East*, p. 134.

36   ibid., p. 137.

37   Bobrick, *East of the Sun*, p. 411.

38   ibid., p. 147.

39   Cited in Stephan, *The Russian Far East*, p. 159.

40   ibid., p. 200.

41   ibid., p. 197.

42   ibid., p. 198.

43   Smith, *Vladivostok Under Red and White Rule*, p. 104.

44   The first communist secret police force, the Cheka, was replaced in 1922 by the GPU, or the State Political Administration, which was technically subordinate to the NKVD. Both were headed by Feliks Dzerzhinsky, a political agitator of noble Polish ancestry who also had been chief of the Cheka. The GPU became the OGPU ('O' for *Ob'edinyonnoye*, or 'unified'). Following the assassination in 1934 of Stalin's close associate Sergei Kirov, the OGPU was subsumed into the new All-Union NKVD, which became the country's main spy agency and secret police service. The system was reorganised in 1941, and in 1946 a second restructuring of the security services took place with the MGB (Ministry of State Security) becoming responsible for counter-espionage and the MVD (Ministry of Internal Affairs) in charge of internal security. After Stalin's death

in 1953, the system was overhauled once again, and in 1954 the *Komitet Gosu-darstvennoy Bezopasnosti* (the Committee for State Security), or the KGB, became responsible for state security, including foreign intelligence.

45   Stephan, *The Russian Far East*, pp. 212–13.
46   Bobrick, *East of the Sun*, p. 422.
47   ibid., p. 424.
48   Robert Conquest, *Kolyma: The Arctic Death Camps*, The Viking Press, New York, 1978, pp. 35. See also pp. 25–9.
49   Mark Galeotti, 'The rise of a criminal superpower: organized crime in Russia', report prepared for the US Department of Defence, Dec. 1995, p. 2.
50   Karlo Stajner, *Seven Thousand Days in Siberia*, Farrar, Straus and Giroux, New York, 1988, p. 203.
51   Galeotti, 'The rise of a criminal superpower', p. 1. See also Judy Mogck, 'Former Soviet-Union-based organized crime'.
52   Conquest, *Kolyma*, p. 30.
53   Stephan, *The Russian Far East*, p. 231.
54   ibid., p. 232.
55   Bobrick, *East of the Sun*, p. 445.
56   Galeotti, 'The rise of a criminal superpower', p. 2.
57   Mark Galeotti, 'Mafiya: organized crime in Russia' *Jane's Intelligence Review Special Report No. 10*, 1996, p. 5.
58   See note 41.
59   Friedman, *Red Mafiya*, p. 109.
60   Galeotti, 'Mafiya,' p. 5.
61   Mogck, 'Former Soviet-Union-based organized crime', pp. 5–6.
62   Galeotti, 'Mafiya,' p. 5.
63   Sophie-Quinn Judge, 'Siberian spring' *Far Eastern Economic Review*, 10 Sept. 1987, p. 95.
64   Stephan, *The Russian Far East*, p. 296.
65   *Asia Yearbook* (the *Far Eastern Economic Review*) 1993, p. 195.
66   Stephen Handelman, 'The Russian "Mafiya"' *Foreign Affairs*, March–April 1994, pp. 83–95.
67   Arkady Vaksberg, *The Soviet Mafia*, St Martin's Press, New York, 1991, pp. 232–3.
68   Finckenauer and Waring, *Russian Mafia in America*, p. 112.
69   James Finckenauer and Elin Waring, 'Russian emigré crime in the United States: organized crime or crime that is organized?' in Phil Williams (ed.), *Russian Organized Crime: The New Threat?* Frank Cass, London & Portland, 1997, pp. 139–55.
70   Handelman, *Comrade Criminal*, p. 243.
71   Dorinda Elliot and Melinda Liu, 'Hostile takeover: the Russian mafia goes global' *Newsweek* (European edition), 2 Oct. 1995.
72   Galeotti, 'Mafiya', p. 19. See also Finckenauer and Waring, *Russian Mafia in America*, pp. 113–14.
73   Friedman, *Red Mafiya*, p. 139.
74   Galeotti, 'The rise of a criminal superpower', p. 6.
75   Quoted in 'Redfellas' *The Economist*, 15 Mar. 1997, pp. 37–8.
76   Galeotti, 'Mafiya', p. 15.

77   For a succinct description of this development, see Lev Timofeyev, *Russia's Secret Rulers: How the Government and Criminal Mafia Exercise Their Power*, Alfred A. Knopf, New York, 1992.

78   LD 3009130197 Moscow Radio Rossii Network (in Russian), 1000 GMT, 30 Sept. 1997.

79   J. Michael Waller and Victor J. Yasmann, 'Russia's great criminal revolution: the role of the security services' *Journal of Contemporary Criminal Justice*, Dec. 1995.

80   Stephen, *The Russian Far East*, p. 288.

81   Mark Galeotti, 'Mafiya', p. 14.

82   Mark Galeotti, 'The Russian Wild East: a complex criminal threat' *Jane's Intelligence Review*, Sept. 1998.

83   Jonathan Manthorpe, 'Organised crime well beyond control of law' *The Vancouver Sun*, 16 May 2000.

84   Elizabeth Wishnick, 'Where the grass is greener: Russia's new Chinese immigration problem' *The Asia-Pacific Magazine*, Nos 6–7, 1997, pp. 54–9.

85   ibid.

86   Mark Galeotti, 'The Russian Wild East' *Jane's Intelligence Review*, Sept. 1998, pp. 3–4.

87   *Vladivostok News*, 29 Mar. 1996.

88   'Drug Trafficking in Russia' DEA Working Paper, July 1996.

89   See Bertil Lintner, 'The Russian Mafia in Asia' *Tokyo Journal* March 1996, pp. 24–7. The information was relayed to the author by a senior western law enforcement official.

90   *Segodnya*, 16 June 1994.

91   ibid.

92   Stephan, *The Russian Far East*, p. 299.

93   *Vladivostok News*, 11 and 30 Oct. 1996.

94   ibid.

95   Galeotti, 'The Russian Wild East'.

96   ibid.

97   Bobrick, *East of the Sun*, p. 461.

98   Communication with a Moscow-based journalist, 18 Oct. 1998.

99   Jonathan Manthorpe, 'Organised crime well beyond control of law'.

100   ibid.

101   Stephan, *The Russian Far East*, p. 296.

CHAPTER 5

1   Chou Ta-kuan, *Notes on the Customs of Cambodia*, Social Science Association Press, Bangkok, 1967, p. 40.

2   J.S.M. Ward and W.G. Stirling, *The Society of Heaven and Earth*, The Baskerville Press, London, 1925, p. 7.

3   Ker Munthit, 'Boonma Fires off Complaint to RAC' *Phnom Penh Post* 18 April–1 May 1997, pp. 1, 13.

4   Anthony Paul, 'Wild Theng' *Fortune*, 21 July 1997.

5   'College revokes honorary degree', *Associated Press*, 10 Jan. 1998.

6   'United States revokes visa of wealthy Cambodian', Reuters, 14 Aug. 1997.

7   Paul, 'Wild Theng'.

8   Robin McDowell, 'Tycoon suspected of drug trafficking helped finance Cambodia's coup' *Associated Press*, 13 Aug. 1997.

9   'A maverick hits back' *Asiaweek*, 30 Nov. 1994.

10   'Special report: the drug trade in Southeast Asia' *Jane's Intelligence Review*, April 1995.

11   Imran Vittachi, 'Tamil Tigers shopping for arms in Cambodia' *Phnom Penh Post*, 20 Sept.–3 Oct. 1996, pp. 1, 3, and Anthony Davis, 'Tigers Inc.' *Asiaweek*, 26 July 1996, pp. 30–8.

12   John C. Brown, 'North Korean envoys in stand-off after harbouring wanted man' *Phnom Penh Post*, 5–18 April 1996.

13   ibid.

14   Communication with Phnom Penh-based journalist, 5 Feb. 2001. For more background about 'Dry Duck', see Sterling Seagrave, *Lords of the Rim: The Invisible Empire of the Overseas Chinese*, Bantam Press, London, New York, Toronto, Sydney, Auckland, 1995, pp. 245, 249.

15   Ker Munthit, 'Citizenships up for sale: $400 000' *Phnom Penh Post*, 26 July–8 Aug. 1996.

16   Chea Sotheacheath and Tricia Fitzgerald, 'Chinese illegals "tip of iceberg"' *Phnom Penh Post*, 10–23 Jan. 1997.

17   The literal rending of 'Nanyang' is 'Southern Ocean', and it used to be the Chinese term for the countries around that ocean, i.e. what we now call Southeast Asia. However, in more recent years, the term 'Nanyang Chinese' refers to Chinese who have settled in Malaysia, Singapore, Indonesia and the Philippines, places reached by the South China Sea. See Lynn Pan (ed.), *The Encyclopedia of the Chinese Overseas*, Archipelago Press, Landmark Books, Singapore 1998, p. 16.

18   See Bertil Lintner, 'The third wave' *Far Eastern Economic Review*, 24 June 1999, pp. 28–9, and Ko-lin Chin, *Smuggled Chinese: Clandestine Immigration to the United States*, Temple University Press, Philadelphia, 1999.

19   For an excellent account of Chinese migration to Hungary, see Pal Nyiri, *New Chinese Migrants in Europe: The Case of the Chinese Community in Hungary*, Ashgate Publishing, Aldershot, 1999.

20   Nyi Pu Lay, 'The Python', in Anna J. Allott (ed.), *Inked Over, Ripped Out: Burmese Storytellers and the Censors*, Silkworm Books, Chiang Mai, 1994, p. 85–101.

21   Lintner, 'The third wave', pp. 28–9.

22   'Chinese using Thailand as stopover base' *Bangkok Post*, 10 May 2000.

23   Interview with Kent Wiedeman, US ambassador to Cambodia, Phnom Penh, 1 May 2000.

24   William H. Myers III, 'Of *Qinqing, Qinshu, Guanxi*, and *Shetou*: The dynamic elements of Chinese irregular population movement', in Paul J. Smith, *Human Smuggling: Chinese Migrant Trafficking and the Challenge to America's Immigration Tradition*, The Center for Strategic & International Studies, Washington DC, 1997, p. 120.

25   Miro Cernetig, 'Chinese media silent on deportations' *The Globe and Mail*, 13 May 2000.

26   Ko-lin Chin, *Smuggled Chinese: Clandestine Immigration to the United States*, Temple University Press, Philadelphia, 1999, p. 42.

27   Nate Thayer, 'Chinese city of dreams' *Phnom Penh Post*, 12–25 Aug. 1994, pp. 1, 8.
28   Communication with Hong Kong-based law enforcement officer, 6 Feb. 2001.
29   Thayer, 'Chinese city of dreams'.
30   Interview with Kent Wiedeman, US Ambassador to Cambodia, Phnom Penh, 1 May 2000. See also W.E. Willmott, 'Cambodia', in Pan, *The Encyclopedia of the Chinese Overseas*, p. 150.
31   Bruce Gilley, 'The Exiled Resurgent' *Far Eastern Economic Review*, 8 Jan. 1998, pp. 22–7.
32   Bruce Gilley, 'A democratic donor's Cambodian connection' *Far Eastern Economic Review*, 15 Jan. 1998, pp. 14–16.
33   Bruce Gilley, 'Rising by degrees' *Far Eastern Economic Review*, 20 Aug. 1998, p. 27.
34   ibid.
35   Gilley, 'A democratic donor's Cambodian connection'.
36   ibid.
37   For a brief overview of Chinese migration to Malaya, see Victor Purcell, *The Chinese in Modern Malaya*, Donald Moore, Singapore, 1956.
38   ibid., p. 4.
39   ibid., p. 5. *Thian Ti Hui* is, of course, *Tiandihui* in *pinyin*.
40   *Kongsi* is *Gongsi* in *pinyin*, but the local Nanyang pronunciation and spelling of this term have passed into common usage. See David Ownby and Mary Somers Heidhues (eds), *'Secret Societies' Reconsidered: Perspectives on the Social History of Modern South China and Southeast Asia*, M.E. Sharpe, New York and London, 1993, p. 115.
41   ibid., pp. 74–5. See also Irene Lim, *Secret Societies in Singapore*, National Heritage Board, Singapore History Museum, 1999, p. 15: 'The Ghee Hin Kongsi . . . was formed in Singapore in 1820. Like other secret societies, it began as a self-help organisation aimed at assisting Chinese immigrants. However, from the mid-nineteenth century, secret societies began to engage in illegal activities, such as smuggling and extortion, and the fiercest of them was the Ghee Hin. It is thought that the Ghee Hin in Singapore was linked to the secret societies in Penang. Superintendent Caunter of the Police Force in Fort Cornwallis noted that in 1825 there were three significant secret societies operating in Penang: Ho Seng, formed in 1810; Ghee Hin, formed in 1801; and Hai San, formed in 1823. These represented, respectively, the first, second and third lodges of the Tiandihui.' Membership of the Ghee Hin in 1830 was estimated at 2500–3000 of a total population of 16 634 registered residents. Some 39.4 per cent, or 6554, of them were Chinese, so nearly half the Chinese population of Singapore at the time belonged to that group alone, which makes the term 'secret society' something of a misnomer.
42   Michael Dillon ed., *China: A Cultural and Historical Dictionary*, Curzon, Richmond, Surrey, 1998, pp. 370–1.
43   Ownby and Heidhues *'Secret Societies'*, p. 215.
44   ibid., p. 81.
45   ibid., p. 85.
46   Purcell, *The Chinese in Modern Malaya*, p. 7.
47   *Outline of a Background to the 'Chinese Triad Societies'*, mimeographed internal police manual dated Kuala Kangsar, 26 Oct. 1946, p. 5.

48 L.F. Comber, *Chinese Secret Societies in Malaya: A Survey of the Triad Society from 1800 to 1900*, J.J. Augustin Inc., New York, 1959, p. 1.

49 Purcell, *The Chinese in Modern Malaya*, p. 29.

50 Wilfred Blythe, *The Impact of Chinese Secret Societies in Malaya*, Oxford University Press, London, Kuala Lumpur and Hong Kong, 1969, pp. 280–1.

51 Gene Z. Hanrahan, *The Communist Struggle in Malaya*, University of Malaya Press, Kuala Lumpur, 1979, p. 30.

52 Blythe, *The Impact of Chinese Secret Societies in Malaya*, p. 423.

53 Michael Backman (ed.), *Overseas Chinese Business Networks in Asia*, East Asia Analytical Unit, Department of Foreign Affairs and Trade, Canberra, 1995, p. 184. 'Tun' is a Malay honorific.

54 Blythe, *The Impact of Chinese Secret Societies in Malaya*, p. 482.

55 Michael Backman (ed.), *Overseas Chinese Business Networks in Asia*, p. 73.

56 For a concise history of Bangkok's Chinatown, see Bertil Lintner 'Bangkok's Chinatown' in *Look East* (a Bangkok monthly), Oct. 1994, p. 55.

57 McCoy, *The Politics of Heroin: CIA Complicity in the Global Drug Trade*, Lawrence Hill Books, New York, 1991, p. 101.

58 ibid., p. 101. See also Suehiro Akira, *Capital Accumulation in Thailand 1855–1985*, Silkworm Books, Chiang Mai, 1996: 'The four most important tax farming items were opium, spirits, gambling and lotteries. In 1863 opium, spirits, and gambling alone produced a revenue of 1,273,000 baht, contributing around one-third of the total state revenue' (p. 77).

59 ibid., pp. 101–2. See also J.N. Scott, *The White Poppy: A History of Opium*, Funk & Wagnalls, New York, 1969, p. 136: 'A fifth of Thailand's total revenue of about £7,000,000 in 1922–3 came from opium.'

60 McCoy, *The Politics of Heroin in Southeast Asia*, Harper & Row, New York, 1972, p. 67.

61 McCoy, *The Politics of Heroin: CIA Complicity in the Global Drug Trade*, p. 103.

62 Scot Barmé, *Luang Wichit Wathakan and the Creation of a Thai Identity*, Institute of Southeast Asian Studies, Singapore, 1993, p. 24.

63 ibid., p. 129.

64 Kobkua Suwannathat-Pian, *Thailand's Durable Prime Minister: Phibun through Three Decades 1932–1957*, Oxford University Press, Kuala Lumpur, Oxford, Singapore and New York, 1995, p. 108.

65 Quoted in Robert Taylor, *Foreign and Domestic Consequences of the Kuomintang [Guomindang] Intervention in Burma*, Cornell University Southeast Asia Programme, Ithaca, Data Paper No 93, p. 42.

66 McCoy, *The Politics of Heroin: CIA Complicity in the Global Drug Trade*, pp. 167–8.

67 US Congress, House Committee on Un-American Activities, 23 April 1958, *International Communism (Communist Encroachment in the Far East)*: 'Consultations with Maj.-Gen. Claire Lee Chennault, United States Army', 85th Cong., 2nd sess, 23 Apr. 1958, pp. 9–10.

68 For a detailed account of the Guomindang's 'secret war' in the Golden Triangle, see 'The secret war' in Bertil Lintner, *Burma in Revolt: Opium and Insurgency Since 1948*, Silkworm Books, Chiang Mai, 1999, pp. 125–57.

69 Elaine T. Lewis, 'The Hill peoples of Kengtung state' *Practical Anthropology* vol. 4, no. 6, Nov.–Dec. 1957, p. 226.

70 See Alfred McCoy, *The Politics of Heroin: CIA complicity in the Global Drug Trade*, pp. 167–8, 469–70.

71 McCoy, *The Politics of Heroin in Southeast Asia*, Harper & Row, New York, 1972, p. 136, and Catherine Lamour, *Enquête sur une armée secrète*, Éditions du Seuil, Paris, 1975, p. 42.

72 G. William Skinner, *Leadership and Power in the Chinese Community of Thailand*, Cornell University Press, Ithaca, 1958, pp. 99–100.

73 *In Memory of Chin Sophonpanich* (special supplement to the *Bangkok Post*, 9 April 1988), pp. 7 and 12.

74 ibid., p. 12. See also Lamour, *Enquête sur une armée secrète*, p. 109: 'Le président de l Bangkok Bank lui est aussi totalement dévoué. C'est lui qui avance a Phao les fond nécessaires pour financer le commerce de l'opium.' In 1955, Chin Sophonpanich also founded the pro-Taiwan Chinese language newspaper *Universal Daily News*, which is still being published in Bangkok.

75 Quoted in Maung Maung, *Grim War Against the Kuomintang* (Guomindang), Nu Yin Press, Rangoon, 1953, pp. 70–1.

76 *Hearings*, 100th Congress, 1st Session, US House Committee on Foreign Affairs, 30 June and 15 July 1987, p. 61.

77 Melinda Liu, 'The Triangle's Pecking Order' *Far Eastern Economic Review*, 14 Sept. 1979.

78 A Thai lawyer and legal expert, who prefers to remain anonymous, once told me that 'the reason why Asian crime gangs such as the Triads and the Japanese *yakuza* have never managed to entirely control drugs, prostitution and similar activities in Thailand was because they were up against an even better organised gang here: the Thai police'. This does not exclude the fact that Thailand has had honest and dedicated policemen as well, but their survival (professionally as well as physically) has often depended on the protection and support they have received from foreign colleagues. For an account of the Chiu Chao (Teochew) underworld, see Sterling Seagrave, *The Soong Dynasty*, Sidgwick & Jackson, London, 1985, pp. 19–20. He adds: 'When Westerners imagined wicked Chinese pirates smuggling gold, drugs, and frightened maidens, and lurking in the dark recesses of the Spice Islands, they were picturing the *chiu chao*. To this day *chiu chao* kingpins heading major banks in the region control the international narcotics trade from the Golden Triangle ... through Bangkok to Amsterdam and other drug centres. Western drug-enforcement agencies look the other way.'

79 ibid., pp. 62–3.

80 ibid., p. 63.

81 David Morell and Chai-anan Samudavanija, *Political Conflict in Thailand: Reform, Reaction, Revolution* Oegeschlager, Gunn & Hain Publishers, Cambridge, Mass., 1981), pp. 50–1.

82 ibid., p. 52.

83 Surachart Bamrungsuk, *United States Foreign Policy and Thai Military Rule 1947–1977*, Editions Duang Kamol, Bangkok, 1988, p. 77.

84 D.G.E. Hall, *A History of Southeast Asia*, Macmillan, London, 1981, p. 948.

85 ibid., p. 949.

86 Charles F. Keyes, *Thailand: Buddhist Kingdom as Modern Nation-State*, Editions Duang Kamol, Bangkok, 1991, p. 113: 'The size of direct US military aid and

military investment in Thailand was enormous, totalling over US$2 billion for the period between 1951 and 1971.'

87   Silverstein, *Burma: Military Rule and the Politics of Stagnation*, Cornell University Press, Ithaca and London, 1977, p. 175. During my trek through the hills north of Kengtung in March–April 1987, I interviewed numerous villagers who vividly described the PLA intervention in 1961. Acting on reliable intelligence, the PLA targeted all major Guomindang camps in the hills around Möng Yang and Möng Wa. The villagers said casualties were heavy on the PLA's side, but the determination of the Chinese communists to press on was unmistakable. The Guomindang was beaten despite the PLA's heavy losses. See also *National Intelligence Estimate, No. 50–61, 28 March 1961: Outlook in Mainland Southeast Asia* (US intelligence document, declassified on 6 March 1990):

> Acting under a secret agreement providing for joint action to protect the teams engaged in demarcating the Sino-Burmese border, the Chinese Communists launched an attack into Burma against the Nationalist [Guomindang] units in December 1960. The Burma Army later joined in. By February 1961, the forces of the two countries had succeeded in capturing the major Nationalist bases and driving most of the irregulars across the Mekong into Laos and Thailand, although this was apparently done at the cost of severe casualties to the Burmese Army. Substantial quantities of Nationalist arms and equipment, much of it US made, were captured by the Burmese ... the fact that Chinese Communist troops helped the Burmese Army in the attack on the irregulars has been kept from the Burmese public and U Nu has publicly and emphatically denied the presence of any Chinese Communist troops on Burmese soil.

88   Central Intelligence Agency, Office of Current Intelligence, *Chinese Irregulars in Southeast Asia*, NLK-77-320, 29 July 1961.

89   ibid.

90   Catherine Lamour, *Enquête sur une armée secrète*, p. 204.

91   Interview with Bill Young, former CIA officer in Laos, Chiang Mai, 3 June 1992. Interview with Chang Shu-chuan (aka Sao Hpalang), a veteran of BS 111, Möng Mai 14 Dec. 1993. See also Lamour, *Enquête sur une armée secrète*, p. 210.

92   ibid., pp. 217–18.

93   The Wei brothers, operating through Wa mercenaries, later became leaders of one of the most powerful drug trafficking networks in Southeast Asia.

94   Lamour, *Enquête sur une armée secrète*, p. 218.

95   *Weekend Telegraph* (London) 10 Mar. 1967.

96   Paul Handley, 'Chonburi Chieftain' *Far Eastern Economic Review*, 18 April 1991.

97   Pasuk Phongpaichit and Sungsidh Piriyarangsan, *Corruption and Democracy in Thailand*, Silkworm Books, Chiang Mai, 1994, pp. 65–6.

98   Paul Handley, 'Chonburi chieftain'.

99   ibid.

100   'Saen Sukh up for international award' *Pattaya Mail*, 27 Mar. 1998.

101   Shawn Crispin, 'Twilight of a Godfather' *Far Eastern Economic Review*, 25 Jan. 2001, pp. 59–60.

102   Officially, Non-Performing Loans (NPLs) make up 19.28 per cent of total loans from Thai commercial banks (*Bangkok Post*, 25 Feb. 2001), but that figure

does not include NPLs which have been taken over by Asset Management Corporations, or AMCs.

103 Bertil Lintner, 'End of innocence' *Far Eastern Economic Review*, 1 April 1999, pp. 52–3.

104 Shawn Crispin, 'Twilight of a Godfather', and 'Power broker Sia Leng falls prey to crisis' *Bangkok Post*, 22 Dec. 2000.

105 Crispin, 'Twilight of a Godfather'.

106 'Kamnan Poh eyes 10 seats at election' *Bangkok Post*, 1 Oct. 2000.

107 'Is the Russian Mafia moving in?' *Bangkok Post*, 22 April 1998.

108 According to a Bangkok-based Russian journalist.

109 'Thaniya Road: playground for the Japanese' *Bangkok Post*, 21 Oct. 1990.

110 'Alleged Yakuza man arrested' *Bangkok Post*, 19 Sept. 1992.

111 'Daichi Group to develop future city for Rangoon' *Bangkok Post*, 19 April 1994.

112 Diplomatic cable from Rangoon, 8 Nov. 1991.

113 A copy of the brochure is in my possession.

114 *Financial Times*, 25 April 1990.

115 Interviews with Japanese Foreign Ministry officials, Tokyo, December 1990.

116 For a history of this development, see Bertil Lintner, *The Rise and Fall of the Communist Party of Burma*, Cornell University Southeast Asia Programme, Ithaca, 1990.

117 For a biography of Khun Sa, which is based on several long interviews with him, see Bertil Lintner, 'Lord of the Golden Triangle' in *Caravan* (a Bangkok monthly), May 1994, pp. 68–76.

118 ibid. See also McCoy, *The Politics of Heroin in Southeast Asia*, pp. 322–8.

119 Interviews with veterans of the 1967 Opium War, Shan state, April 1981.

120 ibid.

121 I visited Homöng in December 1993 and March 1994.

122 I have interviewed both Zhang Suquan and Liang Zhongyin. See also Bertil Lintner, *Burma in Revolt: Opium and Insurgency Since 1948*, Silkworm Books, Chiang Mai, 1999, pp. 303, 324 and 526.

123 *Caravan*, May 1994.

124 *International Narcotics Control Strategy Report*, US Department of State, Washington, 1987, 1988 and 1995.

125 Ten kilograms of raw opium, plus chemicals, are needed to produce 1 kilogram of heroin. The estimate of Burma's 'potential heroin output'— 54 tonnes in 1987 and 166 tonnes in 1995 (instead of 83.6 tonnes and 234 tonnes; 10 per cent of 836 and 2340 tonnes) is based on the assumption that approximately one-third of the opium is consumed locally, and never converted into heroin.

126 For an overview of the mutiny and its aftermath, see Bertil Lintner, *The Rise and Fall of the Communist Party of Burma*.

127 ibid., pp. 39–46.

128 'The Return of Lo Hsing-han' *Focus* (Bangkok), August 1981.

129 Reuters, 22 and 23 April 1999; also personal communication with David Brunnstrom, the Reuters correspondent who attended the event.

130 ibid.

131 *Far Eastern Economic Review*, 25 Mar. 1999, p. 8.

132 Maung Aung Myoe, *Building the Tatmadaw: The Organisational Development of the Armed Forces of Myanmar, 1948–98*, Australian National University, Strategic and Defence Studies Centre, Working Paper No. 327, p. 27.

133 Dennis Bernstein and Leslie Kean, 'People of the opiate: Burma's dictatorship and drugs' *The Nation* (USA), 16 Dec. 1996.

134 Anthony Davis and Bruce Hawke, 'On the road to ruin: Narco-dollars lure Burmese junta toward heroin dependency' *Jane's Intelligence Review*, Mar. 1998, pp. 26–31.

135 *It Myanmar*, Oct. 1996.

136 *Die Presse*, 28 April 1997 and 30 July 1997.

137 For a discussion about these issues, see Bertil Lintner, 'Burma and its neighbours', in Surjit Mansingh (ed.), *Indian and Chinese Foreign Policies in Comparative Perspective*, Radiant Publishers, New Delhi, 1998.

138 Bertil Lintner, 'Enter the dragon' *Far Eastern Economic Review*, 22 Dec. 1994, pp. 22–7.

139 ibid. This article is based on interviews with numerous people in Ruili, Mangshi, Kunming and Jïnghong in Yunnan.

140 Rodney Tasker and Bertil Lintner, 'Danger: road work ahead' *Far Eastern Economic Review*, 21 Dec. 2000, pp. 26–7.

141 See Craig Skehan's article about Möng La in the *Sydney Morning Herald*, 7 April 2000.

142 Communication with Ko-lin Chin, an expert on smuggling of illegal aliens, Jan. 1994. Also interviews with people from the former CPB base areas, Ruili, Yunnan, Dec. 1994.

143 *Far Eastern Economic Review*, 11 Mar. 1999, p. 8.

144 *The Myanmar Times & Business Review* 14–20 Feb. 2000.

145 'Junta serious about speed and opium, UN confirms' *Bangkok Post*, 24 Jan. 2001.

146 Bertil Lintner, 'Tracking new tracks' *Far Eastern Economic Review*, 18 Mar. 1993, p. 25. The article is based on numerous interviews with people from Lin's area.

147 'Wa link to Triads confirmed' *Bangkok Post*, 22 Dec. 2000.

CHAPTER 6

1 Quoted in John Pemberton, 'Open secrets: excerpts from conversations with a Javanese lawyer, and a comment', in Vicente L. Rafael (ed.), *Figures in Criminality in Indonesia, the Philippines, and Colonial Vietnam*, Southeast Asia Programme Publications, Cornell University, Ithaca, 1999, p. 194.

2 Michael Vatikiotis, *Indonesian Politics Under Suharto: Order, Development and Pressure for Change*, Routledge, London, 1994, p. 17.

3 I was that foreign journalist outside the polling booth in Becora, Dili on 30 Aug. 1999.

4 Damien Kingsbury, 'The TNI and the militias', in Damien Kingsbury (ed.), *Guns and Ballot Boxes: East Timor's Vote for Independence*, Monash Asia Institute, Clayton, 2000, p. 77.

5 Damien Kingsbury, 'Conclusion', in Kingsbury, *Guns and Ballot Boxes*, p. 185.

6 John McBeth and Dan Murphy, 'Double whammy' *Far Eastern Economic Review*, 23 Sept. 1999, pp. 8–10.

7 Kingsbury, 'The TNI and the militias', p. 71.

8   Peter Bartu, 'The militia, the military and the people of Bobonaro District', in Kingsbury, *Guns and Ballot Boxes*, p. 84.

9   Bartu, 'The militia', p. 85. For an account of the murder of the journalists, see Desmond Ball and Hamish McDonald, *Death in Balibo, Lies in Canberra: Blood on Whose Hands?* Allen & Unwin, Sydney, 2000.

10 Bartu, 'The militia', p. 85.

11 After the UN intervention, that old hotel where Guterres' thugs used to torture and kill people was renovated, taken over by an Australian expatriate, renamed the DownUnder Bar and has become a favourite hangout for UN workers and other expatriates in Dili.

12 Kingsbury, 'The TNI and the militias', p. 86.

13 ibid., p. 71.

14 I was in East Timor during the August 1999 referendum and met Eurico Guterres and his men. Many local residents in Dili told me about their involvement in illegal activities. See also Vaudine England, 'Manufactured monster?' *South China Morning Post*, 19 Oct. 2000.

15 John G. Taylor, *East Timor: The Price of Freedom*, Zed Books, London and New York, 1999, p. 227.

16 Interview with documentary film-maker David O'Shea of Special Broadcasting Service (SBS), Sydney, 5 Sept. 2000.

17 England, 'Manufactured monster?'

18 Loren Ryter, 'Pemuda Pancasila' *Indonesia 66*, Fall 1998, p. 55. This 70-page article gives an excellent account of rise and role of the Pemuda Pancasila during the Suharto regime.

19 Wagstaff, 'Youth group attempts to shed its bad-boy reputation' *Asian Wall Street Journal*, 25 May 1999.

20 For a detailed account of the birth of the Pemuda Pancasila, see Ryter, 'Pemuda Pancasila', pp. 18–22. Most of the information below comes from Ryter's article.

21 Adam Schwarz, *A Nation in Waiting: Indonesia's Search for Stability*, Allen & Unwin, Sydney, 1999, p. 10.

22 For a detailed account of the part the youth groups played in these massacres, see Robert Cribb (ed.), *The Indonesian Killings of 1965–1966: Studies from Java and Bali*, Monash University Centre of Southeast Asia Studies, Clayton, Vic, 1990.

23 Ryter, 'Pemuda Pancasila', p. 26.

24 *Soeharto: Otobiografi: Pikiran, Ucapkan, dan Tindakan Saya [Autobiography: My Thought, Speech and Acts]*, edited by Dwipayana and Ramadhan K.H., PT Citra Lamtoro Gung Persada, Jakarta, 1988, p. 364. Quoted in James T. Siegel, 'A New Criminal Type in Jakarta', in Rafael, *Figures of Criminality*, p. 227.

25 Ryter, 'Pemuda Pancasila', pp. 44–5.

26 *Inside Indonesia* no. 53.

27 ibid.

28 ibid. See also Ryter, 'Pemuda Pancasila', p. 52.

29 Ryter, 'Pemuda Pancasila', pp. 3, 54.

30 Wagstaff, 'Indonesian youth group attempts to shed its bad-boy reputation'.

31 Ryter, 'Pemuda Pancasila', p. 56.

32 ibid., pp. 46, 49

33 ibid., p. 47.

34 ibid., pp. 4, 47, 49.

35 Wagstaff, 'Indonesian youth group attempts to shed its bad-boy reputation'.

36 'Thugs for hire: a brief history of premanism' *Laksamana.Net*, 29 April 2001.

37 Ryter, 'Pemuda Pancasila', p. 11.

38 'Thugs for hire' *Laksamana.Net*, 29 April 2001.

39 Interview, *Matra* (an Indonesian magazine) Jan. 1993. Quoted in Ryter, 'Pemuda Pancasila', pp. 12–13.

40 Robert Cribb, *Gangsters and Revolutionaries: The Jakarta People's Militia and the Indonesian Revolution 1945–1949*, University of Hawaii Press, Honolulu, 1991, p. 15.

41 ibid., p. 52.

42 ibid, pp. 72–3.

43 Robert Cribb, 'Opium and the Indonesian Revolution' *Modern Asian Studies* vol. 22, no. 4 (1988), pp. 702–3.

44 ibid., pp. 714–15.

45 Leo Suryadinata, *Prominent Indonesian Chinese: Biographical Sketches*, Institute of Southeast Asian Studies, Singapore, 1997, p. 221.

46 Cribb, *Gangsters and Revolutionaries*, p. 97.

47 Carl Trocki, 'The Rise and Fall of the Ngee Heng Kongsi in Singapore', in David Ownby and Mary Somers Heidhues (eds), *Secret Societies Reconsidered: Perspectives on the Social History of Modern South China and Southeast Asia*, M.E. Sharpe, New York, 1993, p. 93.

48 There are many books about the 'white rajahs' of Sarawak. Some of the most comprehensive are Colin N. Crisswell, *Rajah Charles Brooke: Monarch of All He Surveyed*, Oxford University Press, Kuala Lumpur, 1978 and, for the colourful story, Sylvia Brooke, *Queen of the Headhunters: The Autobiography of Sylvia Brooke, Wife of the Last White Rajah of Sarawak*, William Morrow & Co., New York, 1972.

49 ibid., p. 71.

50 ibid., p. 75.

51 Leo Suryadinata, *The Culture of the Chinese Minority in Indonesia*, Times Books International, Singapore and Kuala Lumpur, 1997, p. 27.

52 For a history of the opium trade in the Dutch East Indies, see James R. Rush, *Opium to Java: Revenue Farming and Chinese Enterprise in Colonial Indonesia, 1860–1910*, Cornell University Press, Ithaca and London, 1990.

53 Suryadinata, *Prominent Indonesian Chinese*, pp. 114–15, and Suryadinata, *The Culture of the Chinese Minority in Indonesia*, p. 28.

54 Suryadinata, *The Culture of the Chinese Minority in Indonesia*, p. 148.

55 ibid., p. 141.

56 Mary Somers Heidhues, 'Indonesia', in Lynn Pan, *The Encyclopedia of Chinese Overseas*, Archipelago Press, Landmark Books, Singapore 1998, p. 158.

57 Michael Backman (ed.), *Overseas Chinese Business Networks in Asia*, East Asia Analytical Unit, Department of Foreign Affairs and Trade, Canberra, 1995, pp. 37, 40–1.

58 Suryadinata, *Prominent Indonesian Chinese*, pp. 139–40.

59 Heidhues, 'Indonesia', p. 159, and Schwarz, *A Nation in Waiting*, p. 109.

60 Backman, *Overseas Chinese*, p. 45.

61 Suryadinata, *Prominent Indonesian Chinese*, pp. 136–7.

62 Keith Loveard, 'Is Lippo in Trouble?' *Asiaweek*, 10 Nov. 1995.

63 Suryadinata, *Prominent Indonesian Chinese*, p. 137.

64   Communication with a criminal investigator in Hong Kong, 1 Nov. 1997.
65   *The China Connection: Summary of the Committee's Findings Relating to Efforts of the People's Republic of China to Influence US Policies and Elections*, undated mimeograph, p. 18.
66   John Colmey and David Liebhold, 'The family firm' *Time*, 24 May 1999, pp. 16–29.
67   ibid.
68   Ryter, 'Pemuda Pancasila', p. 2.
69   Special Broadcasting Service, *Indonesian Chinese: Living in Fear*, 8 Aug. 1998.
70   See the Indonesia chapter in *Asia Yearbook 1999*, Review Publishing, Hong Kong, 1999, pp. 124–31.
71   Ryter, 'Pemuda Pancasila', p. 63.
72   Wagstaff, 'Indonesian youth group attempts to shed its bad-boy reputation'.
73   I was outside the parliament when the Pemuda Pancasila marched into the compound in May 1998.
74   David Bourchier, 'Skeletons, vigilantes and the armed forces' fall from grace', in Arief Budiman, Barbara Hatley and Damien Kingsbury, *Reformasi: Crisis and Change in Indonesia*, Monash Asia Institute, Clayton, 1999, pp. 158–9.
75   'Jakarta's hoodlum cleanup operation targets poor street traders' *Laksamana.Net*, 25 April 2001.
76   ibid.
77   Ryter, 'Pemuda Pancasila', p. 69.
78   'Piracy and armed robbery against ships: annual report 1 January–31 December 1999', the International Maritime Bureau, London, Jan. 2000.
79   Pamela Pun, '13 pirates executed for ship murders' *Hong Kong Standard*, 29 Jan. 2000.
80   Bertil Lintner, 'The perils of rising piracy' *Jane's Defence Weekly*, 15 Nov. 2000, pp. 18–19. The article is based on interviews with personnel from the International Maritime Bureau in Kuala Lumpur, 23 Oct. 2000, and IMB reports. See also Dana R. Dillon, *Piracy in Asia: A Growing Barrier to Maritime Trade*, paper produced by the Asian Studies Center and published by the Heritage Foundation, Washington, 22 June 2000.
81   Andreas Harsono, 'Alliance rules the high waves' *The Nation* (Bangkok), 13 April 1999.
82   For an excellent critique of official policies, see Peter Mares, *Borderline: Australia's Treatment of Refugees and Asylum Seekers*, University of New South Wales Press, Sydney, 2001.
83   'Two officers arrested over boat disasters' British Broadcasting Corporation, 26 Oct. 2001.
84   Seth Mydans, 'Afghans, hoping to get to Australia, are trapped in Indonesia' *International Herald Tribune*, 26 Nov. 2001.
85   Michael Winchester, 'The "travel agents"' *Asiaweek* 19 Jan. 2001, pp. 26–31.
86   ibid.

CHAPTER 7

1   Alfred W. McCoy, *Drug Traffic: Narcotics and Organised Crime in Australia*, Harper & Row Publishers, Sydney, 1985, p. 102. The rhyme may be of English

origin, and even predate the establishment of the penal colonies in Australia, but in an Australian context it has a very special meaning.

2   This description of the drug seizure near Port Macquarie on 14 October 1998 is reconstructed from Greg Bearup's excellent reporting in the *Sydney Morning Herald* at the time—for instance, 'Biggest heroin haul: police set up ambush on sand', 15 Oct. 1998, and 'Slaying the dragon', 17 Oct. 1998.

3   *Sydney Morning Herald*, 16 Oct. 1998.

4   'Drug suspect "a syndicate boss"' *Hong Kong Standard*, 14 Oct. 1998.

5   According to court documents I have been shown.

6   'Ethnic gangs raise concern in Australia', a dispatch from Agence France-Presse (AFP), published in *The Nation* (Bangkok), 13 Mar. 2001.

7   I visited Cabramatta in February 1997, and this account of the situation there is based on interviews with local residents and shop owners. Additional information was provided by law enforcement officers in New South Wales, and Lisa Maher, a prominent Sydney criminologist.

8   Communication with a Vietnamese diplomat in Bangkok, 17 Mar. 1997.

9   Interview with Ray Tinker, the Australian Federal Police Eastern Region, Sydney, 10 Feb. 1997.

10   ibid.

11   Nancy Viviani, *The Indochinese in Australia 1975–1995: From Burnt Boats to Barbecues*, Oxford University Press, Sydney, Auckland, New York, 1996, p. 130.

12   'Gang civil war' *Daily Telegraph* (Australia), 8 Aug. 1995.

13   Quoted in Viviani, *From Burnt Boats to Barbecues*, p. 131.

14   Tran's name seems to have been adapted for westerners; in Vietnamese, it would be Tran Tri Minh (Tran being his family name). On second reference, Vietnamese are usually called by the third and last part of the name—in this case, Minh. But the Australian media have always called him 'Tran', so to avoid confusion I use the same style here.

15   For an excellent background to the 5T gang and Tran's life, see Philip Cornford, 'Street gang's culture of violence' *Sydney Morning Herald*, 12 Aug. 1995. This description of the gang is based on that article, and several interviews with Lisa Maher, Sydney, Feb. 1997.

16   Philip Cornford and Col Allison, 'Killing ends reign of young 5T boss' *Sydney Morning Herald*, 9 Aug. 1995.

17   Interviews with Lisa Maher, Sydney, Feb. 1997.

18   McCoy, *Drug Traffic*, p. 22.

19   Jonathan Kwitny, *Crimes of Patriots: A True Tale of Dope, Dirty Money and the CIA*, Simon and Schuster, New York, 1987, p. 66.

20   ibid., p. 66.

21   McCoy, *Drug Traffic*, p. 175.

22   Rodney Tiffen, *Scandals, Media, Politics & Corruption in Contemporary Australia*, University of New South Wales Press, Sydney, 1999, pp. 38, 131.

23   Kwitny, *Crimes of Patriots*, p. 66.

24   For a detailed account of the rise and fall of the BCCI, see Peter Truell and Larry Gurwin, *False Profits: The Inside Story of BCCI, the World's Most Corrupt Financial Empire*, Houghton Mifflin Company, Boston and New York, 1992. Similarities to the Nugan Hand Bank are discussed on pp. 124–5.

25   Malcolm Brown, 'The restaurateur who may have known too much' *The Age*, 26 July 2000.

26   Tiffen, *Scandals*, p. 70.

27   *The Age*, 26 July 2000.

28   'No licence for Saffron' *Daily Telegraph* (Sydney), 15 Mar. 2001. See also S.D. Harvey, *The Ghost of Ludwig Gertsch*, Pan Macmillan Australia, Sydney, 2000, p. 183. Harvey's book gives an excellent account of Saffron and his role in the Sydney underworld in the 1970s and 1980s.

29   McCoy, *Drug Traffic*, p. 99.

30   Manning Clark, *A Short History of Australia*, Penguin Books, Ringwood, 1995, p. 177.

31   McCoy, *Drug Traffic*, p. 113.

32   See Chapter 2.

33   John Pilger, *A Secret Country: The Hidden Australia*, Alfred A. Knopf, New York, 1991, p. 211.

34   Evan Whitton, *The Hillbilly Dictator: Australia's Police State*, ABC Books, Sydney, 1989, p. 159.

35   Marian Wilkinson, 'Clean-up team carries some heavy baggage' *Sydney Morning Herald*, 16 May 1997.

36   For an excellent account of Australia's crime scene, see Richard Hall, *Disorganised Crime*, University of Queensland Press, Brisbane, 1986.

37   Greg Bearup and Kate McClymont, 'Organised crime in the '90s' *Sydney Morning Herald*, 27 Oct. 1997.

38   Richard Hall, *Tiger General: The Killing of Victor Chang*, Pan Macmillan Australia, Sydney, 1995, p. 115.

39   Irene Lim, *Secret Societies in Singapore*, National Heritage Board, Singapore History Museum, Singapore, 1999, pp. 34–5.

40   ibid., p. 35.

41   ibid.

42   Gordon P. Means, *Malaysian Politics*, Hodder and Stoughton, London, Sydney, Auckland, Toronto, 1976, p. 397.

43   ibid.

44   See Hall, *Tiger General*, pp. 9–10.

45   Pilger, A *Secret Country*, p. 94.

46   Lynn Pan, *Sons of the Yellow Emperor: A History of the Chinese Diaspora*, Little, Brown and Company, Boston, Toronto, London, 1990, p. 57.

47   Hall, *Tiger General*, p. 40. See also 'Australia' in Lynn Pan (ed.), *The Encyclopedia of Chinese Overseas*, Archipelago Press, Landmark Books, Singapore 1998, p. 274. In 1861, 3.3 per cent of Australia's population of 1 168 149 were Chinese. This decreased to 1 per cent in 1901, when the Commonwealth of Australia was created.

48   McCoy, *Drug Traffic*, pp. 72–3.

49   Hall, *Tiger General*, p. 73.

50   ibid., p. 11.

51   ibid., p. 258.

52   Interview with local law enforcement officers who have requested anonymity, Bangkok, Feb. 2001.

53   *Australian Illicit Drug Report 1995–96*, Australian Bureau of Criminal Intelligence, Canberra, December 1996, p. 60.

54   Interview with Ray Tinker, Sydney, 10 Feb. 1997.
55   Brett Martin, 'The Battle for Redfern' *The Bulletin* (an Australian newsweekly), 11 Feb. 1997, pp. 16–19.
56   Interview with Ray Tinker, Sydney, 10 Feb. 1997.
57   Denis Warner, *The Last Confucian*, Angus & Robertson and Penguin Books, Sydney and Ringwood, 1964, p. 94.
58   A. Viollis, Indochine S.O.S., quoted in *Association culturelle pour le salut du Viet-Nam, témoinages et documents française au Viet-Nam*, Hanoi, 1945.
59   Alfred McCoy, *The Politics of Heroin in Southeast Asia*, Harper & Row, New York, 1972, p. 94.
60   Warner, *The Last Confucian*, pp. 96, 105.
61   Dr V.N. Kolotov, 'The role of the religious sects in the collective security system' *Nordic Newsletter of Asian Studies* (Copenhagen) no. 2, July 1999, pp. 21–4.
62   McCoy, *The Politics of Heroin*, pp. 125–6.
63   ibid., pp.159–65. McCoy's book remains the most authoritative account of the drug trade during the Vietnam War era.
64   Quoted in James Olson (ed.), *Dictionary of the Vietnam War*, Peter Bedrick Books, New York, 1987, p. 304.
65   Warner gives a vivid account of the birth of Cao Dai in *The Last Confucian*, pp. 96–7. See also Gabriel Gobron, *History and Philosophy of Caodaism: Reformed Buddhism, Vietnamese Spiritism, New Religion in Eurasia*, published under the auspices of His Excellency Tran-quang-Ving, Major-General of the Caodaist Troops, Minister of the Armed Forces of the Government of Vietnam, Saigon 1950.
66   I visited the Holy See in Tay Ninh in December 1995.
67   Ann Caddell Crawford, *Vietnam: Customs and Culture*, Charles E. Tuttle Co., Rutland, Vermont and Tokyo, 1966, pp. 81–3. See also Warner, *The Last Confucian*, pp. 97–9.
68   Warner, *The Last Confucian*, p. 98.
69   'Buddhist woman torches herself' Agence France-Presse, Hanoi, 21 Mar. 2001, and British Broadcasting Corporation, 25 Mar. 2001.
70   Les Kennedy, 'Gagged by inquiry: boy "drug runner" is ready to tell all' *Sydney Morning Herald*, 8 May 2001.
71   Kate McClymont and Greg Bearup, 'Unmasked: our new drug bosses' *Sydney Morning Herald*, 27 Oct. 1997.
72   Niall Fraser, 'The Chinese connection' *South China Morning Post*, 17 Oct. 1998. The paper gives the value of Australia's heroin trade in Australian and Hong Kong currencies: A$3 billion and HK$15.6 billion.
73   *Drug Intelligence Brief: The Price Dynamics of Southeast Asian Heroin*, Drug Enforcement Administration (DEA), United States, Feb. 2001.
74   Information gathered during several visits to Sydney (including Cabramatta) in 1998–2000.
75   Interview with Ray Tinker, Sydney, 10 Feb. 1997.
76   *Australian Illicit Drug Report 1995–96*, p. 59.
77   Michael Backman, *Asian Eclipse: Exposing the Dark Side of Business in Asia*, John Wiley & Sons [Asia], Singapore, 1999, p. 327. See also Chapter 2.
78   *Australian Illicit Drug Report 1995–96*, p. 59.

79   Greg Bearup and Kate McClymont, 'Uncle Six: from refugee to high roller' *Sydney Morning Herald*, 27 Oct. 1997, and Hugh Martin, 'Heroin man gambled $94 million at casinos' *The Age* (Melbourne), 25 Apr. 2000.

80   See Bertil Lintner, 'Global Reach: Drug Money in the Asia Pacific' *Current History* April 1998, pp. 179–82.

81   Editorial in the *Sydney Morning Herald*, 28 April 2000.

82   'Casino went to Cabramatta to woo high-rollers' *Rolling Good Times OnLine*, 14 July 2000.

83   Peter Olszewski, 'Tattoos in the sun: Japanese gangs move into Australia' *Cross Section* (Australia), Summer 1994.

84   ibid.

85   'Asian organised crime in Australia', *Discussion Paper by the Parliamentary Joint Committee on the National Crime Authority*, Parliament of the Commonwealth of Australia, February 1995.

86   Bertil Lintner, 'Paradise for crooks' *Far Eastern Economic Review*, 6 Nov. 1997. The article is based on numerous interviews I did with bankers, lawyers and law enforcement officers during a visit to Australia and Vanuatu in February 1997, pp. 31–3.

87   For an account of the New Hebrides 'pandemonium', see Father Walter Lini, *Beyond Pandemonium: From the New Hebrides to Vanuatu*, Asia Pacific Books, Wellington, 1980 (Father Lini was Vanuatu's first prime minister after independence in 1980), and Stephen Henningham, *France and the South Pacific: A Contemporary History*, Allen & Unwin, Sydney, 1992, pp. 24–46.

88   For a full account of the uprising, see Richard Shears, *The Coconut War: The Crisis on Espiritu Santo*, Cassell Australia, Sydney and Melbourne, 1980.

89   Ben Davis, 'Vanuatu: The serious side of paradise' *Euromoney*, Aug. 1996.

90   Interview with Tim Morris of the Australian Transaction Reports and Analysis Centre (AUSTRAC), Sydney, 10 Feb. 1997.

91   According to a handout called *Company Formation Package* from International Finance Trust Company Limited, Port Vila, Vanuatu, 1997.

92   See 'Statement by Special Agent Harold D. Wankel, Chief of Operations, the Drug Enforcement Agency, US Department of Justice, regarding Money Laundering by Drug Trafficking Organizations', Washington, 28 Feb. 1996.

93   'Estimates of the extent of money laundering in and through Australia' *Australian Transaction Reports and Analysis Centre* (AUSTRAC), Sydney, Sept. 1995.

94   See Lintner, *Current History*, April 1998.

95   Davis, *Euromoney*, August 1996 and Lintner, *Far Eastern Economic Review*, 6 Nov. 1997.

96   Richard Borsuk, 'Jakarta cracks down on mystery bank' *Asian Wall Street Journal*, 17 June 1996.

97   'Dragon Bank's licence revoked' *Vanuatu Trading Post*, 31 Jan. 1997.

98   Interview with Thomas Bayer, Port Vila, 20 Feb. 1997.

99   Nelson Eustis, *The King of Tonga*, Hyde Park Press, Adelaide, 1997, pp. 178–9.

100 Giff Johnson, 'Moon's Pacific rising' *Pacific Magazine with Islands Business*, April 2001.

101 Quoted in ibid.

102 ibid.

103 Michael Perry, 'Pacific Islands Tackle Russian money laundering' Reuters, 9 Feb. 2000.

104 Jack Hitt, 'The billion-dollar shack' *New York Times*, 10 Dec. 2000.

105 For an account of Nauru's economy and tax haven, see Helen Fraser, 'Preparing for economic life after phosphate', and Robert Keith-Reid, 'Tax havens under scrutiny' *Islands Business*, April 1999, pp. 24–9, and Robert Keith-Reid, 'Under the spotlight' *Islands Business*, Feb. 2000, pp. 26–7.

106 Robert Keith-Reid, 'Revolt looming in Nauru' *Pacific Magazine* with *Islands Business*, Nov. 2001, p. 25.

107 'US declares war on EnenKio' *Bangkok Post* quoting *Associated Press*, Auckland, 2 Nov. 2000.

108 Sue Kendall, 'OECD lists 35 states as tax havens', Agence France-Presse, Paris, 26 June 2000.

109 'Sanctions for islands accused of mafia links', Agence France-Presse, Auckland, 9 Dec. 2000.

110 Marc Roche, 'US banks crack down on the world's smallest tax haven' *Guardian Weekly*, 15–22 Feb. 2001.

111 For a colourful description of this deal, see Paul Theroux, *The Happy Isles of Oceania: Paddling the Pacific*, Hamish Hamilton, London, 1992, p. 267.

112 'Troubled times ahead for Tonga: hunt on for missing trust fund' *Pacific Magazine* with *Islands Business*, Nov. 2001, p. 22.

113 Interview with Marie-Noelle Ferrieux Patterson, Port Vila, 19 Feb. 1997. See also her detailed 'Report Regarding Passports Issued to the Family of Jian Peng Chen', the Office of the Ombudsman, Vanuatu, 1997.

114 Communication with Leung Yat-chan, a Hong Kong crime reporter, 28 Mar. 2001.

115 Communication with Robert Keith-Reid, a Fiji-based journalist and editor, 16 Mar. 2001.

116 Communication with Bangkok-based law enforcement officers, 25 Mar. 2001.

117 'Laos consolidates relations with Vanuatu' *Vientiane Times*, 20–22 Feb. 2001.

118 Lintner, *Far Eastern Economic Review*, 6 Nov. 1997.

CHAPTER 8

1 Ko-lin Chin, *Smuggled Chinese: Clandestine Immigration to the United States*, Temple University Press, Philadelphia, 1999, p. 111.

2 A copy of the report is in my possession.

3 There are many accounts of the arrival of the *Golden Venture*—for instance, Paul J. Smith, 'Chinese migrant trafficking: a global challenge', in Paul J. Smith (ed.), *Human Smuggling: Chinese Migrant Trafficking and the Challenge to America's Immigration Tradition*, The Center for Strategic and International Studies, Washington DC, 1997, pp. 1–22. See also Anthony M. DeStefano, 'Crew told: ram ship' *Newsday*, 7 June 1993. Court documents from the subsequent trial of the human smugglers are also in my possession.

4 For an account of the reaction of the media and the public to the arrival of the *Golden Venture*, see Chin, *Smuggled Chinese*, p. 152, and Smith, 'Chinese migrant trafficking', p. 3.

5 Interviews with the crew of the *Gina-III*, Songkhla, August 1993.

6   Smith, 'Chinese migrant trafficking', p. 2, and 'Immigration and Naturalization Service, US Department of Justice, Chinese alien smuggling by sea: Chinese organized crime and illegal migration on boats', paper presented at the 15th International Asian Organized Crime Conference, Las Vegas, 28 Mar.–3 April 1994.

7   Tom Fennell, 'Snakehead country' *South China Morning Post*, 18 Dec. 1999 (reprinted from *Macleans* magazine, Canada). See also David W. Chen, 'Smugglers use Indian reservation to sneak Chinese into US' *New York Times*, 19 Dec. 1998, and Shawn Crispin, 'Overland bridge: illegal Chinese migrants find new route to US' *Far Eastern Economic Review*, 21 Jan. 1999, pp. 26–7.

8   Smith, 'Chinese migrant trafficking', p. 1.

9   Communication with an officer from the US Immigration and Naturalization Service (INS), April 1998. See also Chin, *Smuggled Chinese*, pp. 62–78.

10 Communication with an INS officer, April 1998.

11 Chin, *Smuggled Chinese*, p. 74.

12 ibid., pp. 101–10.

13 ibid., p. 143.

14 Interview with US law enforcement officer, Bangkok, 15 May 1998. See also ibid., p. 7, and Crispin, 'Overland bridge'.

15 I visited New York's and San Francisco's Chinatowns on several occasions during the period 1991–99 and interviewed many people, old-timers as well as newcomers, at random.

16 Jeff Wise, 'The Dragon's teeth: a new generation of brutal gangs is poised to take over New York's Chinatown' *Far Eastern Economic Review*, 13 June 1996.

17 Peter Kwong, *The New Chinatown*, Hill and Wang, New York, 1996, pp. 174–5.

18 Amy L. Freedman, *Political Participation and Ethnic Minorities: Chinese Overseas in Malaysia, Indonesia, and the United States*, Routledge, New York and London, 2000, p. 160.

19 Kwong, *The New Chinatown*, p. 13.

20 ibid., p. 7

21 ibid., p. 14.

22 ibid., p. 92.

23 Peter Huston, *Tongs, Gangs and Triads: Chinese Crime Groups in North America*, Paladin Press, Boulder, Col., 1995, p. 46.

24 Kwong, *The New Chinatown*, p. 97, and Huston, *Tongs, Gangs and Triads*, pp. 74–5.

25 Kwong, *The New Chinatown*, pp. 109–10.

26 Him Mark Lai, 'The United States', in Lynn Pan (ed.), *Encyclopedia of the Chinese Overseas*, Archipelago Press, Landmark Books, Singapore, 1998, p. 265.

27 ibid., p. 267.

28 Communication with law enforcement officer in New York, 8 April 2001.

29 Kwong, *The New Chinatown*, p. 49.

30 Joel L. Swerdlow, 'Trying to fit in' *National Geographic*, Aug. 1998.

31 Kwong, *The New Chinatown*, p. 111.

32 Ko-lin Chin, *Chinatown Gangs: Extortion, Enterprise & Ethnicity*, Oxford University Press, New York and Oxford, 1996, p. 117.

33 ibid., pp. 110–11.

34 Huston, *Tongs, Gangs and Triads*, p. 94.

35 Hall Leiren, 'Friends in vile places: reasons Canada refused entry to a Hong Kong "businessman"' *British Columbia Report*, 29 Aug. 1994.

36   Kwong, *The New Chinatown*, p. 116.
37   Leiren, 'Friends in vile places'.
38   ibid. The summit is also mentioned in the Introduction to this book.
39   ibid.
40   Wise, 'The Dragon's teeth'.
41   For a brief but succinct account of Ah Kay and the Fuk Ching, see Melinda Liu, 'The fall of the Fuk Ching' *Newsweek* (Asian edition), 13 Sept. 1993, pp. 18–19.
42   Seth Faison, 'Suspect in smuggling of Chinese eluded the US immigration net', *New York Times*, 10 June 1993.
43   Liu, 'The fall of the Fuk Ching'.
44   Seth Faison, 'Gang leader is arrested in Hong Kong' *New York Times*, 29 Aug. 1993.
45   Liu, 'The fall of the Fuk Ching'.
46   ibid.
47   Seth Faison, 'Young toughs of Fuk Ching gang mourn 4' *New York Times*, 7 June 1993.
48   Faison, 'Gang leader is arrested in Hong Kong'.
49   Liu, 'The fall of Fuk Ching'.
50   For a public statement on both arrests, see 'Statement by US Consul General Michael Klosson on the Arrest in Hong Kong of Cheng Chui Ping', Hong Kong, 19 April 2000.
51   Chin, *Smuggled Chinese*, p. 41.
52   ibid., pp. 29 and 45.
53   ibid., pp. 34–5.
54   ibid., p. 31.
55   ibid., p. 152. The original says 'illegal immigration', but since the official was based in Fujian, he must have meant 'illegal emigration' or 'illegal migration'. The quote is reproduced with permission from Ko-lin Chin, and he is aware of my changing 'immigration' to 'migration'.
56   Marlowe Hood, 'Sourcing the problem: why Fuzhou?', in Paul J. Smith (ed.), *Human Smuggling: Chinese Migrant Trafficking and the Challenge to America's Immigration Tradition*, Center for Strategic & International Studies, Washington, 1997, pp. 78–9.
57   See Chapter 1.
58   Kari Huus, 'Plant a tree in America', *Newsweek* (Asian edition), 16 Aug. 1993, p. 21.
59   Foreword to Chin, *Smuggled Chinese*, p. xiii.
60   See Pal Nyiri, *New Chinese Migrants in Europe: The Case of the Chinese Community in Hungary*, Ashgate Publishing, Aldershot, Hampshire, 1999.
61   Kwong, *The New Chinatown*, p. 113, and William Kleinknecht, *The New Ethnic Mobs: The Changing Face of Organized Crime in America*, The Free Press, New York, 1996, pp. 89–90.
62   Michael Daly, 'The War for Chinatown' *New York*, 14 Feb. 1983, p. 33. Also quoted in Kleinknecht, *The New Ethnic Mobs*, p. 92.
63   Kwong, *The New Chinatown*, p. 115.
64   ibid., p. 114.
65   ibid., p. 114.
66   ibid., p. 118.

67   ibid., p 170.
68   Kleinknecht, *The New Ethnic Mobs*, p. 89.
69   The photo is reproduced in Martin Booth, *The Dragon Syndicates: The Global Phenomenon of the Triads*, Doubleday, London and New York, 1999, opp., p. 192.
70   According to *Asian Organized Crime*, a US document from an unspecified criminal intelligence organisation, May 1992.
71   David Hogben, 'Japan's Mobsters Slipping Quietly in Business Suits into B.C.' the *Vancouver Sun*, 6 May 1993.
72   *Asian Organized Crime*. See also US Department of Justice, *Vietnamese Criminal Activity in the United States: A National Perspective*, Organized Crime/Drug Branch, Criminal Investigative Division, Mar. 1993, p. 3.
73   Patrick Du Phuoc Long with Laura Ricard, *The Dream Shattered: Vietnamese Gangs in America*, Northeastern University Press, Boston, 1995, pp. 155–6.
74   *Vietnamese Criminal Activity in the United States*, p. 12.
75   Kleinknecht, *The New Ethnic Mobs*, p. 181. For Nguyen Cao Ky's involvement in the drug trade during the Vietnam War, see Alfred W. McCoy, *The Politics of Heroin in Southeast Asia*, Harper & Row, New York, 1972, pp. 166–70.
76   Kleinknecht, *The New Ethnic Mobs*, p. 181. See also 'America Targets the Asian Connection' *Asiaweek*, 22 Mar. 1985.
77   James O. Finckenauer and Elin J. Waring, *Russian Mafia in America: Immigration, Culture, and Crime*, Northeastern University Press, Boston, 1998, pp. 75–6.
78   ibid., pp. 75, 76.
79   James O. Finckenauer and Elin J. Waring, 'Russian émigré crime in the United States: organised crime or crime that is organised?' in Phil Williams ed., *Russian Organised Crime: The New Threat?* Frank Cass, London and Portland, 1997, p. 152.
80   ibid., pp. 152–3.
81   Finckenauer and Waring, *Russian Mafia in America*, p. 75.
82   Finckenauer and Waring, 'Russian émigré crime', p. 152.
83   Garry W.G. Clement and Brian McAdam, *Triads and Other Asian Organized Crime Groups*, Royal Canadian Mounted Police manual, Hong Kong, 1993, p. 21.
84   Howard O. DeVore, *China's Intelligence and Internal Security Forces*, a Jane's Special Report from Jane's Information Group, Oct. 1999, p. 101.
85   John Byron and Robert Pack, *The Claws of the Dragon: Kang Sheng, the Evil Genius Behind Mao and His Legacy of Terror in People's China*, Simon & Schuster, New York, 1992, p. 211.
86   There are other explanations of the origin of the name of the gang, but this version, which appears the most credible, comes from James Dubro, *Dragons of Crime: Inside the Asian Underworld*, Octopus Publishing Group, Markham, Ontario, 1992, p. 12. Another version has it that the gang is named after the circle of army camps that surrounded Guangzhou during the upheaval of the 1960s, see Clement and McAdam, *Triads*, p. 58.
87   Clement and McAdam, *Triads*, p. 58.
88   DeVore, *China's Intelligence and Security Forces*, p. 102.
89   ibid., p. 102.

90   For a detailed account of the transformation of Taiwan, see Hung-Mao Tien, *The Great Transition: Political and Social Change in the Republic of China*, SMC Publishing Inc., Taipei, 1989.

91   Allen T. Cheng, 'Taiwan's Dirty Business', *Asia Inc.*, April 1997, pp. 16–23.

92   ibid.

93   ibid.

94   For a succinct history of the United Bamboo Gang, see David E. Kaplan, *Fires of the Dragon: Politics, Murder and the Kuomintang*, Atheneum, New York, 1992, pp. 366 ff.

95   Cheng, 'Taiwan's dirty business'.

96   ibid.

97   Angelina Malhotra, 'Shanghai's Dark Side' *Asia Inc.*, Feb. 1994.

98   Bertil Lintner, 'The drug trade in Southeast Asia', *Jane's Intelligence Review Special Report No 5*, April 1995, p. 18.

99   Government Information Office, Taipei, 'The war on drugs in Taiwan, ROC', Dec. 1993, p. 2.

100 Ma Ying-jeou, *War on Drugs: The Experience of the Republic of China*, Ministry of Justice, Taipei, 1996.

101 Rodney Tasker and Bertil Lintner, 'Danger: road works ahead' *Far Eastern Economic Review*, 21 Dec. 2000, pp. 26–7, and 'Nasty job for Task Force 399' *Far Eastern Economic Review*, 19 April 2001, pp. 24–5.

102 DeVore, *China's Intelligence and Internal Security Forces*, p. 101.

103 From a source close to the Macau Triads, Macau, 28 July 2001.

104 Fabian Dawson, 'US Probe Links Lai to Election Offences' *The Province* (Vancouver), 6 Dec. 2000.

105 Susan V. Lawrence, 'A city ruled by crime' *Far Eastern Economic Review*, 30 Nov. 2000, pp. 14–18. 'Phnom Penh court frees Taiwanese' *The Nation*, Bangkok, 11 Aug. 2001.

106 Sangwon Suh, 'Smuggler No. 1' *Asiaweek*, 22 Dec. 2000. See also the Introduction.

107 Interview with western intelligence officer, Bangkok, 10 Jan. 2001.

108 *The Sunday Province* (Vancouver), 22 April 2001.

109 Andrew Mitrovica, 'PM's Trip to China Behind Delay in Spy Report' *The Globe and Mail*, 30 Aug. 2000.

110 According to 'Sidewinder', a copy of which is in my possession.

111 For a detailed account of Chinese arms smuggling to the United States, see Howard Blum, 'The trail of the dragon' *Vanity Fair*, Dec. 1997.

112 See 'Sidewinder'.

113 Mark Galeotti, 'Canada: soft target for crime' *Jane's Intelligence Review*, Feb. 2001, pp. 10–11.

114 Simon Romero, 'Technology espionage charges add to China tension' *Sydney Morning Herald*, 5 May 2001, and Kevin Coughlin and Joseph R. Perone, 'Espionage at Lucent: three accused of slipping software to firm in China' *The Star-Ledger* (Newark), 4 May 2001.

115 Jerry Seger, 'FBI arrests two Lucent scientists, trio charged with sending high-tech gear to Beijing' *The Washington Times*, 4 May 2001.

116 Frank Ching, 'China maligned' *Far Eastern Economic Review*, 29 July 1999, p. 28.

117   Robin Munro, 'Syncretic Sects and Secret Societies: Revival in the 1980s'
      Chinese Sociology and Anthropology, vol. 21, no. 4, Summer 1989, p. 3.
118   *Falun Gong: The Real Story*, pamphlet published by Falun Gong practitioners in
      North America, Nov. 1999.
119   Harald Bruning, 'Falun Gong finds few friends in bastion of patriotism' *South
      China Morning Post*, 12 May 2001.

APPENDIX

1   Garry, Clement and Brian, McAdam, *Triads and Other Organized Crime Groups*
     manual prepared for the Royal Canadian Mounted Police, 1993, pp. 35–7. For
     what appears to be a more original version of the same 36 oaths, see Murray,
     The Origins of the Tiandihui, pp. 239–41.

BIBLIOGRAPHY

CHINA, TAIWAN, HONG KONG AND MACAU
Books

Alley, Rewi. *At 90: Memoirs of My China Years*. New World Press, Beijing, 1986.

Backman, Michael. *Asian Eclipse: Exposing the Dark Side of Business in Asia*. John Wiley & Sons (Asia), Singapore, 1999.

—— (ed.). *Overseas Chinese Business Networks in Asia*. East Asia Analytical Unit, Department of Foreign Affairs and Trade, Canberra, 1995.

Black, David. *Triad Takeover: A Terrifying Account of the Spread of Triad Crime in the West*. Sidgwick & Jackson, London, 1991.

Beeching, Jack. *The Chinese Opium Wars*. Harcourt Brace Jovanovich, San Diego, New York and London, 1975.

Blyth, Ken. *Petro Pirates: The Hijacking of the Petro Ranger*. Allen & Unwin, Sydney, 2000.

Booth, Martin. *The Triads: The Chinese Criminal Fraternity*. Grafton Books, London, 1990.

—— *Opium: A History*. Simon & Schuster, London, 1996.

—— *The Dragon Syndicates: The Global Phenomenon of the Triads*. Doubleday, London & New York, 1999.

Bonavia, David. *China's Warlords*. Oxford University Press, Hong Kong, 1995.

Bresler, Fenton. *The Chinese Mafia: The Most Frightening New Organization in International Crime*. Stein and Day, New York, 1981.

Byron, John and Pack, Robert. *The Claws of the Dragon: Kang Sheng, the Evil Genius Behind Mao—and His Legacy of Terror in People's China*. Simon & Schuster, New York, 1992.

Chesneaux, Jean. *Secret Societies in China in the 19th and 20th Century*. Heinemann Educational Books, London, 1971.

Chiang Kai-shek. *Soviet Russia in China*. China Publishing Company, Taipei, 1969.

Chu, Yiu Kong. *The Triads as Business*. Routledge, London, 2000.

Collis, Maurice. *Foreign Mud: Anglo-Chinese Opium War*. Graham Bash, Singapore, 1980.

Davis, Fei-Ling. *Primitive Revolutionaries of China: A Study of Secret Societies in the Late Nineteenth Century*. Routledge & Kegan Paul, London and Henley, 1977.

Eftimiades, Nicholas. *Chinese Intelligence Operations*. Naval Institute Press, Annapolis, 1994.

Ezpeleta, Mariano. *Red Shadows over Shianghai*. Zita Publishing, Quezon City, 1972.

Faligot, Roger and Kauffer, Rémi. *The Chinese Secret Service*. Headline Publishing, London, 1989.

Fei Chengkang. *Macao 400 Years*. The Academy of Social Sciences, Shanghai, 1996.

Glick, Carl and Hong Sheng-hwa. *Swords of Silence: Chinese Secret Societies Past and Present*. McGraw-Hill Book Company, New York and London, 1947.

Guedes, João. *As Seitas: Histórias do Crime e da Política em Macau*. Livros do Oriente, Lisbon, 1991.

Gunn, Geoffrey C. *Encountering Macau: A Portuguese City-State on the Periphery of China, 1557–1999*. Westview Press, Boulder, Col., 1996.

Hahn, Emily. *The Soong Sisters*. Doubleday, Doran & Company, New York, 1944.

Hawks Pott, F.L. *A Short History of Shanghai*. Kelly & Walsh Ltd, Shanghai, 1928.

Hershatter, Gail. *Dangerous Pleasures: Prostitution and Modernity in Twentieth-Century Shanghai*. University of California Press, Berkeley, 1997.

Kaplan, David E. *Fires of the Dragon: Politics, Murder, and the Kuomintang*. Atheneum, New York, 1992.

La Motte, Ellen N. *The Opium Monopoly*. Macmillan, New York, 1920.

Lilius, Aleko E. *I Sailed With Chinese Pirates*. Arrowsmith, London, 1930.

Ljungstedt, Anders. *An Historical Sketch of the Portuguese Settlements in China and of the Roman Catholic Church and Mission in China & Description of the City of Canton*. Viking Publications, Hong Kong, 1992 (reprint; first edition by James Munroe & Co., Boston, 1836).

Lodl, Ann and Zhang Longguan eds. *Enterprise Crime: Asian and Global Perspectives*. The Office of International Criminal Justice with the Shanghai Bureau of Justice and The East China Institute of Politics and Law, Chicago, 1992.

Martin, Bernard. *Strange Vigour: A Biography of Sun Yat-sen*. Heinemann, London, 1944.

Martin, Brian G. *The Shanghai Green Gang: Politics and Organized Crime 1919–1937*. University of California Press, Berkeley, 1996.

Massonnet, Philippe. *The New China: Money, Sex, and Power*. Tuttle Publishing, Boston, Rutland and Tokyo, 1997.

Merwin, Samuel. *Drugging a Nation: The Story of China and the Opium Curse*. Fleming H. Revell Company, London and Edinburgh, 1908.

Morgan, W.P. *Triad Societies in Hong Kong*. Government Press, Hong Kong, 1960.

Murray, Dian H. *Pirates of the South China Coast 1790–1810*. Stanford University Press, Stanford, 1987.

—— *The Origins of the Tiandihui: The Chinese Triads in Legend and History*. Stanford University Press, Stanford, 1994.

Ownby, David and Heidhues, Mary Somers eds. *'Secret Societies' Reconsidered: Perspectives on the Social History of Modern South China and Southeast Asia*. M.E. Sharpe, Armonk, New York and London, 1993.

Pan Ling (Pan, Lynn). *Old Shanghai: Gangsters in Paradise*. Heinemann Asia, Singapore, 1984.

—— *Sons of the Yellow Emperor: A History of the Chinese Diaspora*. Little, Brown and Company, Boston, Toronto and London, 1990.

—— *In Search of Old Shanghai*. Joint Publishing, Hong Kong, 1991.

—— *Shanghai: A Century of Change in Photographs 1843–1949*. Hai Feng Publishing, Hong Kong, 1993.

Pan, Lynn ed. *The Encyclopedia of Chinese Overseas*. Archipelago Press, Landmark Books, Singapore, 1998.

Pawley, Tinko. *My Bandit Hosts*. Stanley Paul & Co., London, circa mid-1930s.

Perry, Elizabeth J. *Shanghai on Strike: The Politics of Chinese Labor*. Stanford University Press, Stanford, 1993.

Porter, Jonathan. *Macau: The Imaginary City*. Westview Press, Boulder, Col, 1996.

Posner, Gerald L. *Warlords of Crime: Chinese Secret Societies, the New Mafia*. Penguin Books, New York, 1990.

Robertson, Frank. *Triangle of Death: The Inside Story of the Triads—the Chinese Mafia*. Routledge & Kegan Paul, London and Henley, 1977.

Seagrave, Sterling. *The Soong Dynasty*. Sidgwick & Jackson, London, 1985.

—— *Lords of the Rim: The Invisible Empire of the Overseas Chinese*. Bantam Press, London and New York, 1995.

Sergeant, Harriet. *Shanghai*. John Murray, London, 1998.

Smedley, Agnes. *The Great Road: The Life and Times of Chu Teh*. Monthly Review Press, New York, 1956.

Wakeman, Frederic Jr. *The Shanghai Badlands: Wartime Terrorism and Urban Crime 1937–1941*. Cambridge University Press, Cambridge, 1996.

—— *Policing Shanghai 1927–1937*. University of California Press, Berkeley, 1995.

Wakeman, Frederic Jr. and Wen-hsin Yeh. *Shanghai Sojourners*. Institute of East Asian Studies, Berkeley, 1992.

Wang, Alexander Zhicheng. *A History of the Russian Emigré Community in Shanghai* (in Chinese). Sanlen Publishing House, Shanghai, 1993.

Ward, J.S.M. and Stirling, W.G. *The Hung Society or The Society of Heaven and Earth*, 3 vols. The Baskerville Press, London, 1925.

Wasserstein, Bernard. *Secret War in Shanghai: Treachery, Subversion and Collaboration in the Second World War*. Profile Books, London, 1998.

Weidenbaum, Murray and Hughes, Samuel. *The Bamboo Network: How Expatriate Chinese Entrepreneurs are Creating a New Economic Superpower in Asia*. Martin Kessler Books/The Free Press, New York, 1996.

Papers and selected articles

Cheng, Allen T. 'Taiwan's dirty business'. *Asia Inc*. April 1997, pp. 16–23.

Cheng Chung-hsin. 'On the problem of hoodlums, underworld gangs and the organized crimes in the Republic of China: a current survey and counter measures'. Investigation Bureau, Ministry of Justice, the Republic of China. Paper submitted to the 15th Annual International Asian Organized Crime Conference, Las Vegas, March 1993.

Chin Ko-lin. 'Triad societies in Hong Kong'. Paper submitted to the 15th Annual International Asian Organized Crime Conference, Las Vegas, March 1993.

Clement, Garry W.G. and McAdam, Brian. *Triads and other Asian Organized crime groups*. The Royal Canadian Mounted Police, 1994.

DeVore, Howard. 'China's intelligence and internal security forces'. A Jane's Special Report, Jane's Information Group, October 1999.

Dobinson, Ian. 'Pinning a tail on the dragon: the Chinese and the international heroin trade'. *Crime and Delinquency*, July 1993.

Munro, Robin. 'Syncretic sects and secret societies: revival in the 1980s'. *Chinese Sociology and Anthropology*, vol. 21, no. 4, Summer 1989, pp. 3–103.

Royal Hong Kong Police. 'Narcotics bureau: aide memoire'. Paper submitted to the 15th Annual International Asian Organized Crime Conference, Las Vegas, March 1993.

JAPAN
Books

Buruma, Ian. *Behind the Mask: On Sexual Demons, Sacred Mothers, Transvestites, Gangsters, and Other Japanese Cultural Heroes.* Pantheon Books, New York, 1984.

Deacon, Richard. *Kempeitai: The Japanese Secret Service Then and Now.* Charles E. Tuttle, Tokyo, 1982.

Dower, John W. *Embracing Defeat: Japan in the Wake of World War II.* W.W. Norton & Company/The New Press, New York, 1999.

Jennings, John M. *The Opium Empire: Japanese Imperialism and Drug Trafficking in Asia 1895–1945.* Praeger, Westport and London, 1997.

Kaplan, David E. and Dubro, Alec. *Yakuza: The Explosive Account of Japan's Criminal Underworld.* Addison-Wesley, Reading, Mass., 1986.

Lamont-Brown, Raymond. *Kempeitai: Japan's Dreaded Military Police.* Sutton Publishing, Gloustershire, 1998.

Saga, Junichi. *Confessions of a Yakuza: Life in Japan's Underworld.* Tokyo, Kodansha International, New York and London, 1991.

Seymour, Christopher. *Yakuza Diary: Doing Time in the Japanese Underworld.* The Atlantic Monthly Press, New York, 1996.

Weiner, Michael ed. *Japan's Minorities: The Illusion of Homogeneity.* Routledge, London and New York, 1997.

Whiting, Robert. *Tokyo Underworld: The Fast Times and Hard Life of an American Gangster in Japan.* Pantheon Books, New York, 1999.

Wolferen, Karel van. *The Enigma of Japanese Power.* Vintage Books, New York, 1990.

Papers and selected articles

Bremner, Brian. 'Yakuza and the banks'. *Business Week*, 29 Jan. 1996, pp. 15–18.

Delfs, Robert. 'Power to the yakuza'. *Far Eastern Economic Review*, 21 Nov. 1991, pp. 28–35.

Hirsh, Michael. 'Tokyo's dirty secret: banks and the mob', *Newsweek*, 18 Dec. 1995, pp. 42–43

Kaplan, David E. 'Japanese organised crime and the bubble economy'. The Woodrow Wilson Center, Asia Programme: Occasional Paper no. 70, 13 Dec. 1996.

—— 'Yakuza inc'. *US News & World Report*, 13 April 1998, pp. 41–7.

Katayama, Hans. 'The man who tried to buy respect'. *Asia Inc.*, March 1994, pp. 34–7.

Marshall, Andrew. 'In the name of the godfather', *Caravan* (Bangkok), Dec. 1994, pp. 83–9.

Wanner, Barbara. 'More Eyes on *yakuza*'s role in the Japanese economy'. *Japan Economic Institute*, 8 May 1992, http://members.tripod.com/~orgcrime/japeconomy.htm

RUSSIA AND THE RUSSIAN FAR EAST
Books

Barron, John. *KGB Today: The Hidden Hand.* Hodder & Stoughton, London, 1983.

Becker, Jasper. *The Lost Country: Mongolia Revealed.* Hodder & Stoughton, London, 1992.

Bobrick, Benson. *East of the Sun: The Epic Conquest and Tragic History of Siberia*. Poseidon Press, New York, 1992.

Forsyth, James. *A History of the Peoples of Siberia: Russia's North Asian Colony 1581–1990*. Cambridge University Press, Cambridge, 1992.

Handelman, Stephen. *Comrade Criminal: The Theft of the Second Russian Revolution*. Michael Joseph. London, 1994.

Hopkirk, Peter. *Setting the East Ablaze: On Secret Service in Bolshevik Asia*. Oxford University Press. Oxford, 1984.

Knight, Amy. *Spies Without Cloaks: The KGB's Successors*. Princeton University Press, Princeton, 1996.

Sergeyev, Victor M. *The Wild East: Crime and Lawlessness in Post-Communist Russia*. M.E. Sharpe, Armonk and London, 1998.

Smith, Canfield M. *Vladivostok under Red and White Rule: Revolution and Counter-revolution in the Russian Far East 1920–1922*. University of Washington Press, Seattle and London, 1975.

Stajner, Karlo. *Seven Thousand Days in Siberia*. Farrar Straus and Giroux, New York, 1988.

Stephan, John J. *The Russian Far East: A History*. Stanford University Press, Stanford, 1994.

Thiel, Erich. *The Soviet Far East: A Survey of its Physical and Economic Geography*. Methuen, London, 1957.

Timofeyev, Lev. *Russia's Secret Rulers: How the Government and Criminal Mafia Exercise Their Power*. Alfred A. Knopf, New York, 1992.

Vaksberg, Arkady. *The Soviet Mafia*. St Martin's Press, New York, 1991.

Williams, Phil ed. *Russian Organized Crime: The New Threat?*. Frank Cass, London and Portland, 1997.

Papers and selected articles

Babbs, Gareth. 'Organized crime in Russia: working with the Russian police'. Paper for a conference organised by the Royal Institute of International Affairs and Control Risk Group, March 1995.

Baranovsky, Igor. 'Organized crime in Russia: the Russian viewpoint'. Paper for a conference organised by the Royal Institute of International Affairs and Control Risk Group, March 1995.

Bosworth-Davies, Rowan. 'Organized crime in Russia: crime and the law'. Paper for a conference organised by the Royal Institute of International Affairs and Control Risk Group, March 1995.

Bray, John. 'Organized crime in Russia: political and economic analysis'. Paper for a conference organised by the Royal Institute of International Affairs and Control Risk Group, March 1995.

Centre for Strategic and International Studies. 'Russian organized crime and corruption: Putin's challenge'. Global Organized Crime Project, 2000.

Crothers, Richard. 'Organized crime flourishes in Russia, or is it just an old tale with a new twist?' *Platypus Magazine* (The Journal of the Australian Federal Police), December 1996, p. 9.

Galeotti, Mark. 'Mafiya: organized crime in Russia'. *Jane's Intelligence Review*, Special Report No. 10, June 1996.

—— 'The Russian wild East: a complex criminal Threat'. *Jane's Intelligence Review*, September 1998.

—— 'The political view: organized crime's influence on politics and vice versa'. Paper for a conference organised by the Royal Institute of International Affairs and Control Risk Group, March 1995.

—— The rise of a criminal superpower: organized crime in Russia. A report for the US Department of Defense, December 1995.

Handelman, Stephen. 'The Russian "Mafiya"'. *Foreign Affairs*, March–April 1994, pp. 83–96.

Koletar, Joseph. 'Organized crime in Russia: financial crimes committed by Russian organised crime'. Paper for a conference organised by the Royal Institute of International Affairs and Control Risk Group, March 1995.

March, Sally. 'Organized crime in Russia: counterfeiting products'. Paper for a conference organised by the Royal Institute of International Affairs and Control Risk Group, March 1995.

Merlino, Paul. 'Organized crime in Russia: crime and risk management'. Paper for a conference organised by the Royal Institute of International Affairs and Control Risk Group, March 1995.

Mogck, Judy. 'Former Soviet-Union-based organized crime. a historical perspective'. *Gazette* (a Royal Canadian Mounted Police publication), No. 10, 1996, pp. 4–10.

Surikov, Anton. 'Crime in Russia: the international implications'. The Centre for Defence Studies, London, 1994.

US Department of Justice, Drug Enforcement Administration. 'Country briefs: Armenia, Azerbaijan, Belarus, Estonia, Georgia, Latvia, Lithuania, Moldova, Russia, and Ukraine'. Working Paper, 1996.

—— 'Drug trafficking in Russia'. Working Paper, July 1996.

—— 'Money laundering in Russia'. Working Paper, February 1995.

—— 'The newly independent states and the drug trade'. Working Paper, September 1995.

Waller, Michael J. and Yasmann, Victor J. 'Russia's criminal revolution: the role of the security services'. *Journal of Contemporary Criminal Justice*, December 1995, http://www.afpc.org/pubs/crimerev.htm.

Wishnick, Elizabeth. 'Where the grass seems greener: Russia's new Chinese immigration problem'. *The Asia-Pacific Magazine*, Nos. 6 and 7, 1997, pp. 54–9.

SOUTHEAST ASIA
Books

Andreyev, M.A. *Overseas Chinese Bourgeoisie—A Peking Tool in Southeast Asia*. Progress Publishers, Moscow, 1975.

Blythe, Wilfred. *The Impact of Secret Societies in Malaya*. Oxford University Press, London, Kuala Lumpur and Hong Kong, 1969.

Budiman, Arief, Hatley, Barbara and Kingsbury, Damien eds. *Reformasi: Crisis and Political Change in Indonesia*. Monash Asia Institute, Clayton, 1999.

Cribb, Robert. *Gangsters and Revolutionaries: The Jakarta People's Militia and the Indonesian Revolution 1945–1949*. University of Hawaii Press, Honolulu, 1991.

Descours-Gatin, Chantal. *Quand l'opium finançait la colonisation en Indochine*. Editions L'Harmattan, Paris, 1992.

Hicks, George L. ed. *Overseas Chinese Remittances from Southeast Asia 1910–1940*. Select Books, Singapore, 1993.

Kingsbury, Damien ed. *Guns and Ballot Boxes: East Timor's Vote for Independence*. Monash Asia Institute, Clayton, 2000.

Lamour, Catherine. *Enquête sur une armée secrète*. Éditions du Seuil, Paris, 1975.

Lamour, Catherine and Lamberti, Michel R. *The Second Opium War*. Allen Lane. London, 1972.

Lim, Irene. *Secret Societies in Singapore*. National Heritage Board, Singapore, 1999.

Lintner, Bertil. *Burma in Revolt: Opium and Insurgency Since 1948*. Westview Press, Boulder, Col., 1994. Second edition: Silkworm Books, Chiang Mai, 1999.

McCoy, Alfred W. *The Politics of Heroin in Southeast Asia*. Harper & Row, New York, 1972.

—— *The Politics of Heroin: CIA Complicity in the Global Drug Trade*. Lawrence Hill Books, New York, 1991.

Phongpaichit, Pasuk and Piriyarangsan, Sungsidh. *Corruption and Democracy in Thailand*. Silkworm Books, Chiang Mai, 1996.

Phongpaichit, Pasuk and Baker, Chris. *Thailand's Boom and Bust*. Silkworm Books, Chiang Mai, 1998.

Pongpaichit, Pasuk, Piriyarangsan, Sungsidh and Treerat, Nualnoi. *Guns Girls Gambling Ganja: Thailand's Illegal Economy and Public Policy*. Silkworm Books, Chiang Mai, 1998.

Rafael, Vincente L. ed. *Figures in Criminality in Indonesia, the Philippines, and Colonial Vietnam*. Cornell University South East Asia Programme Publication, Ithaca, 1999.

Rush, James. *Opium to Java: Revenue Framing and Chinese Enterprise in Colonial Indonesia 1860–1910*. Cornell University Press, Ithaca and London, 1990.

Suriyadinata, Leo. *Prominent Indonesian Chinese Biographical Sketches*. The Institute of Southeast Asian Studies, Singapore, 1997.

McVey, Ruth ed. *Southeast Asian Capitalists*. Cornell University Southeast Asia Program, Ithaca, 1993.

Skinner, G. William. *Leadership and Power in the Chinese Community in Thailand*. Cornell University Press, Ithaca, 1958.

Trocki, Carl A. ed. *Gangsters, Democracy, and the State in Southeast Asia*. Southeast Asia Programme, Cornell University, Ithaca, 1998.

Warner, Dennis. *The Last Confucian*. Angus & Robertson, Sydney, 1964.

Papers and selected articles

Cribb, Robert. 'Opium and the Indonesian revolution'. *Modern Asian Studies*, vol. 22, no. 4, 1988, pp. 701–21.

Dillon, Dana R. 'Piracy in Asia: a growing barrier to maritime trade'. Paper produced by the Asian Studies Centre and published by the Heritage Foundation, Washington, 22 June 2000.

Lintner, Bertil. 'The drug trade in Southeast Asia'. *Jane's Intelligence Review, Special Report No. 5*, April 1995.

—— *The Politics of the Drug Trade in Burma*. Indian Ocean Centre for Peace Studies Occasional Paper no. 33, University of Western Australia, Nedlands, 1993.

McFarlane, John. 'The Asian financial crisis: corruption, cronyism and organised crime'. *Defence Studies Working Paper No. 341*. The Australian National University, Strategic and Defence Studies Centre, Canberra, October 1999.

Purcell, Victor. *The Chinese in Malaya*. Background to Malaya Series No. 9, Donald Moore, Singapore, 1956.

Ryter, Loren. 'Pemuda Pancasila: the last loyalists free men of Suharto's order?' *Indonesia 66*, October 1998, Corell Modern Indonesia Project, Ithaca, pp. 45–73.

Taylor, Robert. *Foreign and Domestic Consequences of the Kuomintang Invasion of Burma*. Cornell University Southeast Asia Programme Data Paper No. 93, Ithaca, 1973.

AUSTRALIA AND THE SOUTH PACIFIC
Books

Hall, Richard. *Disorganized Crime*. University of Queensland Press, Brisbane, 1986.

—— *Tiger General: The Killing of Victor Chang*. Macmillan Australia, Sydney, 1995.

Harvey, S.D. *The Ghost of Ludwig Gertsch*. Pan Macmillan Australia, Sydney, 2000.

Jayasuriya, Laksiri and Kee Pokong. *The Asianisation of Australia? Some Facts about the Myths*. Melbourne University Press, Mebourne, 1999.

Kwitny, Jonathan. *The Crimes of Patriots: A True Tale of Dope, Dirty Money, and the CIA*. Simon & Schuster, New York, 1987.

Lennox, Gina and Rush, Frances. *People of the Cross: True Stories from People who Live and Work in King's Cross*. Simon & Schuster, Sydney, 1993.

McCoy, Alfred W. *Drug Traffic: Narcotics and Organized Crime in Australia*. Harper & Row, Sydney, 1980.

Patience, Allan. *The Bjelke-Petersen Premiership 1968–1983: Issues in Public Policy*. Longman Cheshire, Melbourne, 1985.

Pilger, John. *A Secret Country: The Hidden Australia*. Alfred A. Knopf, New York, 1989.

Shears, Richard. *The Coconut War: The Crisis on Espiritu Santo*. Cassell Australia, Sydney, 1980.

Tiffen, Rodney. *Scandals, Media, Politics & Corruption in Contemporary Australia*. University of New South Wales Press, Sydney, 1999.

Viviani, Nancy. *From Burnt Boats to Barbecues: The Indochinese in Australia 1975–1995*. Oxford University Press, Melbourne, 1996.

Whitton, Evan. *The Hillbilly Dictator: Australia's Police State*. ABC Books, Sydney, 1989.

Papers and selected articles

Australian Bureau of Criminal Intelligence. *Australian Illicit Drug Report 1995–1996*. The Australian Federal Police, Dec. 1996.

Davis, Ben. 'Vanuatu: the serious side of paradise'. *A Supplement to Euromoney*, August 1996, http://www.euromoney.com/contents/ publications/euromoney/.

National Crime Authority. 'Asian organised crime in Australia'. Discussion Paper, Parliament of the Commonwealth of Australia, Feb. 1995.

Lintner, Bertil. 'Global reach: drug money in the Asia Pacific'. *Current History*, April 1998, pp. 179–82.

—— 'Paradise for crooks'. *Far Eastern Economic Review*, 6 Nov. 1997, pp. 31–5.

Olszewski, Peter. 'Tattoos in the sun: Japanese gangs move into Australia'. *Cross Section* (Australia), Summer 1994, pp. 14–18.

Walker, John. *Estimates of the Extent of Money Laundering in & through Australia*. Australian Transaction Reports and Analysis Centre, Sept. 1995.

ASIAN AND RUSSIAN ORGANISED CRIME IN THE UNITED STATES AND CANADA, AND ILLEGAL MIGRATION

Books

Chin Ko-lin. *Chinatown Gangs: Extortion, Enterprise & Ethnicity*. Oxford University Press, New York and Oxford, 1996.

—— *Smuggled Chinese: Clandestine Immigration to the United States*. Temple University Press, Philadelphia, 1999.

Dubro, James. *Dragons of Crime: Inside the Asian Underworld*. Octopus Publishing Group, Markham, Ontario, 1992.

Finckenauer, James O. and Waring, Elin J. *Russian Mafia in America*. Northeastern University, Boston, 1998.

Freedman, Amy L. *Political Participation and Ethnic Minorities: Chinese Overseas in Malaysia, Indonesia, and the United States*. Routledge, New York and London, 2000.

Friedman, Robert I. *Red Mafiya: How the Russian Mob has Invaded America*. Little Brown and Company, Boston, New York and London, 2000.

Huston, Peter. *Tongs, Gangs, and Triads: Chinese Crime Groups in the United States*. Paladin Press, Boulder, Col., 1995.

Kerry, John. *The New War: The Web of Crime That Threatens America's Security*. Simon & Schuster, New York, 1997.

William Kleinknecht. *The New Ethnic Mobs: The Changing Face of Organized Crime in America*, The Free Press, New York, 1996.

Kwong, Peter. *Forbidden Workers: Illegal Chinese Immigrants and American Labor*. The New Press, New York, 1997.

—— *The New Chinatown*. Hill and Wang, New York, 1996.

Long, Patrick Du Phuoc and Ricard, Laura. *The Dream Shattered: Vietnamese Gangs in America*. Northeastern University Press, Boston, 1996.

Nyiri, Pal. *New Chinese Migrants in Europe: The Case of the Chinese Community in Hungary*. Ashgate, Aldershot, 1999.

Smith, Paul J. ed. *Human Smuggling: Chinese Migrant Trafficking and the Challenge to America's Immigration Tradition*. Washington: The Center for Strategic & International Studies, 1997.

Papers and selected articles

Daly, Michael. 'The war for Chinatown'. *New York*, 14 Feb. 1983.

Galeotti, Mark. 'Canada: soft target for crime'. *Jane's Intelligence Review*, Feb. 2001, pp. 10–11.

Leiren, Hall. 'Friends in vile places: reasons Canada refused entry to a Hong Kong "businessmen"'. *British Columbia Report*, 29 August 1994, pp. 8–9.

Liu, Melinda. 'The fall of the Fuk Ching', *Newsweek* (Asian edition), 13 Sept. 1993, pp. 18–19.

Nyhuus, Ken. 'Chasing ghosts: Asian organised crime investigation in Canada'. *Gazette* (Royal Canadian Mounted Police journal), vol. 60. nos, 9 & 10, September–October, 1998.

Royal Canadian Mounted Police and the Canadian Security Intelligence Service. *Sidewinder: A Secret Report*, 24 June 1997, http://www.intellnet.org/resources/sidewinder/side002.html.

Swerdlow, Joel L. 'Trying to fit in'. *National Geographic*, August 1998, pp. 62–77.
US Department of Justice. *Vietnamese Criminal Activity in the United States: A National Perspective*. Organised Crime/Drug Branch, Criminal Investigative Division, March 1993.
Wise, Jeff. 'The dragon's teeth: a new generation of brutal gangs is poised to take over New York's Chinatown'. *Far Eastern Economic Review*, 13 June 1996, pp. 50–2.

INDEX

Brooke, James, 291–2
Brunei, 291–2
Brüner, Jules Johann, 190
Bryner & Co., 190
Bryner, Yulius Ivanovich *see* Brüner, Jules Johann
Brynner, Yul, 190, 234
Budapest, Hungary, 366–7
Bungei Shunju (magazine), 171, 173
burakumin, 147–8, 176, 180
Burama, Ian, 176
Burma: attempts to expel Guomindang, 238; balance of payments discrepancies, 267–8; build-up of armed forces, 266; China attacks Guomindang in, 246–7, 418n; Chinese migration to, 222; Committee for Drug Abuse Control, 265; cross-border trade with China, 270–2; devaluation of currency, 270; Directorate of Defence Procurement, 269; ethnic dissident armies, 260; export of heroin from, 274, 275; foreign investment in, 270; former insurgents support military, 263; government conned by *yakuza*, 254–5; Great Golden Peninsula, 271; Guomindang in, 236–40, 242, 246–9, 256, 258; heroin trade, 258, 263, 270, 274–5, 307, 322, 328, 333, 378; illegal migration from, 272–3, 348–9; invites press to witness 'drug eradication' efforts, 264–5; jade trade, 268; Mekong River Operation, 247; methamphetamine production in, 259, 270; military coups, 255; opium trade, 240, 242–3, 247–9, 256–60, 263–7; popular uprising (1988), 260, 271; Royal Myanmar Casino, 272; State Law and Order Restoration Council, 261, 266, 267; State Peace and Development Council, 264, 266; UN International Drug Control Programme, 386; *yakuza* in, 254–5
Burswood Casino, Perth, 117
Bush, George, 369
bushido, 147
Butterfield and Swire, 17

Cabo Verde, 108
Cabramatta, Sydney, 309–11, 324, 331–2, 334
Cali cartel, 373
Calvani, Sandro, 273
Cambodia: arms dealing, 218–19; Chinese and Taiwanese gangs in, 10–11, 219–20, 220, 225; Chinese migrants in, 223–4; counterfeiting, 219; as a haven for illicit trade, 218; heroin trade, 274; illegal immigration from, 220–1, 223–4; Macau gangsters in, 80; Triads in, 376; UN supervises election (1993), 217; Vanuatu's 'honorary consuls' in, 345, 346
Cambodia-China City Company, 224
Cambodian People's Party, 217
Can Tho, Vietnam, 330
Canada: assists White Russians, 193; Chinese attempts to influence, 348, 382; Chinese criminals in, 381; Chinese efforts to obtain technology of, 348; heroin trade, 375; illegal immigration into, 223, 351–2; in the Korean War, 161; Triads in, 374–5; *yakuza* in, 140, 370
Canadian Security Intelligence Service, 381
Cannon Agency, 159
Cannon, J.Y., 159
Cao Dai, 328–9, 331
Capone, Al, 32, 64
Carrascalão, Manuel, 280
Carrascalão, Manuelito, 280
Carter, Jimmy, 170
Carvalho, José Nobre de, 107
Casino Control Authority, New South Wales, 334–5
Casino (film), 73
casinos *see* gambling
Castro, Fidel, 240
Cathay Hotel, Shanghai, 18, 29
Ceausescu, Nicolae, 323
Central Intelligence Agency, United States, 163, 240, 247–8, 249, 265, 313–14
Centre Français du Commerce Exterieur, Paris, 267

Centurion Bank, 346
Cepeda, Ussulau de Jesus, 276–7
Chalerm Yubamruang, 251
Chan, Eddie T.C. *see* Chan Tse-chiu ('Fast Eddie')
Chan, Elsie, 129–30, 134
Chan Lo, 232
Chan Tse-chiu ('Fast Eddie'), 12, 360–1, 368–9, 371
Chan Wing-po, 13
Chang Pao, 96, 97
Chang Sheng (ship), 2, 303
Changsa, China, 37
chao pho, 236, 249–52
Chaozhou, China, 227
Charoen Patanadamrongkit *see* Sia Leng
Chase Manhattan Bank, 344
Chat Thai Party, Thailand, 250
Chateaubriand, René de, 329
Chatichai Choonhavan, 251
Chea Sim, 220
Chekhov, Anton, 190
Chen Chi-li 'Dry Duck', 219–20, 225, 376, 377
Chen Hung Kee, 345–6
Chen Jianpeng, 345
Chen Kai-kit, 129–30, 132, 133–4, 226, 380
Chen, Peter *see* Chen Hung Kee
Chen Qimei, 37, 56
Chen Shichang, 32
Cheng Chui Ping 'Sister Ping', 364–5
Cheng I Sao, 96, 97
Cheng Yu-tung, 112
Cheng Zhen Shu, 134
Chengdu, China, 3
Chennault, Anna, 132–3
Chennault, Claire, 63, 237, 238, 386
Cherry Society, 152–3
Chesneaux, Jean, 49
Cheung Leung-shing, 124
Chiang Ching-kuo, 376, 377
Chiang Kai-shek: background, 36–7; cracks down on vice and crime, 66; death, 376; fails to govern effectively, 54; flees to Taiwan, 16, 64, 162, 236; helps create anti-communist league,

166; interest in Macau, 98; links with criminals, 373; links with secret societies, 37–8, 60–1; massacres communists, 231; robs Shanghai's bank vaults, 65
Chiang Mai, Thailand, 223, 242, 243
Chiang Rai, Thailand, 257
Chien, Nancy, 226
child labour, in Shanghai, 20
Chin Ko-lin, 223, 348, 365
Chin Sophonpanich, 241, 244, 245
China: amphetamine production, 158; animosity towards the West, 384; approves overseas travel for citizens, 179; banditry (1930s), 57; as a base for drug trafficking, 212; birth of Communist Party, 35–6; Britain in, 23–7; campaign against Falun Gong, 331, 385–6; Chiang Kai-shek's purge of communists, 39; China Lobby in America urges war with, 237, 238; Chinese banks in Vanuatu, 7; Chinese gangs in Cambodia, 11; Chinese in Australia, 308–9, 321–2; Civil War, 57–8, 63–4; Communist China's foothold in the United States, 369; corruption in, 380–1, 386; cross-border trade with Burma, 270–2; Cultural Revolution, 107, 255, 374; Dai Huen Jai syndicate, 8; economic reforms (1990s), 78; executions in, 1–2, 3, 66, 83; Five Antis Campaign, 68; Fujian province, 44–6, 233, 349, 355, 361, 363, 365–6, 381; funnels money to US presidential candidate, 130–1, 380; gangsters flee after Communist victory, 121; government links with organised crime, 9, 13, 31–2, 373–6, 379–80, 386–7; Guangdong province, 233; interference in Canadian affairs, 348, 382; involvement in Donorgate scandal, 127–31, 225, 226–7, 296–7, 380, 383; Japanese forces in, 52–3, 58, 61, 149–50; links with Burma's drug traffickers, 272, 379; links with Chinese Americans, 360; Manchuria, 58, 149–50, 153, 162, 222; migration

Communist Party of Burma, 255–6, 258, 260–3, 265, 270–1, 274, 378
Communist Party of China, 35–6, 38–9, 58, 67–9, 130, 369
Communist Party of Malaya, 231–2
ComTriad Technologies, 383
Confucianism, 293
Continental Finance, 296
Continental King Lung Group, 12
Conway, Hudson, 117
Cook Islands, 343
Cook, James, 337
coolies, 91–2
Coronel, Pastor, 167
COSCO, 382
Cossacks, 187, 196, 210
counterfeiting, 219
Cowdery, Nicholas, 308
credit card fraud, 207, 373
Cribb, Robert, 288–9, 290–1
Cuba, 240
Cuellar, Javier Perez de, 170
Cunning Kin, 127
Cuomo, Matilda, 369

Dai Huen Jai, 8, 79, 374
Dai Li, 61–2, 63
dai siu (game), 92–4
Daichi (company), 254–5
Daley, Robert, 360
Darip, Haji, 289, 290
Dark Ocean Society, 150–1, 153
Dark Side, 371
Datang Telecom Techology, 383
David Sassoon (company), 28
de Leeuw, Hendrik, 70
Deacon, Richard, 150
Decembrists, 189, 200
Dekabristy, 189
Deloitte Touche Tohmatsu, 252
Democratic Action Party, Malaya, 319
Democratic Party-Struggle, Indonesia, 281
Democrats, United States, 128–9, 130, 225, 380
Deng Lin, 224
Deng Xiaoping: entrepreneurial son-in-law, 382; family connections with

Triads, 224; fraud committed against daughter, 375; introduces economic reforms, 82, 126, 221, 227, 355, 360; money laundering for family of, 133; on 'patriotic' Triads, 9, 369; reduces aid to Burmese communists, 256
Denmark, in Korean War, 161
Deordienko, Igor, 88
Descartes, René, 329
Dialogue of Nations (company), 86, 89
Dili, East Timor, 277–9, 281
Domican, Tom, 316
Dong Hwa (company), 169
Dong Thap province, Vietnam, 330
Donorgate scandal, 127–31, 225, 226–7, 296–7, 380, 383
Dostoyevsky, Fyodor, 191
Double Swords, 49
Dragon Bank scandal, 340–1
drugs: amphetamine trade, 157–8, 259, 270; cocaine smuggling, 208; drug abuse in China, 3, 374; drug smuggling by Russian gangs, 8; drug smuggling in Far Eastern Russia, 211–13; production of heroin from opium, 419n; trafficking by North Korea, 179; UN International Drug Control Programme, 273, 386; *see also* heroin; opium
Du Yuesheng: crushes labour movement in Shanghai, 39, 172; description of, 38; dies in Hong Kong, 121; lends armoured car to American officer, 63–4; links with Guomindang, 39–40; mansion on Rue Wagner, 38; massacres communists, 231; moves to Hong Kong, 67, 121; relationship with de facto wife, 33; relationship with Inspector Huang, 32; secures protection for heroin laboratories, 55; ships opium via Green Gang, 61; supplies opium to Japanese, 162; thousands pledge loyalty to, 57
Duan Xiwen, 247, 248, 249, 256
Duanhua School, Cambodia, 224
Duke of Edinburgh's Award International Foundation, 111

Gable, Clark, 19
gali-gali, 284
gambling: Australia, 109–10, 117, 316;
business interests of Stanley Ho,
109–10; Japan, 144, 146, 166; Macau,
76–7, 79, 84, 92–4, 104–7, 112–13,
116–18; Philippines, 76, 84, 110;
see also names of individual casinos
Garcia, António, 73
Gelaohui (Elder Brothers Society), 58–60
Gempur, 289
General Association of Korean
Residents in Japan, 137, 177
Genyosha, 150–1
Gerakan Party, Malaya, 232, 319
German Nazis, storage of gold in
Portugal by, 99, 103
Ghee Hin society, 49, 229, 415n
Ghee Hok society, 49
Ghosh, Amarenda Nath, 346
Ghost Shadows, 13, 359, 370
Gina-III (ship), 350
giri, 147
Gladstone, William, 25–6
glasnost, 184
Glen Shipping Line, 17
Goglidze, Sergei, 202
Gold Coast, Australia, 336–7
gold trade, 99–101, 107
Golden Coins, 49
Golden Triangle: control of by
Communist Party of Burma, 255–6;
control of by renegade army, 237;
export of heroin from, 275, 307;
heroin production in, 258, 322, 328,
333, 378; involvement of
Guomindang in opium trade, 238–40;
involvement of Teochew Chinese in,
312; links with Australia, 321–2;
secret agents in, 246; as a source of
opium, 212; UN International Drug
Control Programme, 386
Golden Venture (ship), 348–9, 351–3,
362, 363, 364–5
Goldfinger (Fleming), 101
Golkar, 284, 286
Good Shan Brothers International Ltd,
269

Gorbachev, Mikhail, 182, 184, 185,
205, 206
Gore, Al, 225
Gough, Sir Henry, 25
GPU (secret police), 411n
Grace Hotel, Bangkok, 323
Grande Hotel, Macau, 94–5
Grande Monde casino, Cholon, 326
Graves, William S., 195, 196
Great Golden Peninsula, 223
The Great Terror (1937–38), Russia,
199
Greece, in Korean War, 161
Green Gang: activities of, 54, 56; Big-
Eared Du joins, 32; Chiang Kai-
shek's links with, 37–8; control over
labour unions, 62; crushed after
Communist victory, 68; in Hong
Kong, 121–2; infiltration of by
Communists, 36; origins, 30, 56;
relations with Pock-Marked Huang,
31; in Shanghai, 118; structure of, 54
Grosse, Victor, 34
Group of 7, 343
Group of the Four United, 79, 127
GST Bank, 346
Guam, 354
Guangnan Holdings, 134
Guangzhou, China, 3, 26, 49, 82, 374
Guardian Angel's Convent School,
Burma, 239
Gui, Miss, 33
Guimaraes, Isidoro Francisco, 93
Guinea-Bissau, 88, 108
Guiuan Island, 65
Gulag Archipelago, Russia, 201
Guo Dongpo, 11, 225
Guo Liangqi *see* Ah Kay
Guomindang: 1st Independent Unit,
248; 3rd Army, 247–8; 5th Army,
248; American support for, 62–3;
Bataillon Spécial 111, 248, 258; in
Burma, 236–40, 242, 246–9, 256,
258, 418n; connections with Tung
family, 114; as a democratic party,
376; establishes government at
Nanjing, 39; flees Shanghai, 16;
formation of, 54; interest in Macau,

98; introduces new currency, 65; involvement in opium trade, 55, 61, 238–40, 242, 244, 247–8, 249, 257; joint control of Chinese Consolidated Benevolent Association, 357, 359; links with criminals, 9, 10, 40, 120, 373; marginalised in US Chinatowns, 369; massacres labour activists, 39; Red Army formed to fight, 57; relations with Communist Party, 36–7, 38, 39, 58; resists liberalisation of Taiwan, 376; sets up Opium Suppression Bureau, 55; in Singapore and Malaya, 231, 232; in Thailand, 241, 247

gurentai, 155

Guterres, Eurico, 280–1

Habibie, B.J., 278, 279, 300

Hadisiswoyo, Subagyo, 279

The Hague, Netherlands, 29

Hai Lok Fung, China, 74

Hai San, 415n

Hall of Mirrors, Saigon, 326

Hamengkubuwono, Sultan, 276

Han Dok Su, 177–8

Hand, Michael, 313–14

Hang Seng Bank, 101

Hangzhou, China, 376

Hankook (company), 169

Hanoi, Vietnam, 325

Hanson, Pauline, 308, 347

Haq, Zia-ul, 110

Harbin, China, 33, 88

Hardoon, Silas, 28

Hariyadi, Siti Hediati 'Titiek', 298

Harjoyudanto, Sigit, 298

Harris, Townsend, 149

Harsono, Andreas, 303

Harun bin Haji Idris, Dato, 320

hatamoto-yakko, 143

Hatanaka, Sumitomo, 141

Hatem, George, 59

Hattori Kikan, 159

Hattori, Takushiro, 159

He Jingsheng, 83

He Long, 60

He Ping, 382

He Shen, 44

He Yaba, 91

Heaven and Earth Society *see Tiandihui* (Heaven and Earth Society)

Heavenly Kingdom of Great Peace, 50

Heavy Club, Macau, 77

Heidhues, Mary Somers, 230

Heifeng, China, 75

Heihachiro, Togo, 192

Helliwell, Paul, 240

Heo Young Jong, 174

Hercules (street thug), 282, 298

heroin: Australia, 305–8, 312, 322–4, 332–4, 349–50; Burma, 258, 263, 270, 274–5, 307, 322, 328, 333, 378; Canada, 375; discovery of, 54–5; early marketing of, 55; Hong Kong, 322, 328; price of, 333; production of from opium, 419n; Russia, 212; smuggling of by Russian gangs, 210, 212; Taiwan, 378–9; Vietnam, 327–8

Heung, Charles, 9–10, 112

Heung Chin, 124

Heung Chin-sing, 124

Heung Wah-yim, 124–6

Hinze, Russell, 316–17

Hip Sing, 357, 359, 367, 368

Hip Sing Credit Union, 359

Hiraoka, Kotaro, 150–1

Hirohito, Emperor, 154

Hiroshima, Japan, 153

Hitler, Adolf, 165

HIV, 379

Hla Min, 265

Hmong people, 235

Ho Chi Minh, 329

Ho Chi Minh City, Vietnam, 325–6

Ho, Edmund, 70, 114–15, 135

Ho Hung-sun *see* Ho, Stanley

Ho Sai-kwong, 109

Ho Seng, 415n

Ho, Stanley: attempts to have floating casinos banned, 113; bids for casino franchise, 105–6; business ties with Yip Hon, 112; buys Seng Heng Bank, 128; criticises police and judiciary, 81; as director of STDM, 76, 108, 112;

people smugglers, 303–4; Chinese community in, 291–4; Chinese *kongsi* in, 291–2; Crystal Night (1997), 299; Dragon Bank scandal, 340–1; under Dutch rule, 287–90, 292–4; effects of Asian economic crisis (1997), 298–9; Islam in, 301–2; under Japanese occupation, 288, 289–90, 293; links between nationalists and gangsters, 288–9; murder of petty criminals, 284; nationalists fight for independence, 288, 289–90; new militias form after Suharto's demise, 300–2; opium trade, 289–90, 292; *pancasila* code, 283; *petrus* campaign, 284; piracy in, 291–2, 302–3; *preman*, 287–8, 299, 301–2; protection rackets, 282, 283, 284, 286, 301–2; slaughter of suspected communists, 283; Stanley Ho's business interests in, 110; Suharto regime collapses, 278, 283; tax farming system, 292; Triads in, 291–2, 293; troops fire on student protesters, 298; use of thugs for political ends, 282, 283–8, 300–2; *see also* East Timor
Indonesian Democratic Party, 285
Indonesian Nationalist Party, 283, 290
Indonesian People's Brigade, 289
Industrial Workers of the World, 197
Industry and Commerce Bank Corp., 380
Infanta, South Africa, 351
INTERFET, 278, 281
International and Inter-religious Federation for World Peace, 341
International Daily News, 226
International Federation for the Victory over Communism, 168
International Forces to East Timor (INTERFET), 278, 281
International Monetary Fund, 99, 267
International Opium Commission, 29
International Refugee Organisation, 65
Internet, use of to move money, 7
IPKI, 283
Iran, 109–10, 162, 244, 304
Iran-Contra affair, 313
Irian Jaya, 300

Irkutsk, Russia, 190, 196
Iron Guards, 167
Ishii, Susumu, 140
Islam, in Indonesia, 301–2
Italy, in Korean War, 161
Ittiphol Khunpluem, 250
Ivankov, Vyacheslav 'Yaponchik' Kirillovich, 183–5, 199, 204–5, 206–8, 372
Ivashov, Petr, 211

jade trade, Burma, 268
Jakarta Tourist Industry Association, 285
Jakrin Patanadamrongkit, 252
Japan: American occupation, 154–5; amphetamine use, 157–8; annexes Korea, 149, 152; anti-gang legislation, 137–8, 142–3; assists White Russians, 193; in China, 52–3, 58, 61, 162; Chinese in, 179–80; collapse of bubble economy (1990), 138–41; development of black market, 155; development of fascism, 152–3; establishes military police, 151; fur traders clash with Russians, 191; gambling, 144, 146, 166; 'helps' Pacific nations, 341; intelligence services, 150–1; Koreans in, 176–9; in Macau, 120; Meiji Restoration, 149, 150; military expansion, 149–50; prostitution, 156–7, 159, 179, 180, 214; real estate boom (1980s), 5; role of Emperor, 150; Self Defence Force, 173; Sino-Japanese War (1894–95), 50; supports Russian counter-revolutionaries, 195, 196; surrenders in World War Two, 153–4; Tokugawa shogunate, 143, 144, 145, 149; transformation from feudal society, 148–9; types of organised crime in, 4–5; uses Triads as informers and enforcers, 120; in Vietnam, 330; war with Russia (1904–05), 149, 151, 192; withdraws from Siberia, 197; *see also sokaiya; yakuza*
Japan Shipbuilding Industry Foundation, 166, 170

Russia, 199; *see also* North Korea; South Korea

Korean Residents Union of Japan, 137, 177

Korkov, Gennadiy 'Mongol', 183, 203, 204

Kosai zendo, 162

Kot Siu Wong, 122

Kowloon Peninsula, 26–7, 119

Koxinga, 45

Krasnodar, Russia, 203

Krasnoshchekov, Alexandr Michailovich, 197, 199

Krasnoyarsk, Russia, 205

Kuala Lumpur, Malaya, 231, 319–20

Kuala Pilah, Malaya, 231

Kuboki, Osami, 168

Kudus, Indonesia, 294

Kulikov, Anatoliy, 209

Kunming, China, 3

Kupang, West Timor, 281

Kurile people, 186

Kuzuo, Yoshihisa, 153

Kvantrishvili, Otari 'Otarik' Vitalievich, 204–5, 208

Kwee Hing Tjiat, 293

Kwong Kwok-leung, 127

Kyaw Myint, 269

Kyaw Thein, 265

Kyaw Win, 268–9

Kyi Myint *see* Zhang Zhiming

Lahu people, 237

Lai Changxing, 380–1

Lai Choi San, 97

Lai Tung-sang, 75, 79–80, 127

Lakatani, Sani, 344

Lam, Duncan, 332

Lam Sak-cheung *see* Lam, Duncan

Lamour, Catherine, 249

Langbaiao, 90

Laos: Burmese export heroin to, 274; devaluation of currency, 270; Guomindang in, 247, 248, 249; illegal Chinese in, 223; Khun Sa attempts to transport opium to, 256–7; Mountainous Areas Development Corporation, 274;

Vanuatu's 'honorary consuls' in, 346

Lapps, 186

Las Vegas, 113

Lashio, Burma, 271

Lasykar Jihad, 302

Lasykar Rakyat Jakarta Raya, 289

Lauer, Tony, 317

Law, Steven, 263, 268

Law Yuk-kai, 11

Le Quang Liem, 330

Le Van Vien, 326–7

League of the Supporters of Indonesian Independence, 283

Lebanese, 308, 323

Lebedeva, Nina, 196

Lee Jai Hyon, 168–9

Lee, James, 28

Lee Kuan Yew, 318

Lee Man-cho, 296

Lee Teng-hui, 376

Lee, Tun Sir Colonel Henry H.S., 232

Leek, Alan, 310

Leite, José Amaral, 279

Leng Seün *see* Liang Zhongyin

Lenin, Vladimir Ilyich, 187, 191, 192, 197

Leong Yew Koh, 233

Lewinsky, Monica, 380

Lewis, Elaine T., 239–40

Li Bai *see* Riady, James

Li Chi-keung, 80

Li Ching-hsi, 60

Li Hongzhi, 385

Li Mi, 236, 246

Li Qihan, 36

Li Ruihuan, 227

Li Teng, 248

Li Wen-zheng *see* Riady, Mochtar

Li Wenhuan, 247, 248, 256

Li Xinwen, 83

Lian Chen, 357

Liang Zhongyin, 258

Liberal Democratic Party, Japan, 14, 163, 177

Lie Mo Tie *see* Riady, Mochtar

Liem Sioe Hie, 294

Liem Sioe Liong, 294–5, 297, 299

Romanians, in Australia, 323
ronin, 143
Roosevelt Club, Sydney, 312
Roosevelt, Franklin D., 202
Roosevelt, Theodore, 29
Royal Air Cambodge, 216
Royal Canadian Mounted Police, 370, 381
Royal Commissions, Australia, 313, 317
Ruddock, Philip, 12
Ruhsmanhadi, General, 279
Rukmana, Hardiyanti 'Tutut', 282, 298
Russell & Company, 24
Russia: Chinese in Far Eastern Russia, 211; collapse of communism, 182–3, 184, 185, 205, 206; contact with American Indians, 187; crime in the Russian Far East, 186, 191; criminals in the Russian army, 202; export of prostitutes, 5–6, 85–9, 180, 211, 214, 253; Far East development scheme, 205; gangster summits, 182, 203–4; heroin trade, 212; internal organisation of gangs, 204; links between criminals and security forces, 201, 203; Maritime District, 188; negotiations with China, 187, 189; opium trade, 198, 212; organised crime under communism, 201; penal colonies, 190, 199–202; prison system, 203, 204; proclaims Far Eastern Republic, 197–8; protection rackets, 185; Red Army massacres Japanese, 196; release of criminals after Stalin's death, 203; relinquishes claim to rights in Manchuria, 36; Revolution (1917), 192–6; rise of organised crime, 4; Russian-designed submarines in Colombia, 7–8; Russian organised crime in the US, 206–7, 371–3; Russian refugees in Shanghai, 33–5, 65; Russians in the South Pacific, 7, 336, 342, 343; 'scab wars' in Russian prisons, 203; secret police, 199, 203, 209, 372, 411n, 412n; secures lease for Dalian peninsula, 192; sells Alaska to America, 188; Stalin's mass purges,

199, 200; SVR, 209; Triads in, 211, 215; war with Japan (1904–05), 149, 151, 192; *yakuza* in, 206, 214, 215; *see also Mafiya*
Russian-American Company, 188
Russian Orthodox Church, 189
Ryan, Morgan, 313
Ryan, Peter, 308, 314, 317, 334
Ryter, Loren, 283

Sacco, Nicola, 200
Sacco (prison ship), 199–200
Saen Sukh municipality, Thailand, 250
Saffron, Abraham Gilbert, 312–13, 314–15, 325
Sagawa Kyubin Co Ltd, 140
Sagoya, Yoshiaki, 166
Sai Lin *see* Lin Mingxian
Saigon, Vietnam, 325–6
Saishikai, 166
Sakhalin Island, Russia, 190, 214
Sakura society, 152–3
Salim, Sudono *see* Liem Sioe Liong
Salween Village, Burma, 262
Samaranch, Juan Antonio, 12
Sambath, Uy *see* Uy Sambath
Samoa, 343
Samofalova, Natalia, 6, 87–8
Samoyed people, 186
samurai, 143, 146, 147
San Cha-Kung, 77
San Francisco, United States, 355, 357, 360
San Kin Yip (company), 129
San Lwin, 348–9
Santos, Antonio Lopes dos, 106
Sao Hpalang *see* Zhang Suquan
São Tomé e Príncipe, 108
Sao Tuen-sung, 249
Sarawak, 291–2
Sarit Thanarat, 241, 244–5, 246
Sasakawa Foundation, 170, 259
Sasakawa, Ryoichi, 161, 164–8, 170–1, 259, 341
Sasakawa, Yohei, 171
Sassoon family, 18, 28, 29
Schlegel, Gustav, 228
Schreiber, Mark, 156

Sliva, Vyacheslav, 208
Small Sword Society, 48–50, 52, 53
Smedley, Agnes, 59
Smith, Arthur 'Neddy', 318
Smith, Stan 'the Man', 318, 325
'smurfing', 339
snakeheads, 180, 349, 365–6
Snow, Edgar, 16, 69, 81
Soares, Mário, 115–16
Sociedade de Turismo e Diversoes de Macau (STDM): celebrates 35th anniversary, 81; China negotiates control of, 116; Fok as financier and first director of, 113; formation of, 105–6; monopoly ends, 78–9; obliged to disclose books, 110; opens VIP rooms, 76; Stanley Ho as director of, 70–1; survives relinquishment of Portuguese sovereignty, 108; transforms gambling in Macau, 107; Yip Hon's stake in, 112
Society of the Celestial Salvation of the Oppressed, 151–2
Socrates, 286
Soerjadi, Mr (PDI chairman), 285
Soerjosoemarno, General, 284
Soerjosoemarno, Yapto, 284–6, 287–8, 298
sokaiya, 5, 174
Solntsevskaya, 183
Solomon Islands, 336, 341
Solzhenitsyn, Alexandr, 201
Somboon Rahong, 252
Somchai Khunpluem, 250, 252
Somsak Prisnanuntakul, 252
Songkhla, Thailand, 350
Sonthaya Khunpluem, 250
Soong Ai-ling, 397n
Soong, Charlie, 55
Soong Chin-ling, 397n
Soong May-ling, 397n
Soong, T.L., 397n
Soong, T.V., 55, 62, 397n
Sope, Barak, 346
South Africa, in Korean War, 161
South Korea: amphetamine production in, 158; business interests in Russia, 213; Korean Central Intelligence

Agency, 167–8, 177; Moon's Unification Church, 167–9; Republic of Korea established, 160
South Pacific Forum, 336
South Sathorn Planner, 252
Southeast Asian Treaty Organisation, 245
Souza, Leonel de, 90
soviets, 193
Sri Bintang Pamungkas, 285
S.S. Group, 226
Stajner, Karlo, 200–1
Stalin, Josef, 160, 191, 198–200, 202, 203, 213
Standard Chartered Bank of London, 134
Star City Casino, Sydney, 334–5
STDM *see* Sociedade de Turismo e Diversoes de Macau (STDM)
Stephens Inc., 296
Stephens, Jackson, 128, 296, 340
Stephens, Jimmy, 338
Stilwell, 'Vinegar Joe', 62–3
Stirling, W.G., 216
Subianto, Prabowo, 282, 298, 299
Sudarno, Tiasno, 279
Sugamo Prison, Tokyo, 154, 161, 165
Suharto, President: allows Stanley Ho to operate *jai-alai* stadium, 110; corrupt activities of brother-in-law, 341; discriminates against Chinese, 294; gives Pemuda Pancasila his blessing, 285; patronage of Liem and Riady, 296, 297; presides over kleptocracy, 297–8, 302; regime collapses, 278, 283, 299–300; seizes power (1965), 283, 294–5; Sultan Hamengkubuwono on, 276
Sukarno, President, 283, 288, 295
Sukarnoputri, Megawati, 281, 285
Sullivan, Kathy, 336
Sumatra, Indonesia, 283
Sumiyoshi-kai, 172
Sun Yat-sen: Chinese Thais seek to emulate, 235; commemoration of first Chinese revolution of, 123, 361; as first president of Chinese republic, 36; Indonesian supporters of, 293;

links with secret societies, 52–3, 61,
119; revolt in Guangdong fails, 118;
seeks aid from overseas Chinese, 231;
as spiritual guide in Cai Dai, 329;
visits Malaya, 231

Sun Yee On: Albert Yeung as member
of, 85; attends 1992 summit in Hong
Kong, 13; brutality of, 124–5;
Charles Heung as member of, 10;
involvement in heroin trade, 334;
lack of central structure, 375; links
with Chinese authorities, 373–4;
membership of, 125; mentioned in
'Sidewinder' report, 382; retains
traditional rituals, 124; in Taiwan,
375; terrorises residents of New
Territories, 11; Yip Hon as member
of, 112

Surachart Bamrungsuk, 244

Surinam, 354

Sutiyoso, Governor, 300–1

Sweden, in Korean War, 161

Syafe'i, Imam, 289, 290

Syahnakri, Kiki, 279

Sydney Harbour Casino see Star City
Casino, Sydney

Ta Thang, 379

Tachilek, Burma, 268, 274

Tai Fung Bank, 102, 114–15

Tai Hing Company, 94, 102

Tai Ping Shan Sports Association, 120

Taipa, 91, 96, 107, 112

Taipei, Taiwan, 354, 377

Taiping Rebellion, 221

Taishan, China, 356

Taiwan: amphetamine production in,
158; *Anti-Hooligan Law*, 377; Chiang
Kai-shek flees to, 16, 64, 162, 236;
Chinese POWs settle in, 248;
Coordinating Council for North
American Affairs, 368; gangsters flee
to from China, 121; heroin trade,
378–9; illegal immigration from, 354;
Japan captures, 149; liberalisation of,
376; links with Chinese Americans,
360; Operation Chih Ping, 377–8;
Portuguese in, 45; returned to China
after Japanese leave, 63; in the
seventeenth century, 45–6; Taiwanese
banks in Vanuatu, 7; Triads in, 123,
375–8; United States' immigration
quota from, 358; see also Guomindang

Takenaka, Masahisa, 174

Takeshita, Noboru, 164

Taksin, King, 233–4

Takumi, Masaru, 140, 175, 336–7, 370

Talented Dragon (company), 132

Taliban, 304

Tam Ngob, Thailand, 247, 248, 257

Tameo, Shirai, 168

Tamil Tigers, 218–19

Tampa (ship), 304, 343

Tan Piak Chin see Chin Sophonpanich

Tanaka, Kakuei, 173

Tanaka, Yoshimi, 219

Taniyama (company), 254

Tao Changzhang, 53

Tao Siju, 8–10, 126, 374, 375

Taoism, 47

Taoka, Kazuo, 152, 153, 162–3, 171,
172, 174

Tartars, 187

Tata, Sam, 16

Taufa'ahau Tupou IV, King, 341, 344

Tavares, João, 279

Tavares, Panglima, 279

tax evasion, 7, 173

Tay Ninh province, Vietnam, 328, 329

Taylor, Elizabeth, 170

Teixeira, Manuel, 111

tekiya, 145–6, 148, 155

Teng Bunma, 11

Tenyukyo, 151–2

Teochew Chinese, 234, 242–3, 312,
398n

terrorism, 85

Thai Financial Syndicate, 241

Thai Rak Thai Party, Thailand, 251,
252

Thailand: abolishes Royal Thai Opium
Monopoly, 246; activities of the *chao
pho*, 236, 249–52; changes names
from Siam, 235; Chinese community
in, 233–4, 236, 245; Chinese illegal
immigrants in, 222–3; Communist

Trie, Charlie, 127–9, 130, 134, 380
Trihatmodjo, Bambang, 298
Tropical Hotel, Dili, 280
Trotsky, Leon, 191, 197
Truman, Harry S., 160, 238
Trump, Donald, 113
Trump Plaza Casino, Atlantic City, 113
Tsai Kuan-lun, 377–8
Tsuji, Karoku, 163
Tuchman, Barbara, 63
Tumasik, 227
Tung Chee-hwa, 113–14
Turalu, 345
Turkey, in Korean War, 160
Tuvalu, 7

U-paing Company, 268, 269–70
Uchida, Ryohei, 151, 153
Ukraine, 133–4
Ulan Bator, Mongolia, 195
Uncle Seven *see* Ong Kai-sui
Ungern-Sternberg, Roman ('Mad Baron') Fyodorovich von, 194–6, 210
Uniana (ship), 305–8, 332, 349
Unification Church, 167–9
Union of Myanmar Economic Holdings, 268, 269–70
United Bamboo gang, 10, 13, 123, 376, 377
United Front Party, China, 38, 58
United Kingdom *see* Britain
United League, 53
United Nations, 238, 262, 267, 273, 386
United Orient Bank, 359, 360, 369
United States: assists Russian counter-revolutionaries, 193, 196; Bureau for International Narcotics and Law Enforcement Affairs, 264, 342; buys Alaska from Russia, 188; Central Intelligence Agency, 163, 240, 247–8, 249, 265, 313–14; in China, 62–4; Chinatowns in, 354, 355, 356, 357–62, 367–9; Chinese at American universities, 355; *Chinese Exclusion Act*, 356, 358; Chinese street gangs in, 357–9, 362–4; conference of godfathers (1957), 185; Donorgate

scandal, 127–31, 225, 226–7, 296–7, 380, 383; Drug Enforcement Administration, 208, 212, 258, 268; embassy in Rangoon, 267; Federal Bureau of Investigation, 208, 382; gang warfare in, 363–4; history of Chinese migration to, 356; illegal immigration into, 348–55, 363, 365–6; indicts On Leung, 360–1; Industrial Workers of the World, 197; interns Japanese in World War Two, 383; involvement in opium trade, 24; occupation of Japan, 154–5; Organisation of Strategic Services, 167; Presidential Commission on Organised Crime, 362; protection rackets, 357, 359, 362, 371, 372, 373; Rico *(Racketeer Influenced and Corrupt Organisations Act)*, 362; Russian organised crime in, 206–7, 371–3; treaty with Japan (1853), 149; Triads in, 369; Vietnamese gangs in, 370–1; *yakuza* in, 140, 369–70
United Wa State Army, 261, 264, 266, 272, 275, 378–9, 386
United World Chinese Association, 361
UNTAS, 281
Urga, Mongolia, 194–5
Ustasha movement, 167
UWSA (United Wa State Army), 261, 264, 266, 272, 275, 378–9, 386
Uy Sambath, 218

'Vachigan' (crime boss), 208
Vajiravudh, King, 235
Valta Trading, 88
Vanuatu, 7, 296, 336–41, 345–6
Vanzetti, Bartolomeo, 200
Vanzetti (prison ship), 199–200
Vasin, Evgeny 'Jam' Petrovich, 210, 215
venereal disease, 21–2
Vereenigde Oost-Indische Compagnie, 287
Victoria, Queen, 25
Vidthaya Khunpluem, 250
Vieira, Vasco Rocha, 70
Viet Ching, 324, 370
Viet Minh, 326, 329, 330

Won Pak-kam, 80
Wong Man-fong, 9
Wong Siliang, 303
Wong Sing-wa, 132, 133, 296
Wong Wong Kit, 120–1
Woo, S.B., 368
Wood Royal Commission, Australia, 317
World Anti-Communist League, 167
World Group, 269
World War Two, 153, 154, 202
Worthen Bank, 128, 296
Wrest Point Casino, Hobart, 109–10, 117
Wright, C.E., 54–5
Wu Jianchang, 224
Wuhan, China, 37
Wynn, Steve, 113

Xi Lu people, 41
Xiamen, China, 380
Xianfeng, Emperor, 188
Xiao Zhang, 66
Xinhua (news agency), 9
Xu Axie, 43–4
Xuanzong, Emperor, 25

Yah Kee (company), 55
Yah Lin Trie see Trie, Charlie
Yakult Honsha Co., 174
yakuza, 137–81; absorbs bike gangs, 180; anti-foreign sentiments of, 155; in Australia, 335–6; in Burma, 254–5; in Canada, 370; compared with Indonesian militias, 290–1; control of prostitution, 157; displacement of by Chinese gangs, 179; effect of anti-gang legislation on, 137–8, 142; effect of collapse of bubble economy on, 138–41; ethnic Koreans in, 176; foreign areas of operation, 90; harassment of tenants by, 138–9; as a haven for outcasts, 176; identifies with disadvantaged, 147–8; inter-gang warfare, 171, 174, 180–1; involvement in amphetamine trade, 157–8; Kodama attempts to unify, 172; links between occupation forces

and, 159–60; links with politics and business, 13–14; links with Russian gangs, 5; membership statistics, 4; mobilised to protect Eisenhower, 171–2; monopoly on labour contracts, 152; origins, 143–5; overseas investments of, 140; overview of, 4–5; place in Japanese society, 141; post-war revitalisation of, 155, 237; punishments for offences, 146–7; rituals and traditions, 144, 146–7, 174–5; in Russia, 206, 214, 215; in Shinjuku area of Tokyo, 155–7; tattooing of members, 147; in Thailand, 253–4; in the United States, 369–70; youth training, 168; *see also* Yamaguchi-gumi
Yamaguchi-gumi: activities of, 4; alliance with Kakuji Inagawa, 172; benefits from new criminal order, 162–3; in Canada, 370; challenges constitutionality of anti-gang law, 142–3; distributes aid after earthquake, 137; as a haven for outcasts, 175–6; involvement in car theft, 214; involvement in gang warfare, 174; leader buys house in Australia, 336; membership statistics, 4; monopoly on labour contracts, 152; organisational structure, 175; publishes own magazine, 141; raises funds for politicians, 14; Taoka as head of, 171; Watanabe's accession ceremony, 175
Yamaguchi, Noboru, 152, 162
Yamaichi Securities, 174
Yamanouchi, Yukio, 176
Yan Yan (cloth seller), 44, 47
Yang Jingtao, 1–2
Yang Jinxiu see Yang, Olive
Yang Kyin-hsui see Yang, Olive
Yang, Olive, 239, 262
Yang Shangkun, 13, 133, 360
Yangon Airways, Burma, 269
'Yaponchik' see Ivankov, Vyacheslav 'Yaponchik' Kirillovich
Yaponchik, Mishka, 183